in the
sweet kitchen

in the
sweet kitchen

THE DEFINITIVE
BAKER'S COMPANION

REGAN DALEY

ARTISAN

NEW YORK

Published by Artisan
A Division of Workman Publishing Company, Inc.
708 Broadway
New York, New York 10003-9555
www.artisanbooks.com

Library of Congress Cataloging-in-Publication Data

Daley, Regan
In the sweet kitchen : the definitive baker's companion / Regan Daley.
p. cm.
ISBN 1-57965-208-5
1. Baking   I. Title
TX763 .D25 2001
641.8'15—dc21   2001041289

Photography: Rob Fiocca Photography
Food styling: Lasha Andrushko
Prop styling: Catherine MacFadyen
Jacket and interior design: Sharon Foster Design

Printed in the United States of America

10 9 8 7 6 5 4 3 2 1

To Rob and Liam and Finn

ACKNOWLEDGEMENTS

THIS BOOK, like most books, is a result of the efforts, generosity, instruction, assistance, support, kindness and enthusiasm of many.

To Alison Fryer and Jennifer Grange of The Cookbook Store in Toronto, thank you for more things than I could ever count, but especially for what manifests itself as delicious eagerness to share the secrets you've learned. Without both of you, this book would never have been written.

To Denise Schon, for having first blind faith, and then confidence in my abilities, and for her mentorship and guidance.

Doug Pepper, a consummate foodie then at Random House Canada, listened to a complete unknown and decided she had a good idea, and for that I am forever grateful.

Random House Canada has overwhelmed me with trust and faith—in a project that at times bore a striking resemblance to Frankenstein's monster. Thanks to Jennifer Shepherd for enormous dedication and perseverance, and for gamely smuggling brownies across international borders on my behalf. Thanks to Anne Collins, for her warmth and constant support, as well as an honest opinion when it counted. Thanks also to Dave Schimpky, Teresa Pavlin, Scott Sellers, Lorraine Symmes, Matthew Sibiga, Marlene Fraser and Alan Terakawa. And a special thank you to David Kent, for always cooing at my children.

This book was a monumental undertaking for my editor, Tanya Trafford. Her insights were considerable, her instincts remarkable, and there is no one anywhere I would rather have had at the helm. Tanya, you are a wonderful guide, advocate and friend. Thank you.

Thank you to my agent, Susan Lescher, who took a risk on a first-time author from Toronto and who is constant, genuine, personal and honourably professional.

I am grateful to Sharon Foster, whose brilliant and beautiful design not only made sense of over 700 pages of *stuff*, but gave every idea, every word, its right and proper home.

In the Sweet Kitchen is a book that needed images, and in my wildest dreams I could not have imagined more beautiful, more perfect photographs than those realized by Rob Fiocca. Thank you, Rob—it was an honour. And an enormous thank you to Lasha Andrushko, for making my desserts look so good that I could feel the honey on my tongue; and to Catherine MacFadyen, for setting each scene with elegance, earthiness and Zen-like simplicity.

Thank you to Diane Hargrave, publicist extraordinaire, for her efficiency and creativity.

To Elizabeth Baird, Donna Bartolini and Kim Mason from the Canadian Living Test Kitchen, for their help and advice, in matters as varied as organic flour to wild berries.

Much of the inspiration for this book, in the form of wonderful ingredients and products, came from the Bonnie Stern Cooking School Shop, and I am grateful to Bonnie Stern and Maureen Lollar for their knowledge, service and friendship. Oh, and the gossip.

To Don and Tony and the staff at The Kitchen and Glass Place in Toronto, for always being eager to help locate a certain piece of equipment or give honest advice about another. Or gossip.

To Naomi Duguid and Jeffrey Alford, for their generosity, advice, candour and guidance.

To Julia Child, for demonstrating without a doubt that finding joy in food is noble and life-giving, and for her overwhelming kindness and support of *In the Sweet Kitchen*. Thank you, Julia.

To Marion Cunningham, Flo Braker, Rose Levy Beranbaum, Nick Malgieri and Emily Luchetti, for being silent and unknowing guides and mentors.

To chef David Van Den Driesschen, for his profound instruction, patience and faith, and for his gentle but unwavering insistence on perfection in all things pastry; and chef Chris McDonald, for his infectious passion for the best of everything culinary. Thank you both for inviting me to work and letting me play and taste and explore, and for being truly gifted teachers. I will always be a better cook and baker because of you.

I am grateful to everyone who tasted and tested the recipes over the months, including Sarah Phillips, Tony Grace and Jonelle Moore, Steve Baisley and Stacy Clark-Baisley, Yona Lunksy, Leslie-Ann Boctor, Naomi Theodor and

Jennifer Fagan; and everyone who joined us for our pastry parties, for giving me such insightful feedback on the nights' offerings.

To my family: Heather Bennett, Rachel Daley, Frank Daley, Patti-Anne Fitzpatrick-Daley, Annette and Gerrit DeBoer, Michelle and Kevin Tohivsky, and Christine and Rich Rorden, for understanding (or pretending to!) that staying home to write about the expiration dates of cornstarch or to bake six different versions of the same cookie is a valid and worthy pursuit, and for being eager and happy guinea pigs for more desserts than they could count. Thanks to my parents especially—one of the greatest gifts you gave me was the love of food.

To my sweethearts, Liam and Finn, for making me see things I have never seen and for teaching me that things do taste better when they're messy...

And finally, to my love, my flame, my Rob, without whom I would be a very unsatisfied cook, and with whom I find the greatest sweetness in my life.

Contents

DEAR READER,

I live in the city of Toronto, in the province of Ontario, and as far as distance goes, I'm a very close neighbor: I can drive to the U.S.-Canada border in less than two hours, and fly to New York City in less than one. Our two countries are very good friends and are so similar in many ways, but we do have our differences, many of them subtle and small: For example, our Thanksgiving turkey graces our table in October, and we do tend to say "please" and "sorry" an awful lot!

The first edition of *In the Sweet Kitchen* was published in Canada and was written as I speak; that is to say, by a Canadian. For this, the first American edition, I wanted to make sure that differences in terminology or ingredients would not hinder your use and enjoyment of the book. To that end, certain things have been changed: what I called *icing sugar* is now called *confectioners'* sugar, and every effort was made to ensure that ingredients and products described are readily available in this country. But I have not changed spellings, as I trust no one will get overly confused seeing the word *savoury* instead of *savory*!

My intention when writing *In the Sweet Kitchen* was to create a book that would be a reliable, accessible, easy-to-use and relevant resource for people who love to make sweet things. It is a book meant to get splattered with batter and thumbprinted with chocolate, a book to be well used. I hope it answers your questions, helps to solve those little problems we all face in the kitchen and, above all, inspires you, even if it comes seasoned with a little Canadian *flavour*! My best wishes for great fun and success.

Regan Daley

Toronto, September 2001

INTRODUCTION

My first encounter with a vanilla bean was an epiphany. Strange, perhaps, but for me it marked the moment when I realized the difference good ingredients can make. The heady aroma was intoxicating, and made the bottled stuff I was used to seem briny and stale. Why had none of the books I'd read prepared me for this? How had I managed to go through a rigorous and, I believed, thorough professional training program with master pâtissiers from all over the world and never experience the considerable gap between these two forms of the same ingredient? Naturally, a crème anglaise made with vanilla extract could not compare to one infused with the dark seeds of a fat, sticky bean.

After graduating from cooking school, I came under the wing of chefs David Van Den Driesschen and Chris McDonald at the Delisle Bistro and Wine Bar. These two visionaries encouraged all of us to explore the different facets of food preparation, and I honed my skills in both the sweet and savoury areas, eventually fitting into the role of pastry chef. David and Chris were the very best mentors and guides—both fanatic perfectionists, demanding only the best from their staff, they were especially fanatical when it came to the ingredients used in their kitchen. For me, it was a culinary utopia: pungent fresh truffles, smuggled in their rice cloaks; herbs I had never even heard of; raw-milk cheeses; magnificent wines. And on the sweet side of the kitchen, perfect fruit, stone-ground cornmeal, glorious crème fraîche and chocolate to make me forget every chocolate I had known before.

Later, when Chris opened the now-celebrated Avalon restaurant, I was encouraged to develop a short, simple dessert list that would complement the constantly changing menu of exquisitely prepared, but ultimately pure and unornamented ingredient-driven food. It was food that relied solely on an expert hand in the kitchen and the very best raw materials, and the desserts had to be in kind. Fortunately, this suited my dessert style perfectly. I was given carte blanche to experiment. If the best vanilla beans came from Mexico, then those were the ones I used. I quickly discovered that some ingredients were more appropriate for certain preparations, and not for others: for example, the slightly sweeter Callebaut bittersweet chocolate was actually better for *Really, REALLY Fudgy Brownies* than the more expensive extra-bitter Valrhona. We would order both, and then use the Valrhona for the desserts where it would be most appreciated, as in my *Molten Chocolate Cakes*.

My senses awakened, I began to actively explore the realm of ingredients open to the pastry cook, both amateur and professional. It became clear that this was the variable, the element that made the greatest difference between a nice dessert, and one that was explosively flavourful and truly memorable. But I was surprised by how little information was available to even a professional in terms of navigating the sea of choices. There was virtually no reference, no handbook or guide, aside from a few pages in the better books on baking technique, available to bakers to define and explain ingredients and their functions.

A familiarity with the vast range of ingredients and raw materials is an integral part of great baking. Identifying these ingredients and selecting the most appropriate variety, however, has been something that until now only the very obsessed or highly trained could do. Of course, a knowledge of the techniques and basic processes is necessary, and there are many excellent books on baking and pastry that clearly and expertly explain these. Some of my favourites are listed at the back of this book, and I encourage you to read and experiment with as many as you can. Good technique allows the baker to expand the complexity of their repertoire, to prepare more elaborate desserts and more delicate constructions. But without the proper and preferred ingredients, even the most sophisticated dacquoise will be mediocre, at best. To that end, I've included many of my own dessert creations, sumptuous yet simple recipes that use ingredients to their best advantage.

For those already expert in the sweet kitchen, this book will serve as a comprehensive, professional-quality reference for ingredients from basic to rare. For the novice, it's a practical and palatable guide to the once mysterious art of baking.

tools
&
techniques

TOOLS FOR THE BAKER

LIKE ANY GOOD CHEF, the home baker needs a well-stocked equipment pantry. The following is an outline of the more common and a few lesser-known tools used by bakers and pastry cooks. Not every baker will need every tool—some are used for one purpose only, and if you never make that particular dessert, you will never miss the tool! Judge for yourself which are necessary for you. In some cases, I have taken the liberty of designating certain tools essential, others simply nice to have, or optional. The dollar signs beside each description refer to the price range one should aim to pay for that particular tool. For example, apple corers may range in price from $3 or $4 to $20; a single dollar sign suggests buying an apple corer at the lower end of this scale. This is only a rough guide: if you make ten apple pies a week, you may want a more durable, fancier corer.

$ There is no need to spend a great deal of money on these tools; they can be bought inexpensively with no risk of inferiority. When it comes down to it, there is little difference, besides the aesthetics, between the least and most expensive versions.

$$ Buy neither the cheapest, nor the most expensive version of these tools; the best value lies somewhere in the middle-price range.

$$$ Buy the very best you can afford; you will be rewarded with tools of the highest quality, best performance and longest life.

Some of the more basic tools and equipment, such as mixing bowls, spoons, spatulas and even bakeware, are available at department stores and modest kitchenware shops. For many of them, however, the best sources are specialty cake decorating, baking supply and restaurant supply stores. Most cities and even smaller communities have a few of these outlets, and they are a resource every committed home baker should become familiar with. Restaurant supply stores often sell many baking tools and equipment, and their prices are generally very reasonable, as they are geared towards a wholesale market and don't normally deal in big-budget brand names. The products are always durable and usually come in a wide range of styles and sizes. I buy virtually all my equipment, from wooden spoons to specialty tart tins, from this type of store and am always confident I am getting not only a good deal, but a product of excellent quality. Check your local yellow pages or ask professional cooks and bakers in your area where they buy their tools.

Mixing, Portioning, Scraping and Spreading Tools

HANDS! Believe it or not, your hands are the best tools in so many situations. From folding the flour into a delicate egg-white foam for an angel food cake to forming cookies, your hands are more sensitive, exacting and efficient than any piece of equipment. If you aren't already, start using them—get gooey, floury, sticky, even mucky; your baking will no doubt improve, and you'll have a ball in the process.

TONGS Probably my favourite kitchen tool of all, I use these whenever I would like to use my fingers, but can't: for lifting hot custard cups out of their water bath, for example, or for transferring caramelized apple pieces from the pot to the cake pan. The small 6-inch size is most convenient for me, but bakers with larger hands may prefer the medium-length tongs. They should be stainless steel, and the sort with two solid scalloped-edged blades, for accurately pinching and holding. **$**

WOODEN SPOONS OF VARIOUS SIZES Spoons made from boxwood are the best, as they are less likely to warp or splinter. You should have at least one each of small, medium and large, for mixing batters, creaming butter and sugar, folding fruit, chocolate and nuts into stiff batters, and stirring crème anglaise and other cooked custards and puddings. You can never have too many! **$$**

FLEXIBLE RUBBER SPATULAS Have at least two, one medium, one large, preferably heat-resistant with durable handles. Don't be tempted to buy cheap or "bargain" spatulas, as the rubber almost always starts to melt upon contact with heat and can start to chip and flake off into your desserts. **$$**

PALETTE KNIFE OR METAL SPATULA This metal spreader or lifter looks like an artist's tool. It may be perfectly flat or bent at the mid-point; if bent, it is called an *offset spatula*. The offset type is excellent for delicate spreading jobs and for added leverage when lifting fragile items. Available in many different lengths. I find one large (10- to 12-inch) and one small (4-inch) straight palette knife and one medium-length (6- to 9-inch) offset spatula is ideal. Use them to spread icing and fillings, lift cookies and pastries from their sheets and transfer rolled-out cookie dough, baked cakes and baked pastries from one surface to another. The straight edge also makes a perfect leveller for measuring dry ingredients. **$**

WIRE WHISKS While it is true that beaters or a stand mixer can do the same job as a whisk faster and effortlessly, sometimes a strong steady arm and the right whisk can do it, well, better. There are two main types of whisks available, with dozens of variations. The *sauce whisk* is long and narrow, often with thick, stiff wires and a tapered bottom. It is designed to blend mixtures with a minimum of air incorporation, such as butter or flour into a sauce. The *balloon whisk* is made of finer, more flexible wires and, as the name implies, balloons out at the bottom. It is used for aerating mixtures such as egg whites or sabayons. The more wires, the more air is incorporated with fewer strokes; the longer the whisk, the easier it is on your arms for jobs. Essential: one sauce whisk, for getting the lumps out of mixtures such as sauces or custards, or for blending ingredients, and one 10-inch balloon whisk (also called an egg whisk). I also find a 6-inch fairly wide-looped and thick-wired whisk useful for mixing certain ingredients that I don't really want to aerate, but do want to blend thoroughly. **$$**

SLOTTED SPOON This should be made of stainless steel, not plastic, as the former has much sharper and more precise edges. Use it for removing dumplings from boiling water and poached fruit from its syrup, fritters and doughnuts from hot oil, for portioning compotes and similar tasks. **$**

SAUCE LADLES Available in all sizes, these are excellent for lifting delicate fruits out of poaching liquids, spooning sauces and glazes over cakes and other desserts, and skimming and serving all manner of sauces, syrups and compotes. One 4-ounce (½-cup) ladle and one 1- or 2-ounce serving ladle will cover most jobs; they should be stainless steel, not plastic, as the latter will stain and can absorb flavours and odours. **$**

ICE CREAM SCOOP For serving frozen desserts, nothing beats the simple, one-piece metal scoops whose handles are filled with a non-freezing liquid. These scoops glide effortlessly through even the firmest sorbet! **$**

HINGED SCOOPS Although not great for all but the softest ice creams, these scoops come in a wide variety of sizes, from about 1 inch to 3 or 4 inches in diameter, and are great for portioning all sorts of desserts and confections. They are made of stainless steel, with a little curved blade that sweeps the inside of the scoop. They are not essential, but the tiny 1-inch size makes forming truffles wonderfully quick and easy, with a minimum of mess and waste, and a 2-inch scoop makes perfectly portioned cookies. **$$**

Measuring and Gauging Tools

A note about liquid and dry measuring cups: Make sure the cups you buy are properly calibrated; I was horrified to discover that many measuring cups are off by up to several tablespoons! Test the capacity with another measure (a scale would be best) to make sure the 8-ounce mark is actually 8 ounces.

LIQUID MEASURING CUPS Although these are also available in plastic and metal, glass is best; it is inexpensive, very durable and easier to read (and therefore more accurate). You should have one 2-cup and one 4-cup, preferably marked with both metric and imperial measurements. **$$**

DRY MEASURING CUPS Graduated sets come with ¼-cup, ⅓-cup, ½-cup and 1-cup measures; a ¾-cup measure is handy, but is rarely included in a set. Stainless steel is much better than plastic, as the plastic can crack, melt or warp. Choose measures that have perfectly straight rims, to allow you to sweep a flat edge across the top to measure ingredients accurately. I have two sets, and find this extremely convenient when preparing certain recipes, because I don't have to stop what I'm doing to wash out a cup. **$$$**

MEASURING SPOONS The best value is a durable set of stainless steel spoons that includes ¼-teaspoon, ½-teaspoon, 1-teaspoon and 1-tablespoon measures. I also have a ⅛-teaspoon measure and a 2-tablespoon measure, which come in handy. (Some sets also come with a ½-tablespoon measure, which I have never, EVER used.) Like the dry measuring cups, the rims of the measuring spoons should have straight rims, to allow ingredients to be levelled off evenly. **$$$**

CANDY AND DEEP-FRY THERMOMETER This is essential for cooking sugar syrups, caramel and candy mixtures, as well as gauging the temperature of fat for deep-frying. Choose a sturdy, professional-looking thermometer that has a foot that rests on the bottom of the pot; the versions that have only a clip to hold the thermometer to the side of the pot are awkward and rarely sit securely. **$$**

OVEN THERMOMETER Almost all domestic ovens are off by several degrees. It's essential that you know by how much your oven varies, and where its hot or cold spots are. If your oven is off by 50 degrees or more, have it recalibrated. I keep an oven thermometer in my oven at all times, and use that to judge the heat, not the dial. Choose a sturdy model that hooks onto the top shelf of the oven, or sits on a lower rack. **$$**

INSTANT-READ THERMOMETER This type of thermometer is often used to judge the internal temperature of roasts and other meats, but is very useful too for gauging the temperature of yeast, yeast doughs, sensitive batters and chocolate mixtures. **$$**

SCALE While you can get by without one, this tool should be in every serious baker's kitchen, to accurately weigh chocolate, butter, nuts, even dry ingredients. Many European and professional recipes are based on weight measurements, not volume, and a reliable scale is essential. The newer digital scales are excellent, not terribly expensive and much more accurate than the average plastic "dieter's scale" available in most kitchenware stores. The best are still the huge, old-fashioned balance scales, but these are becoming increasingly rare, and the ones you do find are very expensive. Consider yourself lucky if one is included in your inheritance! **$$**

12-INCH OR 16-INCH METAL RULER Preferably with both centimetres and inches, for measuring baking pans, rolled out pastry and dough, for marking dough and pastry for cutting and for creating a neat, straight cutting edge. **$**

PORTABLE KITCHEN TIMER Absolutely necessary for about 99.9 percent of bakers. A portable model lets you take it with you throughout the house, so you don't have to strain to hear the bell. Some digital timers come with nifty options like a pause button to let you check your cake partway through baking, then continue from the time you opened the oven door. I prefer the digital timers to the rotary type; not only do they come with bonus features, but they are generally more accurate and reliable. **$$**

Bowls, Strainers and Sifters

GRADUATED SIZES OF MIXING BOWLS You will need bowls of at least three sizes, but extra large and extra small bowls are very useful. Many glass and stainless steel bowls are available in sets of three, five or seven; if the price is good, buy the larger sets, as the extra bowls will always come in handy. They're available in many different materials, each with its own benefits and drawbacks (see below). I recommend investing in a set of five stainless steel bowls, one small glass bowl for melting ingredients in the microwave and one large glazed ceramic bowl for mixing heavy batters and proofing yeast doughs.

STAINLESS STEEL BOWLS Excellent for most uses, these are light, easily stackable, inexpensive, available in dozens of sizes and extremely durable. As stainless steel does not retain heat well, they have the added advantage of being able to quickly heat up or cool down, making them able to function as a double boiler when set over a pot of simmering water, for melting chocolate or making a sabayon. Once the bowl is removed from the heat, it immediately begins to drop in temperature, preventing overcooking. **$**

CERAMIC BOWLS These may be durable, but they are extremely heavy and cumbersome for use as all-purpose mixing bowls. They are also slow to heat up and retain heat extremely well, making them inappropriate for temperature sensitive mixtures. They cannot be used as a double boiler as their thickness makes this impractical, but they are good for insulating proofing yeast doughs and mixing stiff, large and heavy batters and doughs. **$$**

CERAMIC PUDDING BASINS Made of ovenproof glazed ceramic clay, these deep bowls come in a wide range of sizes and are designed for cooking traditional steamed puddings. The batter is poured into the bowl, covered with a layer of parchment paper or cheesecloth, then steamed in a bain-marie. Not essential, but perhaps more practical than the traditional steamed pudding moulds (page 36) for the occasional pudding-maker, as they can also be used as mixing bowls. **$$**

GLASS BOWLS Better than ceramic, but not as good as stainless steel. They are inexpensive, but somewhat heavy and clunky, and only moderately sensitive to temperature, making working with delicate mixtures such as chocolate or egg custards trickier. Glass is, however, the best medium for microwave cooking. **$**

PLASTIC BOWLS are generally unsuitable and should be avoided for most baking and dessert-making applications.

COPPER BOWL For beating egg whites, cooking sabayons and other egg mixtures, nothing beats copper. Egg mixtures whipped in copper have more stability and volume than those prepared in any other material, due to the interaction of the copper with the proteins in the eggs. **$$$**

WIRE MESH SIEVES OR SIFTERS These come in all sizes, but two are particularly important to have in your kitchen: one fine-mesh sieve to use as a sifter for dry ingredients and one with a larger mesh and a fairly big bowl for straining out bubbles in melted chocolate or filtering out solids from a poaching liquid. I also find a very small (½-cup to 1-cup) fine sieve is great to have on hand for sifting small quantities of ingredients such as baking soda, baking powder or cocoa into batters. Do invest in sieves with stainless steel mesh, as other metals tend to rust badly; look for models with a minimum of seams, nooks and crannies (they'll trap food that can spoil) and with strong, securely attached handles. **$$ to $$$**

COLANDER Used for washing and draining fruits, this could be enamelled, crockery or stainless steel. Buy one large enough to hold at least a pie's worth of fruit! The best have handles on either side and a pedestal or ring base so the colander stands on its own. **$**

Baking Accessories

CAKE DOME Although these can be very ornate and beautiful, made of glass or even crystal, I find the best for actually storing cakes are the plastic domes that seal perfectly around the base. They are inexpensive and excellent for keeping cakes, as well as pies and tarts, fresh without damaging their surfaces with clinging plastic wrap or aluminum foil. Buy a tall dome with space for a cake of at least 10 inches in diameter to accommodate even the largest layer cakes. **$**

CAKE INSULATING STRIPS These aluminized fabric strips can be moistened and wrapped around the sides of most round cake pans. They insulate the pan, preventing the sides from overheating, which produces a more evenly baked, level cake. The strips come in several lengths and are reusable. Look for them at cake-decorating and specialty stores. I use these often, especially for very large cakes. **$**

CAKE SPREADER Also called an *angel food cake cutter*, this handy tool looks something like a long-handled hair comb, with thin, long, evenly spaced teeth made of metal. When lowered into an angel food cake as though it were a knife, it severs the piece from the whole without crushing the delicate fluffy crumb. Cake spreaders can be found at cake decorating and specialty stores. **$**

DREDGER Also called a *powdered sugar duster* or *cocoa duster*, this is a small canister with a fine-mesh lid used for dusting cakes, pastries and other desserts. It can also efficiently dust a work surface with a fine coating of flour when you're kneading or rolling out pastry or dough. **$**

DOCKER This medieval-looking tool comes in a variety of sizes, with a rolling cylinder and 1-inch spikes all over. It is used for perforating, or docking, pastry to allow air to escape during blind baking, thus preventing the pastry from rising. While this tool is a great help to professionals who have to dock acres of pastry at a time, it is definitely not essential for the home baker—a good fork will do just fine. **$**

PASTRY BLENDER This hand-held tool, with a semicircular row of metal wires or bars, is used for blending fat into flour in the making of pastry doughs. In spite of its old-fashioned reputation, I still find this the best method for making a perfectly delicate and flaky pastry dough. Make sure the one you choose feels good in your hand and has a non-slip handle. **$**

PASTRY BRUSHES Buy high-quality brushes with natural bristles; cheaper brushes have the annoying habit of shedding bristles and hairs into glazes, syrups and egg washes on pie crusts. The better the brush, the longer it will last, and the better it will work. One for melted butter and oil, and for applying melted glazes, and one for dry brushing are essential; size isn't critical, but I find one 1-inch and one 2-inch brush very convenient. **$$$**

PASTRY CRIMPER WHEEL This hand-held tool looks something like a pizza or pastry wheel. The stainless steel wheel at the end of the handle is about half an inch thick, with cut-out spaces like treads. When it is rolled over the edge of a raw pie crust, it crimps it decoratively, sealing it. Definitely not necessary, but if you are after *perfectly* crimped edges, they're fun. **$**

PASTRY SCRAPER Also called a *bench scraper* or *dough scraper*, this metal sheet of about 4 x 6 or 5 x 7 inches, with a wooden or rounded metal handle on one side, is wonderful for scraping a work table after rolling out sticky dough and for transferring pie and bread doughs from one place to another. The sharp edge is great for neatly dividing bread, cookie and pastry doughs. **$**

PIE OR CAKE SERVER For removing slices of these desserts from the whole without making a great mess of it all. **$**

PIE WEIGHTS These are used to hold down the pastry when blind baking, to prevent it from rising and to encourage the pie or tart shell to bake flat. You can buy ceramic or metal pie weights (they are about the size of sweet peas, and are sold in amounts of enough to fill one average-sized pie shell), but dried beans or peas work every bit as well. The beans can be reused for years if you keep them in an airtight jar, but don't try to make a soup with them after designating them for weights! Let the weights or beans cool completely before storing. **$**

STRAWBERRY HULLER Like a staple-remover without the teeth, this V-shaped metal tool acts as a pair of tongs or tweezers and can be pushed into the stem-end of a fresh strawberry and twisted, in order to pluck out the stem and hull. A sharp paring knife works pretty well, too. **$**

WIRE COOLING RACKS OF VARIOUS SIZES Racks should be good-quality stainless steel or non-stick material and must be level, with no bumps or kinks that might dent or break baked goods. Have at least one large rack to accommodate a 9 x 13-inch pan or a large cookie sheet, two round or square racks of at least 10 inches in diameter for cake layers and at least one with a fairly tight weave, for cooling small cookies, biscuits and confections (so they don't fall through the cracks and break). $

WOODEN AND METAL SKEWERS Simple wooden skewers are the best cake testers; thin metal skewers are better for testing baked custards (for years, I have used one of those tiny poultry trussing pins as a metal tester; they are just the right size!). $

Cooking Pots, Saucepans and Skillets

There are several things to look for when choosing cookware. Of course, the design, shape and size of the pots must suit you, but the most important factor is the material out of which they are made. How well a given material conducts heat determines how well it will perform. Poor conductors such as *stainless steel* will heat slowly and unevenly, retain heat poorly and tend to scorch foods. Good conductors such as *copper*, on the other hand, heat evenly and rapidly, and respond to even small changes in heat, allowing the cook more control over the cooking process. All cooking pots and pans should be heavy-bottomed, to distribute heat evenly, and made of a non-reactive material (in other words, *not* untreated aluminum.) Although it is a good conductor, *aluminum* reacts with acidic solutions, alcohol-based poaching liquids or cooked fruit compotes, for example, to produce a detectable metallic flavour. In addition, untreated aluminum pots tend to turn pale custards and sauces an unappetizing shade of grey. Recently, *anodized aluminum* has become popular for domestic cookware. The aluminum for this material has been electrochemically sealed, making it non-reactive, non-porous and extremely hard. Anodized aluminum pots are excellent heat conductors, with none of the disadvantages of untreated aluminum. The surface of anodized aluminum is effectively non-stick, but not prone to scratching or peeling. For this best of all worlds, however, be prepared to pay dearly! Definitely recommended, but not within everyone's budget. Beyond anodized aluminum, there are several good options.

❖ *Stainless steel* conducts heat relatively poorly, but is inexpensive, easy to care for and attractive. The best stainless steel pots are either fortified with copper bottoms or made of two layers of stainless steel sandwiching a layer of aluminum. Choose according to your budget; either is a good, all-purpose choice. Unfortified stainless steel heats unevenly and can scorch delicate mixtures like crème anglaise, but is acceptable for poaching, or warming thin sauces.

❖ *Copper* conducts heat better than virtually all other materials and is wonderful for cooking egg dishes. It is however, torturous to keep clean and shiny, and more expensive than remodelling your kitchen. Something to aspire to for the serious cook or baker, but definitely not essential. As a baker, if you want to start collecting, start with a copper bowl, then perhaps a small saucepan.

❖ *Enamelled cast iron* cookware is a traditional favourite in many parts of France and the rest of Europe, and I love it. It is somewhat slow to respond to changes in temperature, but once it reaches the right temperature it retains heat better than any other material. This makes it excellent for deep and shallow frying, and for poaching and other types of long cooking as well. It is, admittedly, fabulously heavy, making it impractical for some uses, but I do recommend buying a large, enamelled cast iron Dutch oven.

The term "pots" generally refers to vessels without long handles, but with two short ones close to the body of the pot; "saucepans" have one long handle. All should have lids that fit securely. Saucepans should be light enough that when filled they can still be easily lifted without strain. Handles should ideally be made of a solid piece of ovenproof material and welded directly onto the pot, to lessen the chances of them becoming loose or warped. Do some research before you invest, but buy the very best you can afford—you will be rewarded with good performance and long life (from your pots, that is). The minimum requirements for baking would be at least one small (4-cup) saucepan, one medium (2-quart) saucepan and one Dutch oven (4½ to 6 quarts). **$$$**

DOUBLE BOILER This is an insert, usually made of stainless steel, but occasionally of porcelain or copper, that sits over the mouth of a large saucepan of water.

It heats gently without exposing mixtures to direct heat; essential for sabayons or melting chocolate. If you do not have a double boiler (and after all these years, I still don't!), a stainless steel bowl set over the mouth of the saucepan works equally well. **$** for stainless steel; **$$$** for porcelain or copper.

SKILLETS You should have one large skillet, for sautéing and caramelizing fruit, and one small, for toasting nuts and spices, reducing glazes or warming small quantities of liquid. My favourite small skillet is non-stick, which is excellent for many delicate jobs, and can double as a crêpe pan. Your larger skillet should not have a non-stick finish, as the coating tends to prevent proper caramelization of sugar and fruit. As for pots and saucepans, copper is ideal, but impractical for most; anodized aluminum is excellent; stainless steel, fortified with good copper bottoms, is an adequate medium; and untreated aluminum is not suitable. **$$$** for the large skillet; **$** for the small (if it is non-stick).

CRÊPE PANS The classic crêpe pan is a shallow round pan, usually made of carbon steel or anodized aluminum with a long handle to allow the cook to tilt the pan to ensure the batter coats the bottom as thinly as possible. The sides are gently sloped (some pans are almost flat) so the crêpe can be slid over the entire surface as it cooks. A newer type of crêpe pan, and one which I have used with great success, looks more like a lid than a pan. It is made of seasoned cast iron and is a convex, rather than concave, shape. This strange form is designed to be dipped into a shallow bowl of batter, necessarily picking up only a thin coating, then quickly returned to the heat. The crêpe cooks on the curved surface as it would on any other pan or griddle. Once you get the hang of it, you can make the most delicate, paper-thin pancakes imaginable! Neither pan is absolutely necessary for the occasional crêpe-maker—a small non-stick skillet works just fine. If you love crêpes, however, think about investing. **$$**

Rolling Pins and Boards

CUTTING BOARD RESERVED FOR BAKING I prefer wooden boards, but a durable plastic one is fine. Do try to keep one cutting board for pastry and baking uses, as products like chocolate, nuts and pastry doughs absorb other odours readily. At very least, make sure that the board you use for baking ingredients is not the one used for chopping garlic, onions or chilies! Have at least one large board, but a small one for little jobs is handy too. **$$**

MARBLE PASTRY BOARD Really nothing more than a slab of polished marble, this is extremely handy when making pastry. You can pre-chill the board in the refrigerator before you roll out the dough, which helps keep the dough at a workable cool temperature. It's also the ideal surface on which to do chocolate or sugar work, as well as other confectionery such as making almond paste or marzipan, as its constant temperature and beautifully finished surface keeps the products tempered and smooth. The most useful of these are big enough to accommodate a large piece of rolled-out pastry dough and have four rubber feet to prevent the board from slipping out of place. **$$**

ROLLING PIN My favourite rolling pins are the straight, French solid boxwood pins, about 16 to 18 inches long, and 2 or 2½ inches in diameter. They are excellent for most general uses, from pie crust to tart and even puff pastry, and their length makes rolling out even large quantities of dough easy. Most home bakers, however, prefer the familiar two-handled pins. The handles on many are fixed, but the best roll on ball bearings. The body of these pins should be at least 14 but preferably 16 inches long, and they should have nylon bearings for durability. Another type of French pin is tapered at both ends, very long and rarely more than 1½ or 2 inches in diameter. It is efficient for rolling out thin circles of delicate pastry dough, but is not appropriate for every use and definitely not essential. Whichever type of wooden pin you choose, it should be heavy and at least 2 inches wide, with no nicks or gouges on its surface. Wooden pins should never be soaked in water or even washed with soap: to clean them, just dust with a little flour and wipe the length of the pin with a soft clean cloth after each use. Stainless steel, marble and the new non-stick pins are good for very sticky doughs such as Danish or puff pastry, but are also optional, although a good marble pin is wonderful as it can be chilled to keep doughs from warming and becoming tacky. Cookware shops also sell specialty pins for specific uses: grooved ones for flatbreads, notched ones for almond paste and marzipan, and pins decorated with beautiful embossed or carved Christmas designs for making the German holiday cookies called springerle. **$** for plain wooden pins; **$$$** for ball-bearing type; **$$** for specialty pins.

ROLLING PIN SLEEVE AND PASTRY BOARD CLOTHS These elastic cotton gauze cloths are designed to keep pastry dough from sticking to the rolling pin or work surface. The sleeve is a cylinder of gauze that fits over the pin; the cloth is simply a large square that covers the area of counter or cutting board on which you are rolling. While not necessary for all doughs (a light dusting of flour should keep the dough from sticking), these cloths are useful for particularly delicate doughs that should absorb as little excess flour as possible. **$**

Knives

As with pots and pans, buy the very best knives you can afford, and do some research before investing. Look for forged handles and stainless steel blades that extend down the full length of the handles. Make sure every knife, especially chef's and paring knives, feel balanced and comfortable in your hand; don't be afraid to hold as many as you need to before you decide. A good knife will last a lifetime, and you should enjoy using it. Keep all of your knives razor-sharp by using a steel before each task (your knife merchant can show you how to use this correctly) and store them in way that protects the blades, as well as your hands. Magnetic wall racks are very good as long as there are no young children in the house; otherwise drawer or counter-mounted wooden knife blocks are very good. Hundreds of styles, sizes and specialty knives are available, but the following are essential for the baker.

HEAVY-DUTY CHEF'S KNIFE Depending on your hand, either an 8-, 10- or even 12-inch chef's knife is essential for cutting and chopping fruits, chocolate and nuts. **$$$**

PARING KNIFE A 3- or 3½-inch knife is versatile, comfortable and practical—for peeling and paring fruits, cutting small pieces of fruit, cutting decorations from pastry and loosening cakes and other baked goods from their pans. **$$$**

SERRATED BREAD KNIFE Ideally one with at least a 10-inch blade, for cutting cake layers in half, slicing breads and some cakes and tarts. Don't spend a great deal of money on this knife, as you can't resharpen a dull one, but should replace it instead. **$**

THIN-BLADED SLICING KNIFE This knife has a very long, very thin, slightly serrated blade and is generally used for slicing roasts and other meats, but is excellent for slicing dense tortes and rolls of chilled cookie dough too. **$$ or $$$**

Other Cutting, Paring, Grating and Shredding Tools

SCISSORS OR KITCHEN SHEARS These come in handy for thousands of uses, from simply cutting through plastic bags and string to neatly trimming the overhang from a double crust pie. Make sure the shears you choose are rustproof, as they will need to be washed and dried often, and have comfortable, non-slip handles for safety. A good set should last years. **$$**

PIZZA WHEEL This has a plain, very sharp disc-shaped blade suspended on a hinge, with a short handle for ease of use. It's wonderful for cutting raw pastry dough into large shapes and long strips and is the best tool to cut through sheets of puff pastry, as it won't crush or tear the pastry as a regular knife would. Scalloped-edged *pastry wheels* are considerably less sharp and should not be used on puff pastry, but are fun for adding a decorative touch to pie crusts, sweet ravioli or dumplings and even cookies and confections. **$**

VEGETABLE PEELER My favourite kind has a plastic handle and looks like the letter "Y," with the blade crossing the top, although the even cheaper old-fashioned metal potato peeler takes a thinner pare off the fruit or vegetable, something that is usually desirable. Regardless of the shape, don't spend a lot of money on this tool—peelers have a funny habit of getting thrown out with the peelings and should be replaced as soon as they lose their edge. Do, however, buy one that feels good in your hand. **$**

BOX GRATER These free-standing graters can have four or six sides (most of which you will likely never use!). I don't like the little sharp poked-out hole sides, but prefer my grater to have both small and large shredding planes, for finely grating lemon or orange zest, as well as cheeses and chilled butter. Choose a grater made of sturdy stainless steel, with large and small shredding sides, as well as a tiny grating side for ginger or even nutmeg in a pinch. **$$**

MICROPLANE GRATER OR MICROPLANE RASP Recent additions to kitchenware shops, these hand-held graters are fantastic. Little more than the wood plane rasps used in carpentry, they are perfect for citrus zest, hard cheeses, even chocolate and ginger. Some models look virtually identical to the woodworker's rasp, long and straight, while others are shorter and have a convenient handle. **$$**

NUTMEG GRATER This is a hand-held rasp with a curved or flat plane, usually with a little compartment at one end for storing the whole nutmegs. Whether made of tin, stainless steel or plastic, they are inexpensive and, I think, essential for anyone who even occasionally uses this sweet spice. **$**

CITRUS ZESTER This hand-held little gadget has a row of tiny sharp-edged holes at its end, which thinly pare just the outer coloured zest from lemons, limes, oranges and other citrus fruits in fine threads. Select one that feels comfortable in your hand and has a stainless steel end. **$**

APPLE CORER Choose one that is made of heavy-duty stainless steel, with a well-attached and comfortable handle and a sharp blade. **$**

MELON BALLER Perfect for coring apples and pears, forming tiny truffles and other confections, as well as scooping balls of melon and other fruits. Choose one with large and small sharp-edged, stainless steel scoops at either end and a preferably wooden handle that feels comfortable in your hand. **$**

POTATO MASHER One of the old-fashioned stainless steel mashers with a wooden handle is perfect for mashing soft fruit like ripe bananas before it is added to batters, custards, sauces and fillings. **$**

Big and Small Machines

OVENS This could be an entire chapter in itself! But for practicality's sake, here are some brief points. All the recipes in this book (and in most others) were tested in a conventional 24-inch-wide gas or electric oven. Personally, I have a gas range, but have baked with both extensively and find there is less difference between the two types as there is between a good version of each and a poor one. As far as recipes go, these two are generally interchangeable. That said, I much prefer a gas stove-top to electric. The type of oven you have depends on many things: budget, whether you rent or own, what came with the house, etc. If at all possible, try a few different types of ranges before purchasing. In trying to work best with an existing oven, an oven thermometer is your best ally. I keep one in my oven at all times and check it regularly. Not only does this tell you if your oven tends to run hotter or cooler than the dial indicates (and they virtually all tend one way or the other!), it can also be used to determine where the actual hot and cool spots are.

If I had my dream combination, it would be a gas range stove-top, with a convection oven. Convection ovens have a fan that circulates the hot air to every corner of the oven, eliminating hot and cool spots and creating extremely even heat. This means you can load up the racks with baking pans and sheets, filling every shelf and into the corners without worrying about over- or under-baking. There is one caveat: unless you are using a recipe developed for convection ovens, you should reduce the suggested oven temperature by 25 degrees and reduce the baking time by 10 to 20 percent, depending on the product. The first time you try a new recipe, just keep an eye on things to determine whether it is closer to 10 or 20 percent. Baking in a convection oven is wonderful—cakes are even, not domed, muffins have lovely rounded tops, not ones that list to one side, and cookies are evenly baked no matter where they were on the sheet. **$$$**

MICROWAVE OVEN I don't recommend cooking or baking in the microwave, but even a small model is great for melting butter and small quantities of chocolate (see page 234). Cold butter can be softened in a microwave in seconds if you forget to leave it time to temper. Chilled sauces and syrups can be quickly and gently heated and served from the same containers. You can get by without one, but they do come in handy! **$$**

FOOD PROCESSOR These days, many recipes assume every baker has access to a food processor, and can be difficult if not impossible to prepare without one. I highly recommend investing in one. For some things, like finely grinding nuts or quickly and efficiently making pastry dough, it is indispensable. Shop around before you buy—talk to friends and professionals about their preferences and buy from a reputable distributor who can give you information on the different options. Choose a brand with a very sturdy and powerful motor, and a bowl large enough to accommodate at least one, if not two, recipes of pastry dough—about 1½ to 2 quarts. **$$$**

STAND MIXER I got along for years without one of these, but from the day I finally brought one home, I haven't been able to remember life without it. Although there are certain tasks only a stand mixer can perform, such as beating a large quantity of one mixture while another is carefully added, for the most part stand mixers simply facilitate your life in the kitchen. They whip faster, beat longer, knead more evenly, cream tirelessly and basically do everything you do, faster, smoother and, best of all, they free up your hands, enabling you to make delicate mixtures such as certain meringues and icings that require two things to be done at once. Preparing these types of desserts without a stand mixer would be more than tricky, requiring the juggling skills of a circus performer and the precision and timing of a surgeon. Although there are several companies making stand mixers, the KitchenAid model is unquestionably the most versatile (with dozens of attachments for everything from grinding your own grains to making pasta) and the most durable. They are not cheap, but will last you a lifetime. The most popular size for home bakers is the 4½-quart, but a 5-quart unit is also available and perfect for anyone who regularly prepares very large quantities of bread dough, icing or cake batter. **$$$**

A TIP: Buy an extra bowl—it will save you having to do a great deal of transferring and washing between tasks. And for the baker who has everything, copper stand mixer bowls are also available from KitchenAid!

HAND-HELD ELECTRIC MIXER Contrary to popular belief, this old favourite is not entirely obsolete if you invest in a stand mixer. For certain jobs, such as seven-minute or boiled frosting, its portable nature makes it the ideal tool, sparing your arms and producing an especially fluffy and shiny frosting. It is not absolutely necessary, and I don't use mine all the time, but once in a while I wonder what I would do without it. Buy a sturdy model with a good warranty and a durable motor, and make sure it feels comfortable in your hand, with 3 speeds and buttons and dials in sensible places. **$$**

STOVE-TOP OR ELECTRIC KETTLE Ideal for heating small quantities of water rapidly. **$$**

ICE CREAM MAKER The hand-cranked models of our grandmother's era have been replaced with easier and less complicated units that require neither salt nor ice to work. The best machines are the electric models, but these are often in excess of $300 or $400 and are large, heavy and certainly not necessary unless you are in the habit of making ice cream several times a week. For most home pastry cooks, the inexpensive and non-electric freezer insert-type ice cream makers are perfectly acceptable—the ice cream and sorbet recipes in this book were all devised and tested using one of these. This type of unit comes with a freezer insert chamber filled with a super-coolant liquid and must be frozen at least overnight before the ice cream can be made. The insert is then placed in a plastic casing, the chilled custard added and a small paddle attachment is turned with a hand crank every few minutes for about 20 minutes. The soft-set ice cream can then be transferred to a freezable container and frozen for several hours to firm it up. These machines are easily found at department and kitchenware stores, usually cost less than $80 and make creating homemade ice creams, frozen yogurts, sorbets and gelati as easy as pie! Buy a reputable brand-name machine and read the instructions carefully, as each machine is slightly different. **$$**

FOOD MILL This is a hand-cranked food processor with a conical bowl and a handle off one side. When the crank is turned, a blade smears food over one of several perforated discs, grinding, ricing or even puréeing it. Food mills are excellent for making fruit soups, sauces, coulis and fillings, as well as all manner of savoury foods. They're available in several sizes, from 1- to 4-quart capacities. I recommend about a 3-quart, or mid-sized, model. They are available in stainless steel or heavy-duty plastic; both work well if they are sturdy and well made, but make sure the blades are stainless steel and that the unit can be assembled and cleaned easily. **$$**

COFFEE AND SPICE MILL The small, inexpensive electric coffee bean grinders so common nowadays are perfect for freshly grinding spices, as well as grinding small quantities of nuts or chocolate. If you regularly grind fresh coffee at home, have a separate mill reserved for spices. They are easily cleaned with a few bits of torn fresh bread or a handful of uncooked white rice: simply put the bread or rice in the bowl and spin the grinder. Any traces of spices will cling to the bread or rice, leaving the grinder bowl and blade perfectly clean. **$**

DEEP FRYER Anything can be deep-fried without one of these machines, but deep fryers are excellent for achieving and maintaining accurate temperatures. The cool-wall electric countertop versions available today are not expensive and are very safe; the special fine filters also prevent everything in your kitchen from becoming covered with a greasy film! Look for a model with a removable inner chamber for ease of cleaning and dials that allow you to set the exact temperature of the oil. There is an unfortunate trend in the latest models to have no actual temperature gauge, but rather little pictures of chickens, fish and doughnuts, which keep bakers completely in the dark about the temperature of the fat. Very silly, and not very helpful. **$$**

BLOWTORCH Yes, a blowtorch. A small, hand-held butane torch costs less than $25 at any hardware store and is standard equipment in most professional pastry kitchens. It can also be used in all sorts of ways by the amateur pastry chef, from caramelizing the tops of crème brûlée, curd and fruit tarts and sugar-topped pastries like napoleons to gently darkening meringue toppings and baked fruit. Home broilers are awkward and inaccurate, and are often not hot enough, causing delicate products like lemon curd tarts or sugared custards to overcook or even curdle before their tops are properly caramelized—a small torch gives you perfect control. Make sure to read all instructions carefully and use caution whenever operating a torch. **$**

Juicers and Pitters

CITRUS REAMER There are two versions of this tool: a hand-held, ribbed, wooden, dowel-shaped tool; and a bowl-shaped model with a moat around the reamer. Both make quick work of juicing lemons, oranges, limes and other citrus fruits, and the type with a reservoir neatly collects the juice. Make sure the ribs on whichever version you choose are rounded, not sharp, as the sharp edges could scrape the bitter white pith into the sweet juice. **$**

JUICER Old-fashioned as I am, I do prefer the manual crank or pump versions of this tool to the modern electric juicers. Either works, and I suppose the electric models are much more versatile, able to extract juice from virtually any fruit or vegetable, from oranges to carrots, but I like the control and precision I have with the traditional countertop type. Neither is essential; a simple reamer works well enough for citrus fruit, but for unusual juices such as pomegranate, a juicer saves a great deal of time and effort. **$$**

CHERRY PITTER Also called an *olive pitter*, this is a small, hand-held, spring-loaded tool that neatly extracts the pit from cherries with a single squeeze, leaving your hands and clothing relatively unscathed. Whether made of stainless steel, aluminum or plastic, the cheaper versions are perfectly acceptable. **$**

Disposable and Staple Supplies

KITCHEN TOWELS, AND A GOOD SET OF POT HOLDERS OR OVEN MITTS Kitchen towels should be clean, 100 percent cotton and of a durable weave. Oven mitts should be thick, and should fit well, not be overly large. And please— replace them when they get thin and worn. **$$**

PARCHMENT PAPER Also known as *silicone paper*, this is a non-stick, heatproof paper that is a baker's secret in itself. Its seemingly endless uses include lining cake tins, brownie pans and cookie sheets (no greasing, and no more cookies sticking to the sheet). It is clean, neat, and your products come out of their pans beautifully. It is also reusable, if it gets a wipe with a damp cloth after use. (Discard it once it becomes dark and brittle.) It comes in large sheets that can be cut to fit any pan, and some specialty stores sell it pre-cut for standard-sized pans. **$$**

REUSABLE NON-STICK SHEET LINERS Also referred to by their brand name, most commonly Silpat, Exopat and the Canadian Pantec, these rubberized silicone sheets (available in formed muffin tray liners too) can be used in place of parchment or silicone paper. Not only are they environmentally friendly, but they also work beautifully. **$$**

CARDBOARD CAKE CIRCLES I find these extremely handy, especially for layer cakes that need to be decorated or cakes that are to be transported. Available in many sizes from cake decorating and baking supply stores, they are inexpensive, but can also be made at home from the clean tops of empty pizza boxes. **$**

CHEESECLOTH This wide-woven cotton cloth is familiar to jam- and jelly-makers, and anyone who habitually makes their own savoury spice bags and bundles for stews, soups and sauces. Its uses in the sweet kitchen include straining sauces, coulis and jellies, as well as holding sweet spices and aromatics to infuse sauces and poaching liquids. Layers of cheesecloth are also useful for covering steamed puddings before they are baked and fruit during poaching, to ensure the fruit remains submerged in its syrup. **$**

ALUMINUM FOIL Buy heavy-duty foil, not the bargain brands, as these rarely hold up with handling. **$$**

PLASTIC WRAP Curiously, I find most brands of this wrap absolutely useless, unable to seal, stick or stretch, regardless of the name! Find a brand that does work, and stick to it. **$$**

PAPER TOWELS For draining deep-fried foods, blotting dry fruit, etc. **$$**

PAPER OR FOIL CANDY, CAKE AND MUFFIN CUPS For baking, make sure the cups are heat-safe. These are wonderful for truffles, to keep each chocolate separate and protected, and greatly reduce clean-up time for muffins and cupcakes. **$**

Decorating and Garnishing Tools

LAZY SUSAN OR ROTATING CAKE STAND While not essential, a rotating cake stand is excellent for decorating cakes and pastry constructions. Several models are available: the standard cast iron professional models stand about 5 inches off the counter and rotate very smoothly, but are as heavy as they are expensive! Most good cake decorating and baking supply stores also sell good-quality plastic versions; at about one fifth the price, these are perfectly good as long as they feel solid and balanced, and rotate smoothly. Some people prefer the height (or lack thereof) of the flat Lazy Susans, which also rotate on ball bearings, and these are widely available in kitchenware and department stores. $ or $$, depending on how often you decorate cakes!

CAKE COMB This is a triangular flat scraper with three different serrated edges for decoratively finishing the sides and tops of iced cakes. Cake combs may be metal or plastic; I would avoid the latter, as the triangular teeth can warp, chip and crack. They are fun, but definitely not essential, as a plain fork or serrated knife can do the same thing! $

PIPING TIPS, PASTRY BAGS, COUPLING UNITS Pastry bags are great tools for forming loose-battered cookies and biscuits, as well as truffles and other confections; decorating layer cakes and tortes; even portioning churros and other fritters. Two 12-inch bags will do for most jobs, but smaller and larger bags come in very handy; smaller for delicate decorating work and larger for stiff cookie doughs. Make sure the bags are of professional-quality plastic-coated canvas, lined on the inside to make them watertight, and with sturdy stitching. Cheap bags often leak through the stitches when squeezed, and unlined fabric is sometimes porous, leaving a messy goo on your hands. Some bags come with a plastic coupling unit, a small attachment that secures the tip to the bag; buy one or two separately if you have to, as they prevent a great deal of hassle with bags and tips coming apart at inopportune times. Wash pastry bags well in hot, soapy water immediately after each use. Dry them standing erect with the insides loosely stuffed with a few sheets of crumpled paper towel. If a pastry bag ever develops a musty or mildewy odour, discard it. Stainless steel pastry tips can be bought in sets; a plain-tip set (rounded with no fluting) and a star-tip set (rounded with jagged edges) are ideal, but you can start smaller, buying the tips one by one. Among the plain tips, one each of a large (⅔- to ¾-inch aperture), medium (½-inch aperture) and small (¼-inch aperture), plus one medium (½-inch aperture) star tip is a great start and will see you through most tasks. The fancier decorative tips are usually sold individually and you can acquire them as you need them. Buy professional-quality tips (Ateco is a reliable and widely available brand); cheap tips often rust and dent easily. Cake decorating or baking supply shops are good sources for both pastry bags and tips. $$

BISCUIT CUTTERS These round cutters can be fluted or plain-edged and often come in sets of three; small (1½ to 2-inch), medium (2 to 2½-inch) and large

(3, 3½, or 4-inch). They should be made of stainless or tinned steel, with sides at least 1½ to 2 inches in height for cutting through thick biscuit or scone dough. They also come in handy for cookies, doughnuts and fritters, pastry cut-outs and even yeast dough buns. **$**

DOUGHNUT CUTTER This stainless steel cutter looks like two concentric biscuit cutters attached across the top with a handle and is designed to form the familiar ring shape in a single motion. It should be tinned or stainless steel and feel fairly sturdy. **$**

DECORATIVE COOKIE CUTTERS A few basic shapes are necessary to make rolled cookies, but there are hundreds of shapes available; I collect farm animals and once had a big cutter in the shape of the state of Texas. Go nuts. Choose stainless steel cutters and dry them thoroughly after each use. Keep them in an aerated container and dust them with a little cornstarch before storing, to absorb any moisture and prevent rusting. Another trick I use is to store them with one or two silica gel packets or capsules, the sort that come in vitamin bottles. Just make sure the packets are intact. **$**

COOKIE PRESSES OR PLUNGERS These are hollow metal or plastic cylinders, with a plunger at one end, and come with a variety of discs that fit over the other end. The tube is filled with cookie dough, and the plunger is depressed to form identical cookies in attractive shapes. These presses are used for several traditional types of European cookies and are fun for children. They can be used with many different sorts of doughs and there are a number of different versions available, from inexpensive plastic models to professional-quality metal presses with dozens of different discs. If you do decide to try it, don't feel you have to buy the most expensive model—purchase one that is modestly priced and upgrade in the future if you find you are getting a lot of use out of it. **$$**

WOODEN COOKIE PRESSES OR MOULDS Many traditional European cookies, such as Scottish shortbread and German springerle cookies, are beautifully formed in ornately carved wooden moulds. The raw dough is pressed into the moulds, then turned out, sometimes after a brief chilling, and baked. Although the old-fashioned designs are still available, this tradition has led to many new designs and to the use of moulds for all sorts of cookie doughs. The best moulds are expensive, as they are hand-carved, but will last a lifetime and even become heirlooms. Also available is a variation on the flat mould, in the form of a rolling cylinder, much like a stamped, carved rolling pin, which creates its design on the dough as it rolls over it. These pretty moulds also make lovely gifts, either alone or with the cookies they shape! **$$$**

CERAMIC SHORTBREAD MOULDS These beautiful, unglazed ceramic or stoneware forms can be used in several ways. The raw shortbread dough can be pressed into the form, chilled and turned out, then baked on a baking sheet; or the dough can be baked directly in the moulds. They come in various sizes and shapes, from a 6- or 8-inch round, marked with the traditional thistle design, to individual squares and rounds stamped with everything from Santa Claus to dreidels and menorahs for Hanukkah. I have found these wonderful for holiday shortbread and like the way the dough bakes in the ceramic. Read the instructions carefully, as some types recommend reducing or increasing the oven temperature slightly; in addition, some are ovenproof, some are not. **$$**

Porcelain and Ceramic Baking Dishes and Moulds

COEUR À LA CRÈME MOULDS Made of glazed white porcelain, these come in several sizes, from small individual portion moulds to larger 6- or 7-inch moulds that yield enough for about six people. The moulds are heart-shaped, with perforated bottoms, and are designed to make one special dessert called Coeur à la Crème. A soft, lightly sweetened fresh cheese is pressed into the moulds, which have been lined with several layers of dampened cheesecloth, and is left to drain, usually overnight. The whey drains away, leaving a sweet, firm, cream-cheese-like dessert often served with a fresh raspberry coulis. The moulds are not expensive, and the dessert is a cinch to prepare not to mention wonderful to eat! Look for a recipe in a good classic French cookbook. **$**

GRATIN DISHES AND CERAMIC BAKING DISHES These come in virtually every size and shape, and are the perfect vessels for baking sweet and savoury gratins, as well as all manner of fruit crisps, cobblers, bettys, crumbles and buckles. They are shallow, to allow for maximum browning and crust; gratin dishes are distinguished by their gently sloping sides, which expose as much of the filling as possible to the heat, and their two handles; larger baking dishes look like shallow casseroles. All should be made of porcelain-enamelled cast iron, or good-quality glazed earthenware, and have unglazed bottoms to allow the heat to penetrate and bake the products evenly. Although you can buy very inexpensive dishes of this sort, I was surprised to find that, in general, the more expensive the dish, the better it performs, with the best, usually from France, heating the most evenly and cleaning the most easily. To start, choose one 12-inch oval dish and four or six small, individual gratin dishes. **$$ or $$$**

PORCELAIN SOUFFLÉ DISH These straight-sided round white dishes are available in capacities of 1, 1½ and 2 quarts and are the traditional vessels for hot soufflés, as well as parfaits or frozen soufflés. They must have completely smooth interiors, so that nothing will prevent the soufflé from climbing as high as possible. Although soufflés can be made in other dishes, the true soufflé dish is slightly shorter than it is wide to allow the centre of the soufflé to remain soft and moist. These versatile dishes can also be used to bake some cakes and breads, and come in handy for decoratively holding frozen desserts and large quantities of mousses or puddings. **$$**

RAMEKINS OR INDIVIDUAL SOUFFLÉ DISHES The best are made of good-quality porcelain and are often from France. They are not expensive and can be used for crème caramel, custards, pots de crème, mousses, puddings, even cakes and other individual baked goods. For single-serving soufflés, make sure the dishes are straight-sided; for other desserts, ramekins with slightly sloping sides are fine. **$**

CERAMIC QUICHE OR TART PAN Made of white ovenproof porcelain, this fluted pan is the traditional dish for preparing quiche, but can be used for other open-faced tarts, as a gratin dish or as a dish for fruit crumbles and other baked fruit dishes. The bottom of the pan is unglazed, to allow the bottom crust of even thick or dense tarts to bake thoroughly. These pans are not expensive and are wonderfully versatile, as well as attractive. Ceramic tartlette dishes are also available, great for individual fruit gratins. **$**

Baking Pans

Regardless of the sort of pan, try to use what the recipe specifies. Many recipes might require time and temperature adjustments to work with pans of other sizes and materials. Baking pans are measured across the top, not the bottom, from one inside edge to the other. Fluted baking moulds, such as brioche moulds or tart tins, are measured from the inside edge of one outer curve to the inside edge of the curve directly facing it. To substitute one pan for another, consult the Baking Pan Substitution Chart on page 41, taking care to use a pan of the same material, with the same volume capacity and similar depth.

In terms of materials, heavier is always preferable, as it retains the heat better and won't buckle or warp in the oven. Some materials conduct heat, others reflect it—each of these properties will affect your product differently. In general, shiny or pale materials reflect heat and will produce tender, delicately crusted and lighter-coloured pastries. Dark, non-stick or glass bakeware will produce a thicker, crisper, darker crust, as they tend to retain heat, not reflect it. I like to reserve these materials for products like fruit pies, where the extra crispness prevents the crust from becoming soggy, and prefer to bake delicate-crumbed cakes and sweet-pastry-crusted tarts in lighter, shinier pans. Ceramic pie plates and bakeware are good for crustless fruit pies, crumbles, crisps and other baked fruit desserts, as they are slow to heat and prevent the fillings from scorching. Experiment, by all means—sometimes the most appropriate pan for the job is a highly personal choice and will vary from baker to baker, from recipe to recipe. You may find you need to reduce the oven temperature by 25 degrees when using a dark, non-stick or glass pan when another is specified. Baking pan materials include heavy-gauge aluminum, cast iron, ovenproof glass, stainless steel, carbon steel and ceramic.

A word about non-stick bakeware: true, your baked goods won't stick to these pans. But there ends their merits. Non-stick pans are generally very dark compared to aluminum or stainless steel and do not reflect heat. This means your products will bake faster on the bottom and sides, perhaps burning by the time the middle is done. (Fortunately, your pan is non-stick, so prying the charred cake from the bottom will be relatively easy …) I prefer conventional bakeware to the non-stick type, but if you do use the dark non-stick pans, reduce the oven temperature by 25 degrees to prevent or at least minimize the over-darkening and keep a close eye on the baking.

There is a new type of non-stick bakeware on the market now that has a semi-shiny, lighter, silvery finish than the standard non-stick pans. Not only do they perform much more like traditional materials, but they do not scratch as easily as the dark-finished pans. I have had good luck with these, even without reducing the oven temperature. The crust is still darker than with shiny pans, but not nearly as thick or dark as with conventional non-stick surfaces. I still recommend aluminum, tinned steel or glass over any form of non-stick—any good-quality pan, if properly prepared (greased and possibly floured), should release its correctly baked contents easily. If you are addicted to non-stick, though, and can't quit cold turkey, or if the pan you are looking for is simply not available in any other material, buy the lighter-coloured non-stick pans.

Dark-finished non-stick pans must be treated carefully, as their surface is actually a coating on the metal that can be scratched off by any metal implements or even scrubbed off if scoured or washed when hot. Use only plastic or wooden utensils and allow the pans to cool completely before washing. Lighter-coloured non-stick pans are much more durable, as the finish is part of the material of the pan, not simply a coating. With all bakeware, but especially aluminum pans, make sure all pans are thoroughly washed and completely dried before storing.

Baking Sheets

COOKIE SHEETS When choosing cookie sheets, also called baking sheets, make sure the sheets are at least 1⁄16 inch thick, to ensure they don't buckle in a hot oven. Sheets with only three raised sides (no more than 1⁄2 inch high) are great for sliding cookies and pastries smoothly onto cooling racks. For cookie sheets in particular, avoid dark non-stick finishes, as the added heat retention can do nasty things to cookies, over-darkening the bottoms before the insides have baked properly. The newer *insulated cookie sheets* have just the opposite effect, producing cookies that may be underbaked and doughy. They are fine for some soft, cakey cookies, but shouldn't be used for crisp cookies. For most purposes, medium- to heavy-gauge aluminum is best, and is inexpensive. A minimum of two large (14 x 16-inch) and one or two small (10 x 13-inch) is essential, but cookie sheets are some of those things I never seem to have too many of—having at least four is great when baking large batches: two can be in the oven while the other two are cooling and being re-stocked. **$ to $$**

JELLY ROLL PAN Also called a *sheet pan*, this versatile pan can double as a cookie sheet, as well as being the traditional pan for making sheet and roll cakes. Choose seamless, heavy-gauge aluminum pans that are of a durable thickness and weight, and have at least 1-inch sides. 10½ x 15½-inch and 11 x 17-inch are the sizes commonly found in kitchenware shops and department stores, but I recommend buying your sheet pans from restaurant supply stores. The size you will likely find there is about 12 x 18 inches, slightly bigger than the conventional pans, but not so much that your baking will be affected. Simply shorten the baking time of sheet cakes by a few minutes. I recommend one of the 10½-inch pans, as well as one of the professional 12 x 18-inch pans. Nice to Have: several of each for baking cookies, large galettes and pastries. **$$**

Cake Pans

LAYER CAKE PANS Most recipes call for pans 8 or 9 inches in diameter, but they are also available in larger and smaller sizes from baking supply stores. Make sure the pans you choose have sides at least 2½ inches high (while most layer cakes will not reach this height, it makes the pans very versatile, able to be used for single-layer cakes, tortes, even crostatas). Choose pans with no seams on the inside and a good, heavy feel to them. Aluminum is the very best material, but these pans are also available in stainless steel and non-stick (look for the light-coloured finish). Also available are layer cake pans with removable bottoms, good for heavy tortes and other dense cakes, or those you do not want to invert, such as some fruit-topped cakes. These are handy, but not essential, as springform pans serve the same purpose. Two pans are essential, but I recommend buying three; they are not expensive, and some elaborate recipes have three layers. Nice to Have: additional pans of various sizes, larger and smaller, for versatility. **$$**

SPRINGFORM PANS These are round pans with a spring-loaded hinge on the side, which releases the sides of the pan, leaving the contents resting simply on the bottom. Cakes that cannot be inverted, such as cheesecakes and some fruit-topped cakes, are usually baked in springform pans. These pans are often sold in sets of three, in small, medium and large sizes, but the best-quality pans are usually sold individually. The most commonly used size is 9 inches in diameter, with sides of about 2½ to 3 inches, and will do for most tortes and cheesecakes. Springform pans are available with a non-stick finish, but heavy-gauge tinned steel is preferable. **$$**

SQUARE BAKING PAN Choose a metal pan, either aluminum or light-coloured non-stick, and make sure there are no seams on the inside of the pan. For brownies and other bar cookies and simple cakes, an 8- or 9-inch square metal pan with 2-inch-high sides is essential, but a glass version comes in handy for small batches of fruit desserts. **$**

RECTANGULAR BAKING PAN The classic rectangular baking pan is 9 x 13 x 2 inches and is available in both glass and aluminum. I recommend getting one of each—an aluminum pan for brownies and other large recipes for bar cookies, snack cakes and gingerbreads; and a glass pan for large fruit crumbles and other fruit desserts, as well as baked custards and bread puddings. **$$**

TUBE PAN, ANGEL FOOD CAKE PAN Easily recognized by their high centre tube and squared-off bottom, these round pans come in a variety of sizes; one of 10 inches in diameter is a good all-purpose size. Shiny aluminum is my preference, as it keeps the crust of the cake soft and light, but it is becoming difficult to find these outside cake decorating and baking supply stores. The current trend seems to be for non-stick tube pans, but these can drastically over-darken delicate products like angel food cake; the new light-coloured non-stick finish is preferable. Look for a tube pan that has three little "feet" that stand an inch or two off its rim—these are extremely useful for cooling the cake in its pan. If the pan doesn't have feet, make sure the hole in the tube is large enough to accommodate the neck of a wine bottle (simply place the pan on the bottle neck to cool). **$$**

BUNDT PAN OR FLUTED TUBE PAN Both of these pans are shaped like tube pans, with a tall centre tube, but are decoratively fluted around the edges. The Bundt pan is used for traditional Austrian, German and Alsatian cakes and sweet breads, but can be used for many other types of cakes. Fluted tube pans, sometimes referred to as a Kugelhopf mould, are generally shallower than the deep Bundt pans, with a simpler design. Both are available in several materials; I have not been able to find fluted tube pans in any other form than non-stick for years, but I have had good results with the light-coloured pans. The best Bundt pans come from France or Germany, and are made of very heavy aluminum or cast iron. Look for them in baking supply stores and specialty kitchenware shops. Unless you bake a lot of formed cakes, coffee cakes or sweet yeast breads, a 9- or 10-inch size of one or the other of these pans will do for most recipes. **$$ or $$$**

KUGELHOPF OR KUGELHOPF PAN Very similar to a Bundt pan, this deep round tube pan has ornate fluting and a distinctive rounded pyramid shape when inverted. It is widely used in Austria, Germany, Poland and France to bake the traditional Kugelhopf, a sweet, yeast-risen cake studded with raisins, nuts and candied fruit. I use mine all the time in place of a fluted tube or Bundt pan for its beautiful design. It is very important, though, to be militant about preparing this pan before adding a batter—every groove must be thoroughly buttered and floured to make sure the cake will unmould cleanly. Try to find a heavy, solid tinned-steel pan; they're not cheap, but are worth it. **$$$**

MUFFIN PANS These are metal tins for baking cupcakes, muffins and other small cakes. They are available in three standard sizes: mini-muffin tins usually come in sheets of 6 or 12, with a capacity of about 1½ tablespoons; regular-sized muffin tins are most commonly sold in trays of 12 and have about ½-cup capacity; large or jumbo muffin tins are usually sold 6 to a tray, with a 1-cup capacity. Aluminum is best, but the light-coloured non-stick trays make unmoulding the cakes simple and clean. I usually bake muffins in a large 6-muffin tray, because the muffins are such a satisfying size. Most standard muffin recipes call for 12 regular-sized tins, but will also fill 6 large cups or 24 mini cups, but the baking time will need to be adjusted. I usually increase the baking time by 10 to 15 minutes for my large muffins and reduce it by at least 10 minutes for mini muffins. I recommend one tray each of the regular and large sizes. Nice to Have: two 12-muffin mini-muffin trays, for little cakes, deep-dish bite-sized tartlettes and tea-party treats. **$**

LOAF PANS Loaf pans are measured across the top, from inside edge to inside edge. Darker loaf pans are good for crusty yeast breads, but can overdarken sweet and quick breads. I prefer aluminum to glass or non-stick surfaces, but the choice is personal. For certain yeast-raised breads, I love the crust that a clay or crockery loaf pan produces. Mini loaf pans in various sizes are inexpensive and widely available, and are great fun for making individual muffins, cakes, sweet breads, and for gifts. I recommend at least one each of 9 x 5 x 3 inches (often 9¼ x 5¼ x 3) and 8½ x 4½ x 2¾ inches, in aluminum or a good light-coloured non-stick material. Nice to Have: an additional pan of each of the larger sizes and several mini pans. **$$**

Specialty Baking Pans and Moulds

MINI CAKE PANS Small, plain, ¾- to 1-cup (6- to 8-ounce) aluminum moulds are ideal for individual cakes and small baked goods. Available in many cooking and baking supply stores, they are inexpensive and turn out beautiful cakes. Mini Bundt and tube pans are also available, often in connected sheets of 4 or 6, and are usually non-stick. None of these is absolutely essential, but great fun. **$$**

BABA MOULDS These are straight-sided round bucket-shaped moulds about 1½ to 3 inches in diameter and 1½ to 4 inches in height and are designed for the classic yeast-raised sweet cakes called babas. Available in specialty shops, the best moulds are made of aluminum, but stainless steel moulds are also available. For the best quality, look for pans made in France. These moulds are not essential, unless you make this type of dessert frequently, but I find them very useful as forms for other sorts of desserts, such as individual parfaits, mousses and even ice cream. **$$**

STEAMED PUDDING MOULDS These high, round, often decoratively fluted metal moulds usually have a centre tube and a watertight lid that clamps securely to the sides. The batter is poured into the mould, which is then covered and placed in a pan of water and then into a slow oven. The batter steams inside the mould, and the resulting cake is dense, moist, chewy and beautifully shaped when it is turned out. Seek out these moulds at specialty kitchenware shops, as well as antique markets. Obviously, not an essential piece of equipment for every baker, but well worth having if you like the traditional steamed pudding. **$$ to $$$**

MADELEINE MOULDS These beautifully scalloped shell-shaped moulds are designed for the traditional sponge cake biscuits called madeleines. I have also used them to make other formed cookies, such as shortbread, as well as tiny muffins and petits fours. They are available in trays of 12 standard-sized tins or 24 mini-madeleine tins. Choose heavy-duty trays, ideally made of tinned steel or aluminum. Non-stick trays seem attractive, but if the plain metal pans are properly buttered and floured, and the cookies well baked, the madeleines should unmould cleanly, without having the thick, overbaked crust you get with non-stick pans. These pans are not essential, but are more versatile than you might think initially, and madeleines are divine and easy to make! **$$ to $$$**

CHARLOTTE MOULD This round tinned steel mould shaped like a straight-sided bucket is used for the various classic desserts that fall under the name charlotte. For these, the moulds are usually lined with bread, cake or sponge fingers, then filled with a mixture of fruit, like a pie, or with a mousse or gelatine-and-cream mixture. Charlotte moulds are available in a range of sizes, from individual 6-ounce moulds to 1, 1½, 2 and even 3 quarts. I find a mould of about 6 inches in diameter across the top, with a capacity of 1½ quarts, serves well for most recipes. Although these moulds are rare in North America, they are sometimes available from specialty kitchenware stores and mail-order companies. If you cannot find one, an Italian *pannetone mould* of a similar size can be substituted. Don't buy one that is not made of heavy tinned steel; the best are from France and will last a lifetime, but cheaper versions from China and Portugal may be easier to find. **$$**

BRIOCHE MOULDS These deep, beautifully fluted round moulds are best made of tinned steel and are designed for baking the traditional French knot-shaped brioche loaf. They are surprisingly available in North America and come in many sizes; the tiny ones are lovely for small cakes, muffins and individual sweet breads, and the larger ones make spectacular brioche and other sweet loaves. One or two 8-inch moulds will do for most brioche recipes. Although none of these is essential, I use my little brioche moulds for everything from shortbread, to tarts, to muffins and cakes, even jellies. (As with other small pans, don't buy fewer than 6 or 8, so you can make an entire recipe.) **$$**

GELATINE MOULDS These may be made of tinned steel, anodized aluminum or even copper and may be as plain as a simple domed melon shape or elaborately indented with beautiful designs. They are meant for sweet and savoury gelatins, but can double as ice cream moulds and forms for semi-solid mousses and bavarians. The best of these are rarely found in North American kitchenware stores, but some specialty shops sell a few. Do some research, and ask the shop owner for advice on the various materials and shapes. **$** to **$$$**, depending on your budget, and passion for gelatine desserts.

RING MOULDS OR ROUNDED TUBE PANS Like Bundt and fluted tube pans, these ring-shaped cake pans have a centre hole to allow the interior of the cake to bake at the same rate as the exterior. Shallower than Bundt or angel food cake pans, they are often used for coffee cakes and other plain cakes and may be made of aluminum or non-stick material. I prefer aluminum, as it encourages a more delicate crust, but the newer light-coloured non-stick finishes are fine if aluminum is not available. See the section below on the savarin mould for other uses for ring moulds. A 9- or 10-inch pan should do for most recipes. **$$**

SAVARIN MOULDS A savarin mould is basically a ring mould with an extra-large hole in its centre. Most commonly made of aluminum or tinned steel, savarin moulds come in many sizes, from 3- or 4-inch individual moulds to standard versions of 6, 8 or 10 inches. Specifically meant for the classical French dessert for which they are named (a light, yeast-risen sweet cake soaked with a spiked syrup, much like a Baba au Rhum), the moulds can be used for many other cake and quick-bread batters and can double as forms for ice creams, mousses and jellies. **$$**

Pie and Tart Pans

GLASS PIE PLATES An excellent medium for most pies, glass produces a crisp, golden crust. One 9-inch durable ovenproof glass plate is essential, and will serve for most pies. I recommend buying at least two, even three, especially if you are to come into a bushel of perfect cooking apples or if you've been elected to bake the blueberry pies for the family picnic. Nice to Have: a 10-inch deep-dish plate for specialty pies. **$**

CERAMIC PIE PLATES I love these heavy glazed plates for baking, as they are un-equalled in their ability to retain heat and bake evenly. They often have lovely fluted edges, making crimping and decorating your pies unnecessary. Make sure the bottoms are unglazed, and the pans are of a standard size. Not essential, but definitely a favourite piece of any pie baker's arsenal. **$$**

METAL PIE PLATES Darkened metal pans can be used for most pies, but shiny aluminum or stainless steel plates should be avoided, as they reflect heat, producing an inferior pie with a soggy and underbaked crust. If you do use a metal plate in a recipe that calls for one made of glass, you may need to increase the oven temperature by 25 degrees to compensate for any heat reflection. Nonstick pie plates are totally unnecessary. If you have several glass plates, metal ones are not essential, but one or two 9-inch metal plates can supplement your collection. **$** to **$$**

FLUTED TART PAN WITH REMOVABLE BOTTOM This classic pan for French and European tarts, and even some cakes, allows the baked product to be carefully unmoulded. Most are made of tinned steel, and should feel heavy and strong. One round 9½ or 10-inch pan is essential, and the standard size for most sweet tarts. Nice to Have: one round 11-inch pan, and some smaller, deeper round tins (6 or 8 inches in diameter, 2 inches deep) for savoury quiches and tarts. Square (9-inch) and rectangular (8 x 12 or 4 x 14-inch) tart tins with removable bottoms are also available and make beautiful and unusual desserts. **$$**

ROUND TARTLETTE PANS Designed to make individual tarts, or tartlettes, these are fluted tart pans with removable bottoms about 4 to 4½ inches in diameter. They should be made of durable tinned steel, but some good-quality non-stick tins are available. Buy at least 6, as this is usually the number used to replace one large tart recipe. These are not absolutely essential, but are lovely for specialty tarts, as well as individual cakes and muffins. **$**

SPECIALTY TARTLETTE PANS Plain or fluted boat-shaped tins, often called *barquettes*, are only one example of the many specialty tins—round, rectangular, trapezoid, even triangular—that are available for making decorative tartlettes, both sweet and savoury. The best are made of tinned steel and from France, but you can sometimes find good-quality tins from China or Portugal. Buy at least 6, or even 12, especially if the tins are very small, as one recipe of pastry and filling will fill at least that many. **$$**

FLAN OR TART RINGS Made of tinned steel and sometimes coated with a non-stick finish, these look like cookie cutters with reinforced sides. They are available in many shapes and sizes, from tiny tart circles to large rounds or rectangles, and are used directly on a baking sheet to form the container for tarts and other pastries. They are used extensively in many professional kitchens and bakeries, but are surprisingly expensive and may be difficult to find. As they are not fluted like most tart tins, they make distinctive-looking tarts and are fun to use, but are definitely not necessary for most home bakers. **$$**

BAKING PAN SUBSTITUTION CHART

WHENEVER POSSIBLE, try to use the size and type of pan specified in the recipe. The recipe has been formulated and timed for a pan with a very particular depth, shape and dimensions. But use the chart below to find an acceptable alternative. Substitute a pan with the same volume as the original, and of similar depth (or within half an inch of the suggested pan). With some substitutions, the baking time may have to be adjusted: decreased for shallower pans, extended for deeper ones. To find the volume of a given pan, fill it with water, then carefully pour the water into a measuring cup. The volumes given below are for level capacities of all pans.

DIMENSIONS OF PAN (sides by depth, in inches)	SHAPE	VOLUME
1¾ x ¾	mini muffin cup	2 tablespoons, ⅛ cup
2¾ x 1⅛	shallow muffin cup	4 tablespoons, ¼ cup
2¾ x 1⅜	standard muffin cup	scant ½ cup
2¼ x 4 x 1¼	mini loaf pan	⅔ cup
3 x 1¼	large (jumbo) muffin cup	⅝ cup to 1 scant cup
8 x 1¼	pie plate	3 cups, ¾ quart
6 x 2	round cake pan	3¾ cups
8 x 1½	pie plate	4 cups, 1 quart
9 x 1¼	pie plate	4 cups, 1 quart
9½ x 1½	round fluted ceramic tart pan	4 cups, 1 quart

continued on page 42

8 x 1½	round cake pan	4 cups, 1 quart
6 x 3	springform pan	4 cups, 1 quart
8½ x 2¼	tube pan	4½ cups, 1⅛ quarts
9 x 1½	pie plate	5 cups, 1¼ quarts
7 x 2½	springform pan	5½ cups
6½ x 3½	Bundt pan	5½ cups
8 x 2	round cake pan	6 cups, 1½ quarts
9 x 1½	round cake pan	6 cups, 1½ quarts
8 x 8 x 1½	square cake pan	6 cups, 1½ quarts
7 x 11 x 2	rectangular baking pan	6 cups, 1½ quarts
7½ x 3	tube pan	6 cups, 1½ quarts
7½ x 3	Bundt pan	6 cups, 1½ quarts
8½ x 4½ x 2½	loaf pan	6 cups, 1½ quarts
10 x 1½	pie plate	6½ cups
9½ x 2	deep dish glass pie plate	7 cups, 1¾ quarts
8½ x 3½	Bundt pan	7 cups, 1¾ quarts
11 x 2	oval ceramic baking dish	7 cups, 1¾ quarts
8½ x 2½	springform pan	7½ cups
9 x 2¾	ring mould (Savarin mould)	7½ cups
9 x 2	round cake pan	8 cups, 2 quarts
9¼ x 2¾	tube pan (wide funnel)	8 cups, 2 quarts
9½ x 3	tube pan (narrow funnel)	8 cups, 2 quarts
8 x 8 x 2	square cake pan	8 cups, 2 quarts
9 x 9 x 1½	square cake pan	8 cups, 2 quarts
9 x 5 x 3	loaf pan	8 cups, 2 quarts
9 x 3	Bundt pan	9 cups, 2¼ quarts
9½ x 2½	springform pan	9 cups, 2¼ quarts
8 x 3 to 3¼	tube pan	9 cups, 2¼ quarts
8½ x 3½	fluted tube (Kugelhopf) pan	9 cups, 2¼ quarts
9 x 9 x 2	square cake pan	10 cups, 2½ quarts
8 x 3	springform pan	10 cups, 2½ quarts
9½ x 2½	springform pan	10 cups, 2½ quarts
11¾ x 7½ x 1¾	rectangular baking dish	10 cups, 2½ quarts
13 x 8 x 2¾	oval ceramic baking dish	11 cups, 2¾ quarts
9 x 3	springform pan	11 cups, 2¾ quarts

10 x 2	round cake pan	11 cups, 2¾ quarts
10 x 3½	Bundt pan	12 cups, 3 quarts
9½ x 3	tube pan (extra-wide funnel)	12 cups, 3 quarts
9 x 13 x 2	rectangular baking pan	12 cups, 3 quarts
10 x 2½	springform pan	12 cups, 3 quarts
13 x 9 x 3	rectangular baking pan	14 cups, 3½ quarts
10 x 4	tube pan	16 cups, 4 quarts

A Few Tips
and Techniques for
Better Baking

Preparing to Bake

READ THE ENTIRE RECIPE at least once before beginning to bake! Make sure you understand all techniques, have the right equipment and are familiar with the ingredients. Have all the ingredients properly measured and at hand, and any equipment you will need to complete the recipe clean and dry. Fumbling at the last minute to grease a pan or find the baking powder can take just enough time to ruin some sensitive recipes. Clear your workspace of all unnecessary packages, canisters and equipment. I always keep a clean, damp towel close by to wipe sticky fingers and gooey counters. You certainly don't have to be a fanatically neat baker, but a clear workspace and a lack of extraneous clutter will prevent a huge percentage of baking disasters right off the bat! Follow the recipe as it is written, in the given order, at least the first few times you try it. Skipping ahead, or juggling the quantity or type of ingredients, can ruin the delicate and very exact formula for many desserts and pastries.

Preparing Baking Pans

Before starting to mix ingredients, prepare your pans and preheat your oven. Always begin with cool, dry baking pans; if you are baking in relays, as is often the case when baking several batches of cookies, cool the hot sheets under cold running water then dry well before continuing. Pans may be greased with either butter, vegetable shortening or a good all-vegetable non-stick cooking spray, depending on the recipe. For delicately flavoured products such as madeleines, fine cakes and cookies, only unsalted butter should be used. Make sure the butter is at room temperature and use a small pastry brush to lightly coat the entire interior surface of the pan. You can use butter to grease most pans, but for products that are baked at very high temperatures, or endure long baking times, solid vegetable shortening or all-vegetable non-stick cooking spray may be preferable, as they are less likely to scorch or burn. I was very reluctant to try the non-stick cooking sprays, but once I did, I was pleasantly surprised. For long-baked cakes, such as heavy fruitcakes, and quick breads baked in small moulds, such as muffins, these sprays are quite good, saving the baker not only the time of laboriously greasing every nook and cranny in the tins, but also the expense of the excess butter wasted in the process. Read the label—buy only all-natural sprays and follow the directions before using. A word of caution: cooking sprays can sometimes leave a sticky film on dark non-stick pans that is difficult to wash away. If possible, avoid using these types of sprays with dark non-stick bakeware; the lighter coloured non-stick pans don't seem to be affected.

In addition to greasing, some recipes call for the pans to be floured or sugared. Coating the greased interior of a pan with a fine layer of flour is added insurance against sticking and gives cakes a slightly thicker, more coloured crust. When flouring greased pans, always use all-purpose white wheat flour, even if the flour in the recipe is of a different sort. All-purpose gives the best coating: fine and even, not clumping and thick. Add a small amount of flour to the pan and shake it about, turning the pan so the bottom and sides are completely covered. Invert the pan over another pan or a sheet of parchment paper and tap out the excess flour (the extra flour can be reused). Sugaring a greased pan gives the cake or bread a sweet, crunchy golden crust. Sugar pans in exactly the same way you would flour them, again tapping out the excess. White granulated sugar is most commonly used, but the recipe should specify a type of sugar.

If the recipe calls for a greased or greased and floured pan to then be lined with a paper liner, cut a sheet of parchment paper in the dimensions specified and press it into the pan. For round pans, use round liners that fit into the bottom of the pan (use the bottom of the pan as a stencil to trace out a customized shape, then trim to fit). For square and rectangular pans, I like to cut a sheet of parchment to fit the width of the pan, but overhang the two long edges by an inch or so. This overhang makes it easy to unmould the product after is it baked. Some recipes call for the paper to be greased as well. In cases where a paper liner is recommended, wait until the paper is in the pan before flouring the pan.

Measuring

Just as everyone thinks they have a good sense of humour, every baker thinks they can measure properly. And some people would be wrong, on at least one count. In baking, more things go wrong as a result of inaccurate measuring than probably any other reason. Different ingredients must be measured different ways, and even a slight imprecision can sometimes drastically alter the outcome of the final product. The following tips will help you achieve perfectly accurate measurements:

❖ Regardless of whether you are working in metric or imperial measurements, the key is to stick with one or the other all the way through a recipe. Equivalents are merely rough approximations, and flipping back and forth between the two will cause more than a few problems.

❖ Liquid ingredients should be measured in glass liquid measuring cups with accurate markings. Rest the measure on a flat surface and let the liquid inside stop swishing around before gauging what level it is at. Use the smallest measure you can that will hold the desired amount; larger measuring cups can become inaccurate when filled less than ¼ full.

❖ Dry ingredients should be measured in cups specifically meant for dry goods, preferably made of stainless steel. The cups should have perfectly straight rims, so ingredients can be levelled off with a straight edge.

❖ Very small quantities of both liquid and dry ingredients can be measured in sturdy stainless steel measuring spoons.

❖ Take careful note of how the measurements are worded in the recipe. "1 cup sifted confectioners' sugar" means 1 cup of confectioners' sugar that has already been sifted before you measure it. "1 cup confectioners' sugar, sifted," however, means you should measure out 1 cup of confectioners' sugar, then sift it before using it in the recipe. The difference is significant. The same convention applies to any chopped, ground, sliced, grated or otherwise treated ingredient.

❖ Measure flours by lightly spooning them into the measure until it is heaped, then sweeping a straight edge, such as the side of a metal spatula or a metal ruler, across the top, levelling off the mound. (Do this anywhere but over the mixing bowl! The excess flour can be reused if you do it over a sheet of parchment or waxed paper.) Do not use the measure as a scoop, as this can pack the flour into the cup and give you more than you need. Shaking the measure, tamping the flour down or rapping the cup on the counter also only serve to pack the flour, resulting in an inaccurate reading.

❖ To measure granulated and other free-flowing sugars, as well as cornmeal, oats, nuts and seeds, use the dry measuring cup as a scoop, mounding the sugar, then level it off.

❖ Always tightly pack brown and raw sugars into a dry measure. Keeping them in the original plastic bags allows me to scoop the sugar directly from the bag, then use one hand on the outside of the bag to firmly press the sugar into the cup. Otherwise, use the back of a tablespoon to pack the sugar in.

❖ Chopped or sliced fresh fruits can be measured in liquid or dry measuring cups, depending on the amount. Dried fruits should be measured in dry measuring cups, and packed down to get an accurate amount.

❖ Liquid sweeteners such as honey, corn syrup, molasses and other sticky syrups can be easily measured by lightly greasing the liquid measure with vegetable oil first. The syrups slide out beautifully, giving you an accurate amount and a very unsticky measuring cup. (My grandmother taught me this.)

❖ Butter and other solid shortenings can be measured in several ways. All solid shortenings, chilled or softened, can be measured using an ingredients scale, by converting volume measurements, such as cups and tablespoons, to weight measurements, such as ounces and pounds. Softened butter or shortening can be packed tightly into dry measuring cups and levelled off with a straight edge. Firm or chilled solid shortenings can be measured accurately by suspending them in a large glass liquid measuring cup partly filled with cold water. (My grandmother taught me this too. She also taught me to always remember to clean the very tips of wooden spoons—you'd be surprised how often you forget this.) If the recipe calls for ½ cup cold butter, pour 1 cup water into the measuring cup, then add shortening or butter until the water level reaches 1½ cups.

❖ If a recipe calls for a weight rather than volume measurement, such as 6 ounces chocolate, use an accurate scale or reliably portioned ingredients. Chocolate can be purchased in 1-ounce squares, but most of the best varieties come in blocks of various amounts—a small kitchen scale is an excellent investment.

Sifting

Although most all-purpose flour sold in North America has been pre-sifted, it tends to settle and pack with time, and should be stirred in its bag or canister before it is measured out. Do not, however, sift all-purpose flour before measuring. Cake flour and confectioners' sugar should always be sifted before using; some recipes call for a quantity pre-sifted ("1 cup sifted cake flour"), others specify an unsifted amount ("1 cup cake flour, sifted") and require it to be sifted after measuring.

Get into the habit of sifting easily clumping powders such as cornstarch, cocoa powder, baking powder and baking soda before adding these to mixtures that will not be sifted later. I find this helps to ensure an even distribution and a mixture free of lumps. When cornstarch, flour or other starch is used to thicken pie or tart fillings, sift it into the fruit mixture or stir it into the sugar to make sure any lumps are broken up.

Use a wire mesh sieve, or a flour sifter, and read the recipe carefully to make sure you are sifting at the appropriate point!

Creaming

The aim when creaming two ingredients together, such as butter and sugar, is to create a soft, evenly blended, malleable mixture while incorporating air. The grains of sugar trap air that becomes suspended in the fat molecules of the butter. This air will later serve to aid in leavening the product, be that a cake, cookies or even the crust for bar cookies. Several factors can help ensure maximum aeration and a smooth, creamy mixture. Always make sure that your butter is at room temperature—no warmer, no colder. Butter that is overly soft is oily and will not retain much air as its structure has begun to break down. The resulting product will be too dense and heavy, and likely have a greasy feel due to the poorly distributed fat molecules. Butter that is too cold is too firm to cream and will neither blend nor aerate. Creaming can be done by hand with a wooden spoon, or with a stand mixer using the paddle attachment. Place the butter in a large bowl and begin by beating the butter until it is smooth. Add the sugar. If creaming by hand, use the flat side of the wooden spoon to smear the butter and sugar together in broad, smooth strokes, using a vertical circular motion somewhat similar to whipping. This will spread the mixture over the bottom and up one side of the bowl, incorporating air into the mixture with each stroke. Using the paddle attachment of the stand mixer on medium or medium-high speed will achieve a similar effect. The mixture is well creamed when it is a pale yellow and light and fluffy, almost whipped, in texture.

Folding

Folding is a process of gently mixing a batter, or incorporating ingredients into a batter in such a way as to not deflate any air suspended in either mixture. Nuts, fruit and pieces of chocolate are often folded into cake and quick bread batters just before baking; whipped egg whites and whipped cream are folded into batters and custards; and flour is folded into whipped egg mixtures. This can be done with a large rubber spatula, a large, broad spoon, or even the flattened palm of your hand. In every case, it is a smooth, gentle motion: start with the spatula or spoon flat against the bowl's nearest inside edge. Sweep the flat side of the utensil down through the centre of the mixture, bringing it up on the opposite side of the bowl and literally fold the batter over onto itself to one side. Turn the bowl about ¼ turn, and repeat the same motion until the two elements are just combined. It sounds much more complicated than it is—just keep in mind that you want to blend the mixture thoroughly and gently, in as few broad strokes as possible.

Citrus Tips

The coloured part of the rind or peel of citrus fruits is called the *zest*. As it contains the highly flavoured citrus oils, with none of the bitterness of the white pith that lies just underneath it, this zest is one of the most versatile and effective flavourings in the sweet kitchen. It can be finely grated and added to batters, doughs, custards, mousses, cakes, muffins, pie and tart doughs, ice creams, even compotes and sauces, as a delicate or potent flavouring; or pared off in wide strips or fine strands and caramelized or candied. Candied peel or zest (see recipe on page 634) can be used as an ingredient in much the same way as fresh zest and can also serve as a decoration or garnish.

If you wish to impart a particular citrus flavour to a dessert, look to zests. Most citrus juices will only give a very subtle flavour virtually undetectable in the presence of stronger flavours, but will add acidity, especially in the case of lemon juice. If a dessert needs a hit of acidity, add a few drops of lemon juice, but if it's the lemon flavour you're after, add some finely grated lemon zest.

Tools can make the difference between getting a nice clean zest and a bitter combination of zest and pith that will add an unpleasant edge to your baking. Vegetable peelers are potentially good, but make sure yours doesn't remove too much of the rind—many types take quite a thick strip off their victims and are inappropriate for zesting. A better tool by far is the zester, a hand-held implement with a little row of tiny holes with sharp edges that takes beautiful strips off just the top part of the rind. The finest holes on a box grater do an admirable job too, when finely grated zest is called for in a recipe—make sure you carefully scrape out the inside of the grater to get all of the bits.

If you're planning to use the zest of any citrus fruit, try to buy organic fruit, as the other kind has been subjected to a barrage of potentially harmful pesticides, wax and even dyes. When buying organic is impossible, wash the fruit thoroughly in warm running water with a mild dishwashing detergent or antibacterial hand soap and a vegetable scrub brush. It may sound extreme, but it is much healthier and may even mean the difference between a fresh lively fruit flavour and an unpleasant chemical one.

To get the maximum juice from a lemon, lime or other citrus fruit, use room temperature fruit or even fruit that has been submerged in warm water for a few minutes. Roll the whole fruit on a hard surface, pressing very firmly, then cut it in half across its middle and squeeze by hand or over a simple citrus juicer. The rolling crushes the membranes and starts the juice flowing inside the fruit, so it is softer and much easier to squeeze. And remember—if a recipe calls for both zest and juice, zest first! It's really hard to grate half a lemon!

Cutting and Chopping Fruit

FRESH FRUIT Make sure the knife you are using is made of stainless steel, not carbon steel. Carbon steel will react with the acid in citrus fruits and apples— the knife will discolour and the cut fruit may pick up an odd metallic flavour.

DRIED FRUIT Due to its very high sugar content, dried fruit tends to make a terrible mess of the knife as you chop, leaving it gummy, sticky and difficult to use. To avoid this, simply coat the blade with a mist of vegetable oil cooking spray (or brush it with a little vegetable oil)—it will glide cleanly and effortlessly through piles of prunes, dates, even apricots!

Testing Cakes for Doneness

There are three ways to judge the doneness of cakes: with a "cake tester" in the form of a wooden skewer, with the touch of your hand and by judging the appearance of the cake's surface. Cakes should be tested with wooden skewers, if possible; depending on the type of cake, these should come out clean or with a few crumbs clinging to them. Use your hand to lightly touch the top of the cake—some will be very springy, others dense and firm. Finally, look at the surface and edges of the cake: the top may be golden, shiny, smooth, cracked and/or risen; edges often begin to pull away from the sides of the pan when the cake is properly baked. The following are generally good gauges of doneness:

❖ Brownies, flourless chocolate cakes and other dense tortes and bars should be set in the centre, but often still a little shiny. A wooden skewer inserted near the centre should come out with a few moist crumbs clinging to it, and the edges of the cake should be just beginning to pull away from the sides. Some tortes should have large cracks on their surfaces.

❖ Sponge cakes should be risen and golden, with tops that spring back when lightly touched. A wooden skewer inserted in the centre should come out clean.

❖ Pound cakes should be firm and nicely coloured, and a skewer inserted in the centre should come out clean. The edges should be just beginning to come away from the sides of the pan.

❖ Angel food and chiffon cakes should be well risen and golden, often with a large cleft on their surfaces. A skewer inserted in the centre of the cake should come out clean, but the cake should still be moist, its surface springing back when lightly pressed.

Always keep in mind that the baking and cooking times given in most recipes are approximate and should not be adhered to religiously. Use them as rough guides, but always trust your own judgement when determining the doneness of cakes, pies and tarts, cookies and other desserts. The best recipes give not only time estimates, but other flags of doneness: a springy top and golden colouring, a crisp crust and bubbling juices, lightly coloured bottoms and still-soft tops. Use these as indicators of doneness perhaps more than any time suggestion. If after the 45 minutes given in the recipe, your pie still looks pale and you see no bubbling juices, bake it a little longer!

Unmoulding Cakes

Most cakes and quick breads should cool for between 5 and 15 minutes in their pans before they are turned out. Some denser cakes, tortes and brownies, however, should be left to cool completely in their pans—the recipe should tell you which is appropriate. To unmould a cake from its pan, run a thin-bladed sharp knife around the edges of the cake, keeping the knife perpendicular to the counter so you don't shave off little slices of the cake. Place a wire rack over the top of the pan and invert the cake onto the rack. If the cake is one that must be cooled right side up, place a sheet of parchment paper over a flat plate or cardboard cake circle and place this over the top of the cake pan. Turn the cake out onto the paper, then place a wire rack on the top (which is really the bottom) of the cake and invert it once more, setting it right side up again.

A TIP: If you forget to unmould a cake from its pan within a few minutes of baking, and it cools completely in a pan without a removable bottom or sides, there is a simple way to extricate it neatly from its pan. Pop the whole cake and pan into a preheated 325 to 350-degree oven for 3 to 5 minutes. Remove it, run a thin-bladed knife around the edges of the cake, then invert it onto a serving platter or cake circle.

Icing and Assembling Layer Cakes

Before you begin to assemble a layer cake, have all the tools you will want for decorating and frosting nearby: a dry pastry brush, a metal palette knife or offset spatula, a rubber spatula, a small bowl for portioning working batches of icing, a Lazy Susan or rotating cake stand and a cardboard cake circle or platter. Make sure the cake layers are cool and trimmed if necessary. Whatever icing you are using should be at the proper temperature and consistency to make the process as easy as possible.

Portion an amount of frosting into a small bowl. For the first stage, use only this bowl, adding more from the master batch as needed (this keeps the main quantity of frosting from becoming contaminated with crumbs). Begin by smearing a dab in the middle of the cake circle or platter to anchor the first layer. Place a completely cooled cake layer on the circle or platter and use the pastry brush to sweep any loose crumbs off the sides and top of the layer. Now spoon a generous dollop of icing onto the layer, and use the palette knife or offset spatula to spread it evenly to the outside edges. Settle a second layer directly on top of the first, pressing gently to secure it to the icing; brush off the excess crumbs. Repeat with any other layers until all of the layers are stacked. If the cake is particularly high, or very dense and heavy, you may want to chill the cake between layerings to allow the icing to firm up enough to support the structure.

With the palette knife or offset spatula, spread a very thin layer of icing on the sides and top of the cake. This undercoating, called the crumb coat, serves to plaster any loose crumbs to the cake and provide a smooth, even surface for the icing. Use the icing in the small bowl for this task, and use separate utensils to portion from the large and small containers. Continue portioning only small amounts into the separate bowl, as once it gets crumby, it cannot be used for the main coat. Chill the crumb-coated cake in the refrigerator for 10 to 30 minutes before you ice the top and sides of the cake with the reserved icing, then decorate as you wish.

Cutting Cakes

It's *really* important that cakes (of all types) are completely cool before you attempt to cut them, as they can tear or crumble if cut too soon. A long, thin-bladed slicing knife works well for most layer, sponge and pound cakes. For dense tortes and flourless chocolate cakes, warm the blade under hot running water and dry it between each slice—the heat of the water will be transferred to the metal and the blade will slide through the cake without pulling, gumming up or crumbling the cake. Angel food cakes are notoriously tricky to slice, often crushing and flattening under the pressure. The best tool for the job is a cake spreader, which looks like a long-toothed comb, with thin evenly spaced metal prongs of about 3 or 4 inches. It gently separates a wedge of angel food cake from the whole by prying it away from top to bottom. The same effect can be achieved by using two table forks. Place the forks, one in each hand, back to back. Line the row of prongs up with the line where you want to divide the cake and insert the prongs about 1 inch into the cake. Gently pull the cake apart, alternately pushing the prongs into the cake and separating the forks, as though you were uncovering a small treasure buried just beneath the surface. Cheesecakes are best cut not with a knife at all, but with a clean piece of fishing line or dental floss (unflavoured!). Hold the line or floss taut along the diameter of the cheesecake and lower one hand to the surface the cake is set on. Slowly lower the other hand, slicing through the dense filling. If necessary, you can finish cutting through the crust with a long thin-bladed slicing knife moistened with a little warm water.

Using a Pastry Bag

First of all, insert the tip and attach the coupling unit. (Sure, this may sound obvious, but trust me: if you forget, you'll end up having to scrape the icing, batter or other goo out and start again.) To fill the bag, fold the top of the bag over to form a wide cuff; this will protect the edges of the bag from getting covered with icing or batter and keep your hands clean. Twist the end of the bag, just above the rim of the metal tip, and stuff a bit of the fabric into the tip, plugging it up. Place the bag, open end up, in a tall glass to hold it still while you spoon the mixture in. Don't overstuff the pastry bag, especially if the mixture is particularly stiff—it will be too heavy, and you won't have the control necessary for accurate piping. Unfurl the cuff and twist the excess fabric close to the bulk of the filling, squeezing as you would a tube of toothpaste. The twisted part of the bag should sit comfortably in the crook between your thumb and forefinger, leaving your other fingers free to wrap around the bulk and squeeze.

With your other hand, support the tip, and guide it as you gently squeeze the bag to release the mixture. This is one task where practice does indeed make perfect. In cooking school I practised for hours using rehydrated instant mashed potato flakes. For goodness' sake don't eat the stuff, but when mixed with just enough water to make a semi-soft pipable "cream," it's a great stand-in for real icing: cheap, long-lasting and definitely not tempting. If you want to get fancy, invest in a good cake decorating book with illustrations of various piping styles and possibilities with different tips. Then buy your instant Idahoan flakes, and go wild.

Freezing Desserts

CAKES AND QUICK BREADS Wrap cake layers, quick breads, muffins and whole uniced cakes well, first in plastic wrap then in aluminum foil or a sturdy freezer bag. Label with the date and the type of cake, and freeze for up to 4 months. Thaw simple cakes, cake layers, quick breads and muffins for 2 to 4 hours at room temperature, without disturbing their wrappings to prevent condensation from settling on the cake itself.

Even some frosted cakes can be frozen. Buttercream icings freeze quite well, but boiled icings, seven-minute frosting and other meringue icings, and custard frostings and fillings do not fare so well, so should not be frozen. To prevent the frosting from getting ruined, place the entire cake on a parchment-lined baking sheet and freeze it uncovered until the cake and decorations are completely firm. The cake can now be loosely wrapped; I find a cardboard cake box just big enough to fit around the cake is the best way to "wrap" an iced cake. Place the cake in the box, then wrap the box itself in a heavy plastic wrap or bag and label. If you don't have a box, wrap the cake loosely (airtight) in plastic wrap or large plastic bags and label. You can freeze iced cakes for up to 3 months. Thaw iced cakes 4 to 6 hours at room temperature before serving. If the cake is in a box, leave the wrappings intact until the cake is thawed; if the cake is loosely wrapped in plastic, remove the wrappings to thaw so the icing doesn't get soggy.

Cheesecakes, both the baked versions and the unbaked refrigerator cheesecakes, freeze surprisingly well. Do not garnish the cakes with cream, fruit or glazed toppings before freezing, and let baked cakes cool completely before wrapping. Cheesecakes can be easily frozen in the springform or removable-bottom tins in which they were made, or can be made or baked in foil liners, which can be removed from the pans before freezing. For this method, line the tin very well with several layers of heavy-duty aluminum foil; cool the cake, chill it overnight in the refrigerator to firm it up, then remove the sides and bottom of the pan and set the cake in its foil lining on a baking sheet. Freeze the cake uncovered until solid, then wrap in plastic wrap and aluminum foil or a large freezer bag. Cheesecakes can be frozen for up to 1 month. Thaw at room temperature for 4 to 6 hours, or in the refrigerator for 12 to 24 hours, before garnishing and serving.

COOKIES AND COOKIE DOUGH Both raw and baked cookie doughs freeze extremely well, especially those high in butter. Raw dough should be formed into a shape that will be convenient when it is thawed—a log or cylindrical shape is handy, as it can be easily sliced into cookies ready for the sheet. Pack the dough tightly regardless of shape, to minimize the air trapped inside. Wrap cookie dough securely first in plastic wrap then in aluminum foil or a freezer bag and label with the date and type of dough. Cut-out cookies can also be frozen before they are baked: layer the raw shapes between pieces of parchment paper in a freezable container, preferably one that seals well. If you choose a cookie tin, wrap the tin with aluminum foil or place it in a sturdy plastic bag, then label. Freeze raw cookie dough for up to 6 months, then thaw overnight in the refrigerator. Cut-out cookie dough can often be baked right from the freezer; simply add an extra few minutes to the baking time.

Although I don't highly recommend it, baked cookies can be frozen as well. The higher the butter content, the better they freeze; shortbread freezes beautifully! Make sure the cookies are completely cool before wrapping, but for best results, freeze as soon after baking as possible. As with raw cookies, layer the baked cookies between sheets of parchment paper in a sturdy freezable container. If you use a metal tin, wrap the tin well before labelling. Freeze for up to 4 months and thaw frozen baked cookies for 4 to 6 hours at room temperature without disturbing their wrappings.

Baked meringues can be frozen once cool, packed into sturdy tins or boxes with lids to protect the delicate cookies from being crushed. Layer the meringues between sheets of parchment paper and wrap the box well in plastic wrap or plastic bags. Label, date, then freeze for up to 2 months. Thaw meringues at room temperature for 1 to 2 hours in the tin without disturbing the wrappings.

PASTRY DOUGH Raw pastry, pie and tart doughs freeze beautifully. Form the raw dough into the shape you will want it to have when you go to work with it again: a flattened disc is best for round pies and tarts, but squares and rectangles are obviously better for those shaped pans. Wrap the dough well, first in plastic wrap then in aluminum foil or a freezer bag. Label the bag with the date and type of pastry dough, then freeze for up to 6 weeks. Thaw the pastry overnight in the refrigerator without disturbing its wrappings.

Unbaked dough can also be frozen in its pie plate or tart tin, well wrapped, for up to 6 weeks. This makes throwing together a last-minute pie so much easier! Thaw the tins overnight in the refrigerator without disturbing the wrappings, or blind bake, or fill and bake directly from the freezer, depending on the recipe. For double-crust pies and tarts, roll out the pastry on sheets of parchment paper to the right dimensions, then slide the paper onto a baking sheet. If making several batches, repeat this process and stack the circles between sheets of parchment. Freeze the pastry on the baking sheet until frozen, then place the stack in a freezer bag or wrap securely in plastic wrap and aluminum foil; label, date and return to the freezer. You can remove the circles as you need them to cover filled pies and tarts; don't thaw the tops, just take them out of the freezer a few minutes before you need them and cover with a piece of paper towel to absorb any moisture.

Prebaked, unfilled lined tart and pie shells can be frozen once completely cool. Wrap well in plastic wrap, then in aluminum foil or a freezer bag; label, date, then freeze for up to 3 months. The frozen shells can be thawed at room temperature for 2 to 3 hours then crisped in a 350° oven for a few minutes. Cool before filling.

PIES AND TARTS Whole pies and tarts can be frozen before or after they are baked. Unbaked filled double-crust pies should be made with a little additional starch, about 1 extra tablespoon cornstarch or two tablespoons flour, to compensate for the added moisture acquired in freezing and thawing. Do not cut slits in the top pastry, but wrap the pie well and freeze for up to 4 months. Do not thaw before baking. Put the pie directly into a 425° oven for 15 minutes, then reduce the oven temperature to that specified in the recipe and cut three or four slits in the top of the pastry. Bake for a further 35 to 45 minutes, or until you can see the juices bubbling up through the slits.

Fully baked pies and tarts can be frozen once fully cooled. Wrap well, label and date, then freeze for up to 4 months. For best results, thaw at room temperature, then warm in a slow oven for 15 minutes or so.

CRISPS, CRUMBLES AND OTHER BAKED FRUIT DESSERTS Like baked pies and tarts, these freeze very well, although they are so simple to assemble, it is hardly worth it. For best results, freeze the crumble or crisp unbaked. Line the dish with the fruit and sugar mixture, and top with the crumble. Freeze the baking dish, well wrapped and labelled, for up to 3 months. Do not thaw, but bake right from frozen, adding an extra 5 to 15 minutes to the baking time.

Whipping Egg Whites

Depending on the intended purpose, egg whites can be whipped to a soft, floppy semi-stiff stage, or to tall, firm peaks. When whipped with sugar, egg whites will not achieve the same height as those whipped on their own, but will be firmer and glossier, and will better hold their shape. The aim when whipping egg whites for any purpose is to incorporate as much air as possible, without overbeating. The proteins in egg whites expand when beaten and trap air, creating a flexible and somewhat stable foam. The trapped air expands during baking, whether folded into a cake batter, or combined with sugar and used to top a pie or make simple meringue cookies, leavening the product and stabilizing it. Correctly whipped egg whites can make the difference between a well-risen cake or light, puffy meringue and a deflated, damp lump. Keep a few tips in mind and you will always end up happy.

❖ Egg whites hate fat. Not for the same reasons as Californians do, of course, but because lipids inhibit the whites' ability to expand and retain the most air. Make sure all utensils that come into contact with the whites are pristine, free of any traces of grease. For best results, separate eggs when they are cold and be especially careful to avoid getting any yolk mixed in with the white. The best way to do this is to crack the eggs one at a time over a small bowl, make sure the white is free of yolk and shell, then transfer it to the larger bowl with the rest of the whites.

❖ Egg whites whip best if they are at room temperature. But since you've probably separated your eggs cold, the fastest and safest way to temper the whites is to place them in a copper, stainless steel or thin glass bowl set over barely simmering water. Just hold the bowl above the steam for a minute or two, swishing and swirling the whites so they don't begin to coagulate. When they feel about body temperature, remove the bowl from the heat and whip. For maximum volume, I always warm egg whites slightly before whipping, even if the recipe doesn't suggest it.

❖ Egg whites should be beaten in a large bowl, big enough for them to triple or quadruple in volume. The very best material for whipping egg whites is unlined copper, as the proteins in the eggs react with the metal to whip higher, lighter and to a more stable foam. If you don't have a copper bowl, stainless steel is the next best thing. Do not try to whip egg whites in plastic bowls. (Unless you are camping, and ambitious.) When beating by hand, use a large balloon whisk—the finer and more plentiful the wires, the faster and lighter the whites will whip. The whip attachment on stand mixers also does a good job of whipping whites, but you may want to do the last little bit of whipping by hand to make sure they don't get overbeaten. Hand-held electric beaters produce a heavier, less voluminous foam, and should not be used for recipes in which a very light, high foam is critical.

Whip whites in a stirring motion, or on medium speed with the stand mixer, until the whites become a loose foam. If using a copper bowl, begin using a large, circular whipping motion with the whip until the whites hold very soft floppy peaks. If not using a copper bowl, you can help your whites along by adding an acid, most often in the form of cream of tartar, which firms the proteins in the whites, allowing them to retain more air. Add the cream of tartar, about ¼ teaspoon for every 5 or 6 whites, when the whites are loose and foamy, then use long circular whipping strokes, or the whip attachment of the stand mixer on medium speed, until the whites hold very soft peaks. Any sugar can be added gradually from this point, and the whites beaten until they hold stiff peaks.

I would venture to say that most whites used in home baking are overbeaten, especially when whipped with electric beaters or stand mixers. People see the phrase stiff peaks and whip until the whites are so firm they have begun to dry out. Overbeaten whites look grainy, lumpy and dry. They may even begin to separate, and even when only slightly overbeaten will present problems when you try to incorporate them into other mixtures, remaining lumpy and distinct, rather than smoothly absorbed. Stop at the point you think you are *almost* there—the whites are probably perfect. If the whites are to be folded into cake batters or other relatively heavy mixtures (see page 49), whip them to softly stiff peaks that are still shiny and moist. Whites for meringues and toppings tend to be whipped with more sugar than those for incorporation into baked goods and will be stiffer, glossier and more stable.

Whipping Cream

When whipped cream is the aim, heavy or whipping cream with at least 35% butterfat is the cream to use. For best results, the cream and all utensils, including bowls and whips or beaters, should be as cold as possible. Keep the cream in the coldest part of your refrigerator and pre-chill the equipment for half an hour or so before whipping. Cream whips quite quickly, and can go from perfect peaks to a sloppy mess in a frustratingly short time. Overbeating, beyond the fluffy, billowy, smooth cloud stage, will render the cream lumpy and grainy and, as my husband was delighted to discover, eventually produce butter. Perfectly whipped cream will not be very stiff, but will stand in soft, floppy mounds. If you begin to see a distinct texture or notice a graininess in the cream, it has been overwhipped. Slightly overwhipped cream can some-times be rescued by adding a few tablespoons of fresh cream to the foam, and re-whipping. Keep your eye on the cream as it begins to stiffen and never beat beyond the smooth and shiny peak stage. Whipped cream looses its volume with standing, but can be re-whipped to regain its height just before serving.

Rolling Out Pastry Dough

All pastry dough should be chilled between the mixing and rolling out stages. This allows the gluten that was developed in mixing to relax and will prevent the dough from tightening and toughening during baking. Shape the mixed dough into a flattish disc shape, wrap in plastic film and place in the refrigera-tor for at least 30 minutes, or up to 24 hours. Allow the dough to warm a lit-tle at room temperature before rolling, otherwise it will require so much effort in rolling that it will become overworked and, consequently, tough. Lightly flour a smooth, non-stick working surface, such as a marble pastry slab, a smooth wooden board or smooth countertop. Stainless steel is a wonderful surface for rolling pastry, but not easily found in most home kitchens! Use as little flour as possible, scattered in a fine dusting in the centre of the work sur-face. Excess flour can make your pastry tough and chewy. Position the pliable dough on the work surface and sprinkle the top with a bit more flour. Lightly flour your rolling pin and keep it dry when rolling to prevent sticking. Always beginning in the centre and rolling towards the edges, roll the dough in smooth, long, evenly pressured strokes, easing up before your pin reaches the edge to avoid crushing and pinching the dough. Gently turn the dough a quarter turn every few strokes, and sprinkle the underside with a little extra flour only if it sticks. Properly made dough at the correct temperature should need a minimal amount of flour, but do use enough to prevent the dough from sticking. If dough does stick in a few places, dust a palette knife or pastry scraper with flour, gently scrape the dough cleanly off the board or table and sprinkle the gummy area with a little flour. Roll dough into a circle, always keeping an eye on the size of tin it needs to fit—so often I have rolled absent-mindedly, only to realize I've rolled the dough much larger than it should be, and so thin I can almost see through it! In general, try to get the dough uniformly about ⅛ inch thick and a couple of inches larger than the tin, to allow for depth, overhang and decorative crimping. If your pastry tears as you are rolling it out, just wet your finger with a little water, moisten the area around the gash and patch with a piece of dough from the outside of the circle. Patching is infinitely better than re-rolling: never re-roll a whole round of pastry dough—you will end up with a tough crust so shrunken and cracked it won't hold any filling! When the circle is the right size and thickness, lightly place the rolling pin across the centre of the circle and drape half the dough over the pin. Hold the edges of the pin and transfer the dough to the pie tin, then unfold the dough. I find tapping the whole tin once or twice on the counter helps to ease the dough smoothly into shape. Use a scrap knob of dough or your fingertips to ease the dough perfectly into the corners. For best results, cover the shell and chill again at least 30 minutes or up to overnight before filling or blind baking. Roll out top crusts in the same way.

Blind Baking Pastry for Pies and Tarts

Blind baking is a method used for prebaking a crust, either partially or completely, before filling. For fillings that don't require a long baking time, custards, for example, partially baking the crust in advance ensures it will be crisp and flaky, not undercooked and soggy. Partially baked crusts are actually minutes away from being fully baked—they should be dry and lightly coloured. For pre-cooked or raw fillings such as fruit curds, mousses or fresh fruit, a fully baked shell is necessary. The crust should be golden brown and crisp all over. Both partially and fully baked crusts must be completely cool before the filling is added—adding a filling to a still-warm shell will trap steam in the pastry, resulting in a soggy crust.

TO BLIND BAKE

Preheat oven to 350°. The raw pastry shell should have been resting in the refrigerator for at least 30 minutes, and up to overnight. Remove the shell from the refrigerator and prick it all over, including up the sides, with a fork. Line the shell with a circle of aluminum foil or parchment paper about 2 inches larger than the rim of the pan. Fill the liner with pie weights (see Tools, page 13) or dried beans. There should be enough weights to support the sides of the crust while baking, to prevent it from collapsing inward.

Bake in the centre of the oven for 10 minutes, then rotate the shell. Bake for 5 more minutes, then carefully lift a corner of the foil or paper to check that the bottom is beginning to dry a little. If not, leave the liner and weights in place, and check again after another 5 minutes. When the edges are barely beginning to colour, remove the liner and weights. Return the empty shell to the oven and bake for 5 minutes, then check to make sure the crust isn't puffing up anywhere. If it is, use a clean kitchen towel to gently tamp the bubble down or pierce the pastry again with a fork or the tip of a sharp knife. You may have to repeat this deflating several times. Continue to bake, checking often, until the crust is dry and barely golden for a partially baked crust or dry with hues of gold for a fully baked crust. A cautionary note: the times given above are approximate only—the actual timing will depend on the heat and evenness of your oven and the type of pastry. In general, pie crust doughs bake faster than tart doughs and those rich in butter and sugar brown quite quickly once they begin to colour (so keep a close eye on them!). Consult the recipe for each type of pastry for more specific baking times.

Deep-Frying

Deep-fried desserts, when done well, are among the most satisfying and addictive of all desserts—light, crisp and delicate. When done poorly, however, they can be greasy, heavy and most unappetizing. Deep-frying must be done properly, or not at all. Fortunately, it is relatively easy to do when you keep a few points in mind:

❖ The fat you choose for deep-frying is critical. For sweet fritters and pastries, the oil should be pale and extremely mild in flavour, such as canola. It must have a high smoke point (the maximum temperature to which it can safely be heated), as fats with low smoke points will scorch and break down at the high heat of deep-frying. Neither animal fats, such as butter or lard, nor olive oil should be used for deep-frying, as these fats tend to have either strong flavours or low smoke points.

❖ The fat must be clean and fresh. All fats eventually go rancid, and repeated frying accelerates their deterioration. Salt, water, particles of food and blending with other fats also compromise the integrity of frying fats and cause them to break down. If the fat is treated with care, it can be used for frying several times. When using new oil, smell it first to make sure it is not rancid.

❖ Do not combine old and new frying oil, and do not blend two types of vegetable oils to use as frying fat.

❖ If using a countertop deep fryer, make sure it is one with an actual temperature gauge (see page 24) so you know the true temperature of the fat. If you're deep-frying the old-fashioned way, like I do, using a large kettle, pot or Dutch oven, make sure the vessel is heavy, non-reactive (not aluminum) and large enough to accommodate 3 to 4 inches of fat with another 3 to 4 inches of headspace for foaming and spattering. Always use an accurate deep-fry thermometer (also called a candy thermometer; see page 9) and position the thermometer in the oil *before* you begin heating it. The best thermometers have a metal foot that rests on the bottom of the pot; if you are using one that clips onto the side of the pot, make sure the sensor is not touching the side or bottom, but is suspended about midway into the fat.

❖ Heat oil slowly and carefully, allowing it to come up to the desired temperature gradually, always watching to make sure it does not overheat.

❖ For most doughnuts and other fritters, a temperature between 360° and 375° is generally best. Do not overload the fryer, as this will lower the temperature of the fat and prevent it from recovering quickly. The resulting fritters will absorb too much oil and have a greasy taste and feel. Too high a temperature will cause the outside to cook before the inside is done, leaving the fritters gooey and raw. If your oil seems a few degrees too hot, add another fritter or two to the pot, thereby lowering the temperature. If it is more than 10 degrees over temperature, lower the heat and wait until the temperature drops.

❖ To extend the life of your frying fat, make sure anything to be deep-fried is free from surface water, and use only dry utensils around the fat. Keep salt away from the oil and use a fine hand-held strainer to skim the loose crumbs from the fat between batches.

❖ Use only stainless steel utensils in the hot fat, as wooden and plastic tools can scorch or melt.

❖ Lower items into the hot oil carefully, but quickly, so each fritter in the batch cooks for approximately the same amount of time. Don't overload the fryer—3 to 6 fritters, depending on the size, is ideal. Turn them over once or twice during the frying to make sure they cook evenly and remove them with a slotted spoon or a pair of tongs. Drain hot fritters on a plate or platter lined with several layers of paper towel and change the towel if it becomes saturated with oil.

❖ Allow the oil to recover its temperature between batches of frying. Failing to do this will cause the temperature to remain too low and result in greasy, heavy fritters.

❖ After each use, let the oil cool completely, then strain it through a coffee filter or a fine-mesh strainer lined with several layers of cheesecloth. This oil can be stored in an airtight container in a cool, dark place and reused for another round of deep-frying as long as it still smells fresh and is clear and light in colour. If the oil looks dark golden or amber, cloudy or smells or tastes "off," discard it and begin with fresh oil. When products are lowered into fresh fat, it should bubble with clear white bubbles. If the oil foams with yellow bubbles or smells strongly when heated, allow it to cool then discard.

❖ Clean the frying kettle or pot well between each use with hot, soapy water and rinse thoroughly with hot water. Dry the kettle completely before storing or filling with oil.

CAKE TROUBLESHOOTING CHART

WELL, IT HAPPENS TO THE BEST OF US. It's four o'clock and the guests are due in an hour. At the ding of the timer you open the oven to retrieve your masterpiece but in its place is something that looks more like a four-year-old's mud pie than dessert. Cakes are sensitive things, prone to little fits of wilfulness every now and then. There is always method in their madness, however; instead of writing it off as a cruel bit of misfortune, use the chart below to understand what went wrong, and prevent it from happening again.

FOR CREAMED BUTTER AND SUGAR BATTERS (POUND AND BUTTER CAKES)

BATTER SEEMS TO CURDLE AFTER THE EGGS ARE ADDED

- The ingredients were not at room temperature. Eggs must be room temperature, not cold, and butter for creaming should be malleable—not cold and firm, but not overly soft and oily either.
- The butter and sugar were not creamed well enough. The creamed mixture should be very light, thick, pale and fluffy.
- The eggs were not added one at a time or were not fully blended into the batter between additions.

CAKE IS DENSE, HEAVY AND FLAT

- Not enough air was incorporated into the butter and sugar mixture, from either too little sugar or insufficient creaming.
- The eggs were not beaten thoroughly into the batter.
- Insufficient baking soda was used or there was not an acid present in great enough quantity to activate it.
- Insufficient baking powder was used or it was old and had lost potency.
- The cake batter was placed in the oven too long after the baking powder or baking soda was added—the leavener was all or partly exhausted.
- Air volume was lost when dry ingredients were folded into the creamed batter too roughly.
- Too much flour was incorporated, causing the batter to be too heavy and dry.
- The batter was overbeaten, causing too much gluten to develop in the flour.
- The pan used was too small.
- The oven temperature was too low.

TOP OF CAKE APPEARS DOMED AND CRACKED

- The oven temperature was too high, causing the periphery of the cake to bake faster than the middle, forming a thin crust. As the centre cooked, it burst up through this crust, hence the peak.
- Too much baking powder or baking soda was used.
- Too little sugar was incorporated into the batter.
- Too many eggs or too much liquid was mixed into the batter.
- The pan was placed too close to the top element of the oven, causing the top to bake faster than the rest.
- The flour used had a very high gluten content (hard or bread flour was used instead of all-purpose or cake flour), creating too much strength and structure, which produces an overly risen and tough cake. This can sometimes happen when a delicate cake from a Southern or British recipe is made with all-purpose flour; to prevent this, substitute at least half the all-purpose flour with cake flour (see page 101).

continued on page 68

FOR WHISKED EGG-SPONGES AND EGG WHITE-LEAVENED BATTERS (CHIFFON, SPONGE AND ANGEL FOOD CAKES)

CAKE IS DENSE, HEAVY AND FLAT

- The egg whites may not have been whipped high enough or air was lost when they were folded into the batter too roughly.
- Melted ingredients, such as chocolate or butter, were too hot when added to the egg and sugar mixture; air volume was lost as the batter was dampened and deflated.
- Too few eggs were used or the eggs were too small.
- The batter deflated when flour was added too roughly or overmixed after the flour was folded in.
- Too much flour was incorporated, causing the batter to be too heavy and dry.
- The batter was overbeaten, causing too much gluten to develop in the flour.
- The pan used was too small.
- The oven temperature was too low.

TOP OF CAKE APPEARS FALLEN OR COLLAPSED

In some cakes, this is desirable and intended—many flourless tortes, for example, are meant to have this appearance. If, however, this is not a flourless cake ...

- The oven temperature was too high.
- The cake was removed from the oven too early and is underbaked.
- The pan was knocked about at some point in the baking, deflating the air trapped in the batter.
- The oven door was opened too early during baking, creating a draught and collapsing the structure before it had a chance to firmly set. Don't open the oven door during the first half of the estimated baking time, and only when absolutely necessary after that. Instead, check the cake's progress through the oven door window.

- Too much leavener was used (baking powder, baking soda or beaten egg whites), causing the cake to rise too quickly and collapse before the batter was firm enough to support the structure.
- Not enough flour was added, so the batter did not have the strength to support the structure.
- Too much sugar was added, causing the batter to retain too much moisture, making it heavy and incapable of supporting its own weight.

FOR ALL CAKES

CAKE SURFACE IS UNEVEN

- The flour was not incorporated thoroughly enough, creating a batter with pockets of strength and pockets of mostly liquids.
- The sides of the pan were not evenly prepared: greased or greased and floured.
- The oven temperature was too high.
- The oven temperature was inconsistent throughout baking time, or varied from place to place in the oven and the cake pan was not rotated for even baking.
- Cake pans were placed too close together or too close the sides of the oven, preventing air from circulating around the pans.

CAKE IS OVERLY TENDER AND FRAGILE

- The cake was not completely cooled when handled.
- Too much leavener was used (baking powder, baking soda or beaten egg whites).
- Too much sugar was incorporated into the batter.
- The oven temperature was too low.

FRUIT SANK TO THE BOTTOM OF THE BATTER

- Fruit preserved in syrup can slip through the batter to the bottom. You can prevent this by rinsing the fruit and thoroughly drying it before adding it to a cake batter.

continued on page 70

* The fruit was not dusted with flour before being folded into the batter. A fine coating of flour allows fresh or dried fruit to remain suspended in the batter.
* The oven temperature was too low, causing the fruit to sink through the softened batter before it was firm enough to support the fruit.
* Too much leavening agent was added, causing the batter to rise too quickly and the fruit to drop through the soft structure.

BOTTOM OF CAKE IS OVERBAKED OR BURNT

* The baking pan was too thin or too dark. Avoid using thin, cheap bakeware; when using dark bakeware, reduce the oven temperature by 25 degrees, line the pan with parchment paper and check the cake occasionally to ensure it does not overbake.
* The pan lining was incomplete or incorrect—for example, parchment paper was recommended but not used.
* The pan was placed too near the bottom of the oven.

BATTER OVERFLOWED THE SIDES OF THE PAN DURING BAKING

* The pan was too small; if substituting another pan than the one specified in a recipe, consult the Baking Pan Substitution Chart on page 41. In any recipe, batter should come no more than ⅔ up the side of the pan.
* Too much leavening was added, either in the form of baking soda, baking powder or beaten egg whites.
* The batter was overbeaten, which allowed too much air to be incorporated.

SURFACE OF CAKE APPEARS SPECKLED AND UNEVEN IN COLOUR

* The batter was not thoroughly blended, so pockets of flour, baking powder or soda and/or egg white remain distinct and suspended in the batter.
* The sugar did not completely dissolve, usually a result of using too coarse a grain. If a recipe calls for superfine sugar and you have only regular granulated sugar, spin the granulated sugar in a food processor fitted with a steel blade for a few moments to reduce the size of the granules.

- The batter did not contain enough liquid, preventing the dry ingredients from being fully distributed and dissolved.

SURFACE OF THE CAKE IS OVERBROWNED AND THE CRUST IS DARK AND CRISP

- The oven temperature was too high.
- Too much sugar was added to the batter.
- The cake is overbaked.

SUGAR SYRUP COOKERY CHART

Sugar syrup, whether very light and aqueous or cooked to a glossy amber caramel, is a key component in countless desserts. The sugar density, or thickness, of the syrup depends on its intended use. If the syrup is to become the base for a poaching liquid for fruit, it should be relatively thin, as more evaporation will take place during the poaching—a ratio of at least 1 part sugar to 2 parts water is standard. For a syrup to be flavoured with a liqueur and brushed on sponge cake layers before frosting (or other similar uses), the syrup should be of medium thickness, with a ratio of about 1 part sugar to 1 part water. For situations in which the syrup must act as a powerful sweetener without adding a great deal of liquid, such as in many cooked meringues and buttercream frostings, it should be higher in sugar than water, anywhere from 2 parts sugar/1 part water to pure cooked sugar.

When a sugar and water syrup is cooked long enough, it will reach a temperature of 212°F, at which point the water evaporates. If the sugar, now in liquid form, is cooked further, it will reach various key temperatures before finally scorching (sugar cooks extremely quickly once the water has dissipated). If the cooking is halted at any one of these points, the cooked sugar will behave in a very particular way and can be used for specific purposes. There are two methods for determining the stage of the cooking sugar: by the touch method and with a thermometer. The touch technique involves dropping little bits of the molten sugar into a bowl of cool water, then testing its texture and firmness between your fingertips. While this method has been used for centuries, it is a little fiddly and not always reliable for the novice. As you're determining the stage of the test batch, the remaining sugar continues to cook. The most accurate way of cooking sugar is with a good candy thermometer (also called a deep-fry thermometer) that registers the temperature of the syrup as it cooks (see page 9).

A Few Safety Tips for Working with Sugar

- Have all ingredients, equipment and tools assembled and within reach before you begin to cook the syrup.
- Move smoothly and carefully when working with or transferring hot sugar syrup.
- Wear long sleeves.
- When adding a new element, such as a liquid or fruit to be caramelized, to a boiling sugar syrup, wrap a kitchen towel around your hand to prevent burns.
- Always keep a bowl of ice water next to or on the stove in case you do get splattered with bits of the molten sugar. Hot sugar should never be wiped or brushed off, as this will only increase the area of the burn. Instead, plunge the affected area into the ice water (or press a piece of ice onto the skin) to stop the burning, then remove the hardened sugar from your skin.

How to Cook Sugar

❖ Use a very clean, heavy-bottomed pot with smooth, straight sides. The best pots for sugar work are made of unlined copper, but any non-reactive pot will do if it is sturdy and heavy.

❖ Make sure your thermometer is accurate; you can check this by placing it in a pot of water and bringing the water to a boil—water boils at 212°F, or 100°C at sea level (see page 662).

❖ Add just enough water to the sugar to dissolve it, about ¼ to ⅓ cup water for every cup of sugar, as the water will be evaporated quickly.

❖ Place the pot over low heat and stir the mixture until the sugar dissolves. With a very clean pastry brush dipped in a bowl of cool water, wash down the sides of the pot to clean them of the crystallized sugar syrup. After this point, do not stir the mixture again—you'll only wash more syrup onto the sides and the syrup will cook unevenly and possibly burn.

❖ Once the sugar has completely dissolved and the sides are clean, increase the heat to medium and bring the syrup to a boil. Lower the thermometer into the syrup. Ideally, it is a model with a metal foot that rests on the bottom of the pot. If you are using one that clips onto the side of the pot, make sure the sensor is not touching the side or bottom, but is suspended about midway into the syrup.

A TIP: Adjust the height of the clip before beginning to cook the syrup.

❖ Allow the syrup to boil undisturbed until it reaches the desired stage or temperature, then use it immediately. There is sufficient heat retained in the molten sugar and the pot to continue the cooking even after you have removed the pot from the heat. You can use this to your advantage, taking the pot off the heat just before the sugar reaches the desired temperature, slowing its progress slightly to avoid overcooking it. To quickly halt the cooking of the sugar at a desired temperature, immediately place the bottom of the pot into a large bowl of ice water.

SUGAR COOKERY STAGES

- **Simple Syrup (212°F, 100°C)** The water in the syrup will have just reached a boil, but will not be completely evaporated. Simple sugar syrups can be used as the base for poaching liquids, brushing and soaking syrups, and sweetening for sorbets, ices and other frozen desserts.
- **Thread Stage (223° to 234°F, 106° to 112°C)** Dip the tip of a metal teaspoon into the boiling syrup, then cool this in a bowl of cool water. Pick a small amount of the syrup off the spoon and pinch it repeatedly between your thumb and index finger; it should form a thin thread, about 1 to 2 inches long. If the syrup is simply dropped into the water, it cannot be gathered into a blob, but remains in loose rivulets. Syrup at this stage is excellent for making fruit and other preserves.
- **Soft Ball Stage (234° to 240°F, 112° to 116°C)** When a small amount of syrup is dropped into the cool water, it can be gathered into a very soft,

pliable ball with your fingertips. The ball will flatten on the bottom of the bowl if left alone. Sugar at this stage is commonly used for fondant, candy-making and other confectionery such as fudge and for Italian or cooked meringue.

- **Firm Ball Stage (242° to 248°F, 116° to 120°C)** The globule of sugar in the cool water can be rolled into a ball that is firm but still pliable and retains its shape when released in the water. Sugar at this stage can be used for certain soft toffees and other sugar confections.
- **Hard Ball Stage (250° to 265°F, 121° to 129°C)** Sugar will readily roll into a sturdy ball, but will still be slightly pliable when pinched and can be used to make caramels and soft nougat including the Southern favourite, divinity.
- **Soft Crack Stage (270° to 290°F, 132° to 143°C)** When poured into cool water, sugar will separate into threads or globs that harden instantly, but are still malleable and tacky. At the soft crack stage the sugar can be used to make hard nougat and torrone, butterscotch and pull taffy.
- **Hard Crack Stage (300° to 310°F, 149° to 154°C)** If sugar is boiled beyond the soft crack stage, it reaches a point when the threads produced in the cool water become glass-like and brittle. Sugar at this stage is often used for advanced sugar work decorations, spun sugar and other confectionery, as well as for glazing fruits and nuts.
- **Light Caramel (320° to 338°F, 160° to 170°C)** At somewhere between 310° and 320°F, sugar begins to take on an amber colour, and becomes caramel. Light caramel is used for confections such as praline, nut brittle, and for glazing fruit, choux pastries and other desserts.
- **Dark Caramel (338° to 350°F, 170° to 180°C)** Dark caramel is a deep rich amber colour, and has a dark, almost burnt flavour. Sugar cooked to this point is ideal for lining crème caramel moulds, as well as for flavouring sauces and icings. Always cool a small amount of dark caramel in a little cool water and taste it to ensure none of the caramel has burnt; you will taste a distinctly acrid flavour if it has. Watch closely, as sugar very quickly goes from dark caramel to the next, always undesirable stage ...
- **Black Jack (350°F and up, 180°C and up)** Sugar cooked to the black jack stage is easily identifiable by a pungent scorched aroma, a deep brown or black colour and a great deal of smoke. Unfortunately, if your sugar reaches this point, it is burnt, and must be discarded.

A Simple Guide to Garnishing

Desserts, perhaps more than any other part of a meal, are savoured first with the eyes, then with the mind and, finally, and most satisfyingly, with the mouth. My best desserts have never been elaborate, gravity-defying creations—I leave that to the frustrated architects among my professional colleagues. Rather, they are both familiar and elegant, and garnished with simple additions that add to the balance of textures, flavours, colours and ingredients. The fact is, a piece of flourless chocolate cake looks pretty darn good just plain sitting on the plate, alone, crumbs and all. Most desserts can sell themselves without a great deal of gilding; too much ornamentation can actually detract from a dessert's appeal. Achieving the perfect balance between frumpy and frou-frou is easy: just keep the garnish simple, suitable and, above all, taste-full!

Ice creams, biscuits, sauces, coulis and other dessert elements can be used as garnishes, to accent different elements of a dessert or make a simple product more elaborate. Use the Flavour Pairing Chart on page 352 for suggestions and always consider the effect of the combination of flavours. A lemon curd tart will seem light and tropical when paired with a coconut sorbet, but may seem comparatively tart and bright in flavour when accompanied by a blackberry ice.

Consider the occasion and the degree of formality of the entire meal, as well as the dessert itself. A complex, towering creation with shards of caramel and fourteen different coulis may be a tad overwrought for a casual dinner in the backyard. Similarly, if the first six or seven courses were all quite elaborate, a single scoop of ice cream sitting in a plain white bowl may seem a little wanting. Let the style of the meal suggest not only what dessert you serve, but also the degree of garnishing you apply to it.

In every case, whether formal or casual, be as simple in your garnishing as you can. As with so many other things, less is more; you want to highlight the dessert, not obliterate it in a blinding display of decoration.

Play with the four non-flavour elements of your dessert: texture, colour, shape and temperature. In general, opposites complement each other: creamy with crunchy or firm; rough with smooth; cold with hot; light with dark. This is why a good sundae is as sublime and as satisfying as any fancy-schmancy restaurant creation: cool velvety ice cream; warm, thick, rich hot fudge; soft, smooth, light whipped cream; and brittle, crunchy, buttery nuts. Each element complements the others and none is there with no relation to the whole. When a wedge of chocolate torte is paired with a creamy pour of crème anglaise, the smoothness of the sauce caresses the palate as it mingles with morsels of the dense, rich cake. With smooth or creamy desserts, introduce an element of brittleness or crunch with a sugar cookie or a shard of praline; with large, sturdy cakes, use a dollop of whipped cream to soften the effect and provide lightness and a change of texture. Add a splash of colour to a bowl of ice cream or a yellow cornmeal pound cake with a fresh blackberry sauce or a handful of sliced strawberries.

You can alter the appearance, flavour and overall effect of a dessert just by varying the garnish or accompaniment. The dark chocolate torte made richer and more luxurious with the addition of the crème anglaise can be made brighter, lighter and more bold in flavour when paired with a fresh raspberry coulis. Or, serve it slightly warm, with a good mocha or praline ice cream—the contrasting temperatures are divine and the ice cream will melt into a rich, dreamy sauce.

Perhaps the most common mistake made in garnishing, by both professionals and home bakers alike, is forgetting the element of flavour. Sounds silly, doesn't it? But how many times have you seen a sprig of mint used to garnish a bowl of ice cream, or a plate of cake or slice of tart? Countless, no doubt. But how many times has that dessert actually been mint-flavoured? Maybe never. Certainly the mint adds a bit of colour, but it also adds a distinctive perfume, one which might not match the dessert at all. And once the diner appreciates the appearance of their plate, they pick up the sprig, set it aside and proceed to completely ignore it. What's the point? Its only function is to add colour and it does nothing to enhance the enjoyment of the dessert. A garnish should complement the dessert in as many ways as possible, especially in flavour. The pretty sprig of mint so inappropriate beside a wedge of mocha walnut cake or on a coupe of butterscotch ice cream would be perfect beside a chocolate cake with a mint crème anglaise or atop a bowl of lemon-mint sorbet.

The aim of garnishing is to accent perfectly the dessert you have prepared, simply and naturally. Keep in mind the textures, shapes, colours, temperatures and, especially, flavours of your desserts, and you will find enhancing them easy and great fun.

The following are a few simple, fast and versatile ideas for garnishing all sorts of desserts:

Sauces: Custards, Coulis and Ganache

Many cakes, tarts and frozen desserts are wonderful on their own, but can be made extra-special when paired with a suitable sauce. Varying the flavour and type of sauce can provide an entirely new experience of the original dessert.

CRÈME ANGLAISE is a creamy, cooked custard sauce traditionally flavoured with vanilla and served cold. It is one of the most versatile and delicious sauces in the sweet kitchen and can be paired with dense chocolate cakes, fruit tarts, warm pies, nut pies and tarts, warm steamed puddings and crisp pastries. The basic sauce can be flavoured with almost infinite variation; see the recipe on page 649.

FRESH FRUIT COULIS are bright, intensely flavourful sauces made by puréeing fruit flesh with enough sugar to make them dessert-like. Some coulis are strained, making them perfectly smooth and fairly runny; others are only partly puréed and left thick and chunky. To vary and deepen the flavour, add a splash of a fruit liqueur or eau-de-vie. Fruit coulis are excellent over a simple ice cream and make a great alternative to crème anglaise with dense cakes and tortes. Their vibrant colours and endlessly variable flavours can accent almost any flavour, from chocolate and vanilla to complex tropical tastes. See recipes for *Raspberry* (and other berry) *Coulis* on page 643 and *Mango-Orange-Passion Fruit Coulis* on page 644.

CHOCOLATE GANACHE, when warm and thick, makes a dynamite and dead easy hot-fudge-like sauce for draping over ice cream or pooling beside a dense chocolate torte, a crisp fruit tart or even certain mousses and puddings. Both dark and white chocolate ganache are wonderful; for a beautiful and decadently good accompaniment to chocolate or vanilla desserts, serve both! See recipes on page 647.

SYRUPS, from the simplest drizzle of maple right out of the jug to a wonderfully complex reduction of caramel and fruit juice, can be used to accompany all sorts of desserts. They can be perfectly smooth or chunky with nuts or fruit; they can be served cold (think of cold syrup on hot pancakes) or warm (perfect on an ice cream sundae). Most syrups start with a base of sugar and liquid (water, wine, alcohol or fruit juice) or are reductions of unadulterated fruit juice. The flavours are endlessly variable—caramel, liqueurs, nuts, virtually all types of fruit, even coffee and spices.

Chocolate

MELTED CHOCOLATE can be drizzled decoratively over cakes, fruit tarts, cookies and bars for a simple and fast garnish. For a casual, random drizzle on a cookie you can let the chocolate fall from a teaspoon, but for better control and accuracy, use a small piping bag or a plastic squeeze bottle. If the chocolate is going over whipped cream, buttercream or other soft frosting, make sure it is only barely warm or it will melt and mar the icing or glaze (see page 233 for tips on melting chocolate).

Melted dark, sweet or white chocolate, when drizzled on a piece of parchment paper in *decorative patterns or shapes* and left to cool, can be a lovely, unusual and professional-looking garnish for cakes, mousses and frozen desserts. You can drizzle freehand or use a template. Draw the design on a piece of parchment paper with a dark marker, then cover the sheet with another sheet of parchment; you should still be able to see the outline through the top sheet and can move and reuse the template under as many sheets of decorations as you want.

Warm melted chocolate can be poured onto a marble pastry board or a metal baking sheet, left to cool slightly and then scraped with the edge of a bench scraper or a palette knife to form *curls and shards*. For large, rounded curls, scrape the chocolate when it is still fairly soft; for shards, let the chocolate cool a little longer. This is not at all an exact science—it takes practice, and the best results are sometimes a surprise! Don't be overly anxious about what you are aiming for, but allow yourself the freedom to see what develops. Use the curls to garnish cakes, tarts, cream pies, puddings, mousses and parfaits.

You can make *smaller curls and shavings* by gently warming a vegetable peeler and scraping it along a thick block of chocolate. Very warm, the peeler will make larger curls; cool, you will have a lovely mess of delicate little shavings. These are particularly good on mousses, custards and as decoration for iced cakes and cookies.

Caramel and Praline

CARAMEL SYRUP is a wonderful accompaniment to ice creams, parfaits, simple cakes and many tarts and pies. Heat at least 1 cup sugar plus 3 tablespoons of water in a heavy-bottomed saucepan and stir until the sugar dissolves. Bring the mixture to a boil, then cook until the syrup becomes a dark golden amber colour or reaches about 335 degrees. Immediately add about ¼ cup water (Stand back! The addition of the water will cause a great deal of splattering and the molten sugar is dangerously hot). When the action in the pot has subsided, transfer the hot syrup to a heatproof container and let it cool. The syrup will thicken as it cools; you can adjust the consistency by adding more warm water if necessary. This simple sauce can be used warm or cool and can be enhanced with the addition of almost any liqueur or spirit (see page 223). When left fairly thick, this clear golden syrup makes beautiful patterns when drizzled on a plate and lusciously coats ice cream and other frozen desserts. For a richer sauce and to adjust the sauce's consistency, use heavy cream in place of the water added to the hot syrup.

SOLID CARAMEL SHAPES AND DECORATIONS are a popular garnish for all sorts of desserts in professional kitchens and are wonderfully simple to prepare at home. Use the recipe and procedure above, but have a large bowl of ice water nearby, large enough for the bottom of the caramel pot to sit comfortably in. When the caramel syrup reaches the lovely amber colour, or about 335 degrees on a candy thermometer, don't add any liquid, but immediately remove the pot from the heat and place it into the bowl of ice water. After a minute or so, dribble the caramel from the pot or use a stainless steel utensil to carefully drizzle onto a prepared surface. A parchment lined baking sheet is a good surface for making flat decorations and shapes; for more three-dimensional shapes, lightly coat a stainless steel utensil, bowl or other form with vegetable oil, then drizzle or pour the caramel over top. Pastry chefs love using the backs of ladles for this purpose, creating beautifully wound caramel cages. Play with the things you have on hand; inverted bowls, stainless steel rolling pins, even the backs of cake and pastry tins are just a few ideas. Let the hot caramel cool, then remove the shapes. They should not be made more than a few hours ahead, as they get sticky and lose their shape; warm humid days will accelerate this demise! Try to make caramel on dry days, and as close to the time of serving as possible. These decorations can ornament mousses, ice creams, cakes, even simple fruit or custard desserts.

PRALINE, a simple nut and caramel brittle, can be used in many ways as a creative and flavourful garnish for all kinds of desserts. With the recipe for basic praline on page 633 made with the nuts of your choice, you can make shards by simply breaking the sheet of cooled praline into irregular pieces. As a garnish for cakes, mousses and custards, these are dramatic and beautiful. If the shards are spun in a food processor until chunky, so that some larger pieces of nuts are still visible, the praline becomes a versatile confection, great for topping ice cream sundaes and iced cakes. When finely ground, it becomes a sparkling golden dust, wonderful sprinkled on puddings, ice creams, mousses, iced cookies and even as a side and top dusting for iced cakes.

Cream

In many parts of the world, the most perfect accompaniment to rich cakes, pies and tarts is nothing more than a pour of a good, fresh, thick cream. In North America, most of us don't have access to cream with a higher butterfat content than 35%, which can be a little runny on its own, so we generally whip the cream before pairing it with our desserts (see below). We can improvise, however, by whipping the cream until it is only very slightly thickened and then using it as is so common in Europe, simply poured over a slice of *Tarte au Sucre d'Érable* (page 461), or warm apple crumble. Heavy cream served this way is a rewardingly different experience than the common stiffly whipped version, one particularly suited to rustic and homey desserts.

The thicker creams of Europe can be otherwise imitated: the glorious French *crème fraîche* is not available unpasteurized in North America, and the pasteurized imported brands are prohibitively expensive. Good crème fraîche can be easily be "faked" at home, though, following the simple recipe on page 651. This fabulously rich, slightly tangy cream can be served plain or lightly sweetened with sugar or honey, with cakes, tarts, pies and fruit desserts and compotes. The luxuriously creamy Italian *mascarpone cheese* is another versatile and unusual accompaniment for tarts, baked fruit desserts and compotes. It can be sweetened with a little sugar or honey and flavoured with vanilla or a liqueur as well.

Plain, unsweetened whipped cream is a classic and much overlooked garnish for all sorts of desserts, especially those that are particularly sweet or rich on their own. The lightness and smooth, cool, gentle flavour of a dollop of plain whipped cream balances desserts such as dense chocolate tortes or intensely sweet and gooey pecan pies. Use 35% (whipping or heavy) cream, as cold as possible, and whip just until the cream stands in soft, floppy peaks.

Whipped cream can also be *lightly sweetened* with sugar, honey or maple syrup and can be flavoured with virtually any extract or liqueur. The classic Chantilly cream is made by whipping heavy cream with a little sugar and pure vanilla extract. Experiment with more unusual liqueurs and flavourings; try pairing a simple almond cake with cream whipped with lavender honey and a few drops of a French lavender eau-de-vie—definitely not for every dessert, but original and absolutely sublime. Plain or flavoured whipped cream can be served in dollops or mounds beside rustic or simple desserts, such as pies and some cakes, or can be decoratively piped, using a pastry bag and a star tip, onto or beside more elaborate or sophisticated desserts, such as layer cakes, cupcakes and mousses or puddings.

Powders

CONFECTIONERS' SUGAR, COCOA POWDER, even POWDERED SPICES such as cinnamon sifted over cakes, tarts, cookies, pastries or the plates on which desserts are served is a simple and colourful way to garnish many sweet dishes. You can dust the whole surface of the dessert with the powder, or just one area. Many tarts and pastries look lovely with confectioners' sugar dusted just around the edges, and you can retain the appearance of the dessert by dusting just one side with cocoa or sugar. Use a little canister called a dredger, which has a fine wire mesh top, or use a very fine mesh sifter or sieve to sprinkle the dessert with just a light dusting. Just invert the dredger or hold the sieve over the area to be dusted and lightly tap the edge to distribute the powder onto the dessert in a fine, even layer. For a more professional and dramatic effect, play around with stencils; cut shapes and reliefs out of the thin plastic tops of margarine tubs or coffee tins and dust the powder through the cut-outs. The stencils can also be made out of cardboard, but plastic stencils are much more durable and can be washed and reused.

If you are dusting with cocoa, use a Dutch-process cocoa, as these are much less bitter than natural cocoas. Be very sparing if you dust with cinnamon, as it is a strong spice and will dramatically alter the flavour of the dessert; blending it with confectioners' sugar will achieve a pretty colour, but a milder taste.

If you decide to dust the plate with sugar, cocoa or cinnamon, please practise restraint! Great sprinklings of powder around the edges of the plate seem to end up more often on guests' sleeves and can actually detract from the dessert itself.

Using Creative Plating to Showcase Desserts

Restaurants have long known the value of attractive plating—arranging the food in a manner that best showcases it. There are all sorts of rules of thumb: the highest point on the plate should be at least 3 inches high (the recent trend towards towering food has greatly extended that height!); have at least three colours on the plate; have one main point of focus, preferably off-centre. These rules may be fine for restaurant chefs, but are mostly unnecessary for the home dessert cook. Personally, I don't pay much attention to them, preferring, as you likely will, to let the simplicity and beauty of the dessert itself dictate its plating. In your own home, the most important aspect of any dessert is the flavour, and your guests' enjoyment of it. A slice of homemade cake looks lovely by itself on a plain white plate; to elevate the presentation, use a coloured plate, a dusting of confectioners' sugar or a dollop of whipped cream. Coloured, decorated and unusually shaped plates or serving dishes can go a long way towards making plain and simple desserts look more exciting. I caution against using them with elaborate or highly decorated or intricate products, however, as the result can be a too-busy and unfocused presentation. Large white plates focus the eye on the dessert itself. It is better to have an overly large plate than one too small, as the latter tend to make desserts look awkward and out of proportion. Sauces and other garnishes show up more clearly on white plates, but some light or pale products, such as angel food cake or other light cakes, look quite beautiful on a coloured plate. Of course, use what you have on hand, but get creative— you don't have to use dessert plates or bowls! Dinner plates, goblets, wine glasses, salad bowls, even unusually shaped bakeware and ramekins are all possible serving dishes for desserts.

Edible Flowers

Many flowers, such as roses, pansies and nasturtiums, are edible as well as exquisitely beautiful and can be used plain or lightly sugared to garnish all sorts of desserts. The flowers must be naturally grown, without the use of sprays, pesticides and synthetic or chemical fertilizers. Make sure that any flower or petal that comes into contact with food has been untreated and never use a flower you are not positive is safe to eat. Flowers sold in florists' shops are almost always treated and should not be used for garnishing desserts or savoury foods. Many specialty fruit markets sell organically grown edible flowers and any you have grown yourself without the above influences are ideal, and perfectly safe.

Store edible flowers and petals in the refrigerator in a moist container or plastic bag, and garnish the dessert as close to serving as possible, as many flowers are very delicate and wilt quickly, especially on hot or humid days. (I once made a large wedding cake for an August outdoor wedding. I delivered the cake several hours before the dinner, but by the time guests began arriving, every flower on the cake had begun to droop! I was saved by a devoted young waiter who kindly spent twenty minutes running all over the grounds picking pansies and other wild edibles to replace my poor little casualties!)

Most edible flowers and even individual petals can be dusted with a light coating of sugar, leaving them icy-looking and sparkling. Lightly beat one or two egg whites, at room temperature, in a small bowl until frothy. Place a cup or two of superfine sugar in a small bowl, along with a teaspoon. Make sure the flowers or petals are perfectly clean and dry. Have a baking sheet lined with parchment paper nearby to place the flowers on as they are finished. With a pair of tweezers held in one hand (your left, if you are right-handed), pick up one flower by the very base of the blossom. With a small, soft paint brush (a child's tiny watercolour brush works perfectly!), coat the entire surface of the flower, top and bottom of each petal, with the egg white in a very thin film. If the white seems too thick, add a few drops of water to the bowl. Working over the sugar bowl, spoon the sugar over the damp petals, making sure every surface is covered. Gently shake off the excess sugar by tapping the tweezers on the edge of the sugar bowl and set the flower, blossom up, on the baking sheet. Repeat with the other flowers and let the sugared blossoms dry for at least an hour before using to garnish cakes, ice creams, mousses, puddings and other desserts. Sugared flowers should be stored in a single layer or in several layers separated by shredded waxed or tissue paper, in an airtight container. They have a wonderful shelf life, lasting a year or more if properly stored.

SOME EDIBLE FLOWERS COMMONLY AVAILABLE IN NORTH AMERICA

acacia blossoms	English primroses	pansies
almond blossoms	freesia	peach blossoms
apple blossoms	geraniums	plum blossoms
banana blossoms	gladioli	roses and wild roses
baby's breath	hibiscus	sage blossoms
borage	hollyhock	snap dragons
calendula petals	honeysuckle	squash blossoms
carnations	Johnny-jump-ups	sweet peas
chamomile	lavender	violets
chive blossoms	lemon balm	wild radish
cornflowers,	lilac blossoms	
bachelor's buttons	marigolds (petals only)	
(blue, white and pink)	mimosa	
daisy petals	nasturtiums	
day lilies	orange blossoms	

Fruit

FRESH FRUIT used to garnish cakes, tarts, ice cream, custards and pastries is an easy and endlessly variable way to make your desserts look colourful, attractive and unique. There are only two rules of thumb. First, the fruit you choose must be fresh and beautiful—I am always amazed at how often I get a few anemic-looking strawberries or slices of wilted starfruit in even good restaurants! Second, use only fruit that is appropriate to the dessert, not a slice of kiwi or a wedge of melon with a peanut butter chocolate tart! The flavours of the fruit should accent and complement the flavours in the dessert itself. Use the Flavour Pairing Chart on page 352 for hints on which fruits marry well with which flavours and ingredients. You can play with the way you arrange the garnish—nestle a cluster of tiny Zante grapes beside a maple walnut tart, fan out a few bright strawberries on top of an almond pound cake, scatter a hand-ful of wild blackberries around a tangy lemon tart. Don't overdo it—one or two perfect pieces of fruit are all you need.

SUGARED FRUIT, like sugared flowers and petals, is a beautiful and very simple garnish too. The colours of the fruit come through the sparkling coating, look-ing glassy and delicate. Small, firm, whole, smooth-skinned fruits are best: in-dividual or clustered grapes, cherries, strawberries, fresh currants, small apricots and plums, kumquats and even tiny lady apples and sugar pears are all good candidates. Make sure the fruit you choose for garnishing is completely intact, with no cracks, splits, bruises or soft patches. Proceed exactly as for sug-ared flowers, above, using the tweezers to hold the stem or other "handle," if there is one, or to gently grip the fruit itself, rotating the fruit so its entire sur-face gets covered with both the egg white and the sugar. Let the sugared fruit dry for an hour or two, then use within several hours. Perfect for garnishing light cakes, pastries, wedding cakes and other delicate desserts.

FRESH AND DRIED FRUIT DIPPED IN DARK OR WHITE CHOCOLATE (I don't rec-ommend using milk chocolate, but it's up to you!) can be served as a confection on its own or as a garnish for other desserts. Melt at least 4 ounces of finely chopped chocolate in a small bowl in the microwave or in a bowl set over a pot of barely simmering water (see page 233 for tips on melting chocolate). Mean-while, make sure the fruit you have chosen is very dry, and at a cool room temperature. Strawberries, slices of candied orange peel, whole grapes, cherries, blackberries and dried fruits such as apricots, dates, figs, banana chips, even dried mango and other tropical fruits are excellent for dipping. I love cherries, grapes and dried dates dipped in white chocolate, and berries, candied orange peel and banana chips in a rich bittersweet chocolate. Lower the dry pieces of fruit into the chocolate one at a time—dipping just halfway lets the fruit's original colour and texture contrast with the smooth chocolate. If the chocolate begins to thicken too much, return it to the heat to soften, then continue dipping. Set the dipped pieces on a parchment-lined baking sheet and let the chocolate set for 1 to 2 hours before using or storing the fruit. Chocolate-dipped fresh fruit should be used as soon as possible, but dried fruit coated with chocolate can be layered between sheets of parchment or waxed paper in an airtight container and stored at room temperature for up to 2 days.

CANDIED CITRUS ZEST AND PEEL are also wonderful accents, glossy and jewel-like in colour, and fantastically flavourful, especially when homemade. Use for garnishing cakes, compotes, tarts, pastries and ice creams with orange or citrus flavours (see recipe on page 634).

Nuts

WHOLE, HALF, SLIVERED, SLICED, CHOPPED AND GROUND NUTS can all be used to garnish desserts, from whole walnuts perched atop a row of buttercream rosettes on petits fours to sliced almonds nestled into a lemon tart to ground pecans pressed onto the sides of a iced layer cake. A light toasting does wonders for most nuts (see page 253 for tips on toasting various nuts), bringing out their richness, sweetness and unique flavours.

SPICED OR SUGARED NUTS are a simple and effective garnish for many fruit and chocolate desserts. The recipe for *Maple Sugared Pecans* on page 636 can be amended to use any type of nuts, and any kind of sugar—adding a pinch of cinnamon, nutmeg, ginger, mace, cloves, even black or white pepper further changes the flavour, allowing you to customize the nuts to whatever dessert they are to accompany. Serve these alongside a chocolate-nut torte, a walnut layer cake, coffee-flavoured desserts or even a simple fruit compote.

CHOCOLATE-DIPPED NUTS are a great (and really yummy) decoration for special cakes and other showcase desserts. Use dark, white or even milk chocolate depending on the type and flavour of dessert and follow the instructions for fruit, above; store as for dried fruit.

OTHER NIFTY THINGS TO USE FOR GARNISHING

- Crushed cookie and biscuit crumbs, applied to the iced sides or tops of cakes to add colour, flavour and texture
- Store-bought cake decorations, such as silver or gold dragées (tiny metallic candy balls) and candy or chocolate vermicelli (sometimes called chocolate jimmies)
- Crystallized violets, roses, mimosa, mint leaves and angelica
- Crystallized sugar, rock sugar, raw sugar and coloured sugar
- Candied and crystallized ginger
- Dark chocolate coffee bean candies and chocolate-covered coffee beans
- Edible gold and silver leaf, available at specialty food stores and cake decorating shops

---

the
ingredients

INGREDIENTS IN THE
SWEET KITCHEN

LIKE MANY PEOPLE, some of my earliest memories of food are of desserts and sweet things. I can vividly recall my grey-haired, rosy-cheeked Gran making her banana pudding or showing me what just the right shade of beige the icing for her famous mocha rolls should be; and my Grandma baking wild blueberry pies in her big kitchen in Northern Ontario. I can still taste those childhood treats as if I had them in my mouth a moment, not decades, ago.

Since then, I have eaten in some of the most celebrated restaurants in the world, enjoying desserts so glamorous and complicated that their very names occupied a good three or four lines on a menu. And make no mistake, they were often wonderful creations—wildly original and decadent. But none was better than a bite of the soft cake, sweet icing and crunchy nuts of a mocha roll or a melting mouthful of blueberry pie made with wild blueberries hand-picked and still warm from the sun. The best of all of these desserts, plain or fancy, were good for two very simple and unmysterious reasons: they were well prepared by someone who understood what they were doing and who used proper ingredients of the highest quality. No matter how many squiggles of how many different sauces are on the plate, no matter how long the name, how exorbitant the price or how tall the creation, without careful and precise preparation and good basic ingredients, no dessert can succeed.

The wonderful flip side to this is that anyone, whether a complete culinary virgin, a gourmet cook making their first foray into the sweet kitchen or an accomplished dessert-maker, *anyone* can make a fantastic dessert. In fact, anyone can make a dessert as good as the best in the world. Sound crazy? The simple fact is, in the sweet kitchen there are relatively few ingredients to play with. While the composition of savoury dishes varies wildly from dish to dish, cuisine to cuisine and culture to culture, the basic ingredients in the sweet kitchen are fairly constant: flour, sugar, butter, eggs. From all or some of these four ingredients you can make delicate puff pastry, tender shortbread, moist pound cake, light and airy angel food cake, crisp cookies, chewy meringues, pie crusts, tart pastry, gooey blondies, even a simple egg foam or luxurious sabayon. Add chocolate, cocoa, milk or a simple flavouring and the list of possible recipes multiplies fourfold; add two or more of these ingredients and you can make literally hundreds of desserts, all different, all wonderful and all infinitely variable.

What makes the pound cake from the corner bakery so divine in contrast to the last one you may have made is nothing magical, but likely due to a marked difference in ingredients. With so much of the success of most desserts relying on so few and such simple ingredients, the ones you choose must be absolutely fresh, seasonal and of the highest quality you can find or afford. The difference is unimaginable: a lemon curd made with bottled juice and old eggs will seem limp and bland compared to the same recipe made with fresh, fat lemons and fresh eggs; the lifeless pound cake, now made with fresh flour, good butter and fresh eggs, will be stellar (and probably better than any you could buy in a shop). Just as you would never make roast potatoes with green, sprouted potatoes, don't settle for slightly rancid butter or steroid-enhanced bland and pulpy strawberries for your shortcake. There is no magic—there is only knowledge about the raw materials and a sense of integrity.

This section on ingredients has been designed for easy access, whether you are looking for information quickly while in the middle of baking or you have a few minutes to browse before going to the market. At the start of each chapter is information on the roles those ingredients play in various types of sweet products. You'll find this helpful when it comes to understanding what went wrong, for substituting one ingredient for another or when striking out on your own and trying new ideas. When it comes to flexibility and variation, we must understand the role of ingredients in baking in the first place or our hands are tied. The rest of each chapter is devoted to exploring the different products available in each category.

What is the difference between *semisweet* and *bittersweet* chocolate? How much difference does real vanilla make? What is *caster sugar*, anyway? Read on, and use these pages as a guide—a good excuse to head out in search of sweet treasure. Every locality has its own specialties—explore what is available to you, not just in supermarkets and gourmet shops, but in ethnic markets, specialty food shops, health and natural food stores, farmers' markets, even your own garden. See, and taste, what a different place the sweet kitchen can be.

FLOURS, GRAINS AND GELLING AGENTS

Role of Flour

FLOURS ARE COMPOSED of starches, which can be broken down to complex carbohydrates or even simple sugars, and proteins. Each of these components behaves in a specific way when combined with other ingredients, manipulated a certain way and subjected to different temperatures. It is common knowledge that flour is one of the most important ingredients in the sweet kitchen, providing structure and texture, as well as flavour. But flour's many roles in baking extend beyond these obvious duties.

❖ Flour binds to the liquids and fats in batters and doughs, creating a uniform and homogeneous mixture and ensuring that all of the ingredients in the recipe are evenly distributed.

❖ Flours and starches can be used to thicken the juicy fruit fillings of pies and tarts, as well as pastry creams, puddings and sauces. When moistened, the starches in flours such as wheat flour begin to expand, forming a web of starch molecules that can absorb liquids and fats. This web gets stronger as the mixture is heated, becoming fully potent just below the boil. At a certain temperature, depending on the other ingredients in the mixture and the proportion of flour in relation to them, the starches stop absorbing and gel or set, much as eggs coagulate, thereby suspending the trapped liquid in the web. The thickening power of flours and starches varies from type to type and may be influenced by various external factors. White flour, for instance, commonly used to thicken both pastry creams and pie fillings, is a reliable starch for thickening, but has several peculiarities. Mixtures thickened with

93

white flour will have a cloudy appearance—not noticeable in opaque custards or puddings, but perhaps undesirable in a raspberry pie. Wheat flour
can be rendered almost powerless as a thickener by some fruits with exceptionally high acid contents, as they cause the gelled starches to break down.
So much flour would be needed that the flavour and texture of the pie would
be compromised. Wheat flour also tends to leave an unpalatable, and indi-
gestible, floury taste if not cooked sufficiently. For mixtures that don't require much cooking, but do need a great deal of thickening power, this can
be a problem. Cornstarch or tapioca are often good alternatives. Both of
these starches thicken at about double the power of flour, so half the amount
can be used for the same volume of liquid. They do not leave a detectable
taste and thicken to a beautifully clear gel. (See the section on specialty flours
and starches for more information on these and other alternatives.)

❖ Just as they serve to thicken liquid mixtures such as pie fillings and custards,
the strong mesh created by cooked starch molecules supports the structure
created by the leaveners in cakes, cookies, yeast and quick breads. This web
enables the trapped air to remain suspended, and so contributes to the tenderness of the baked product. In the heat of the oven, having been moistened
with the liquid or fat ingredients in the batter or dough, the mesh of starch
molecules sets exactly as it would in a liquid mixture, effectively thickening
or creating structure where there was none and creating a strong framework
for the leavening.

❖ Flour adds a desired texture and crumb to baked goods, with each flour providing its own characteristics. Whole wheat flour adds a coarse, slightly
chewy texture to breads and cakes, cornmeal yields a product with a pleasant crunch and soft, bleached cake-and-pastry flour gives angel food and
chiffon cakes their light and delicate crumb.

❖ Flour can be used to prevent doughs and batters from sticking to surfaces,
as it is when dusted on a work surface before kneading bread dough or
rolling cookies, or dusted onto cake pans before adding the mixed batter.
For rolling and dusting pans, unless specified, always use all-purpose flour,
even if the flour in the main recipe is bread or cake—it will provide the best
buffer without being absorbed. Some bread recipes do call for cornmeal or
whole wheat flour to be used when rolling or shaping the dough and for lin-

ing the baking sheet before baking the bread. This will give the finished loaf a characteristic appearance, flavour and texture, as well as prevent the dough from sticking to the work surface or pan.

❖ Flour is often used to dust fruits and nuts before they are added to a cake batter, thus keeping them from clumping together and preventing them from sinking to the bottom of the batter during baking.

❖ Flour adds nutritional value to baked goods, in the form of vitamins, minerals, carbohydrates, protein and even fat, depending on the type of flour used.

❖ Flour, either dusted on the product before frying or as the main ingredient in a batter, contributes to a crisp, tender crust in fried desserts such as pancakes, doughnuts and fritters. The sugars in the flour caramelize with heat, becoming golden and crisp.

❖ The caramelization of these natural sugars also contributes to the crust colour and texture of baked goods such as breads, cakes, cookies and pastries.

❖ Gluten-free starches, such as cornstarch, tapioca, rice flour and potato flour, add tenderness and delicacy when used to replace some of the wheat flour in certain recipes for delicate baked goods such as shortbread and shortcrust pastry. The starches effectively counteract some of the power of the gluten in wheat flour, creating a more fragile, less securely bound if you will, structure.

❖ Many flours add a distinct flavour to baked goods, such as the rye flour in a sweet gingerbread, the cornmeal in a polenta cake or the graham flour in the *S'mores Roulade*, page 399.

❖ Flours, specifically high-gluten flours, contribute to a high, tender and fine-textured bread. The proteins in high-gluten flours, such as wheat and kamut, when lubricated by a liquid and agitated with a vigorous motion such as mixing or kneading, combine to produce a protein called gluten. Gluten forms a strong and elastic web of strands that traps the carbon dioxide produced by the active yeast and supports this structure until the starches in the flour have set in the heat of the oven. The higher the proportion of gluten in a flour, the stringier this web, and the more air the dough will be able to hold. Gluten is what gives leavened breads their characteristic springiness, elasticity, chewy texture and lightness. Breads made with very low-gluten flours, such as rice flour or soft wheat flour, will be dense, tough and very heavy, as there is insufficient gluten to support the action of the yeast, so the breads do not rise much at all.

Selection and Storage

Buy all flours and grain products from a reputable source with a high turnover and clean, cool, dry storage. If you buy in bulk, inspect the bins for insects and smell the products for freshness. Once you find a good supplier, bulk is often the more cost-efficient way to purchase your ingredients, as you are free to buy only as much as you need, and the prices are almost always better to begin with!

Store white flours and degerminated flours and grains in a cool, dry place, away from light, heat and moisture, and strong odours. Fresh white flours should keep for up to 1 year this way. Whole grains and whole-grain flours should be stored in the refrigerator or freezer to prevent rancidity and to extend their life to between 5 and 8 months, depending on the freshness when bought and type.

Organic Flours in Baking

Today, virtually all types and grades of flours and grains are available in organic form from health and natural food stores, and some bulk shops. Many books of bread recipes are now recommending organic flours be used, especially in the case of sourdough starters, as they tend to be more flavourful and have better texture and character. While these naturally grown and produced flours are subject to the same standards and regulations as commercially produced varieties, they can behave slightly differently in certain products. Yeast breads in particular can illustrate the slight differences between organic and non-organic flours. The dough produced with all organic flour will be softer, stickier and floppier than one made with standard flour and may be more difficult to shape and knead. Organic flour lacks the acidity of standard flour, acidity that is contributed by chemicals in the refining process. To compensate for this difference, add a few drops of lemon juice, vinegar or ascorbic acid, in the form of vitamin C powder (available in health and natural food stores), to the liquid ingredients before mixing them into the flour. This should help firm the dough, making it easier to shape, and it should keep its form throughout the rising and baking.

Baking with Flour

Humidity is often blamed for poor or inconsistent results when baking with flour. The theory is that the amount of flour specified in the recipe may be inadequate in humid weather, or excessive in dry conditions. In fact, variations in the air humidity affect the outcome of your baking very little. The most common error is not using the appropriate flour to begin with. Most recipes were devised with a very specific type of flour in mind: hard wheat for a chewy, high-risen multigrain bread; soft, Southern wheat for a batch of fluffy traditional biscuits; or dark rye flour for a hearty black bread. Using a different flour can radically alter a recipe, sometimes beyond recognition.

The proteins in flour, when combined with liquid in a recipe, form a new protein called gluten. This protein, when wet, binds the flour and water to form an elastic and flexible dough. Flours made from different grains, different types of the same grain or grain milled at different stages or times of the year can have greatly varying gluten contents. (Wheat gluten differs from the proteins of other grains, though many nutritionists tend to lump all grain proteins together under the term. Some people who are intolerant of wheat gluten can tolerate a certain amount of other grains such as rye and kamut.) Gluten is what enables a flour to retain liquid, and become elastic and springy. More gluten means the dough will be able to support the structure of the final recipe. Flours with high gluten contents can support more liquid and will produce chewier, springier products. Low-gluten flours, such as Southern flour, have poor retention qualities and will not become elastic and strong with beating, but can therefore produce very tender, delicate products. Using a hard bread flour to make an angel food cake or those fluffy biscuits will be disastrous, resulting in a dense, dry cake and tough, heavy biscuits. Likewise, the soft Southern flour would produce a floppy, dense, damp bread that would hardly rise at all. It is important to understand the role each type of flour plays in the final product and to use the type specified for best results.

Wheat Flour

Wheat flour has become the most popular grain flour in the world for breads and other leavened baked goods such as flaky and puff pastries, as well as cakes and biscuits. It has a pleasant, nutty, mild flavour and can have a high gluten content, making it capable of producing both delicate shortbread and tender, high-risen breads.

The wheat kernel is made of three parts: bran, germ and endosperm. The bran is the tough outer shell of the kernel and contains most of the fibre. The germ is the kernel's nucleus and is high in protein, oil, thiamine, vitamin E and minerals. The endosperm is the starchy bulk of the kernel from which most flour is made. It contains most of the protein, carbohydrates and some B-complex vitamins. The bran and the germ are removed to make white flour, but are retained when whole wheat flour is milled. The bran and the germ may also be added to a recipe separately.

Today, three types of common wheat are grown. *Hard red winter wheat* is planted in the spring or fall and harvested in the fall or late spring. It has a very high gluten content, about 12.5 to 13.5%, and is milled for bread flour. *Soft red winter wheat* is planted in the fall and harvested in late summer. It has a relatively low protein content, about 7 to 8%, and is milled for cake and/or pastry flour. (Some all-purpose flours are a combination of hard and soft wheat, yielding a flour with between 9 and 11% protein content, making it a good general flour for most baking.) *Durum wheat* is the hardest wheat of all and is used almost exclusively in the making of pasta and some breads, although it is difficult to knead the dough for a 100% durum bread into a homogeneous mass.

Flour in Regional Recipes

North American flour is, bar none, the best in the world. Reliable, consistent and always of extremely high quality, it is one of our largest and most important crops, exported all over the world. Most often, baking recipes work perfectly well when made with all-purpose flour, as much of the flour produced in the United States is of good quality and of similar gluten content. Occasionally, however, a recipe devised in the South with local flour does not turn out properly when made with all-purpose flour. This happens more frequently with delicate products such as chiffon cakes, some sponge cakes, biscuits and delicate cookies. The reason lies in the protein content of the flour. In the South, the most common flour used is a very soft flour, comparable to cake or pastry flour, with a gluten content of about 8%. The recipe may very well not state that a low-gluten flour is used, especially if it is a local cookbook or a regional recipe, but may simply call for white or regular, even all-purpose flour. If all-purpose flour is used, the result may be tough, heavy, dense and dry. I usually substitute all cake or pastry flour and find the results very close to the original. (See also All-Purpose Flour, page 101.)

Types of Wheat Flour

HARD FLOUR OR BREAD FLOUR is made from hard red winter wheat and has a very high gluten content, between 12.5 and 14%. It is perfect for supporting the structure of yeast breads, puff pastry, strudels, Danish pastry and cream puff pastry—doughs that need the structure from the high gluten content to support the many layers of fat and air. While bread flour used to be available only to professional bakers, some national brands such as Gold Medal, King Arthur Flour and Pillsbury now mill flour with a high protein content, made specifically for bread baking. Bread flour may be white or whole wheat, bleached or unbleached, and can also be organic. It is best used in yeast bread and flaky pastry recipes, as its high gluten content can toughen and dry out other more delicate baked goods such as cakes or cookies.

CAKE, PASTRY AND SOUTHERN FLOURS are all types of *soft flours*, made from low-gluten soft wheat or a combination of soft and hard winter wheat. Soft flour is suitable for light cakes and delicate pastries, as its low gluten content does not interfere with chemical leaveners, such as baking powder or baking soda, and will ensure a tender, delicate texture for the final cake. Soft flour is better for light, white cakes with few additional or heavy ingredients, like melted chocolate or cocoa, as melted chocolate is quite heavy, and cocoa replaces some of the flour in a cake recipe—the batter for these cakes requires more strength to support the additional weight. For the same reason, do not use soft flours for breads, or for cakes or quick breads containing a lot of moist, chunky or heavy additional ingredients. Angel food and chiffon cakes, however, should be made with nothing else. Soft flour is available in white or whole wheat, bleached or unbleached varieties, but Southern flour is always white, and bleached.

All soft flours tend to clump with sitting and should be well sifted, several times in some cases, before being used. Some recipes call for pre-sifted flour, ("1 cup sifted cake flour"), while others suggest sifting after measuring, ("1 cup cake flour, sifted"). Even if the recipe does not specify, always sift your soft flour before proceeding.

Cake flour is a type of soft flour with about 8% gluten and which has been chlorinated. The chlorination serves two purposes: first, to bleach the flour a pure white, particularly desirable for angel food and other white cakes; second, to thicken the batter, which is especially important in industrial applications. The bubbles encounter less resistance and deflate less, creating a tender, delicately crumbed cake with maximum volume. Cake flour, such as Softasilk or Swans Down, is usually packaged in 2-pound boxes and is found in most supermarkets.

Pastry flour is similar to cake flour, but has a slightly higher gluten content, about 9%, and has not been chlorinated. It is rarely available from sources other than professional suppliers and is used mainly by professional bakers and pastry chefs. Organically grown pastry flour is sold in health food stores, but it is often made from whole wheat. Be careful not to use whole-grain pastry flour unless it is called for in the recipe. You can substitute all-purpose flour in a recipe calling for pastry flour or, for an approximate equivalent, blend your own by mixing one part cake flour with three parts all-purpose.

Instant-blending or gravy flour such as Wondra is usually made from soft wheat and has a gluten content of about 8 to 10%. Always white, it is also usually bleached. It has been well sifted and may have had an anti-caking agent, such as cornstarch, added to keep it smooth-pouring and to prevent it from clumping. It is used as a thickener for sauces and gravies, and for coating foods to be fried, but is rarely used in baking.

Southern flour is extra soft, milled from very soft winter wheat, and bleached. Often labeled *plain flour,* brands of flour milled and sold exclusively in the South, such as White Lily, have an extremely low gluten content, about 7 to 8%. Baking powder biscuits and other delicate Southern pastries are made wonderfully tender and light. You can bake these products with nationally available brands of all-purpose flour, but they won't be nearly as delicate!

Cake, pastry and all-purpose flours are all also available in *self-rising varieties*. These flours have had baking powder and salt added in regulated proportions, which enables the cook to measure all the dry ingredients for a recipe at once. To substitute regular soft flour for self-rising, use 2 teaspoons baking powder and 1 teaspoon salt for every 2 cups of flour.

ALL-PURPOSE FLOUR In America, because we are blessed with the finest flours in the world, our all-purpose flour is of exceptional quality. A blend of hard and soft wheat, it is the most commonly used flour for home bakers and, as the name implies, can be used to make anything from flaky pastry doughs to various breads. National brands such as Gold Medal, Pillsbury and King Arthur have a gluten content of 9 to 11%. As the protein content in wheat is affected by climate, seasonal changes and weather, brands of all-purpose flour will vary slightly in their protein content. To determine the protein content of a particular flour, read the nutritional facts on the package. Take the number of grams per serving size (often 3) and divide it by the number of grams per serving (for example, 31). That number represents the percentage of protein in the flour (in this example, 9.6%). All-purpose flour can be purchased either bleached or unbleached. Bleached flour is thought to be better for making cookies, cakes and pastry, while unbleached flour is often considered desirable in making yeast dough.

SEMOLINA Semolina is not a variety of wheat, but rather durum wheat that has been relatively coarsely ground, then sifted to remove the fine flour. Its graininess or sandiness make it the best choice for satisfyingly al dente pasta and gnocchi, as well as many traditional Italian breads, custards, puddings and even soups. It should be used in recipes only when specified and can be found at Italian groceries as well as some natural food stores.

WHITE WHEAT FLOUR For white flour, the bran and the germ are removed during the milling. After milling, it is called *unbleached white flour*. *Bleached flour* is made when chemicals such as chlorine dioxide, benzoyl peroxide or acetone peroxide are used to treat the flour, giving it an ivory-white colour and a slightly more delicate flavour and texture. Some of the vitamins (such as E and B-complex) that may have been retained after milling are destroyed in this process, so government regulations require vitamins to be added, producing *enriched flour*. A very small percentage of the general population claim they can detect a slightly bitter flavour in products baked with bleached white flour, but for most palates, the difference is too subtle to notice. Although they can be used somewhat interchangeably, I prefer using unbleached flour for yeast breads and heartier cakes and quick breads, and bleached flour for cakes, pies, cookies and as a thickener. All-purpose flour is pre-sifted, but can settle, so I generally sift all my flours before using.

WHEAT GLUTEN, ESSENTIAL WHEAT GLUTEN, VITAL WHEAT GLUTEN The same starch inherent in wheat flours, vital or essential wheat gluten is isolated and removed from the flour by a process of washings and rinses. It is used in combination with low-gluten flours or in doughs containing very large amounts of non-flour ingredients in relation to the wheat flour, to provide the extra strength, structure and support necessary for the bread to rise high and tender. Many good bread recipes with alternative flours call for additional wheat gluten, and if you become creative with substituting specialty, alternative and low-gluten flours for the bread flour in your favourite recipes, you may find adding a little of this product will produce a bread more close in texture to the original than one made without it. Vital or essential wheat gluten can be found in most heath and natural food stores and should be stored in the refrigerator, in an airtight container.

WHOLE WHEAT FLOUR To make whole wheat flour, also known as *wholemeal flour* in Britain and Australia, the entire grain of wheat is milled, including the bran and the germ. These components give it a speckled cream-and-brown appearance and a coarser texture than white flour. Rich in fibre and highly nutritious, whole wheat flour contributes a nutty, toasted flavour to breads, quick breads and even some cakes and cookies. Like white flour, whole wheat flour can be made from hard or soft wheat and can be labelled bread, all-purpose or pastry flour. The gluten contents are the same as those of the same types of white flours.

The fat in the wheat germ component of whole wheat flour becomes rancid very quickly, within three to four months of milling, depending on the season and humidity. Buy all whole grain flours from a supplier with a high turnover, to ensure they are fresh, and store them in the refrigerator, away from strong odours and chemicals. Properly stored, whole wheat flour should last six to eight months. Rancid flour will not harm you, but it will contribute a bitter, stale flavour to your baking. Flour that is too old will have a distinctly rancid or pungent smell and should be discarded. Buy only in small quantities and check for freshness before using.

Whenever possible, especially for yeast breads and hearty quick breads, buy *stone-ground* whole wheat flour. Stone-ground flours have been ground between one stone that rotates and another that remains stationary. This process retains maximum nutrients in the wheat and gives the flour a wonderfully nutty, full flavour, as well as a more interesting texture than regular-milled flours.

Baked goods made with whole wheat flour will be more chewy, nutty-flavoured and heavier than those made with white flours. If you substitute whole wheat flour for all of the white flour in a yeast bread recipe, expect a significantly heavier, denser texture. Many people find this type of bread a little hard to negotiate—a ratio of about 60% whole wheat and 40% white flour is generally preferred. In lighter baked goods, such as cakes and quick breads, unless the recipe specifically calls for whole wheat flour, replace no more than half of the white flour with whole wheat, or you may be unhappy with the results. If you do want to replace all of the white flour in a cake or quick bread with whole wheat, I find substituting whole wheat cake-and-pastry flour for white all-purpose works quite well, as the lower gluten content compensates somewhat for the increased texture and strength of the whole flour.

WHEAT GERM Highly nutritious, wheat germ is the isolated germ of the wheat grain. On its own, it can be added to almost any cake, bread, quick bread or cereal to increase the nutritional value. It will add a distinctly nutty, whole-grain taste, not appropriate for every dessert, but breakfast breads and muffins are perfect vehicles for this healthy addition. Wheat germ spoils very quickly if not refrigerated, but properly stored, it should keep about 3 months, and is widely available in supermarkets, as well as in health and natural food stores.

WHEAT BRAN Like wheat germ, wheat bran is isolated from the wheat grain during the milling of white flour. Bran is the outer layer of the wheat kernel and is very high in carbohydrates, calcium and fibre. It is coarser and darker than the germ and is often added to muffins and quick breads to increase their fibre content and nutritional value. Available in the baking section of most supermarkets, as well as from health and natural food stores, whole bran can be stored in an airtight container in a cool, dark place for up to 6 months.

GRAHAM FLOUR When first devised in the 1840s, graham flour was a coarse whole wheat flour made by removing the germ and bran, then adding the bran back in a higher than usual proportion. Today, graham flour may also be a blend of whole wheat flour and whole rye flour. It is most famous as the characteristic flavour in graham crackers and cookies, but is also an excellent addition to breads, muffins, cookies, pancakes, waffles or anywhere whole wheat flour is called for. It is very high in fibre and, because it does not contain the fat from the germ, keeps longer than conventional whole wheat flour. Stored in a cool, dark place it will keep about 6 months, in the refrigerator it will stay fresh up to 1 year.

Specialty Flours, Grains and Starches

With the growing awareness of ethnic cuisines and ingredients, as well as food and nutritional allergies, alternative flours are being incorporated more often into everyday cooking and baking. Health and natural food stores, and vegetarian cookbooks are great sources for recipes using alternative flours and grains. These newcomers, as well as traditional flours and grains, are discussed below.

AMARANTH Amaranth was a staple in the diets of the Aztec and Incan cultures. The seeds are small, pale, lentil-shaped grains with a sweet and nutty flavour and they can be ground to a flour for use in batters and doughs. However, the flour should replace no more than 50% of the wheat flour in yeast doughs, as it has little or no gluten. Amaranth flour is best used for hearty whole-grain quick breads, cookies, bars and baked goods other than yeast breads. It will actually increase these products' moisture-retaining ability and shelf life. Amaranth grains can also be popped like corn and will expand to about ten times their original volume. The popped grain is slightly sweet and toasty in flavour and, since it's high in fibre and iron, can be used to enrich products like granola bars or other nut and seed cookies. When boiled, amaranth becomes quite gelatinous and viscous, thanks to a starch present in the grain that is activated by moisture and heat. When used as an ingredient in pectin-free fruit preserves, it aids in the thickening naturally, allowing for a minimum of sugar as well. Amaranth can be stored at a cool room temperature, in a dark, aerated place.

ARROWROOT, ARROWROOT FLOUR Arrowroot, also called arrowroot flour, is not the product of one single plant or root, but rather a combination of starches from several tropical roots. The roots are dried and finely ground, yielding a powdery starchy flour much like rice flour or cornstarch. Its most common use is as a thickener and an ingredient in puddings, biscuits and crackers. Like cornstarch, arrowroot thickens to a clear gel and has about double the thickening power of wheat flour. Unlike both wheat flour and cornstarch, however, arrowroot does not impart a floury taste to the product if slightly undercooked. It can be used to replace cornstarch, rice flour, potato flour or tapioca flour in pie and tart fillings, as well as in delicate shortbread and some cakes. As arrowroot is very easily digested, arrowroot products are often served to the very young, very old or the infirm. Available in some supermarkets, as well as health and natural food stores, arrowroot is also commonly found in many Asian, Latin and South American markets. It should be stored in a cool, dark place for up to 2 years.

BARLEY Barley is an extremely hardy ancient grain, dating back over 4000 years. It has been used for millennia to make breads and other simple baked goods, as well as hearty hot cereals. And, of course, there's the beer! Barley is harvested with the hull intact, and although whole-grain barley (with the bran) can be found in health and natural food stores, most of the barley available in North America has been degerminated and is called *pearl barley*. Barley's slightly sweet flavour makes it a versatile ingredient in cooking, and it is often added to stews and soups to extend them and add texture and flavour.

Barley flour is milled from pearl barley and can be used in baked goods such as breads and some simple cakes and cookies. Low in gluten, it can be used to replace up to 25% of the wheat flour in yeast breads, but the result will be heavier and more coarsely textured. Added to baked goods, barley adds moisture and improves shelf life.

Store pearl barley and barley flour in airtight containers in a cool, dry place for up to 1 year.

BUCKWHEAT Buckwheat is not properly a grain, but is actually the seed of a herb. Buckwheat honey is made from pollen gathered from the fragrant flowers of this plant, and the flour and other products made from the seeds are as darkly flavourful as this pungent honey. Although buckwheat is nutritionally similar to wheat, it is unrelated, and many people who cannot tolerate wheat have no trouble with buckwheat products.

Buckwheat groats are sold two ways, roasted or raw. *Kasha* is made from roasted buckwheat groats and is used commonly in Eastern European and Russian cuisines. *Buckwheat grits* are coarsely ground groats, also used in many Eastern European cuisines to make baked goods, porridges and stews.

Finely ground groats are called *buckwheat flour*, and it is this form we are most familiar with in North America, particularly in pancakes. Buckwheat flour is available in *dark* or *light* varieties, the dark having retained more of the hull in the milling process and being a somewhat better source of protein. Baked goods made with buckwheat flour have a distinct, dark, malty and faintly bitter flavour.

Buckwheat products should be stored in the refrigerator for up to 6 months and checked periodically for evidence of rancidity.

CORNMEAL (POLENTA, MAIZE MEAL) Cornmeal, called *polenta* in Italy and *maize meal* in other parts of the world, is made from ground, dried corn kernels. Although yellow and white are the most common varieties, it may also be blue, even red. Most of the cornmeal available outside Mexico and South America has had the germ removed during the milling process to prolong its shelf life. While this type of meal has the ability to make a very smooth porridge or cooked polenta and is unobtrusive when added to baked goods, I think it lacks character, flavour and texture. *Stone-ground cornmeal*, a coarser grind of the entire grain, is far preferable for baking and cooking, contributing a nuttier, more "toasted corn" flavour and a pleasantly crunchy, nibbly texture. It is also more nutritious than regular cornmeal, as it still contains the corn bran.

Blue cornmeal makes interesting and unusual baked goods, with a slightly sweeter flavour and crunchier texture than yellow or white cornmeal. You'll have to add slightly more fat and liquid when substituting for yellow or white cornmeal, though, as it eventually absorbs more of both, resulting in a drier product if no compensation is made.

Cornmeal absorbs liquid much more slowly than wheat flour, but if the batter or dough is allowed to rest, from 5 to 10 minutes for time-sensitive batters made with baking powder or beaten egg whites to up to 1 hour for doughs or batters such as tart crusts or breads, the liquid will be satisfactorily incorporated. Alternatively, the cornmeal can be moistened ahead of time, like oatmeal often is, before it is added to the rest of the ingredients. Products baked with cornmeal will tend to be crumbly and slightly crunchy, depending on the coarseness of the grind.

Store stone-ground and blue cornmeal in the refrigerator for up to 4 months and regular cornmeal in a cool, dry place for up to 1 year.

Corn germ is the isolated germ of the corn kernel. It is extremely high in fibre and can be used to replace wheat germ in many recipes. It has a lovely toasted corn flavour and adds a crunchy texture to baked goods when added in small amounts. Available in some health and natural food stores, corn germ should be purchased in small quantities, stored airtight in the refrigerator and used within 2 months of purchase, as it spoils quickly.

Masa harina is a very finely ground yellow cornmeal from the southwestern United States and Mexico, used to make delicate tortillas, tamales, breads and some traditional baked sweets. It should only be used in recipes specifically calling for masa harina and not substituted for any other form of cornmeal.

Hominy is whole-kernel yellow or white corn that has had the germ removed and is then soaked in lime. It is most often sold canned, but is also available dried and ground. Ground, it is called *hominy grits* or simply *grits* and is used to make spoonbread, porridge and griddle cakes. *Instant grits* are also widely available and need only a brief rehydration and cooking to make a porridge-like dish. Hominy and grits figure prominently in the cooking of Mexico and Central and South America, but are rarely, if ever, used in baking and dessert cookery outside of these cuisines.

Johnnycake meal is similar to regular white cornmeal, but its grains are milled flat, rather than rounded. It is used almost exclusively to make johnny-cakes—cornmeal griddle cakes that may be as thin and delicate as French crêpes or as puffed and thick as traditional North American pancakes. A batter of johnnycake meal, sweet milk, salt and a little melted butter are combined and fried on a griddle, and the hot cakes are usually eaten with butter, maple syrup or thick cream. Johnnycake meal may be difficult to find outside Rhode Island and the surrounding states. It can be stored airtight in a cool, dry place for up to 1 year.

CORNSTARCH (CORNFLOUR) *Cornstarch* is the ground starch isolated from the whole corn kernel (called *cornflour* in Britain and Australia, it should not be confused with other cornmeal products, though some Mexican, Latin and South American recipes may use the term cornflour when masa harina or cornmeal is meant). Cornstarch is an excellent thickener and is commonly used in the sweet kitchen to thicken pie and tart fillings, puddings, custards, sauces and glazes. It has twice the thickening power of wheat flour and thickens to a clear, not cloudy, gel. Unlike tapioca (see page 113), cornstarch can thicken the fillings of open-faced or lattice-crust pies and tarts. Like wheat flour, however, cornstarch must be thoroughly cooked in a mixture or it will leave an unpalatably chalky taste in the mouth.

Stove-top cooked mixtures thickened with cornstarch, such as some puddings, pastry creams, sauces and custards, must be carefully timed to achieve the best consistency. Cornstarch granules swell to their full capacity at the boiling point and may be boiled for 1 minute beyond boiling to thicken the mixture. However, if boiled longer than that, the granules will begin to collapse and break down and the mixture will thin out irreversibly. Similarly, if the mixture is stirred too vigorously, the granules will also collapse, with the same result.

Although it is regarded most often as a thickening agent, cornstarch can be used in combination with wheat flour to produce a desired tenderness and delicacy in certain baked goods. Many recipes for shortbread, including mine, replace up to 25% of the total amount of flour with cornstarch to yield a more delicate, fragile biscuit, and some cakes and tortes call for cornstarch to contribute a particularly fine-textured crumb. Rice and potato flours can be used in the same way, and all three are generally interchangeable. Cornstarch should be stored in a cool, dry place, for up 2 years.

KAMUT Kamut is the ancient Egyptian word for wheat and is the ancestor to our modern strains of this grain. Ancient indeed, kamut was a dominant crop from 4000 BC until the late Roman Empire and was called the "Grain of the Pharaohs." It fell out of favour, however, when the Greeks and Romans developed the close relatives of our durum wheat. Today, kamut is regaining popularity thanks to its high nutritional profile and its rich, full and nutty flavour. Although the two are distantly related, many people who are mildly allergic to common wheat can tolerate small amounts of kamut in their diets. It's relatively high in gluten, and many people feel it makes a superior pasta to that made using durum wheat. It can be used to replace the whole wheat flour in many recipes and will produce a slightly heavier, fuller-flavoured product. It is best to use a combination of kamut and white wheat bread flour for a more palatable and finely textured bread. Kamut flour can also be used to add flavour to quick breads, muffins and pancakes. Store in the refrigerator for up to 6 months.

MILLET Millet is the tiny round yellow seed of a cereal grass, not properly a grain. In North America, almost the entire crop is used as the main ingredient in bird seed, and only a tiny portion of the harvest is allocated for humans. In many other cultures, however, millet is used as commonly as rice or barley, added to casseroles, soups, stews, even stuffings for vegetables and meat. Millet is very easy to digest and is the least allergenic of any cereal or grain. Although quite bitter when raw, millet is related to sorghum, a grain from which a sweet, molasses-like syrup is made, and develops a sweet, nutty flavour when baked into muffins, soft cookies, health bars and quick breads.

Millet flour is simply ground millet and can be used to replace some of the wheat flour in breads and other baked products. Although millet is high in protein, it does not contain gluten. While this means it can be tolerated by people who cannot digest wheat or other glutinous grains, millet flour cannot be used on its own to make yeast breads, as the dough will not hold together properly and will fail to rise. Millet flour can be substituted for up to 25% of the wheat flour in breads and other baked goods, but there will be a noticeable difference in the texture and flavour of the product. Store whole millet in an airtight container in a cool, dry place for up to 4 months or refrigerate for up to 6 months. Millet flour should be refrigerated for up to 4 months.

OATS, OATMEAL Oats have the dubious distinction of being, until recently, the only whole grain consumed in any quantity by North Americans. In most oat products, all three parts of the grain are used: the bran, germ and endosperm. Oats are harvested with the hulls intact, then the hulls are removed and the remaining grain is called an *oat groat*. To enable the oats to retain all of their elements without spoiling quickly, the groats are treated with heat to kill the enzyme *lipase*, which causes the breakdown of fats. This heating enables oats and oatmeal to be stored at room temperature and also gives the oats a delicious, faintly toasted flavour.

Many different forms of oats and oatmeal are available, both from supermarkets and from health and natural food stores. I strongly recommend buying organic oat products whenever possible, as the flavour and texture are far superior to the commercially produced varieties.

The term *oatmeal* can mean the cooked cereal or the oats themselves, as in *old-fashioned oatmeal*, *Scottish* or *Irish oatmeal* or *instant oatmeal*. In baking recipes, "oatmeal" will always refer to the raw product, unless otherwise specified. Perhaps surprisingly, all of the various forms and types of oatmeal, regardless of the degree and method of processing, have the same nutritional value.

Steel-cut oats, also called *Irish* or *Scottish oats*, are oat groats that have been cut horizontally with a heavy steel blade. Preparing these oats for a breakfast porridge requires overnight soaking and a lengthy cooking, but nothing makes a more satisfying, chewy and wonderfully flavourful oatmeal! They are not generally suitable for baking, but I have seen some Irish and Scottish recipes using the cooked porridge to enhance breads and scones.

Large flake rolled oats, or *old-fashioned oats,* are groats that have been heated to soften them, then rolled flat. They only require about 5 minutes of cooking to make a hot cereal and are excellent for baking, producing chewy, coarse-textured cookies, cakes and quick breads with a full, nutty, oaty flavour.

Quick-cooking rolled oats are rolled thinner and need only about 1 minute of cooking to make a hot cereal. In a pinch, they can be used for baking, but I do not recommend them. They produce a much drier, crispier cookie than large-flake oats and tend to disappear in breads, cakes and quick breads.

Instant rolled oats are steamed, cut into small flakes, steamed again and then rolled, requiring nothing more than rehydration in a hot liquid to make a ready-to-eat porridge. Their lack of texture and bland flavour make them unsuitable for baking.

Oat flour is nothing more than very finely milled oat groats. It can be used in some baked products, but is very low in gluten, so mustn't be used to replace all of the wheat flour in breads. Substitute 25 to 50% of the wheat flour with oat flour in cakes, muffins and quick breads, but be aware that the substitution will affect the final product, and you may have to try the recipe several times before you find the right balance. In leavened breads, substitute up to 25% of the total flour with oat flour, keeping in mind that the low gluten content of the oat flour will produce a slightly heavier, denser, chewier bread that will not rise quite as much, or retain as much air.

Oat bran, like wheat bran, is the isolated hull of the groat. High in fibre and much lighter in flavour and texture than wheat bran, it is popular today as an addition to baked goods, and as a hot cereal. It can be added in small quantities to enhance yeast and quick breads, cakes, cookies, pancakes, crêpes and waffles.

All oat products, unless otherwise stated on the package, should be stored in a cool, dry place for up to 1 year.

POTATO FLOUR (POTATO STARCH) Made from potatoes that have been cooked, dried and ground, potato flour, also known as *potato starch*, is used in baking to add a characteristic tenderness and delicacy to biscuits and cakes where a fine, moist crumb is desired. It can be substituted for up to 25% of the total flour in a shortbread recipe and can be used interchangeably with cornstarch and rice flour in most baking recipes. Potato flour can also be used as a thickener in soups, sauces and other dishes. Potato flour should be stored in a cool, dark, dry place for up to 2 years.

PSYLLIUM Psyllium seeds and husks are considered one of the very best intestinal cleansers on earth. Their flavour is mild and nutty, not unlike that of wheat bran, and either form can be used in hearty yeast and quick breads, as well as breakfast cereals. Extremely high in insoluble crude fibre, psyllium should be used with caution, as it can cause gastrointestinal discomfort in those who are not used to eating it. The seeds and husks are also available ground into a powder; all forms can be found at good health and natural food stores and should be stored airtight in the refrigerator for up to 4 months. While it can be added in small quantities for extra fibre or flavour, do not use psyllium to replace wheat bran or any other grain or flour product in baked goods.

QUINOA Like amaranth, quinoa (pronounced "KEEN-wa") was an ancient staple of the Incas, together with corn, beans, squash and potatoes. Though quinoa is properly a herb, not a grain, the plant's seeds resemble grain and are treated in the same way. The seeds look like tiny rounds disks when raw, and round, semi-transparent globules when cooked. They can be ivory, yellow, orange-brown, even almost red. The outer hull of the quinoa seed contains an element called *saponin*, a very bitter, resinous material that lends an acrid, soapy taste to the finished product if left intact. Depending on the preparation and the type of seed itself, quinoa can benefit from as many as five or six rinsings under cold running water before cooking. With each rinsing, the grain becomes milder and sweeter.

Quinoa seeds can be cooked whole, sprouted or ground into *quinoa flour* (also called *quinoa meal*) for use in baked goods such as pancakes, waffles, muffins, quick breads and yeast breads. Because quinoa is very low in gluten, when used in a yeast bread it should replace only up to 25% of the wheat flour. Store all quinoa products in the refrigerator for up to 6 months.

RICE FLOUR (RICE STARCH) Rice flour, also called *rice starch*, is simply rice that has been ground to a very fine powder. It is usually made from white rice, but brown rice can also be used. It can add desired tenderness to products such as shortbread and some fine-crumbed cakes. Rice flour can be substituted for up to 25% of the total flour in a biscuit or shortbread recipe and can replace cornstarch or potato flour in most baking and dessert recipes. In Japan, the sweet glutinous mochi rice is used to make rice flour, predominantly for thickening sauces and soups. Many other Asian cuisines also use glutinous rice flours in this manner. Store rice flour in a cool, dark, dry place for up to 2 years.

RYE History has proven rye flour second only to wheat for bread baking. It makes the characteristically dark and rich black breads of many parts of Europe, and its distinct and earthy flavour is still very popular in European communities. Rye flour does contain some gluten, but it is of a poorer quality than that found in wheat flour, and breads made exclusively with rye have a characteristic dense, heavy and damp texture. For a more conventional leavened bread, use rye for no more than 25% of the total flour, with white or whole wheat making up the balance. Rye flour's strong flavour makes it unsuitable for most desserts, but there are several traditional recipes, such as the French Pain d'Épices or delicate buckwheat crêpes, that capitalize on its nutty, slightly bitter flavours.

Dark or whole rye flour is milled from the whole rye kernel. The kernels for *light rye flour* have had the germ and/or the bran removed during milling. Dark rye retains much more of the protein, vitamins and minerals than light rye.

Rye flakes and *cracked rye* are other rye products, but are not commonly used in North American cuisine.

All whole rye products are prone to rancidity and should be stored in the refrigerator.

SAGO A granular starch resembling tapioca but with smaller grains, sago is commonly used in Asian cooking. It can be used as a thickener in savoury recipes or as the primary ingredient in a tapioca-like pudding. Although rarely called for in North American recipes, sago can be found in some Asian markets.

SPELT Spelt is one of the most ancient grains known, harvested in Europe over 9000 years ago, and in Asia long before that. It lost favour in Europe during the mid-nineteenth century, but has come back into vogue recently for its nutritive and culinary virtues. Related to wheat, a grain of spelt looks much like one of hard winter wheat. It is exceptionally hardy and flourishes in harsh climates, often without need of pesticides, fertilizers, even much warmth. It is among the most nutritious grains, being higher in protein, carbohydrates, iron, thiamine, riboflavin, niacin and other vitamins and minerals than whole wheat. Spelt does contain gluten, but it differs from that of wheat, and some people who cannot tolerate wheat may not be allergic to spelt. One of spelt's most appealing qualities is its taste. Rich and nutty, it is more robust than wheat and can enhance breads, muffins, quick breads, even pancakes or waffles. Leavened bread can be made exclusively from spelt, although it will be much heavier and denser than one made with white bread flour, similar to a loaf made only with whole wheat or rye flour. Spelt flour can be substituted for the whole wheat flour in a part-whole wheat and part-white flour yeast bread or can replace up to about half the white flour in a white bread recipe, but expect a change in the delicacy of the crumb, the density and the flavour. Spelt flour should be stored in the refrigerator for up to 6 months.

TAPIOCA Tapioca is made from dried manioc, the starch from the root of the tropical cassava or manioc plant. Available in several different forms, tapioca is mainly used to thicken savoury and sweet sauces, fillings, soups and stews, but instant or pearl tapioca can also be used to make a sweet, mild-flavoured custard dessert.

Tapioca flakes are not widely used, but are available in health and natural food stores. The tiny-grained *instant tapioca*, also called *minute* or *quick-cooking tapioca*, has been precooked, much like parboiled rice, then dehydrated and formed into tiny pellets. It requires no soaking, and a short exposure to moisture and heat activates it. It is a highly convenient form of the starch and, like cornstarch, thickens clear, making it a good choice for fruit pie fillings and sauces. It does retain a softly beaded texture and is most appropriate paired with fruit with a similar texture, such as blueberries or raspberries. The soft granules will be more noticeable and may be distracting in an apple or peach pie, for instance. Tapioca cannot be used to thicken the fillings of open-faced or lattice-crust pies and tarts, however, as the starch must be completely surrounded with liquid and heat to gel properly. The exposed tapioca starch will not dissolve properly, and the filling will not thicken uniformly.

Although it can be used for the traditional tapioca pudding custard, instant tapioca doesn't make a custard as voluptuous and roundly textured as large pearl tapioca would (see below). Use a ratio of 1 part quick-cooking tapioca to 4 or 5 parts water or milk to make a pudding. Instant tapioca should be stored in a cool, dry place for up to 2½ years.

Large pearl tapioca is primarily used to make tapioca pudding, rather than as a thickener, and indeed makes the most wonderfully chewy, creamy, comforting version of this childhood dessert. It must be presoaked in cold water for about 2 hours, then drained and cooked using a ratio of 1 part tapioca to 8 parts liquid (milk or water) to make a pudding. The starch and liquid is best cooked in a double boiler until the mixture is clear, before the other ingredients and flavourings are added, to ensure the starch is properly rehydrated and the liquid absorbed. Pearl tapioca is widely available in most supermarkets and also comes in flavoured varieties. Ignore these, as they usually have more chemicals and additives than flavour. Store pearl tapioca in a cool, dry place for up to 2½ years.

Tapioca flour, also called *tapioca starch*, is a finely ground dried starch most often used as a thickener for sauces, soups, fillings and puddings. It can be used in place of cornstarch, rice flour and potato flour in most recipes, including those for shortbread and fine cakes. Store tapioca flour in a cool, dry place for up to 2 years.

TRITICALE Triticale is an exceptionally hardy hybrid grain created by Canadian agricultural scientists by crossbreeding varieties of wheat and rye. It was developed to enable people living in less fertile areas of the world to grow a nutritious, versatile grain. Triticale tastes of both wheat and rye and can sometimes have a slightly sour flavour, not unlike that of many rye flours. It can be used alone or in combination with other grains in yeast breads and some other whole grain baked products. Bread made entirely with triticale requires less and gentler kneading, as its gluten is softer than wheat gluten, and will need only one rising. Experiment a few times to get the feel of the dough and the timing right. An easier way to begin incorporating this new grain into your baking is to replace up to 50% of the total wheat flour in a yeast bread recipe with triticale flour. As it is a whole grain flour, triticale should be stored in the refrigerator for up to 6 months and checked periodically for signs of spoilage.

Other Specialty Flours

BEAN FLOUR (see also Soy Flour) Made from finely ground soy, romano or garbanzo beans (chickpeas), bean flours can be used in bread doughs, cakes and other baked goods, but only in recipes specifically calling for them. Specialty cookbooks, as well as health and natural food stores that sell the flours themselves, are good sources of such recipes. Bean flours are nutritious, high in fibre and protein, but are not recommended to replace wheat or other flour in most recipes. Store all bean flours in airtight containers in the refrigerator for up to 6 months.

MATZOH MEAL (MATZOH FLOUR) Matzoh bread is a crisp, unleavened flatbread made for the Jewish feast of Passover, during which leavened bread of any kind is forbidden. Made from white or whole wheat flour, water and sometimes salt, it's very similar in appearance and flavour to cream crackers or saltines. Matzoh bread can be ground into a fine meal and used in cakes and other baked goods during that holiday. Many classic recipes for tortes (cakes in which the flour is all or mostly replaced with ground nuts, bread crumbs or cake crumbs) can very successfully be made with matzoh meal. Feel free to replace the bread crumbs in torte or pudding recipes with matzoh meal. It can be purchased already ground, as matzoh meal, or you can simply crush the matzoh yourself.

SOY FLOUR Made from milled soy beans, soy flour is highly nutritious, as it is extremely high in protein, cholesterol-free and full of a host of vitamins and minerals. It is usually deodorized before being sold for use in doughs and other preparations, as it has a strong, not terribly desirable odour that can be imparted to the finished product. Soy flour is most often blended with other flours when used in baking, as it does not behave as a conventional flour. It is commonly used in Asian cuisine as a thickener for sauces and as a base for sweet confections, bean curd cakes and candies. It can be used in recipes specifically calling for soy flour, but I do not recommend using it to replace any of the wheat flour in most recipes. Store soy flour in an airtight container in the refrigerator for up to 4 months.

Gelling Agents

AGAR-AGAR Also called *agar, kanten, Japanese gelatine, Japanese moss* and *Ceylon moss*, agar-agar is an Asian product extracted from dried seaweed. Neutral in taste and with a more efficient thickening power than gelatine, it's used for many Asian fruit puddings, jellies and other gelatinous desserts. It can be found in Asian markets and should be stored in a cool, dry place.

GELATINE Gelatine is a protein, traditionally extracted from the tendons, bones and cartilage of beef and veal, but today more commonly made from pig skin. Colourless, clear-setting and tasteless, it has been a popular thickener for sweet and savoury jellies, such as aspics, glazes and moulded desserts, for hundreds of years. It is available in two forms—powder and leaf. Do not confuse the sweetened, artificially flavoured powdered gelatine dessert mixes available with unsweetened pure gelatine products.

Powdered or granulated gelatine is the most popular form used in North America. The gelatine is dehydrated and finely ground, producing a pale yellow-ivory powder. It is widely available in standardized ¼-ounce envelopes, but can also be purchased in bulk. It requires a brief softening in cold liquid for 3 to 5 minutes before being added to the warm liquid of the recipe. This soaking plumps the dried granules, enabling them to dissolve evenly.

Leaf or sheet gelatine is less commonly available, but is preferred by chefs and European cooks because it is easier to use than powdered gelatine and absorbs less of its soaking liquid. It can be purchased in specialty food stores, baking supply shops and many European delicatessens. Each thin, fragile sheet of leaf gelatine is about 3 inches wide by 6 inches long and is perfectly clear. Leaf gelatine needs to be soaked longer than granulated, about 10 minutes, then gently squeezed to release any excess liquid. It can then be melted into the other ingredients of the recipe and performs in exactly the same way as powdered gelatine. In general, 4 sheets of leaf gelatine have the equivalent thickening power of one envelope of granulated gelatine.

Gelatine, either alone or in the context of a recipe, should never be frozen or heated to above 150 degrees, as at these extreme temperatures it begins to lose its strong, mesh-like structure and becomes impotent.

One envelope (¼-ounce or about 1 scant tablespoon) powdered gelatine or 4 sheets leaf gelatine is often recommended to thicken 2 cups of liquid. I have found that this proportion is appropriate for moulded desserts that are to be turned out, therefore requiring more setting power. For gelatine desserts that are to be eaten from a coupe dish or a glass, I prefer a ratio of ¼ ounce or 4 sheets to 3 cups of liquid. This results in a more delicate, wonderfully jiggly dessert, one that feels smoother on the tongue. A high proportion of sugar, alcohol or fruit can also weaken the setting capabilities of gelatine, so if you are creating your own recipes, you may find you need to use more gelatine in desserts where these are present.

Gelatine will continue to set for up to 2 days after its initial incorporation, so you can play with the texture and solidity of your dessert by serving it earlier or later. I generally leave the dessert to set for between 4 and 6 hours, depending on the size and depth of the mould. Leaving the dessert too long will give you a fairly bouncy product, while not enough setting time will make turning the mould out impossible and give non-moulded gelatine desserts a consistency similar to a slightly thickened sports drink. The ideal texture is firm enough to jiggle teasingly on the spoon, but soft enough to melt on your tongue and slip seductively down your throat.

Some fruits contain an enzyme called a *protease*, which directly attacks the protein that enables the gelatine to set. Pineapple, honeydew melon, papaya, fresh figs, mango, guava, kiwi fruit and passion fruit are among the most common fruits that present this problem. However, cooking the fruit pulp above 170 degrees neutralizes this enzyme, so the fruit can be used with gelatine. Canned varieties of these fruits have been cooked to at least that temperature and may be used as well, although in some cases, the flavour and/or texture may be somewhat compromised.

ISINGLASS Isinglass is a very pure form of gelatine obtained from the bladders of sturgeon and other cold water ocean fish. Although it was very popular in the last century for the preparation of all manner of sweet and savoury jellies and aspics, it fell out of favour with the introduction of more easily acquired and conveniently used forms of gelatine, and is rarely used today.

PECTIN Pectin is a complex carbohydrate that occurs naturally in the seeds, peel, rind and flesh of many fruits. When cooked, pectin thickens liquids and pulps into jellies and jams much the way gelatine would. Some fruits, like apples, citrus fruits and quince, are high in natural pectin and will set up beautifully on their own, while others are relatively low and need the assistance of added pectin. Commercial pectin is a flavourless and odourless substance that dissolves easily in water and other liquids, then thickens to a clear gel. It is used for jams, jellies, glazes and other preserves made with fruits low in natural pectin, such as peaches or apricots.

Commercial pectin is available in two forms, and both work equally well. *Liquid pectin* is derived from apples, while *dry, granulated* or *powdered pectin* can be made from apples or from various citrus fruits.

While commercial pectin's strongest selling point is the speed with which it can set a mixture, thereby greatly reducing the time it takes to make jam or jelly, I, along with many expert preservers, find it of dubious value. The quality and flavour of a jam or jelly depends on the flavour of the fruit being allowed to come through, unmasked by a great deal of sugar. For commercial pectin to be effective, the mixture must have a certain proportion of added sugar—a ratio in the neighbourhood of 60% sugar to 40% fruit, juice or other liquid if you observe the manufacturers' directions. This proportion not only makes a cloyingly sweet preserve, but can also the render the fresh taste of fruit or juice quite fake and artificial. A far preferable method of preserving is to use the natural pectin present in fruit such as apples and lemons to boost the pectin levels of low pectin fruits. A few strips of lemon peel, or the cores and peels of several apples, combined with fruits such as peaches or a fruit juice, then cooked long and slow will produce a deeply flavoured, softly set jam or jelly that retains the wonderful taste of the original fruit. Many good preserving cookbooks are available today that advocate this natural preserving method and are well worth seeking out!

Sugar and Other Sweeteners

Role of Sweeteners

As with most ingredients in the sweet kitchen, sugar and other sweeteners are marvellously accomplished role players, often performing a variety of functions in a single product. Of course, they most often sweeten everything from baked goods to frozen desserts to meringues, candy and preserves. But if you were to simply replace them with a product that does nothing but add sweetness, your cake would most likely fall, your ice cream crystallize, your meringues deflate, your candies become lumpy and your jelly refuse to thicken. Below, the myriad functions of sugar and other sweeteners.

❖ As well as contributing sweetness, many sweeteners impart flavour to baked goods and desserts. All sugars develop a richer, darker, often toffee-like flavour when exposed to heat, because the heat causes them to caramelize. Even relatively flavourless refined white sugars contribute a depth of flavour in desserts that are cooked or baked. Some sweeteners, such as honey, molasses and brown sugar, have an inherent flavour all their own, which is imparted in some degree to the final product, regardless of whether or not it is cooked.

❖ Sweeteners often add colour to many desserts and baked goods, either from their own natural colour or due to caramelization. Sweeteners such as molasses, dark corn syrup, maple syrup and brown sugar add an element of colour to even uncooked or lightly cooked mixtures, such as icings and frostings. All sugars, as they caramelize, take on an increasingly darker golden amber colour. It is the caramelization that contributes to the golden crust of cakes, cookies and other baked goods.

❖ Sugars of all kinds feed the yeast in yeast doughs, enabling fermentation and thereby allowing the breads to rise. Often, a pure sugar such as honey or granulated white or brown sugar is added to the warm liquid ingredients at the beginning of the preparation of a dough to encourage the yeasts to begin fermenting. While this may be the only added sugar in the recipe, the yeast quickly consumes it and begins to convert the starch in the flour to sugar as well. This provides enough food for it to perform properly, producing the carbon dioxide gas that will ultimately leaven the bread.

❖ Sugars form the foundation of many icings and frostings, candies and confections. In addition to adding flavour and sweetness, they often act as the main body of the preparation, as in confectioners' sugar-based frostings, syrup-based or cooked-sugar icings and glazes and caramel toppings and glazes.

❖ Granular sugars aid in the aeration of cake, cookie and quick bread batters, thereby enhancing their tenderness and texture. When granulated sugar is creamed with butter or eggs, air becomes trapped between the grains and the surrounding material. Other ingredients in a recipe ensure this air remains suspended in the batter, expanding during baking, making the resulting product risen and tender. Granulated white sugar is most commonly used, but some varieties of brown granulated sugar can also perform this function. Very fine grained sugars, such as fructose or superfine sugar, however, are not appropriate, as their grains are too small to create the necessary friction.

❖ Some sweeteners, such as brown sugar, molasses, maple syrup and many grain syrups, are acidic in nature, and often act as the acid necessary to activate the baking soda in recipes for baked goods. They must be present in a large enough quantity, however, to have sufficient acidity to react with the baking soda; otherwise, another acidic ingredient must be used as well, such as buttermilk or lemon juice.

❖ Many sweeteners enhance the texture and crumb of even those baked goods that do not rely on the creaming method of leavening. Liquid sweeteners such as honey add a rich moisture and velvety texture to cakes and quick breads such as gingerbread, producing a denser, more moist cake with a tighter crumb than the same cake made with a granulated sugar. Superfine sugar contributes to angel food cake's lightness, fine crumb and delicate texture.

Brown sugar produces a chewy, soft cookie, while granulated white sugar will make the most crisp, dry and delicate of cookies.

❖ Sugar is hygroscopic, meaning it attracts and retains moisture. This characteristic allows all forms of sugar to extend the keeping qualities of baked goods, adding moisture and tenderness, and allowing the products to retain necessary moisture so they remain fresher, longer. Although any type of sugar performs this function to some degree, liquid sweeteners contribute the most moisture, being about 20% water themselves. Soft sugars, such as brown and raw sugars, are second in terms of moisture at about 3 to 5% water and granulated white sugars have the lowest inherent moisture.

❖ Sugar's hygroscopic nature also allows it to act as an effective preservative for fruits, as in the case of jams, jellies and other compotes. Sugar draws moisture away from bacteria and yeasts, killing or sterilizing them, allowing the fruits in the solution to remain "fresh" for much longer than they would naturally.

❖ Liquid sweeteners such as honey and corn syrup function as invert sugars and are often used to delay crystallization of other sugars in syrups, icings, candies and confections. Invert sugars are formed of much smaller crystals than granulated sugars and act upon other sugars present to ensure a smooth, fluid, viscous product, with no crystalline lumps.

❖ Sugars of all kinds, but particularly liquid sweeteners such as honey or corn syrup, give ice creams, sorbets and gelati a characteristic smooth and luxurious texture. Sugar freezes at a lower temperature than water and when thoroughly incorporated into a custard, cream or fruit mixture effectively lowers the freezing temperature of the mixture itself. When the mixture is placed in the freezer, it becomes firm and cold, but not rock hard the way water, milk or fruit juice would naturally. The inherent sugar in alcohol performs the same function. Liquid sweeteners, acting once again as invert sugars, add to the smoothness and creaminess of the final desserts by preventing the mixture from becoming icy and crystalline when frozen.

❖ Granulated sugar aids in making light and voluminous cooked mousses and egg creams, for two reasons. First, when sugar is whisked with eggs, the granules provide friction for the eggs, trapping air and contributing to the lightness and volume of the mixture. Second, sugar delays the coagulation of eggs, giving mixtures such as cooked mousses, meringues and sabayons more time to incorporate air before setting, resulting in a thicker, foamier dessert.

❖ When sugar is used in the preparation of whipped egg whites, it adds stability and structure, allowing the foams to be held longer and mixed more vigorously than possible without the addition. The sugar first delays the foaming of the whites. While this also means it decreases the ultimate volume the foam can achieve, it means the foam is unlikely to be overwhipped, a boon when mixing small amounts of whites, or using an electric mixer. Sugar also enables the foam to retain moisture in the oven, providing stability until the proteins of the whites can solidify and support the structure of the foam themselves.

❖ The small amount of cornstarch in confectioners' sugar helps stiffen and stabilize egg white foams, whipped cream, meringue icings and many uncooked candies and confections.

❖ In the making of jams, jellies and preserves, sugar activates commercial pectin, enabling it to quickly set a liquid mixture. The ratio of sugar to fruit or liquid must be very high, however, in order for the pectin to work. By comparison, the natural pectin in fruits such as apples, blueberries and citrus fruits needs a relatively small amount of sugar, often little more than is naturally present in the fruits, to produce a thick, set preserve. Preserves made this way (see page 117) do require a considerably longer cooking time than those made with commercial pectin (but it's worth it!).

❖ Sugars can be used to control the thickness and consistency of gelling in preserves and compotes. The more the mixture is reduced, and its inherent moisture evaporated, concentrating the sugar, the thicker, more viscous and more jellied the mixture will be. In other words, the higher the proportion of sugar in a given mixture, the thicker the final result. This can be used to an advantage in syrups, sauces and poaching liquids, as well as all manner of sweet preserves such as jams, jellies and compotes.

❖ Sugars and other sweeteners can be used as a garnish, to enhance the appearance of myriad desserts and baked goods. From a very simple dusting of confectioners' sugar on a cake or a topping of sparkly crystal sugar on a puff pastry turnover to a more elaborate caramel cage over an ice cream bombe or even artistic sugar work mouldings as a centrepiece for a wedding cake, sugar and its variations can be beautiful and decorative.

❖ The granular quality of white sugar can be used to prevent dry ingredient mixtures from clumping together, for an even distribution of all ingredients. A good example is the preparation of a quick bread, for which all the dry ingredients in the recipe are combined in one bowl and all the wet ingredients combined separately. The two are mixed together all at once, just enough to moisten the flour, but not overwork it and develop unwanted gluten. To achieve a well-blended batter with this bare minimum of mixing, thorough blending of the dry ingredients beforehand is essential, in order to keep the batters light and the texture of the final product tender. Sugar provides friction, allowing the other dry ingredients to be evenly dispersed and distributed.

❖ While most forms of sugar, including the so-called raw varieties, are dubious sources of nutrients, they do provide energy in the form of carbohydrate calories.

❖ And, of course, the addition of sugar and other sweeteners to many recipes is what distinguishes them as desserts! Perhaps it goes without saying, but the primary function of sugar and other sweeteners is to add sweetness! However, each type of sweetener has a different sweetening power, as well as other characteristics that make it more or less appropriate for different products. Read on to discover each sweetener's individuality.

Sugars

All sugars should be stored in airtight containers, in a cool, dry, place. Moisture can attract yeasts and moulds to all types of sugars, so make sure they are kept well sealed. Stored properly, most sugars should last at least 2 years. Honey will keep even longer, but maple syrup has a shorter shelf life, which can be prolonged to about 1 year by storing it in the refrigerator in a sealed jar or tin. In all cases, if white, furry or odd-smelling things begin to appear in your honey, syrup or sugar, don't take any chances—discard it immediately.

SUGAR SWEETNESS REFERENCE CHART

Type of Sugar: Sweetness Level
Sucrose: 1
Fructose: 1.7
Dextrose: 0.6
Glucose Syrup: 0.5
Maltose: 0.3 to 0.4

SUGAR CANE AND SUGAR BEETS Sugar can be obtained from many sources, including most fruits and even starches. The two most common sources of refined sugars are *sugar cane*, a woody, bamboo-like tropical plant, and *sugar beets*, a form of beet particularly high in natural sugars. While beet sugar is rarely used to make molasses and molasses-type sugars, it is more widely used than cane sugar in the production of white and regular brown sugars, as it is more prolific, easier to grow and much cheaper. Cane sugar, however, in its raw state, has a more pleasant, less harsh flavour than that of beet sugar. This flavour is relatively immaterial in white sugars, as these are so refined that little or none of the original flavour remains. Molasses and brown sugars are most often made of cane sugar, however, as the residual molasses material carries a significant flavour. The rarer refined white cane sugar (as well as all manner of brown, molasses and raw sugars) is often available at Caribbean, Creole or Latin American groceries, but will usually be significantly more expensive than its beet counterpart, and the discernible difference is negligible.

GRANULATED SUGAR (*White Sugar, Table Sugar, Fine Granulated Sugar*) Granulated sugar is the most common form of sugar used today, excellent for both cooking and baking. It is the final product of the sugar refining process. Juice from the beets or sugar cane is put through a centrifuging process, during which the molasses and other impurities are removed. The resulting syrup is clarified, then put through a charcoal filter to make it a pristine white, as well as remove any residual mineral salts. The sugar is then forced to crystallize, drying into the familiar fine grains. It is free-flowing, lumping only if it comes into contact with moisture. Granulated white sugar is approximately 99.9% sucrose, a very sweet disaccharide, or double sugar, composed of glucose and fructose. Granulated sugar can be made from sugar cane or beets, and likely you will not even know which one you are using. Unless the package is labelled "Pure Cane Sugar," it is likely beet sugar. The medium-fine grains of regular granulated sugar allow it to act as a good source of friction for creamed mixtures such as cake and cookie batters, yet ensure it will readily dissolve in most solutions. It is the most widely used form of sweetener in baking, playing a vital role in all manner of desserts. It has little distinct flavour when raw and primarily contributes pure sweetness, but when caramelized on its own or in baked goods takes on a toffee-like flavour and colour. Keep in mind when substituting other sweeteners for granulated sugar that most alternatives will not have granulated sugar's sweetening power and therefore will have to be used in somewhat greater quantities to achieve the same result.

SUPERFINE SUGAR (*Instant Dissolving Sugar, Castor Sugar, Caster Sugar*) Superfine sugar has exactly the same composition and sweetness as granulated sugar, simply ground into smaller grains. This fine texture enables it to dissolve almost instantly, important for products such as fresh fruit sauces and other uncooked mixtures. It can be smoothly blended into mixtures where a smooth dough is desired, as in the case of shortbread. It incorporates easily into delicate batters, incorporating a minimum of air in the process. The grains are also lighter than the grains of regular granulated sugar, so it can be better suspended in light batters, such as that of an angel food cake, without weighing down the mixture and causing it to lose precious volume. Superfine sugar is not appropriate in situations where air incorporation is demanded, as the granules are too small to create the necessary friction. For this reason, it should never be substituted for granulated sugar in creamed batters and other situations where aeration is important, such as sabayons, fruit curds and mousses or foams. Superfine sugar tends to clump, so should be sifted before using. To keep superfine sugar free-flowing, some manufacturers add anti-caking agents, such as cornstarch. These starches, however, can negatively interfere with the chemical balance of a recipe: in the case of meringues, for example, cornstarch would prevent the egg whites from expanding to their full capacity. For this reason, be sure to purchase superfine sugar to which nothing has been added. You can prepare your own by spinning regular granulated sugar in a food processor until it is very finely ground.

CONFECTIONERS' SUGAR (*Powdered Sugar, Icing Sugar*) Confectioners' sugar is granulated sugar that has been powdered or pulverized. Because sugar in this state tends to attract so much moisture, a maximum of 5% anti-caking agent is added, most often in the form of cornstarch. Confectioners' sugar is therefore not appropriate as a substitution for granulated or superfine sugar, nor can it be replaced with any other product in most recipes. Confectioners' sugar is most often used as an ingredient in icings and frostings or as a garnish on its own for cakes, pastries and other baked goods and confections. It can also be used as a sweetener in fruit sauces, in which it dissolves quickly and smoothly, and aids in the thickening. In shortbread, shortcrust pastry and other delicate baked goods in which a very delicate, fine texture is desired, the fine grains and small amount of cornstarch dissolve into the dough without leaving large crystals, contributing to the tenderness of the biscuit. The cornstarch in confectioners' sugar can also be used to an advantage to help stiffen meringues and other egg white-based confections, such as royal icing.

Confectioners' sugar must be stored airtight, as it tends to cake in spite of the cornstarch. It should be well sifted before using and often before measuring, depending on the recipe.

GLAZING SUGAR Glazing sugar is basically confectioners' sugar minus the cornstarch. It is used commercially and by specialty bakers in icings, glazes and confections. It can be purchased from some specialty cake decorating companies, but is rarely called for in home use.

COARSE SUGAR, CRYSTAL SUGAR, ROCK SUGAR These forms of cane or beet sugar are rarely used in baking for their sweetening power, but often as a garnish or decoration. They are all examples of sugar that has been left in large crystals and may be white, blond, brown or even artificially coloured every hue of the rainbow. Although not recommended for use as a sweetener, these sugars can add an appealing crunch and attractive sparkle to the tops of yeast and quick breads, cakes, cookies, pastries and other baked goods and confections. They are available in gourmet and specialty food shops, as well as baking and cake decorating supply shops.

SANDING SUGAR This large-crystalled sugar, usually clear but sometimes amber or coloured, is used predominantly by commercial bakers as a topping for pastries, sweets and other confections, lending a pretty sparkle and pleasant crunch.

FRUCTOSE *(Fruit Sugar)* Although fructose occurs naturally in all fruits and in honey, commercial fruit sugar is actually made by dividing sucrose (regular white sugar) into its two components: fructose and glucose. Crystalline fructose looks similar to white granulated sugar, with somewhat finer granules. It has the same nutritional profile, even the same number of calories as sucrose by volume, but is about twice as sweet as granulated sugar. This means less can be used to achieve the same sweetness—great for those trying to control their weight or for diabetics because it is metabolized more slowly than granulated sugar. However, it's not generally recommended for dessert recipes. In fact, fruit sugar is usually not a suitable replacement for granulated sugar, unless the recipe specifies. It is available in some supermarkets and in health and natural food stores, and is often considerably more expensive than granulated sugar.

DEXTROSE Dextrose is a form of glucose, produced when enzymes act upon cornstarch, breaking it down into a simple sugar. Crystalline dextrose looks very similar to granulated sugar, with free-flowing, fine white grains. Only about 65 to 80% as sweet as sucrose, it is not an efficient sweetener. However, dextrose is widely used in the commercial baking industry to aid in the fermentation of yeast doughs, and its ability to enhance the flavours of other ingredients in a product without adding an overly sweet taste has also made it valuable as an ingredient in packaged and prepared foods. It is not recommended as an ingredient in most domestic baking and dessert recipes.

MALTOSE *(Malt Sugar)* Maltose is a sweet disaccharide (double sugar) that occurs naturally when enzymes act on starches to break them down. Maltose is produced this way in active yeast doughs and contributes a slight sweetness to the finished breads. It is widely used in alcohol fermentation, promoting the yeast's development. Although rarely used in baking in Western cuisine, maltose has a distinctive and pleasant taste, with a sweetening power of about 30% of that of sucrose, making it somewhat sweeter than barley malt extract. It is used more frequently in Asian cooking and can sometimes be found in Chinese and Asian groceries, as well as in health and natural food stores in either syrup or crystalline form. Maltose should be used only in recipes where specified, as it does not perform the way granulated or other sugars do and can drastically alter the chemistry of a recipe.

FRUITSOURCE A relatively new alternative sweetener, FruitSource is a patented natural product made by thoroughly blending concentrated grape juice, naturally high in sugars, and whole grain syrup through a process of vacuum pressure. Available in liquid or granulated form, it has approximately the same sweetness as brown sugar. FruitSource in granulated form can be substituted for granulated or brown sugar in some recipes, but does not cream well or dissolve in the same way. For these reasons, it is best substituted in cases where the sugar's function is simply as a sweetener. If liquid FruitSource is used to replace other liquid sweeteners, such as maple syrup or barley malt syrup, the other liquids in the recipe should be reduced, or the flour increased, by a margin, or the batter or dough will be too wet. For best results, follow the manufacturer's recommendations. FruitSource is available in many health and natural food stores.

SUCANAT Like FruitSource, Sucanat is a brand-name patented natural sweetener that is becoming increasingly popular as an alternative to refined white sugar. Really nothing more than crystallized molasses, it is made by extracting molasses from cane sugar syrup and drying it under carefully controlled conditions to encourage crystallization into large, toffee-coloured grains. It has an intense, almost burnt, distinctly molasses flavour, not appropriate for all recipes. It can be substituted for granulated white or brown sugar in some cases where the sugar functions mainly as a sweetener. I would recommend spinning it in a food processor first, though, to produce a finer grind. Sucanat is also available in a thick syrup and in a diluted liquid form; all forms can be found in many health and natural food stores.

DATE SUGAR Dates are one of the most intensely sweet natural foods available and have been used in sweets and confections, not to mention savoury foods, since long before other forms of sweetener were available. With date sugar, their natural sweetening power is harnessed by reducing dried dates to a cooked paste, dehydrating the mixture and breaking it down into granules. Zahidi dates, plump, large and ultra-sweet, are most often used, as their high invert sugar content allows them to impart an intense sweetness to mixtures quickly and efficiently. Although pleasantly flavoured and quite sweet, date sugar does not dissolve the way other sugars do (it's basically just ground dates). It is also prone to scorching and burns at a lower temperature than sucrose or other sugars. For these reasons, it is best used in dried fruit fillings, icings and baked goods where the role of the sugar is simply as a sweetener and where the rich flavouring would be appropriate. Date sugar is very expensive, available in health and natural food stores.

BROWN SUGAR Originally, brown sugar was semi-refined white sugar, in which some of the natural molasses remained. These days, the refining process for most sugar is so extensive, the molasses must be re-added afterwards! It has a very moist, cakey texture. Its granules are smaller and softer than those of white sugar, making it inappropriate for some creaming and aerating preparations. This moisture means brown sugar produces chewier cookies and softer, more tender, moist baked goods than white sugar. Both light and dark brown sugar are almost as sweet as white sugar, at about 96% sucrose, and can be substituted in equal amounts for granulated sugar in some recipes. When measuring, pack the measuring cup tightly, as the sugar is quite soft and inconsistent in volume if simply scooped or spooned. Recently, liquid and dry granular versions of brown sugar have become available, but should only be used in baking where specified and never to replace other forms of brown or granulated sugar, or other liquid sweeteners. Brown sugar tends to dry out rapidly when exposed to air; keeping it in a strong plastic bag, usually the one it came in, keeps it moist for months. If yours does become as hard as a rock, don't despair: there are several remedies, such as adding a wedge of fresh apple to the bag to restore some lost moisture. Kitchenware and gift shops often sell discs of unfinished terra cotta that can be moistened and stored with brown sugar to prevent hardening. Alternatively, place the hard sugar in a shallow baking dish and sprinkle it with a few drops of water. Cover the dish with aluminum foil and place the dish in a preheated 250° oven for 3 to 5 minutes or until the sugar is soft and moist again. These techniques can be used with any variety of brown or raw sugar.

Light Brown Sugar (*Golden Sugar, Brilliant Yellow Sugar*) Light brown sugar is made by adding small amounts of molasses and other sugar refinery syrups to refined sugar, to give it a pale yellow colour and a slight caramel flavour, milder than dark brown sugar. It adds a subtle caramelized flavour to baked goods such as many cakes and quick breads, in cookies where a chewy, soft texture is desired and in many icings and confections for flavour and colour.

Dark Brown Sugar *(Old-Fashioned Brown Sugar)* Dark brown sugar is made the same way as light, with more molasses added. It has a darker brown colour and a deeper, richer, more toffee-like flavour than light brown sugar. Dark brown sugar is often used in dark spice and fruit cakes and fillings for flavour and in cookies and other baked goods to add a moist, soft, chewy texture. Light and dark brown sugars can often be used interchangeably if a slight change in colour and flavour in the product are acceptable.

RAW SUGARS Raw sugars are what remains when the molasses is removed from the sugar cane and the sugar is processed into crystals. In their unadulterated states, raw sugars have some, albeit slight, nutritional value in the form of minerals and vitamins. At one time, raw sugars were truly raw; today, however, sugar marketed in North America as "raw" has been purified and sterilized to remove any impurities and kill any harmful moulds that may be present. This processing effectively reduces the nutritional profile of these sugars to that of super-refined white sugar. Raw sugars are similar in appearance and sweetness to brown sugar, but have unique flavours and textures.

Demerara Sugar From the Demerara region of Guyana, demerara sugar is amber-brown, coarse-grained and relatively dry. With about 15% of the natural molasses remaining, it has a deep toffee-like flavour and can be substituted for dark brown sugar in many baked goods and fillings, though its sandy texture makes it inappropriate for most creaming applications. Its relatively large crystals make it useful as a decoration, in toppings and crumbles, and in baked products in which it has the opportunity to melt into the batter.

Muscovado Sugar *(Barbados Sugar)* Very moist, dark and fine-grained, this "raw" sugar has a rich, distinct molasses flavour. It is about as sweet as dark brown sugar and is best used in fillings and baked goods that echo its strong flavour, such as spice cakes, fruit cakes and rich fruit fillings.

Chinese Rock Sugar *(Chinese Sugar)* This "sugar" is actually a blend of several refined and raw sugars and honey. Its beautiful giant-crystal form makes it the perfect choice for garnishing sweets and drinks, but its primary use in the

Chinese kitchen is to add a mellow sweetness to savoury dishes such as braised pork or duck and soups. It can be used in desserts in which it will be melted down, such as poached fruit or custards, and lends a mild, slightly honeyed flavour. It can be found in Chinese and other Asian markets.

Jaggery *(Palm Sugar, Coconut Sugar, Java Sugar)* Jaggery is a dark "raw" sugar popular in Indian, Thai and other Asian cuisines. It is usually made from the sap of various palm trees, but can also be made from the juice of the sugar cane plant. It is widely used to add a distinctive flavour and perfume, as well as sweetness, to both sweet and savoury dishes. It comes in two forms: the smooth, thick paste has a consistency like creamed honey and is usually used as a sweet spread rather than as an ingredient in cooking and baking. The more common granulated form resembles coarse-crystalled light brown or golden sugar and has a similar sweetening power. It may be sold in traditional blocks of bricks, which can be crumbled, then spun in a food processor before use. It can be used to replace brown sugar in many recipes, but will add a significantly different, slightly smoky flavour. Jaggery is available in many Indian, Thai and other Asian groceries, as well as some health and natural food stores.

Piloncillo *(Panela, Panocha)* A traditional Mexican sugar available at Latin American markets, piloncillo is cane juice that has been boiled down to a thick syrup and poured into moulds. The cone-shaped loaves are staples of Mexican cooking; chunks broken off may be added to sauces, salsas and soups, as well as sweet dishes. Dark and flavourful, piloncillo can be used as a decoration or in crumbles and toppings when coarsely ground and in much the same way as Demerara sugar when ground more finely. To break it down, place the cone on a firm, secure surface, cover it with a kitchen towel and hit it with a mallet until it breaks into shards. The pieces can then be processed in a food processor before use.

Turbinado Sugar Turbinado sugar is raw sugar that has been steam-cleaned, then dried into large crystals. The cleaning removes most of the molasses, but the small amount that remains gives the sugar its light amber colour and caramel flavour. Its coarse grain makes turbinado sugar inappropriate for some preparations, but it is well used in many cookies, quick breads, fillings and cakes. Although it is softer and more moist, it can often be used to replace dark brown sugar, as it has a comparable sweetness.

Artificial Sweeteners

Artificial sweeteners such as *aspartame, Acesulfame-K* and *saccharin* are sold under a plethora of brand names. There are several other products in development, and others still that have fallen out of favour, either for flavour deficiencies or for questionable safety.

ASPARTAME, commonly known as NutraSweet, is approximately 160 times sweeter than sugar, but tends to have a distinctive aftertaste. Marketed under several product names, such as *Equal,* it is used commercially in baked goods, candies and soft drinks. It is also popular as a coffee sweetener and as a sugar replacement for home baking.

ACESULFAME-K, also called *Ace-K,* is 200 times sweeter than sugar. Sold as *Sunette* or *Sweet One,* it can have a bitter aftertaste when used in large amounts. Ace-K is widely used in non-dairy creamers, chewing gum and beverage mixes.

SUCRALOSE, sold as *Splenda,* is not yet as popular, being used in only a few soft drinks and juices at this time. Although it is not entirely calorie-free, at about 6 calories per scant teaspoon, it has about 600 times the sweetening capacity of sugar, with a more subtle flavour than NutraSweet.

SACCHARIN, the popular brand names of which are *Sweet'n Low* and *Sugar Twin,* is used to sweeten numerous commerical foods and beverages. With only ⅛ calorie per teaspoon, it is said to be 300 times sweeter than sugar. A bitter aftertaste is especially noticeable when a food sweetened with saccharin is heated. Current research supports saccharin's safety, despite previous concerns.

Although these and other products are becoming increasingly popular and versatile, I strongly urge you to use real sugar or alternative natural sweeteners in your baking and dessert preparations. The results will be more flavourful, nutritious and infinitely more satisfying. Choose to have one piece of wonderful chocolate cake every now and again, rather than two sugar-free brownies every day. You will develop a healthier eating pattern and enjoy your food a thousand-fold more. If you must bake with artificial sweeteners, contact the manufacturers to obtain replacement guidelines, recommendations and recipes designed to be used with that particular brand. Do not expect the replacement, however, to fulfill any or all of the functions that natural sugar would in the same product. Compensation will likely have to be made in order for the outcome to be similar.

Liquid Sweeteners

BARLEY MALT SYRUP *(Barley Malt Extract, Malt Extract)* Not to be confused with *maltose* or *malt sugar*, barley malt syrup is a sweet, thick, brown syrup made from malted barley. Pure barley malt syrup is considerably less sweet than sugar—at about 65% maltose, it is about 75 to 80% as sweet as honey. Barley malt syrup may be made exclusively from malted barley or a combination of barley and corn grits, and some varieties have glucose added for increased sweetness. It has a distinct malty, barley flavour, excellent for use in many yeast and breakfast breads, but not recommended for delicately flavoured baked goods and desserts. It is widely used in prepared health foods as an alternative to sugar, but should not be substituted for other forms of sweetener unless specified in a recipe. Barley malt syrup is available in two styles: a plain variety and a hop-flavoured variety that is less sweet and has a strong, slightly bitter flavour. If using the syrup in baking and dessert cookery, be sure to buy the plain type. Barley malt syrup should be heated slightly before using in a recipe to enable it to blend smoothly with the other ingredients. If you do decide to experiment, substituting barley malt syrup for another sweetener in a recipe for baked goods, add ¼ teaspoon baking soda to the batter to counteract the acidity in the syrup and reduce the liquid in the recipe by ¼ cup for every 1 cup syrup used. If there is no other liquid called for, increase the flour by ¼ cup for every cup of syrup, or the batter will be overly wet. Barley malt syrup is usually sold in jars and can be found in health and natural food stores.

BROWN RICE SYRUP Also known as *yinnie* in Asian cuisine, brown rice syrup is made when brown rice is ground to a fine meal and cooked. Enzymes are added that break down the starch in the slurry to sugar, in the form of maltose. The resulting liquid is boiled down to a thick, brown syrup with about the same sweetening power as barley malt syrup. It is becoming more widely used in commercial health and natural food products as an alternative to refined sugar, but, as it is considerably less sweet and of a significantly different composition, it should not be substituted for other forms of sweetener in most baking and dessert recipes. The exception is in recipes calling for barley malt syrup, as the two can be used interchangeably. Rice syrup has a unique and distinctive flavour, not appropriate in many delicately flavoured products, but quite at home in some yeast, grain and breakfast breads. It is widely used in Chinese and other Asian cuisines to add a subtle sweetness and a rich, grainy flavour to both sweet and savoury recipes. Like barley malt syrup, brown rice syrup should be heated before being used in a recipe (see Barley Malt Syrup for recipe modifications). It is available in most health and natural food stores, as well as many Chinese and Asian groceries.

CANE SYRUP Widely used in Caribbean, Creole and South American cuisine, cane syrup is made by reducing cane sugar to a very thick, and extremely sweet, clear syrup, thicker and sweeter than corn syrup. Cane syrup is available in Caribbean markets and can be used in desserts and baked goods where a powerful sweetness and slight molasses flavour is desired, but should not be used in equal proportion to replace any other form of sweetener.

CORN SYRUP Corn syrup is not a naturally occurring sugar and must be artificially engineered by introducing an enzyme to cornstarch that converts the starch to sugar. Other ingredients are added to refine and enhance the final syrups. Available in both light (clear) and dark (golden) varieties, the composition of corn syrup varies widely within these categories. Dextrose, the form of sugar in corn syrup, is in fact a form of glucose, enabling it to delay the crystallization of sugar in syrups, icings and glazes, as well as keep ices and sorbets smooth and non-crystalline when frozen. Manufacturers can alter the moisture content, sweetness, flavour and colour of corn syrups to suit the purpose, contributing one or more of these assets in as great a proportion as desired. The corn syrup that is available to the general public is a fairly standardized, balanced blend of flavour, sweetness, and moisture.

Light corn syrup is actually a combination of dextrose (glucose) and a high fruit sugar (fructose) syrup, often flavoured with vanilla or artificial vanillin. It has been clarified to be completely clear and can be substituted for glucose when making certain pastes, icings and sugar confections. It is mildly sweet and very delicately flavoured, and used most often to contribute moisture to baked goods and to delay the crystallization of sugar in cooked syrups, compotes and frozen desserts.

Dark corn syrup is a mixture of light corn syrup and refiners' syrup (a by-product of the cane sugar refining process), with caramel flavour and colour added. It has a more pronounced vanilla and butterscotch flavour than light corn syrup and contributes a golden colour to light mixtures. Light and dark can be used interchangeably in situations where a difference in flavour and colour is acceptable. Both light and dark corn syrup are widely available in most supermarkets.

GLUCOSE (see also Dextrose) Glucose is a simple sugar, occurring naturally in the form of dextrose in grape juice, honey and corn syrup. On its own, glucose is a very thick, viscous gel, perfectly clear and colourless. It is about half as sweet as sucrose and is rarely used as a sweetener in baking, but is an important ingredient in cooked sugar and moulded chocolate confectionery, many syrups and compotes, as well as frozen desserts and other products where a smooth, malleable, flowing or creamy consistency is desired. This is mostly due to its resistance to crystallization—when glucose is present in a sugar-rich syrup, it delays or prevents the other sugar from reverting to a crystalline state as the mixture cools. Icings and glazes are free of grains of sugar crystals, and sorbets and ices stay smooth and creamy. Glucose is widely used commercially for its moisture and texture-enhancing properties, not its sweetness, but may be difficult to find in retail stores. It is available from good cake decorating and baking supply shops, but for many applications light corn syrup is a perfectly acceptable substitute, functioning almost identically, though it is not quite as sweet.

GOLDEN SYRUP *(Light Treacle)* Like molasses (which is often simply referred to as *treacle* in Britain), golden syrup is a happy by-product of the cane sugar refining process. It is a viscous, golden liquid, very similar in appearance and flavour to golden (dark) corn syrup and, in fact, the two are completely interchangeable. It appears commonly in steamed puddings, cookies and light spice cakes and gingerbreads, as well as being a popular table syrup for pancakes, toast and biscuits. Because of its British heritage, golden syrup is readily available throughout most of Canada, but also in some supermarkets in the United States, as well as in specialty and gourmet shops under such brand names as Lyle's.

HONEY It is as common around the world as rice or bread, yet it may be made from the nectar of millions of different flowers. And try as we might, we humans don't do a thing to improve it besides bottle it.

Forager honeybees collect several substances on their daily journeys from the hive. Nectar, gathered from flower blossoms, is the only one that can be transformed into honey. The sucrose in the nectar is broken down by an enzyme in the bees' stomachs into glucose and fructose. Back at the hive, the liquid is transferred to other bees, then deposited into single cells in the elaborate system of beeswax chambers known as the comb. The beating of thousands of wings fans the moisture from the liquid, concentrating its sugars and resulting in honey, just as we know it.

When harvested, the honeycomb is spun in a simple centrifuge to release the honey. Any crystals, bubbles and minute impurities are then strained out, and the honey is ready for packaging.

Honey is not pure sweetener. It is made up of about 18% water, with dextrose, fructose and traces of vitamins and minerals making up the balance. It has fewer calories by weight than sugar, but is not as sweet, at about 75 to 80% the sweetening power of sucrose. Honey's high water content allows it to add moisture to baked products, such as muffins, cakes and cookies, and baked goods made with honey often have a longer shelf life than those made with granulated sugar. Honey also adds a characteristic flavour and a natural, mellow sweetness to all types of desserts. It caramelizes at a lower temperature than sugar, so recipes glazed with honey or containing large amounts of honey should be baked at lower temperatures. High in glucose, honey is a natural invert sugar and will delay the crystallization of syrups and other liquid sugar mixtures, as well as assist in keeping sorbets, ices and other frozen desserts smooth and creamy. Honey's smooth, viscous texture enables it to bind other ingredients together, sometimes functioning as the only liquid in a recipe, as in many gingerbreads and honey cakes. Baked goods made with honey will tend to be slightly heavier, denser and more moist than those made with dry sugars.

The flavour and colour of the honey is determined wholly by the type of blossom that yielded its nectar. All over the world there are regional specialty honeys, from the intensely sweet and perfumed French lavender honey, to the earthy, resinous and almost bitter Italian chestnut honey to the dark and fragrant Greek honey made from wild thyme.

Commercially mass-produced honeys are usually blends of several different honeys, combined to retain a uniform and consistent product. Unfortunately, they are often bland and uninteresting, as well. They are frequently pasteurized, a process that dampens the flavour and can add a slight aftertaste to baked goods.

On the other hand, honeys made from the nectar of a variety of blossoms, blended by the bees themselves, if you like, are called multi-blossom honeys. These, such as forest, meadow and wildflower honeys, can have wonderfully complex and varied flavours, depending on region and season.

The most unique and flavourful honeys, though, are those for which the nectar is collected from a single type of blossom. Within the single-blossom varieties, there is almost infinite variety, from delicately flavoured honeys like the clear, pale yellow acacia, through every shade of yellow, orange and brown to the pungent and almost black buckwheat honey. As a rule, the darker the honey, the more pronounced the flavour. Often the honey tastes faintly of the fruit or leaves of its mother blossom as well, such as orange flower honey and wild thyme honey. Some herbal honeys are more suited to savoury preparations, such as glazing meat or poultry. Very strong honeys such as buckwheat are best used with a judicious hand and palate, as their strong flavours can overpower subtler ingredients, and the honey can end up dominating the dessert. Unless I want that intense signature flavour, I prefer to use slightly less powerful honeys, but dark, fragrant and flavourful ones nonetheless.

Make honey a hobby—collect different varieties from places you visit and try new types as often as possible. They are a wonderful and easy way to vary your baking, not to mention your breakfast! There are over 300 varieties of honey produced in North America alone, to say nothing of the delicious European varieties; experiment with as many as you can.

Comb honey is the rawest form of honey, with the golden syrup still suspended in the wax comb. It is not appropriate for baking, but is a delicious accompaniment to dried fruits, nuts, fresh fruits and a selection of cheeses, and is a chewy, sweet and delicious treat on its own.

Creamed honey is made by combining crystallized honey and liquid honey, blending until a uniform consistency is obtained. It is often pasteurized and therefore slightly less nutritious than regular honey. Thick, sticky and spreadable, creamed honey is not usually appropriate for baking or cooking, but is popular as a spread on toast and makes a mean peanut-butter-and-honey sandwich.

Honey has remarkable, almost incomparable, keeping abilities, retaining its colour, flavour and aroma for years, if stored correctly. In time, most honeys will begin to crystallize, but can be re-liquefied by submerging the container in a pan of warm water for a few minutes. Honey should be stored at room temperature, as refrigeration accelerates crystallization. Store honey well sealed, as it attracts moisture from the air and can develop moulds and yeasts.

Honey should not be given in any form to children under 1 year, the very elderly, the infirm or those with immune deficiencies, as it may contain a form of botulism spore that may be very harmful, even deadly, to those individuals.

INVERT SUGAR *(Liquid Invert Sugar)* Invert sugars may be naturally occurring, such as glucose or the dextrose in honey, or may be produced by introducing an acid, such as lemon juice, to a liquid sucrose (a sugar syrup). The crystals in invert sugar are much smaller than those of sucrose, making it exceptionally useful in products such as sugar candies and confections, as well as creams and syrups. The fine crystals ensure that these products remain smooth, without becoming studded with recrystallized sugar molecules. Invert sugar is naturally produced in the process of jam and jelly-making when acidic fruits interact with a sugar syrup, keeping the preserve viscous and the thickened juices smooth. Corn syrup, honey and acidulated sucrose syrup can all perform as invert sugars, however, and pure invert sugar is rarely called for in domestic baking and dessert recipes. Pure or liquid invert sugar can be difficult to find, but is available in many cake decorating and baking supply shops.

MAPLE SYRUP Pure maple syrup is the sap of the sugar maple tree, with most of the water evaporated. It is a sweet, dark amber liquid, more fluid than either corn syrup or most honeys, with a unique and distinctive flavour. It tastes of wood and earth, subtly of sweet caramel and even ripe fruit. Some grades are light and as nuanced in flavour as wine; others are dark, less sweet and powerfully flavoured. The denser the syrup, or the more of the sap's water is evaporated, the darker and more concentrated the flavour. Maple syrup has been used for centuries in the northeastern part of North America to enhance dishes both savoury and sweet, from baked beans to sticky tarts. It also makes one of nature's best dessert accompaniments completely on its own—dribbled over ice cream or a still-warm apple cake—and is virtually indispensable when pancakes, waffles or French toast are involved. It shares many of the characteristics of honey, being an effective sweetener and flavouring and enhancing the moisture and keeping qualities of products such as cakes and quick breads. Like those made with other liquid sweeteners, baked goods sweetened with maple syrup have a dense, moist crumb and tend to be slightly heavier than those made with dry sugars. Maple syrup is slightly less sweet than granulated sugar—1½ cups of maple syrup will sweeten to the same degree as 1 cup of granulated sugar. I do not recommend replacing more than half the total sugar in a recipe with maple syrup, however, as the very different composition can drastically alter the outcome of the product. If you do substitute maple syrup for a dry sweetener in a recipe, decrease the amount of liquid in the recipe by ¼ cup for every 1 cup syrup used or increase the flour by ¼ cup. In addition, add ⅛ teaspoon baking soda for every cup, to counteract the acidity in the syrup.

Within the denomination of pure maple syrup, there are wide-ranging variations. Syrup tapped and produced earlier in the season, when the weather is colder, tends to be lighter and more delicately flavoured than that produced later in the spring. The most full-flavoured syrups are usually produced during the warmer weeks. Maple syrup is carefully controlled and graded in Canada and the northeastern United States.

Grade A, Fancy, Extra-Light or Canada #1 is very light, the most refined and delicately flavoured grade. It is also the most costly type, best for consuming straight, poured over breakfast cereals, pancakes and desserts.

Grade A Medium Amber or *Dark Amber* and *Medium* are all slightly darker syrups, with a somewhat more robust maple flavour.

Grade B or *Amber* syrup is darker and more strongly flavoured still and is excellent for baking, as its assertive flavour can stand up to combination with other flavours and ingredients.

Finally, many health and natural food stores sell a fourth grade, *grade C*, which is most commonly used for commercial flavouring, as it is almost as dark as black molasses. It has a wonderfully strong maple flavour, and I find it to be perfect for many baked goods, as it has a robust, rich flavour that comes through even in the presence of other ingredients such as toasted nuts and dried fruits.

A word of caution: beware of very inexpensive syrups labelled "maple syrup" and syrups with the word *flavoured* anywhere on the label. These are likely synthetic blends—some may not contain any real maple syrup at all. Read labels carefully and avoid any products that are not 100% pure.

Maple sugar is simply maple syrup, dried and crystallized into fine, tawny-blond granules. It is available in both solid block form, which must be grated before use, and as a fine powder. It is intensely flavoured, and dear in price, and should be used sparingly, for flavour rather than the dominant sweetener. The exceptions are cases such as the traditional *Tarte au Sucre d'Érable* (page 461).

Maple butter is a delightfully addictive confection—not actually butter at all, but maple syrup spun and beaten to the consistency of a sticky, thick, churned honey. Its scarcity outside maple-producing regions means it is rarely called for in baking, but I find it wonderfully versatile, for everything from folding into a cake or quick bread batter, icing or frosting or all by itself as a rich filling for a delicate layer cake. And there is simply no better topping for toast, pancakes, waffles or your index finger.

Most New Englanders have at least one bottle or tin of maple syrup somewhere in the pantry, but spring is really the best time to buy fresh maple syrup. It is expensive, but well worth the price, as a little flavours a long way. (Having said that, a lot can go a short way, too, if you live in my house. That is why they sell it in those oil can-sized drums. For me. Not for institutions, not for sharing, but for lots and lots of French toast.)

MOLASSES Molasses is a by-product of the sugar refining process, removed from the raw cane sugar juice or sugar beet juice at various stages of processing, leaving the base for white sugar. It is most often made from cane sugar; although beet sugar molasses does exist, its flavour is harsher and less pleasant than that of cane molasses, and it is reserved almost exclusively for commercial use, most often in animal feeds. Molasses contains minerals and trace elements such as iron and calcium, but in such minute quantities that it cannot truly be considered any more nutritious than brown or white sugar. Molasses adds a characteristic flavour and colour to desserts and baked goods, but also enhances the tenderness and moisture of baked goods due to its approximately 20% moisture content. It is an acidic compound and, when present in sufficient quantity, can be used to activate baking soda in cakes, quick breads and cookies. If molasses is substituted for non-liquid sweeteners in a recipe, the liquid in the recipe should be reduced by ¼ cup for every 1 cup molasses used (or increase the flour by ¼ cup if no other liquids are present), and ¼ teaspoon baking soda should be added to counteract the acidity. When substituting molasses for non-acidic liquid sweeteners, simply add the ¼ teaspoon baking soda.

Sugar undergoes three refining stages, and a different grade of molasses, each with its own sweetness, colour and flavour, is produced with each stage:

Light molasses, also called *Barbados* or *table molasses*, results from the initial refining. It is a dark amber colour, with a sweet, burnt-sugar flavour, perfect for drizzling on toast, pancakes and scones.

Dark molasses is produced from the second refining, and is not as sweet as table molasses. It has a darker, richer, slightly more bitter flavour, perfect for baking and cooking.

Blackstrap molasses is the very dark syrup that remains after the final refining. It has a strong, only slightly sweet and quite bitter taste, and while it is definitely not the molasses to spread on your morning toast, it can be used to great advantage in baking such things as dark gingerbread, certain spice cakes, as well as icings, candies and other confections. It should never be used as the primary sweetener in a recipe or to replace any other product, but is best used in combination with other sweeteners, to add flavour and moisture.

Unsulphured molasses is simply molasses of any grade that has been produced without the use of sulphur. It has a lighter, clearer, appearance and a purer flavour than sulphured varieties. Happily, more and more producers are ceasing to use sulphur in the production of their molasses, as it is highly allergenic and can add a distinctly "off" flavour when present in too high a proportion. Read the label and avoid sulphur-treated varieties.

Light and dark molasses are available in most supermarkets; blackstrap and unsulphured molasses can be found in health and natural food stores.

PANCAKE SYRUP This table syrup is usually a base of golden corn syrup, with artificial flavourings added to simulate a maple or butterscotch flavour. It should never be used in baking or dessert cookery, and if you are a purist, its value as a topping for pancakes, waffles or French toast should be questioned too!

SORGHUM SYRUP *(Sorghum, Sorghum Molasses)* Sorghum is a highly nutritious cereal grain, widely grown in North America for export and animal feed. Although little of the grain crop makes it to North American consumers, a thick, sweet syrup produced from the plant's sugar cane-like stalks is popular in many regions as a table sweetener, as well as an ingredient in baking and dessert cookery.

TREACLE In its native Great Britain, the word treacle can refer to two different products: golden syrup or light treacle and proper or dark treacle. This thick, dark, mildly sweet and slightly bitter syrup is almost identical to North American dark molasses, and the two are completely interchangeable in most recipes. Dark treacle is a beloved spread for toast and griddle cakes and an important ingredient in many steamed puddings, cakes, gingerbreads, pie fillings and yeast and quick breads. It is quite bitter, significantly less sweet than sugar, so is often combined in a recipe with another form of sweetener, and relied upon mostly for flavouring and colour. It may be difficult to find outside gourmet shops specializing in imported British products. Dark molasses is a perfectly good substitute.

FATS

Role of Fats

IT IS NO DOUBT QUITE OBVIOUS by this point that this is not a low-fat cookbook—a fact of which I am proud, however unfashionable that may be. Fats and good pastries, baked goods and desserts are inseparable, and the role of butter, shortenings, lard and oils in these products should be respected and honoured. To ignore or downplay the various functions of fats is to discount one of the most critical elements in most desserts, and the resulting product can only be a vague imitation of the original. The function of fat in a given recipe depends on the type, form and quality of fat used. Although different types of fat often perform similar functions, they are rarely interchangeable without a distinct alteration in the finished product. In all cases, poor-quality ingredients can drastically affect the outcome of the dessert. As with every ingredient, choose your butter and other fats very carefully, opting for the best products you can afford; in most cases, a bargain is often an indication of an inferior product. Large supermarkets can be the most cost-effective sources for common fats used in baking, with prices generally lower than specialty shops for the same products. For more information on the characteristics of each type of fat, see the specific section in the pages that follow.

A note about saturated fats: Much attention has been focused in recent years on the healthfulness of various fats from the point of view of saturated fats, mono- and polyunsaturated fats, etcetera. These fancy terms refer to the molecular structure of a given fat and, in particular, the quantity of hydrogen atoms present. The more hydrogen atoms, the worse the fat, so current wisdom dictates. Fewer hydrogen atoms enable the fat to more easily combine with other elements, including those in the body, such as oxygen, so the fats are more completely assimilated and beneficially used. Saturated fats, those with the highest percentage of hydrogen atoms, are today virtually condemned, while the healthier polyunsaturated and monounsaturated fats are heavily favoured. While some oils, such as coconut and palm, are naturally high in saturated fat, others, like olive oil, are high in monounsaturated fats, making them nutritionally superior. The process of hydrogenation, however, can reduce even relatively healthful fats such as canola to primarily saturated fats. Hydrogenation involves injecting the natural oil with a large number of hydrogen atoms in order to keep it solid at room temperature. The elevated hydrogen content transforms the once healthful fat to a saturated fat, making it every bit as damaging as one naturally high in saturates.

But back to baking! The roles of fat in baking and dessert cookery are many and varied:

❖ Products like puff pastry and those gloriously flaky Danish pastries get their characteristic flakiness from fat. Without it, they would be nothing more than tortillas or pita bread! The fat plays much the same role in these doughs as it does in pie or tart pastry, but in a much more specific and complex fashion. Chilled, solid fat, usually butter, but sometimes vegetable shortening, is carefully layered into the dough by a systematic process of repeated folding, rolling, chilling and resting, then folding again, etc. The fat separates the dough into layers, sometimes as few as six or seven layers or, in the case of traditional puff pastry, as many as a marvellous *729 layers of fat and pastry!* When the moisture in the dough expands in the heat of the oven, it pushes up against pockets created by the now melted fat, creating larger pockets. The result is an extremely tender and delicate pastry, with layers and layers of flaky sheets separated by tiny air pockets.

❖ Fat makes pie crusts tender and flaky. The fat in pie dough has a similar effect to that in puff and Danish pastry, but rather than being very methodically layered into the flour dough, the fat in this simple dough is worked in very roughly, with the aim of creating a marbled effect. The result is a more randomly layered dough, with larger patches of fat, which create larger air pockets in the oven. For this reason, the best pie crusts are extremely flaky and too delicate to stand on their own without the support of the pie tin. In comparison, puff and Danish pastries have many more, and smaller, pockets and are therefore more sturdy. Solid fat is used in pie doughs and should be cut into the dry ingredients in a way that allows it to remain as intact and unabsorbed as possible. Chilling the fat, in fact chilling all the ingredients, helps keep the fat from blending into the dough. It should be cut into the dry ingredients just until the largest pieces are about the size of fat peas. From that point, great care must be taken to keep these pieces intact. Lard produces absolutely the most delicate and flaky crust and has a subtle but distinctive flavour that is excellent in some cases, but not desirable in others. Vegetable shortening is a close second in terms of flakiness, but is terribly lacking in flavour and makes a bland crust. All-butter pie crusts have a lovely rich flavour, but are not very flaky, as the moisture in the butter is quickly absorbed into the flour, making a tougher crust. A combination of butter and one of the other fats is often used to get a compromise in flakiness and good flavour.

❖ In traditional shortcrust doughs and shortbread-type cookies, butter is always the fat of choice. It functions both as a flavouring and as a fat, creating a delicate, crisp pastry. Rather than remaining in solid pockets as in pie dough, the fat in tart doughs is more thoroughly blended into the dry ingredients. The result is a less flaky, but very rich, short and tender pastry, similar to a shortbread. In cookies and biscuits, fat creates a tender, crumbly or short texture, as well as contributing flavour. The more fat in the dough, the more like shortbread the result will be, and the more the baked pastry will "melt in your mouth." Cookies with less fat will be chewier, but can be tougher and sometimes even stale-textured if insufficient fat has been used.

❖ Solid fats, such as butter and vegetable oil shortening, act as a leavener in baked goods when creamed with sugar. The granular quality of the sugar traps air as it is creamed into the soft fat. The fat molecules hold the air in the batter, and expand when the heat of the oven reaches them. The result is a risen and tender product. Cakes that begin with a creamed butter and sugar mixture are lighter and more tender than those made solely with chemical leavenings such as baking powder or baking soda.

❖ Many fats, especially those from animal sources, contribute a richness in flavour to baked goods and other desserts. Butter is no doubt the most familiar of this group, often playing the role of a primary flavouring ingredient in products such as shortbread, tart crusts, icings and frostings and many cakes and biscuits. Lard imparts a rich, distinctive flavour to pie crusts, mincemeat fillings and many steamed puddings and pastries. Unfortunately, it has fallen out of favour over the last twenty years, but is still used for many traditional desserts, as well as savoury pastries. Some vegetable oils have a rich and distinctive taste that can be used to flavour all manner of desserts. Nut-derived oils, such as hazelnut, walnut and almond oils, and seed oils, such as sesame, have wonderfully rich, smooth, intense flavours and are more often used as flavourings rather than fats.

❖ Fats add moisture to baked goods, imparting tenderness and enhancing the texture of the products, but also extending their keeping abilities. Butter, vegetable oils, shortenings and even margarine fulfill this role, supplying moisture, making the texture of the baked products more tender and yielding and keeping them fresh for longer than drier, less rich products.

❖ Solid fats, such as butter and shortenings, impart a smooth, creamy, voluminous quality to creamed icings, frostings and fillings, acting as both the flavour and structural base. Butter will always yield a more delicious product, but is sometimes too rich or heavy and is prone to melting or weeping in delicate icings and fillings. For that reason, vegetable shortening is often blended with butter to create a more stable cream.

❖ Fats contribute a distinct and appealing texture to baked goods such as cakes, quick breads and biscuits. Each type of fat will yield a different grain, crumb and texture: vegetable oils tend to give a very moist texture, with a large crumb and a pleasant springy quality, characteristic of carrot cakes, many gingerbreads and breakfast muffins. Melted butter has a similar effect, but with a finer crumb, a cakier texture and a richer flavour. Batters made from soft or creamed butter will have a fine, velvety crumb, a very tender, delicate texture and a rich full flavour, much more cakey than most quick breads and muffins. Vegetable shortening can perform in baked goods much the same way as butter and can yield a product with an even more velvety, tender, fine crumb. The drawback, however, is in flavour, as vegetable shortening has virtually none to speak of and can produce an unpalatably bland cake. Some recipes compromise by calling for a combination of both soft butter and vegetable shortening.

❖ Fats prevent batters and doughs from sticking to pans, moulds and baking sheets. Greasing the forms allows the baked product to be removed easily and cleanly, without tearing or breaking, because the fat creates a slippery surface difficult for the batter or dough to adhere to. In the case of angel food cakes, this lubrication is not desired, as it would prevent the cake from climbing as high and attaining maximum volume.

❖ Fats of all kinds, solid or liquid, help develop the gluten in yeast doughs. They contribute to the dough's elasticity and flexibility, which support the role of gluten in achieving an elastic and springy product.

❖ Fat is a very efficient heat conductor and acts as the main cooking medium for sautéed and deep-fried desserts. The type of fat used is critical, as is the freshness and quality. Heat rapidly accelerates the deterioration of fats (some break down faster than others) and most frying fats can only be used a few times before they become stale and need to be discarded. Every fat also has what is known as a smoke point: the maximum temperature it can reach before it begins to break down or burn. Some fats, such as nut oils and toasted sesame oil, have very low smoke points and are not suitable for even light cooking, let alone deep-frying. The best oils for frying, such as peanut oil or canola oil, have relatively high smoke points.

❖ When used in cakes and quick breads, butter gives the product a rich but non-greasy texture and flavour. Other forms of fat, such as oils and shortening, do not dissolve or melt completely into the batter, and the result can be a slightly oily, heavy and crumbly product. Butter's low melting point ensures it will dissolve completely into the batter, producing a cake with a tender and delicate crumb, and no greasy-mouth feel.

Solid Fats

BUTTER It has no equal, no substitute. It is, quite literally, the crème de la crème, for butter at its simplest is nothing more than the richest part of freshly churned cream. The result of enough agitation is two distinct elements: the creamy rich butterfat and the whey, or buttermilk. Today, commercially produced butterfat is washed to remove any impurities and kneaded to achieve a uniformly creamy consistency. The composition of butter in the United States and Canada is carefully regulated, with both maximum and minimum percentages specified for moisture content, salt content and colourings. Within these guidelines, how-ever, is a wide range of qualities, from high-moisture, high-salt butters that are inexpensive but perform poorly to relatively high-quality butters with low mois-ture contents, little or no colour and no salt added. The cream used for butter-making in North America has been pasteurized to inhibit the growth of bacteria. And although butter can be and is made from the milk of goats, sheep, horses, yaks, camels, even buffalo, we are, for baking purposes, interested in butter from the cow.

Butter's flavour and colour are directly affected by the cow and her diet. Certain regions, those with particularly rich pasture lands, are said to produce the best butter in the world, and butter produced from spring milk is thought to be more flavourful and rich than from milk at any other time of the year. Spring and early summer butter is made from the milk of cows able to graze freely on rich, fresh grass, which contributes a richness of flavour, but also a dis-tinctly yellow hue, due to the natural carotene present in the grass. In the win-ter, the cows' diets consists mainly of dried grasses and grains, which produces a firmer, less pliable butter with a much paler, creamier colour. To maintain a consistency in appearance, many manufacturers add a natural colouring called annatto to their winter butter to please a public they fear will be alarmed at any slight change. Carotene itself may also be used. The colourings are totally harm-less, but I find it disappointing that we are so far removed from the origins of what we eat that we need to be placated into thinking even natural products are totally unchanging.

Butter is available in both salted and unsalted varieties. *Unsalted butter*, also called *sweet butter*, has a delicate, nutty and faintly sweet flavour that lives up to its name. *Salted butter* has a more pronounced flavour, but the percentage of salt can vary from brand to brand, anywhere from 1.5 to 3% and may not be appropriate for every recipe. Although you can use salted butter in baking recipes and reduce the amount of salt you add, I strongly recommend using un-salted butter whenever possible. Its flavour is sweeter, and you can better con-trol the amount of salt in your recipe. Salted butter is more likely to be coloured during the late fall and winter than unsalted.

North American butter must have a minimum 80% butterfat and a maxi-mum 16% moisture, 1.5% milk solids and 2.5% salt. The vast majority of com-mercial producers do not exceed the minimum levels for butter fat and do not have less than the maximum moisture content in their butter. In other words, it is easy to buy a butter inferior to the standard, but almost impossible to buy one that exceeds it, unless you manage to find a source for the wonderfully rich European butters. In recent years, however, smaller domestic dairies have started producing premium-quality butters, with sometimes as much as 88% butterfat. Available in good natural food stores, farmers' markets and specialty shops, these low-moisture, high-fat butters are well worth seeking out. They will reward you with more tender shortbread, crisper pastry and creamier icings that will tend to separate less.

Feel the butter before you buy it—different brands and even the same brands at different times of the year will feel different; buy the firmest butter you can find. Softness is a factor of moisture content: the higher the percentage of water in butter, the softer it will be, even when chilled. All butter is approximately 16% moisture, but some producers blend even more water into their butter to reduce the overall expense. Higher moisture levels in butter make for tougher pastries, inefficient creaming abilities and a host of other disappointing results. This is one of the most common reasons that baked goods fall short of expectations, as many people buy cheap butter, which tends to have considerably more moisture than their higher-priced counterparts. The firmer the butter, the more air it will be able to hold and the more tender and flaky the resulting pastries will be.

Don't become loyal to a fault: the moisture and even ingredient content of butter can be altered at different times of the year as a result of changes in season, feed and other influences. The brand that worked beautifully in July may have added colour and more water in January, and another brand may be preferable at that time of year.

Good butter should be perfectly dense, with no holes or air bubbles inside. It should break and cut cleanly, without crumbling. There should be no dew or other moisture evident on the surface of the butter, or once it has been cut. Excessive moisture in the butter can affect the way it melts, blends, creams and bakes, but it will also cause the butter to spoil faster, as the moisture creates conditions for bacteria to develop.

Like most dairy products and fats, butter absorbs other flavours and aromas very easily, which is great if those flavours are in a cake batter, but not so great if they are onions or last night's curry. It should be stored, well-wrapped in foil or plastic, away from strong odours or flavours, light and heat. And not in that little butter box in the door of your refrigerator, where it is more likely to be exposed to changes in temperature and moisture, and will oxidize and go off more quickly. The middle of the fridge is perfect.

Butter should smell sweet and fresh. "Off" butter will have a rancid odour and should be discarded. Salted butter keeps longer than unsalted, about 5 months if refrigerated. Store unsalted butter in the refrigerator until needed, only taking out enough for your immediate purpose. Properly stored, unsalted butter will keep about 3 months. Keep it at room temperature for no longer than 4 or 5 days, even fewer in hot weather.

Butter for general use, such as on sandwiches and vegetables, can be frozen and thawed overnight in the refrigerator, but I do not recommend using previously frozen butter for baking and desserts. Freezing can alter the moisture content of the butter and can affect its texture. Frozen butter, once thawed, can appear grainy, dewy or even slightly curdled, especially if it is unsalted. To minimize the risk of getting a poor result, only use fresh butter for baking.

If a recipe calls for soft butter, leave the butter out at a cool room temperature for several hours or overnight. Soft butter should still be cool (about 65° is ideal), and firm enough that if you push a finger into it, the impression is clean and crisp. It should never reach the point of being oily or sloppy. Soft butter is malleable and will incorporate a maximum amount of air. Cold butter, such as is called for in many pastry doughs, allows the butter to remain intact in the mixture, producing a tender and flaky pastry when the heat from the oven expands the moisture trapped in the butter, creating layers and pockets of air. Cold butter also enables the dough to be worked and rolled out more easily, without a lot of excess flour, which toughens doughs.

Although you can soften butter in the microwave to use in a recipe calling for room temperature butter, it is best to allow the butter to temper naturally, as microwaves can be uneven in their heating. If you do have to use the microwave, cut the butter into small, even-sized pieces and heat on medium power in increments of 30 to 45 seconds, checking after each period. The butter should be just malleable, not overly melted or soft.

Butter is the most delicate fat used in baking when it comes to heat, with a very low smoke point. In other words, it burns easily. This feature is often used to an advantage, as in recipes calling for browned butter, or those that call for ingredients such as fruits or bread to be sautéed in butter to create a crisp, brown, caramelized coating. Butter is soft but solid at cool room temperature, which makes it perfect for creaming into batters, doughs, icings and fillings. Butter is solid at and below about 50°F. At about 105°, butter liquefies, at 212° it foams as the inherent water evaporates and at about 380° and beyond, the milk solids quickly scorch and turn the butter from golden to brown, to black.

Whipped butter, as the name implies, has been whipped, often with nitrogen gas to ensure it retains a maximum volume. It is easier to spread than regular butter, even when cold, and often has sugar and flavourings added, such as fruit purées or honey.

Light or low-fat butter must contain at least 52% fat to bear the butter label. The remainder of the compound is made up of stabilizers, emulsifiers, gums, whey, milk solids and even dry milk powder. *Light, whipped, and low-fat butters* are unsuitable for most desserts and baking recipes, unless specifically called for. (Don't expect to find any such recipes in this book!) In addition to being whipped for a more voluminous, less dense texture, most of these products have a long list of artificial and foreign ingredients added to compensate for the reduced fat (see above) and neither taste nor perform like good butter.

Cultured butter is made from milk or cream to which active lactic bacterial culture has been added, creating a very minimal degree of fermentation. The resulting butter is very rich in flavour and slightly tangy, similar to the European varieties and to butter made with cream left up to a week before churning. It is wonderful in simple cakes and biscuits where the rich flavour can be appreciated.

Blends of butter and margarine or vegetable shortening are becoming increasingly available and are popular with those who favour the flavour of butter, but are trying to reduce the amount of cholesterol in their diets. These blends should not, however, be used to replace butter or vegetable shortening in baking or dessert cookery.

Clarified butter is butter that has had the milk solids removed, leaving only the pure butter fat. It is a simple process, and the clarified butter keeps much longer than whole butter, as the milk solids accelerate the deterioration. To clarify butter, gently heat butter (working with at least 1 cup at a time makes the process easier) in a small pot, until it is completely melted and slightly foamy on the surface. Pour the melted butter into a tall glass or glass measuring cup and let stand for several minutes. It will separate into three distinct layers. Skim off and discard the foamy surface layer. Very carefully pour the yellow liquid below the foam into a clean container, leaving behind the milk solids, which will have formed a sediment on the bottom. The yellow liquid will lose its cloudy appearance as it cools, becoming clear and golden. You can store this in an airtight container in the refrigerator for up to 6 months. Clarified butter has a much higher smoke point than whole butter and, in fact, does not brown at all, as it is the milk solids that scorch when butter is overheated. Unfortunately, without the milk solids, clarified butter has much less flavour than whole butter.

Butter's richness and unique flavour are its glory, but may not be appropriate in every dessert. In products such as pound cakes, butter creams and tart crusts, best-quality butter is essential to the success of the final dessert. In other cases, however, butter can lead to an overly heavy texture and an over-powering flavour, as with many lighter quick breads and muffins and with certain pastry doughs. If you are substituting any fat for another in baking, do so thoughtfully and be aware that the replacement may alter the final product.

VEGETABLE SHORTENING *(Hydrogenated Vegetable Shortening)* Made from liquid vegetable oils that have undergone a chemical process called hydrogenation to transform them into a solid state, vegetable shortening is a solid fat with a consistency somewhere between that of butter and lard. While this process produces a very useful fat for the baker, hydrogenation also negates any benefits the vegetable oils may have had in their original state, as it converts all oils into saturated fats. It is an opaque white in colour and is virtually odourless and tasteless. This blandness makes shortening a poor choice when a rich flavour is desired, but it has other useful qualities. Unlike liquid oils, it can be creamed into batters, icings and fillings. Cut into pie doughs, it approaches lard in terms of tenderness and flakiness and it creams very well when used at room temperature, producing more stable icings and buttercreams less prone to weeping than those made exclusively with butter. Vegetable shortening can be stored in a cool, dry, dark place or in the refrigerator for up to 1 year. Like butter and other fats, shortening picks up strong flavours and odours easily, so keep it well wrapped and away from such influences.

MARGARINE Although margarine was developed over 100 years ago, it has come into its own over the last twenty years as people have become obsessed with avoiding cholesterol. Margarine is made from vegetable oils that undergo various degrees of hydrogenation to transform them from a liquid to a solid, spreadable state. (Unfortunately, as with shortening, this process also transforms beneficial polyunsaturated fats into harmful saturated ones, thereby reducing the product to about the same nutritional value as butter.) The hydrogenated fat is then enhanced with flavourings, both artificial and natural, in the form of milk solids and other dairy ingredients. Stabilizers, emulsifiers, gums and colourings are also added in an attempt to make the margarine appear and taste more like butter. Anyone who has tasted the two side by side, however, knows margarine tastes about as much like butter as sparkling grape juice tastes like a good champagne. Today, there are literally hundreds of variations on the theme, from whipped margarine to butter-margarine blends to partially hydrogenated rather than totally hydrogenated types to dairy-free margarine—and the list goes on. I will not go into detail about each of these categories, for one simple reason: I do not recommend using any type of margarine in baking, as it is unreliable, unnatural and woefully lacking in flavour. In many cases, margarine is not more beneficial nutritionally than other forms of fat and often produces less than satisfactory results when substituted for them. Unless a recipe has been developed specifically with a certain type of margarine in mind, don't risk the flavour, texture or success of your baking.

LARD The nutrition police may strike me down for saying this, but there is simply no better fat for delicate, flavourful and divinely flaky pie crusts than lard! Lard is higher in fat and lower in moisture than other solid fats and therefore makes the most tender crusts and the flakiest biscuits. Made from pork fat that has been rendered and clarified, lard is relatively unpopular today as a cooking fat for dietary reasons, and many people do not use it for religious ones. It is still, however, used in many traditional recipes in Great Britain and the rest of Europe, as well as in the province of Quebec and throughout the American South.

Fat from different areas of the animal produce lard of varying qualities. *Leaf lard*, universally considered to be the best, is derived from the fat surrounding the kidneys, like suet in beef. In our grandmothers' time, the lard used to make the daily biscuits and pastries was usually rendered at home from the excess fat from the week's butchery. The difference between this lard and the processed lard we buy today is little more than a matter of consistency in quality and texture. Unrefined lard will work just as well as the processed variety, but has a much stronger, more distinctive and not always appropriate flavour. Commercially produced lard undergoes a number of refining treatments—trace impurities are removed, the lard may be partially hydrogenated to maintain the uniformly solid state and may be bleached to render the fat an opaque white colour similar to that of vegetable shortening. It has a much milder flavour than that of unprocessed lard and a longer shelf life. Unless you are an old hand at rendering and cooking with lard, I strongly recommend using only the commercially processed kind. Choose a reputable brand and read the label for information on how to store the fat—some lard may be kept at room temperature, but others require refrigeration. Keep all lard well wrapped and away from light, heat and strong odours and flavours.

SUET Suet is a solid fat derived from the fat around the kidneys of beef cattle, and occasionally sheep and other animals. It is rich in fat and flavour and is often used in recipes for traditional British and European puddings, cakes, pastries and even candies. It is also an essential ingredient in authentic mincemeat and in many steamed puddings. Sold in block form or already grated and ready for use, fresh suet is available in delis, specialty shops and in some supermarkets, especially around Christmastime. Store suet well wrapped in the refrigerator, away from strong odours and flavours.

COCOA BUTTER Cocoa butter, and its primary role as an ingredient in fine chocolate, is discussed in more detail in the section on Chocolate (page 229). It is a hard, pale yellow fat extracted during the grinding process of dried, fermented and roasted cocoa beans. Although cocoa butter *should* be used in the manufacturing of all chocolate, it is expensive, and many producers extract as much of it as they can from the rough chocolate matter and replace it with cheaper vegetable oil substitutes. The valuable cocoa butter is then sold to the highest bidder, usually a cosmetic, rather than a comestibles, company. Cocoa butter can be found in almost every type of cosmetic and lotion on the market, prized for its luxurious smoothness and emulsifying abilities. The best brands of chocolate contain a high percentage of cocoa butter, and *couverture*, a type of chocolate specially designed for coating or incorporation with other ingredients, has extra cocoa butter added to increase its smoothness, flexibility and gloss. At one time, cocoa butter was added to baked goods in order to extend their keeping abilities, but its high cost has encouraged the use of cheaper shortenings and fats instead.

COCONUT FAT *(Coconut Oil)* Coconut fat is extracted from pressed, dried coconut flesh. Besides being widely used in myriad cosmetics, lotions and soaps, it is a popular frying fat due to its very high smoke point. As a culinary fat, it has excellent stabilizing and lubricating abilities and was often used to replace cocoa butter in the processing of inferior chocolates. It has long been used by many commercial manufacturers of baked goods and confections as an ingredient in cakes, cookies, biscuits and crackers, even candies and other sweets, but has fallen out of favour in recent years for nutritional reasons. Coconut fat is one of the only non-animal sources of saturated fat and cholesterol and has been replaced in many products with more healthful fats. It can be purchased in hydrogenated or natural form from Asian specialty shops, as well as health and natural food stores. It has an appealing coconut aroma and flavour and should be used only where specified in baking and dessert cookery.

NON-STICK COOKING OR BAKING SPRAY These can contain a wide variety of ingredients and be based on mild-flavoured vegetable oils such as canola or a blend of vegetable and pure or extra-virgin olive oil. Some have artificial flavours added to simulate the flavour of butter, but I find these to be unpalatably fake-tasting. Look for a minimum of ingredients: a non-hydrogenated vegetable oil, grain alcohol to preserve the oil's colour and integrity, lecithin to act as an emulsifier and a propellant. I don't recommend these sprays for all greasing tasks, but for small, intricate moulds, such as small muffin or cake tins or little petit four tins, it saves a great deal of time and wasted butter. For especially fine-flavoured cakes, breads and pastries, however, butter imparts a far superior flavour.

Oils

Vegetable, nut and seed oils are used in baking for two reasons, for flavour and for their role as a fat. Flavouring oils in baking tend to be nut oils, such as almond or walnut, or seed oils, such as toasted sesame or sunflower. They are usually used in small quantities and rarely are the sole fat in the product. Oils used as fats in baking are there primarily to supply moisture, tenderness and lubrication. They cannot be used as a creaming fat, as butter can be, as their liquid form does not allow for any retention of air.

Oils are extracted from seeds, nuts, vegetables, and fruit such as avocados by one of several processes. The most common and cost-effective methods are "hot" pressing or the use of solvents. These methods are usually followed by various refining and purification processes, including bleaching, deodorizing and sometimes partial hydrogenation. While these processes are efficient in their extraction, the heat used destroys both the beneficial vitamin E naturally found in the raw oils and a great deal of the inherent flavour. An alternative is the "cold" pressing method, which enables the oils to retain their vitamin E content and produces a flavourful, delicate and aromatic oil. Extra-virgin olive oil is a popular example of a cold-pressed oil. They rarely require further processing, but have a naturally shorter shelf life than their processed cousins. Cold pressing yields a much lower rate of extraction than conventional methods, making the resulting oils more expensive. In addition, they are not appropriate for heavy cooking, sautéing and frying, as heat destroys both the vitamin E and the delicate flavours of these oils. These very flavours make most cold-pressed oils too obtrusive to be used as an all-purpose oil in baked goods and confectionery.

Oils used in baking and pastry should be mild in flavour. They must be fresh, not old or rancid (all oils will eventually go rancid, some faster than others). Unrefined oils usually contain vitamin E in large quantities, which acts as a natural preservative (wheat germ, corn and safflower oils are high in vitamin E) but refining makes the addition of preservative chemicals, such as BHA, BHT or citric acid, necessary. Keep that in mind when you're choosing your oils! Heat, light and oxygen promote deterioration of all oils, so they are best stored in an airtight container, preferably in opaque non-porous bottles, in a cool, dark, dry place.

Rancid oils smell musty and slightly foul and can taste mouldy or bitter. Refrigeration prolongs the life of most oils, but there are a few too delicate to withstand it, such as walnut and some other nut oils. Cold temperatures can render some oils thick and cloudy, but they will liquefy and return to their original clarity once back to room temperature.

Vegetable oils are derived from many natural sources—grains such as linseed (flax), pumpkin seeds, grape seeds, sesame seeds, sunflower seeds and corn; nuts such as almonds, hazelnuts, walnuts, peanuts and macadamia nuts; and fruits and vegetables like olives and avocados. The characteristics of some of the more common oils are discussed below.

ALMOND OIL Sweet and aromatic, almond oil was long ago adopted by the cosmetic and soap industry for its moisturizing and scenting properties. As a culinary oil, it is best used as a flavouring, rather than as a cooking oil, although it can be heated gently without much of a loss to its delicate flavour. It is a medium to pale amber colour and can range from being almost tasteless to rich with the flavour and scent of sweet almonds. In baking, I use it to enhance the flavour of almond desserts, such as cakes, biscuits and even ice cream. For the best flavour, seek out a high-quality (read: expensive!) oil with a full aroma.

Most of the best examples are produced in France. Buy it in small quantities and store this special ingredient in a cool, dark place for up to 4 months or in the refrigerator for up to 7 or 8 months.

AVOCADO OIL This clear, pale oil is used primarily in North America, specifically the southern and southwestern United States, as a cooking oil. Curiously, it has a very faint anise flavour and is best used as a dressing or light cooking oil for savoury dishes. I do not recommend it for baking or sweet cookery.

CANOLA Canola oil, also known as refined rapeseed oil, is a relatively recent addition to the culinary scene, but has made a huge impression. It was developed in Canada to be especially high in polyunsaturated fatty acids, making it the healthiest cooking oil next to olive oil. There are a host of other ways canola oil is a superior fat to most other oils, nutritionally speaking: it is high in the much-touted omega-3 fatty acids and is significantly lower in saturated fat than comparable oils such as peanut or palm oils. It is mild-tasting and pale, with a high smoke point, and is an excellent all-purpose oil for baking, cooking and frying. I use it almost exclusively for sautéing, frying and baking when a non-assertive flavour is desired. All of the recipes in this book using vegetable oil were tested with canola oil. Store airtight at room temperature in a cool, dark place for up to 1 year.

CORN OIL Corn oil has long been a favourite cooking oil in much of North America, still in favour today thanks to its high levels of polyunsaturated fats. It is a heavy, golden oil with a mild flavour of the grain from which it is extracted. For this reason, it is excellent for use in dishes where the flavour of corn can be echoed, such as corn bread, muffins and dumplings or fritters. It has a very high smoke point, making it a good choice for sautéing and deep-frying. The subtle but distinct flavour of this oil is not always appropriate, however, so use it thoughtfully. In delicately flavoured desserts, a lighter, blander oil is usually a better option. Unrefined corn oil is a dark amber colour and has a strong toasted-corn aroma and flavour. The refined oil, the variety most commonly available, is a pale gold and has a milder flavour. Store in a cool, dark place at room temperature for up to 1 year.

COTTONSEED OIL This clear, viscous oil obtained from the cotton plant is rarely sold in retail stores, but finds its way into many blended oils, shortenings and margarine. It has a high smoke point and is inexpensive, so is also a commonly used fat for commercial deep-frying. Rarely used domestically in this country, it is sometimes called for in Middle Eastern cuisines.

GRAPESEED OIL Grapeseed oil is among the most popular cooking oils in much of Europe, and most of the available supply in North America comes from France, Italy or Switzerland. As the name implies, it is derived from grape seeds and, indeed, some examples have a distinctly fruity flavour. Most of the stronger-flavoured types remain in Europe, however, as the North American preference seems to be for a blander taste. Grapeseed oil is a very pale and delicate oil and does not thicken or cloud when refrigerated. For this reason, it is an excellent choice for many vinaigrettes and emulsified sauces such as mayonnaise. It is excellent as a general salad and dressing oil and has a very high smoke point, making it a good choice for sautéing and shallow frying. It should be stored airtight at cool room temperature for 7 to 8 months or in the refrigerator, where it will keep for up to 1 year.

HAZELNUT OIL Unquestionably one of my very favourite flavouring oils, hazelnut oil is an amber-hued oil with the rich flavour and aroma of toasted hazelnuts. It is expensive, as are most nut oils, and is best used as a flavouring for both sweet and savoury dishes rather than as a traditional cooking fat. Although direct heat, such as sautéing or frying, destroys its delicate flavour, it can be used with great success in baked goods or added to sauces or dressings at the end of cooking. I love adding a few drops to a pancake batter, then folding in finely chopped, roasted hazelnuts or using it to flavour cakes, cookies and confections like ice cream. France is by far the largest producer of hazelnut oil, but it is imported from around the world. It is available in many specialty food stores, as well as some health and natural food stores, in tins or small bottles. Buy only as much as you need, as it does not keep well. Hazelnut oil should be stored in a cool, dark place for up to 3 months or in the refrigerator for up to 6 months.

OLIVE OIL Perhaps the most celebrated oil of the '90s, olive oil burst onto the North American supermarket scene in huge quantities after being identified as a healthful and potentially healing ingredient. Fortunately for those of us who are as passionate about our taste buds as we are about the rest of our bodies (or more so!), it is also a wonderfully complex, versatile, varied and rewardingly flavourful oil that has proven itself in myriad applications. There are several distinctions in the category of olive oil: *extra-virgin olive oil* is a result of the first cold pressing of the olives and is the most complex and flavourful. It is best used to anoint foods such as fresh vegetables or bread, or in vinaigrettes and dressings that will not be exposed to heat. *Virgin olive oil* is also a result of this first pressing, but has a slightly higher acidity than the Extra grade. *Pure olive oil* is the product of subsequent pressings and can be a blend of several lots, even of several grades. With a less pronounced flavour and a higher acidity, it is perfectly good for cooking and frying. Recently, a new denomination called *light* or *extra-light olive oil* has appeared. In spite of the moniker, it is no lighter in fat or calories than any other oil, but has been carefully refined and filtered to make it especially mild-flavoured, with a higher smoke point. This new oil is a boon to bakers, as we can now reap the health benefits of olive oil without tainting our delicate sweet foods with a distinctly savoury flavour. Good brands of light olive oil should have little or no discernible flavour or aroma and can be used in place of any mild-tasting oil in cooking or baking. With the exception of the light variety, olive oil should only be used in baking where specified, such as in an Italian olive-oil cake or pastry dough. Care should be taken to use the grade specified, usually extra-virgin, as it is the most flavourful and least acidic. Olive oil should be stored airtight in a cool, dark place for up to 6 months for extra-virgin and virgin, 8 to 12 months for other grades.

PALM OIL, PALM KERNEL OIL Extracted from the African oil palm, palm oil is a strongly flavoured golden oil popular as an ingredient in West African and South American cuisines. *Palm kernel oil* is a different oil, made from the nut or kernels of the same palm trees. With a milder flavour and paler colour than palm oil, it was once widely used in commercial baked goods and processed foods. It has been blacklisted by the nutrition police recently, however, as it is extremely high in saturated fat, and many manufacturers have replaced it with more healthful oils. It has a high smoke point and pleasant, mild flavour, but a very short shelf life, making it generally a poor choice for home use.

PEANUT OIL North American peanut oil is a pale, mild-flavoured oil, used as a cooking and salad oil but especially favoured as a deep-frying fat due to its high smoke point. *Chinese peanut oil* is often cold-pressed and tends to have a much richer peanut taste, but can be used for the same purposes. When using peanut oil, however, be careful to warn any guests who may suffer from nut allergies, as even a little can be dangerous. Store airtight at cool room temperature in a dark place for up to 2 years.

PINE KERNEL OIL *(Pine Seed Oil)* Produced almost exclusively in France, where it is favoured for its decidedly pine-scented flavour, pine kernel oil is a wonderfully unique flavouring oil. It is very expensive, and its delicate flavour does not stand up well to heat, making it a poor choice as an all-purpose oil. It does, however, make a distinct and delicious addition to light vinaigrettes, dressings and dipping sauces. While not appropriate for most dessert cookery, pine kernel oil is worth seeking out if you are as passionate about savoury food as you are about sweet!

PUMPKIN SEED OIL Dark, almost opaque and vaguely green, this richly flavoured oil extracted from roasted pumpkin seeds is an excellent addition to many traditional Mexican and Latin American dishes. It can be used in sauces, vinaigrettes and dressings, often in combination with a milder-flavoured oil, as it can be overpowering. With a moderately high smoke point, it can also be used for cooking, but only in situations where its characteristic flavour is appropriate. I do not recommend it as a general purpose oil for baking and sweet cookery, unless specified in the recipe.

SAFFLOWER OIL Extracted from the seeds of the safflower (also known as the *saffron thistle* or *bastard saffron*), safflower oil has gained popularity recently for its nutritional profile. It is higher in polyunsaturates than any other oil, although even the unrefined oil does not contain vitamin E. The unrefined oil is a dark golden colour, with a full, nutty flavour, but the refined version is clear yellow and virtually tasteless. Safflower oil has a high smoke point and is an excellent all-around choice for cooking, baking and frying. Store in a cool, dark place in an airtight container for up to 1 year.

SESAME OIL Sesame oil is one of the most widely used Asian ingredients, often playing the roles of both a flavouring and a fat. Derived from sesame seeds, sesame oil is available in two forms. The pale, slightly nutty-flavoured sesame oil produced in North America and Europe is good for vinaigrettes, dressings and sauces. With a high smoke point, it can also serve as a sautéing or deep-frying fat. The darker golden *Asian sesame oil*, also known as *toasted sesame oil*, is made from seeds that have been roasted to develop a deeper flavour. It has a wonderfully rich, highly aromatic taste and is predominantly used as a flavouring for stir-fries, salads and dressings. Toasted sesame oil should not be limited to savoury dishes, however—its intense, dark and delicious flavour can add a wonderful dimension to cookies, cakes, even ice creams. It has a relatively low smoke point, and the rich flavour dissipates with prolonged exposure to heat, so the oil is often added at the end of cooking or to raw dishes. This sensitivity seems to be less of a problem with baking, and I have used it with great success in biscuits and cakes. Toasted sesame oil is considerably more expensive than most other vegetable oils, but it should be treated more as a flavouring or essence than as a fat. Stored in an airtight container, it will keep in a cool, dark place for up to 1 year.

SOYBEAN OIL This nutritious, versatile and adaptable oil has long been used in Chinese and other Asian cuisines and is becoming increasingly popular in North America. Soy beans are extremely high in fat, but it is predominantly the healthful mono- and polyunsaturated varieties. Unrefined, soybean oil is highly flavoured and should be used only in dishes in which a strong soy flavour is appropriate. Refined, it is a pale yellow, with a mild, pleasant flavour and has an extremely high smoke point. It is a good choice for most cooking and frying applications and can be used in all but the most delicately flavoured baked goods. It is inexpensive and can be stored in a cool, dark place for up to 2 years.

SUNFLOWER OIL This light, clear oil extracted from sunflower seeds is a highly nutritious and flavourful one. Unrefined, it is a medium amber colour and has a lovely, distinctly sunflower-seed taste. It has a relatively low smoke point, which makes it inappropriate for sautéing and deep-frying, but can be used successfully in baking and dessert cookery. The refined oil is a very pale yellow, with a mild, delicate flavour, and is excellent for vinaigrettes and dressings and as a general, all-purpose oil. I like the subtle flavour in whole-grain yeast and quick breads, where it echoes the flavours of the flours, grains and even nuts in the bread. It can be stored at room temperature, airtight, in a cool dark place for up to 1 year.

WALNUT OIL Like almond and hazelnut oils, walnut oil is a richly flavoured dark amber oil. Carefully, almost painstakingly, produced in France, it shares those oils' high price tag, but also their consistently high quality and exceptionally full flavour. Walnut oil can be used as a flavouring for both sweet and savoury foods, but should not be exposed to excessive heat. The flavour of walnuts in all types of salads and cold dishes are enhanced with a few drops of this potent oil, and it is wonderful added to cake batters, cookie doughs and even custards and ice creams. Walnut oil should be stored in a cool, dark place, but not in the refrigerator. It does not keep long, about 4 months at best, and should be bought in small quantities.

Dairy Products

Role of Dairy Products

Dairy products are the renaissance men (and women!) of the sweet kitchen, with the ability to function as liquids, fats and flavourings. Consult these sections to get an even more comprehensive view of the roles dairy products can play in baking and dessert-making. (For information on butter, see page 146.)

❖ In cakes, quick breads, yeast breads and other baked goods, milk's primary function is to act as a liquid, lubricating the dry ingredients in the batter or dough, binding ingredients together and providing the right consistency.

❖ The inherent fat in milk, yogurt and sour cream adds moisture and prolongs the shelf life of baked goods.

❖ The sugar in dairy products, specifically milk, caramelizes upon baking and gives a pleasant crust to baked goods such as cakes, breads and cookies.

❖ This sugar, called lactose, feeds yeasts in the preparation of yeast breads, encouraging fermentation.

❖ The acid present in buttermilk, yogurt and sour cream reacts with baking soda to activate it, leavening baked goods such as cakes, quick breads and cookies.

❖ Liquid dairy products aid in the activation of baking powder, acting as the liquid necessary to release the carbon dioxide gas from the compound.

❖ Dairy products contribute richness and flavour to baked goods and other desserts in several ways. The fat in products such as cream, sour cream and whole milk carry and enhance the flavours of other ingredients. The inherent flavours of buttermilk, yogurt and sour cream add a characteristic tang to baked goods, and milder products such as heavy cream contribute a sweet, rich flavour to creams, ice creams, puddings and custards.

❖ Dairy products provide the structure, foundation and texture in preparations such as puddings, custards, creams and frozen desserts.

❖ Milk and cream can serve as the liquid required to develop gluten in yeast breads. The proteins in flour need the lubrication of a liquid to begin developing gluten, which ultimately provides structure and texture for the bread.

❖ Dairy products enhance the nutritional profile of desserts and baked goods. Milk and other dairy products are high in protein and carbohydrates, as well as being rich in many vitamins and minerals, most notably calcium.

❖ The protein in dairy products bind with fat to enable it to be more evenly dispersed, providing a velvety, rather than greasy, texture in baked goods.

❖ Due to their fat and protein contents, dairy products contribute a fine and tender crumb to cakes and quick breads.

Milk

It is one of the most nutritious and versatile natural food products in the world, and almost every culture has used the milk of one animal or another to enhance their diets and their lives. Cows, goats, llamas, horses, sheep, buffalo, camels, yaks and even reindeer have long been kept for the rich milk they produce. North America and Western Europe are almost unique in their dependency on milk as a drink by itself, but milk is still an important ingredient in the sweet and savoury cuisines of cultures all over the globe. In the West, we rely almost exclusively on the milk of dairy cows, bred and raised specifically for their milk.

With only a few exceptions, all milk in North America is heat pasteurized to kill any bacteria present, such as salmonella and hepatitis, and homogenized to ensure the cream and milk do not separate as they would if left naturally. Raw milk is sometimes available in health food stores and has a more pronounced, richer flavour. Many supporters claim raw milk is more nutritious, as the naturally occurring vitamins and enzymes are left intact (pasteurized milk is fortified with vitamins A and D, though).

Fresh milk should be purchased as long before the best before date as possible and stored in an opaque carton or container in the refrigerator. Exposure to light rapidly deteriorates the nutritional value of milk and even an hour or less at room temperature can greatly shorten its (refrigerator) shelf life. Make sure the carton closes securely and store milk, and all dairy products, away from strong odours and flavours—it tends to absorb these like a sponge and "garlic milk" may not always suit your purpose. Most major milk producers are conservative with the best-before dates on their milk, and the milk should be safe for consumption for up to 1 week past the date. Get into the habit of smelling the milk before using it in a recipe, to make sure it is fresh, and discard it if it begins to assume a foul or bitter aroma.

For the purpose of clarity, milk of any fat content, but not buttermilk, may be called "sweet milk."

WHOLE MILK (*Homogenized Milk*) Milk comes from the cow at approximately 3.5% butterfat. After being strained, pasteurized and homogenized, it is sold as whole or homogenized milk. Though out of favour these days as a drinking milk, whole milk is by far the best to use for baking. The elevated fat content adds a smoothness and richness lacking with lower-fat varieties. Due to its high fat content, whole milk has a lovely opaque, rich white appearance and a longer shelf life than lighter milk.

PARTLY SKIMMED MILK (*2%, 1% milk*) Partly skimmed milk contains 2% butterfat. The most popular type of milk for straight consumption, 2% milk can be used successfully in baking and dessert-making, but should not be used where whole milk is specified or in recipes that rely on a certain richness, such as ice creams and custards.

1% milk has gained popularity in recent years, but is generally unsuitable for most baking. It can, however, be successfully substituted in recipes calling for skim milk.

SKIM MILK *(Non-Fat Milk)* An excellent product for the health conscious, skim milk contains all of the nutritious elements of whole milk, but has virtually no fat. For baking, however, it should be reserved for recipes specifically calling for low- or non-fat milk, as it does not contribute the same richness, moisture and keeping qualities that higher-fat milks do. Due to the absence of fat, skim milk appears semi-transparent, almost bluish in hue, and has a relatively short shelf life.

FLAVOUR-ENHANCED MILK *(Filtered Milk)* Several large dairies have recently developed varieties of milk engineered to taste "fresher" or richer than other examples of the same grade. Many companies claim their newly created fat-free and 2% milk tastes like traditional whole milk. There are a number of ways dairies create these enhanced milks—the more common, but expensive, is a complex process of cold filtration. Some of the liquid is removed, giving the milk a richer, creamier taste. It takes five quarts of raw milk to get four quarts of flavour-enhanced milk. With the milk less watery, not only is the mouth-feel richer, but the nutrients in flavor-enhanced milk, such as protein and calcium, are more concentrated. An easier process, and one some smaller, less wealthy dairy companies have adopted to compete with the filtered milks, is to enhance the taste of the milk with the addition of dry milk solids: There is likely to be a noticeably higher price tag than for regular milk. My dairy-addicted Dutch husband claims there is no comparison between the filtered milk and the regular stuff, renouncing the milk solids-enhanced variety as "very odd-tasting." Feel free to use the filtered type in any recipe calling for milk of the same fat content, but be careful when using the added milk solids variety—it may not behave reliably in certain situations.

BUTTERMILK Originally, buttermilk was the thin, cultured milk left over when butter was churned from whole cream. Today, it is produced by adding active cultures to low- or non-fat milk, sometimes with milk solids added for enhanced flavour. It has a thick, creamy texture and a pleasantly tangy, sour taste. It has long been used as an ingredient in baking, adding a slight acidity and an old-fashioned, homey flavour to baked goods such as pancakes, biscuits, cakes, fritters and frostings. In recipes using baking soda, the acid in buttermilk reacts to activate it as a leavener. Buttermilk should not, however, be substituted for regular milk. Available in low- or non-fat varieties, it is also sold in powdered form.

ULTRAPASTEURIZED MILK Appropriate only in situations where refrigeration is delayed or unavailable, ultrapasteurized milk has been heated to over 300°F, killing all living organisms, but also giving the milk a distinctly boiled taste. It is sold in small tins or cartons and has excellent keeping abilities. It is generally not appropriate for baking.

EVAPORATED MILK, CONDENSED MILK Now available in whole, partly skimmed and even non-fat varieties, this unsweetened product is milk that has had about 60% of the water extracted, leaving a thick, syrupy liquid. It can be used straight from the can, lending a creamy, rich flavour and texture to sweet and savoury recipes. When combined with an equal amount of water, it can be used to re-place milk, although it does have a slight "tinned" and cooked flavour not appropriate for some dishes. Although evaporated milk and unsweetened con-densed milk are the same product, the term "evaporated" generally applies to the unsweetened version, while sweetened condensed milk is the most com-mon term for the sweet stuff. Store unopened tins indefinitely at cool room temperature, but refrigerate once opened and use within 3 to 5 days.

SWEETENED CONDENSED MILK, SWEETENED EVAPORATED MILK Sweetened condensed milk is whole evaporated milk combined with an almost equal amount of sugar. Sticky, thick, creamy and intensely sweet, it is a key ingredi-ent for sweet bars, custards and other confections. Store unopened tins at cool room temperature for 6 to 8 months, then refrigerate after opening and use within 4 days.

CHOCOLATE MILK One of the best products to ever emerge from a dairy, this is milk to which sugar, cocoa or chocolate flavouring and often gums or stabiliz-ers have been added. Although it is an incomparably good addition to a six-year-old's lunch, it is generally not used in baking.

LACTOSE-REDUCED MILK Fortunately, for the huge number of people who can-not digest lactose (also called *milk sugar*), many large dairies have developed milk that has had up to 99% of the lactose removed. The result has a slightly sweeter taste, but can be substituted in baking for regular milk of the same fat content with excellent results.

DRY MILK, POWDERED MILK Available in whole and partly skimmed varieties, including buttermilk, powdered milk is milk from which all of the moisture has been removed, leaving an ivory-coloured powder. It is excellent for situations where refrigeration is limited or unavailable. Dry milk powder can also be added in small amounts to enhance the nutritional value of milk shakes, baked goods and ice creams. Although the rehydrated milk is virtually identical to fresh milk, it is not recommended as a substitute for milk in baking recipes unless absolutely necessary, as it has a slightly stale flavour and a different consistency. The powder can be stored indefinitely in a cool, dry place, but the rehydrated milk must be refrigerated and should be used within 3 days.

WHEY POWDER Whey powder is a by-product of the cheese-making process. The thin milky whey is separated from the cheese curd and dehydrated. Whey powder is used in the making of many commercially processed and packaged foods, but can also be found at health and natural food stores. It can be used in baked goods to add nutritional value and imparts a slight sweetness to the product at the same time. Whey powder should be stored airtight in a cool, dry place.

GOAT'S MILK Goat's milk has gained favour in recent years, first as an easier-to-digest alternative to cow's milk, but more recently for its own merits: the tangy, bright flavour that it lends to cheese and yogurt, as well as to the milk itself. It can be used to add a distinct taste to certain desserts, but should be used only where specified, or where you are willing to experiment! It is available in health food stores and should be kept refrigerated.

SHEEP'S MILK Sheep's milk cheese is available in North America, but sheep's milk has not yet caught on as a raw ingredient, although there are several small producers in the United States and Canada with thriving cottage industries. Its applications in baking are the same as those of goat's milk, above.

SOY MILK Soy milk is the product of pressed, cooked soy beans and has been a staple in the diets of many Asian cultures for millennia. It is low in fat, calcium and sodium, but high in protein and iron and is cholesterol-free. Now widely available in health food stores and most supermarkets, it is an excellent milk substitute for those who are allergic to cow's milk or who are lactose-intolerant, and many brands are now being fortified with calcium and other vitamins and minerals. Although it can be used to replace milk in many recipes for baked goods such as cakes and quick breads, soy milk does not work reliably in mousses, creams or custards, in part because of its distinctive flavour. Soy milk also tends to curdle in the presence of acidic ingredients. It is available in plain, low-fat and sweetened, flavoured varieties such as vanilla and chocolate. When substituting for milk, take the flavour of the particular soy milk into consideration. Some have a stronger soy taste, while others are milder and less distinctive. I have actually had very good results using a sweetened vanilla soy milk in place of regular milk in baked goods—the sweetness mimics the slight sweetness of cow's milk, and the vanilla flavour tends to mask the inherent flavour of soy.

Soy milk is available in long-lasting Tetra Pak cartons that can be kept at room temperature for up to 1 year, then opened, refrigerated and used within 1 week. Regular cold-stored cartons of soy milk should be used by the best-before date and, once opened, consumed within 1 week.

Dried soy milk or *soy milk powder* is much like dried cow's milk in appearance and uses. It is made by dehydrating plain soy milk and can be rehydrated with the addition of water and consumed on its own as a beverage. The dry powder can be used in the sweet kitchen to enhance the nutritional profile of products such as cakes, quick breads and other baked goods, as well as ice creams and custard, but as it does have a rather pronounced flavour, I would recommend using soy milk powder only in recipes specifically calling for it. Available in health and natural food stores, it should be stored airtight in a cool, dark, dry place.

NUT MILKS Made from ground nuts, usually mild-flavoured almonds, soaked in water, pressed, drained and fortified with other ingredients such as stabilizers, gums and sweeteners, nut milk is high in protein, carbohydrates and vitamins. Like soy milk, nut milks have increased in availability at the demand of those who cannot tolerate cow's milk. It is not recommended for general baking, although it can be substituted for cow's milk in some simple recipes, such as pancakes and quick breads—expect a difference in flavour and texture, however.

OAT MILK Similar to nut milk, oat milk is made from whole oats that have been cooked, soaked in water, pressed and drained. The result is a milky liquid high in iron and sometimes enhanced with other vitamins and minerals. The same recommendations and cautions with regard to its use in dessert cookery apply as for nut milks, above.

Cream

The very mention of cream conjures up images of rich and decadent desserts. Indeed, cream holds a valued and irreplaceable place in the sweet kitchen, with the power to create, accompany and enhance everything from a simple fruit tart to a rich custard to a frothy cool sabayon.

Natural cream is the layer of thick, rich substance that rises to the top of fresh dairy milk if the milk is left to separate, leaving skimmed milk below. Commercial cream is separated from the raw milk by a process of centrifugal force. As are all commercially produced dairy products, most cream produced in North America is pasteurized. Today, most dairies have implemented a process of ultra-pasteurization, to extend the lifespan of cream. Ultra-High-Temperature (or UHT, as it is often labelled) cream tastes less sweet and is thicker when unwhipped than its natural counterpart. To compensate for the lack of sweetness and textural differences, sugar, in the form of dextrose, and carrageenan, a natural seaweed extract that increases the cream's smoothness and viscosity, are added. The main benefit of UHT cream is its extended shelf life, but the drawbacks for the baker are many. Aside from the slight difference in taste, UHT cream behaves somewhat differently from natural cream. It does not whip as light or to the same volume, and I have experienced brands that do not whip at all! Most cream on the market today has been ultra-heat treated, although some brands may not be labelled as such. It is becoming difficult to find a source for natural or single-pasteurized cream products, but some dairies still distribute these products to certain regions, and many health food stores across North America are beginning to carry organic and natural dairy products. If you can, splurge for these varieties when cream plays a major role in the dessert. The rest of the time, buy cream, milk and butter from a reputable dairy, test the products for quality and be loyal to the brands you find that work.

HEAVY CREAM, WHIPPING CREAM *(36% butterfat)* These terms are used to refer to several different products. In Europe, some whipping creams have a butterfat content of between 36 and 40%, while heavy cream can be as rich as 48%. In the United States, cream containing at least 36% butterfat is called *heavy cream* or *heavy whipping cream*. Products labeled *whipping cream* or *light whipping cream* contain up to 30% butterfat. When air is beaten into heavy or whipping cream, it becomes *whipped cream*. Because light whipping cream has a lower fat content than heavy cream, it is not as stable once it is beaten. Thick, slightly sweet and buttery-rich, heavy cream can be used plain or whipped, as an ingredient or as a garnish for desserts. It can also play a big role in rich sauces, pastas and soups. In general, heavy cream whips to about double its original volume, attaining maximum volume if the cream, bowl and beaters or whisk are very cold. If overbeaten, whipped cream will break down into a mess of butterfat clumps and a thin, curdled buttermilk. Do not mistake sweetened whipped toppings or already-whipped cream products for heavy cream, as these are strictly for the accompaniment of desserts, and should not be used as ingredients themselves. Heavy cream is sold in cartons of various sizes and should be kept in the coldest part of the refrigerator.

LIGHT CREAM *(18% butterfat)* Light cream is used mainly as an addition to coffee, hence its other common name, *coffee cream*. Although rarely specified in recipes, light cream can be substituted for half-and-half cream or even whole milk in some recipes for custards or sauces where a richer flavour and creamier consistency are desired.

HALF-AND-HALF CREAM *(10.5% butterfat)* A mixture of heavy cream and whole milk, half-and-half has been homogenized to keep it from separating. It is a useful ingredient in making ice creams and custards, as it is richer than milk alone, but can be more vigorously stirred, beaten or agitated than whipping cream without becoming overworked or separating.

SINGLE CREAM *(5% butterfat)* Single cream was developed to be a slightly richer alternative to whole milk for adding to coffee. It can be used to replace whole milk in recipes for sauces, custards and ice creams, with similar but slightly richer results. (At this time, single cream is available only in Canada.)

DOUBLE CREAM *(48% butterfat)* Unfortunately for gourmands, pastry chefs and the dairy-addicted, double cream is not widely available in North America. In Britain, however, it is virtually a national dish! Thick, wonderfully rich and sweet, it is the perfect accompaniment to fruit tarts and compotes. If you live near a small artisan dairy and can persuade the farmer to sell you some, indulge in this treat once in a while. Store this, like all creams, in the coldest part of the refrigerator and use within 3 days.

CLOTTED CREAM, DEVON CREAM, DEVONSHIRE CREAM *(minimum 55% butter-fat)* The ultimate in devastatingly rich dairy foods, the traditional accompaniment to High Tea's scones and jam, this decadent cream is tragically not available in North America. Clotted cream is produced by warming raw whole milk until a thick layer of cream forms on the top. Once cooled, the spreadably rich cream is skimmed from the surface, and it is said one can stand a spoon upright in the cream. Clotted cream has a sweet, faintly cooked taste and a slightly longer shelf life than raw cream. If you are lucky enough to acquire some, keep it refrigerated and use within 5 days.

"READY-WHIPPED CREAM," "REAL WHIPPED CREAM," PRESSURIZED WHIPPED CREAM These are dubious products, designed to save the host the two or three minutes it takes to hand-whip a bowl of heavy cream. Even the brands labelled "Real Cream" contain only a small portion of any recognizable dairy product, bolstered by a combination of vegetable oils, synthetic ingredients and sugars. They are a poor substitute for real whipped cream, from the point of view of both flavour, texture and nutrition, and should be avoided. In particular, they should never be used as an ingredient in baking.

WHIPPED TOPPING Tubs of this product are widely available, now in both regular and low-fat versions. They frequently have not a drop of real cream in them, but are based on a host of synthetic ingredients. As with the "whipped cream" preparations discussed above, I urge you to steer clear of this and similar wolves in sheep's clothing. Use the real thing: you will be rewarded!

NON-DAIRY WHIPPED TOPPING Made from "edible oil products." Need I say more? Although great for those who cannot tolerate dairy products, this whippable thick liquid tastes alarmingly unlike cream and should never be used in recipes.

SOUR CREAM Regular sour cream has about 14% butterfat and has lactic acid culture added for a pleasantly sour flavour and a thick creamy texture. It is most often used as an accompaniment to savoury dishes, but makes an excellent ingredient in many baked goods, lending a slightly tangy taste and a moist texture. It can often be used to replace buttermilk or yogurt in baking, and these products can often work in its stead, as well. It is also available in low-fat and fat-free versions, but these should be avoided in baking unless specified, due to the addition of stabilizers, gums and other ingredients (not to mention the overwhelming lack of taste!). Store sour cream in a closed tub in the refrigerator and use within 1 week of the best-before date. If mould or yeasts develop anywhere in the container, discard the cream.

CRÈME FRAÎCHE Crème fraîche may be France's most generous contribution to the world of dairy products. Authentically, it is made from unpasteurized cream left to ferment naturally with the action of inherent bacteria. The slightly soured cream thickens to a consistency at least as thick as sour cream, and thick enough to spread like butter if left long enough. In North America, where raw dairy products are strictly regulated and mostly banned, crème fraîche must be made by adding a lactic culture to pasteurized heavy cream. There are commercial brands of crème fraîche available in specialty food shops and gourmet dairies, but it is unreasonably expensive and you can make it at home (see the recipe on page 651). It makes a wonderful addition to savoury sauces, as it doesn't curdle when heated like whipping cream tends to do, and there is nothing more delicious as an accompaniment to fruit tarts and bread puddings than plain or lightly sweetened crème fraîche. It keeps very well, for 10 days or more in the coldest part of the refrigerator, but should be discarded at the first sign of mould.

CAJETA, CAJETA DE LECHE Cajeta is a rich, sweet, completely addictive caramel-like cream confection used in many Latin American cuisines. Although it was originally made from goat's milk, cow's milk is often used today. It is very thick, more of a fudge-like paste than a thick cream, and is used exclusively in desserts (or even as dessert!), confections and sweet drinks. It is available in many Latin American groceries and markets and may be caramel-flavoured, or flavoured with fruit.

DULCE DE LECHE This thick sweet cream is made by boiling milk, usually cow's but sometimes goat's, with sugar. It is almost identical to cajeta, but is thinner, always pourable and sometimes no thicker than maple syrup. It is used extensively in Latin American desserts and drinks and can be found at the same types of markets as cajeta.

YOGURT *Plain yogurt* is a creamy, slightly tangy thick dairy product originally made by allowing non-harmful "friendly" bacteria to become active in milk over a period of time, causing the milk to thicken and partly sour. It was most likely developed by nomadic Balkan tribes as a way of preserving precious fresh milk. Today, commercial yogurt is made by adding several particular strains of bacteria to whole, partly skimmed or skimmed milk and controlling the degree of fermentation. Fermentation, or the lifespan of the bacteria, is often ceased artificially, to achieve a consistent product in terms of taste and texture. The longer a live yogurt is allowed to ferment, the more sour and thicker it will naturally become. Several styles of plain yogurt are widely available in North America, differing slightly in flavour and consistency. Yogurt is an excellent ingredient in baking, adding a wonderful moistness and a pleasant tang to pancakes, coffee cakes, yeast breads and quick breads. Be sure to use a yogurt with the fat-content called for in the recipe. If none is specified, use whole (3 to 5%) or partly skimmed (2 to 3%) yogurt.

Live culture or *active culture yogurt* has live bacterial cultures, most often friendly lactobacillus Bulgaricus and acidophilus, still in the yogurt when packaged. This type of yogurt is extremely nutritious, as these strains of bacteria can provide many health benefits for the intestinal and other systems in the body. Active culture yogurt will continue to thicken as it ages, even after purchase, and by the best-before date it may be considerably thicker than when you first bought it. Although many supermarkets are now carrying varieties of this type of yogurt, you'll have no trouble finding it in heath and natural food stores. Available in plain as well as sweetened and flavoured varieties, live culture yogurt is often lower in fat than whole plain yogurt. The plain varieties are perfectly good to use as an ingredient in baking, in any recipe calling for plain yogurt.

Flavoured and sweetened yogurts are made when sugar, fruit, fruit juices or purées and other ingredients are added to plain yogurt. Often these varieties have had various gums and stabilizers added to make the yogurt less "yogurty," and more like a mild-flavoured pudding. Indeed, many examples of this type of yogurt resemble a dessert custard more than a yogurt, with flavours like cappuccino, crème caramel and cherries jubilee. However delicious, these yogurts are not appropriate for baking.

Fat-free and very low-fat yogurts have little in common with their nutritious cousins. Full of sugar, gums, stabilizers, thickeners and flavours, both artificial and natural, they are poor substitutes in terms of both flavour and satisfaction and should never be used in baking.

Goat's milk yogurt is available in many health and natural food stores and has a pleasantly tangy, unmistakably "goaty" flavour. It is excellent in many savoury dishes, and I have made wonderful frozen yogurt from it to accompany fruit and nut tarts or pies. Do not substitute it for cow's milk yogurt in a recipe, however, unless you are prepared for the striking flavour difference.

Soy yogurt is made by adding active cultures to soy milk. It may be plain or flavoured and sweetened and can be found in health and natural food stores. Although it can be used in place of regular yogurt in the odd recipe with success, its more watery and less creamy texture and strong soy flavour generally make it a poor substitute. Use your own discretion—if you can find a mild-flavoured variety, it may be acceptable in small quantities in recipes for baked goods. Unopened cartons of soy yogurt should be consumed before the best-before date; once opened, they should be used within 5 days.

Cheese

With the exception of rare finds in gourmet and specialty cheese shops, all cheese sold in North America has been pasteurized. If you are fortunate enough to live in a region where there are a number of artisanal cheese makers or, as in the case of the province of Quebec, one that commonly disregards the pasteurization laws, do take advantage of the phenomenal cheeses out there. Unpasteurized cheeses have a depth of flavour, aroma and complexity incomparable to those of their heat-treated cousins. Seek out the best type of each you can afford—you will be rewarded with a deeply flavourful dessert, satisfying both to the tongue and the taste buds.

Store all cheese in the refrigerator, well sealed or wrapped. If mould develops on ripened or hard cheese, such as cheddar or Parmesan, cut the offending part away cleanly and continue to use the cheese. Fresh or soft cheeses, such as ricotta or mascarpone, that develop moulds, funky odours or unexpected colours should be immediately and completely discarded.

Some cheese commonly used in dessert cookery are discussed below.

RICOTTA A fresh, rich cow's milk cheese, with creamy white curds smaller than those of cottage cheese. Ricotta was originally made from the whey drained off in the process of making other cheeses, such as mozzarella and provolone. Today, however, most ricotta is made from a combination of whey and milk. Ricotta actually means "re-cooked"—the whey is cooked first as part of the original cheese and then again when the ricotta is created. As such, ricotta is really a cheese by-product, rather than a cheese proper. It has a creamy, mild and faintly sweet flavour that makes it a natural addition to many traditional and unique desserts, from Italian cheesecakes and tarts to soufflés and ice creams. Lightly sweetened with honey, it makes a lovely accompaniment to fresh fruit. Unless the recipe states otherwise, use whole-milk ricotta, also called full-fat ricotta. It is the most creamy and ultimately the most satisfying. Lower-fat varieties have a higher water content and may adversely affect the outcome of the recipe. Buy ricotta from a good delicatessen or cheese shop, rather than in the supermarket—the flavour is much better. Ricotta must be absolutely fresh when it is used. Purchase it as close to the time of use as possible and use any leftovers within a day or two. If left beyond that time, it has a tendency to acquire an acrid aftertaste and will contaminate the flavour of anything it is paired with. Store in an airtight container in the refrigerator.

FRESH UNRIPENED GOAT'S CHEESE (*Chèvre*) While goat's milk cheeses come in myriad ages and forms, flavours and textures, the type most suited to dessert-making is the fresh, unripened variety. This creamy, slightly cakey, moist white cheese is becoming widely available in North America, with several excellent domestic producers in both Canada and the United States. Choose varieties not flavoured with herbs, peppercorns or other savoury elements, for obvious reasons. Its tangy, distinct flavour combines well with tannic fruits and nuts, such as grapes, plums, walnuts and pecans, as well as with citrus fruits and many liqueurs. Apples, pears and other orchard fruit also make good partners. Fresh goat's cheese makes a delicious addition to cheesecakes and tarts, as well as to many pastries and fruit desserts. It is most commonly sold in vacuum-sealed plastic cylinders in most supermarkets and delis. Store well wrapped in plastic in the refrigerator and use leftovers within 5 days.

MASCARPONE One of the most voluptuous, rich, double- or triple-cream cheeses, Italian mascarpone is actually a cream to which cultures have been added. Thick, smooth and almost custard-like on its own, mascarpone needs little more than a bowl of fresh berries to make an instant dessert. When combined with other ingredients, its mild flavour and luscious texture enhance classic desserts such as tiramisu and make it a perfect accompaniment to fruit, tarts and pastries. Though not cheap and, at an arresting 90% butterfat, not the cheese for the faint of heart, it is worth its weight in gold as a luxury ingredient—nothing replaces mascarpone satisfactorily. Though thicker and richer than all of them, it can often be substituted for whipped heavy cream, cream cheese or ricotta, depending on the recipe and situation. Take care when mixing, however, as mascarpone can separate as easily as heavy cream if overworked. There is very good domestically produced mascarpone available, at prices lower than their imported counterparts. Store in an airtight container in the refrigerator and discard at the first signs of mould.

CREAM CHEESE A nineteenth-century American invention, cream cheese is a smooth, white, slightly tangy cheese made from cow's milk. Regular cream cheese contains a minimum of 33% milk fat, but can sometimes have as much as 73%, and most commercial brands have added gum arabic as a stabilizer. This type of cream cheese is thick and dense, but spreadable. Fresh cream cheese, without the added gum arabic, is readily available in bulk from delis and cheese shops, but be warned: although you'd think more natural would be desirable, I have had difficulties in preparing recipes using this variety. Most North American recipes have been tested using popular brands such as Philadelphia Cream Cheese that have natural gums added to ensure consistent texture and stability. The bulk type of cheese is not as carefully regulated for fat and moisture content, and I have found wide inconsistencies in the results when I have used it in cheesecakes, icings and tarts. What is better on the bagel is not necessarily better for baking! *Whipped cream cheese* has been aerated to lighten the texture, making it less caloric by volume and easier to spread when cold. It is not appropriate for baking, however, and cannot be substituted for regular cream cheese. *Light, low-fat* and *fat-free cream cheeses* are also inappropriate as substitutes—their very low fat contents are compensated for by the addition of chemicals, stabilizers and gums, all of which behave erratically when heated and combined with other ingredients. Save them for the breakfast table, and then only if you feel you must!

COTTAGE CHEESE A fresh curd cheese made from cow's milk, cottage cheese is available in whole, partly skimmed and skimmed varieties. It is a very moist, large-curd white cheese with a bland flavour. If left to drain, the curds condense to create *pot cheese*; drain completely and you get *farmer's cheese*. Cottage cheese became popular as a diet food, as it is generally lower in fat than many other fresh cheeses. *Low-fat cottage cheese* and *fat-free cottage cheese* are also available, but in baking, I find only the whole-milk cottage cheese is reliable when the product is called for, such as for certain cheesecakes. Other varieties tend to be so high in water they upset the balance in most recipes. In general, I don't recommend cottage cheese as a substitute for other curd or fresh cheeses, unless stated in the recipe.

CHEDDAR, PARMESAN, ROMANO, ROQUEFORT and GORGONZOLA are other traditionally savoury cheeses sometimes used in dessert preparations, particularly in French and Italian recipes.

EGGS

Role of Eggs

EGGS ARE A VITAL and irreplaceable ingredient in many baked goods and dessert preparations. They perform a wide variety of functions, from adding moisture to providing leavening and flavour. Listed below are some of their primary roles.

❖ Both egg whites and yolks can aid in the leavening of baked goods, each in a different way. Egg yolks and whole eggs are excellent emulsifiers, with a great capacity for entrapping and holding air. When egg yolks are beaten with sugar to a thick, pale cream, as is often the case with many cake batters and creams, air is trapped between the grains of sugar and suspended in the expanded egg yolks. When the batter is baked, the trapped air expands, leavening the product. Such leavening is the sole form used in traditional pound cakes. The wonderfully creamy French sabayon or Italian zabaglione relies on a similar principle. Egg yolks are combined with sugar and a small amount of liquid, usually in the form of alcohol, and beaten over simmering water. The sugar and egg yolks trap air as they would for a cake batter, and the liquid extends the mixture slightly. As the temperature of the mixture rises, the yolks coagulate (at between 80°F and 85°F, to be technical!), creating a firm structure for the trapped air and ensuring that the mixture will remain thick and voluminous once whisking ceases.

❖ Egg whites leaven in a slightly different way. When whites are whipped to stiff but still moist peaks and then carefully folded into a batter, the air trapped in the whites expands in the heat of the oven, leavening the product. The same principle applies in the case of soufflés and soufflé-type desserts.

❖ Eggs give structure to baked goods. Even when incorporated into a batter or dough, eggs coagulate at a relatively low temperature. Although it may be slightly delayed or accelerated by the presence of ingredients such as sugar or salt, this coagulation occurs earlier than the stabilizing or gelling of the starch in the flour providing the main structure for the product. The co-agulated eggs support the structure until that time, enabling it to retain the trapped air and not deflate before the starches have had a chance to set and become firm.

❖ Whole eggs and egg yolks provide a velvety smoothness to everything from tender cakes and quick breads to creamy custards, curds, puddings and mousses. This is because egg yolks contain the emulsifier lecithin. Emulsifiers bond to both fats and water and can therefore bind ingredients that normally repel. The result is a smooth, homogeneous mixture, be it a cake batter or a crème brûlée custard. In baked goods, egg yolks enable fat to be evenly dis-tributed throughout the batter or dough, suspended in tiny particles. This means there won't be a greasy, oily or heavy feel to the finished product, but rather a tender, fine-flavoured and delicate crumb. In creamy desserts such as custards and curds, their power as an emulsifier enables eggs to bind fats to liquids, to create wonderfully smooth, satiny mixtures. The higher the pro-portion of yolks to other ingredients, the more voluptuous and silky the cus-tard will be, and the more velvety the crumb of the cake.

❖ Eggs can hold up to four times their own weight in moisture upon coagula-tion, which makes them a very good thickener for many custards, sauces and curds. These mixtures must be handled carefully, as eggs are delicate when it comes to heating. Eggs that are subjected to high heat without being constantly stirred will coagulate in large, uneven curds, becoming nothing more than scrambled eggs floating in whatever liquid. The mixture must be stirred or whisked constantly until it reaches the right temperature, then cooled slightly to cease the cooking. You can do this by transferring the hot custard to a new container or by immersing the bottom of the bowl or pot in ice water. The cooked mixture must then never be heated above about 90 degrees or the coagulated yolks may curdle. For this reason, custards that cannot be constantly stirred, such as oven-baked bread puddings, are often cooked in a water bath, preventing the temperature of the mixture from rising too quickly or reaching the boiling point. Even these carefully cradled mixtures will curdle if left in the oven too long, but they are less prone to doing so than those cooked in "naked" dishes! The degree of thickening and binding depends on the proportion of eggs in relation to other ingredients in a mixture. The higher the ratio of eggs to liquid and sugar, the thicker the final mixture will be. Mixtures with a great deal of sugar will require more eggs or yolks to thicken them, as sugar retards coagulation. Conversely, those mixtures that contain a starch, such as flour or cornstarch, will need fewer eggs, as these starches contribute to the binding and thickening process.

❖ Eggs' remarkable ability to retain moisture upon coagulation is not wasted on baked goods, where their coagulation is not as specifically noticeable. By retaining valuable moisture, allowing the finished products to remain tender and moist, eggs greatly prolong the freshness of baked goods such as cakes, yeast and quick breads and cookies.

❖ Eggs contribute a distinct colour to many different desserts and baked goods, from the pure white of an angel food cake made with only egg whites to the bright yellow of a rich lemon curd, not due to the lemons, but to the number of egg yolks used. Pound, butter and yellow cakes also get their characteristic golden hue from egg yolks. The chemical responsible for egg yolks' orange or yellow colour is called *carotene*. Carotene is also the chemical that gives fresh butter its yellow colour (and makes carrots bright orange!). The amount of carotene present in the hen's diet will determine the intensity of the colour of the yolks. The carotene content of eggs can vary quite widely and is usually higher in natural, free-range eggs from chickens fed a diet high in natural foods. Corn-fed chickens are themselves slightly yellow, and their yolks are often a bright, deep orange. Organic eggs will tend to have brighter yolks than mass-produced eggs, and for those products you wish to have a particularly vivid colour, such as lemon, orange or passion fruit curd, they are worth seeking out.

❖ Eggs can be used to add colour and gloss to the crust of cookies, pies and tarts, scones, biscuits, breads and buns. Both the yolks and the whites of eggs are rich in protein, which browns well when exposed to heat. Products brushed with egg-based glazes take on a rich, glossy sheen when baked. Eggs can be used whole or in their parts, on their own or combined with other ingredients such as water, cream, milk, even alcohol, to form a glazing medium called an *egg wash*. This glaze can be brushed on the raw products before they are baked or may be brushed on just as the product comes out of the oven, depending on the desired effect.

❖ Eggs can be used as a glue to seal two pieces of dough or pastry together, as in a pie crust top and bottom or a decorative garnish made of pieces of dough on the top of a pie crust. An egg wash brushed on the surface of an unbaked loaf of bread forms a sticky surface to which seeds, grains or other pieces of dough can adhere.

❖ Finally, the mild and versatile flavour of eggs provides the base of flavour for desserts such as custards, creams, mousses, sabayons and puddings. Eggs alone are rather bland and in desserts must be enhanced with other, stronger flavourings and sweeteners. Think of them as an impressionable canvas, capable of supporting and enhancing the flavours of other ingredients.

All About Eggs

> NOTE: The eggs used in the recipes for this book were grade A large eggs. I try to buy corn-fed or organic eggs, as they are more flavourful and probably healthier.

Eggs have been a staple food for humans for millennia. The eggs of virtually any bird can be eaten, but it is the egg of the domesticated chicken that is most often meant in Western cooking when the term "egg" is used. I don't recommend using eggs from other birds in baking and dessert cookery, for several reasons. The chemistry of carefully balanced recipes does not take well to even slight alterations, and non-standardized eggs such as those of geese, ducks or game birds may vary considerably in composition from those of domesticated chickens. In addition, some birds' eggs have distinct flavours that are rarely desirable in baked goods. Duck and goose eggs, especially, tend to have an oily, pronounced flavour and should only be used very fresh, for savoury dishes.

It may surprise many people to know that, originally, chicken hens produced only three to five eggs per year, solely for the purpose of reproduction. Strategic handling and cross-breeding have led to domestic breeds of chicken that can lay that many in a week. The quality of commercially produced eggs is relatively high, but can vary to some degree depending on the habitat, feed and breed of the chickens.

When the eggs are collected from the laying hens, they are first graded according to quality. A process called *candling* is used to evaluate the quality of uncracked eggs. The eggs are examined in front of a bright light, which allows the form and colour of their interiors to be seen through the translucent enamel of the shell. Misshapen yolks, overly large air sacs and obvious defects or blood spots are grounds for removing the eggs from the lots for general sale. Only eggs of very high quality, labelled grade A, are packaged for commercial sale— the lower grades are reserved for the wholesale or processed food markets. A grade A egg will have a clean, smooth and evenly oval shell, with no blemishes. The yolk is very firm and round, the white dense and thick, and the air sac at the softly rounded end of the egg small and centred. Lower grades will tend to have thinner whites, less firm yolks and may have uneven, blotchy or even slightly cracked shells.

The eggs are then sorted according to size: jumbo, extra large, large, medium, small and peewee, a size not available in every store. A hen will lay eggs of various sizes, but for purposes of consistency of product, the eggs are sold according to a standardized size system. A large egg weighs about 2 ounces, or 60 grams. The shell accounts for 10 to 12% of this weight, the white for about 60% and the yolk for about 30%.

Contrary to any romantic notions that brown eggs are better for you than white, both colours and in fact even the candy-hued eggs of specialty breeds contain the same proportions of nutrients and have the same composition. In other words, don't pay more for brown eggs!

Eggs have a complex composition, consisting of protein, fat, moisture and trace minerals and carbohydrates. The fat is found almost exclusively in the yolk (a fact that has led to the alarming and unfortunate trend of the "egg-white omelette"). The white is slightly higher in moisture, while the yolk has slightly more protein. Each of these elements contributes to the egg's valuable place in baking and dessert cookery.

Egg Products

Recently, producers have engineered several new types of eggs, in the interest of lowering their overall fat and/or cholesterol content. *Small-yolk eggs* have a disproportionately large white in relation to the yolk and *low-cholesterol eggs* have been laid by chickens fed a diet designed to reduce the eggs' saturated fat content. While I have used the second type of egg with good results, I do not recommend using the small-yolk variety in egg-based dessert cookery, as most recipes rely on a standard ratio of white to yolk.

Another recent introduction to supermarket shelves are various *egg-white only* products. Usually nothing more than already-separated eggs, without the yolks, these gelatinous liquids must be measured out to be substituted for fresh whites. I have had good success using these products in recipes calling for egg whites that do not need to be whipped for volume, such as for macaroons or frangipane. They did not seem to whip as high or as firmly as fresh whites, however, so I would not recommend using them for cakes and meringues in which the end result relies heavily on the volume of the whipped whites for leavening.

Powdered egg products include whole eggs, yolks and whites and are available from baking and cake decorating specialty stores. They are generally used in large-scale and wholesale production, as they have a much longer shelf life than fresh eggs, but can also be used by the home baker. Although they are dried, these eggs must still be stored and handled with care, as they are prone to mould, rancidity and developing "off" flavours. They should be stored in well-sealed containers, in a cool, dry place well apart from any strong flavours or odours. Read the manufacturer's instructions carefully with regard to reconstituting the products—sufficient time is needed in order for the powder to properly absorb the water or the resulting "egg" will be runny, poorly blended and of little use in baking. In my experience, the only dried egg product worth using for the home baker is a high-quality dried egg white, actually preferable to fresh whites in certain cases. For sugar-coating flowers and fruits, for example, dried whites blend perfectly with water without becoming thick or gelatinous. This means they can be applied in a very thin film over the delicate petals of a flower without weighing it down or tearing it. Dried whites also make an excellent dense meringue and are often found already combined with superfine sugar in powdered form, sold as meringue powder. Used widely in cake decorating to make royal icing and other meringue-based confections, it rehydrates to a perfectly balanced meringue base, ready to be beaten. Although not recommended for general use to replace fresh whites, these powders are a good time- and money-saving option for anyone doing a great deal of cake decorating or fine confection work, providing reliable results without the expense of leftover yolks.

Storage and Handling of Eggs

If you buy natural, organic or free-range eggs from a natural food store, farmers' market or directly from a farmer, several extra steps must be taken to ensure safety. Do not wash the eggs until you are ready to use them—the shells of natural eggs are protected by a thin coating that makes them impervious to air. Commercially produced eggs are rinsed with a bactericide to remove any harmful bacteria present, but are then coated with a film similar to mineral oil, which serves the same purpose as the natural coating. Raw natural eggs are covered with potentially harmful dirt and bacteria, however, and care should be taken to keep them from contacting other foods. Always wash your hands with an antibacterial soap after handling natural eggs in their shells, and when you do use them, wash the shells thoroughly with the same antibacterial soap. Obviously you are not going to eat the shells, but when an egg is cracked, some contact between the shell and its contents is unavoidable, so the shells must be clean. If you happen to crack an egg accidentally, use it at once or freeze it whole or in parts to be used when you need them.

A NOTE ABOUT RAW EGGS: There has been some concern of late about the use of raw eggs in cooking and baking, with salmonella being the main fear. In fact, in the United States only one in 20,000 eggs is contaminated with the bacteria, and the ratio is even lower in Canada. As well, the vast majority of occurrences of illness caused by contaminated eggs happen in commercial settings, such as institutions and restaurants, where the eggs may not be properly stored, handled or prepared, NOT in home kitchens. If you store and handle your eggs properly, keeping them cold until ready to use, and don't use old or broken eggs, the risk is infinitesimal. Young children, pregnant women, the elderly and those with compromised immune systems, however, should refrain from eating dishes containing uncooked eggs.

Uncracked eggs have marvellous keeping abilities and can even be stored at room temperature for up to a week or so from the time they are laid. Commercial manufacturers take advantage of this quality, however, and by the time eggs reach supermarket shelves, they are often at least that old. For this reason, it is best to store eggs in the coldest part of your refrigerator, where they will often keep for a week or more past the date stamped on their carton. Although many refrigerators have special egg trays on the insides of their doors, this is not the ideal place to keep eggs, as it is one of the warmest areas in the unit. A better choice is to keep the eggs in their original carton at the back of one of the middle shelves. To be safe, never keep an egg at room temperature for longer than 2 hours.

Leftover raw egg whites and yolks can be refrigerated in small, airtight containers for up to 2 days. Cover the yolks with a little water to prevent them from forming a skin or drying out. Whites, yolks and even whole cracked eggs can be frozen for up to 3 or 4 months, then thawed and used as fresh. To freeze whites, place them in a freezable container just large enough to hold them, to minimize the amount of air trapped with the whites and prevent freezer burn. Using masking tape and a good marker, note the date, and the size and number of whites before freezing. Whites can also be frozen individually in ice cube trays, then transferred to a plastic freezer bag once solid. This way, you can add a few here and there until you have a need for them and keep track of how many you have frozen. When freezing yolks, add a little sugar to prevent the yolks from becoming grainy and lumpy when thawed. Using a ratio of about 1 teaspoon of sugar for every 3 yolks, whisk the two together until just blended, then transfer to a small freezable container. Whole eggs should be lightly beaten to blend the whites and yolks, then frozen in small containers, with the date, size of the eggs and number noted on the outside. To thaw the frozen whites, yolks or whole eggs, refrigerate the container for 12 to 24 hours, then use as you would fresh eggs. If the amount of egg you need is less than the total amount you have thawed, use the following measurements as a guide:

1 large egg white = about 2 tablespoons liquid whites
1 large egg yolk = about 1 tablespoon liquid yolks
1 large whole egg = about 3 tablespoons liquid whole eggs

While frozen egg products are reliable and perfectly sound for cooked dishes, they should not be used in raw dishes such as meringue toppings for pies and uncooked glazes. Even for baking and cooking, they are rarely preferable to fresh eggs, and the fact that they can be frozen should be used as a method of saving extra whites, yolks and whole eggs, but not as an excuse to buy more than you need!

Judging Freshness

Oxygen is the main cause of spoilage in eggs. Eggshells are porous and over time they allow the carbon dioxide in the eggs to escape, to be replaced with oxygen. All eggs contain a small air sac, which you can best see in eggs that have been hard cooked. In a perfectly fresh egg, this sac is located at the very end of the larger curve of the egg and is relatively small. As the egg ages and dehydrates, the air sac becomes larger and begins to spread outward and upward, creating a larger space for bacteria to breed. You can judge the size of the air sac, and the freshness of the egg, by placing the raw, uncracked egg in a glass of water. A very fresh egg will sink quickly, while a spoiled or very old egg will float. How quickly the egg sinks is an indication of its age and condition. Once cracked, eggs spoil very quickly. The bacteria that thrives on eggs spreads very rapidly to other foods and to other eggs. You should never buy an egg with a cracked shell, nor replace the cracked egg in the carton with a sound one before purchasing.

A fresh egg should have a firm, high-standing yolk that appears round and compact. The white should be as thick as possible, although even a very fresh supermarket egg may have started to develop two parts to the white, a thick area surrounding the yolk, and a slightly thinner, looser part towards the outside. The yolk of a not-so-fresh egg will be flatter and more flaccid and the white, too, will tend to spread easily, appearing more liquid than gelatinous. These older eggs are not unusable, but should not be used in egg-based recipes. They are fine to use in baked goods or cooked and eaten as a savoury food.

Tiny red or brown flecks, called *blood* or *meat spots*, may occur in any type of egg, but do so more often with organic or naturally produced eggs, as commercial processing plants often weed out these eggs before packaging. These spots are completely harmless and, in fact, will disappear with age.

Using Eggs in the Sweet Kitchen

For eggs to provide the maximum benefit to a given product, several things must be considered. The most appropriate part of the egg must be used, be that whole eggs, yolks or whites. The eggs must be used at (and heated to) the right temperature, and they must be properly combined with other ingredients, by creaming, whipping, folding, beating or otherwise blending. All of these factors will heavily influence the success of the final product.

Freshness is essential when it comes to eggs in baking. For some purposes, such as a good fruit curd or a custard, the fresher the eggs, the better they will hold and thicken the mixture. For other applications, such as some meringues and other egg-white foams, slightly older whites are preferable, as they have loosened up and are more flexible and expandable.

To fully appreciate and understand the amazingly varied role eggs play in the world of baking and dessert cookery, it is best to look at the egg not as a single unit, but as two distinct elements—the white and the yolk—each with very different compositions, abilities and tendencies.

Lecithin, the main emulsifier in eggs, is found in the yolks, not the whites. Lecithin enables egg yolks to absorb fat, while whites become dry with cooking, despite whatever ingredients they may be combined with. For this reason, whites alone should not be substituted for whole eggs or egg yolks in the interest of reducing the cholesterol or fat content of a finished product without considering how the texture and quality will be affected. Whereas whole eggs and yolks will have the desired emulsifying effect, whites alone can produce a drier, tougher texture and, ironically, a heavier feel, due to the poorly distributed and suspended fat particles.

The proteins in egg whites straighten and expand when beaten or whipped, creating a strong and flexible mesh of strands that entrap and hold air. This expands with the heat of the oven, making the whites excellent mechanical leaveners (see Whipping Egg Whites, page 58).

The proteins in egg yolks, however, are more fragile. While their role as an emulsifier gives them a great capacity for binding and thickening various mixtures, their proteins break down with exposure to high heat, causing the yolks, or the mixtures in which they are smoothly suspended, to curdle. Custards, sauces and other mixtures based on egg yolks must therefore be handled carefully around heat, and not heated above certain temperatures.

Egg whites do not contain lecithin and are completely free of fat. With heat, they provide strength and support to cakes and other baked goods, but not the same smoothness or moisture of yolks. Baked goods made with too many whites will be dry, tough and overly firm. This dryness can be used to an advantage, though, in cases where too much moisture weighs down the product or prevents it from baking properly. With some fritters and choux pastries, a higher proportion of whites ensures the pastries will cook thoroughly, without remaining gooey or underbaked in the centre. Many fritter batters and coatings for fried or deep-fried foods are made with egg whites, as whites do not absorb much fat and will puff and fry to a crisper, drier, lighter coating. More yolks will lead to a heavier product, one that may absorb too much fat during cooking. Whites will yield a lighter, crisper fritter, with no greasy or oily aftertaste.

Cold eggs are much easier to separate than warm ones. A good habit to get into is separating your eggs one at a time into a small, very clean bowl, then transferring each egg white to a larger bowl. This way, if a yolk does break and touch the white, it won't contaminate the entire batch. Unless you are extremely deft, keep the theatrical one-handed egg cracking for omelettes. I find the best and safest way to separate eggs is to use my hands. Crack each egg over the small bowl, then turn the egg's insides into your palm, letting the white fall through your fingers into the bowl, continuing to cradle the intact yolk in your hand. (If the yolk breaks and some of it gets into the bowl, you can use a little piece of plain bread to absorb the yolk, then add the clean white to the larger bowl.) The yolks may be refrigerated, well covered, for several days, or frozen for several months.

Whipping Egg Whites

When egg whites are whipped and folded into cake batters, the air trapped in the foam expands with the heat of the oven and provides volume and height for the finished cake. The proteins in egg whites are formed in tight coils. When the whites are beaten, these coils gradually straighten out, forming a tight, strong protein web, capable of entrapping and retaining air. For the best results, the whites must be whipped to high, stiff peaks, incorporating the maximum volume of air, while still remaining flexible and moist. For cakes, mousses and soufflés, the whites should be beaten to what are called "soft peaks"—the whites form floppy mounds that come to a peak when the whisk is lifted, but are still moist and soft. For firm meringues, angel food cakes and other foam-based cakes, the whites should be beaten to "stiff peaks"—very glossy, pure white foam that stands stiff and remains peaked when the beater is lifted. Regardless of the intended use, if whites are overbeaten, they will look dry, grainy and flaky and will be difficult to fold into the batter smoothly. They will not have the strength to hold as much air and will deflate quickly. In effect, overbeaten whites are "cooked," their potential exhausted. The heat of the oven will only serve to deflate the air and further dry out the whites, creating a tough, poorly risen product. If you do overbeat your egg whites, add another white and continue beating gently until the foam comes together again and looks moist and glossy.

For best results, whites should be at least three or four days old, as the coils of proteins will have relaxed slightly and will expand more easily, but will still be strong and elastic. Unfortunately, this is not an issue for most, as the eggs available in the supermarket are likely at least a week old. If, however, you buy your eggs as I do, from a farmers' market, try to use eggs of less than a week, but more than a few days old. Egg whites should beaten at room temperature or slightly warmer. They will be more elastic and will expand to a larger web, incorporating more air. Whole eggs are separated most easily when cold, so I generally warm my whites (after separating) over a bowl of warm water, swirling the whites in their bowl until they are just about body temperature, keeping them moving to prevent any premature coagulation.

Egg whites must be kept completely apart from any fat, or they will not whip to nearly as great a volume and may in fact not whip at all. Be careful when separating the whites from the yolks, as even a speck of yolk, which is high in fat, can contaminate the whites. Sharp edges in the eggshell-to-eggshell method can pierce the yolk, but soft and sensitive hands are much more gentle. Be sure that all equipment—bowl, whisk, whip or beater attachment, even spatula—are perfectly clean and grease-free. A quick rinse under very hot water is a good safety measure for tools you think are clean, but have been sitting around a busy kitchen. Finally, the material of the bowl in which the whites are whipped contributes to the success of the final product. The very best material for any type of egg beating or whipping is copper. The natural acidity in copper strengthens the proteins of the raw whites and enables them to expand to a greater volume without collapsing. Whites whipped in a copper bowl will whip to about 1¼ times the volume of whites beaten in a stainless steel or glass bowl. The copper also seems to effectively raise the temperature at which the whites coagulate, allowing the air they have trapped to continue to expand for a longer time than if they had coagulated earlier. Adding cream of tartar, an acidic element, to egg whites before they are beaten has a similar strengthening effect, enabling them to retain more air and remain more stable once beaten. In fact, any acid, such as lemon juice, will do what the cream of tartar does and can be added even when a copper bowl is used. If you don't have a copper bowl, beat the whites in a stainless steel or glass bowl and always use the largest, finest-wired balloon whisk you can find. Whipping by hand will yield a higher volume, while beating with an electric or stand mixer provides a denser, slightly more stable foam. I use the whisking-by-hand method for soufflés and mousses, where a maximum volume is desired, and the stand mixer for meringues and cake batters that require a glossier, stiffer and stronger foam.

When sugar is added to egg whites as they are whipped, it creates a thick, stiff and glossy foam, denser and much more stable than egg whites alone. For a very stiff meringue, the sugar is gradually beaten into the whites, a little at a time, beginning once the whites have reached a slightly loose foamy state. The sugar must be added slowly enough that it can dissolve in the whites before the next bit is added. Some bakers favour using a superfine sugar for making heavily sugared meringues, as the smaller granules dissolve quickly, but others feel that these fine grains do not provide enough resistance and friction, thereby producing a lower foam, and prefer to use regular granulated sugar. I have used both and find that for most meringues, either makes a good choice. If the recipe specifies one or the other, try to be faithful.

Folding Whipped Whites into Batters

Folding whipped egg white foam into batters must be done gently and with as little extraneous movement as possible, to avoid deflating the whites. If the batter is particularly dense and heavy, it is a good practice to stir a small amount of the foam into the batter to lighten it first, before adding the rest. The remainder of the whites should be folded into the batter in two to four stages, each being almost incorporated before the next is added. To fold, use a large flat rubber spatula for the best coverage of the entire bowl and a scooping and folding motion. Begin with the spatula flat against the side of the bowl nearest you and scoop it away from you, making sure the spatula scrapes the very bottom and centre of the bowl. When it reappears on the other side, fold over the mass of batter you have scooped up to one side, turning the bowl a little as you do. Continue until the whites are gently blended. It sounds complicated, but is in fact a very natural movement. Just remember to use very broad, slow motions, covering as much area as possible, trying not to stir, crush, or jiggle the batter in the process. The aim is for the whites to be suspended in the batter, but not so completely incorporated that they lose the air they have trapped. It is far preferable to have a few little pockets of unincorporated whites in the batter than to so vigorously blend the two elements as to deflate the whites.

When whipped egg whites are folded into a batter for the purpose of leavening and lightening it, they are not also able to provide structure. In other words, if no other eggs—whole, yolks or unbeaten whites—are used in the batter, the cake will indeed rise to great heights, then immediately fall as it begins to cool, because there is nothing to support the structure of the trapped air. For this reason, egg yolks are often beaten into the batter before the whipped whites are added, providing structure and form until the starch in the flour can set. In cakes with little or no flour, more egg yolks must be used as they must assume full responsibility for the structure of the finished cake. In the best of these cakes, some falling will occur when the cake is removed from the oven, but the final product is a moist, evenly aerated and tender cake. If you find that a cake using a large number of whipped whites is falling more than you'd like it to, try adding a few yolks or unbeaten whites to the batter. They should provide sufficient structure to support the leavening from the whipped whites and keep the cake high and tender even when cooled.

Combining Egg Yolks and Other Ingredients

Egg yolks, like whites, must be treated with respect when combined with other ingredients. Certain elements, sugar and acids among them, can cause the yolks to "burn," or form tiny, hard granules. These will not ruin the dessert, but they will not disappear with stirring or cooking and can lend a slightly grainy texture to mixtures that should best be perfectly smooth. To avoid this, add sugar or acidic ingredients, such as lemon juice or other fruit juices, to egg yolks only at the last minute, to avoid the yolks sitting with the undissolved or incompletely blended ingredients for any length of time. Whisking the ingredients into the yolks, keeping the mixture moving until the two elements are combined, will prevent the little beads from forming, keeping the egg mixture smooth.

LEAVENERS

Role of Leavening Agents

LEAVENING AGENTS ARE USED in baking to create pockets of gas that expand before and during baking and are ultimately supported by the structure of the baked good. The makeup of the bubbles depends on the type of leavening agent used, but is one or a combination of steam, air and carbon dioxide. The leavening agents fall into three categories as well: mechanical, chemical and natural. Each is used to achieve a specific type of result. These agents are sometimes used in combination, but cannot be used interchangeably.

Mechanical leavening occurs when ingredients are combined by the baker in a way that incorporates air into the batter, with creaming and whipping being the most effective. The process of creaming ingredients, most often sugar and butter or eggs, uses the friction between the ingredients to generate pockets of air. The air becomes trapped in the fat and proteins of the batter and expands in the oven, leavening the product. The longer and more thoroughly a mixture is creamed, the more air will be incorporated.

Another kind of mechanical leavening occurs when air is whipped into egg whites, as for a soufflé or cake, or heavy cream, as in a parfait or mousse. The proteins in the whites and the fat molecules in the cream hold a great volume of air when whipped properly. When the aerated foam is carefully combined with the other ingredients of a recipe, the air becomes permanently trapped and serves to lighten or leaven the product.

Mechanical leavening also occurs in the making of products such as Danish pastry and puff pastry. Through the repetitive process (called *laminating*) of rolling and folding the dough over the first layer of fat, usually butter, layers upon layers are created, the integrity of each preserved using regular chilling to prevent the fat from melting into the dough. When the dough is baked, the inherent moisture in the butter expands, creating steam. The pockets of steam are supported by the strong dough, and the end result is a delicate, crisp, flaky pastry with a great network of air pockets (see page 143 for more detail).

With mechanical leavening, many factors can influence the level of aeration. The quality, freshness and temperature of the ingredients; the type and condition of all equipment used; the degree of creaming, whipping or mixing; and the time elapsed between aeration, incorporation of other ingredients and baking all contribute to the success of the finished product. Good recipes will alert the baker to any specifically delicate points, such as the best temperature for the ingredients or the cleanliness of the tools, and any tips offered should be observed!

Chemical leavening occurs with the use of baking soda, baking powder or, in some cases, ammonium bicarbonate. These products are used in recipes that are not suitable for natural leavening (yeast) and may require more extensive or more reliable leavening than could be achieved with mechanical leavening alone. Many products leavened with chemical leavening agents also use some form of mechanical leavening, such as creaming, beating or whipping, to ensure an even lighter, more tender product.

Natural leavening occurs with the use of yeast in a recipe. The range of products in which this form can be employed are limited as yeast requires very specific conditions to thrive, namely moisture, sugar and warmth, as well as time to produce the carbon dioxide necessary to leaven a product.

Chemical Leaveners

BAKING SODA (*Bicarbonate of Soda, Sodium Bicarbonate*) Baking soda is commonly used as a leavener in baked goods such as cakes, quick breads and cookies. By itself, it has no leavening power, but must be activated by the presence of an acid and a liquid. In combination with these elements, baking soda releases carbon dioxide in the form of air bubbles. Suspended in the structure of a cake or quick bread, these bubbles leaven the product and give it a characteristic airiness and tender crumb.

Acids with the power to activate baking soda include cream of tartar, buttermilk, yogurt or sour cream, molasses, dark brown sugar, maple syrup, lemon, lime or orange juice or even non-alkalized cocoa powder. In some cases, although there is a moderately acidic ingredient in the recipe, it may not be acidic enough or present in sufficient quantity to provide the necessary leavening with baking soda. Honey, brown sugar and cocoa may sometimes fall into this category. In these cases, a combination of baking soda and baking powder is often used to ensure the proper degree of leavening.

Because baking soda begins to release carbon dioxide as soon as it is moistened in the presence of an acid, it should be thoroughly blended into the dry ingredients in a recipe and combined with the liquid ingredients at the last minute, then quickly mixed and placed in the oven. If too much time elapses before the mixture is baked, the gas will dissipate before the other ingredients can support the structure, and the product will not rise, or at least not properly.

If you replace the acidic ingredient in a recipe calling for baking soda as the leavener with a non-acidic ingredient, you must introduce another acid or replace the baking soda with baking powder. A tablespoon of lemon juice or vinegar added to a cup of sweet milk can be used to replace buttermilk, but sweet milk alone lacks the acid necessary to activate the baking soda. Similarly, if Dutch-process cocoa, which has been treated to neutralize most of the acid naturally present, is substituted for natural cocoa in a recipe with baking soda as the leavener, and no other acid is present, baking powder should be used to replace the soda.

A secondary function of baking soda is to neutralize or dampen acidic ingredients. For this reason it is sometimes used in recipes with a high proportion of ingredients such as lemon juice, buttermilk or other sour flavours. When replacing sugar with a large amount of an acidic sweetener, such as honey, molasses or barley malt syrup, ½ teaspoon of baking soda should be added to the recipe to account for the increased acidity, even if baking powder is the principal leavener.

The substitution ratio for baking soda and baking powder is 1:4. Therefore, if a recipe calls for 1 teaspoon of baking soda, you can substitute 4 teaspoons of baking powder. Keep in mind the other properties of baking soda—if there are any highly acidic ingredients in the recipe, baking powder will not dampen their sting as well as baking soda, and the acidic flavour may be more prominent in the final product than is desirable.

Baking soda keeps 9 to 12 months, depending on how fresh it was when purchased. To test the potency of baking soda, combine a small amount with at least an equal quantity of vinegar. Fresh baking soda will bubble vigorously. It should be stored in a cool, dry place and kept airtight if it is to be used for baking, as it tends to absorb odours extremely well. This characteristic makes it ideal for use as a deodorizer, in cupboards, refrigerators and freezers. Do not, however, use the baking soda that has been inhaling strange aromas in the back of your refrigerator for your next cake!

BAKING POWDER Baking powder is a compound originally made of bicarbonate of soda (baking soda) and acid, in the form of tartaric acid (cream of tartar) and a moisture-absorbing starch, usually cornstarch. When combined with a liquid, baking powder releases carbon dioxide, generating air bubbles that, if properly supported in the structure of a batter, leaven the product. The tartaric acid provides the necessary acid in the right proportions to activate the baking soda, so baking powder can be used in recipes that do not call for acidic ingredients. As with baking soda, this type of baking powder, called *single-action*, begins to release carbon dioxide bubbles as soon as it is moistened.

There were two problems with this compound, however, as a commercial product destined for mass consumption. First, producing tartaric acid is laborious, making it fairly expensive. Second, the single-action compound gives the baker a relatively short time to get the product into the oven before the gas is completely released. For these reasons, the old baking powder has been replaced with a new *double-acting*, or continuous-action, variety. Two different acid salts are used to replace the tartaric acid. One of these acids reacts with liquid, creating a small network of bubbles in the batter. The second acid reacts with the heat of the oven, expanding the bubbles at a time when the structure of the surrounding batter can support them. Monocalcium phosphate and sodium aluminum sulphate are most commonly used in commercial baking powders today, giving the baker more time to prepare the recipe without losing volume in the final product. Virtually all baking powder sold in North American supermarkets is double-acting whether or not it states so on the label. This type of baking powder is slightly less time-sensitive than baking soda, although it is still best to work quickly once the dry ingredients have been moistened.

The "improvements" to the old-fashioned single-action baking powder, however, have led to some controversy. Aluminum is generally thought to be best avoided as a foodstuff, and many people have difficulty tolerating sulphates of any kind. Some people can detect a metallic taste in products with relatively large amounts of commercial baking powder, such as biscuits and scones. Many bakers also feel these highly engineered baking powders do not produce as delicate and tender a product, sacrificing maximum leavening for ease of use. Some health and natural food stores have begun selling *aluminum-free* (or *non-alum*) *baking powder*. It tends to be expensive and does not keep well, but is far preferable to the commercial sort.

Fortunately, excellent baking powder is easy to make at home. For every teaspoon of baking powder called for in a recipe, combine ¼ teaspoon baking soda, ½ teaspoon cream of tartar and ½ teaspoon cornstarch. Blend well and use immediately, as this mixture loses potency with prolonged storage.

Keep baking powder airtight in a cool, dry place, as moisture causes the powder to go flat. To test the potency of your baking powder, place ½ teaspoon into a small quantity of warm water. If it fizzes and bubbles happily, it is still good. Properly stored, baking powder should last about 1 year.

AMMONIUM BICARBONATE (*Carbonate of Ammonia, Powdered Baking Ammonia, Hartshorn*) Although rare today in North America, this compound was the first chemical leavener to be used in baking. It is still used in many parts of Europe and may be called for in some traditional recipes, especially ones for crisp cookies and biscuits. It tends to create a very crisp product and must be very carefully measured to exert maximum potency. If used in incorrect proportions, it can lend a distinctly ammonial aftertaste, which is why it has been eclipsed by baking soda and baking powder for home baking. Though my own experience with ammonium bicarbonate has been somewhat limited, I have used it with great success in several biscotti recipes, where it produces a fabulously shattering crunchiness, and in a recipe for springerle, the highly spiced German Christmas cookie. Ammonium bicarbonate can be purchased from pharmacies and will likely need to be ground to a fine powder with a mortar and pestle. I have also found it in Eastern European and Greek groceries, already powdered.

CREAM OF TARTAR Cream of tartar is made from tartaric acid, a sediment left in wine bottles after fermentation, which has been isolated, purified and ground to a fine white powder. It is often used to give stability and strength to whipped egg whites, the acid helping to firm the proteins in the white, allowing them to hold maximum shape and volume. (The acid in lemon juice sometimes performs the same function.) It is also one of the key components of baking powder and is sometimes used to supplement the acid present in ingredients in a recipe containing baking soda, in order to activate the baking soda to release carbon dioxide and leaven the mixture. When a non-acidic or alkaline ingredient is used to replace an acidic one in a recipe containing baking soda, such as sweet milk for buttermilk, cream of tartar should be added to ensure there is sufficient acid present to activate the baking soda. Cream of tartar tends to clump, so I always sift it before use, even though recipes rarely specify doing so.

BAKEWELL CREAM Bakewell Cream is a traditional New England term for a powdered acid, most likely cream of tartar, which would have been combined with baking soda to act as the leavener for baked goods. It is little referred to today, but should you come across a traditional or historical recipe calling for it, you can substitute as follows: for each 2 teaspoons Bakewell Cream plus 1 teaspoon baking soda, substitute 2 teaspoons baking powder.

Yeast

Yeast is a living organism that thrives under warm, moist conditions, feeding on simple sugars and producing energy in the form of alcohol and carbon dioxide. Centuries ago, humans realized this process could be harnessed and controlled, improving the quality of breads and enabling the making of wine, beer and other liquors.

Wild yeasts are present in almost every natural environment in the world, with each climate, region and even micro-climate (such as your kitchen!) harbouring a different balance of strains and densities. Originally, all bread was made from wild yeasts. Known as the *sourdough method*, a "sponge" of flour, water and often a little sugar or fruit is left to attract the naturally occurring yeasts from the air. This starter is fed with more flour and kneaded to develop the gluten. The gas produced by the yeasts is trapped in the complex web of gluten strands, and the bread becomes risen and tender. The benefits of relying on wild yeasts are a unique flavour, ranging from pleasantly tangy to downright sour, and the ease of being able to make leavened bread virtually anywhere, with a minimum of ingredients.

There are drawbacks to this method, however. Sometimes a sour taste is not desired, and in some regions the wild yeasts present in the air produce inconsistent results or unappealing flavours. While sourdough breads are still very common, especially in parts of Europe, a more reliable type of yeast, designed to produce a mild-flavoured, consistent and rapidly made bread, was developed in the mid-nineteenth century, as a result of the work of Louis Pasteur. *Baker's yeast*, as it is commonly known, is the result of careful fermentation of a pure, reliable and pleasant-tasting strain of yeast, processed to forms that can be used immediately, and under many different conditions. When using baker's yeast, you do not need to wait for a sponge or starter, and the long rises that must follow. Some bakers, however, like the effect using a starter and a prolonged rise have on a bread, namely a less yeasty flavour and a larger-holed, airier crumb. These bakers, though, may not want the tang of a sourdough. In these cases, the baker's yeast can be used in a smaller than usual amount to make a starter, and the dough can be given several long rises to develop superior flavour, effectively behaving like a sourdough. Most often, however, people use baker's yeast to enable the entire process, from combining the first ingredients to enjoying hot, crusty bread, to be completed in a matter of hours, not days.

Like all living organisms, yeasts thrive under some conditions, but are threatened by others. Yeasts love sugar, but can be killed by direct contact with salt. Direct contact with fat may smother the yeast, preventing it from being able to feed and ferment. Yeast is also very sensitive to temperature. Slow fermentation, the sort that produces the best texture and flavour in a product, occurs at about 65°F. A good average temperature for most doughs is 80°F, and between 90° and 100°F is appropriate for doughs requiring a fast fermentation. Temperatures above 140°F have a fatal effect on yeast. Yeast can be refrigerated to retard its development and fermentation, and can even be frozen, alone or in yeast doughs. Defrost in the refrigerator and use immediately upon thawing.

FRESH YEAST *(Compressed Yeast)* To make the fresh form of baker's yeast, a pure, active strain of yeast is introduced to a hospitable environment and allowed a controlled amount of fermentation. The culture that develops is washed, producing a yeast cream, and the cream is then compressed to remove excess water. The resulting moist, creamy mass is called *compressed yeast*. Fresh compressed yeast should break cleanly, smell sweetly of yeast and be uniformly moist, creamy and even-coloured. If the yeast is crumbly, funky-smelling or dark in places, it is likely past its prime.

Fresh yeast is highly perishable and is most commonly used by professional bakers and large manufacturers who use large quantities of yeast and can be sure to use it before it spoils. It must be stored in the refrigerator, well wrapped, and used within 2 or 3 weeks of the date on the package.

Fresh yeast should be "proofed," to make sure it is potent. Dissolve the quantity called for in the recipe in a small amount of warm (105° to 115°F) water and add a pinch of granulated sugar. Leave the mixture in a warm, draught-free place for about 5 minutes. At the end of that time, it should be foamy and pleasantly yeasty-smelling. If it is not, discard it and begin with a fresh batch.

Fresh yeast is available in bulk in large blocks or in small cakes. One 0.6-ounce cake can be substituted for one standard envelope (¼-ounce or about 2¼ teaspoons) of active dry yeast, but fresh yeast does not need to be rehydrated.

ACTIVE DRY YEAST To make active dry yeast, the cake of fresh compressed yeast is pressed into thin filaments and dried in a controlled environment to a moisture content of 5 to 8%. This dehydration gives active dry yeast a much longer shelf life than its fresh counterpart and has made it overwhelmingly more popular with North American bakers. The yeast cells are dormant until activated by contact with a warm liquid, and when rehydrated perform exactly the same way as fresh yeast.

Active dry yeast is commonly available in ¼-ounce packets (about 2¼ teaspoons) and in 4-ounce tins. I suggest buying the tins only if you go through a large quantity of yeast in a short period. Although dehydrated, active dry yeast is not everlasting and deteriorates rapidly once exposed to air. Take care when buying active dry yeast that the expiration date has not passed. These days, many stores sell so little yeast that their stocks may be woefully out of date!

Active dry yeast sold in foil packets is packaged under the pressure of nitrogen gas and does not need refrigeration. Loose, bulk or tinned active dry yeast should be stored airtight in the refrigerator, away from moisture, heat and light. Unopened, it should keep about 9 or 10 months, but always go by the date stamped on the packet and proof your yeast before proceeding with a recipe.

To proof active dry yeast, scatter the yeast over a small amount of lukewarm water and let the mixture sit in a warm place for up to 10 minutes, to allow the yeast time to rehydrate. If it foams and develops a yeasty aroma, it is live. If not, throw it away and begin with a new batch.

INSTANT YEAST (Fast-Acting Active Dry Yeast, Quick-Rising Active Dry Yeast) To create this relatively new form of dried yeast, fresh compressed yeast is further dehydrated than it is for regular active dry yeast. It comes in the form of tiny granules that do not require rehydrating, but can be immediately combined with the dry ingredients in a recipe before the liquid and fat are added.

Although this type of yeast has become quite popular in this age of instant everything, I don't use it and find it to be of dubious value for anyone who truly appreciates good bread. Because the yeast works so quickly, the dough does not get a chance to develop its own flavour, and the flavour of the yeast remains overpowering in the finished bread. The greatly reduced rising time also means that more yeast must be used in the dough, producing a floppy, overly risen dough and a poorly crumbed and unevenly textured loaf.

Instant dry yeast is available in foil packets and in small tins and can be stored in a cool, dark, dry place if unopened. Refrigerate the tins once opened and always note the best-before dates on the packages. The foil packets should be very hard to the touch before opening, indicating a good vacuum.

BREWER'S YEAST, ENGIVITA YEAST, FLAKED NUTRITIONAL YEAST and TORULA YEAST are all forms of cultured nutritional yeasts popular for their health benefits and for flavouring processed foods, but cannot be used to leaven baked goods. None should be substituted for any form of baker's yeast, and they should be used only where specified in a recipe.

LIQUIDS IN BAKING

LIQUIDS FULFILL A VARIETY of functions in baking and dessert-making, but not every liquid will satisfy the requirements of any recipe. For this reason, it is important to understand how a particular liquid functions in a given recipe before you set about substituting it.

Role of Liquids

❖ Liquids of all kinds supply moisture to baked goods, contributing to their tenderness and prolonging their shelf life.

❖ Every liquid, even plain water, adds flavour to all types of desserts, from poached fruit to cakes to custards to jellies and more. The better the flavour of the liquid on its own, the better the flavour of the finished dessert.

❖ Liquids supply the moisture necessary to activate baking powder and baking soda, thereby contributing to the leavening of baked goods.

❖ In yeast breads, the proteins in the flour need a liquid to enable them to develop gluten, the protein ultimately responsible for the breads' elasticity, tenderness and crumb. Water most commonly plays this role, but in some recipes milk, beer or even fruit juice may be called for.

❖ Sweet milk, buttermilk, cream and semi-liquid dairy products like yogurt, sour cream and crème fraîche contribute richness to many baked goods, custards, creams and puddings due to their various fat contents. The thicker and richer the ingredient, the more moisture and richness it will impart to the final product. Lower-fat products should not be substituted for regular or whole-fat ingredients, as the success of the recipe likely depends on the integrity of the original ingredient. In some recipes, a product with a slightly higher fat content can be used to replace another, but added richness and perhaps a slight change in texture should be expected. For example, a recipe in which the buttermilk is replaced by yogurt or sour cream will work, but will be somewhat richer and possibly heavier.

❖ Liquids lubricate other ingredients in batters and doughs, assisting in the distribution of other ingredients and developing the proper texture and consistency in the finished dessert.

❖ Liquids sometimes form the basis of certain desserts, such as the fruit juice or wine in a jelly or the milk or cream in a custard. The type of liquid is critical in these cases, and substitutions should be as close to the original ingredient as possible.

❖ Many liquids provide considerable sweetness, as well as characteristic flavours, to desserts such as cakes, quick breads, sauces, syrups and compotes. Fruit juices, wine, liqueurs and spirits are all naturally sweet and may be used alone or with additional sweeteners to flavour desserts.

❖ Some liquids, in certain desserts, even contribute colour, as is the case in many compotes and syrups. Fruit juices and wine, in particular, are often of vivid shades that colour the mixtures into which they are incorporated. The colours are not usually noticeable in baked goods if the liquids are present in small quantities, but keep the colour in mind when substituting.

Liquids Commonly Used in the Sweet Kitchen

Sweet milk, buttermilk, cream and semi-liquid dairy products are discussed in detail in the Dairy section (pages 162–77).

FRESH FRUIT JUICES are an excellent addition to many baked goods, adding moisture, sweetness and flavour. Because fruit juices contain no fat or protein, they are limited in their function in baked goods and often need to be supple-mented with milk or another dairy product.

Fruit juices form the base for many jellies, sorbets, ices and curds, where their flavour, liquid and sweetness are key. These desserts are generally very lean, with little or no added fat, and use the sugar naturally present in the fruit juice to help achieve the desired texture. A simple gelatine dessert can be made of nothing more than fruit juice and gelatine, although a bit of extra sugar en-hances the flavour of the fruit and makes it more dessert-like.

Whenever possible, use fresh juices, preferably freshly squeezed, especially in the case of citrus juices. These in particular tend to assume a very canned or cooked flavour when they are from concentrate or have been packaged and pas-teurized. Fresh citrus juices lose flavour very quickly and should be squeezed as close to the time of use as possible. Today, the juice of almost any fruit can be found, in health or natural food stores if not the supermarket. The juices of par-ticularly pulpy or creamy fruits, such as apricots, mangoes or pears, often called nectars, are a gold mine for the baker, adding rich, pure flavour and great mois-ture to muffins, cakes and sauces.

When thickened with a little cornstarch, arrowroot or fruit purée, many fruit juices can form the basis of thin, flavourful sauces, perfect with tarts, ice creams and rich cakes.

Many recipes have capitalized on the concentrated flavours that *frozen juice concentrates* can give. These should be used undiluted for best potency and have the advantage over fresh juices in that they provide a maximum of flavour with-out a lot of liquid.

WATER, often overlooked, plays an enormous part in baking and dessert cook-ery. From moistening the flour and yeast for a bread dough to serving as a warm liquid in which to dissolve instant espresso powder or cocoa powder for a sauce or a cake batter to being the base of the sugar syrup for poaching fruit or mak-ing cooked meringues and icings, water is a critical and versatile ingredient. Water as an ingredient is a bit of a foreign concept to many people, perhaps be-cause most of us have come to take it quite for granted, thinking of it as more of a utensil or tool, rather than as a component in a recipe. In fact, water can have a powerful effect on the flavour of the finished product and should con-sidered as important as the flour, butter or chocolate. In many regions, tap water is perfectly good, with a pleasant, neutral flavour, and serves most of our pur-poses well. In others, tap water may be tainted with detectable flavours and odours, not welcome in a drink, let alone a dessert. *Bottled spring water* and *filtered water* are widely available and many of us drink little else. Yet when it comes time to poach the pears for dessert or make a starter for a loaf of bread, we reach for the tap. In fact, as with many flavours in baking and dessert-making, the "flavour," or aftertaste, of water becomes concentrated with cooking or baking, as the pure water is evaporated and the residual elements remain. For this reason, only water you would happily drink should ever be used in preparing desserts. Even in the case of those who have inoffensive tap water, many bakers suggest using bottled spring water for the preparation of bread doughs, as the action of the yeast can aggravate any impurities and "off" flavours in the water. I have baked identical loaves of white bread, one using Toronto tap water, hailed as the safest and most drinkable tap water in the country, and the other using bottled spring water and, indeed, I did taste a slight difference. As with all ingredients, if you are going to the trouble and expense of making your bread, pastries or dessert from scratch, don't compromise the outcome by using less than pure ingredients. It's not worth it!

LIQUID FLAVOURINGS, such as *wines*, *liqueurs*, *spirits*, *extracts*, *essences* and *flower waters*, disperse evenly and quickly into a mixture. As they are very concentrated flavours, and little is needed, the liquid form allows them to thoroughly saturate the entire mixture without leaving some pockets unflavoured or others too concentrated. These ingredients function more as flavours, rather than liquids in the traditional sense. They may serve to replace a small amount of the main liquid in a recipe such as a cake batter or mousse, but if left out, usually the only discernible difference would be in the flavour of the product, not the texture or structure. For this reason, they are very easily substituted for one another, enabling the flavour and accents of many desserts to be slightly or significantly varied. (See also Flavourings, page 209.)

SALT

SALT HAS RECEIVED a bad rap in the last few years. I don't know how many people have confessed to me that they rarely or never add salt to recipes even when it is called for, including those for baked goods. I am always dismayed, as it is one of the most important elements in any baked product and cannot be replaced or omitted if a successful product is to be achieved! Unless the recipe is specifically a low- or no-salt recipe, salt should never be left out! It has numerous functions in the sweet kitchen:

❖ The primary function of salt in any recipe, sweet or savoury, is to enhance the flavours of the other ingredients and to heighten the overall taste of the product. Salt itself should not be a discernible flavour. In desserts such as cakes and cookies, salt enhances sweetness and highlights the flavour of the other ingredients. In plain baked goods, such as simple breads and pastries, omitting the salt can make the product all but inedible. More than once I have made a huge batch of baked breads for the evening meal at a restaurant, left out the salt and had to start again from scratch. Salt adds a depth of flavour and complexity to otherwise bland products, giving them life and brightness.

❖ Salt has a regulating effect on the development of yeast in doughs. It slows the rate of fermentation by inhibiting the yeast slightly. The dough rises more slowly, but has a tighter gluten structure, enabling it to spring higher in the oven and have a more elastic and pleasant texture when baked. Unsalted doughs have a tendency to be airy and flaccid when rising and don't bake as high and tender. Although salt should account for only about 2% of the total weight of flour in a yeast dough recipe, it is an exact proportion and should be measured carefully, as too great a quantity can kill yeast.

❖ Salt has a strengthening effect on proteins, including gluten. In a yeast dough, this means it gives support and structure to the loaf, particularly important in free-form loaves.

❖ Salt gives the crust of yeast breads and other baked goods a golden colour and a delicate crispness. If the salt is omitted, the crust is often dull and pale.

❖ As with the protein in flour, salt strengthens the proteins in egg whites, making them better able to achieve and hold their whipped volume and shape.

❖ Salt inhibits the growth and development of bacteria, moulds and harmful yeasts in the same way that it slows the development of the yeasts in bread dough, acting as a preservative and prolonging the life of many products.

❖ Coarse salt is often used as a decoration for yeast breads and rolls, as well as savoury baked goods such as pretzels and crackers.

In yeast doughs, particular attention must be paid to the manner in which salt is incorporated, as well as to the amount of salt used. It is a powerful ingredient and should be treated respectfully! Salt can kill live yeast if the two come in contact directly. Therefore, it should only be added to a yeast batter or dough after being well blended into the dry ingredients, namely the flour, to protect the yeast. This is generally a safe way of incorporating salt to ensure even distribution, although it can also be added to the butter or shortening before creaming them with sugar. Measure flour carefully if a specific quantity is stated, especially in yeast doughs, as the amount of salt is critical to the flavour and texture of the finished product.

There are several ways of processing salt for the kitchen, each of which can alter its flavour slightly.

IODIZED TABLE SALT is mined from the earth, then purified in water if necessary to make it safe for consumption. This is the least expensive method of salt production, and most of the salt used industrially and commercially in North America is of this type. It is available in fine, coarse and very coarse grinds and has the benefit of being fortified with iodine, an essential element many of us would lack without the addition. "Conditioners," in the form of anti-caking agents, are also added to table salt to prevent packing of the salt with time and exposure to moisture, to keep it free-flowing. These additives give common salt a coarse, bitter flavour, however, and this harsh taste can be imparted to delicately flavoured baked goods and desserts.

PICKLING SALT is an additive-free version of table salt, ground extra-fine to enable it to thoroughly dissolve in brines and pickling solutions. It should be reserved for pickling, and not used in sweet cookery.

SEA SALT is made by evaporating large quantities of salt water by one of several methods, then purifying the salt residue in the same manner as for mined salt. Sea salt is available in various grinds, from coarse crystals meant for cooking and home grinding to fine grinds suitable for the table. Neither iodine nor anti-caking chemicals are added, so sea salt should be kept fairly airtight to keep it from clumping. Sea salt has a smooth, fine, unbitter taste and is generally preferred by cooks and bakers. It costs somewhat more than regular salt, but is worth it. Fine-grind sea salt can be substituted in equal volume for table salt.

KOSHER SALT is a coarse-grained mined salt that has no additives of any kind. It is popular with cooks and bakers, who appreciate its superior texture and flavour. It can be used widely in cooking and baking, often without further grinding. If substituting for table salt, use 1¾ to 2 teaspoons of kosher salt for every 1 teaspoon of table salt called for.

ROCK SALT is a coarse, greyish mined salt, usually reserved for use as a base for cooking, such as under baked potatoes or for raw oysters and other seafood. It is also the salt of choice for the old-fashioned hand-crank model ice cream machines. Rock salt gets its characteristic grey colour from harmless residual minerals and impurities left in the salt after mining. It is not suitable for baking.

SOUR SALT, also called *citric salt*, is derived from citrus fruits and is used exclusively as a seasoning for certain traditional savoury recipes. It should not be used in baking.

SALT SUBSTITUTES, most often a blend of various herbs, spices, flavour-enhancers and yeast extracts, are not suitable for baking or dessert cookery.

Flavourings

Extracts, Essences, Flower Waters and Coffee

ESSENCES AND EXTRACTS Essences and extracts are concentrated liquid flavourings, made by macerating or distilling the essential flavours from a variety of ingredients, including plants, fruits, nuts and compounds such as coffee and spirits. They are used for their flavour, not their colour, though many of the extracts available in supermarkets have had harmless dyes added to impart a "suitable" colour. (This is purely in the interest of marketing.) The best extracts are derived from completely natural sources and have the most complex, delicate and pure flavours. Natural extracts are fairly expensive to produce, however, and many companies count on the consumer not demanding the better product, so they can synthesize an artificial approximation of the flavour. Coal tar, petroleum and other equally unappetizing substances make up much of the imitation flavourings available. Artificial extracts have a coarse, one-dimensional flavour, often tasting very "fake," and can all but ruin a dessert. Seek out the natural products—they keep almost indefinitely if stored in a cool, dark place, and you'll reap the rewards in your baking. Using the artificial extracts in a product you have taken the time and care to bake yourself is like using fat-free margarine to make shortbread. Just not right.

Natural extracts are available in a multitude of flavours, all of which add a wonderful depth of flavour and pure taste to cakes, chocolate ganache and fillings, icings, creams, mousses, custards, bars and cookies. Pure fruit extracts can be made from fruits such as raspberries, blackcurrants, strawberries, pomegranates, bananas, pineapples, apricots, oranges, lemons and peaches; rich nut extracts from hazelnuts, almonds, black walnuts and coconut; and compound extracts from such products as coffee and maple syrup. Vanilla extract is familiar to most of us, but a surprising number of even accomplished bakers have never experienced the real thing (see page 214 for lots of information on vanilla).

Almost any dessert can be enhanced with the addition of an essence or extract, but they are very potent and are best used judiciously, and in small quantities. Used indiscreetly, they can easily overpower other flavours and lend a distinctly one-dimensional taste to the dessert. Use extracts in baked goods, icings and frostings, ice creams and other custards, even cookies, bars and fruit compotes—either to add a hint of a new flavour, such as mint extract in a chocolate brownie, or to echo a flavour already present in the dessert, such as a raspberry extract in the filling of a fresh raspberry pie.

Citrus oils are similar to other fruit extracts, but are derived from the essential oils found in the skins of lemons, limes and oranges. They are very powerful, with an intense citrus flavour. Used sparingly, they can be used as any other extract would be used or in place of finely grated lemon, lime or orange zest in mixtures that will not undergo further cooking. The delicate oils in these flavourings are dissipated by direct heat, so they should be used carefully. They are perfect for flavouring icings, fillings, puddings and custards that have already been cooked. I have used them successfully in baked goods as well, but found that I had to use more than the suggested amount on the bottle. Most brands suggest ½ teaspoon of oil to replace the zest of one lemon, a ratio that works well in uncooked recipes, but seems shy in a cake or quick bread. I used up to 3 times that amount before I got the full, delicate citrus flavour I wanted. Once you find the right proportions, however, the convenience of these oils make them a great asset to the busy cook!

Some extracts, such as mint, vanilla, almond and even orange and lemon are available in most supermarket baking sections. Rarer extracts and citrus oils can be found in good baking supply stores and many specialty food shops. Stored in a cool, dark place, extracts will keep indefinitely. If, however, you begin to notice a change or weakening in the aroma, it is probably time for a new bottle.

FLOWER WATERS Flower waters are dilute extracts made from the blossoms of fragrant edible flowers, mainly roses and orange blossoms. *Rose flower water* (*rose water*) is derived from attar of roses, or rose oil. It has long been used as a flavouring for sweet dishes and confections in India and the Middle East. As unusual as it may seem to us today, it was the flavouring of choice in early North American baking, before exotic vanilla became common. It has a delicate, rose-scented flavour and aroma and is often called for in traditional desserts such as Turkish delight and baklava. I have used it to flavour ice creams, parfaits and mousses, often adding pesticide-free rose petals for a pretty garnish. It has a particular affinity with honey, sugar syrups, strawberries, pistachios and cinnamon, but can also be used on its own to give a subtle and unique perfume to delicate baked goods such as angel food cake and madeleines. A few drops added to mascarpone cheese or whipped cream make a lovely accompaniment to almond or pistachio desserts, or light fruit salads.

Orange flower water is distilled from the fragrant and sweet blossoms of the orange tree. Like rose water, it has been used in Eastern and Middle Eastern cuisines for centuries, in salads, sweets and beverage infusions. Orange flower water is slightly stronger than rose water and, as you'd expect, tastes of oranges, with a beautiful, complex floral aroma. It is best in dishes containing this fruit, such as compotes and fruit salads, but is also good in ice creams, syrups and confectionery.

Although less concentrated than other fruit extracts, flower waters are powerful flavourings and should be added with care. In too great proportions, they can make many desserts taste slightly medicinal. Be sure of two things when you purchase flower waters: first, that they are pure, not artificially derived, and second, that they are intended for use as a comestible, not cosmetic product (some are perfectly safe for both uses). Flower waters should be stored in a cool, dark place, preferably in dark glass bottles. If the product you buy comes in a plastic bottle, transfer it to one that is opaque and glass, as the liquids can leech chemicals and "off" flavours from plastics over time. Stored properly, they should keep several years. Replace them when the aroma begins to wane.

COFFEE Much like chocolate, coffee is a relatively new flavour to European cooking, originating in Africa and adopted by medieval monks who found they were less prone to drowsing off after drinking a brew of coffee beans! Since then, it has become one of the most universally loved flavours, appearing in many desserts and confections, as well as in savoury dishes such as barbecue sauce, gravies and even beer. Coffee has a marvellous affinity with chocolate, caramel and other flavours and is a natural ingredient in the sweet kitchen. When brewing coffee for drinking, great exactness is necessary to achieve the perfect balance of flavour, acidity, fruitiness, bitterness and mellowness. Fortunately for the baker, no such pains need to be taken when using coffee in baked goods and other desserts. What is desired is the pure flavour of the beans, and this is easily achieved through a variety of methods. Brewed coffee often has too gentle, too dilute a flavour to impart a sufficiently intense taste to most desserts. For that reason, brewed espresso, a darker roasted bean with a more concentrated flavour, is a good option. For a particularly pronounced flavour with a minimum of liquid, the espresso is brewed double-strength and further strengthened by being reduced on the stove until it becomes concentrated, more like other flavouring extracts. In this way, only a few drops are needed to impart a rich, pure flavour, without affecting the consistency of the batter or mixture. In some recipes, brewed coffee can serve as the liquid in a recipe, such as a cake or quick bread, or a granita or sorbet. In these cases, a less concentrated form of coffee is appropriate, and strong brewed coffee can often be used without reduction. Reducing brewed double-strength espresso is not the most convenient, or fastest way of deriving a good coffee flavouring, however, and for many people, espresso machines are not among the usual batterie de cuisine. Do not despair, as there is a foolproof, inexpensive, instant method, one preferred by many of the best pastry chefs in the world. *Instant espresso powder* is commonly available in specialty food and gourmet shops, Italian groceries and even many large supermarkets. Not to be confused with instant regular coffees, instant espresso has a far superior flavour and is generally of excellent quality. Buy Italian brands, such as Medaglia D'Oro, for the best flavour. Instant espresso is made by high-heat drying brewed espresso coffee. (*Freeze-dried coffee* is a similar product, often said to have a superior flavour, but in the case of espresso, I have found little difference. Freeze-dried coffee is produced by freezing the brewed coffee before dehydrating it and can be slightly more expensive.) When used in baking, the espresso powder is usually dissolved in a small amount of warm water or other liquid, creating a dark, intensely flavoured and bitter paste or liquid. The consistency and intensity of the flavouring can be adjusted to suit any palate, any dessert and any situation—from a very mild, almost imperceptible hint of flavour in a dark chocolate mousse to a dark, strong coffee flavour in a rich mocha ice cream or sauce. Instant espresso powder keeps very well, stored in its original jar or container, in a cool, dark cupboard.

Sticky Spiked Double-Apple Cake with a Brown Sugar-Brandy Sauce (page 441)

Classic Brioche (page 619)

Sweet Polenta Crostini with Mascarpone, Raspberries, Pistachios and Wild Forest Honey (page 628)

Black Chocolate Espresso Cake with Bittersweet Glaze (page 412)

Armagnac Parfait with Agen Prune and Apple Compote in Vanilla and Earl Grey Tea (page 564)

Double-Crust Deep Red Raspberry Pie (page 465)

Food Colourings and Dyes

Food colourings are natural or artificially derived dyes used to tint icings, candies and confections, white chocolate and sometimes even batters and doughs. Virtually all of the commercial food colourings and pastry tints are artificial, as they are a great deal cheaper to produce than those from natural plant and insect sources and are more consistent and reliable. Red, blue, yellow and green are the most common colours, but many baking supply shops are now selling mixed tints, such as purple, pink, turquoise, brown and orange, even grey and black. Most widely available are *liquid dyes*; these are likely all that will be stocked by your neighbourhood supermarket. They are perfect for adding to stable mixtures that will not be damaged by contact with a small amount of liquid. Batters, icings and other liquid mixtures are ideal for colouring with liquid dyes. Sensitive elements, such as melted white chocolate and marzipan or almond paste, should be coloured with *paste* or *powdered dyes*. Available at specialty baking and cake decorating shops, these are really just partially or completely dehydrated liquid colourings, designed to provide desired colour in mixtures where the addition of a liquid is not recommended. For example, melted chocolate will seize and become unusable if it comes in contact with even a drop of moisture, so paste or powdered colourings are used. All food colourings are very concentrated—a drop or two of liquid is likely enough to give a good colour. Start with one drop (most brands come in tiny eyedrop-like bottles and are good for meting out small amounts) and mix this in well before judging if you need more. In the case of paste colourings, use a toothpick to scoop up a tiny amount of paste and stir or knead it into the mixture being dyed. With any type of dye, be conservative! You can always add more, but once your icing is fluorescent green, it's impossible to go back to the shade of a pale leaf. The dyes are tasteless and odourless and can be stored indefinitely in a cool, dark place.

Certain commercially made baked goods use colourings and dyes that are not available to the general public. The deep brown colour of pumpernickel bread, for instance, comes from a product called *baker's caramel*, derived from the sugar-cooking process. Sugar is cooked to the black jack, or burnt, stage, then is processed to remove the scorched flavour. What is left is an intense colouring used to darken doughs and batters. Most of these breads and baked goods originally got their characteristic hue from a particular ingredient, such as unsweetened cocoa powder, but today shortcuts like baker's caramel are most often used in the interest of saving money. Most home recipes for these baked goods have either returned to the traditional ingredients or have substituted something easily found in its place. Although products such as baker's caramel and others like it are occasionally available at bakery supply shops, the average home baker would be hard-pressed to find a worthwhile recipe to use them in. Don't worry—most commercial products have sacrificed much more than traditional colourings in their quest for mass production; they should not be emulated!

Vanilla

Whoever coined the term "plain vanilla" had obviously never experienced the real bean. This I know, for after one encounter, they would have used words like magnificent, peerless and indispensable. The second most costly spice in the world, vanilla beans are actually the fruit of a climbing orchid native to Central America. It was cultivated and processed by the Aztecs, who developed a process of alternately sweating and drying the beans to develop on them the white crystalline substance *vanillin*, which gives the beans their flavour and perfume. The exquisite blossoms open only one day a year, and then for just a few hours. Their only natural pollinators, the Melipona bee, a few species of ants and hummingbirds, are all native to Mexico (and not terribly reliable workers!), so the orchids must be hand-pollinated in order to bear a bean, hence their hefty price tag. The beans are green and odourless when picked, gradually becoming dark brown, almost black, as they undergo a lengthy fermentation—alternately dried in the sun during the day, then sweated under heavy blankets at night. This process continues for three to six months; the beans are then aged for up to two years.

Like chocolate, vanilla was brought to Europe via Spain by Cortés, but for almost 100 years, was used only in chocolate and perfumes. Finally, an English apothecary in the royal court suggested its use as a flavouring. It became all the rage, and was even considered a powerful aphrodisiac by the elite of European society.

Vanilla is perhaps the most versatile flavouring in the sweet kitchen. In small amounts, it has the ability to blend with and support myriad other ingredients, mellowing harshness and deepening the richness of other flavours. It can be a perfect and equal partner or even a primary flavour all on its own. Although vanilla is often used in recipes as a supportive flavour, not detectable in the final product, it can also be used to create a new spin on a recipe—a cornmeal cake that calls for a teaspoon of vanilla becomes a cornmeal-vanilla cake when the vanilla is increased to two or three teaspoons. I occasionally use up to twice as much vanilla as is called for in a recipe if vanilla would really complement the other flavours in the dessert, or if the dessert is quite plain. Vanilla in all of its forms is great for enhancing recipes that have little sweetness and/or fat, as it imparts a distinct richness and voluptuous flavour.

Vanilla pairs beautifully with chocolate—it was a key ingredient in the warm chocolate drink *xocolatl* so adored by the Aztecs; their king Montezuma is said to have drunk fifty goblets a day! This perfect marriage has withstood the test of time—the best chocolates are today made with pure vanilla, and almost every good chocolate dessert also calls for some form of the bean. Rich nuts such as toasted hazelnuts and almonds; caramel; coffee; tropical fruit, as well as fruits such as pears, peaches, and raspberries; cinnamon, ginger and other sweet spices; even alternative grains and flours such as cornmeal and oats, all are enhanced with a benediction of vanilla.

Vanilla's immense popularity has led to its production in four major regions around the world, each producing a distinctive variety. Like coffee beans and chocolate pods, vanilla beans' flavour is deeply affected by the climate and soil in which they are grown.

MEXICAN VANILLA BEANS are thick and dark, with a strong, intense fragrance and a flavour that is deeper and more robust than that of other vanilla beans. They are quite scarce today, but are considered by many to be the finest vanilla beans in the world. Sadly, some Mexican producers have recently begun to compromise their vanilla extract with the addition of *coumarin*, a potentially toxic substance that has a similar aroma to vanilla but that is illegal in the rest of North America. To be safe, buy Mexican vanilla products only from a reputable supplier.

BOURBON VANILLA BEANS are grown off the coast of Africa on the island of Madagascar, as well as on the neighbouring isle of Réunion. Also called *Mada-gascar* or *Bourbon-Madagascar vanilla beans*, they are smooth, rich and sweet, the slenderest variety of vanilla bean. Madagascar vanilla makes up more than 70 percent of the world's vanilla, making it much more widely available and generally less expensive than its Mexican or Tahitian counterparts.

INDONESIAN OR JAVA VANILLA is the second most commonly available type of vanilla in the world. Its flavour is smooth and earthy, with a slightly smoky note.

TAHITIAN VANILLA BEANS are the darkest of the three and are longer and fatter than their Mexican or Madagascan cousins, with a complex, floral aroma. Not as intense as the other two varieties, their delicate and slightly fruity flavour is perfect for using in poaching syrups and light desserts with fruit, fragile pastry and other subtle tastes.

Several forms of vanilla are available, each with its own suitability and uses in baked goods and desserts. *Vanilla beans* are the most costly form of the flavouring, but are without question the best. I love splitting open a fat bean in front of friends and watching their faces as they are overwhelmed by the aroma. This is an opponent worthy of chocolate! Though their flavour is very rich and mellow when baked, a fresh vanilla bean's aroma is powerful: sensuous and intoxicating, and deliciously warm. This form has the added advantage of being able to be used in many different ways, and more than once. Scraped-out seeds can be used to flavour cakes and puddings; hulls can be used to infuse milk or cream for custards or sugar syrups for poaching fruit. Whole beans can be used to flavour liquids, then rinsed, dried and reused, sometimes several times.

When buying vanilla beans, look for dark brown, almost black beans that are plump, tender, shiny, and that feel moist and even sticky to the touch. They should not be leathery and dry—if they are they have been improperly stored or are past their prime. They should be supple and very fragrant. A dusting of white crystalline dust on the beans is not a sign of deterioration, but is actually desirable.

To use in cakes, doughs and cookies, split the bean lengthwise and with the tip of a small knife scrape out the mass of sticky black seeds into the batter, reserving the hulls for another purpose. Hulls can be used to flavour custards for ice cream, soufflés and desserts such as crème brûlée. Place one or both halves of a scraped out hull in the milk before scalding, then let it infuse anywhere from 5 to 20 minutes, or until the custard is strained. Using beans in these two different ways will allow you to get the most value for your investment. Vanilla beans and scraped out pods should be wrapped in plastic wrap and placed in a sealed glass jar at room temperature, in a cool dark place. Stored this way, they should keep for 6 months. If a recipe does not require the bean to be split, it may be rinsed after infusing, dried and stored for reuse.

Pure vanilla extract is made by macerating crushed or chopped beans in an alcohol-water solution for several months. The dark clear liquid that results is rich, intensely flavoured and highly aromatic. Vanilla extract is the most commonly used form of the flavouring used in North America and has become an essential ingredient in almost every cake and cookie recipe! However, its deep, rich fragrance and flavour are easily dissipated by direct or prolonged heating, making it unsuitable for long-cooked dishes such as poached fruit. It does retain its potency when used in baked goods, though, and has the advantage over vanilla seeds in that it disperses thoroughly throughout a batter. When buying vanilla extract, look for products bearing the label "Pure," "Real," or "Natural." Vanilla extract may be stored indefinitely in an opaque, airtight bottle in a cool, dark cupboard.

Vanilla essences, also called *double-* or *triple-strength extracts*, are products usually available only to professionals. They are highly concentrated forms of vanilla extract, so intense that only a drop or two may be needed to impart a strong vanilla flavour. They are particularly useful in industrial and professional kitchens, where their high potency and concentrated form mean fewer steps in the preparation of large recipes. Vanilla essence and high-strength extracts can sometimes be found at bakery or cake decorating supply stores and through some professional mail-order sources.

Imitation or artificial vanilla extract contains no real vanilla at all. It is made from 100% artificial ingredients, mostly by-products of the pulp and paper industry, that have been treated with chemicals and supplemented with feeble flavourings. Artificial vanilla has a harsh, one-dimensional flavour that can come across as medicinal, cloying and even almost bitter in some cases. At best, it is rough and dull and absolutely incomparable to any other form of real vanilla. Avoid it at all costs, as it will do neither you nor your precious baking any good! If you have only ever used the artificial stuff, the difference pure vanilla will make to your favourite recipes is worth the price of this book, not to mention the vanilla itself.

Vanilla powder is made by pulverizing the whole dried beans to a fine powder. Read the list of ingredients to make sure it is pure, as sweeteners and fillers are sometimes added. Vanilla in this state is well suited to incorporation into liquid-sensitive mixtures, such as some icings and melted chocolate, where even a small amount of liquid could create a problem; and into uncooked mixtures in which vanilla seeds would not have a chance to impart their flavour evenly and thoroughly. In addition, the flavour of vanilla powder is more intense than that of most extracts and does not dissipate even with prolonged cooking. For these reasons, it can be used to an advantage in many cooked custards, sauces and baked goods. Vanilla powder will keep indefinitely, stored in an opaque, airtight container in a cool, dry place.

Vanilla sugar is a lovely, fragrant product, easily made by burying one bean in two cups of granulated or superfine sugar for at least two weeks. I like to store my scraped out vanilla bean hulls in a canister of sugar, replenishing the sugar as I deplete it and adding new hulls when I have them left over. Vanilla sugar is a luxurious sweetener for coffee or hot chocolate and a great addition to all sorts of baked goods and desserts. I love using it as a garnishing sugar, sprinkling it on cookies, cakes, pie and tart crusts, as well as confections. For a simple, easy and divinely flavoured summer dessert, toss fresh berries or peaches in a little vanilla-scented sugar and serve with a little vanilla sugar-sweetened whipped cream. Divine! Vanilla sugar will keep indefinitely, stored in an airtight container.

Liqueurs and Spirits in the Sweet Kitchen

The use of liqueurs and spirits in baking and dessert-making has a long and established history. From the first cakes made over 10,000 years ago and flavoured with sweet wine to the brandy- (or whiskey, or rum ...) soaked puddings and trifles of the Victorians to today's fashionable champagne granitas and spiked ice creams, liqueurs and spirits add depth, dimension and complexity of flavour (not to mention a pleasant little kick, where desired). Virtually every spirit can work its way into one recipe or another, from biscotti to cakes, to pie fillings to ice creams, to compotes and preserved fruit. Although they can be the primary flavour, they are more often used as complementary flavourings, much like vanilla or coffee.

WINE is often used as a poaching medium for pears, quinces, peaches and other fruit and can also be added to biscotti and some cakes to lend a round, fruity flavour. Wines and fortified wines are unusual and delicious additions to ice creams, able to gently support the flavours of nuts, and fresh and especially dried fruit. In the case of poached fruit, the flavour of the wine is critical—different wines will yield very different results. Flavourful, off-dry (slightly sweet, with a sugar code of 1 or 2) whites like *Gewürztraminer* and *Riesling* are particularly suited to pears and peaches and will contribute complex, fruity or floral tones. Sweet wines, like *Beaumes de Venise* or *Sauternes*, enhance the natural sweetness in the fruit and the syrup but balance it with a necessary acidity, making the final dessert rich and full-flavoured, not cloying. Young, fruity reds like *Beaujolais* are good for late-season pears, balancing a deep sweetness in the pears with a light, fruity acidity. Robust reds can turn a simple dessert of poached fruit into a sophisticated end to a fall or winter meal. *Fortified wines* like *port* and *sherry* are also good poaching mediums, very intense if used in high proportion to sugar syrup, and more delicately flavourful if used as an accent along with a lighter wine.

In every case, taste the wine or be familiar with its quality and characteristics before using it in a dessert, even if only a small amount is needed. Unlike liqueurs and other spirits, wines are not consistent, varying widely in quality from one variety to another, from producer to producer, even year to year. Only a wine you would like to drink should be used in any recipe, as the flavour of the wine will be imparted to the product. (This is particularly important if the wine will be subjected to heat—once the alcohol is evaporated all that will remain is the inherent flavour.) If the recipe does not specify a type of wine, consider several things: the body or weight of the wine should match the other ingredients and the final dish. If the dessert is a light sorbet to accompany grilled peaches, a very robust, tannic red would overpower the rest of the dish. A young, fruity *Beaujolais* would be lovely, as would a sweet white, flavourful on their own, but able to allow the delicate flavour of the peaches to come through.

The next consideration should be the inherent flavours in the wine. Wine experts have an entire vocabulary, almost incomprehensible to the outsider, to describe the flavours and aromas of a wine. The jargon isn't important, only that you know generally what are the main, perceptible tastes and flavours present in a wine. These flavours will be concentrated by cooking and should suit the other tastes present in a dessert. A wine with plummy, spicy, peppery and woody notes would be perfect to make a mulled wine sauce, but would be inappropriate in the syrup for banana fritters. Similarly, a late-harvest *Vidal* with overtones of caramel, tropical fruit, toasted nuts and citrus, would be wonderful with the bananas, but make the mulled wine sauce taste, well, awful! If you haven't tried the wine before, ask someone at the liquor store to give you an idea as to its character, then make an educated decision. The quantity of wine will also be a key factor in determining its effect on the final dessert. In the case of poached fruit or a wine jelly, the wine is a primary flavouring and will be tasted as such. In a custard or cake, however, the wine would be used in a smaller amount, playing much the same role as other liquid flavouring, such as vanilla or almond extracts. It will add subtle nuances to the flavour of the dessert, but will not dominate.

Champagne and other sparkling wines have a noble place in dessert-making, but must be used deliberately in order to get the maximum benefit. Their unique bubbliness is often desired in granitas and gelatine desserts, where the dessert will be eaten within a short time of being prepared, so the wine does not lose its fizziness. As very good champagne is correspondingly expensive, it need only be used in cases where the wine will play a major role, such as a granita. In desserts such as sabayons, where only a small amount of sparkling wine is called for, a good substitute may be used instead (Spanish *Cava* wines are often very tasteful and of a very good quality, at a fraction of the cost of French champagne). In many cases, a still wine can be substituted for a sparkling one, and vice versa; you can vary the flavour and the overall character of desserts such as sabayons, custards, sauces and syrups for poached fruit simply by using a different wine.

SPIRITS *Rum* has a natural affinity with other sweet things, as it is made from pure sugar cane itself. It marries well with many fruits, such as bananas and apples, as well as with most nuts, chocolate, coffee, maple and other flavours. Finding a truly good rum, sadly, can be difficult, as much of the rum available in many liquor stores is of a terribly average quality. As with any other ingredient, the quality of the spirit is critical. In general, the best rum for baking is dark and rich. Jamaica and Cuba are good producers; for the very best, look for the famous Demerara Rum from Guyana.

Whiskey is used mostly in recipes from Scotland, Ireland and Britain, but can be very effective in recipes containing chocolate, fruit and grains. *Bourbon*, an American whiskey made from corn, is especially good in desserts hailing from the South, such as pecan or sweet-potato pie, as well as bread puddings and custard sauces. Ice creams enhanced with bourbon or *single-malt Scotch* are divine as accompaniments to pies, tarts, plain cakes and fruit compotes.

Brandy is not so much a single spirit as a family of them, made by distilling wine, cider or other fruit juices. Brandies made from wine, such as *Armagnac* or the quintessential *Cognac*, are luxurious liquids able to elevate a simple dessert to the realm of the sophisticated and a complex one to the sublime. Armagnac has had a long and blissful love affair with the wonderful dried prunes of France, one of the truly inspired combinations in the culinary world. Ice creams, truffles, parfaits, cakes and tarts can be enhanced with an ounce or two of Armagnac, or its cousin Cognac. Other brandies, such as the apple cider-derived *Calvados*, have deliciously unique fruit flavours, quite unlike any other spirit. Calvados is marvellous in recipes using apples, such as custard and fruit tarts, cakes and ice creams. Pear brandies should be used in the same way, to deepen the flavour of pears in desserts such as baked or broiled pears or tarts.

Eaux-de-vie are clear, colourless brandies distilled from fruit. They are often enjoyed straight as an aperitif or digestif in Europe, as are Calvados and Armagnac, and are some of the pastry cook's most treasured ingredients. Finely and purely flavoured, the best examples taste strongly of the fruit from which they are made, adding a more complex and textured flavour than many extracts. The alcohol inherent to the eau-de-vie is often evaporated in the preparation of a dessert, such as a cake or cooked tart filling, but can be retained to give an added and decadent dimension to desserts by adding the brandy after cooking. Many cakes can be brushed with a simple syrup of sugar, water and an eau-de-vie before being served or decorated, adding a wicked and profoundly interesting accent.

Some of the more common eaux-de-vie used in the sweet kitchen are *Framboise*, a raspberry brandy; *Poire Williams*, made from pear; and *Kirsch*, the famous cherry liqueur from Austria. Each eau-de-vie, of course, marries seamlessly with its own fruit, and you can't go wrong including a splash of Kirsch in a cherry compote or Framboise in a raspberry pie filling. But many eaux-de-vie also have the power to highlight and accent other ingredients: use berry eaux-de-vie in berry dishes, but also in those based on all types of chocolate and try a few drops of Kirsch in the frangipane mixture for an almond tart. Most eaux-de-vie are delicious with nuts and chocolate and can make a simple truffle endlessly variable. Some small boutique wineries and distilleries in Canada and the United States are beginning to produce some very good eaux-de-vie, usually far less expensive than their European counterparts.

LIQUEURS are made by combining a spirit, such as a brandy, with an extract, infusion or essence of fruits, herbs, spices or nuts. Also called *cordials* or *ratafias*, they are most often sweet and so are natural ingredients in desserts. A word of caution: many cheaper liqueurs today rely on coarse artificial flavourings. As they keep indefinitely, it's worth investing in those of quality. Liqueurs can be divided into two basic categories: those with one or two dominant flavours and those based on a complex recipe of ingredients. The first group are the ones best for baking and sweets, whereas the second often have very herbal, sometimes spicy, medicinal or powerfully unique flavours, making them distinctly savoury and difficult to blend successfully with baking ingredients. Almost any single-flavoured sweet liqueur can be married to chocolate or vanilla, and to many types of nuts as well. Experiment—the flavours of these sweet spirits are so pure, so marvellous, you'll want to use them wherever you can!

Sweet liqueurs can be divided yet again into three main groups, based on their main ingredients: fruit liqueurs; liqueurs based on nuts, beans, and seeds; and herb and spice liqueurs. *Fruit liqueurs* are made in a similar manner to eaux-de-vie, but are sweetened with sugar and are usually artificially coloured. Raspberries, currants, figs, apricots, pears, peaches, cherries, bananas, pineapple—in fact, virtually every fruit has been honoured in some part of the world with a liqueur. Citrus-based liqueurs, such as the famous *Grand Marnier*, are often made from a combination of several fruits, such as oranges, tangerines, lemons and limes, and add a brightness and depth to many citrus-based recipes. Rather than the juice, the oil-rich peel is used, often contributing a tangy accent to the liqueur. Citrus liqueurs usually blend well with stone fruits, such as apricots, and many tropical fruits. They also have an affinity with many nuts, especially almonds and walnuts. White chocolate and coffee are good counterpoints for these flavours, conspiring to make a complex but harmonious overall effect. Liqueurs made from fruits are perfect in support of the fruits they contain, and of similar fruits—use a blackcurrant liqueur (such as *Cassis*) with blackcurrants or redcurrants, or to deepen the flavour of a recipe containing raspberries or blackberries. Apricot or peach liqueurs can be used successfully in recipes calling for any stone fruit and often work well with oranges and almonds as well.

Nut-, seed-, and bean-based liqueurs are made by macerating crushed ingredients in a sweet brandy or other spirit. Nut-based liqueurs are perhaps my favourite, with a marvellously rich, sweet, toasty flavour, often harbouring notes of caramel, vanilla and sweet spices. I use *Frangelico*, a hazelnut liqueur, in everything from ice creams to hazelnut-chocolate cake to fruit and hazelnut tarts and more. It is fantastic with pears, and makes a plain biscotti something to sing about. Almond liqueurs such as *Amaretto* are of course perfect in almond-based desserts, but also have a great affinity with many fruits, particularly oranges, peaches, apricots, nectarines and cherries. Coffee beans have been used to give their rich, dark flavour to many liqueurs, such as *Tia Maria* and *Kahlúa*. Even seeds such as caraway have been used as the primary flavours in liqueurs, and perhaps the most popular flavour for liqueurs in the world is anise seed. Almost every European country has their own special anise-flavoured liqueur, such as the French *Pernod* and the Greek *Ouzo*.

Herbal and spice liqueurs are usually reserved for savoury recipes or cocktails, but there are several that can wind their way into the sweet kitchen very gracefully indeed. The Scottish *Drambuie* is a sweet honey- and herb-based liqueur that is lovely in many traditional sweet recipes, but can also be added to desserts containing honey, soft fruit or white chocolate.

In recipes that undergo cooking or baking, the alcohol evaporates, and what is left is a pure flavour. In the case of a flambé, the alcohol in the liqueur is what allows the dish to be ignited, but it quickly evaporates to leave a benign but beautifully flavoured dish. In uncooked desserts such as fresh fruit and ice cream, or those in which the spirit or liqueur is added after baking or cooking, such as sabayon, the alcohol remains, adding a distinctly "adult" dimension to the dessert.

In every case, whether the liquor be wine, rum, Cognac or Framboise, always buy the very best you can afford. There is a remarkable variation in the quality of wines, spirits and liqueurs, and a poor-quality product will offend your dessert. If you cannot afford the very best, do a little research to determine what are the better bargains, and which labels are most respected. Sometimes you will be pleasantly surprised—small, unknown producers can often almost match the quality of their huge, world-famous competitors. Your investment is not at risk for spoilage any time soon, if stored in a cool, dry, dark place, and you will be amazed by how much you can improve your cooking as well as your dessert-making with the occasional benediction of a truly good liqueur or spirit.

Liqueur Flavour Chart

Ever wonder what liqueur would suit a banana soufflé? Or what the name of the wonderful walnut-flavoured liqueur you had with your gelato in Italy was? Or whether Crème de Cassis is the same thing as Cassis? The chart below is a brief guide to the most common liqueurs used in the sweet kitchens of the world, with a word of two about their flavours and origins. You can use it to help choose a liqueur as an ingredient by pairing its primary flavour with the flavours in the dessert. (See also the Flavour Pairing Chart on page 352.)

LIQUEURS

Advocaat (Advokaat) (Netherlands): Like a spiked eggnog made with brandy, sugar and egg yolks

Amaretto (Italy): Bitter almond extract, apricot pits (see page 277), brandy

Anise, Anisette (Spain, called Anis; France, called Anise): Aniseed or star anise

Aurum (Italy): A luxurious blend of orange and other citrus fruit with brandy

Bénédictine (France): Cognac-based liqueur tasting of citrus peel, herbs and spices, originally made by members of a cloistered monastery according to a complex, and secret, herbal formula (it's still a secret)

Chartreuse (France): Like Bénédictine, a secret formula of more than 120 herbs and other ingredients; yellow or golden version, coloured with saffron, is milder and sweeter than the green, chlorophyll-tinted type.

Cheri Swisse (Switzerland): Chocolate and sweet cherries

Cointreau (France): Colourless, slightly herbal orange liqueur

Curaçao (Netherlands): May be clear or vibrantly coloured (blue, red, green or orange); is flavoured with the peel of bitter oranges grown on the Caribbean island of the same name

Drambuie (Scotland): Scotch whiskey, heather honey and herbs

Frangelico (Italy): Hazelnuts and vanilla

Galliano (Italy): Anise, licorice, vanilla

Glayva: (Scotland) Scotch whiskey, heather honey, orange peel and wild herbs

Goldschläger (Switzerland): cinnamon schnapps with edible gold leaf

Goldwasser (Danziger Goldwasser) (Poland): Aniseed, caraway seed and mixed citrus rind, with tiny flakes of edible gold leaf

Grand Marnier (France): Orange peel and top-quality Cognac

Herbsaint (New Orleans): Anise

Irish Mist (Ireland): Irish whiskey and heather honey

Kahlúa (Mexico): Coffee

Kümmel (mainly Holland but also various Eastern European producers): Caraway, cumin, anise or fennel seed

La Grande Passion (France): Passion fruit

Malibu (Caribbean): Coconut, rum

Mandarine Napoléon (France, Italy): Tangerines and Cognac

Maraschino (Italy): Wild Italian Marasca cherries and crushed cherry pits

Midori (Japan): Honeydew melon—the liqueur actually tastes more like a blend of tropical fruits

Nocino, Nocciole, Nocello (Italy): Walnuts

Noisette (France): Hazelnuts

Ouzo (Greece): Anise

Pastis (France): Anise, licorice

Pernod (France): Anise, licorice

Poire Williams (France, Switzerland): Actually an eau-de-vie, made from pears

Prunelle (France): Wild blackthorn plums (sloes) and brandy

Punsch (Sweden): Sweet spices (cinnamon, cloves) and rum

Sabra (Israel): Chocolate and orange

Sambuca (Italy): Aniseed, elderberries

Sloe Gin (Britain, US): Moderately sweet liqueur made by pricking wild plums (sloes) in gin for several months, then straining

Southern Comfort (St. Louis, Missouri): Peaches, bourbon, oranges

Strega (Italy): Complex formula of flowers, herbs and citrus fruits

Tia Maria (Jamaica): Dark-roast coffee and rum

Triple Sec (France): Clear version of Curaçao, flavoured with bitter orange peel

Vandermint (Holland): Chocolate and mint

CREAM LIQUEURS

Irish Cream (Ireland): Coffee, chocolate, cream, whiskey

White Chocolate (such as Godiva) (US among others): White chocolate, vanilla, cream, brandy

Chocolate (such as Cadbury) (Britain): Chocolate, cream, brandy

CRÈME LIQUEURS

Not to be confused with cream liqueurs, those labelled "crème" do not contain any cream at all. The term was originally used to denote very sweet single-flavoured liqueurs. They are often fruit-based and are usually coloured appropriately. Virtually all are produced in France.

continued on page 226

crème d'abricots: apricots

d'amande: almonds

d'ananas: pineapples and vanilla

de banane: bananas

de cacao: cocoa beans and vanilla

de café: coffee

de cassis: blackcurrants

de cerise: sweet cherries

de fraises: strawberries

de framboise: raspberries

de mandarine: tangerines

de menthe: mint

de myrtille: bilberries

de noix: walnuts and honey

de noyau: apricot and other stone fruit kernel pits, tasting very much like sweet almonds

de rose: rose petals and vanilla

de thé, de Recco: black tea leaves and brandy

de vanille: vanilla beans

de violette (de Yvette): violet blossoms

LIQUEUR BRANDIES

Made by combining a fruit liqueur with a wine brandy, these are usually French and are always sweet. The most common flavours are apricot, peach and cherry.

Chocolate

In the realm of the sweet kitchen, chocolate is unquestionably king. In fact, its botanical designation is *Theobroma Cacao*, from the ancient Greek for "god" and "food." Chocolate is made from cocoa beans, which grow on large tropical trees native to Central and South America, and the quality of a chocolate is hugely dependent on the bean from which it is derived. Winemakers may be highly skilled, but if the grapes are only satisfactory to begin with, the wine will be no better than average. Similarly, a good chocolate, although the manufacturing process and the additional ingredients are important (and indeed have the power to ruin a chocolate), cannot result from inferior beans.

Three types of trees produce cacao pods: the Forastero, the Criollo and the Trinitario. (In general, the term *cacao* refers to the tree and sometimes the bean, and the word *cocoa* applies to the products of the beans.) *Forastero* trees account for over 90% of world production and are cultivated mainly in Africa and Brazil. The Forastero is a good basic bean, though not one with any exceptional qualities. *Criollo* trees are native to Venezuela and produce the most flavourful, complex and delicate chocolates. The trees are very fragile, however, and expensive to harvest, so chocolate made exclusively from Criollo beans is quite rare. The *Trinitario* is a cross between the first two and has characteristics of both parent trees—sturdier and more prolific than the Criollo, but approaching it in subtlety and flavour. Some chocolates are blends of more than one type of bean; the blends with a higher percentage of Criollo or Trinitario beans will be more unique, flavourful and aromatic than those made primarily of Forastero beans.

Cocoa beans, like coffee beans, are bitter and totally unpalatable when raw. They must be carefully fermented, roasted and aged before they'll begin to develop the characteristic flavour and aroma of chocolate. The roasted beans are shelled, then ground in a heavy press or mill. The heat from this process releases the beans' natural fat, called *cocoa butter*. This is removed, leaving a dark chocolate paste known as *cocoa liquor*. It is this paste that contains the flavour and aroma of the chocolate.

NATURAL COCOA POWDER is produced if virtually all of the cocoa butter is removed from the cocoa liquor, leaving a dry cake that is then ground to a fine powder. Very bitter on its own, it imparts a deep, fudgy chocolate flavour to baked goods and desserts. Natural cocoa powder is also quite acidic, so can be used as the necessary acid to activate baking soda in leavened baked goods, if present in sufficient quantity. Because of its high acidity and unpalatable bitterness, natural cocoa powder is best used only in baked or cooked desserts. It is widely available in North American supermarkets and the well-known brands such as Hershey's or Ghirardelli are generally of high quality, but do avoid the no-name brands and bulk versions, as these are likely to be inferior and impure.

DUTCH-PROCESS COCOA has been treated with a small quantity of an alkaline solution to reduce the natural acidity. The process darkens the cocoa's colour, making it a richer, often redder brown, and gives it a smoother, more mellow flavour. Also called *alkalized cocoa powder*, it is usually of very high quality, especially that which is produced in and imported from Holland. Look for brands such as Droste or Valrhona.

Both natural and Dutch-process cocoa have had about 75% of the cocoa fat removed. Do not confuse either of these types of cocoa with the sweetened cocoa powder drink mixes used for making hot chocolate! They are unsweetened, unless otherwise specified, as in the case of Ghirardelli's Sweet Cocoa Powder.

Although some recipes, such as those for certain cookies and sauces, can be made with either form of cocoa powder, many rely on the properties of one or the other. For this reason, be careful when substituting Dutch-process for natural cocoa, or vice versa. In recipes for baked goods using baking soda as the leavener in which no other acid is present, Dutch-process cocoa is not appropriate, as it does not contain sufficient acid to activate the baking soda. (You could use Dutch-process for natural cocoa, but an additional acid such as cream of tartar would need to be added.) Similarly, using natural cocoa powder in a recipe originally calling for a large amount of Dutch-process cocoa may cause the mixture to become overly acidic. Adding a small amount of baking soda, or increasing the amount already called for, will compensate for this. If the amount of cocoa is small, the effects of the increased or decreased acidity will be negligible. Regardless of the chemical effects, be aware that each type of cocoa powder has its own very distinct flavour and may be more or less appropriate in various situations.

Natural cocoa has a darker, fudgier, more intense flavour, better for most American-style desserts such as brownies, old-fashioned chocolate cakes and simple chocolate cookies. Dutch-process cocoa, more palatable than natural cocoa when raw, is good for icings, custards, creams and sauces that will not undergo further cooking. It has a more subtle, delicate flavour, one well suited to many elegant European-style cakes, biscuits, pastries and creams, and in any recipe where an overt, sharp chocolate flavour would overpower more delicate flavours. It is very good in nut cakes and ice creams, where a refined, un-bitter chocolate taste can complement the soft flavours of the other ingredients. If the cocoa will be tasted raw, as it is when dusted on cakes, cookies or truffles, opt for Dutch-processed. If the recipe is for a traditionally rich and fudgy baked good, use the stronger flavour of natural cocoa.

COCOA BUTTER itself is an expensive and valuable product, with numerous uses in both the confectionery and cosmetic industries. For these reasons, it is often completely extracted from the chocolate compound during the grinding process. Ideally, in the making of chocolate, some cocoa butter is added back to the cocoa liquor. Unfortunately, many producers substitute hydrogenated and other vegetable shortenings for the prized cocoa butter, so they can sell the pure cocoa butter at a high cost. The resulting chocolate is of poor quality in terms of both flavour and texture. Cocoa butter has a very subtle, mellow flavour that naturally complements that of cocoa liquor. Vegetable shortenings, on the other hand, have little or no inherent flavour and can dull and dampen that of the cocoa liquor. The more critical difference, however, is in the texture of the chocolate. Part of the reason good chocolate is so divine to our senses is because cocoa butter has a melting point that is exactly that of our own internal body temperature. So when you put a piece of excellent dark chocolate on your tongue, it melts immediately, becoming creamy, smooth and sensually liquid. Vegetable shortenings have a much higher melting point, and chocolate made with them does not have the same creaminess, richness or sexy "mouth-feel" and often seems thick, bland and waxy on the palate (for more information on cocoa butter see page 153).

If the processing continues, and a measure of the cocoa butter (or a replacement fat such as vegetable shortening) is returned to the cocoa liquor, a thick paste is formed. This paste can be augmented with the addition of sugar, pure or artificial vanilla, perhaps milk solids and other flavourings. It then undergoes a process called *conching*. Named for the original shell-shaped machine first used by Charles Lindt, conching kneads, grinds and aerates the chocolate mixture, making it luxuriously glossy and smooth. This can take anywhere from a few hours, in the case of inferior chocolates, to several days, for the best chocolate in the world. A short conching time results in a coarse-grained chocolate with a rough, raw, unsubtle flavour, which is usually compensated for by adding artificial and extraneous flavourings. The best chocolate needs only time to develop its full potential of nuances, accents and aromas.

When the conching process is finished, the warm, liquid chocolate is carefully cooled, or *tempered*, and set into moulds before packaging. Tempering, like conching, has a great effect on the quality of the final chocolate—if the chocolate is cooled too quickly or heated to too high a temperature in the first place, it can develop a crumbly texture, white patches known as *oysters* or *bloom* on its surface and can present problems when melted and tempered by the consumer later. Manufacturers of better brands will take more care, and will therefore charge a little more. As with many things, there are few true bargains, and you most often get what you pay for.

UNSWEETENED CHOCOLATE, also called *baking* or *bitter chocolate*, is what you get if nothing except cocoa butter is added to the chocolate liquor before it is conched. It is very intensely flavoured, but as bitter as cocoa powder.

BITTERSWEET CHOCOLATE is the result if some sugar and a little pure or artificial vanilla is added with the cocoa butter. This is the best type of chocolate for baking, with a dark, intense flavour but just enough sweetness to make it palatable and smooth. The higher the cocoa liquor (also called *cocoa solids*) content, the more flavourful and rich the chocolate will be. The minimum percentage of cocoa solids in bittersweet chocolate is a paltry 35% in North America and 43% in Britain. The best for baking are between 65 and 70%. I wouldn't recommend using a chocolate with less than 55% cocoa solids in a recipe calling for bittersweet chocolate, or you'll be disappointed by the lack of "punch."

SEMISWEET CHOCOLATE is very similar to bittersweet, but has more sugar added. It has the same minimum requirements for cocoa solids as bittersweet; in fact, there is no official designated difference between the two. While a good bittersweet chocolate has about 55% to 75% cocoa solids, semisweet generally has between 35 (43% in the UK) and 54%. Although semisweet chocolate is a versatile baking chocolate, it is also the most popular type of chocolate for straight eating in many parts of the world. It is sweeter and more mellow than bittersweet chocolate and will not impart as intense a flavour to most baked goods. I prefer using semisweet chocolate in preparations where it will be eaten pure, such as the chips or chunks in cookies, in frostings and icings, in fillings and in ice creams and custards.

SWEET CHOCOLATE is used in many commercial chocolate bars and candies in North America, and is even sweeter than semisweet. One brand, German's Sweet Chocolate, was used in the now-famous cake of the same name. In spite of this legacy, I generally find sweet chocolate a little wimpy for most baking applications. There are some cases where its mild but not milky flavour is perfect, however, such as in light icing on a doughnut or when paired with a very delicate flavour in a situation when the intensity of a bittersweet or good semi-sweet chocolate would be overpowering.

COUVERTURE CHOCOLATE is available only in specialty baking shops or from wholesalers and is used almost exclusively by professionals. It is a bittersweet or semisweet chocolate with extra cocoa butter added to give it an especially smooth, silky texture when melted, perfect for coating truffles, candies and other confections. Do not substitute couverture chocolate for other varieties in baking, as the increased cocoa butter will alter the final product, sometimes severely. Couverture must be tempered before using, a process that involves heating the chocolate to 115°F, then spreading it on a cold work surface and keeping it moving by spreading and smearing it until it reaches 80°F. The couverture is then scraped back into the bowl and heated again until it reaches 90°F—it is then ready for use as a moulding or for coating chocolate.

MILK CHOCOLATE is made when milk solids, flavourings and additional fat (usually vegetable shortening) are added to the cocoa liquor in addition to sugar and vanilla, before conching. Since these ingredients make up a great deal of the final product, milk chocolate has a much less pronounced chocolate flavour and is subject to much more variation in quality. In the United States, milk chocolate must have at least 10% cocoa solids, considerably less than even sweet dark chocolate. As this causes it to have an easily masked, unassertive flavour, it is not well suited to most baking and desserts. With each additional ingredient, the flavour of the original chocolate liquor is muted, and the final result is an only mildly chocolatey confection with a very smooth, creamy texture, thanks to the added milk solids and emulsifiers. Milk chocolate should not be used to replace semisweet or bittersweet chocolate in most recipes, although substituting milk chocolate chips for dark ones in cookies won't hurt anyone! When buying milk chocolate for baking, and eating for that matter, read the label and look for pure ingredients such as cocoa butter and vanilla, with no artificial flavourings. European brands are likely to be of better quality, with a higher percentage of cocoa liquor than many of their domestic cousins, but there are several very good American brands, such as Ghirardelli, and even Baker's.

WHITE CHOCOLATE is not, in fact, chocolate at all, but a confection based on cocoa butter. It doesn't contain any cocoa liquor, but is made by adding milk solids, vanilla and emulsifiers such as lecithin to melted cocoa butter or vegetable shortening. The mixture is poured into moulds and cooled. Good white chocolate should contain a high percentage of cocoa butter and no vegetable shortening, but many, if not most, products sold as white chocolate in North America are made with only vegetable oil shortenings and artificial flavours, with not a trace of cocoa butter. Read the label carefully, as the difference in flavour is marked, and only the higher-quality brands will perform properly when melted and cooled. Good examples have a rich, creamy, sweet and mellow flavour and are a deep pale yellow in colour. Poor versions are ivory to completely white, waxy in texture, with a bland and artificial taste, and are often tricky to work with.

Storage

Store all chocolate in a very cool (between 65 and 70°F is ideal), dark place, completely away from heat, light and moisture. A tight wrapping of aluminum foil is the best protection. Some pastry chefs keep their chocolate in the refrigerator, which greatly extends its shelf life, but I do not recommend this for the average baker. Unless you know exactly what you are doing when you wrap, chill and return the chocolate to room temperature, and have perfectly controlled temperature and humidity in your refrigerator, the moisture and severe temperature changes can destroy chocolate's texture and flavour. All types of chocolate are prone to picking up strong odours such as tobacco and onions, even strong-smelling leather. Make sure chocolate is kept well apart from potential contaminants. Unsweetened, bittersweet and semisweet chocolate will keep for up to 18 months, if properly stored. Milk and white chocolate, due to their high milk solids content, have a much shorter shelf life and can go rancid if stored too long or improperly. In fact, much of the white chocolate consumed in North America is likely already rancid. White chocolate, in particular, is extremely susceptible to light and should be carefully wrapped and stored in a completely dark, cool, dry area. Milk chocolate should be used within 6 months, white chocolate within 3 to 4 months.

Bloom

The surface of chocolate can sometimes become marked with a white, powdery-looking substance called *bloom*. Bloom can occur on chocolate that has not been used yet or on chocolate products after they have been prepared, such as dipped confections, truffles and moulded candies. There are actually two different types of bloom, resulting from two different inhospitable conditions. The first type appears as cloudy, grey streaks on the surface of the chocolate and can be wiped off, leaving an oily residue. Called *fat bloom,* or "oysters," this occurs when the chocolate has been heated to too high a temperature or cooled improperly during processing or stored at too warm a temperature. The fat in the chocolate begins to melt and separate from the emulsion of the mixture. This can also occur if cold products such as truffle centres are dipped in warm melted chocolate. The second type of bloom occurs when chocolate has been exposed to too much moisture in storage. It looks very much like fat bloom, but the surface of the chocolate can feel dusty or even gritty, and the cloudiness cannot be wiped or rubbed off. If chocolate has been stored in too cool a temperature and then taken into a warmer environment, condensation can form on its surface, causing this bloom. In some lower-quality chocolate, inferior types of sugar may have been used in production, resulting in the same condition. Neither of these blooms makes chocolate unusable for most baking and dessert applications and will only present problems if the chocolate is to be used in advanced chocolate work or confectionery. In this case, the chocolate would need to be carefully tempered (see Tempering on page 235).

Melting Chocolate

Chocolate has the not-undeserved reputation of being temperamental and unpredictable to work with. In fact, melting chocolate is far from difficult, but must be done with respect and understanding. Regardless of the method used, two things should be kept in mind. First, lower temperatures produce much better results, with far fewer dangers. Chocolate scorches easily and can develop a granular texture if overheated. Second, always chop chocolate to be melted as finely and uniformly as possible, to lessen the time it will need to be exposed to heat, and to ensure it melts evenly. I generally use a chef's knife to chop chocolate, but a good solid serrated knife works very well, too. Perhaps the best tool is the pitchfork-like chocolate fork, available in specialty shops.

There are two acceptable and effective methods of melting chocolate: in the microwave and in a double boiler on the stove, the traditional fashion. I use both methods frequently, though I do find the microwave method works particularly well for small quantities of chocolate. Place finely chopped chocolate in a microwave-safe bowl and heat uncovered on medium or 50% power for dark chocolate and low or 30% power for white and milk chocolate. The time it takes to melt will vary with the size of the pieces, quantity of chocolate and wattage of the oven itself. Start with 30 seconds, then increments of 10 to 15 seconds from there. Remember, chocolate melted in the microwave will retain its shape even after it is melted; stir after every increment and when there are only a few lumps left in the chocolate remove it from the microwave and stir until completely melted. There will be enough residual heat in the chocolate to complete the melting.

To melt chocolate on the stove, pour an inch or two of water in a pot and bring it to a gentle simmer. Place the chopped chocolate in the top portion of a double boiler or in a stainless steel or glass bowl. Set over the mouth of the pot, reducing the heat so the water remains at a bare simmer and making sure the bowl fits well into the opening, sits deep enough in the pot so none of the chocolate is directly over the stove element, but not so deep that the bottom of the bowl touches the water. The water should continue to barely simmer, but not boil. If you are unsure about the heat, err on the side of too low rather that too high. Stir the chocolate frequently as it melts and remove the bowl from the heat when the chocolate is about ¾ melted; the residual heat in the mixture will finish the melting. When melting chocolate alone, be very careful to see that not even a drop of moisture touches it. Even a damp wooden spoon, or a blast of steam from the simmering water can cause the chocolate to seize, becoming tightly clumped, hard, and virtually unsalvageable. (In theory, it is possible to salvage seized chocolate by adding enough additional liquid to restore its creaminess. In practice, however, if chocolate has seized, adding a lot more liquid *would* resurrect the chocolate, but it would still be unusable for that particular recipe!) While small amounts of liquid are lethal, large quantities do not have the same effect, and many recipes call for chopped chocolate to be combined with fairly generous amounts of coffee, cream or other liquid before being placed in the top of the double boiler for melting. In these proportions, the chocolate and liquid melt together smoothly.

White and milk chocolate are even more sensitive to overheating and scorching than dark varieties, due to their high milk solids content. Make sure these chocolates are very finely chopped before melting and keep the heat low. Small quantities melt faster and are less likely to heat unevenly—try to work with no more than a single layer of chopped or white milk chocolate in the bowl at a time. The microwave method works very well for these chocolates. If you are using the stove-top method, bring the water in the pot to a gentle boil, then turn off the heat completely and place the bowl of chocolate over the mouth. Stir occasionally until the chocolate is melted from the steam.

With any type of chocolate, do not substitute chocolate chips for bar chocolate when melting is required. Chocolate chips are designed and engineered to retain their shape even in the heat of the oven during baking and often do not melt smoothly.

Tempering

When good chocolate is processed for sale, it has been properly tempered. The cocoa butter particles in tempered chocolate are aligned in a stable, even arrangement, but can be disturbed by changes in temperature. Out of alignment, they become loose and unstable and can cause the chocolate to develop the grey, greasy streaks of fat bloom when cooled and set. To realign the fat molecules, the heating and cooling process must be carried out slowly and under controlled conditions. In other words, the chocolate must be re-tempered. As are well-tempered children, well-tempered chocolate is well behaved and easy to work with, while out-of-temper chocolate will rarely do anything you want it to.

Tempering *is* critical in the making of glossy confections that are to be stored at room temperature for long periods of time. So, if you decide to make your own Easter treats or filled chocolates, you can use the following method as a guide, ensuring your finished confections have a rich smooth shine and a clean-breaking texture. Keep in mind, however, that every type and variety of chocolate will temper slightly differently, and while the instructions are relatively simple, tempering well takes a great deal of practice.

There are several ways to temper chocolate, some more complicated than others. The following method is one I find extremely reliable. Its only drawback is that the chocolate used must be in good temper to begin with, with no

evidence of bloom. To temper damaged chocolate showing signs of fat or moisture bloom, a more elaborate, thorough process is required, and can be found
in many good books on baking theory and confectionery technique. I have not
included it here, because it is highly unlikely you will ever need to do it yourself. In fact, it is quite possible to be an accomplished baker and pastry chef
without ever having tempered chocolate at all. Although it seems to be per-
ceived as the mark of a true dessert chef in the minds of many amateurs, it is
rarely necessary for home or even restaurant products.

SHORTCUT TEMPERING METHOD: Always work with at least 1 pound of chocolate
at a time—it is virtually impossible to properly temper less, and even easier with
more. Finely chop 1 pound of very good bittersweet or semisweet chocolate.
Place about ¾ of this into a heatproof bowl and set the bowl over a pot of barely simmering water. Be very careful to not allow any moisture to come into contact with the chocolate, or it will seize. Using a candy thermometer, melt the
chocolate until it reaches 115°F, then remove the bowl from the heat. Stir in the
remaining finely chopped chocolate, a little at a time, until the mixture registers
80°F. Return the bowl of chocolate to the top of the pot and stir until the temperature reaches 88°F. The tempered chocolate can now be used to coat candy
or truffle centres, or to glaze cakes, cookies and pastries. For best results, products to be dipped, coated, glazed or covered should themselves be between 75°
and 80°F and should be left to set at between 55° and 60°F.

The Best Chocolate for the Job

By now you have realized that all chocolate is not created equal. Given the vast
range of chocolates that are available, both good and not so good, how do you
decide which one to use when the only stipulation in the recipe is for "dark
chocolate"? A chocolate's suitability to a given dessert depends on several factors: the chocolate's own inherent sweetness, bitterness and flavour; what other
flavourings are included in the product; how prominent the chocolate taste
should be; the richness of the final dessert and whether or not the chocolate is

meant to be tasted alone in the product, as it would be in a chocolate chip or a simple glaze.

Some chocolates are better eating chocolates, some are better cooking chocolates—the sweeter the chocolate, the more palatable it is in its raw state and the darker the chocolate, the more bitter and intense its flavour. Sweet chocolates, such as milk chocolate and sweet dark chocolate, are much better tasted with few other flavourings present, such as in bar form or in simple chocolate confections. Darker, more bitter chocolates with higher cocoa solids content may be a little intense for straight eating, but are ideal for baking, as they have the ability to impart a pure, deep flavour even when combined with other flavours and when present in small quantities.

If the flavour of the chocolate is to be the primary flavour in a dessert, as in a flourless torte or a rich mousse, the flavour of the chocolate itself should be as complex and wonderful as possible. Similarly, if the chocolate is to be simply one of many elements in the final product, as it is in many cookies and ice creams, it should not be so intense that it overpowers subtler flavours, or so weak that it gets lost.

Some bittersweet chocolates, such as those with a cocoa solids content of about 70%, are almost unpalatable on their own, but are exquisite in simple but decadently rich cakes and confections. In these cases, the intensity of the chocolate's flavour is matched by the richness of the dessert. The same chocolate would make a lighter, more casual dessert like a chocolate pudding or a birthday-type layer cake overly intense and not sweet enough, preventing it from being enjoyed the way it was meant to be—in sizable portions! The following recommendations are merely guidelines for selecting the best chocolate for a specific type of dessert.

Unsweetened chocolate is best used in desserts with large quantities of sugar, and often fat as well, such as brownies or dark chocolate cookies. These products would be overly sweet and not fudgy enough in flavour if a milder chocolate such as semisweet were used. It can also be well used to supplement bittersweet or semisweet chocolate in cakes, cookies and other baked goods, to darken and intensify their flavours.

Bittersweet chocolate is best for deeply chocolatey desserts such as a flourless chocolate cake, a French chocolate mousse, a dark chocolate ice cream or a rich chocolate tart, where its depth and complexity of flavour and subtle sweetness can be appreciated. Many of these chocolates are the most flavourful and luxurious in the world, with wonderful nuances of flavour and a serious chocolate kick. These desserts allow the subtleties of the chocolate to come through, as it is not smothered by a great deal of sugar or other flavourings. In comparison, a relatively bland semisweet chocolate would make the flourless chocolate cake a monotonously flavoured, overly sweet and ultimately cloying experience. The darker the chocolate, or the higher the cocoa solids content, and the smaller the proportion of other ingredients such as sugar, the more intense and, usually, complex the flavour of the final dessert will be. The most wonderful thing about baking with bittersweet chocolate is how dramatically the flavours of your desserts can change depending on the particular brand or type you use.

Semisweet chocolate is a good choice for lighter chocolate desserts, and for those in which the chocolate is to be tasted relatively pure, such as in chocolate chip cookies, as glazes on cakes and in sauces. Some ice creams, custards, cookies, icings and frostings and fillings are ideal showcases for good semisweet chocolate, as they allow the simple and smooth taste of the chocolate to be appreciated. The very strong, bittersweet chocolate with 70% cocoa solids, excellent in the flourless torte, would be much too overt for a sweet and creamy custard, and far too bitter for the icing on a layer cake.

Sweet dark chocolate is generally not great for baking, but can be well used in several situations. Because its flavour is about the same weight and sweetness, it's a good alternative for milk chocolate chips or chunks (or peanut butter or butterscotch chips) in cookies or ice creams. Also, in simple icings, frostings and glazes for pastries and confections such as doughnuts, cookies and some cakes where a more bitter chocolate would detract from the gentle sweetness in the pastry itself, sweet chocolate complements it beautifully.

Milk and white chocolate are both much sweeter than any form of dark chocolate and do not have the necessary intensity to impart a good flavour to most baked goods. They can be used to great advantage, however, in delicately flavoured mousses, puddings, and ice creams.

There is no single chocolate that is perfect for every application. There are several excellent brands out there, some domestic and most European, and within this group, most bakers and pastry chefs have their favourites. Often, a chef will prefer one brand or type for her flourless cake, another for her truffles and yet another for ice cream. Partly this is a matter of personal taste and opinion and partly it is a question of which characteristics are best suited to which dessert. Fortunately, the most expensive chocolate is not always the most appropriate—the widely available domestic brand Baker's has been rated among the very best for traditional American-style brownies and fudgy chocolate cakes.

Although this may seem strange, it actually makes a great deal of sense—often the most suitable ingredient for a recipe comes from the same region as the recipe itself!

Taste as many types and varieties of chocolate as you can over time, and if you really want to get serious about it (an absolutely wonderful excuse to consume enormous quantities of chocolate), keep a few notes about each. Consider the type of dessert you are preparing and judge what personality of chocolate would be best. Don't worry if you try the most expensive chocolate you can find and find it too bitter or strong. There is a great deal of variation, and even the best pastry chefs strongly disagree about the merits of each brand or type.

Switzerland, Belgium and France produce what are regarded as the finest chocolates in the world. In general, Swiss chocolate tends to be sweeter, smoother and creamier-tasting than French chocolate, which is darker and usually more bitter—think of French-roast coffee! Ever the middleman, Belgian chocolate is somewhere in between. Lindt is the premier Swiss chocolatier, with a massive range of products, from ready-made truffles and bars available in every corner store to superior professional-quality bittersweet, white and unsweetened chocolates. The Belgian chocolate master Bernard Callebaut produces some of the finest professional chocolate anywhere, and I have used it extensively for years. Perhaps the most specialized and exquisite chocolate is made in France by Valrhona. Valrhona chocolates are all handmade from totally pure and organic ingredients and come in dozens of subtly nuanced varieties, most of them very dark, and very bitter. They are some of the most unique varieties in the world, but some pastry chefs and bakers find them overly bitter for the North American palate, preferring the mellower Callebaut or the slightly sweeter Lindt. A relative newcomer to the world of elite chocolate is the Venezuelan maker El Rey. Available from wholesalers and some professional baking supply mail-order companies, El Rey chocolates can match every step of the more established European houses. If you can find it, it is well worth whatever price you pay!

In general, most pastry chefs in North America would name Valrhona, Callebaut, Cacao Barry, El Rey and Lindt the best imported varieties and San Francisco's Ghirardelli and Scharffen Berger as the best American brands. Of the supermarket chocolates, Baker's is very good, but avoid the cheaper brands. In recent years, some larger supermarket chains have created their own label of imported European chocolates for baking. The bittersweet type of these brands are usually of very high quality and cost significantly less than a comparable

European brand. If the higher cost of the European chocolates seems prohibitive, consider using a combination of a very good domestic brand, such as Ghirardelli, and a little of the really pricey stuff. I often use this technique to achieve a more complex, deeper flavour than I could get from one type alone.

Read the labels of all chocolate carefully—a high percentage of cocoa solids and the presence of cocoa butter are signs of a quality chocolate. European chocolates have the cocoa solids content on the package, but, unfortunately, American ones don't, so you'll just have to taste as many varieties as you need to before you find a comparable domestic brand. Depending on the country of origin, the terms *cocoa liquor*, *cocoa solids* and *cocoa mass* on labels and packages are used interchangeably. In quality chocolate, cocoa butter should be listed high among the ingredients, and there should be no mention of vegetable oil shortening. Bittersweet and semisweet chocolate should contain cocoa solids, cocoa butter, sugar, vanilla (or the synthetic flavouring vanillin) and possibly an emulsifier such as lecithin. Sweet chocolate will have a higher proportion of sugar and may have artificial flavourings added. White chocolate should be made with cocoa butter, not vegetable oil shortenings, and milk solids, vanilla or vanillin and an emulsifier, with little or no other ingredients. Milk chocolate should contain milk solids, cocoa solids, cocoa butter, vanilla or vanillin and an emulsifier.

When tasting and testing chocolate, there are several things to keep in mind. Look for a glossy, richly coloured, smooth surface. In general, with bitter- and semisweet chocolate, the darker the colour, the higher the cocoa liquor content and the more intense the flavour. White chocolate should have the rich pale yellow of pure cocoa butter and not be snow white. All chocolate should break with a good, clean snap, leaving no tiny crumbs or chips. Crumbling or a pasty texture of the broken chocolate is a sign of too little cocoa butter. Use your nose before your mouth—as with so many other good foods, chocolate should have a strong and rich aroma. It should smell deeply of chocolate, not of vanilla or, worse, "off" odours that it picked up in storage. In the mouth, the best chocolate should begin to melt immediately, becoming evenly creamy and luxurious. It should not feel at all dry, waxy, crumbly or pasty. And lastly, the flavour should fill your mouth with a rich, dark sweetness, and no lingering aftertaste. The flavour will depend on the type of chocolate and its origins. Some taste slightly acidic, some are very sweet, and often you'll notice faint overtones of other flavours, such as coffee, wine, cinnamon, vanilla, even chili or saffron. This complexity of flavour is a sign of a high-quality chocolate. Overt sweetness with no hint of acidity is usually the mark of a cheap product, with a great deal of sugar and other additives added to mask poor quality and rushed processing.

Flavoured Chips and Other Special Additions

PEANUT BUTTER CHIPS, BUTTERSCOTCH CHIPS These are two similar products made from milk solids, vegetable shortenings and artificial flavourings, with a consistency similar to white or milk chocolate chips. Available in packages in most supermarkets, as well as in bulk from many bulk food stores, they are used almost exclusively in cookies and bars and should not be used in any other context to replace dark, sweet or other forms of chocolate.

FLAVOURED CHOCOLATE CHIPS Recently, commercial baking supply companies have come out with variations on the traditional chocolate chip. Mint, raspberry, orange and coffee flavourings are added to a sweet dark or milk chocolate base, then packaged as chips. They should only be used in desserts where they can retain their chip form, as in cookies, bars and ice creams, and should never be used to replace other forms of chocolate, as they do not behave like pure forms of chocolate when melted or combined with other ingredients.

TOFFEE BITS These are basically just little bits of English-style butter toffee broken into tiny pieces, the perfect size for adding to cake batters, cookie doughs, ice creams, even as a decoration for finished baked goods and desserts. Skor, the toffee-centred chocolate bar, has lent its name to a brand of toffee bits for baking, and they are available in the baking sections of most supermarkets.

CANDY-COVERED CHOCOLATE PIECES FOR BAKING Many large supermarkets are now selling packages of mini versions of brand-name candies such as M&Ms for use in baking. They are fun as a novelty item, especially in cookies and as a garnish for children's desserts, although the flavor does leave a little to be desired. Use them in place of chocolate chips or nuts in cookies or snack cakes, or to decorate cakes, cookies or sundaes. Use caution when baking, though—they can scorch and burn if heated over 400°.

CRUSHED PEPPERMINT CANDIES FOR BAKING One of the best experiments I ever made was adding a handful of finely crushed candy cane to a batch of plain shortbread cookies at Christmas. The darn cookies were so good they never made it onto a plate, much less into the gift boxes for friends. While you can certainly have it out with some candy, a strong bag and a hefty mallet, ready-crushed peppermint candy is now available in packages in the baking sections of many supermarkets. It is a fabulous holiday addition to cookie doughs, icings and frostings, some ice cream bases, and even some plain or chocolate cakes. In recipes already calling for mint extract, the addition of crushed peppermint candy is an excellent way to layer the mint flavour. As it is basically hard sugar, the crushed candy can burn very easily. Don't be tempted to use huge amounts, and take care to watch cookie bottoms for signs of scorching.

Flavouring Powders

CAROB POWDER Carob powder is the ground, dried pulp of the carob or locust bean, a long, tough-skinned pod with a sweet edible flesh. The pulp can also be eaten fresh, but is most commonly dried, ground, then sold in powdered form. Although similar in appearance to a light cocoa powder, carob powder is higher in natural sugar and lower in fat than cocoa. Carob does have a faint taste of chocolate, making it a popular substitute for chocolate or cocoa products in baking. The amount of sugar in a recipe may need to be reduced and a little more butter or oil added if substituting for unsweetened chocolate or cocoa. Available in health and natural food stores, carob is sometimes called *honey locust*, *locust bean powder* or *Saint John's bread*. *Sweetened carob powder* and powders enriched with powdered milk or other flavourings are also available, but these should be used in baking only where specified.

Carob is also available in other familiar forms, including *carob chips*. These will have vegetable shortening, sugar and often milk solids added and can be used to replace chocolate chips in cookies, bars and some quick breads and cakes, but not to replace any other form of chocolate, especially if it is to be melted.

MALT AND MALTED MILK POWDERS *Malt*, also called *malt powder*, is made from sprouted grain, usually barley, that is dried in a kiln, then ground into a fine powder. It has a lovely mellow, sweet flavour and is often used in warm drinks and baked goods, as well as in the production of vinegar, beer and spirits.

Malted milk powder is a popular malt product, made by combining malt powder with powdered milk and sugar and sometimes additional flavourings such as vanilla or chocolate. It is widely available in North American grocery stores in the powdered beverages section, under names such as Carnation and Ovaltine. Malted milk powders are most often used to make warm or cold beverages and ice cream floats, and the plain or vanilla varieties can be wonderful flavourings for baked goods such as cakes and icings, yeast and quick breads, creams and pie fillings. Be sure to read the carton—some are plain, but others have cocoa added and may not be appropriate for every dessert.

Spices

All spices should be kept for no longer than 3 months. Can't remember when you bought that spice? Replace it! Buy your spices in small quantities from a bulk store with a high turnover to save money and ensure freshness. Many of the commercially produced bottles of spices in grocery stores are already so old they have lost most of their potency and will be more like scented dust than rich flavouring accents. And chances are, the place you are currently keeping your spices is over or next to the stove, for convenience, and they are most likely still in the original clear glass bottles. Unfortunately, this means your spices and herbs are constantly being exposed to not one, not two, but all three of the conditions that cause them to deteriorate: light, heat and moisture. The best place to store spices is in a cool, dry cupboard, in airtight jars. If you prefer the handiness of a spice rack, position the rack on a cool wall and keep the spices in dark, opaque jars. The following are the most commonly used spices in baking.

ALLSPICE *(Jamaica Pepper, Myrtle Pepper)* Contrary to popular belief, allspice is not a blend of many (or all!) spices, but is a single spice with a complex, fragrant flavour. Allspice berries are the fruit of an aromatic tree in the myrtle family. It is native to North and South America, but the spice became popular in the cuisines of much of Europe very soon after it was first imported. The ripe green berries are about the size of peppercorns and become brown and puckered when dried. Allspice is aptly named—its spicy flavour is reminiscent of cinnamon, cloves, nutmeg and even muted pepper. Although allspice is grown in much of Latin America and the Caribbean, Jamaican allspice is by far the most aromatic and flavourful. Fortunately, that country produces most of the world's supply. If possible, buy the whole berries and grind them yourself in a coffee or spice mill; whole berries should last up to 18 months if stored away from light, heat, and moisture. In spite of its complexity, allspice is rarely used on its own to flavour desserts and baked goods, but often in combination with cinnamon, cloves, nutmeg and ginger. It should be used with care, though, as it can be overpowering if used in too great a quantity.

ANISE *(Aniseed, Sweet Cumin)* Anise is one of the most common flavourings in the world, but is still rather underused in North American cuisine. It is related to fennel, dill, tarragon, cumin and caraway, and has a pronounced, sweetish licorice flavour. Anise seeds are tiny, dark-brown curved grains, with a stronger, purer flavour than star anise (see page 249), though I prefer the latter for use in baking and dessert-making. Anise seeds should always be bought whole, then ground as needed with a spice or coffee mill. Ground anise loses its flavour and aroma very quickly, and even the seeds are more perishable than other whole spices. Anise is often used in desserts containing nuts and dried fruits, frequently in combination with other strong spices, such as cloves, cinnamon and ginger. It lends a distinct flavour to cakes, breads, pie and tart fillings and many traditional European confections and candies.

CARAWAY SEED Caraway has been used in sweet and savoury cooking for thousands of years and remains popular today in the cooking of Eastern Europe, especially in Germany and Austria. Many traditional British dishes also call for this sliver of a seed, and it features prominently in such baked goods as seed cakes and soda breads. It has a very distinctive, easily recognizable flavour, familiar to most North Americans as the "other" flavour in seeded rye bread. It is mainly a savoury spice, but can be added to breads, plain cakes and biscuits to give a rustic, hearty flavour. It marries well with lemon and can be added to a lemon pound cake for a good tea-time treat.

CARDAMOM An unfamiliar spice to many North America palates, cardamom has been used in the sweet and savoury dishes of many cuisines since antiquity. Native to India and widely used in Eastern and Asian cuisines, it is grown in many parts of India, Mexico and South America and is a common flavouring in Germanic and Scandinavian cuisine. When ripe, the stem of the cardamom plant produces pale green seed pods, each containing 15 to 20 tiny seeds. The pods can be bleached a creamy white, but these are no different in flavour (*brown cardamom pods* are not the same, but from a closely related plant. They have a coarser, cruder flavour and should be avoided). Both whole pods and ground cardamom are available, but it is far preferable to buy the pods and grind them yourself as needed because, once ground, cardamom loses its flavour and potency very quickly. Lightly crushed pods can be used to infuse liquids, such as custards for ice cream, poaching syrups and mulled wine; while freshly ground cardamom adds a characteristic bright flavour to breads, cakes, buns, pastries and biscuits. Cardamom has a complex, lemony, sweetly spicy flavour and aroma and marries beautifully with other sweet spices, breads and fruit compotes. It has a great affinity for coffee, as well as plums, apricots and other orchard fruit. To accentuate the flavour of the pods, dry-roast them in a skillet for a few seconds until fragrant and warm. Use all forms of cardamom sparingly, however, as a little goes a long way.

CINNAMON *(Ceylon or Sri Lankan Cinnamon)* and CASSIA *(Chinese Kortintje or False Cinnamon)* Cinnamon is perhaps the most loved of the sweet spices. It has a delicate, fragrant warm flavour and aroma. Although many Middle Eastern and Asian cuisines have long incorporated cinnamon into their savoury dishes, it is used almost exclusively as a spice for sweets in the West. Cinnamon is the inner bark of a small evergreen tree native to Sri Lanka. The bark is peeled away from the thin branches, and the outer bark is removed. The inner bark then curls into scrolls, which are either cut and sold as cinnamon sticks, or ground. Cinnamon sticks can be used to infuse warm milk or cream with flavour or can be added to poaching liquids. Ground cinnamon is often added to cakes; cookies; pie, tart and pastry fillings; and baked fruit dishes. Most of the spice sold as cinnamon in North America is actually *cassia*; to get the real thing, seek out a Sri Lankan grocery or a very reputable spice vendor.

Cassia is closely related to cinnamon and is often sold falsely under that name. It is the bark of a tree native to Burma, not Sri Lanka, and can be found in the same forms as cinnamon, as well as being available as tiny buds and leaves. Although it looks almost identical to cinnamon, cassia has a stronger, coarser flavour, more robust aroma and is less sweet. For certain products, I find cassia actually preferable to cinnamon, as it has a more pronounced taste, but I generally prefer the more delicate, nuanced flavour of real cinnamon for more subtle flavouring. The location in which cassia is grown can greatly affect its flavour and intensity. *Indonesian cassia* is most common and is of high quality, but consider yourself lucky to find cassia from Vietnam or China. *Vietnamese cassia* has an incomparably intense flavour, perfect in recipes meant to highlight the taste of cinnamon, such as sticky buns and some coffee cakes. Use a little less than the recipe calls for and you'll still get a real punch of flavour. *Chinese cassia* is perceptibly sweet, almost candy-like in its flavour and aroma. It can be very sharp and overwhelming if used in too great a quantity, but can enhance many confections and sweets where its flavour can stand up to the high sugar content, such as in ice creams and rich icings.

Neither cassia nor cinnamon is inferior to the other; rather, they should be used thoughtfully, in products that best showcase their individual attributes. For delicate biscuits, cakes, creams, custards and mousses, cinnamon's sweet and slightly muted flavour is perfect. For more robust preparations, such as spiced compotes, rich spice cakes and hearty fillings, the more intense and aggressive flavour of cassia is appropriate. If using ground cassia to replace ground cinnamon, use slightly less, as the flavour could be overpowering.

CLOVES Richly spicy, dark and wintery, the flavour of cloves is unmistakable. The unopened bud of an evergreen tree, cloves have been adopted into the cuisine of almost every culture since pre-history. Aside from being a strong accent to many savoury stews and meat dishes, they have found a permanent place in many sweet preparations, such as pie and tart fillings, ginger and spice cakes, yeast and quick breads and fruit cakes. They are sold both as whole dried buds, simply called cloves, and ground. As with most spices, the best way to buy cloves is whole, then grind them as you need them. They marry well with other sweet spices, such as cinnamon, allspice and nutmeg, and are almost never used alone. They should be used very conservatively, as they are extremely potent.

GINGER Ginger has woven its way into almost every aspect of our lives—it is a common ingredient in sweet and savoury dishes all over the world; it is used as a medicinal tonic and remedy; its spicy pungent perfume is used to scent our bodies and our homes and it has even been used as a talisman against evil spirits and bad fortune. For the baker, too, ginger remains a most versatile and rewarding ally.

The gnarled, blond root of a pretty flowering plant, root ginger is available in innumerable forms. *Fresh root ginger* must be very fresh, with taut tan skin covering the pale yellow flesh. Choose firm, unpuckered roots with no blemishes, ones that feel heavy for their size. Larger roots often have a hotter, more intense flavour than younger, smaller roots. Virtually all of the root ginger sold in North America is mature ginger, but occasionally *young* or *stem ginger* can be discovered at Asian groceries. Young ginger is much milder and can be treated almost as a vegetable, rather than a seasoning. Its thin skin doesn't require peeling. The skin of mature root ginger should be pared away with a small knife or vegetable peeler, but only immediately before the root is used, as the flesh loses its flavour quickly. Stringy and pulpy, the inside of the root is often very finely grated before it's added to dishes. Or, the grated pulp can be squeezed to exude a potent juice that can give a tangy, bright taste to recipes. Fine ginger graters, often made of porcelain, are available in kitchen supply stores and many Asian shops and are well worth it if you use ginger often. In general, fresh ginger is not commonly used in baked goods, as its flavour is quite hot and can be overpowering. It makes a good addition to a dark spicy gingerbread, though, and can be complemented with one or two other forms of the root, such as ground or candied. Fresh ginger is preferable to any other form in poaching syrups for fruit and in flavoured sauces, where the heat and intensity of the fresh root can be controlled and is needed to impart as much fresh flavour as possible in a relatively short time. Fresh root ginger should be stored in the refrigerator, wrapped well in paper towel, then sealed in plastic bags. Properly stored, it should keep for about 2 weeks.

Ground ginger is the most commonly used form of ginger in baking. It has quite a different flavour than the fresh root and should never be used to replace fresh ginger. Ground ginger should always be aromatic and fresh, no more than 2 months old for best potency. It adds a smooth, gently sweet-spicy flavour to breads, cakes, cookies and pie and tart fillings and is especially good in combination with dried fruits, nuts and other sweet spices. It is also delicious when paired with cooked apples, pears, rhubarb, figs or oranges.

For information on *candied* or *crystallized ginger* and *preserved ginger in syrup*, see the section on Candied Fruits on page 331.

Pickled ginger is pieces of the root that have been brined in a salt and sweet vinegar. It is not generally used in sweet dishes.

Dried root ginger is a common ingredient in savoury Asian and Eastern cuisines, but is rarely called for in dessert cookery.

MACE *(Blade Mace)* Mace is the lacy, orangy-red covering of the nutmeg seed. The delicate, mesh-like membrane is removed, dried and can be sold whole, called *blade mace*, or ground. Blade mace may be difficult to find in most grocery stores, but good spice shops and Indian groceries are a good source. Mace has a muted, warm flavour similar to that of nutmeg, but with overtones of cinnamon and spice. Although difficult to grind finely at home, freshly ground mace is preferable to the packaged ground powder. Use a spice or coffee mill and sift the powder afterwards to separate the coarser bits out. Ground mace, either homemade or purchased fresh, has better keeping qualities than most ground spices and may be stored in a cool, dry place for up to 3 months.

MINT Not a spice, of course, but a favourite flavouring for desserts and sweets all over the world. Although it is available dried, only the fresh herb or a pure extract should be used for baking and desserts. Peppermint and spearmint are two common varieties, both with a wonderful affinity for all types of chocolate, especially white and bittersweet, as well as berries of all kinds, oranges, grapefruit and cream. Mint is not an appropriate flavour for every dessert, but makes fantastic ice creams and mousses and is good added in extract form to chocolate cakes, brownies, icings and chocolates. A few mint leaves broken over a fresh fruit salad or a plate of candied oranges in syrup are lovely and suit the flavours in the dish, but mint leaves should not be used randomly to garnish every dessert. Like any decoration, it should make sense within the integrity of the whole—if its flavour is not appropriate, use another garnish! (Consult the section on garnishing starting on page 76 for more ideas and tips.)

MIXED SPICE *(Pumpkin Pie or Apple Pie Spice)* *Mixed spice* is a compound of sweet spices and is often called for in British and older North American recipes. *Pumpkin pie spice* and *apple pie spice* are similar, blended specifically for use in those desserts. The following are perfectly good substitutions:

FOR 1 TEASPOON *MIXED SPICE*, SUBSTITUTE:
½ teaspoon ground cinnamon
¼ teaspoon freshly grated nutmeg
⅛ teaspoon ground cloves
⅛ teaspoon ground allspice

FOR 1 TEASPOON OF *PUMPKIN PIE SPICE*, SUBSTITUTE:
½ teaspoon ground cinnamon
¼ teaspoon ground ginger
⅛ teaspoon ground allspice
⅛ teaspoon freshly grated nutmeg

FOR 1 TEASPOON *APPLE PIE SPICE*, SUBSTITUTE:
½ teaspoon ground cinnamon
¼ teaspoon ground ginger
¼ teaspoon freshly grated nutmeg or mace
⅛ teaspoon ground cloves, optional
⅛ teaspoon ground allspice, optional

NUTMEG Nutmeg is the olive-sized kernel of the fruit of an evergreen tree. When the nectarine-sized fruit is ripe, it splits open, revealing a lacy red membrane surrounding a hard oval shell. The lacy covering is called mace and is used as a spice on its own. These two are not identical or interchangeable as many people believe, but are similar in many respects. The hard shell is cracked open to harvest the ash-brown oval nutmeg seed, which is then dried before being sold as a spice. Nutmeg has a warm, woody, mellow flavour that makes it a natural spice for many desserts and baked goods, as well as savoury dishes. Although it is all but ignored in North America, many cuisines rely on nutmeg in much the same way they do salt, to enhance the flavours of other ingredients, sweet and savoury alike. It should *never* be purchased already ground, but always as whole seeds. Special nutmeg graters are very inexpensive, and many have a little compartment to store the extra nutmegs. The flavour of freshly grated nutmeg is infinitely spicier, sweeter and warmer than the dull, dusty and sometimes bitter taste of the bottled ground powder. Nutmeg is often used in combination with other sweet spices, such as cinnamon, ginger, cloves and allspice, but is a lovely flavouring on its own, giving a warmth and depth of flavour to doughnuts, pancakes, pound cakes and biscuits.

STAR ANISE (*Chinese Anise*) Star anise is one of the most beautiful and richly flavoured spices. The dried fruit of a Chinese evergreen, the spice is indeed star-shaped. It is a hard, glossy-brown disc about the size of a nickel, with eight points. Each little arm of the star contains a single glossy seed, milder than the fruit itself. Star anise has a warm, sweet licorice flavour that I find preferable to regular anise for baking as it is richer and more complex. The stars are available whole and ground, but the whole is infinitely preferable, as the ground spice loses its flavour and aroma very quickly. Grinding them yourself in a spice mill will yield a much more flavourful and potent spice. Freshly ground star anise adds a haunting, warm anise flavour to breads, cakes, fritters and cookies. The whole stars can be used to infuse cream or milk for custards and are a delicious addition to the sugar syrup for poaching pears or dried fruit. Return the stars to the reduced syrup served with the fruit for a striking touch at the table.

Nuts, Fruits
and
Sweet Vegetables

Nuts

Nuts are indispensable to the cuisine of almost every culture in the world. Full of protein, vitamins and minerals, they are also extremely high in oils, making them rich and deeply flavoured. They can be used raw to add a subtle flavour to baked goods and other desserts, but are even more wonderful when their flavour is intensified with roasting, making them able to play the feature role in concoctions such as frangipane (a creamy, baked nut filling) or tender nut-flavoured butter cakes.

Lightly roasting or toasting most nuts does something almost magical for their taste and texture. The quick exposure to heat brings out the unique flavours, making them richer and sweeter, masking any bitterness. Like wine grapes, some nuts contain a fair amount of tannin, giving the raw nuts a noticeable bitterness. Walnuts and pecans are good examples. A few minutes in a medium oven toasts the nuts enough to dampen the tannins, making them mellow and full-flavoured. Some nuts have such a high oil content, however, that it is wiser to leave them raw when adding them to a recipe that is to be baked. Macadamia nuts and pine nuts tend to burn quickly if exposed to too much or too high a heat and usually toast just enough during the baking of a recipe to impart a perfect flavour to the finished product. Be suspicious of recipes for cookies or cakes that call for these varieties to be toasted before they are added—I always use them raw if they will be subjected to heat in the recipe. Similarly, if substituting either of these nuts for another variety, such as almonds or hazelnuts, keep their fragile nature in mind and consider adding them raw.

Many nuts can be substituted for one another, allowing the baker to vary their recipes almost infinitely. See the Ingredient Substitution Chart (page 335) for some suggestions.

Selecting Nuts

The best time to buy fresh nuts is in the late fall, when most varieties, such as hazelnuts, pecans, chestnuts and walnuts, are freshly harvested. Unless you are fortunate enough to live in a region that produces nuts, the nuts you will see in the shops will have been dried to enable them to be stored for long periods of time without spoiling. When selecting nuts, buy nuts that are beautiful: hazelnuts and pecans should be shiny and smooth, and all nuts should be free of gouges and marks. In their shells, only peanuts should rattle, and all nuts should feel heavy for their size.

Storing Nuts

The high fat content of nuts makes them prone to becoming rancid quickly if kept improperly or too long. Nuts keep longest if still in the shell, where they are protected from light and heat, and where their oils cannot oxidize. Most nuts can be shelled with the help of an inexpensive conventional nutcracker, although some, like chestnuts and coconuts, require special techniques described below. While this is all well and good in theory, not everyone has the time to shell a pound of nuts just to make some muffins. If you buy shelled nuts (with the shells already removed), make sure your supplier has a high turnover, and that the bins are kept clean and free of little critters. I find buying from a good natural or bulk food store the best way to go, as I can buy only the amount I need and get a good price at the same time. Taste one or two before buying them. Rancid nuts are easy to identify—a nasty, bitter, stale flavour and no sweetness. Raw nuts should very fresh when purchased and stored in airtight bags or in plastic or glass containers. Nuts should never be stored in tin or metal containers, as the metal accelerates their deterioration. Stored in the refrigerator, fresh nuts will keep for 2 to 3 months, and in the freezer for 9 months to 1 year. In both cases, especially in the refrigerator, make sure the nuts are well protected from moisture, as this will quickly encourage moulds and yeasts. Ideally, fresh nuts should be used within 4 to 6 weeks. Roasted nuts can be stored at room temperature, airtight, but should be used within 2 weeks.

The more of the nut is exposed to air, the faster it will deteriorate. For this reason, nuts in the shell will keep the longest, and whole shelled nuts have a longer shelf life than chopped or ground nuts. Even if a recipe calls for chopped or ground nuts, buy them whole and chop or grind them yourself.

Large quantities of nuts are easily and efficiently ground in any food processor. Use the steel blade and process the nuts in short bursts and pulses, rather than long spins of the machine. If the nuts are to be used immediately in a recipe, add a tablespoon or two of the granulated sugar called for in the recipe to the processor with the nuts; the grains of sugar will encourage the nuts to grind into fine but distinct particles. Pulse the processor just until the nuts are a powder, but stop before they begin to become creamy. Overprocessing causes the nuts to release their oils, and you will end up with a lovely homemade nut butter—yummy, but not quite right for cakes and frangipanes. To grind small batches of nuts, invest in an inexpensive coffee grinder, the type that is no bigger than a large tin of coffee. This type of grinder also makes a brilliant spice grinder and will more than pay for itself with the money you'll save avoiding rancid nuts.

Toasting Nuts

To lightly toast most nuts, spread the shelled nuts, skinned if desired, in a single layer on a baking sheet. Place the sheet in a preheated 350° oven and bake until the nuts are fragrant, lightly coloured if they are pale, and warm or hot to the touch. Depending on the richness of the nut, and the recipe for which they are intended, this process can take between 7 and 10 minutes. WATCH CLOSELY! If you are easily distracted, set a timer in very small increments and check the nuts frequently. Shake the tray several times to promote even roasting. Aim for a light, colourless toasting if the nuts are very oily or will undergo further cooking during baking. Hardier nuts like hazelnuts can withstand a slightly longer toasting, becoming golden and very aromatic. A good way to judge is to use your nose and your hand: the nuts should be very fragrant and feel warm to the touch.

NUT BUTTERS Besides the ubiquitous peanut butter, there are many rich and flavourful nut butters available in most health and natural food stores today. In fact, any oily nut, processed finely enough to elicit the natural oils, can be made into a spreadable thick paste. Peanuts may be the most common, but almonds, hazelnuts, walnuts, even buttery-rich macadamias can be the base for a nut butter. While they are usually used as spreads for toast and sandwiches, they can be used in many ways in the dessert kitchen. Many nut butters can be substituted for peanut butter in cake, quick bread, cookie and bar recipes, but be aware that some may be more oily, thinner, thicker, etc., and the recipe may have to be adjusted slightly to compensate. Nut butters can be used in tart fillings, icings and even in ice creams and custards as a way of getting the richness and flavour of nuts without the crunch and texture. Store natural nut butters in a cool, dark place; if you keep them in the cupboard, they will often separate, and a layer of oil will settle on the surface, so stir the contents of the jar well before measuring or using. Keeping the butters in the refrigerator will prevent this separation, but the butters will be very firm and may be difficult to spread or blend easily. At room temperature, most nut butters will keep for about 9 months; refrigerated, they can last up to 1 year. Discard any butter that begins to smell or taste rancid.

NUT FILLINGS Available in many European groceries, *processed, canned nut fillings* are ready-made pastes used for filling tarts, strudels, pastries and cakes. These fillings are made from ground nuts, either a single variety such as almonds, or a blend of almonds, hazelnuts and perhaps walnuts. The nuts are combined with corn syrup, sugar, water, evaporated whole milk, natural and artificial flavourings, salt and citric acid, becoming a thick, sweet, sticky paste. Although these fillings are an easy way to a homemade dessert, they don't have the depth of flavour and subtlety of a freshly made nut paste. They should never be used to replace any other product in a recipe, but feel free to experiment with uses for them!

NUT AND CHOCOLATE SPREADS Sweet, sticky thick spreads made from ground nuts, usually rich hazelnuts, and chocolate or cocoa are a schoolchild's dream sandwich spread. (My best friend's family was French, and she had this sandwich at least three times a week—on white bread even! I have never in my life felt such jealousy.) Although most brands, such as Nutella, are still imported from Europe, these spreads are now commonly available in North American supermarkets and are used almost exclusively as a spread for toast, pancakes and waffles and sandwiches. They should never be used to replace any other product in a recipe for baked goods or desserts, but are quite versatile if used creatively. I have used them in custards, ice creams, icings and fillings and even in sponge cakes and cookies. Unlike plain unsweetened nut pastes, these spreads will contribute a great deal of sweetness to a product, so you may need to reduce or even omit any other sweetener present when using them.

Types of Nuts

ALMONDS Almonds are the seed kernels of a stone fruit similar to peaches and apricots. Two main types of almonds exist, bitter and sweet. *Bitter almonds* contain the unpalatable prussic acid and are never eaten fresh. Their essence is distilled, and they are used as a flavouring for almond extracts and liqueurs. *Sweet almonds* are one of the most familiar nuts to the baker. The raw nuts are chewy and mild, with a elusive perfume that is intensified with light roasting. They can be used whole or chopped in cakes, cookies and other biscuits, pastry crusts and fillings, candies and confections such as nougat or praline, as well as decoration for many desserts. Almonds can also be ground and used in rich tortes, in pastes such as marzipan and the less sweet almond paste and various fillings and creams.

Shelled almonds are available in several forms: whole, sliced (thin, wide slices off the nut), slivered (cut into little wedge-shaped shards) and ground (sometimes called *almond flour* or *meal*). Whole and sliced almonds may be skinned or blanched. Although the papery amber skins are not bitter, they can be tough in certain recipes and the nuts most often called for in recipes are blanched. Many health food and natural food stores sell sliced, slivered and ground almonds with the skins still on.

To blanch (skin) whole almonds, bring a pot of water to the boil, then drop in the shelled nuts for 30 seconds to 1 minute, depending on the freshness of the nuts. Drain, then plunge the nuts into ice water to stop the cooking. When the nuts are cold, about 2 minutes, drain again and simply slip the skins off. The almonds should then be dried without colouring in a preheated 325° oven for 7 to 10 minutes.

Almond paste is a finely blended mixture of ground almonds and sugar. In some cases, glucose or glycerine replaces part of the sugar for a smoother texture.

Almond extract may be added to intensify the flavour. Almond paste is used extensively in many traditional European pastries, baked goods and confections such as frangipane and macaroons. It should be firm but malleable; if it seems too hard to work with, or becomes dry, heat it in a microwave oven on low power for several seconds. Almond paste is available in tins of several sizes, as well as in plastic-wrapped tubes. The tinned variety has a better flavour and is usually softer and easier to work with than the tubes, but may be difficult to find. You'll find it at gourmet and specialty food shops, European delis or groceries and baking and cake decorating supply stores.

Almond paste should not be confused with *marzipan*, a similar paste confection with a higher ratio of sugar to almonds. Marzipan appears frequently in the baking and confectionery of many European cuisines, as a garnish or petit four on its own, incorporated into cake or biscuit doughs or as an ingredient in fillings for cakes, pastries and confections. It is available from many gourmet and specialty food shops, as well as most good European delis. It should be soft, sweet and moist, with a strong perfume and taste of sweet almonds. When called for in a recipe, ignore the coloured, moulded marzipan shapes and candies and buy plain baker's marzipan.

BRAZIL NUTS Buttery-sweet, tropical Brazil nuts are among the most underappreciated of nuts. They grow in clusters of eight to twenty-four nuts inside a pod the size of a coconut. Their high oil content means they turn rancid extremely quickly, and I'll bet that most of the Brazil nuts the average North American has tasted were on their last legs. This is a tragedy, as this hefty nut has a soft, rich flavour that complements many desserts. Brazil nuts are sold either in the shell or shelled, and I urge you to buy the unshelled sort, as you can be sure of their freshness. Crack the shell with a nutcracker, then chop the large, meaty, half-moon shaped nut before adding it to cakes, muffins and quick breads, tart pastry and confections. The thin brown skin covering the ivory-coloured meat is not bitter and should be left intact. If you are buying shelled Brazil nuts, taste a few to be sure they are not at all bitter or foul, but have a full, sweet flavour.

CASHEWS Cashew fruit are fleshy tropical tree fruit that resemble large misshapen apples. Protruding from the bottom of each fruit is a comma-shaped nugget of meat, enclosed in a tough shell. The fruit is much used in Latin American cuisine, and the nut is what we know as a cashew. Cashews are always sold shelled and roasted, as the outer shell contains a toxic oil, and the nuts must be roasted or bleached to destroy any residue. Raw cashews have very little flavour, but once roasted the nuts take on the rich, smooth, buttery flavour that has made them one of the most delicious nuts around. Although cashews are rarely used in baking and dessert-making in North America, their buttery, mellow flavour lends itself well to recipes including other sweet tropical ingredients, such as dried or fresh tropical fruit, coconut, citrus fruit and white chocolate. Their flavour is subtle enough not to overpower other delicate ingredients, and their texture tends to become chewy and quite soft with cooking or baking.

Cashews are available in a variety of forms, but for most baking and cooking applications *roasted unsalted cashews* are best unless otherwise specified and do not need further roasting before use. Roasted unsalted cashews come whole or in pieces (also called *cashew butts*). They can be regular-sized or jumbo, with the latter being more expensive and not always more flavourful. Taste the nuts before you buy them, as cashews are high in oil and are often sold already old or even rancid.

CHESTNUTS The sweet chestnut has been an important addition to the cuisines of many cultures for centuries. Much less oily and more starchy than other nuts, it is often treated as a vegetable or starch, rather than as a traditional nut. Although it is used extensively in the savoury cuisines of many cultures, its mild, subtle flavour is well suited to many sweet dishes and confections. Chestnuts are often combined with other autumnal flavours, such as cranberries, apples, pears and dried fruits, as well as dark chocolate, vanilla and many liqueurs.

Choose fresh chestnuts with richly coloured, glossy shells and no scars or other blemishes. Although local chestnuts are available in some areas, most of the chestnuts sold in markets in North America are imported from Italy. These tend to be smaller than the local variety, with darker, more greyish-brown shells. Either will do well in any recipe calling for fresh chestnuts. Store fresh chestnuts in a cool, dark place for up to 10 days. Once shelled, chestnuts should be refrigerated in an airtight container and used within 2 or 3 days. Fresh chestnuts need to be shelled and peeled before being used in a recipe. The easiest way I have found is to use the microwave, rather than the old-fashioned method of oven-baking them or boiling. With a very sharp paring knife, slice off the very tip of each chestnut. Turn the nuts over and make a slit in the curved side of each, a straight line down to the cut end. Try to slice through both the hard, outer shell and the papery inner skin, but not into the meat of the nut. Place the

nuts in a single layer on a plate and microwave on high power for 2 to 4 minutes. The nuts should be steaming and the shells peeling back slightly. Allow the
nuts to cool, and the shells and skins should come off easily. If you don't have
access to a microwave, you can use the oven. Slit and cut the chestnuts in the
way described above, then roast in a 350° oven for 15 to 20 minutes, or until hot
and steaming, with the skins starting to fold back. When the nuts have cooled,
pare the shells and skins away, with the help of a knife, if necessary.

Although fresh chestnuts are only available from late fall through to late
winter, they are the base for several products that can be used all year long.
Tinned *unsweetened chestnut purée* is a thick, dryish purée of cooked chestnut
meat, with little or nothing added. It makes an excellent addition to savoury
dishes like mashed potatoes, but can also be used extensively in baking cakes,
yeast and sweet breads and preparing creams, custards and sauces.

Sweetened chestnut purée (also called *crème de marrons*, or *chestnut spread*) is
virtually a dessert in a tin—puréed cooked chestnuts are combined with sugar
syrup and pure vanilla to create a thick, sticky paste that can be simply spooned
out of the can onto a dish of ice cream or used as a component in fillings, creams,
custards and confections. It can be quickly combined with a custard sauce or ice
cream base, folded into whipped cream or even layered with other ingredients
for an easy parfait.

Canned whole chestnuts are widely available, but should be used only where
called for and not substituted for fresh peeled chestnuts. The flavour difference
is marked, and the result will likely be a flat-tasting, bland dessert. Some gourmet food shops sell French *vacuum-packed peeled chestnuts*, and these are a good
bit better than their tinned cousins. Even so, they are very expensive and should
only be used in an emergency—when you simply MUST make a certain dessert
and there is not a fresh chestnut to be found.

Whole chestnuts in syrup are sometimes available from fine food shops and
are really a whole version of the sweetened chestnut purée described above.
With a dab of whipped cream and a drizzle of chocolate sauce, they're everything you could desire for dessert.

Candied chestnuts, also called *marrons glacés*, are delightful confections imported from France. They almost always cost more than the rest of the meal put
together, but are absolutely delicious. Whole peeled chestnuts are very slowly
cooked in a heavy sugar syrup until their moisture is entirely replaced with the
sugar. They become candies more than nuts and are most often eaten as petits

fours at the end of a special meal. If you're looking for a little decadence, however, they are a wonderful ingredient in ice creams and other desserts.

Chestnut flour is made from dried chestnuts ground to a fine powder. It is used in many delicate cakes, cooked cereals, fritters, pancakes and biscuits in northern Italy and can be found in health and natural food stores.

COCONUTS Coconuts are the fruit of the coconut palm, native to Asia, but now also grown in India and South America and almost inextricably associated with Hawaii and the South Pacific. Coconuts are almost as versatile as corn when it comes to their ability to be used in different preparations, in different ways and in different forms. They share with corn the ability to be used in their entirety at virtually every stage of their development. Even the hard shells of the mature nuts can be ground and used in the paving of roads and in building mortar in regions that produce coconuts. *Young fresh coconuts* are rarely available in North America, but are very popular in the regions where they are grown. Coconuts at this stage are green on the outside and have a soft skin, unlike the hard shells they develop later. They are often served simply, with a straw to drink the milky juice, and a spoon to eat the sweet jelly-like flesh. *Mature fresh coconuts* are round, softball-sized nuts made up of five distinct layers. The outer layer is a smooth, leathery skin that has almost always been removed by the time the nuts reach North American markets. The familiar hard, hairy dark-brown shell or husk beneath this conceals a thin, brown, papery skin, which in turn covers the moist white meat or flesh. The final "layer" is the thin sweet juice inside the cavity of the nut.

Coconuts at this stage protect their prize well, but you will be well rewarded for your efforts. Fresh coconut meat is rich and mild, with a unique and recognizable flavour. It blends marvellously with other tropical flavours, as well as with any type of chocolate. Choose a coconut that feels heavy for its size and sloshes happily when shaken next to your ear. Check to make sure there are no signs of mildew or mould. Unopened, a fresh coconut can be stored in a cool, dry place for up to 6 months.

There are three dimples at one end of the slightly oval shell that will yield if poked with a metal skewer or screwdriver. To crack the shell, poke two of the little "eyes" and pour out as much of the watery white liquid as you can. Coconut juice is delicious—and can be chilled for a refreshing drink. (Contrary to popular belief, this liquid is not coconut milk, which I will discuss soon.)

There are two ways to open a coconut—the fun way and the quiet way. For the first, wrap the coconut in a towel and hold it down on a very hard surface, like a walkway or very firm floor. With a mallet or hammer, lightly tap the coconut through the towel until you hear a slightly more hollow sound. Then let loose your frustrations—hit the coconut on this fault until it opens. If you have sensitive neighbours, place the drained coconut in a preheated 400° oven for 15 minutes. Remove it from the oven and hit it with a mallet or hammer to break the shell.

Crack each piece into smaller ones of a manageable size. To separate the white meat from the shell, wedge a dull knife, such as a parmesan cheese wedge, or even a flat-head screwdriver between the meat and shell and pry the two apart. The coarse brown skin can be removed with a vegetable peeler, if desired, but in many cases can be left on, adding a pretty accent of colour. The meat can now be rinsed of any debris, then shaved, shredded or used to make coconut milk. It can be prepared up to 4 days ahead of time and stored well-wrapped in the refrigerator. It can also be frozen for up to 6 months.

The flavour of fresh coconut is incomparable to the stuff that comes in the packages, but is not always practical. *Sweetened dried coconut* has been combined with powdered sugar and is best used for cookies, some cakes, icings, decorations and many confections. *Unsweetened dried coconut* can be used in sweet or savoury recipes and is often called for in baked goods. Packaged coconut, sweetened or unsweetened, comes *shredded*, *desiccated* or *flaked* and sometimes toasted. All forms of packaged coconut keep very well, wrapped airtight at room temperature, but should be kept away from moisture and heat and used within 6 months. Taste them before you use them—if there is a dusty, dull flavour rather than a succulent coconut-rich taste, start with a new package.

Toasting coconut brings a buttery richness to its flavour and gives the ivory flesh a beautiful caramel colour. Toast fresh coconut shavings in a single layer on a baking sheet in a preheated 325° oven for 5 to 10 minutes or until lightly tinged with gold. Any variety of packaged coconut can be toasted in the same fashion, but will likely take less time, perhaps 5 minutes. Watch closely, especially with sweetened types, as these will colour faster.

Fresh coconut milk can be made by soaking freshly grated coconut meat in an equal portion of water. The mixture is simmered gently, then strained, and the solids squeezed through several layers of dampened cheesecloth. The result is a thick, rich creamy liquid, with a sweet coconut flavour that marries well with ingredients as disparate as hot chilies, vanilla beans and bananas. *Coconut cream* is simply a richer, thicker version, made by using four parts grated coconut and one part water. Both of these preparations may be further enriched by using cow's milk in place of the water. Neither one keeps well and may separate slightly if left even for a few hours. A good stir will homogenize the milk again, but both fresh coconut milk and cream should be used as soon after they are made as possible. Coconut milk or cream can be used in savoury stews and sauces, as well as in custards, puddings, ice creams, cakes and fillings.

Both coconut milk and cream are available in tins and are usually of high quality. In addition, some companies have recently developed "light" or "low-fat" versions of coconut milk. Although it is acceptable to replace homemade with tinned, do not substitute milk for cream or "light" milk for regular without being prepared for uncertain results. A thick layer of rich coconut cream will settle on the surface of canned coconut milk if the tin is left undisturbed for a day or two. You can choose how you use the contents: stir the milk before measuring to thoroughly blend the thinner milk and the cream or spoon off the thicker layer for a richer more luxurious product. Store tins of coconut milk and cream in a cool, dark place; once opened, refrigerate in a clean container and use the contents within 2 or 3 days.

Cream of coconut should not be confused with coconut cream, as it is quite a different product, and the two cannot be used interchangeably. Cream of coconut is basically coconut cream sweetened with a high portion of sugar and stabilized with the addition of emulsifiers and preservatives. It is used almost exclusively in the making of tropical drinks such as piña coladas and sometimes in frozen desserts. It is widely available in cans, often in the mixed beverage and syrup section of the supermarket. Store cream of coconut at room temperature; once opened, refrigerate and use within 3 days.

Creamed coconut is yet another product with a frustratingly similar name, yet a very different definition and should not be confused with either coconut cream or cream of coconut. Creamed coconut is coconut meat that has been tightly condensed into blocks. It is meant to be grated or crumbled into warm liquids, where it dissolves and becomes rehydrated. It is available in most supermarkets and in Indian, Asian and Caribbean groceries. Sold in small cartons, it can be stored, unopened, at room temperature indefinitely. Once opened, store airtight in the refrigerator and use within 5 days.

Powdered coconut cream (also called *coconut cream powder*) is made by removing all of the moisture from fresh coconut milk or cream and can be reconstituted to any strength, from very weak to almost a paste. Sold in foil packets and available in many Asian and Southeast Asian markets, it's a good addition to many coconut dishes, sweet and savoury. As the fresh products are extremely perishable, this powdered version is a convenient and quite acceptable substitute, good to have on hand for spontaneous moments. There is somewhat of a flavour compromise if the liquid produced is used to replace all of the coconut milk or cream in a given recipe, but if used to augment the coconut flavour, it can add a depth of flavour and smoothness that makes a good dish great. To give an added boost to custards, puddings, ice creams and cakes, blend just enough warm water or milk into the powder to make a thick paste, then combine this with the other liquids in a recipe.

Coconut sugar is a sweet natural sugar obtained from the sap of the coconut palm. It is very moist, more like a paste honey than a traditional granular sugar in consistency. Used mostly in desserts and confectionery, it can be found in Thai and other Southeast Asian groceries and some natural food stores. If a recipe calls for it specifically, but you cannot find it, substitute an equal amount of light brown or granulated sugar.

HAZELNUTS *(Cobnuts, Filberts)* Although the two terms have come to be used interchangeably, filberts were originally a hardier cultivated version of the wild hazelnut. Today, *cobnut* is the British term for hazelnut. Hazelnuts are acorn-shaped nuts with papery dark brown skins clinging to creamy ivory, round centres. Rich in oils and with a robust, deeply satisfying flavour, hazelnuts are one of the most versatile nuts to use in dessert-making. In my opinion, no other nut complements chocolate as well, and they blend seamlessly with almost any fruit, adding a unique smooth flavour while still supporting the delicate taste of the fruit. They are best lightly roasted and skinned before being used in a recipe. Shelled hazelnuts are available whole, skinned or unskinned, as well as chopped or finely ground. In baking and dessert cookery, they are most often called for both toasted and skinned, which is convenient, as one must toast them in order to properly skin them! To toast, preheat the oven to 350° and spread shelled hazelnuts on a large baking sheet in a single layer. Bake for about 7 to 10 minutes or until nuts are hot to the touch and fragrant. Watch closely, as they burn easily, and shake the pan several times. Transfer the toasted nuts to a bowl lined with a clean kitchen towel, bundle the nuts in the towel and set aside just until nuts are cool enough to handle. Rub the nuts in the towel briskly, then open the bundle and use your fingers to rub the papery skins from the nuts. Don't worry if some of the nuts refuse to be totally (or even partially!) skinned—the toasting has made the tannins in the skin less bitter, and a little bit of the skin will add an attractive colour and depth of flavour.

MACADAMIA NUTS Macadamia nuts are native to Australia, but today the largest plantations are in Hawaii. Perhaps the richest nuts anywhere in the world, they're buttery, devastatingly fattening and decadently expensive. This said, they are a baker's dream. Their mellow, full flavour blends beautifully with other tropical ingredients, such as coconut, lime, banana, mango and papaya, as well as chocolate, especially white chocolate.

Larger than a hazelnut and pale yellow-white, their texture is softly crunchy, to the point of almost being creamy, and they have a flavour like a tropical shortbread cookie. Most reasonable recipes don't call for huge quantities, and there really is no other nut than can replace macadamia's luxurious flavour. Believe me, they are worth the expense!

Macadamias are most often sold lightly roasted and salted for use as a cocktail nut, but some nut shops and natural food stores are importing the raw unsalted nuts. These are best, but if only the salted variety is available, just rinse the nuts quickly under cold water and dry thoroughly before using. They are highly perishable and should be very fresh when used. Store them in the refrigerator in well-sealed bags or jars.

PEANUTS *(Groundnuts, Goobers, Goober Peas, Earthnuts)* Though properly a legume, the humble peanut is probably the "nut" most North Americans know best. The peanut is native to North America and was in fact so prized by the ancient Peruvians that it was buried with the dead. The vast majority of the peanuts cultivated today are grown in the southern United States. Unlike true nuts, the peanut is not tough to crack—a rather soft, webbed pod encases two, usually, though often one and sometimes three or four, papery-skinned seeds. The dark skin is tannic and slightly bitter, but is also highly flavourful and may be left intact for some uses in baking. The two most common varieties are the large oval Virginia peanut and the smaller round Spanish peanut.

The peanut is more often eaten as a snack food than used as an ingredient in baked goods and sweets, but can be an element of many desserts and confections, from cookies to peanut brittle. Chopped peanuts can be added to quick breads and biscuits, and ground peanuts, most commonly in the form of peanut butter, are a wonderful addition to cookies, icings, muffins and ice creams.

Peanuts are sold in a multitude of ways, but generally only *whole roasted peanuts*, usually without the skin, and *peanut butter* are of any real interest to the baker. Most recipes calling for forms of peanuts or peanut butter will be very specific about what type is most appropriate. While in most cases, *unsalted peanuts* are preferable, I love the added flavour chopped salted peanuts add to cookies and brownies. (Make sure when you buy *salted peanuts* for baking, salt is the only addition—many "salted" peanuts are actually highly seasoned with spices, sugar and even MSG.) Similarly, the really junky type of peanut butter with sugar and salt added is better for certain recipes. *Natural peanut butter*, which I far prefer to eat, can separate, making the recipe overly oily and heavy. The processed butters also tend to be richer and sweeter, due to the addition of flavour-enhancing ingredients such as sugar and salt. The best brands for baking have molasses added as well as sugar, imparting a wonderful richness and depth of flavour.

PECANS Native to North America, pecans are the pride and joy of the American South and have been thoroughly woven into the rich dessert tradition of that region. They are used almost exclusively in dessert-making, due to their buttery, slightly bittersweet taste and soft texture. The reddish-brown oval pecan shell contains two halves of the nut meat. Shelled pecans are often sold as *pecan halves*, but are also available *coarsely chopped* and *finely ground*. Pecan skins are virtually impossible to remove, but their slight bitterness is sweetened with a little toasting, and even raw pecans can taste distinctly sweet. They must be very fresh, however, or the bitterness becomes dominant. The meat is crisp and yielding, with a buttery, almost caramel flavour, especially when toasted.

Pecans are a key ingredient in traditional Southern sweets like pecan pie and pralines, but are also wonderful additions to ice creams, nut and fruit breads, cakes and tarts.

Soft, meaty nuts like walnuts and pecans do not need to be skinned, but toasting will make the tannic oils in their thin skins mellow and sweet. Even if a recipe does not specifically call for these nuts to be toasted, I often do so anyway, always pleased with the depth of flavour that results!

PINE NUTS (*Pignoli, Chinese Pine Nut, Indian Nut, Pine Kernels*) Pine nuts are indeed the seeds from pine trees, but not the variety that grows rampant throughout much of Canada and the northern United States. The seeds of the stone pine, pine nuts are cultivated in the Middle East, India, Italy and China. The nuts from each region will have a unique flavour, but all are similar.

Most North Americans were introduced to them through Middle Eastern and Italian dishes such as pesto and couscous, but pine nuts' elusive and delicate flavour can enhance many baked goods, from cookies and biscotti, cakes and tart fillings to confections like nut brittle and pralines. They are a wonderful addition to dishes savoury as well as sweet. Small, ivory-coloured and with an elongated teardrop shape, pine nuts have a sweet, slightly resinous flavour that is enhanced with a very delicate toasting. Care must be taken in order not to scorch the nuts, as their high oil content makes them quick to burn. Highly perishable, pine nuts, unfortunately, are often sold already rancid. They are fairly expensive, and many suppliers do not sell them in great enough quantity to keep a fresh store. Try to buy them from vendors that keep them in the refrigerator and sell their stock quickly. Italian groceries are a good place, as the turnover is likely to be high, and the prices should be reasonable. Use fresh pine nuts within 1 month of purchase and keep them airtight in the refrigerator.

PISTACHIOS The multi-hued pistachio is the great beauty of the nut family. When ripe, the almost impenetrable beige shell of the pistachio cracks open to reveal a purple and green nugget of nut meat. They can be used raw or toasted and can be blanched and skinned to preserve their beautiful colour. Raw pistachios are chewy and delicately flavoured.

Commonly used in the cooking and confectionery of many Arabic and Middle Eastern cuisines, pistachios are slowly catching on in the West as a lovely addition to custards, ice creams, fruit and nut breads and cookies. They have a mild, delicate flavour and a soft texture, and are often chopped and used as a garnish for fruit tarts, compotes and chocolate-dipped confections.

Originally from the Middle East, pistachios are today grown in California, as well as Afghanistan and Turkey. I don't find that the American-grown nuts have the depth of flavour and sweetness of the Middle Eastern varieties, although they may be less expensive, larger and "prettier." Try to find a Middle Eastern grocery that sells fresh pistachios—the price is likely to be good, and the turnover should be high.

Not long ago, the only pistachios most of us had ever seen were dyed a glaring red and heavily salted. According to the pistachio producers, the nuts were originally dyed to make them stand out in the nut world, and the practice has continued for the simple reason that many people now associate the colour with the nut. Needless to say, these are not the nuts to use in baking! Buy unsalted pistachios still in the shells and shell them yourself. (Buy a few extra to reward yourself for your efforts.)

To skin pistachios, remove the nuts from the cracked shells and bring a pot of water to the boil. Drop the nuts into the water and boil for 1 minute; drain, then plunge into ice water. Slip the skins off with your fingers (and a small sharp knife if they are stubborn). Dry the damp nuts in a single layer on a baking sheet in a preheated 325° oven for 5 to 10 minutes, without colouring.

WALNUTS The noble walnut has held a place of honour in the cuisines of cultures all over the world since ancient times. They can be used at all stages of their development. Young immature nuts can be pickled whole, shell and all, and can be used fresh in savoury dishes. Even the shells are not wasted—in walnut-producing regions, they are often finely ground and mixed into the mortar of roads and even houses. But it is the ripe fruit of the walnut tree with which we are most familiar, appearing all over the world in sweet and savoury preparations.

English or *Persian walnuts* are by far the most common, available all over North America throughout the year. Most have a thick, hard, mushroom-coloured shell, but there are a few rare varieties with almost paper-thin coverings. While they can be as small as a hazelnut, most are about the size of a small plum, with two gnarled halves of meat inside the hard tan shell. Walnut skins are rich in tannins, and the nuts benefit from being toasted to bring out their deep woody, winey flavour and succulent texture.

Black walnuts, also called *American walnuts*, are darker than their English cousins, with harder shells and a smoother, more pronounced, more buttery flavour. Grown in California, they are used extensively in baking and dessert cookery. Still a boutique ingredient, they may be difficult to find in many parts of the United States and Canada, but are available in the fall and winter from some high-end specialty food shops and fresh markets.

Shelled walnuts are sold *whole*, in *pieces* (meaning broken halves), *chopped* and *ground*. They go rancid very quickly, becoming musty-flavoured and very bitter, so extra care should be taken to ensure they are fresh. As with most nuts, you'll extend their shell life if you buy them whole and chop or grind them yourself.

Seeds

FLAX SEED The prolific flax plant has been used for thousands of years for its stem, the fibres of which can be spun into rope and cloth, and for the oil extracted from its seeds. Flax seeds, also known as linseeds, are tiny, oval, glossy brown seeds that are enjoying a renewed popularity today due to their extremely healthful nutritional profile. They have mild, nutty flavour and are a great addition to many baked goods. Knead a handful into the dough of a yeast bread or add them to whole-grain quick breads, muffins, pancakes, waffles or homemade granola.

Flax meal is simply finely ground flax seeds and can be purchased or made at home in the food processor.

The high fat content of the seeds makes flax products prone to rancidity. Seeds and flax meal should be stored in an airtight bag or container in the refrigerator. The seeds will keep for about 3 months if fresh when purchased, the meal for about 2 months. Only buy as much as you need and smell the seeds or meal before using. If it smells a little musty or rancid, replace it.

POPPYSEEDS While they do indeed come from the opium-producing poppy flower, poppyseeds, some may be disappointed to learn, don't contain the opium alkaloid that gives heroin, morphine and codeine their characteristic powers, so, as my Austrian baking professor used to say, don't get your hopes up with that second slice of coffee cake. Although most of us are familiar with the blue-black colour, poppyseeds are available in a wide range of hues, from shiny black to dark grey to blue and even white. They have a sweet, nutty and pleasant, slightly bitter flavour that is much enhanced with a light toasting. Just set the seeds in a dry pan over low heat until warm and fragrant. If the seeds are to be further cooked or baked, you can omit this toasting, but it prepares them beautifully for sprinkling on a fresh fruit salad. Crushing the seeds brings out their flavour even more. I prefer recipes in which the poppyseeds are crushed, rather than the ones that recommend soaking the seeds in boiling water to soften them. Either method will work, but I think the flavour is better with the first. When used as a filling for pastries and sweet yeasted coffee cakes, the seeds are crushed and mixed with sweet ingredients such as honey or sugar and often citrus rind. These fillings also often call for a small amount of cocoa or chocolate to be mixed with the crushed poppyseeds, and the combination is very good. Poppyseeds can also be used in cake and cookie batters and in the fillings of pies, tarts, strudels and other pastries.

In North America, they are commonly used to decorate breads and buns, like sesame seeds.

Poppyseeds are very high in oil and can become rancid quickly. They should be stored in airtight plastic bags or jars in the refrigerator and used within 3 months.

Poppyseed oil is a mild pale oil, used in Europe.

Poppyseed filling is a canned processed product intended as a ready-made filling for pastries, tarts, cakes, strudels and cookies. Available in many European groceries, poppyseed filling is fine for use on its own as a shortcut to a home-made dessert, but should not be used to replace any other product in baking. Made from poppyseeds, corn syrup, sugar, corn starch, salt, lemon juice, vanilla and other flavourings, it doesn't have nearly the richness and bright flavour of a homemade filling.

PUMPKIN SEEDS *(Pepitas)* Pumpkin seeds are used extensively in Latin American and Mexican cooking and are popular as a snack. Although they are edible, the white hulls are most often removed when the seeds are to be used in cooking or baking. The flat, oval pale green seed inside is sweet and nutty in flavour and can be added to many savoury dishes, as well as granola, health bars, muffins, quick breads and some healthy crunchy cookies. The seeds are available hulled or unhulled, in which case they need to be hulled at home. They may also be salted, but for baking try to find unsalted seeds. The green seeds benefit from a light toasting in a dry pan until warm and fragrant. They can be used with or in place of other nuts or small dried fruits such as raisins or apricots. Do not substitute them for recipes calling for ground nuts, however. Pumpkin seeds, both hulled and unhulled, are widely available in health and natural food stores, as well as Mexican and Latin groceries and markets. Store them in a cool, dark, dry place for up to 2 months and make sure the seeds are fully dried and crisp before storing if you've dried them yourself.

SESAME SEEDS *(Benne Seeds)* Sesame seeds come from beautiful pink flowers that produce a plethora of both black and white tiny seeds. The seeds ripen at different times, meaning the bulk of the crop must be harvested by hand. Called benne seeds in the American South, sesame seeds have been a popular ingredient in traditional dishes both sweet and savoury in the cuisines of Africa, Asia and the Middle East for centuries. Sesame seeds arrived in North America with African slaves and quickly established themselves in the cooking of the South, most notably in the delicate buttery cookies called benne wafers. Middle Eastern cooks long ago discovered sesame seeds' affinity with sweet ingredients—halvah, a rich and flavourful mixture of sesame seeds, honey and nuts, sometimes accented with dried fruits or chocolate, is one example of their ingenuity.

Sesame seeds have a pleasant, nutty taste that can enhance breads, pastries, biscuits and cakes, either as an ingredient in the batter or dough or, very common in North America, as a topping. Although they are sold raw, they benefit from a light toasting, which brings out a delicious, nutty, buttery flavour, but is unnecessary in cases where the seeds will undergo further baking, such as on breads or crackers.

White sesame seeds are available bleached or unbleached. *Bleached seeds* are the creamy ivory-coloured seeds most of us see on our morning bagel and have a buttery, mild flavour. Health and natural food stores often sell the darker beige to brown *unbleached* or *natural seeds*, which have a slightly nuttier flavour, excellent kneaded into whole grain breads and rolls.

Black sesame seeds are rare in North America, but are widely used in Asian cuisines. Although the flavour is virtually identical to that of natural white seeds, their striking appearance makes them somewhat less versatile in baking and dessert cookery and more suited to savoury foods.

Sesame seed are very rich in oils and are prone to rancidity. They should be stored in an airtight container in the refrigerator, where they will keep up to 3 months if fresh to begin with.

Tahini, or *sesame butter*, is a thick, flavourful paste made from raw or toasted white sesame seeds. It is a staple in the savoury dishes of many Middle Eastern cuisines, such as Baba Ghanouj, but is rarely called for in dessert cookery. It is available from many health and natural food stores, as well as Middle Eastern groceries and even some supermarkets. Refrigerate after opening.

SUNFLOWER SEEDS Native to North America, sunflower seeds are the pale greenish-beige, teardrop-shaped seeds of a large bright yellow flower. They are now grown all over the world, from Russia to Central and Western Europe to many regions of Canada and the United States. The seeds themselves are encased in brittle, black and white striped shells that must be removed before eating. They are sold with or without the shells—the former are likely to be fresher, but the convenience of the naked seeds makes them handier for baking. Either form of the seeds may be salted; consult the recipe as to which type is required. Pleasantly crunchy, sunflower seeds are highly nutritious and have a mild nutty flavour and can be a flavourful addition to granola, cookies and bars, muffins and quick breads, as well as to whole grain breads and rolls.

Sunflower seeds have a funny habit of turning some batters a rather alarming shade of green. They contain chlorogenic acid, which reacts with an alkaline environment to produce this colour. The acid is harmless, and the taste of your baking won't be affected, but if you wish to avoid the St. Patrick's Day effect, try making the mixture more acidic by adding a squeeze of lemon juice or using baking powder in place of baking soda. If you prefer to stay with baking soda, try adding a pinch of cream of tartar to boost the acidity.

Store the seeds in an airtight bag or container, in a cool, dry, dark place or the refrigerator, for up to 3 months.

Fresh Fruit

General Tips for All Fresh Fruit:

❖ For all fruit, buy local whenever possible—the flavour will be infinitely better than fruit that has been harvested too early and subjected to a lengthy journey.

❖ Buy seasonal varieties. Apples are available all year long, but the most flavourful varieties usually have a relatively short peak time. They will reward your attention, however, with often unique and delightful tastes.

❖ Don't wash fresh fruit until you are ready to use it, as moisture accelerates most fruits' demise.

❖ Avoid any fruit that smells of mould, is overripe or is showing signs of mould or damage.

❖ Try to use ripe fruit as soon as possible. Refrigeration can slow deterioration, but most types of fruit reach a peak and quickly pass it. Delicate fruit, such as berries or tropical fruits, are particularly sensitive to cold and do not generally take well to refrigeration. If at all possible, avoid introducing these to the refrigerator, but buy them and use them immediately.

Pome Fruit

APPLES You think you know what an apple is, don't you? Well, the number of types of apples you have eaten, even seen, does not even begin to scratch the surface of this fruit's variety in shape, colour, texture and flavour. There are presently no fewer than several thousand varieties of apple cultivated throughout the temperate areas of the world, not to mention innumerable cross breeds, wild species and unique regional specialties. Apples are an orchard fruit, growing on small, gnarled trees and ripening generally in late summer to late fall. Some varieties are best eaten soon after harvest, while other varieties develop a sweeter, more rounded balanced flavour with several months' cold storage. They may be as small as a lime or as large as a fat grapefruit, and their skins can be almost any colour under the sun, from blood-red, to green, yellow, ivory or beautiful blends of all of these. Some have smooth, shiny skin, others have a dull matte finish and still others have a rough, russety appearance. Sour apples, such as the tiny crabapples that grow wild all over North America, are extremely tart and are always cooked with a healthy amount of sugar before being eaten as jelly, in sauces, or baked as an accompaniment to savoury fare. Most apples available in North American fruit markets and groceries are of the sweet variety, but many are better suited to cooking and baking than to eating raw.

Declaring the best eating apple is a delicate matter, as every apple lover will have a favourite. The best apples for baking and cooking, however, are somewhat more agreed upon. I will preface this section by saying that in every region of the United States and Canada, local apples are available and should always be chosen over long-travelled varieties, if possible. They will be more flavourful and have a superior texture. The following are commonly available varieties, and their close relations, and all are generally reliable and good for a range of uses. They are flavourful, with good texture and juiciness, but each has characteristics that may make them more suitable for a particular dessert. Experiment!

Golden Delicious apples have a pale yellow skin and ivory flesh. They are sweet, crisp and juicy, but, unless they are very good local ones, tend to become overly soft and bland when baked or cooked. *Red Delicious* apples are crimson and thick-skinned and are often waxed. They are good, flavourful eating apples if fresh, but can be mealy and bland as the season wanes and are unsuitable for cooking and baking. *Mutsu* apples are large, very firm and slightly more tart relatives of the Golden Delicious, very good for baking and eating. Bright green *Granny Smith* apples are one of the most popular eating apples around, with a white, juicy, sweet-tart flesh. They make excellent juice and are very good in raw salads, chutneys and salsa, but are not the best baking or cooking apple due to their high moisture content. The expanding family of *Jonathan* and *Idared* apples, including the *Jonagold*, *Jonalicious*, *Jonamac*, *Melrose* and *Monroe* apples, are bright red apples with an appealing, slightly spicy, sweet flavour with a hint of acidity. They are good for both eating and cooking, including pies and cakes, but tend not to stand up well when baked alone. *Northern Spys* are perhaps my favourite pie apple. They are large, muted red and green apples, with a full, sweet-tart flavour and a texture that is perfect for pies, cakes and crumbles. They bake beautifully, holding their shape, yet becoming soft, tender and very fragrant. Along with their relatives, the *Prairie Spy*, *Spygold* and other Spys, they are better for baking and cooking than plain eating, as their pronounced acidity can be difficult to digest raw. The large and popular *McIntosh family* includes, besides McIntosh, *Macoun*, *Empire*, *Cortland* and *Spartan*. This group is usually the first to appear fresh from the harvest in early fall, shiny red skins looking as if they are about to burst with juicy flavour. They are excellent eating apples, their snow-white flesh yielding a lovely sweetness and a pleasant astringency. They make very good applesauce and juice, and the hardier members, such as Empire, Cortland and Spartan, are good in combination with other, drier baking apples in crumbles, cakes and puddings. I find they become too soft and lose some brightness of flavour when used in pies or exclusively in these other desserts. Sweet, crisp *Royal Gala* apples are among the very best for just eating, with a purely sweet and apply flavour. They can be used to add flavour to pies, crumbles, cakes and other desserts, but are not an ideal baking apple on their own. *Russet* apples are easily identified, with a dull or matte finish to their skin and rough, tan or brown patches, called russetting, here and there on the surface. They are often an olive green, but can have blushes of yellow or red as well. Some russet varieties are good eating apples and most of them are excellent for cooking and general baking. If you are lucky enough to find them in your supermarket or fruit market, do give them a try. Sadly, they get nowhere near the attention they deserve, due to their rather "homely" appearance! *Winesap* apples are juicy, tart red-skinned apples with a creamy yellow flesh, perfect for pies and excellent for other baking. *Gravensteins*, which are not available in all areas, are grown mainly on the West Coast with a relatively short peak season, lasting about 2 months in late summer. If you have access to them, however, they are among the best baking apples. They are a bright green brushed with red and have a juicy, sweet and pleasantly acidic flesh that is good on its own, but excellent in pies, tarts, cakes and baked. *Rome Beauties* are large, tart-sweet apples with red skin often flecked with yellow. They are among the best baking apples, especially for baked apples and pies, as their dryish texture and full, tart flavour allow them to stand up to the long period in the oven without becoming mushy or bland.

Low-moisture apples (Gravenstein, Rome Beauty and Spy) are better for desserts that are long-baked such as pies, crisps and cobblers, cakes and baked apple dishes. Quick-baked desserts like sautéed apples or caramelized apple slices are best made with higher-moisture apples such as McIntosh, Empire, Granny Smith, Royal Gala and Cortland. I think there's no better pie apple than the Canadian Northern Spy, but occasionally I combine a number of different varieties for a more complex flavour and texture.

Buy apples in season! There are undoubtedly several good, local varieties available at any time of the year in your local market—seek them out, taste as many as you can and experiment. Ask your fruit vendor for advice; any good merchant will gladly tell you which are the best and for which purpose at any given time. In the fall, head for the weekend farmers' markets in your area, and you may find treasures of rare, heirloom or regional varieties, with proud growers anxious to tell you the best way to treat each variety. When buying any apple, look for taut, firm skin, with no bruises or blemishes. Patches of rough russetting are harmless, but avoid fruit with deep gouges or cracks. Soft-type apples will have a delicate scent near the stem. Apples can be stored at room temperature, but they last longer if refrigerated. Once past their prime, the skin will tend to wrinkle as the fruit dehydrates, and the flesh will become increasingly dry, mealy and pulpy.

Apple sauce is a great ingredient in baking, adding a delicate flavour and wonderful moisture to cakes, quick breads, even cookies. The best apple sauces are easily homemade, but there are dozens of good prepared versions on the market. Try to find an unsweetened apple sauce, ideally with no preservatives. Some manufacturers have begun not only to name the variety of apple used in the sauce, but to make several different sauces using various types of apple. This gives the cook (or toddler) the opportunity to choose the flavour they like best for each application.

Dried apples are available in health or natural food stores and are discussed in detail in the Dried Fruits section (page 319).

Apple butter is a thick paste made by slowly cooking down apples, usually without sugar. The resulting spread is amber-coloured and thick enough to spread on toast and is often used as a simple filling for cakes, cookies and other pastries, as well as an ingredient in many baked goods. It is wonderful simply spread on pancakes, muffins, quick breads and toast and makes a great glaze for roast chicken! Apple butter is a popular Mennonite product and is often available in farmers' markets and natural food stores. It is also sold in many good supermarkets as well. Read the label carefully and choose pure products, not those compromised with artificial ingredients.

Fresh apple cider is simply the juice pressed from apples and may be fermented into the spirit known as *hard cider*. Indeed, apple cider ferments very easily and must be very fresh when consumed. It should be pasteurized to kill any bacteria and is best sold and stored in opaque plastic jugs to allow for expansion. Apple cider has a rich, full apple flavour and is usually unsweetened, although it may still be very sweet depending on the type of apples pressed. It is marvellous in desserts of all kinds, as the liquid in cakes and other baked goods or even reduced to a thick sweet syrupy glaze for tarts, pies, even ice cream. The syrup has an intense apple flavour and can be used to flavour mousses, icings, custards and baked goods. For best results, buy cider in the fall from a store with a big turnover or, better yet, from the orchard itself!

PEARS Pears have become one of the most common fruits in the world, with upwards of fifteen hundred varieties available! Indeed, even in North America, there are hundreds of types of pear grown, from the common Bartlett to rare heirloom varieties grown by a few passionate farmers. Pears look similar to apples, but have a lovely plump bottom and a more slender rounded top. They have a thin, edible skin, but this can be pared away easily for recipes where it is not desired, as with poached pears, or in some pie or tart fillings. They should be peeled at the last minute, or dipped in acidulated water or lemon juice to prevent the delicate flesh from turning brown. Pears have a subtle but sweetly perfumed flavour reminiscent of honey, apples and even citrus, that marries well with many flavours, especially chocolate, ginger, nuts, port and other liqueurs and most wines. They are most often cooked when used in desserts; the slightly grainy or pulpy texture of the raw flesh smoothes out beautifully when poached, baked or incorporated into batters and pastries. Look for firm, heavy, unblemished fruit; a ripe pear will yield slightly when pressed, but many pears are only available underripe. They can be ripened at home at room temperature. Refrigerate when ripe to extend the pears' keeping abilities. Harvested during the summer and early fall months, pears are always picked unripe and can be cold-stored in much the same way as apples. For that reason, many varieties are available all year long, although some rarer types may have a more limited season. North American varieties are fresh from about mid-August to late October and from cold-storage from November to January or February.

Although many regions of North America have seasonally available and rare varieties of pears in their fall markets, many of the best varieties for baking and cooking are widely available year-round throughout the United States and Canada. *Bartlett pears* are the perhaps the most popular, both for baking and eating. In fact, they are the pear most of us picture when we think "pear." When ripe, its green skin turns a pale yellow, and it becomes juicy, very sweet and flavourful. *Red Bartlett pears* are similar, but deepen to a bright red when ripe. *Bosc pears* have a mottled greenish-brown skin and a long, slender shape. They are firmer-fleshed and slightly less sweet than other varieties, perfect for cooking and baking into batters and doughs, where their dry, firm texture will not dampen the dough and where they will keep their shape. Lovely *d'Anjou pears* (also called simply *Anjou*) are round and large, with pale yellow-green skin. The flesh is sweet and mild, with a beautiful scent, and is excellent for eating, poaching and in tarts and other baking. *Clapp pears* look similar to Bartletts, but their skin turns a deep gold when ripe. Their flesh is extremely sweet, and they are good all-around eating and baking pears. The tiny Italian *Forelle pears* are delightfully flavourful, with a delicate sweetness, and are made for dessert, either gently poached or just as they are as an accompaniment to cheese, walnuts and port. They are about one third the size of regular pears, with a greenish yellow skin that becomes flecked with red, orange and gold as they ripen. *Flemish Beauty pears* are large soft-fleshed pears with a thick, yellow skin that becomes mottled with red when ripe, and which should be removed before cooking or baking. Small *Seckel pears* are bottle-green and russetted, with a sweet, creamy yellow flesh. They may be hard to find in certain regions, but are well worth the effort. Seckel pears are perfect for poaching and make beautiful tarts.

Pear butter is very similar to both apple and plum butter (see page 325), made from pears that have been slowly cooked down to a thick, sweet paste. It is most often unsweetened, relying on the natural sugars in the pears for sweetness. Wonderful as a breakfast spread on toast, pancakes and muffins, pear butter can also be used as a filling for cookies, cakes, tarts and other pastries. Many traditional Mennonite and other old-fashioned cakes calling for apple butter can be made with pear butter for a slightly different taste. In recent years, all three of these fruit pastes have been incorporated into the world of low-fat baking. They can be used to replace some of the fat such as butter or oil in some (*some*, not all!) recipes for simple cakes and quick breads. The fruit butters add moisture and compensate for some of the tenderness lost in the absence of the fat.

Canned pears tend to be overly syrupy, leaving little room for the real taste of pear, and are often very mealy. They are fine in baked goods such as cakes and quick breads or mashed and used to replace apple sauce or other purées, but should not be used in pies, tarts, crumbles and the like.

Dried pears can be found in health and natural food stores and are discussed in the section on Dried Fruits on page 324.

QUINCES Without a doubt, my favourite fruit. Quinces are large yellow fruits, similar in shape to a very large, slightly fattened apple. They are a rich butter yellow when ripe, usually covered in a fine, white down. Their powerful, intoxicating aroma winds its way through the whole house, perfuming the air with a heady, sweet, almost floral scent. They are totally inedible when raw, however, with a dull, bland flavour and a hard, woody texture. Quinces must be cooked slowly, but will reward you by turning a lovely rosy pink and assuming an even more divine flavour than their perfume promises. They are very high in natural pectin and are often used to make jelly, jam and preserves. They should be peeled and cored before using, but the peels and the core material can be added to the poaching liquid to add pectin and flavour, then strained out. My favourite way of cooking quince flesh is poaching in a sugar syrup flavoured with cinnamon sticks, honey or other sweet or even savoury spices. Poached quince can be used in many dishes, much as one would use poached pears or even a soft raw fruit, like apples. Many savoury ingredients marry beautifully with the slightly spicy, honeyed flavour of the quince, and it is often used in Middle Eastern or Mediterranean cooking. But it truly shines as a fruit for baking. Pies, tarts, bread puddings, pastries, trifles, ice creams, puddings and fruit compotes all show off the rich, sweet, complex flavour of this magnificent fruit. For instructions on preparing and poaching quince, see page 595.

Quinces are available for a relatively brief period during the end of fall and the early winter. Choose firm, heavy fruit with no signs of green or wrinkling on the skin. They should have a pronounced, exotic aroma near the stem, with no bruises or blemishes. Quinces may be stored in a plastic bag in the refrigerator for up to 2 months if very fresh when purchased.

Stone Fruit

APRICOTS Apricots look like tiny oval peaches and have the same velvety skin, with a colour ranging from pale yellow-orange to a vibrant orange-red. They have a large, smooth stone that falls out easily as soon as the ripe fruit is halved along its seam in most varieties, although there are a few rare clingstone types. Apricots may be skinned in the same fashion as peaches (see Peaches). Available for a brief period in June and July, apricots are a fleeting luxury. They are easily damaged and cannot be stored well, so should be taken full advantage of during their brief season. Choose plump, smooth-skinned fruit with a sweet scent that yield slightly to a light touch. They should feel heavy for their size and be a deep, vibrant orange, with no soft patches, bruises or scars. Like peaches, apricots tinged with green or that are very hard will not ripen and will be unpalatably bland or tart. Store slightly underripe fruit at room temperature for several days until slightly soft and aromatic, then refrigerate for up to 5 days. Apricots have a pronounced honeyed flavour, with a marked acidity that makes them excellent for both cooking and baking. They can be poached, used in pies and tarts and cooked into jams, preserves and compotes.

Canned apricots are acceptable in certain recipes in a pinch but only if the fresh fruit is unavailable.

Apricot pits are the small, almond-like centres of apricot stones. Rarely if ever called for in North American recipes, they are a wonderful source of flavour. In fact, Amaretto, the famous almond liqueur, is made from a combination of bitter almonds and apricot pits. Save the stones during apricot season and experiment a little. Finely grated, the pits add a delicious accent to desserts such as cakes, frangipane fillings for tarts and other pastries and muffins. They have a delicate, slightly floral Amaretto-like flavour, which complements apricot, peach, almond and citrus flavours beautifully, and they can be used anywhere ground almonds are combined with fruit. Use a hammer or cleaver to carefully crack open the stones. Grate the pits on the finest side of a box grater and use one or two for a standard frangipane or cake recipe.

For information on *dried apricots*, see Dried Fruits, page 319.

CHERRIES If rhubarb means the end of winter, and the first strawberries mean spring is finally here, then cherries are a joyous sign that summer is upon us. They are one of the early summer fruits, available in most of North America in late spring and often through to late summer. Cherries grow from delicate stems on small orchard trees and are usually between the size of a hazelnut and a walnut. Plump, shiny and nearly perfectly round, they have firm juicy flesh that surrounds a single, hard pit. Cherries can be divided into two categories: sweet and sour, and there are several varieties of each commonly available in most North American markets.

Sweet cherries come in a huge variety of colours from deep, blood-red, chocolate brown or almost black like the delicious *Bing*; to bright butter yellow to the beautiful dual-toned *Royal Ann*, which are mostly yellow with blushes of crimson or orange. Sweet cherries are best enjoyed just as they are, but can be used successfully in many desserts, such as pies, cobblers, ice creams and even quick breads. If you are replacing sour cherries with sweet, add a good squeeze of lemon juice and consider reducing the amount of sugar in the recipe. Choose plump, glossy cherries that are firm to the touch, but evenly deep-coloured. Soft or mushy cherries are either bruised or decaying.

Sour cherries are most commonly used for desserts and other cooking, their bright tangy acidity tempering with cooking and bringing out a deep, fresh flavour. There are two types of sour cherries—those grown on trees like sweet cherries and those that grow on thick bushes. The tree varieties are much more common in North America, with the bush type being cultivated in certain areas of Europe. The richly flavoured *Morello cherry* is often considered to be the king of sour cherries in this part of the world, perfect for pies, cobblers, preserves and the wonderful French custard-pancake *clafouti*. Sour cherries are usually slightly paler than sweet varieties, with shades ranging from crimson to bright orange-red to yellow-orange and even white. Choose firm, shiny sour cherries with no signs of bruising, softness or splitting on the skin. Store both types of fresh cherries loosely covered, wrapped in paper towels, in the refrigerator for up to 3 days.

Canned cherries, both sweet and sour, are available, but are a poor imitation of the fresh fruit, and I don't recommend using them at all.

Preserved sour cherries, usually sold in glass jars or bottles, are often very good on their own, as a dessert topping or a base for a filling or sauce.

Maraschino cherries, otherwise known as *candied* or *glacé cherries*, are discussed in the section on Candied Fruits, page 327.

Dried sweet and *sour cherries* are becoming increasingly available as they rise in popularity and are discussed in the section on Dried Fruits, page 320.

NECTARINES The nectarine is a cross between a peach and a variety of plum, created to produce something that tastes like a peach, without the furry skin. Nectarines are similar to peaches in appearance and flavour, with bright yellow-orange skin that becomes tinged with red when the fruit is ripe. The flesh is firmer than that of peaches and has a slightly more acidic edge and an easily removed stone. Nectarines are hardier than peaches and are often sold ripe, as they are not as prone to bruising. A ripe nectarine will yield slightly to the touch and smell perfumed and sweet. Like peaches, nectarines will not ripen appreciably after they are picked, so avoid those that are tinged with green or overly firm. Store nectarines at room temperature unless very ripe, then refrigerate and use promptly. Nectarines can be stoned and skinned in the same way as peaches (see below).

PEACHES Peaches are one of the most sensuous fruits, with their soft, velvety skin, their abundantly juicy, honey-sweet flesh and their fragrant, summery aroma. Still warm from the sun, heavy in your hand just plucked from the tree, there is no more perfect fruit. Fortunately, they can be almost as good picked by someone else, eaten unadorned or laced with whipped cream or baked into a thick pie or crumble. The average peach is about the size of a medium apple, although some varieties are as small as an egg or as large as a navel orange. All peaches have one large stone at their hearts. Peaches are usually divided into two groups, freestone and clingstone, the difference being how easily the stone is removed from the ripe flesh. Most early harvested peaches are of the clingstone variety, and the flesh will need to be pared away with a sharp knife. Free stone peaches are a cook's delight and make easy work of a good jam or pie. The most common varieties of peaches are yellow-orange in colour, sometimes tinged with green when underripe, becoming a deep gold, orange, even red when fully ripe, with a bright orange flesh, often laced with red right near the stone. *White peaches* are becoming more available for limited periods towards the end of the summer and are divinely delicate, with a sweet, subtle flavour. They are less intensely flavoured than orange peaches, but are wonderful in simple preparations such as poached and served with a syrup or nestled into a buttery tart crust.

Choose heavy, taut-skinned fruit, the larger the better, as larger peaches are generally more mature, riper and sweeter than small examples of the same variety. The colourful blush of many varieties is not an indication of ripeness—

look instead at the paler background colour. This should be rich golden amber on orange-skinned peaches or ivory on white peaches. When ripe, the flesh will yield to the touch, but don't prod your peaches any more than you have to or you will bruise the flesh. Ripe peaches are very fragile and bruise easily. Slightly underripe peaches can be ripened at home at room temperature; refrigerate the fruit as soon as it is fragrant and a little softened, but use as soon as possible. Do not bake, cook or poach underripe peaches, as they do not benefit from it and will remain hard, flavourless and even bitter. Peaches tinged with green are very underripe and will not ripen further off the tree. They should be avoided. Overripe peaches are not much better, becoming woolly and pulpy if left to get too soft.

In general, the early-season peaches are sweeter and less acidic than those available in late July and August and are best for just eating, drizzled with maple syrup or simply sliced as an accompaniment to a fresh pound cake or a good homemade ice cream. Late-season varieties tend to have a better flavour for baking, with the higher acidity balancing the potent sweetness. For pies, cobblers and other baked desserts, nothing beats the fruit that ripens at this time of the year. Try to buy locally grown peaches, as with all fruit. You will be rewarded with a sweeter, juicier, more full-flavoured fruit, and likely less expensive than long-travelled varieties.

Peaches have an indented seam along one side, conveniently located along one edge of their stone. To stone a peach, cut around the fruit beginning on this seam, following the line all the way around. Twist the two halves apart and remove the stone from the side in which it is imbedded. This little trick works only with ripe, freestone peaches; with under- or overripe fruit you may end up with a bit of a pulpy mess.

In most recipes, peaches are called for without the skin. To remove the skin from a peach, submerge it in boiling water for 20 to 40 seconds, depending on the ripeness, then plunge it into a bowl of ice water to stop the cooking. I find this the perfect time to halve and stone the fruit, before the skin is removed, so you can get a grip on the flesh to twist the halves apart. The skin should then slip off easily.

Peaches marry well with other sweet ingredients, such as brown sugar, maple syrup or other sweet fruit, but also stand up to contrasting tart flavours. Sour cherries, dried cranberries, orange and lemon all accent the ripe peach's sweetness and full flavour.

Canned peaches are widely available, and a good brand will make an acceptable pie in a pinch, but they are no match for the fat, sweet, fresh flavour of the real thing.

Dried peaches can be found in health and natural food stores and are discussed in the section on Dried Fruits, page 324.

PLUMS Wild and sweet, plums of hundreds of varieties flourish all over North America. Their complex flavour, sometimes honey-sweet, sometimes citrus-tart, often a delicate balance between the two, makes them one of the most rewarding eating fruits, but also perfectly suited to baking and dessert cookery. Plums are smooth-skinned tree fruit, with one large smooth stone in the centre of translucent, juicy and aromatic flesh. They can be as small as a walnut or as large as a small apple, often with a slightly oval shape, although some types are perfectly round. The thin skin can range from dark blue, to purple, red, yellow, green and pink, and the flesh can be yellow, ivory, dark reddish-blue or green. The flavour of plums can range from syrupy sweet, in what are usually called *sweet* or *dessert plums* to the very acidic bite of *sour plums*. Dessert plums can be eaten raw or used in many desserts, from tarts to crumbles and bettys to ice creams and compotes, and are frequently dried (see Prunes, page 324). Sour varieties are usually reserved for pickling, canning and savoury dishes, as well as in the making of brandies and other spirits. The thin skin of even sweet plums is often much more acidic than the inner flesh and can be left on or removed, depending on the degree of sweetness and tartness desired. Since the skin contains much of the acidic enzymes, it may be pared away before eating raw, if desired, but I don't generally recommend skinning plums for most dessert applications, as so much flavour is lost with the skin. In most situations where the fruit will be cooked or baked, heat neutralizes the strongest acids, leaving a sweet and balanced flavour.

Although plums are available from late May to October, the prime season for local plums is actually quite short, about one month for each variety, and occurs from June through late August. Select plums that are smooth and taut-skinned, with no wrinkled or blemished areas on the skin. They should feel heavy in the hand, a sign of ripeness and juiciness, and give slightly to a gentle pressure, especially near the stem. Overly soft or mushy plums are likely overripe. Store slightly underripe plums at room temperature until they yield to a gentle touch, but don't expect them to ripen much—plums must be mature when they are picked, as they don't develop and sweeten off the tree. Unfortunately, cooking and baking do nothing to bring out the underripe plum's latent sugars, and you'll only end up with a dull-tasting dessert or, worse, a sour one. Keep ripe plums in a plastic bag in the refrigerator and use within 4 or 5 days.

Among the most commonly available varieties in North America is the small, egg-shaped *Italian blue plum*, often falsely labelled *Damson* (true damsons have no centre line and are actually a close cousin to the true plum). Italian blue plums are one of the most popular plums for eating and baking alike. They have a bluish-purple skin and a deep yellow-red flesh. Sweet and nicely tangy, they are excellent in most desserts, from tarts to baked plums to crumbles and pies. *Greengage plums* are available for a brief few weeks at the end of the summer, and are a treat if you can get them. Plump and round with a vibrant green skin, they have a sweet, juicy flesh that is lovely in any recipe calling for plums, especially nut tarts and compotes. *Mirabelle plums* are tiny, fine-flavoured plums with greenish-yellow skin and a perfectly round shape. Available for the same brief period as greengages, they make a wonderful cooked plum, for fillings, purées and compotes.

The variety of plums is so staggering, and varies so widely from region to region, that no list could hope to be complete or very accurate in describing them. The best advice I can give is head to a good fruit market, buy a single plum of several varieties and try them all. Decide for yourself which type you like best for eating, which would make the best pie and which is perfect for jam. Then go back and buy what you need. Be aware that you may have to vary the amount of sugar and acid called for in a recipe depending on the type of plum you use. Very sweet varieties will not need as much sugar, but may benefit from a squeeze of lemon juice, while tart varieties may need extra sweetener, but no additional acid.

For information on *prunes* and *plum butter*, see the section on Dried Fruits, page 324.

Berries and Grapes

If possible, buy locally grown berries. They will undoubtedly be fresher, but also sweeter, juicier and more flavourful than those that have travelled for days or even weeks. In all cases, choose firm, plump berries with no mushy or soft patches and no signs of mould or excessive moisture. If you notice mould on one berry, immediately remove it from the bunch, as mould spreads rapidly.

Washing at the last minute, not as soon as you get them home, is particularly important with berries. Even then, very delicate berries such as raspberries should only be washed if they are dusty or have been sprayed with growing pesticides or other chemicals. To wash berries, simply rinse them quickly under cold running water and immediately blot as dry as possible on paper towels. Berries with the hulls intact, such as strawberries, should be washed before they are hulled, to minimize the amount of water they absorb.

Berries do not ripen after they are picked, so they must be picked when ripe, then shipped, sold and used quickly. Berries that have travelled far are often hardy cultivated hybrids, pumped full of steroids and preservatives to prolong their life. Try to limit your purchase of berries to the short season they are each available locally and freeze them to use throughout the year. Some gourmet and specialty food shops freeze large quantities of local and even wild berries in season, then sell them during the off-months.

Most berries freeze very well, but strawberries tend to become mushy and pulpy when frozen. Freeze fragile berries in a single layer on a baking sheet until solid, then transfer to a freezer bag or a container just big enough to hold them. Seal airtight and use the berries within 6 to 8 months.

If you are not planning to use fresh berries within a day, refrigerate them for up to 3 days, loosely surrounded by paper towel to absorb any excess moisture, ideally in a single layer. Shrivelled or soft berries are too old and very prone to mould.

BLACKBERRIES *(Brambles)* Plump, shiny blackberries have a shape and appearance similar to a magnified black raspberry. They are a glossy purple-black and have a wonderful sweet-tart flavour that gets sweeter as the berry ripens. Wild blackberries are smaller than cultivated varieties, but are becoming almost impossible to buy. Fortunately, wild blackberries flourish in temperate northern climates, such as the northern United States and most of Canada, and the brambly bushes are relatively easy to find and pillage! If picking your own isn't an option, choose fat, evenly dark blackberries whose hulls have been removed, as any that still have the hulls attached were picked underripe and will likely be sour. Check the container for signs of crushed berries, mould or other damage. Blackberries freeze well and can then be used in sauces, purées and even some crumbles, cobblers and pies.

Dewberries are a variety of blackberry that grow on long, hanging vines. They are not cultivated.

Youngberries are a plump dark-red cousin to the blackberry, possibly native to Africa. They have a similar sweet, juicy, tart flesh and can be used in the same way as other types of blackberries.

BLUEBERRIES Blueberries are small, round, shiny dark-purple berries with a juicy sweet flavour and a faint tang. *High-bush berries* are cultivated in New Zealand and other temperate countries and are fatter and lighter in colour than the low-bush variety. *Low-bush blueberries* grow wild in much of the northeastern United States and Canada, and are smaller, sweeter and more intensely flavoured than the large imported berries. *Domestic cultivated blueberries*, also called *hothouse blueberries*, to look at are much like the high-bush type, large and plump with a dusty dark blue colour, but have a disappointingly bland flavour. If possible, ignore the cultivated berries in favour of the fantastic wild type— you will notice the difference in everything from your pancakes to homemade ice cream. Wild blueberries are a hardy bunch, and are usually available locally during July and August, depending on the region.

When buying blueberries, choose plump berries with few or no crushed ones in the carton. They should be evenly dark bluish purple, with a dusting of grey or silver, which indicates freshness. If the berries are labelled as wild, look for a few stems and tiny green leaves among the berries, a sure sign of wild harvest. Store unwashed berries loosely covered at room temperature if they are to be consumed within a day or in the refrigerator wrapped in paper towel for up to 3 days.

Blueberries freeze extremely well—there's nothing like warm wild blueberry muffins or pancakes in the middle of winter! A word of caution: frozen berries have a tendency to turn some batters an odd shade of green. This occurs in alkaline conditions, as in batters with baking powder as the leavener and no acidic ingredients such as buttermilk or lemon juice. You can minimize the problem by making sure the berries are frozen solid and are folded in quickly and gently, but the best prevention is the introduction of an acid: buttermilk or yogurt can be substituted for milk or cream, or lemon juice may be added. To avoid an overly tangy finished product, consider replacing the baking powder with baking soda, using a 1:4 ratio (1 part baking soda for every 4 parts baking powder called for). The acidic ingredient will activate the baking soda, which in turn will neutralize any imbalance in flavour, and your berries will remain true blue. In recipes where you don't want to change the flavours, try to use fresh berries, which are much less

likely to affect the colour if mixed in quickly and delicately. If using frozen blueberries, be aware that they can also break down and turn the batter completely
purple if they are mixed in too much. Do not thaw the berries before adding them
to batters and be very gentle when folding them in. Add them at the last minute
and in the case of pancakes or waffles, wait until the cake is already cooked on one
side before sprinkling the batter with the frozen berries. For information on *dried
blueberries*, see Dried Fruits, page 320.

BOYSENBERRIES A recent addition to the berry family, this hybrid was created
by crossing the raspberry, the blackberry and the loganberry. Boysenberries are
larger than raspberries, with the same plump shape of the blackberry, and a
deep blue-red colour. Their juicy, sweet-tart flavour makes them excellent substitutes for any similar berry, and they are very good on their own. Available
during July and August, boysenberries should be selected, stored and used as
for other berries of the same type.

CAPE GOOSEBERRIES *(Ground Cherry, Physalis, Golden Berry, Poha)* These gol-
den-orange orbs are one of the most elegantly packaged fruits on earth. Each
little berry comes wrapped loosely in a dry, lacy cage, similar to a sheer Chinese
lantern. The leaves of this casing must be peeled back before the fruit can be
plucked out and used, but you will be loath to completely sever the fruit from
its home when you see how exquisite the two look with the filigreed leaves flowering out behind the bright berry. It is for this reason that even during the brief
time fresh cape gooseberries are available, they are most often used as much as a
decoration or petit four on their own, rather than as a traditional dessert ingredient. They can be opened, the leaves of the cage lightly dusted with confectioners'
sugar or the fruit dipped in white or bittersweet chocolate, and served as part of
a fruit and nut platter. They also make spectacular decorations for cakes and
tarts, maximizing the effect of each fruit. They are beautiful enough not to need
a flavour, but they have quite a lovely one, tasting faintly of things tropical,
coconut, citrus, pear and melon. Although they can be cooked and made into
jams, jellies and preserves, as well as pie and tart fillings, I don't find it enhances
their delicate flavour, and it is a shame to waste their unusual beauty.

Local cape gooseberries are available in many parts of North America in late
summer and early fall, but very good imported berries arrive from Hawaii,
Australia, New Zealand and other subtropical regions beginning in March or
April, then disappear around the time the native varieties come out. Choose

plump, shiny berries with the cages intact and use them as soon as possible. If you must, store them very loosely covered in the refrigerator for up to 2 days.

CLOUDBERRIES The golden, raspberry-like cloudberry grows wild in harsh, northern climates in North America such as Newfoundland, as well as parts of Europe, especially Scandinavia. They have a much more acidic tang to their flavour than other similar-looking berries and are always cooked before eating. They make highly flavourful jams and preserves and can be combined with sweet ingredients such as other fruit, honey and maple syrup in pies, tarts, crumbles and fools. Cloudberries are not cultivated, but are sometimes available in farmers' markets. Otherwise, it means a trip to the bush with a basket! Choose deep-golden berries that come off the hull easily, with no signs of mould or shrivelling.

COWBERRIES A wild member of the cranberry family, these are smaller, dark red berries with a similar flavour and acidity. They must be cooked and are most often used in sauces, jellies and pies.

Lingonberries are probably the most famous variety of cowberries, cultivated widely in Scandinavia, but growing wild in many parts of New England, Canada and even Russia. They have a tart, intense cranberry-like flavour and are often used to make sweet and savoury preserves, as well as jams, jellies, juices, cordials and some baked goods. Wild lingonberries should be chosen and stored as for cranberries.

Canned or preserved imported lingonberries are available in some European delis and specialty food stores (and at Ikea!), but are generally reserved for sauces and purées. Prepared imported lingonberry sauces, syrups and jellies are very good, however, and make a nice change from more common types of syrup and preserves.

Partridgeberries, also called *foxberries* or *mooseberries*, are a native variety of cowberry, very similar in appearance, flavour and use to lingonberries. Always wild, they can be substituted for lingonberries or cranberries in many recipes in which the tart berries will be cooked before eating.

CRANBERRIES These hard, round, shiny red berries grow in marshy bogs, covering the entire surface of the water with a tarp of glossy red when they ripen. They are cultivated almost exclusively in North America, although Finland does produce a small harvest. Tart and vibrantly flavoured, cranberries are one of the few berries that absolutely must be cooked before eating. Due to their mouth-puckering sourness, they are often paired with rich savoury fare, such as holiday roasts and heavy sauces. Their fresh, bright flavour makes wonderful desserts, however, especially in combination with sweeter ingredients such as apples, brown sugar, oranges, pears and rich dried fruit.

Cranberry season in North America is between October and December, and standard-sized 12-ounce bags of fresh cranberries are available in most fruit markets and even supermarkets. When buying cranberries, choose bags that have mostly uniformly red berries, as white or green ones are underripe. They should be plump, shiny and firm, not shrivelled or mushy. Cranberries keep beautifully—well-wrapped in plastic, they can be stored in the refrigerator for up to 2 months and can be frozen from 9 months to 1 year.

Frozen cranberries are quite easy to find and make a very acceptable substitute for the fresh berries, as they all need to be cooked or baked anyway.

Canned or frozen cranberry sauce is a prepared product and not intended for baking.

Dried cranberries, sweetened or *natural*, are in vogue these days and are excellent additions to cookies, sweet and quick breads, cakes and compotes. Use them instead of fresh cranberries in muffins, or in place of raisins, currants and other dried fruit. Dried cranberries are further discussed in Dried Fruits, page 321.

BLACK-, WHITE- AND REDCURRANTS The berry type of currant should not be confused with the dried, raisin-like fruit with the same name, actually the dried form of the Zante grape (see Dried Fruits, page 321). Fresh currants may be black, white or red, each with a slightly different flavour. All are small, shiny round berries that grow on beautifully draping little stems, each so heavily laden with berries it looks like a jewelled garland. For this reason, currants are often used plain or dipped in egg white and sparkling sugar to decorate cakes, tarts and dessert platters. Deep indigo-coloured *blackcurrants* are often sold off the stem and have a more tart and astringent flavour than the other two varieties. For this reason, they are virtually always used cooked, in preserves and jams, pie fillings or a cooked purée for fools and ice creams. Their intense flavour is the basis for the famous Cassis liqueur. *Whitecurrants* are almost transparent, with a sheer, pale skin. *Redcurrants* are a bright crimson red and, like whitecurrants, are usually sold on their garland-like stems. The stems should be removed for cooking and eating. Both white- and redcurrants can be eaten fresh-picked, but are very good in preserves, jams or jellies, pie and tart fillings, even fruit compotes and salads. Buy a few extra to use as decoration—you can't make anything this beautiful!

Fresh currants are available from late spring to late summer. Choose plump, shiny berries, with no signs of shrivelling, mould or being crushed. Store loosely covered in the refrigerator for up to 3 or 4 days or freeze as for other berries for up to 6 months. Frozen currants should be reserved for purées, preserves and compotes.

ELDERBERRIES AND ELDERFLOWERS The small, dark purple or blue currant-like elderberries have been an integral part of the British culinary tradition for hundreds of years and are widely used in many other areas of Europe. They are quite tart on their own, but make wonderful jams, jellies, wines and cordials, as well as ice creams and sorbets. Elderberries grow wild in much of North America, but are so little used you will likely have to pick them yourself. Pick firm but very dark berries, as pale or still green ones are underripe. Look for ripe elderberries in wild gardens, on roadsides and in meadowlands during the summer and early fall. The tiny, lacy white *elderflowers* have a highly perfumed aroma, similar to the flavour of lychee and melon. They are traditionally used to make wine, cordial and jellies, but can also be dipped in light batter and deep-fried as a delicate and unusual dessert. The flowers precede the berries by several weeks, usually blooming between early to midsummer and early fall.

Both the berries and the flowers have an affinity for honey, gooseberries and rhubarb and are often paired with these ingredients in desserts, sweets and beverages.

GOOSEBERRIES Much more popular in Europe than in North America, goose-berries are large, tart berries with spidery, ivory-hued veins just visible under the sheer, transparent skin. They can be olive green, white, red and yellow or gold, but the most common is the green variety. In North America, they are available in July and August, but you may have to search farmers' markets or specialty fruit shops to find them, as they are all but ignored here. A shame, considering their success in desserts such as pies, crumbles and the famous gooseberry fool, as well as preserves and jellies. Choose firm, shiny berries of a uniform size, with no signs of wrinkled or crushed skin. Store them loosely covered in the refrigerator for up to 3 days or freeze for up to 6 months.

Frozen gooseberries are available from some upscale fruit markets and groceries and are an acceptable substitute for fresh in sauces, fools and some preserves.

Canned gooseberries are usually overcooked and disappointing when used to replace fresh berries, so reserve them for recipes in which they are specifically requested.

HAWBERRIES The fruit of the wild hawthorn bush, hawberries are tart, bright red berries that grow wild throughout much of Canada's northern regions. They are often used to make jam and other preserves, but can also be added to pie fillings and other sweet dishes. They must be cooked before eating, as they are extremely tart, but have a delicious and unique flavour.

HUCKLEBERRIES Often confused with blueberries, the common blue variety of this small, round North American berry is almost black, with a thicker skin than that of the blueberry and several hard seeds at its core. Not as sweet as either the cultivated or the wild blueberry, huckleberries are a good addition to pies, crumbles and other baked fruit desserts and make fabulous preserves. They are always wild and rarely available in markets and shops. If you know of a patch, or have a friend who does, take advantage! They ripen during the summer months and should be eaten or used as close to the time they are picked as possible, but can be refrigerated for a few days loosely covered, wrapped in paper towel.

Red huckleberries, much less common than their blue cousins, grow wild along the Pacific coast from Alaska to central California. Bright red, they are juicy and tart. Although they can be eaten raw, they are more often used in preserves and pies.

LOGANBERRIES Loganberries are large, jewel-like berries that look like a cross between a red raspberry and a blackberry, with a slightly deeper colour than the first and the plump size of the second. There is, in fact, some debate as to whether they are a unique species or a cross between the two. They are most often wild and are rarely found in markets outside their growing regions, but if you do come across them, by all means pick them up. They have a juicy, sweet-tart taste that can be enjoyed raw, as with raspberries or blackberries, but they're also divine in pies, preserves, crumbles and cobblers and even ice creams. Choose plump, unbruised berries and check the bottom of the container for any mouldy or crushed berries. Store them in a loosely covered container, wrapped in paper towels, in the refrigerator for up to 3 days.

MULBERRIES Several varieties of mulberries exist, all available in different regions. *Black mulberries* are grown exclusively in Europe and are used for preserves and many desserts. *White mulberries* hail from Asia but are rarely exported. The common *red mulberry* grows wild in much of the southern and eastern United States, from New England to the Deep South. They are similar in appearance to a blackberry, with a juicy, mild but sweet-tart taste. Although they can be eaten raw, their somewhat muted flavour is good combined with other berries or fruit, such as apples, pears and peaches. Use them in any recipe calling for similar berries, but consider replacing only half of the total amount of berries with mulberries, supplementing them with a more flavourful variety such as raspberries or blackberries. Select and store as for similar berries.

OLALLIEBERRIES A cross between a loganberry and a youngberry, these look like long, slender blackberries and have a similar flavour. They are grown exclusively on the west coast of North America and are available during the late summer months. Olallieberries can be used in any recipe calling for blackberries or other related berries and can be eaten on their own as well. Select and store as for blackberries.

RED, GOLDEN AND BLACK RASPBERRIES The queen of the berry family, the sensuously juicy, sweet raspberry is widely cultivated, but will easily grow wild in most temperate climates. Shaped like little inverted bells, raspberries are clusters of tiny, spherical lobes, each containing a single yellow seed surrounded by abundant sweet-tart juice. While wild raspberries are, like most wild berries, more intensely flavourful than their cultivated cousins, cultivated raspberries are generally of a consistently high quality. They are larger, milder and sweeter than wild berries, sacrificing a little sparkle and brightness for a consistently palatable smooth sweetness. The best raspberries grow in northern climates, such as those of Canada and the northern British Isles.

By far the most common variety of raspberry is the red, but black and golden berries are also available, often for a much shorter period of time. *Black raspberries* are sometimes confused with blackberries but are much smaller and usually wild. Still sweet, their sweetness is tempered by a pleasant tartness. They have more seeds than the golden or red varieties and are often used for jams and jellies. *Golden raspberries* are juicy, delicately flavoured and very sweet, with a subtler, less tangy taste. While some consider the golden berry to be the most delicious, I'll take a thick pie laden with fresh, ripe red berries any day of the year.

Raspberries are among the most delicate of fruits and must be carefully handled. Choose firm, unbruised and unmushy berries, with the hulls already removed. Occasionally you may see raspberries with the hulls and stems still attached—avoid these, as they were likely picked too early and are underripe. Put your nose close to the berries and inhale: good ripe berries will have a sweet, aromatic scent. While all by themselves raspberries are as close to perfect as a fruit can get, they aren't hurt by a dollop of fresh cream (or a flaky crust, for that matter!). Local red raspberries are available in most of North America from mid-spring to late fall depending on the region; the berries available during the balance of the year are hothouse grown or imported, with a somewhat inferior flavour.

Frozen raspberries, unsweetened or in a light sugar syrup, are widely available and are excellent for making sauces and purées. However, they generally have far too much liquid to make satisfactory pies, tarts and other desserts.

SALMONBERRIES These curiously named berries grow wild throughout the northeastern United States and the Pacific regions of Canada. Related to wild raspberries, salmonberries are tiny versions of this fruit that slip right off the core when ripe. The berries may be yellow, pink, red or a deep salmon orange and have a somewhat bland, juicy and sweet flavour. They are best eaten raw, as their subtle flavour tends to dissipate with prolonged cooking.

SASKATOON BERRIES These sweet, dark berries grow wild throughout much of Canada's western regions. Also called *serviceberries* or *Juneberries*, for the month they appear, they are often used in preserves and pies and can be substituted for blueberries.

STRAWBERRIES Strawberries are one of the most rewarding little mouthfuls in nature's bounty. Their juicy, refreshingly sweet, almost floral flavour harbours a hint of tartness and a memory of other berries. Full of the taste of approaching summer, strawberries are the most popular berry in North America. They can be divided into two categories: garden or cultivated berries and wild berries. *Garden strawberries* are the ones most of us are familiar with, widely cultivated in North America and a favourite eating and dessert fruit. They are plump, shiny, bright-red berries, with a green leafy stem often still attached. This stem and the ¼-inch deep hull it leads to should be removed before eating or using the berries for any purpose. The outside of the strawberry is dotted with tiny yellow seeds that are absolutely edible and give the berries a pleasant little crunch, but may be strained out of purées, sauces and preserves. Garden strawberries should be sweet and juicy, with a moist, evenly red flesh. Many of the strawberries sold in our markets, especially those not grown locally, are terribly compromised by steroids, hormones and dyes—meant to give them perfect beauty and long life—and are often bland, pulpy, even sour, with insides that are a pale white rather than the same rich deep red of their skin.

Although garden strawberries are available all year long, local berries are in season June through September, depending on the region. Like that of other berries, the short life of the local strawberry should be respected, and the imported or hothouse berries should be reserved for no more than plate decoration. If you can find a truly good fruit vendor who brings in flavourful off-season berries, consider yourself lucky. But don't fool yourself into thinking those huge, glossy, plastic-looking things in the middle of January will taste any better than a dishcloth. (Even in summer, the mass-produced varieties hailing from Florida and California are likely to be dull and flavourless compared to local varieties.)

Today's garden strawberries are probably the hardiest of all berries and can be stored longer than their fragile cousins. Choose firm, evenly coloured, deep-red berries with no signs of soft or mushy patches. The leaves should be bright green if attached, and there should be no white flesh near the stem. This indicates the berries were picked too early, and they do not ripen once harvested. Turn the basket or container upside down to make sure there are no green or crushed berries on the bottom. Rinse strawberries, like all berries, just before use. Leave the hulls on the berries until after they have been dried, to keep the porous flesh from absorbing the water. Store strawberries loosely covered in the refrigerator, wrapped in paper towels, for up to 3 days. Unfortunately, strawberries are one of the few berries that do not freeze well, becoming mealy and waterlogged.

Wild strawberries, sometimes called *alpine strawberries*, are smaller, darker versions of their popular cultivated counterparts, with a wonderfully sweet, intense flavour that makes them especially treasured. Some varieties, like the tiny French *fraises des bois*, have a world-famous reputation, so unique is their flavour. Wild strawberries grow in many parts of North America and Europe, flourishing in mountainous, northern regions. The hulls of many wild strawberries, fraises des bois included, can be eaten, as they are soft and moist. A rare find in supermarkets and even specialty shops, wild strawberries almost always have to be a happy accidental discovery!

GRAPES Grapes, like bananas curiously, are actually members of the berry family. They grow in tight clusters on vines in temperate regions all over the world and are most famously used for the production of wine. Table or eating grapes, however, are a popular fruit too and are widely available in several varieties. Most grapes are about the size of olives, with smooth skin and a juicy, gelatinous interior, sometimes harbouring a few seeds. Many varieties of table grapes have been engineered to be virtually seedless, but these are often bland-tasting and insipid, neither very sweet, nor pleasantly sour, nor flavourful. It is worth buying a good pure-strain grape for cooking or baking and spending the few minutes it takes to halve each grape and flick the seeds out with a paring knife. Grape skins are, in spite of that classic Roman request, very edible, often containing much of the flavour. Some varieties are of the slip-skin type, with thickish skins that easily slip off the flesh when pulled. Other varieties have thinner skins that adhere securely to the interior. *White grapes* are actually pale green or yellow, with transparent pale interiors and are frequently called *green grapes*. *Red* or *black grapes* have dark skins, ranging from purple to blue to red to almost black, with translucent bluish or pinkish interiors.

Muscat or *Muscatel* grapes are one of the most flavourful grapes, with hints of nutmeg, honey and citrus. Pale green-gold in colour, they make luscious sweet wines, but are also excellent for eating and cooking. *Concord* grapes are used predominantly for the production of juice, jelly and other conserves, but are also wonderfully flavourful for eating and baking, tasting as grapey as a grape can taste. Tiny, jewel-like *Zante* or currant grapes are only about the size of wild blueberries and are usually dried and sold as currants. If you can find them fresh in an autumn farmers' market, they are a beautiful and delicious addition to fruit tarts, sauces and perfect for garnishing fruit, cheese and nut platters. The number of varieties of table grapes, beyond the ubiquitous "red and green seedless" grapes, available to you will depend on where you live and the season. Virtually all the grapes sold in fruit markets will be good for eating and baking or desserts, so try as many of them as you can.

Choose grapes that are firm, not soft and squishy. Green grapes should have a slightly yellow hue, indicating sweetness and ripeness. Red or black grapes should have no signs of green on them. A thin dusty film on both green and red grapes is normal and can be rinsed off. Store grapes, unwashed, in the refrigerator, only rinsing them just before use. Dry thoroughly on paper towels.

Grapes, especially Concord or other highly flavoured varieties, make wonderful pies, tarts and crumbles or cobblers. I love little custard tarts topped with halved grapes and brushed with a little melted jelly.

Citrus Fruit

In all cases, choose citrus fruit that is heavy for its size, with bright, shiny skin and no soft or bruised areas. Green patches on some varieties of orange do not indicate underripeness, but simply where the fruit was shaded from the sun. Unfortunately, most oranges sold in North America have had their skins injected with bright dyes, to indulge the public desire for beautiful and even-coloured fruit. Store citrus fruit at room temperature for 2 or 3 days or refrigerate for up to 2 weeks. For fruit whose skin is to be zested, candied or otherwise used for flavouring, be sure to wash the skin well to remove any traces of pesticides and other chemicals and impurities. This is especially important for candied peel, where any imperfections will cause the syrup to foam excessively.

Although the juices of many citrus fruits, such as oranges, grapefruit, lemons, limes, even tangerines, are available in bottles, cartons and as frozen concentrates, these are never a good replacement for the real, freshly squeezed juice. Only use the processed juices when called for, as in the case of a cake specifying undiluted frozen juice concentrate, or if the fresh fruit is absolutely unavailable. Fortunately for most North Americans, almost every type of citrus fruit can be readily found year-round.

Citrus fruit loses it flavour, as well as its nutritional value, extremely quickly once cut and exposed to air. Slice or juice these fruits as close to the time of use as possible. For information on candied citrus rind, see the section on Candied Fruit, page 327.

GRAPEFRUIT The result of a cross between a sweet orange and a pomelo, grapefruit range in size from that of a naval orange to about four times that size. Grapefruit should not be confused with pomelos, although *pomelo* is the Spanish name for this large member of the citrus family. Grapefruit have been bred to be sweeter and less acidic in recent years and have come to hold a secure place on the breakfast tables of many North Americans. Two main varieties exist, white and pink. *White grapefruit* have pale yellow skin and white or very pale yellow flesh. They are best for juicing, as their sweetness is accented by a sharp acidity. *Pink grapefruit* have salmon- to orangy-red coloured skin and a pinkish orange flesh. They are much sweeter than their white relatives, and some newly engineered varieties, such as the *Ruby Red*, have virtually no discernible sourness at all. These make the best eating grapefruit, but may not have enough tang for many recipes. For the most part, the two are interchangeable—decide for yourself how much acidity you would like.

KUMQUATS *(Dwarf Oranges, Dwarf Lemons)* The tiniest of the citrus family, kumquats are oval, deep-orange fruit no bigger than a pecan in its shell. Unlike other citrus fruits, the skin of the kumquat is sweet and flavourful, while the flesh inside is tart and not nearly as juicy as that of its cousins. For most uses, the peel and flesh are best kept together, rather than separated. What few seeds they may have are edible, and kumquats are most often eaten whole. Sweet, ripe kumquats can be sliced or wedged and used in fruit salads and compotes, while even slightly underripe fruit can be candied whole. They make very good marmalade and are excellent poached or preserved in syrup and alcohol. Available from mid-autumn to early spring, kumquats are more delicate than most other citrus fruit and should be stored in a plastic bag in the refrigerator, where they should keep for several weeks. Choose firm, unblemished and unbruised fruit.

LEMONS Lemons have become as important as salt and garlic in the cuisines of many cultures around the world. They are grown in warm, temperate and subtropical regions, with most of those available in North America coming from California, Florida and South America. Lemons are the sourest of the citrus family, with a mouth-puckering acidity, but an intense, bright, fruity flavour. Some varieties are slightly sweeter or more pleasantly flavoured than others—I find the Meyer lemon, grown almost exclusively in California and rarely exported outside the state, to be one of the best for baking. Lemons are usually an oval shape, but can be quite round and as small as a lime or as large as a sweet orange, although generally somewhere in between. They have a shiny skin that can be smooth or knobbly and may be as thin as that of a lime or almost as thick as a navel orange. Look for smooth, thin-skinned lemons that are evenly yielding when pressed gently. These will be the most juicy and ripe. Lemons, like oranges, are frequently dyed and often waxed to give a glossy shine to their skins. Avoid the waxed fruit if you plan to use the zest and always scrub the skin of any citrus fruit whose peel will be included in a recipe. Lemons may be seedless, but are rarely labelled as such, so you are just as likely to end up with seeded ones. Although they are available all year in North America, the best season for fresh lemons is summer, and you will find these will be juicier and less sour than off-season fruit.

Store fresh lemons in a plastic bag in the refrigerator for 2 or 3 weeks. Lemons that become soft or mushy have begun to decay and are too old to use.

In baking and dessert cookery, it is most commonly the pungent juice and the flavourful skin of the lemon that are used. There are some unusual recipes out there that call for whole lemons to be baked into pies, cakes or steamed puddings, but these are relatively rare.

A TIP: If a recipe calls for both zest and juice, zest the lemon first, then juice it. That may seem obvious, but I have wasted more lemons forgetting this, trying to do it in the reverse order! *Lemon zest* can be removed with a paring knife, vegetable peeler or citrus zester, which removes only the yellow, oil-rich, outer layer in thin ribbons and leaves the bitter white pith behind. If the method you use removes both the zest and pith, be sure to cut away the pith or you will be surprised with an unpleasantly acrid flavour. The flavour of the lemon rests almost exclusively in the zest, and it is this part of the fruit that should be used when a pure lemon flavour is desired.

Lemon juice is used as an acidic ingredient, to activate baking soda, for example, or to counter intense sweetness. Unless used in enormous quantity, it will not impart a perceptibly lemon flavour, and even in large amounts, its acidity would overpower any pleasant flavour. So when improvising, if it is acidity you are after, try a few drops of freshly squeezed lemon juice; if you are looking for a true taste of lemon, forget the juice and go for the zest. See page 50 for tips on getting the most juice from a lemon. *Bottled lemon juice* is widely available, but is a shameful imitation of the fresh juice—I suggest avoiding it altogether. In some areas, *frozen lemon juice* is sold. Though considerably better than the bottled stuff, it is also a poor substitute for freshly squeezed. Considering the availability of the fruit, it seems a waste to use any form of the processed juice.

LIMES Once relegated to exotic cuisines and domestic cocktails, the fragrant lime has finally found its way into savoury and sweet dishes in North America, to the great delight of food lovers. However, limes are still much less common than the temperately grown lemon, as they grow only in hot, humid regions of the world. Limes are small, round or oval citrus fruit about the size of a golf ball, with thin vibrant green skin and a pulpy pale green flesh. The skin of some limes may be quite russetted, which in no way affects the flavour or indicates decay or damage. Avoid limes with hard, shrivelled or mushy skin, however. Choose ones that are somewhat yielding to a firm squeeze, as these will be the juiciest. A squeeze of lime accentuates the flavour of almost every tropical fruit and marries well with macadamia and coconut, white chocolate, ginger and cream. See page 51 for tips on juicing limes. If very fresh, limes can be stored in plastic bags in the refrigerator for up to 2 weeks.

Two main varieties of lime are available in North America, the most common being the *Persian lime*. In Canada, and most of the United States, this may be the only variety available. The rarer *Key lime* is grown in Florida, from whence it derives its name, and also in California. Key limes are smaller, rounder and more yellow-hued than their Persian counterparts and have a delicate, floral and very perfumed flavour, ideal for baking and desserts. The famous Key lime pie should be made with nothing else.

A third variety of lime is occasionally found in Asian and Middle Eastern markets in North America and is a phenomenal flavouring, widely used in the savoury cuisines of these cultures. *Kaffir limes* are grown almost exclusively in Southeast Asia, but Hawaii is becoming a major competitor. They are small, fig-shaped yellow-green fruit with a thin, bumpy skin. Very flavourful, they are almost exclusively used in savoury dishes.

Kaffir lime leaves are the thick, shiny dark-green leaves of the Kaffir lime tree. They are widely used, both fresh and dried, in much the same way lemon grass or bay leaves are in the savoury cuisines of Asia and the Middle East, as a flavouring herb. Kaffir lime leaves are available in North America in good ethnic markets and some specialty food shops.

Bottled lime juice and *lime juice concentrate* are widely available, but are poor substitutes for the freshly squeezed juice. *Frozen lime juice* is an improvement, but if possible, use the juice from the fresh fruit, as it is infinitely more flavourful and bright.

THE FAMILY OF ORANGES Oranges are a remarkable testament to human creativity and achievement. Originally, all oranges were as sour and acidic as lemons, but have been bred over a period of hundreds of years to accentuate their succulence and sweetness. Today, many varieties of orange are among the sweetest and most loved fruits in the world. They can be roughly divided into two categories, early season and late season. Early-season oranges ripen during the spring and summer and are generally much more sour than their late-season cousins. The bitter but intensely flavourful *Seville* orange is the most famous example of the early type. Grown almost exclusively in Spain, it has a piquant acidity that makes it the very best orange for marmalades and other bittersweet preserves. *Valencia* oranges, sweeter than the Seville and incredibly juicy, arrive next, followed by the powerfully sweet *navel* oranges. These have been bred to have a thick, easily peeled skin, few if any seeds and a full, honey-sweet orange flavour. Navel are the best eating oranges, but for recipes using orange juice, I prefer the Valencia, as its flavour is more astringent and perceptible in a recipe.

Blood oranges are so-called thanks to the red-tinged flesh, sometimes almost completely crimson in colour. Their skin is thinner than that of the navel orange and is sometimes, though not always, blushed with red. Blood oranges are usually available for a limited time during first few months of the year and make fantastic baking and dessert oranges, with a slightly sharp, very intense flavour. Blood orange compotes, candied blood orange or tarts made from this striking fruit are all glorious and unusual.

Tangerines, and the smaller, sweeter *mandarins* are sweet, often seedless members of the orange family, grown in warm, subtropical regions such as South China, Morocco and Spain. They have a thin, easy-to-peel skin and plump, juicy segments, perfect for eating, candying and for fruit salads and compotes. Their taste is often too subtle to replace the orange juice in many recipes, and the fruit should be used whole and raw for the best flavour. Japanese *satsuma* oranges are also members of the tangerine subfamily and are almost exclusively used for canning, in which case they are labelled "mandarins."

Clementines are tiny, bright orange fruits, similar to mandarins, but are a cross between the bitter Seville orange and the tangerine. They are not at all sour, however, but are intensely sweet, almost candy-like when ripe and fresh. They are best eaten on their own, candied whole or incorporated into fruit salads and compotes.

POMELOS *(Shaddock)* and **TANGELOS** Pomelos are a large, sometimes enormous, pear-shaped citrus fruits with thick, soft skin. Also called *shaddock*, they can be pale yellow, pale green, creamy-brown, even pink, and as small as a common grapefruit or as big as a beach ball. Like the grapefruit, thought to be a descendant, the flavour of the pomelo can range widely as well, from quite sweet to very tart and acidic. Pomelos are much used in Asian cuisines, but are virtually ignored by the rest of the world. A shame, as they have a highly perfumed aroma and even the sourest of them has a piquant and appealing flavour. The flesh is satisfyingly dense and firm, perfect for uncooked recipes or simply eating.

The tangelo is a recent cross between a pomelo and a tangerine, as small as a tangerine or as large as a small grapefruit. The skin may be pale to deep orange, and the flesh is sweet with a pleasantly tangy bite. Several varieties of tangelo are available, but the most common is the *Minneola*, distinct with its overt, nipple-shaped end. Available from late fall to early spring, tangelos are best for eating, but can be used in any recipe to replace tangerines.

UGLI FRUIT This amusingly misshapen member of the citrus family (pronounced "ooo-glee") is a relatively recent addition, having been developed in Jamaica around the turn of the century. It is believed to be a cross between a grapefruit and a tangerine, although the pomelo may have played a part in its inception. In an effort to increase its popularity, some vendors have taken to labelling it "Uniq or Unique" fruit—with less than stellar success! Not exactly ugly, the ugli fruit resembles a large, knobbly skinned grapefruit. Its thick skin hangs rather loosely over the pulpy flesh and can be pale yellow to pale green or any combination of the two, sometimes with blushes of orange. The fruit inside is orangy-yellow, with large lobes in each of the segments. Sweeter than a white grapefruit, the ugli makes a good substitute for those who find the grapefruit's acidity unpalatable. In cooking, ugli fruit can be included in fruit salads and juices, but is not widely used in baking. Available in Jamaican, Latin and Caribbean markets and some supermarkets from mid-fall to early spring, ugli fruit should be stored in plastic bags in the refrigerator for up to 2 weeks or at room temperature for several days.

Melons

Melons are a sensualist's dream, tempting the senses with their refreshing coolness in the deepest heat of summer, with exotic and tropical fragrances, and juicy and potent sweetness. They thrive in warm, humid regions, but are today grown in hothouses all over the world. Melons are divided into two categories: sweet melons and watermelons, which are discussed separately below.

SWEET MELONS originated in Asia, but there are varieties available in virtually every region of North America and Europe, imported from Mexico and South America, as well as the Mediterranean, Israel and South Africa. Sweet melons can be divided into smooth- and rough-skinned varieties. Sweet melons range in size from that of a grapefruit to fruit as large as seven or eight pounds. They have a thick, inedible skin and juicy but firm, sweet flesh. In the centre of the melon is a large web of oval seeds, which can easily be scooped out before serving or using the flesh. All melons should be halved and seeded before use. Honeydew, cantaloupe and other sweet melons are often paired with salty and savoury ingredients, such as prosciutto or cured salmon or duck breast, but are divine as, or in, desserts. Their high water content makes them best suited to fruit salads, chilled fruit soups and ices, granitas or sorbets.

Honeydew melons have smooth, pale green or yellow skin and are uniformly hard, even when ripe. The juicy, firm, pale greenish-white flesh is sweet and delicately flavoured. The glorious *cantaloupe* is among the sweetest melons in the world and comes in several varieties. It's a member of the *muskmelon* family, which encompasses sweet melons that have a pale netting that may be smooth or raised, over the smooth skin. Cantaloupes have a greenish yellow skin that turns a pale tan colour when ripe. The skin is rough and mesh-like and the bright orange flesh is juicy and sweet, with a more pronounced flavour than the delicate honeydew. Ripe cantaloupes are heavy for their size with a lovely sweet, honeyed fragrance near the blossom end, and will yield to gentle pressure around this point. Smell your melons! You may think you look silly, but you will be rewarded with a most delicious fruit. Russetting on parts of the skin is harmless, but melons with soft, squishy patches or a mouldy, overripe aroma should be avoided. Perhaps the most revered of the cantaloupe family is the French *Charentais* melon, a small, round fruit with a smooth, grey-green skin when ripe and a deep orange flesh bursting with intense flavour and sweetness. Now available in some parts of North America, they are indescribably good and are often served simply, halved and filled with aged port or alone with a platter of dried fruits and nuts.

The *casaba* melon has been cultivated in the Americas for over a century and is readily available throughout much of this continent. Unlike the ubiquitous honeydew or cantaloupe, however, it is only available for a short time during the early fall. Casaba melons have a smooth, thick, bright yellow skin, with deep rivulets running over it. Like other muskmelons, it should be aromatic and slightly soft at the blossom end when ripe, and the skin may even be slightly puckered. The ivory-hued flesh inside is mildly sweet, similar to a slightly underripe honeydew.

Wonderfully sweet and aromatic *Crenshaw* melons are hybrids, grown extensively throughout North and South America. They have a smooth greenish-yellow skin, faintly laced with tiny raised lines, and a bright orange flesh. They are slightly egg-shaped and very heavy, often reaching eight or nine pounds. Crenshaw melons are in season in much of North America from late summer to early fall and are among the most flavourful melons available.

Ogen melons are small, smooth-skinned hybrids, created in Israel for their succulent sweetness. Their dark-green skin is laced with flat, tan-coloured netting, and the flesh inside is similar in appearance to that of a honeydew. Available in specialty shops and markets from late spring to late fall, they are a treat if you can find them. The *Galia* or *Gallia* melon is closely related and very similar in flavour and aroma.

Local sweet melons may be available during the late summer and early fall, but good honeydew and cantaloupe melons are usually available pretty much all year long. Store sweet melons at room temperature if slightly underripe and refrigerate once ripe. Cut melons tend to lose flavour and nutrients quickly, so use them as soon as possible.

WATERMELONS Watermelons are native to Africa, but are now cultivated in many other countries, including the United States. They are not, however, as highly prized to gourmets and the culinary elite, as their pulpy texture is excessively watery and only mildly sweet and flavourful. But nothing is more refreshing on a swelteringly hot and humid afternoon than a huge slice of watermelon, and they have become inextricably associated with barbecues and picnics in North America. Most watermelons are a dark shade of green, sometimes streaked with yellow or white, with a thick, smooth rind and an oval shape. They range from large to immense, and often weigh in excess of twenty or thirty pounds! The icy-looking flesh is most often red, but can be pale pink, bright yellow and even white. It is bursting with juice and is imbedded with dozens of slippery seeds, which can range in colour from black to brown to green, red and white. While the flesh is what you're really after, picnics would be a little boring without the seeds.

Seedless varieties of watermelon have been recently engineered and are widely available throughout most of North America. Certainly they make preparing a fruit salad less time-consuming, but the trade-off is harsh. Seedless watermelons are impotent, both in fertility and in flavour. They are terribly bland and seem to taste more of stale water than sweet fruit! A few seeds are a small price to pay for a sweet, juicy, true-flavoured fruit.

Although watermelons are available from late spring to early fall, peak watermelon season happily coincides with the heat of summer, during July and August. Choose heavy, evenly shaped watermelons with no dents or soft patches. The skin should have a matte, not glossy, surface, and the whole melon should sound hollow when slapped. If possible, buy whole melons, not the pre-cut portions often sold in markets. These have already begun to deteriorate and may be dehydrated and dull-flavoured. Cut watermelons as close to the time of using as possible, then store in the refrigerator if necessary, for up to a day. The flesh of a ripe watermelon will be dense, firm and deeply coloured, with a sweet, fresh flavour. Pulpy, grainy or dry flesh means the melon is likely old or over-ripe. Store whole, ripe watermelons in the refrigerator, or in a cold storage pantry if you have one, for up to 5 days.

In many parts of the world, including the American South, *watermelon rind* is pickled or used in sweet preserves.

Mature *watermelon seeds* can be toasted like pumpkin seeds, salted, then eaten as a snack.

Common Exotic Fruit

BANANAS One of the holy trinity of childhood fruits (the other two being apples and pears) for most North American children, tropical bananas are cultivated in such variety and in so many regions of the world that they now rank as one of the most popular fruits on earth. Good for the banana! And good for the baker and pastry cook, as creamy, sweet bananas are perfectly suited to desserts.

Grown in huge clusters on tall tropical plants, bananas are usually picked very underripe to ensure the delicate fruit does not become damaged or too ripe before reaching its far-flung consumers. They can be eaten when their pale yellow flesh is still very coloured with green, but will have a chalky, slightly bitter taste. When just ripe, the skins will be a rich yellow, with a few dark brown spots dotting their surface. The flesh will be sweet and full-flavoured, with little or no bitterness. The skin will continue to develop these dark patches as the banana ripens further, finally turning quite black if left long enough. Extra-ripe bananas are the very best for baking and are perfect for cakes, quick breads, custards and ice cream, as the flesh becomes very soft, almost custard-like, and the flavour deepens, becoming aromatic and sugar-sweet.

Baking or roasting bananas is a wonderful way of heightening their flavour and sweetness and can seem to accelerate the ripening of slightly underripe fruit. Simply place several firm, moderately ripe bananas on a baking sheet in a pre-heated 325° oven. Bake until the skins are black, and the bananas are very soft. Cool, then spoon the custard-like flesh out of the skins. This is an outrageously good dessert on its own or gilded with chocolate sauce or maple syrup and a generous dollop of whipped cream; the flesh can also be used as you would ordinary mashed banana pulp in baked goods, creams, custards, sauces and puddings.

Most bananas in North America are from the dessert banana family, cultivated for eating or sweet cooking. The *Cavendish* is the overwhelming favourite, and more than 90% of total banana sales in North America are of this variety. Other varieties available include the tiny *fingerling*, *dwarf* or *baby bananas*, not young bananas at all, but a miniature strain. They have a slightly sweeter flavour than the larger dessert bananas. Stubby, short *red bananas* are also available and have a dark brick-coloured skin when ripe and a sweet flesh similar to the dwarf variety. *Plantains* are large, thick-skinned members of the banana family with a firmer flesh and a mild, almost vegetable-like flavour. They are most commonly treated as a starchy vegetable, similar to a potato, in Mexican, Caribbean, and Latin American cuisine and must be cooked before being consumed. Although most recipes for plantains are for savoury dishes, some desserts incorporate their mild sweetness, in tart or pie fillings or deep-fried fritters. Plantains are sweetest when very ripe, and only ripe fruit should be used in dessert cookery. The skin may need to be pared off and the plantain fruit should be cut into chunks and soaked in cold water for 10 to 20 minutes to purge it of an enzyme that can sting the flesh. Look for plantains in Latin or Caribbean markets, and even in some larger supermarkets.

Banana leaves are also used extensively in Caribbean and Southeast Asia, as well as Central and South American cuisine to encase food during cooking. They're not widely used in baking and sweet cookery, but may be called for in some traditional recipes and can be found at Latin American and Caribbean markets.

Choose firm, unblemished bananas, with a few streaks or spots of brown if you can. Allow bananas to ripen at room temperature. Ripe bananas can be refrigerated or even popped in the freezer to prolong their life and will be fine for cooking after such storage, although the skins will turn dark brown or black. Cold is not recommended for bananas, however, or any other tropical fruit, and should only be a last resort. Better to use the bananas as soon as possible once they are ripe. Peeled bananas brown quickly upon contact with the air and should be used quickly or dipped in acidulated water or brushed with lemon juice to preserve their colour.

Dried bananas are discussed on page 320.

Crisp, fried *banana* or *plantain chips* are a popular ingredient in many trail mixes and make an attractive and crunchy garnish for muffins, quick breads, cakes and pies. They can be easily found at health and natural food stores.

FIGS Figs carry with them almost as much symbolism in history and myth as the pomegranate and the apple. Their powder-soft skin, richly coloured from green to gold to all shades of purple; their succulent, honeyed flesh laden with delicate tiny seeds and their sensuous shape, often compared to a woman's breast, have made them almost deified. Originally native to parts of Asia, they are now grown in the Mediterranean, Central and South America, as well as California, a region that produces much of the North American supply. Figs are tree fruits, belonging to the mulberry family, that develop on mature trees three times each year. The fruit is soft and fragile, however, and figs are often dried to prolong their life. Fresh figs were a revelation to me: sweet, succulent, tasting of honey and sunshine and reminiscent of dates, dried apricots and raisins. Figs come in many colours, from a deep purple-black to a pale green-gold, even almost white. Most are about the size of a small mandarin orange, with a plump, round shape tapering quickly to a little nib of a stem. The skin is luxuriously soft and can be eaten—should be eaten! The inside of the fruit harbours thousands of tiny pale seeds imbedded in flesh ranging from rosy to downright crimson and sometimes pale green blushed with pink.

In general, the fresh figs available in much of North America can be classified into two categories: green and black. *Green figs* have pale rose-coloured flesh and are less sweet than their dark cousins. I prefer using them in savoury dishes, often marrying them with prosciutto or other salty ingredients. *Calimyrna figs* are the most common variety of green fig in this country and are grown in California. The same variety is called *Smyrna* in its native Turkey.

Black figs, such as the deep-purple *Mission figs*, are my favourites for baking, with their heady honeyed sweetness and glorious burgundy flesh. Calimyrna and Mission figs are both widely cultivated and are often sold dried as well as fresh. For a beautiful effect, use both varieties in a tart or compote. Other types you may be able to find in specialty markets are the delicate white-fleshed *Adriatic*, a small firm fig with a pale green skin; the *Kadota*, another small fruit with a slightly thicker green-gold skin, and the *Magnolia*, a beautiful dark gold-tinged fig with a yellow flesh blushed with pink. Many recipes specify which general type of fig to use; if you want to substitute green for black, you may need to add a little more sugar to the recipe.

Fresh figs are best between late spring and late fall, with different varieties flourishing at different times. Choose figs that are plump and pretty, with soft, taut and unblemished skin and no overly soft or oozing patches. Ripe figs should feel heavy in your hand and yield to gentle pressure. Slightly underripe fruit may be stored at room temperature for a few days, but should be used quickly once they ripen. Ripe figs can be kept a day or two in the refrigerator, but cold does them no good in general.

Figs' exotic, sensuously sweet flavours are wonderful with honey, almonds, hazelnuts, walnuts, white chocolate and citrus fruits.

A word of caution: figs contain the same enzyme as pineapple and other fruit that prevents gelatine from properly setting. See the section on pineapple for more information.

For information on *dried figs*, see the section on Dried Fruits, page 322.

KIWIS *(Kiwifruit, Chinese Gooseberries, Monkey Peaches)* Although native to China, the kiwi has become so linked with its largest producer, New Zealand, that its name has come to be a moniker for human inhabitants from the same country. Actually, the name comes from New Zealand's national bird, the Kiwi! The Kiwi fruit is a recent addition to North American fruit stands and breakfast tables, but a welcome one. Most kiwi fruit are about the size of a goose egg, or about twice the size of a chicken egg. The skin of the kiwi is khaki-coloured and covered with a coarse fur or hair. The skin can either be pared off, or the whole kiwi can be cut in half across the centre and the fruit spooned out. The latter is by far the easier method and works beautifully for kiwis that are meant for immediate eating, or those that are going to be mashed, puréed, chopped, or even sliced. To get each half out in one clean piece, use a thin tea-spoon or tablespoon. Kiwi flesh is a bright, almost neon, green, with very soft, totally edible black seeds dotting its pulp. The entire interior should be used, with the seeds adding a distinctive bit of texture and colour to even puréed preparations. The flavour of a ripe kiwi is sweet and tangy, with hints of straw-berries, gooseberries and other sweet-sour berries. There was an unfortunate trend during the Nouvelle Cuisine fad of the early 1980s of incorporating kiwi into everything from soup to meat to pasta dishes; thankfully this has evolved into a more thoughtful use of the fruit, now almost exclusively in des-serts. Kiwis do not stand up well under heat, as their flavour tends to become flat and dull. Use them raw on fruit tarts, in trifles, fools and other creams, as well as in fruit salads.

Kiwis are available from midsummer to early spring. Choose fruit with firm, unblemished skin, and with no soft or bruised patches. Kiwis can be ripened at room temperature over several days, ideally in the presence of apples or pears, which emit the same ethylene gas as the kiwi stalk, necessary for ripening. When ripe, they will yield very slightly to gentle pressure and can be refrigerated, but should be eaten or used as soon as possible.

Kiwis are wonderful eaten simply, with a sprinkling of sugar or a liqueur, in fruit salads, compotes, as well as in fools, raw fruit tarts and fruit gratins. They do, however, contain an enzyme, also found in pineapples, that makes them unsuitable for preparations requiring thickening or gelling. See the section on pineapples for more information on this enzyme.

MANGOES Mangoes are tropical tree fruits, ranging in size from that of a medium pear to a grapefruit. They may be almost perfectly round, oval or even quite flat, depending on the variety. Members of the nightshade family, the mango's skin is toxic and must be pared away with a sharp knife or vegetable peeler. If eaten, mango skin may cause a rash similar to that caused by its dis-tant relative, poison ivy. Ripe mangoes should yield slightly to the touch, like a ripe pear. A dribble of sweet syrup may be visible around the stem end, and the mango should smell sweetish. Mangoes have a voluptuous and exotic, slightly spicy, peach-like flavour, with a shiny bright orange flesh.

Several varieties of mango are readily available in most North American cities from late May to mid- or late September, and some imported varieties are sold throughout the year in specialty markets. The most common is the large *Kent mango*, whose green skin becomes well blushed with deep red-orange and yellow when ripe. It has a juicy but slightly stringy flesh, which can be strained for perfectly smooth sauces and purées. The smaller *Alphonse mango* has a leaner shape and a curved tip. The skin is a pale green, turning a buttery yellow when ripe. The flesh of the Alphonse is, I think, the most exquisite of all, with a honeyed and more delicate flavour than that of Kent mangoes and a very smooth, silky texture. Alphonse mangoes are less common than the larger red varieties, but are often available in Mexican and Chinese groceries.

As they are extremely fragile, most mangoes are shipped underripe and may still be too firm when you find them. Plan ahead and buy heavy, smooth-skinned mangoes with no blemishes or bruises. Let the fruit ripen at room temperature for several days. Only refrigerate mangoes that are too ripe to keep out—tropical fruits do not like cold. Use a ripe mango as soon as possible; it will begin to deteriorate quickly.

The flesh of the mango clings tightly to a fibrous, oval, flattish stone. There are several ways to separate the two. For the first method, begin by peeling the mango, then slicing off the flattish, broad sides, leaving a space of about 1 to 1½ inches in the centre, around the stone. Pare away the rest of the good flesh from the stone; it doesn't come gracefully, but there is a surprising amount of fruit! An easier, but not always appropriate, way of stoning the mango is to leave the skin on and slice off the broad sides in the same way as above. With a paring knife, score the flesh in the cup-shaped bowls of skin into squares, not cutting through the skin. Turn the skin inside out, exposing the cubes of fruit, which can now be gobbled up or properly sliced off.

Ripe mango flesh can be used in many desserts, and its sweet, slightly acidic flavour combines well with those of other tropical ingredients, such as papaya, macadamia and coconut. Mango and cream is a wonderful marriage in any form—ice creams, custard tarts and trifles. Mangoes lose their beautiful flavour quickly when cooked, however, and should be used raw. Puréed sauces made from mangoes may be warmed, but never let them get truly hot.

Underripe mangoes, called *green mangoes*, are used extensively in Southeast Asian, Indian and other Asian cuisines in savoury salads, noodle dishes and stir-fries. They have a fresh, sharp, fruity flavour that is more tangy than sweet.

A word of caution: mangoes contain the same enzyme present in pineapple, which interferes with the setting and gelling of mixtures. See the section on pineapples for more information.

Canned mango flesh is quite readily available, but is usually mushy and either rather bland or cloyingly sweet due to the heavy syrup in which it is packed. I do not recommend substituting this product in any recipe calling for fresh mango.

Dried mango is discussed in the section on Dried Fruits, on page 324.

PAPAYAS *(Pawpaws, Papaws)* Papayas are large, pear-shaped tropical fruits, with pale green skin that ripens to a deep yellow, sometimes tinged with orange. They have a soft, silky, salmon-orange flesh and a dense core of shiny black seeds. The skin should be pared away before eating or using the flesh in baking, but the seeds are harmless and can add a beautiful colour and texture to many dishes. They do have a slightly peppery bite to them, however, which may not be desirable in every recipe. If unwanted, they can be easily scraped out. The sweet flesh is quite mild, sometimes even bland unless very ripe, and marries well with citrus juices, especially lime, which brings out a lovely slightly acidic flavour. Other good pairings are tropical fruits, nuts and white chocolate. Papayas tend to lose much of their potency and aroma when puréed or over-cooked. I prefer keeping it as raw as possible, such as in fruit salads, compotes or added to puddings such as tapioca at the last minute.

Choose heavy, taut-skinned fruit with pale green skin, even yellow if possible. A ripe papaya will yield to a gentle pressure and will have a yellow skin, perhaps with blush of orange or red. Ripen a too-firm papaya in a warm, damp place, not the refrigerator, for several days. As with most tropical fruit, even ripe papaya should be kept away from the refrigerator and used promptly.

A word of caution: papayas contain the same enzyme as pineapples that prevents gelling or setting. See the section on pineapples for more info.

Underripe papaya, like mango, is a popular ingredient in many savoury dishes in Asian and Indonesian cuisines. Called *green papaya*, it is used more as a vegetable than a fruit, its tart, refreshing flavour often acting as a counterpoint to hot and spicy flavours.

Dried papaya is available in health and natural food stores and is discussed on page 323.

PINEAPPLES The divine sweetness and exotic perfume of the noble pineapple have made it one of the most loved fruits in the world. In spite of its rather uninviting, prickly exterior, it is a wonderfully juicy, soft fruit, with a unique and very tropical flavour. Choose a pineapple that feels heavy for its size. A ripe pineapple will have a green rind flecked with gold, yield slightly when pressed and have a sweet, distinctive aroma near the leaves. Some people claim that ripeness can be judged by pulling a few of the smaller leaves—if they come easily, the fruit is ripe. I have found this method to be less than consistent, however, and prefer trusting my hands and my nose.

One American fruit producer has developed a new variety of pineapple, intensely aromatic and even sweeter than the ordinary type. These "new and improved" pineapples are worth the extra few dollars they often cost, as they are almost always perfectly ripe and have the best possible flavour. I rarely recommend highly engineered fruit, but in this case, you couldn't do better. Called *Extra-Sweet*, or *Gold*, pineapples, they are now available in most large supermarkets and many produce stores in Canada and the United States.

To prepare a pineapple for eating or cooking, cut off the leafy top and the stem end or bottom. Set the fruit on one of these now flat ends and slice off the rind in strips. You will be left with a cylindrical yellow fruit, with hard, brown eyes twisting around the cylinder in spirals. These eyes must be removed, as they are tough and inedible. Place the cylinder on its side and with the long blade of a knife cut the eyes out in wedges, a few at a time, trying to follow the natural lines they keep. Then cut out any eyes you missed in the first pass and quarter the cylinder through the core from top to bottom, making four long wedges. Stand each wedge on one end and cut the woody core portion away from the more tender flesh. The pineapple is now ready for eating, slicing, juicing, dicing or anything else.

Whole fresh pineapples can be stored at room temperature to ripen if necessary and should be refrigerated once fully ripe. They do not ripen very quickly, however, and I prefer to leave them at room temperature until I use them, rather than subjecting the flesh to the cold of the refrigerator. Cut fresh pineapple can be stored for a day or two in an airtight container in the refrigerator.

A word of caution: pineapples contain an enzyme that prevents gelling or setting, as in the case of thickened pie and tart fillings, as well as set custards, jellies, mousses and bavarians. Most starches and gelatines are neutralized by the enzyme, and you will end up with a runny mess, rather than a properly firm or thickened product. This enzyme is destroyed with cooking, however, so sautéed, quickly blanched, baked, roasted or otherwise cooked pineapple can be used successfully. Canned pineapple, as it has been heat treated before processing, also works perfectly well in these situations.

Canned pineapple is available as rings, chunks or crushed fruit. In its favour, my grandmother makes a fantastically trashy dessert called Pineapple Guck, of which I am so enamoured I considered including it in this book. It is a wonderfully gooey, sweet concoction of vanilla wafers, sweetened whipped cream, butter icing and canned crushed pineapple, and almost every member of my family would practically forego all other food for a taste of it. That said, I must tell you that for most purposes canned pineapple products are no comparison to the fresh fruit. The one virtue they hold is that the fruit has been cooked—a double-edged sword, as it alters the flavour of the fruit, but neutralizes that troublesome enzyme. Because of that, you may find good recipes calling for canned pineapple. However, I find the same neutralizing effect can be achieved by oven- or pan-roasting the flesh, without sacrificing the flavour. In part, it depends on availability of the fresh ripe fruit and the time available for preparation. Judge for yourself.

For information on *dried pineapple*, see the section on Dried Fruits, page 324; for *candied pineapple*, see Candied Fruit, page 327.

Really Exotic Fruit

CACTUS PEARS (*Prickly Pears, Barbary Figs, Indian Figs*) The fruit from any of several varieties of cactus, the cactus pear is an oval, lemon-sized fruit, with a thick, prickly skin that is green when the underripe fruit is picked, but which becomes a muted red-brown or purple-brown when ripe. Now cultivated in tropical and subtropical regions around the world, such as Australia and the Mediterranean, as well as the Americas, the cactus pear is available in specialty food shops and Caribbean or Latin markets from late August through the winter. The rough skin should be removed by cutting off the ends of the fruit, then making a long incision down the skin from top to bottom and laying the fruit on its side. Slice the skin away from the fruit as you would the skin from a fillet of fish, rolling the fruit until it is free. The pale to golden-green flesh of the cactus pear is mild and sweet, with a slight tang and a faint flavour of pear and papaya, and is imbedded with edible black seeds. Choose fruit with a deep, even colour and that gives slightly when pressed. Store underripe cactus pears at room temperature for several days, then refrigerate for up to 1 week if necessary, although as with any tropical fruit, for best flavour they should be used as soon as they ripen.

CHERIMOYAS (*Custard Apples, Sherbet Fruit*) The custard apple is a member of the anona family, related to pineapples. Somewhat smaller than this cousin, custard apples are usually about the size of a medium cantaloupe and have a slightly oval rounded shape. The thick, leathery, olive-hued skin covers the flesh in what look like flat, overlapping scales, giving the custard apple a distinctly reptilian or prehistoric appearance. The pale ivory flesh, however, quickly dispels any question of the fruit's merits. It is soft and indeed almost custard-like, with a seductively sweet and tropical flavour, reminiscent of pineapple, vanilla, papaya and banana. To eat the fruit on its own, simply scoop the flesh out of the shells with a teaspoon. Any tiny black seeds can be discarded. Divine! In desserts and baking, the silky loose flesh is best used almost as a saucy accompaniment, on its own or augmented with a little sugar and vanilla or even a little cream, served with tropical-flavoured cakes, ice creams and pastries. I have also had great success with custard-apple ice cream and a simple custard-apple tart, using the flesh to replace part of the cream in a traditional custard recipe. Force the flesh through a mesh sieve and discard the seeds before using. Custard apples are available from specialty fruit stores and Latin or Caribbean markets from late fall to early spring. Store them at room temperature until they yield slightly to a gentle pressure, then use promptly or refrigerate for up to 2 days.

DURIANS One has to be terribly committed to uncover the elusive charms of this strange Asian fruit. A durian is large, often weighing up to eight or ten pounds, and looks more like a medieval mace than a fruit, with sharp olive green spikes covering its surface. This dangerous appearance, however, is not what keeps it at bay from most fruit-lovers. No, it's its atrocious, ungodly, decidedly foul aroma! Indeed, the stench of a ripe durian is more akin to something rotten than to a luscious exotic fruit. But for those who steel themselves (or are aromatically challenged), the inside of this repellent package is well worth the quest. The ivory flesh of the durian is creamy and sweet, with a delicate, almost floral flavour and a lovely smooth texture. It is wonderful as an addition to subtly flavoured custards, ice creams and mousses, but, unfortunately, it is rarely used in North America. I understand any reluctance to bring one of these alarming things home, but you won't be sorry if you manage to do so! Don't even bring it into your house—butcher it on the front porch or in the backyard, then use the flesh as you desire. Fresh durian is available in Asian and Indonesian markets.

Preserved *dried durian* is widely used in Asian cooking in both sweet and savoury dishes. Available in Asian groceries, it can be rehydrated and used to replace fresh durian, but does not have the latter's delicate flavour and subtlety. On the other hand, you can keep it and your family in the house at the same time.

GUAVAS *(Goyaves, Guayabas)* Guavas are apple-sized, round tropical fruits, long used for their slightly sweet, pleasantly acidic flavour, not unlike that of quince, papaya and citrus combined. The thin pale orange or salmon-coloured skin must be pared away and the few seeds removed before the soft, juicy flesh can be enjoyed. Guava can be used raw, but benefits greatly from combination with other ingredients, such as ginger, cream, sweet spices, citrus fruit and other tropical fruits and its flavour is enhanced by baking or cooking.

Guava are only available in specialty or Latin markets during the mid to late fall. Choose fruit that feels heavy, with firm, smooth skin, no signs of bruising or mould and a highly perfumed, exotic, almost floral aroma. Leave slightly underripe guava to ripen at room temperature and once ripe use as soon as possible. Like other tropical fruit, guava does not benefit from refrigeration, although ripe fruit can be refrigerated for short periods until it can be used.

Canned guava, usually packed in a thick syrup, is readily available, and some varieties can be quite good. Before replacing fresh guava with the canned variety, however, evaluate the recipe to see whether further cooking is called for, and whether the already cooked canned fruit will stand up to the process. Check the sweetness of the canned guava as well—you may need to decrease the amount of sugar called for in the recipe, depending on the sugar content of the syrup.

LYCHEES *(Litchees, Lichis, Lichees)* and RAMBUTANS The lychee has been cultivated in South China for thousands of years and remains one of China's most popular fruits. They are now grown in many other warm regions, including Indonesia, India, Australia, Brazil and even California. Lychee grow in dense clusters on the branches of a tall shrub. Each fruit is about the size of a large walnut and is wrapped in a rough, easily removed leathery red skin that turns brown with storage. The flesh of the fruit is a translucent, creamy ivory, similar in texture to a slightly dry grape flesh, and is wrapped around a large, shiny brown stone. The flavour is sweet and delicate and has been compared to a cross between that of elderflower, coconut and watermelon—hard to imagine, but quite accurate and truly delicious. Lychee is used in much savoury cuisine in China, but is still very unfamiliar even as an eating fruit in North America. Lychee can be used in creams, ices and fruit compotes and is especially good when paired with ginger, spices and coconut.

Although fresh lychee is only available for a short time in the fall, *canned lychee* is widely available in Asian markets and many supermarkets, and is surprisingly good.

Lychees should not be confused with *lychee nuts*, which are a type of dried lychee with an entirely different texture and flavour. They are rarely, if ever, used in baking.

The rambutan is a close relative of the lychee, but has a hairy red skin that looks more like a sea anemone than a sweet fruit! The flavour is just as sweet and exotic, though finding fresh rambutan in North America may be almost impossible. For recipes that call for rambutan, lychees are a perfect substitute.

PASSION FRUIT *(Granadillas)* What a divine name for such a potent little fruit! Passion fruit is a round, kiwi-sized fruit, with a tough, inedible shell or skin. When ripe, the skin will begin to soften and pucker, and the fruit should be used quickly, as it deteriorates rapidly. An overly wrinkled, soft passion fruit is likely overripe and will not have a bright, sparkling flavour. Inside the shell is a mass of tiny black seeds, each suspended in bright yellow, green or orange gelatinous juice. The seed mass can be easily spooned out of a ripe fruit, though an underripe passion fruit will tend to grip its contents more tightly. The seeds are edible and add a peppery bite and striking visual element to many desserts, but are often removed before the intensely flavoured juice is used. The best way to efficiently separate the seeds from their jelly-like juice is to spin the entire mass very briefly in a food processor, just enough to loosen the seeds from the pulp, but not enough so they start to crack or crush. Push the whole mixture through a fine sieve, discarding the seeds, and you'll end up with a pure, liquid flavouring. If you do not have access to a food processor, simply push the pulp through a sieve, pressing very firmly to extract as much juice as you can. The fresh pulp or juice can be frozen in airtight bags or containers for up to 8 months.

Ripe passion fruit pulp has a vibrant, tangy, off-sweet flavour and benefits from a careful dose of sugar or other sweetener to balance its astringency and bring out the ripe, tropical sweetness. A little goes a long way, and one or two passion fruit can enliven an entire dessert. There is a distinct note of fruity sweetness, but with an astringency reminiscent of lemon juice. The pulp can be used as it is, seeds and all, to enliven a fruit salad or a fruit purée or sauce, and the juice can be used in curds, custards, icings and fillings, ice creams and other desserts.

Look for shiny, smooth-skinned fruit with no blemishes (a few wrinkles, dimples and puckers in the skin indicate ripeness). The pulp of a ripe passion fruit will be full-flavoured and juicy, bright-coloured and intense. Underripe passion fruit can be ripened at room temperature for several days, but ripe fruit should be kept in the refrigerator if necessary, to be used as soon as possible. Choose passion fruit heavy for its size, and you will likely get a fruit with a high ratio of pulp to rind.

The best variety for eating and cooking is by far the purple *granadilla*, a kiwi-sized fruit with dark purple-red skin and a mass of green pulp that be-comes increasingly orange with ripening. The granadilla's flavour is superior, pleasantly sharp, but with an overall sweetness and tropical taste. *Yellow grana-dilla* passion fruit are also available, with a bright, yellow skin tinged with green or orange. The flavour is similar, and just as good. Another commonly avail-able variety is the *Jamaica honeysuckle* passion fruit, grown in South America and the Caribbean. Larger than the granadilla varieties, its skin can range in colour from yellow to reddish orange, and its flavour is less sweet and less pro-nounced.

Passion fruit is available from late March through September, in specialty fruit markets, as well as at many Latin American groceries.

Canned passion fruit is available in some supermarkets, but is a pale and dull imitation of the original.

PERSIMMONS Persimmons are a fruit common in Asian and Mediterranean cuisines, but are quite unfamiliar to most North Americans. Those who hail from British stock may have tasted a persimmon steamed pudding, but that is likely the extent of their experience. A shame, considering the persimmon's sweet, delicate, meltingly juicy, pudding-like flesh. Available in good fruit mar-kets and specialty stores from late fall to mid-winter, they look more like a savoury ingredient, a bizarre exotic tomato perhaps, than a sugar-sweet, gelati-nous dessert fruit. Persimmons range in colour from yellow-orange to a deep flame-orange. Some varieties are squat, tomato-shaped fruit with a similar weight and feel in the hand. Others are larger, taller and firmer, with a denser flesh. Persimmons have a thin, tomato-like skin, which should be pared away before eating or using in baking and desserts. There may be a few shiny black seeds nestled in the jelly-like sweet flesh that are easily removed. Most varieties of persimmon must be eaten completely ripe, or the powerful acidity of the fruit will dominate its sweetness. When ripe, the acidity is all but undetectable, and the flesh candy-sweet. Choose heavy, wonderfully plump, almost bursting fruit and store ripe persimmons in the refrigerator. Slightly underripe fruit can be ripened at room temperature for a few days.

Hachiya persimmons, the most common variety, must be used fully ripe, when they feel very soft and jelly-like under a light pressure. In baking, they are best in dense cakes and puddings, as their very high moisture content has a tendency to dampen many batters. Although they are often combined with heady spices and other highly flavoured ingredients, they do benefit from a delicately flavoured environment, letting their own subtle sweetness come through. Their molten consistency makes them perfect for mousses, fools and creams.

Fuyu persimmons are small, squat and tomato-shaped, with much less acidity than the Hachiya. They can be eaten when still slightly firm, but otherwise taste very similar.

Depending on the season and country of origin, there can be quite a range in flavour and texture within the two varieties above. I have on occasion found a type of persimmon labelled *Vanilla* or *Kaki Vanille*, which is very much like a typical Fuyu persimmon, but with even sweeter flesh and a perceptible hint of vanilla. It is larger and its flesh firmer, and it holds its shape beautifully in batters and doughs. I have even used it to replace apples, pears and other fruits in some recipes. Ask your fruit merchant and try different varieties as they appear.

POMEGRANATES The pomegranate has been celebrated since long before being praised in the Song of Solomon, and for good reason. Its full-figured, rough, crimson exterior harbours a multitude of glistening red and white seeds, each bursting with sweet and tangy flavour. The allusions to fertility are obvious! The pomegranates available in North America are all of the *sweet red* variety, meant for eating, as well as use in certain sweet and savoury recipes. *Sour yellow pomegranates* are common all over the Middle East and are used extensively in savoury dishes, but are unpalatably tart when raw.

Ranging in size from that of an orange to a large grapefruit, pomegranates do not make access to their treasures easy. The seeds are enmeshed in a maze of thin, ivory or yellow membranes, which need to be peeled away to expose the clusters of seeds. I have found no reliable or short way of doing this, but you are welcome to try anything you like! Most "shortcuts" I have tried have resulted in my being covered in the abundant and staining juice, with at least half of the seeds crushed or exploded. Score the thick skin of the fruit in four places and use a sharp knife to help you peel back one section of the rind. You will expose some of the seeds. Pluck these out, one by one or in nice, satisfying clumps, gradually exposing more of the fruit and breaking it down into manageable pieces. This doesn't actually take very long and is the fastest, neatest and most efficient method of seeding the fruit. The seeds themselves have a tissue-thin skin over an almost totally liquid flesh that surrounds an edible ivory-coloured seed. For recipes using just the juice of the fruit, the little seeds can be strained out, but the whole seeds make a jewel-like garnish for fruit salads, tarts, ice creams and parfaits, mousses and custards, adding a big bright flavour.

Pomegranates are available from late August to December, sometimes January if the season is good. Choose firm pomegranates that feel very heavy for their size, with beautiful, evenly dark red firm skin. A little russetting on the skin is fine, but there should be no gouges or deep blemishes. Store pomegranates at room temperature.

Grenadine is a dark red, sweet, concentrated pomegranate syrup used mainly in bartending, but also in some desserts and ice creams. It has a subtle fruity flavour, vaguely reminiscent of pomegranates, but most varieties are so sweet the fruit is all but lost. If you do use it, seek out a brand with pomegranate juice listed high in the ingredients—many are now artificially flavoured or contain largely other fruit juices. Some types also contain alcohol—in general, these should not be used in desserts. Non-alcoholic grenadine is available at most supermarkets and some specialty food stores.

Pomegranate molasses is a thick, dark syrup made by reducing the juice of the sour pomegranate. It is used widely in Middle Eastern cuisine as a piquant and potent flavouring and is a wonderful ingredient in many savoury dishes. Pomegranate molasses is available in Middle Eastern and Arabic groceries, as well as specialty food shops.

Pomegranate juice is a glorious ruby red and is becoming increasingly available in health and natural food stores. It should be used as soon after being extracted as possible to flavour drinks, sauces and desserts.

STAR FRUITS *(Carambolas)* The beautiful and easily identifiable star fruit gets its name from the unmistakable shape of its cut slices. A tropical fruit, star fruit grows in many hot and humid regions, including most Caribbean countries as well as Hawaii. They are about 3 to 6 inches in length, with the larger fruits usually being the sweetest and most flavourful. The thin edible skin of a ripe star fruit is a bright green and ripens to a mellow yellow-green, covering dense, watery flesh about the texture of an abundantly juicy apple. The flesh may contain one or more shiny black seeds, but these are easily removed. Ripe star fruit is crisp and juicy and has a fragrant, sweet flavour. Slightly underripe, however, the flesh can be unpalatably tart or bland. Star fruit is available in specialty fruit markets, as well as Latin, Mexican and Caribbean markets from late summer through mid-winter. Look for fruit with no signs of green on the tips of the ribs or leave these at room temperature for several days until the fruit is evenly yellow-green, then use promptly. Star fruits, like other tropical fruits, do not like cold and should only be refrigerated if in danger of becoming overly ripe. In baking and dessert cookery, they're best used in fresh fruit salads or as a colourful garnish for tropical-themed desserts, ice creams and fruit plates.

SWEET SOPS *(Sugar Apples)* Often confused with the cherimoya or custard apple, the sweet sop is very similar but has distinct, barnacle-like scales on its yellow-green skin. Despite its rather unattractive armour, the flesh is extremely sweet and custard-like, with hints of pear, vanilla and cinnamon. The large black seeds are easily removed, and the fruit may then be eaten raw or used in desserts.

TAMARILLOS *(Tree Tomatoes)* Tamarillos look more like slightly egg-shaped plum tomatoes, with the same thin skin and even a vaguely tomato-like fragrance. Inside is a soft, juicy, jelly-like mass of bright and dark reddish-yellow flesh dotted with tiny black edible seeds. The flavour is elusive—somewhere between a papaya, an apricot and a sweet yellow tomato. Tamarillos are mildly sweet at best, and wincingly tart if underripe. A ripe tamarillo should feel about like a ripe tomato: barely soft, but not mushy or bruised. The skin is edible, but I prefer to remove it before using the fruit in desserts. Do so in the same way as you would peel peaches (see page 280). The best way to eat a perfectly ripe tamarillo is to scoop it out of its skin with a spoon, but the flesh can be used raw or cooked, in fruit salads, sauces, pie and tart fillings, ice creams and custards. One of my favourite ways to prepare tamarillos is to halve the fruit, sprinkle it liberally with sugar and broil or grill it for a few minutes until hot, fragrant and caramelized. Dusted with confectioners' sugar and served with a good vanilla bean ice cream, they are a perfect end to a Latin or Mexican meal. Look for them in specialty fruit stores and Latin, Caribbean or Asian markets from early spring through mid-fall. Store them at room temperature until they yield slightly to a gentle pressure, then use promptly.

Dried Fruits

Though it may sound contrary, dried fruits can and should be fresh. I don't mean originally, but as a dried product they should be treated as perishable ingredients with relatively long shelf lives. In all cases, look for moist, plump fruit, with no signs of very hard, chipped or mouldy bits. Many dried fruits develop a powdery white "bloom" on their surfaces and in the wrinkles and folds, as the naturally occurring sugars crystallize. This bloom is completely harmless and should not be confused with moulds or yeasts. Store all dried fruit in airtight bags or containers at room temperature, away from heat, light and moisture. Stored properly, most should last from 3 months to 1 year, depending on the variety and the freshness when purchased.

When purchasing dried fruit, try to buy in bulk from a good natural food shop or fruit market with a high turnover, instead of grabbing the packaged varieties on the supermarket shelves. This way, you can feel, see, smell and often even taste the fruit to ensure you are buying a fresh, flavourful, moist product. You are also free to buy only as much or as little as you need, which is especially nice when buying pricey fruit such as dried berries or Medjool dates. Health and natural food stores often have very good products in their bulk sections, even offering organic varieties of many fruits. In addition, they sell packaged dried fruits produced by small growers and organic farms that are usually of very high quality. Specialty and gourmet food stores are good sources for imported varieties of dried fruits, such as Agen prunes from France, and while they are likely to be more expensive, the quality of the fruit often makes the price well worth it! If you must buy from a supermarket, read the label and do your best to buy naturally grown, naturally preserved dried fruit.

A word about sulphur and other preservatives used in dried fruits: Many if not most commercially available dried fruits have been treated with sulphur dioxide to retain the original colour of the fruit. Fruits that oxidize easily, such as bananas, pears and apples, turn a medium to dark brown when dried, and manufacturers concerned that the colour will turn consumers off effectively bleach the fruit so it stays a pristine ivory or cream colour. Unfortunately, besides giving the fruit an odd background flavour that many sensitive palates can detect, sulphur and sulphites have been known to cause severe allergic reactions in some people. Although the amount present in most dried fruit is minimal, unsulphured fruit is infinitely preferable (and tastes better, to boot). Unsulphured varieties of most dried fruits can be found in health and natural food stores, and most organically grown dried fruit is also free of sulphur or any other preservative. Unsulphured fruits can be slightly harder than their preservative-enhanced cousins and are often a dull, disappointing shade of brown or gold. These differences may take a little getting used to, but the enhanced flavour and nutritional value you will gain are well worth it.

APPLES Dried apples have been a popular ingredient in cakes, quick breads and even pies for centuries, imparting a mellow, gently sweet flavour and a soft, slightly chewy texture. They are usually sold in rings or slices and can be found with or without the peel. The best dried apples are unsulphured and will have a caramel-brown colour, unlike the stark ivory of their sulphur-treated counterparts. I find them more attractive, actually, and they certainly taste better. Choose plump, very soft dried apple slices, not ones that have become leathery and dry, and use them in cakes, gingerbread, pies, tarts, and even chopped up in cookies and bars.

APRICOTS Dried apricots are almost as popular as fresh in North America and are one of the most luscious dried fruits in the world. They are almost always sold already stoned and can either be whole or in halves. The fat, bright orange apricots that we all know best are one of the most severely preserved fruits, with a very noticeable sulphuric aftertaste. Unsulphured dried apricots are becoming much easier to find, but are quite a shock to the uninitiated. Firm, plump and the colour of burnt caramel, they have a markedly different appearance, but a divine flavour. Intense, concentrated and beautifully sweet with an almost toffee-like flavour, they are much more complex and rewarding to use in sweet cookery than the sulphured variety. As they are not as acidic as the sulphur-treated type, add a squeeze of fresh lemon juice to your recipe. Unsulphured dried apricots may need to be soaked in warm or boiling water for 15 to 30 minutes or more before using in some recipes, until they are soft enough to chop, stuff or purée. They do not store as long as the sulphured variety, about 3 to 4 months in an airtight container, and can take on a strange, almost fermented flavour if stored improperly or too long.

Apricot paste is a wonderful ingredient made from puréed dried apricots. Most varieties are imported from Turkey and are available in plastic-wrapped sheets in Middle Eastern groceries and markets. This thick, sticky, rich orange paste is used for filling pastries, simple cakes and confections and can be tremendous fun. I have used it in fruit bars, spreading it over a layer of crust and topping it with a simple crumble, and it makes a dead easy and deeply flavourful coffee cake filling.

BANANAS Dried banana is an intensely sweet, rich and flavourful product, excellent on its own as a snack, but very good in certain dessert preparations too. Drying intensifies the caramelly sweetness of the ripe fruit, and pieces of dried banana can be used to enhance the flavour of baked goods, ice creams, fruit compotes and even preserves. Look for unsweetened, unsulphured dried bananas, which will have a dark, golden colour and a surprisingly small, shrivelled appearance. They should still be somewhat soft and plump, however. Some producers are using lime juice as a way to preserve the colour of the bananas, creating a more tangy flavour. This variety is delicious, but is better suited to snacking than inclusion in most recipes.

BLUEBERRIES Recently, blueberries have joined cranberries and cherries as the newest thing on the dried fruit scene, showing up in the trendiest scones, muffins, pound cakes, syrups and cookies. Wild berries are usually used, giving a slightly tangy, very flavourful taste to the dried product. Blueberries' natural acidity means they are rarely treated with sulphur or other preservatives and the results are generally of very high quality. They can be quite expensive, but a few go a long way towards making a dessert or baked good unusual and special. Look for plump, soft berries that give slightly when they are pinched. Use them as a substitute for other dried berries or even raisins in baked goods, compotes and even custards, ice creams and sauces.

CHERRIES Dried cherries are one of the most fashionable ingredients these days in dishes both sweet and savoury. They are usually quite expensive, but are bursting with rich, cherry flavour. They can be used in place of fresh cherries in certain recipes or in any situation where other small dried fruit would be appropriate, such as cakes, cookies, bread puddings, pies, ice creams and custards, bars and even sauces or syrups. Both sweet and sour cherries are available in dried form, but the sour variety is more prevalent and better suited to baked goods and desserts, as the flavour of the sweet variety often gets a little lost.

Dried sour cherries have a divinely full flavour and, like blueberries, enough natural acidity for them not to require preservatives. *Dried sweet cherries* are becoming more popular, but are still fairly costly. Plump, intensely flavourful Bing cherries are the most common variety dried, and they're a fantastic addition to many delicately flavoured baked goods and desserts, such as cookies, tarts, cakes and even cheesecake fillings.

Look for both dried sweet and sour cherries in health and natural food stores, as well as in many gourmet and specialty food shops. Buy soft, dark, evenly coloured cherries that give slightly when pinched. Hard or even brittle dried cherries can be rehydrated in boiling water or other liquid for 30 minutes, but try to buy them as fresh as possible.

CRANBERRIES Dried cranberries are a truly wonderful product—the wild, sweet-tart flavour of the fresh berry without the stinging acidity that makes them unpalatable when raw. They can be used in any recipe calling for raisins or other dried berries, and I have used them to great success in baked goods such as muffins and sweet breads in place of fresh cranberries. Look for bright, ruby-coloured berries that are soft when pinched.

CURRANTS Currants are the dried version of the Zante grape, a beautiful, wild blueberry-sized grape with a dark bluish-purple skin and a sweet-tart flavour. Almost the entire crop of Zante grapes is dried, and currants are one of the most popular dried fruits in the world. Cooks in the Middle East and Asia use them widely in savoury dishes, but in the West they are a key ingredient in many desserts, breads and other baked goods. Currant scones, cookies, breads, cakes, and even compotes are wonderful vehicles for these intensely flavoured little fruits. Unless they are very hard, they do not need to be soaked or simmered to rehydrate them before using in a recipe. Use them in place of raisins, dried berries or any other dried fruit in baked goods.

DATES Dates are a plump, sweet tree fruit grown in arid, desert-like areas around the world, including California. Fresh dates are fragile and are rarely exported, but can sometimes be found in specialty markets for brief periods in late summer and early fall. Much of the commercial date crop is dried, though, and bakers, cooks and fruit-lovers alike should rejoice! Fresh dates are already intensely sweet, and this sweetness is only concentrated and enhanced with drying. Dates are among the sweetest, richest and most flavourful dried fruits available, excellent additions to cakes, steamed puddings, sweet breads, tarts, compotes, ice creams and confections. Ranging from about 1 to 3 inches long, dried dates are plump, oval fruits with a smooth, dowel-shaped pit in the centre. This pit is easily removed with a single slit of a sharp paring knife. The skin is papery thin and becomes virtually indistinguishable from the flesh when the fruits are dried.

Several varieties of dried dates are available in most areas of North America, with the most common being packaged *cooking dates*. These have usually been pitted and are an average variety, with a flavour more sweet than complex. Cooking dates are usually chopped or crushed and can also be found in bulk, though be aware that the pits may still be intact. *Honey-pitted dates* are most often whole and meant for plain eating, for confections such as stuffed dates or in recipes calling for whole dates.

Both of these varieties are perfectly satisfactory, but neither can compare to the king of the date family, the colossal *Medjool date*. Medjool dates are plump, large and have a moist, paste-like flesh that is fairly a dessert on its own. Their flavour is incomparable—powerfully rich, sweet and marvellously fruity. They are available in good fruit markets, specialty shops and some natural food stores beginning in late fall, but are staggeringly expensive. The price falls slightly as the winter progresses, but they are never a budget ingredient. In any recipe worth its salt, however, there is simply no better date in the world. If the price is simply prohibitive, consider using a combination of Medjool dates and a good organic variety to get some of the virtues of the first, sustained by the bulk and mild flavour of the second.

FIGS Dried figs are familiar to most North Americans, but few of us have stopped to notice the wonderful variety in colour, shape and flavour available today. Both green and black varieties of figs are commonly found dried, and many ethnic and specialty stores sell rarer varieties and imported figs. *Dried green figs*, such as the fruity *Calimyrna* variety, tend to be slightly less sweet than black ones, with a more delicate, almost floral flavour. *Dried black figs*, such as the almost toffee-like *Mission*, have an intense, chewy sweetness, perfect for rich desserts and baked goods. Dried figs are a good addition to sweet and fruit breads and cakes, as well as compotes, sauces and steamed puddings. They can be cooked and reduced to a sticky paste for use in fillings and topping for cookies, muffins, cakes and even tarts or crostatas. For purées, sauces and spreadable fillings, try soaking the figs in warm water or another liquid (brandy works marvellously!) for about 4 hours or until they are very soft and able to be mashed. This will allow the fruit to retain as much flavour as possible, whereas simmering in liquid that is eventually discarded robs the figs of much of their essence. Look for plump, even-sized fruit that is soft and yielding to the touch. Seek out unusual varieties from Italy, France and the Middle East in specialty, ethnic or gourmet stores. The very best figs I have ever tasted come from France and are widely imported to specialty and gourmet stores. They are dark chocolate brown, almost black, and are fat, incredibly moist and almost syrupy. They are expensive, sometimes as much as $2 apiece, but each exquisite fig is a dessert by itself, ungarnished and even unaccompanied. If you are lucky enough to know of a good source, treat yourself—you will not believe the flavour.

MANGO Dried mango makes a deliciously chewy sweet snack and can also be used as any other dried fruit, in cakes, quick breads, tarts, compotes and preserves. As it is quite tough and leathery, it should be rehydrated in warm water for between 2 and 4 hours or simmered in a light syrup until just tender or completely soft, depending on the intended use. Dried mango has a lovely pronounced flavour that stands up to prolonged cooking, unlike fresh mango. It makes a good addition to light fruit cakes, and in a light gingerbread dried mango and papaya can lend a distinctly tropical flavour, especially if coconut is used as well. Or, combine dried mango with other fresh and dried tropical fruit in a warm compote and serve over vanilla ice cream.

PAPAYA Dried papaya is similar in appearance and uses to dried mango, with a leathery texture and concentrated fruit flavour and sweetness. It can be used as any dried fruit, although it is usually very tough and should be rehydrated in warm water for 2 to 4 hours or simmered in a light syrup until softened. Some dried papaya is sugared on the surface and tends to be softer and more candy-like. This variety rarely needs soaking and can be used like other candied fruits. Dried papaya has a wonderfully bright, very concentrated flavour, not unlike the fresh fruit, but is not quite as complex or subtle. Try pieces of plumped dried papaya stirred into a vanilla custard or tapioca pudding and top with a handful of toasted coconut.

PEACHES Dried peaches are a popular snack in peach-growing regions, with the deep, sweet-tart flavour of caramel, peach and apricot. They are frequently treated with sulphur dioxide, but naturally dried varieties can be found in health and natural food stores. They can be quite tough and leathery and may require soaking or a light poaching to soften them before use in a recipe. Like most other dried fruits, they can be added to cakes, quick breads, pie and tart fillings, compotes, even cookies, as well as being very good all by themselves.

PEARS Dried pears have a wonderful, delicately sweet and rich flavour that makes them better in some cases for baking than fresh pears. They are usually fairly moist for a dried tree fruit, with an addictive chewiness that makes them an indulgent snack. Like peaches, they are available both sulphured and unsulphured, and the latter is far preferable. Some varieties may be slightly tougher than others and may need a short soak in boiling liquid or a light poaching in sugar syrup, but if very fresh and of high quality may be soft enough to be used straight. Dried pears are excellent poached and served warm with ice cream or baked into gingerbread, cakes, quick breads and even pie or tart fillings. Look for the plumpest, softest pears you can find and try not to eat too many before you use them in the recipe.

PINEAPPLE Dried pineapple is a delicious snack, sugary and satisfyingly chewy. It has a pronounced pineapple flavour, with a hint of tanginess. It can be rehydrated in a light sugar syrup, but I prefer to soak it in a bit of rum, brandy or a liqueur. It can be used as any other dried fruit, in cakes, gingerbread, quick breads and muffins, compotes and even ice creams. Dried pineapple is very good in desserts made with fresh pineapple or even the canned variety, such as many carrot cakes, to enhance the flavour of the fruit throughout the dessert and to add a pleasantly chewy texture. It is available in many health and natural food stores.

PRUNES All dried plums are commonly called prunes in English (although the French term for plum is *prune* and the dried version is called a *pruneau* and this all became very confusing in elementary French class ...). Virtually any type of plum can be dried, and there are hundreds of varieties available, with great diversity in appearance, flavour and quality among them. Most of the packaged prunes sold in grocery stores are grown in California and have been treated with sulphur dioxide as a preservative. They are inexpensive, but woefully lacking in flavour. Bulk stores and good natural food stores sell many types of organically grown prunes, usually preserved without chemicals, and these have a good, full, sweet flavour. The very best prunes in the world are reputed to come from the region of Agen in France. *Agen prunes* are available throughout much of North America in specialty or gourmet stores or through mail order from specialty food importers. They are indeed outstanding and make all other varieties pale in comparison. They are plump, even juicy, with a syrupy rich sweetness and a robust sensual flavour that make any references to roughage and bulk fade to black. If you are going to indulge, use Agen prunes where they will be appreciated—combined with apples and vanilla in a simple compote to accompany an Armagnac parfait (see page 564), in a rich custard tart, or all by themselves as petits fours served at the end of a grand meal, perhaps with fresh walnuts, some figs and a glass of Armagnac. When buying prunes, regardless of the variety, look for very plump, moist fruit, with a shiny syrupy glaze, indicating moisture and freshness. Avoid dry, hard and very withered fruit. As with all dried fruit, try to buy prunes in bulk from a natural food store, rather than in the supermarket.

Plum butter, also called *prune butter* or *prune purée*, is a traditional product that has been recently adopted by the low-fat gurus as a fat substitute for baked goods. It has long been used in Eastern European, Russian and Middle Eastern cuisines as an ingredient in cakes and breads and as a filling and topping for cakes, cookies and pastries. It is a thick, sticky, mild-flavoured purée of cooked prunes and adds richness and moisture to baked goods. It can be used to replace some of the fat such as butter or shortening in certain recipes, but be aware that the results can vary widely in flavour and texture. Not all recipes can be tampered with in this manner. Feel free to experiment, however—recipes for many simple cakes, muffins and quick breads can be lightened without too great a sacrifice. Prune purée is available in many supermarkets, occasionally labelled as a fat substitute rather than as a fruit spread. It is also found in health and natural food stores and in many European delis and groceries.

RAISINS A raisin is a dried grape. A dismissive definition, in my opinion, totally unfair to the rich little raisin! Unlike many dried fruits, raisins have a distinctly different flavour than their source, sugary, almost winey, often with strong tones of caramel, toffee, tropical fruits and honey. Although any grape can be dried, the best raisins are made from the most flavourful grapes, such as Thompson and Muscat. California produces almost half of all the raisins sold in the world, but many countries have their own varieties worth seeking out in ethnic markets and specialty food stores.

Dark raisins have been allowed to dry naturally, with the heat of the sun. They shrivel considerably, becoming dark, richly flavoured, with a deep sweetness and a hint of acidity. The same *Thompson* grape produces both the dark, wrinkled raisin, and the plumper golden raisin. *Golden raisins* have been dried artificially, then preserved with sulphur dioxide to prevent them from darkening. They are fatter and slightly sweeter than dark raisins, but have the unfortunate saddle of the sulphur to bear. Fortunately, there is enough natural acidity in grapes that only a minimal amount of sulphur needs be used and in raisins is rarely noticeable. *Sultana raisins*, originally from Turkey but now most often from Australia, are dark golden raisins with a caramelly sweetness and a unique fruity flavour. They are sometimes available unsulphured and are a good substitute for either golden or dark raisins. The intensely flavourful Muscat grape is among the best eating grapes in the world and produces some of the most revered wines and, not coincidentally, some the sweetest, most flavourful raisins as well. *Muscat raisins* are a dark, brownish-black, larger than Thompsons, and are often quite firm and slightly crunchy from the semi-crystallized natural sugars. They have a rich, deep flavour, reminiscent of burnt caramel and honey, and are both dark and sweet with a faintly floral aroma. Often called *Lexia* or *Turkish raisins*, they make the common Thompson raisin seem dull in comparison. They can be used in any dish to replace dark or even golden raisins. A small bowl of good Muscat raisins is a lovely way to end a rich meal, along with some lightly roasted almonds, fresh pears and a glass of something warming and spirited, such as Cognac or Armagnac.

If buying raisins in bulk from a health or natural food store, try to sample a few before deciding. Choose moist, flavourful raisins with no blemishes, and no signs of spoilage or moulds in the bins.

Candied Fruit, Flowers and Chestnuts

Also known as glacé fruits, candied fruit is fruit that has been gently cooked in a sugar syrup until all of the inherent moisture is replaced with the syrup. Often, as is the case with most of the European candied fruit, the process involves repeated poaching in increasingly heavy syrups, to the point when the fruit is plump and firm and has an even, almost fudge-like texture throughout. The painstakingly slow process ensures the delicate flavour of the fruit remains evident and prevents any bitterness or rawness from coming through. The process is highly specialized, and very time-consuming. For these reasons, it is virtually always done professionally, with the exception of citrus peel, which can easily be candied at home. The most commonly candied fruits are described below, but almost any fruit can be treated this way, including pineapple, pears, plums, papaya and figs. Never inexpensive, in general you will pay for quality with candied fruit—cheaper examples may be harshly flavoured and are often dyed. Look for good-quality candied fruit from France, Germany and England, in fine food shops, and perhaps even from specialty local sources.

ANGELICA This "herb of the angels," as it is sometimes known, is actually a member of the parsley family. Fresh, its long green stalks resemble celery, but it is rarely used in its raw state. Instead, it is candied, becoming almost like glassine and retaining a vibrant green colour. Little known in North America, it is used extensively in French and other European cuisines as a garnish and flavouring for desserts and sweets. Although Switzerland is the largest producer of candied angelica, France is by far its biggest consumer, using it to adorn petits fours, cakes, sweet breads and even truffles. Angelica is also used as a flavouring for liqueurs. Available at specialty stores and baking supply shops, candied angelica should be stored in an airtight container at room temperature for up to 6 months.

CHERRIES Also called glacé cherries or Maraschino cherries, candied cherries are sweet cherries that have been pitted, then macerated and cooked in a pleasantly flavoured sugar syrup. The candied cherries are then dyed a bright red or green and either bottled whole, stems and all, for use as a decoration for drinks and sundaes; or halved and packaged, to be used for fruit cakes, holiday breads and as decoration for cookies and other baked goods. Originally made from the rare Italian Marasca cherry, they are now commonly made from sweet Royal Ann cherries. Maraschino cherries should never be used to replace any other type of cherry.

CITRUS RINDS *Orange and lemon peel*, though unpalatably bitter when raw, can be slowly cooked in a sugar syrup, or candied. The intensity of flavour remains, and much of the bitterness is replaced with sweetness. If the thin white under-layer, known as the pith, is left on the outer coloured layer, the resulting candied peel will still retain some bitterness (think marmalade), whereas if only the zest or coloured part is used, the peel will be sweeter and more intensely flavoured.

Used frequently in Italian sweets and breads, candied citrus peel is common in North America in fruitcakes, mincemeat and as a decoration for holiday cookies. Sadly, most of what is sold in packages and in bulk as candied lemon or orange peel is actually candied citron peel, artificially dyed yellow or orange. Laden with preservatives, it would probably outlast the most stubborn fruitcake. I avoid this stuff like the plague, in any form—its flavour is harsh and often acrid, and it has none of the delicate fruity flavour of the real thing. (See Citron Peel, below, for storage tips.) Fortunately, good candied peel is easy to make, keeps ages and is wonderfully versatile. Following the recipe for *Candied Orange Peel* on page 634 you can make delicate candied orange, lemon, grapefruit, and even lime peel. Fruitcake never had it so good!

Citron peel is made from the citron, a large, knobbly lemon-lime hued member of the citrus family that looks like an underripe and overgrown lemon. Indeed, even when fully ripe the citron is about as sour as an underripe lemon. Never eaten raw, it is cultivated almost exclusively for its thick bumpy rind, which is candied and used in cakes, breads and confections. Before being cooked in the sugar syrup, the peel is brined and the highly aromatic oils are extracted for use in liqueurs and perfumes. Although freshly candied citron peel is sometimes available from baking supply shops and specialty stores, the vast majority of it is treated with preservatives to extend its shelf life. Dyes are added: pale green for citron, orange for candied orange peel and yellow for candied lemon peel. The rind is then chopped and sold as all three fruits. By all means, try to find a source for freshly candied citron, then store it well-wrapped in the freezer for up to 6 months. Preservative-added candied citron peel should be stored in an airtight container at room temperature for up to 6 months.

GINGER *Candied* or *crystallized ginger* has been sliced and cooked slowly in a heavy sugar syrup until all of the moisture has been replaced with the sugar. The ginger is then coated with more sugar and dried. It is sweet and tangy and can be eaten plain as a candy, chopped and used as a garnish for cookies and confections or incorporated into many baked goods and desserts to add a rich, warm, sweet ginger flavour. It is nicely chewy and makes a good addition to gingerbread, cookies and many plain, spiced and fruit cakes. The best candied ginger comes from Australia and is often available in specialty and gourmet food shops. Stored at room temperature in an airtight container, it keeps almost indefinitely.

Preserved ginger in syrup is similar to candied ginger, but is suspended in a thick sugar syrup. It is sold in glass jars and can be found in many supermarkets as well as Asian and European groceries. Almost a confection in itself, ginger in syrup is wonderful chopped and spooned with its syrup over ice cream or drizzled over a warm gingerbread. Use a little of the syrup as a flavouring for cakes, quick breads, cookies and compotes and the chopped ginger in the same way or in place of candied ginger in baked goods. It is delicious added to many desserts, and the syrup can be used to flavour cakes, fillings, custards, puddings and ice creams. Store in the refrigerator or in a cool, dark place for up to 6 months.

MARRONS GLACÉS Candied chestnuts, called *marrons glacés*, are among the most costly bonbons around, but their deep, mellow, vanilla-laced flavour makes them worth every penny. They can be chopped and added to mousses, ice creams and batters, and are often used in French and Italian desserts and pastries, but they can also be eaten all by themselves as a petit four or in lieu of truffles or other small confections. Look for tins or shrink-wrapped boxes of imported French marrons glacés in gourmet and specialty food stores, especially around the holidays.

CANDIED (CRYSTALLIZED) ROSES AND VIOLETS The petals of roses and violets are often crystallized and used as a decoration for cakes, pastries and other desserts. You can buy them in cake decorating and specialty food stores, but these are often shattered and broken, and terribly expensive. They are very easy to make, however, and last a year or more if stored properly. See page 84 for instructions on how to crystallize roses, violets and other edible flowers.

Sweet Vegetables

CARROTS Carrot cake, carrot muffins, carrot cookies... Perfect vehicles for cream cheese frosting, to be sure, but great desserts in their own right. Carrots are among the most popular vegetables in the world, and have been for millennia. Rich in vitamins, they are versatile, delicious and widely available year round. For baking, I generally prefer the large, sweet mature variety, often sold in bulk in fresh markets and grocery stores. Their flavour is full and sweet, and much more satisfying than that of the dainty baby carrots. If buying carrots with lacy tops still attached, look for fresh, vibrant foliage and stiff roots. Remove the green tops as soon as possible, as they quickly leach sweetness and nutrients out of the orange root. Avoid carrots that are bendy or blemished, and in general stay clear of pre-cut carrots in plastic packages—most of the nutrients are long gone, and the flesh has more than likely started to deteriorate. If stored in the refrigerator in plastic bags with a few holes poked in them, carrots can last several weeks.(Don't, however, store them near apples, which emit a gas that can turn carrots' flavour quite bitter.) For baking, add carrots raw or, even better, cooked and mashed to batters, doughs and puddings. Larger older carrots should be peeled before use, while young or baby ones are fine with a good scrubbing.

PARSNIPS No, not turnips, *parsnips*. And yes, they are sweet. Not to be confused with the more celery-flavoured parsley root, these long creamy-yellow roots look like white carrots. Despite their mild, distinctly sweet flavour, they have never really caught on in North America as a favourite vegetable. Their sweetness is a result of the first frost, when some of their high starch is converted to sugar. At their peak between mid-fall and late winter, they are perfect candidates for oven roasting and caramelizing, and in turn for use in muffins, cakes and quick breads. They can also be mashed, after either roasting, steaming or boiling, and then added to batters and doughs. They can be used in most recipes where carrots are called for, although a little additional moisture in the form of liquid or fat might need to be added. Choose firm, medium-sized roots and avoid those that are shrivelled, splotchy or limp. Parsnips will last for several weeks if stored in a plastic bag in the refrigerator. In general, they should be peeled before use.

PUMPKINS AND SQUASH Pumpkins and squash are members of a huge family of gourds and are also related to melons. Gourds have a thick, hard, inedible rind protecting dense, often dry flesh, similar in texture to a potato when raw. They are beautiful fruit—some are plump and round, some are long and gently curved, some smooth and glossy and some elaborately decorated with raised ribbons and bumps. Often various shades of orange, yellow and green, the skin may also be red, white, brown and even almost grey. The flesh may be hard and dry, or stringy and moist. It is usually orange or yellow, but may range from as dark as a sweet potato to as pale as a banana.

Most gourds are native to North and South America, and dozens of varieties are available in various regions of Canada and the United States. While most supermarkets carry a good selection, seek out lesser-known and local varieties in farmers' markets and specialty fruit stores in the fall.

Although used more today as savoury vegetables than ingredients in desserts, the sweet mild flavour of many pumpkins and squash make them wonderful additions to the sweet kitchen. Whole, pumpkins and squash keep very well. Stored in a cold storage pantry or at cool room temperature, they will keep a month or so; refrigerated, they will last up to 3 months.

For baking and desserts, a few key varieties stand out. Most common for the traditional pumpkin pie are *sugar* or *pie pumpkins*. These look very similar to the large pumpkins carved at Hallowe'en, but are only about the size of a large grapefruit. They have a smooth, sweet flesh that is much less pulpy and stringy than their jack-o'-lantern brethren and are more manageable due to their size! They are widely available during the fall and early winter and are very inexpensive if locally grown.

Squash are not commonly thought of as dessert fruits, but there are several varieties whose sweet, dense and flavourful flesh make them a wonderful substitute for pumpkin in many desserts, such as pies, tarts, quick breads and cakes. I have also used them either in place of, or in combination with, sweet potatoes to great success. The pale yellow-orange *butternut squash* is a long, club-shaped squash with a hard, waxy rind and a rich orange flesh. When cooked, it has a smooth, creamy texture and a lovely sweet mild flavour. Cut the squash in half through its waist, creating one long cylinder and one bulb. Cut off the top and bottom of the squash and set each half on the flat end. With a very sharp, heavy knife, slice the rind off the flesh, trimming where necessary. The cylindrical neck half of the fruit contains no seeds and is solid, usable flesh. The bulb portion must be halved from top to bottom, then cut into eighths. The stringy seed web can then be cut or spooned out, and the flesh used as for pumpkin.

The fat, stout *buttercup squash* is another good baking squash. Buttercups are related to the *turban squash* and have a similar knobbly green-grey-blue skin, often painted with streaks of grey. Its orange flesh is even sweeter than that of the butternut and makes for divine desserts. The rind of the buttercup is almost rock-hard; be sure to use a very sharp, heavy knife when butchering it and be careful to anchor the squash so it doesn't suddenly roll off your cutting board.

The best way to prepare the flesh of pumpkins and hard-rinded squash such as the buttercup for baking is to steam or bake the fruit with the skin still intact. Cut off the stem end and the flower end, then cut the fruit into wedges, leaving the rind on the flesh. Scrape out the seeds and stringy fibres with a kitchen spoon. Place the wedges in the top of a vegetable steamer, cover, then steam over boiling water until very tender when pierced with a sharp knife. Alternatively, cut the two ends from the fruit, but otherwise leave it whole and bake in a preheated 350° oven for 45 minutes to 1½ hours, or until the fruit feels soft and tender. With either method, cool the cooked fruit slightly, then scrape the soft flesh from the rind. Mash the flesh and force it through a ricer, food mill or a wire-mesh sieve. Allow the flesh to cool before combining it with the remaining ingredients in a recipe or storing. Although it will keep airtight in the refrigerator for about 4 to 5 days, cooked pumpkin or squash flesh freezes beautifully too. Pack it into freezer bags or airtight containers, removing as much of the air as possible, and freeze for up to 8 months. Thaw the flesh overnight in the refrigerator before using in pies, cakes, muffins or breads.

Canned, solid-pack pumpkin is widely available and is one of those rare processed products that is almost as good as fresh. Canned pumpkin purée saves a great deal of effort and can be used at any time of the year. Do not, however, confuse canned, solid-pack pumpkin with *canned pumpkin pie filling*, which has spices and often sugar added. This product is best avoided. Leftover canned solid-pack pumpkin should be transferred to a clean, airtight container and refrigerated up to 1 week or frozen for up to 6 months.

Pumpkin seeds, often called *pepitas*, are a common addition to many Mexican and Latin American dishes. They are delicious dried, then toasted in a moderate oven. They can be salted or left plain and are a great snack (see page 268).

RHUBARB The bright red stalks of rhubarb are more eagerly anticipated in my house than the equally red robin as a herald of spring. Their sweet-tart flavour is a perfect wake-up call to sleepy winter taste buds, and their glorious ruby hue adds a touch of colour to the dull palate of winter. Rhubarb can be divided into two types, hothouse or cultivated rhubarb and wild rhubarb. *Hothouse rhubarb* is available in much of North America throughout the year and is distinguished by its thick pink and green stalks. It has a mild, pleasant flavour, but hardly compares to the wild stuff that appears with the first signs of spring. I have found it lacks the necessary acidity to carry the delicate flavour of the rhubarb throughout a dish, especially in the presence of other flavours. *Field* or *wild rhubarb* has dark red and green stalks, often somewhat thicker than the hothouse variety. Its flavour is intense, with a distinct sweetness and a generous astringency, making it perfect for baking. In fact, so suited is it to certain desserts, it long ago acquired the name "pie plant." It grows eagerly and wild in much of Canada and the northern United States, as prolific as a weed. Many people have rhubarb growing rampant in their backyards, doing nothing to aid or encourage it! Lucky them, for it is a key ingredient in some of the most popular desserts around. Almost always treated as a fruit, rhubarb is used mainly in sweet cookery rather than savoury. Its celery-like stalks can grow as tall as two feet, with great, thick green leaves. The leaves must be discarded, as they are toxic if ingested. Rhubarb must be cooked with a fair amount of sugar before it can be eaten, as it is unpalatably tart on its own. It can be stewed simply, with sugar and nothing more or can be combined with sweet ingredients, such as strawberries or raspberries. It has a particular affinity with cream, ginger, oranges, apples and strawberries and is most often used with these flavours.

Choose firm, unblemished, slender stalks, as the larger ones can be overly stringy and pulpy. Try to buy stalks with a great deal of red or pink, a sign of ripeness and full flavour. The leaves should be intact and healthy looking, not insect-eaten or wilted and brown. Hothouse rhubarb is somewhat hardier than the field or wild varieties, but all rhubarb deteriorates quickly once picked and should be used promptly. Store fresh unwashed stalks, leaves and all, in the refrigerator, well-wrapped in plastic for no more than a day or two. Cooked rhubarb pulp can be frozen in airtight bags or containers, and even the fresh stalks, cut into pieces, freeze fairly well.

Rhubarb, especially the field or wild variety, releases a surprising amount of liquid when cooked. Don't be afraid to discard some of this liquid in cases where the cooked rhubarb is to be added to other ingredients, such as in ice creams or fools. Some recipes for pies, tarts and crumbles call for the rhubarb to be cooked before being combined with the other filling ingredients, but I have found this is rarely necessary and makes for a less pleasant texture. Simply toss the cut stalks with the sugar and the starch or flour in the recipe and let the mixture sit for about 10 minutes so the sugar has a chance to draw out some of the liquid. Add the mixture, juice and all, to the filling, and the result will usually be properly thickened yet juicy. Be wary of recipes that do not call for much or any thickener, though—a ratio of 3 to 4 tablespoons of flour for every 1½ pounds of rhubarb, depending on the other fruits use in the filling, if any, is a good guide.

SWEET POTATOES The rich sweet flavour and creamy texture of cooked sweet potato is tailor-made for desserts. Sweet potatoes make fabulous pies, puddings, custards, cakes, quick breads and even ice cream and are abundant and inexpensive to boot. In areas where they have been a mainstay of the diet for generations, sweet potatoes have become the base for many baked goods and desserts, from the southern U.S. sweet potato pie to light and fluffy sweet potato biscuits. Grown extensively throughout North and South America, the sweet potato is often falsely called a *yam*. Yams, in fact, are a totally different species and are actually quite rare in this part of the world.

Two types of sweet potatoes are common in North America. The *pale sweet potato*, sometimes called the *white sweet potato*, has a light orange or amber skin and ivory-orange flesh. It has a mild flavour and can be used much as a regular white potato. *Dark sweet potatoes* have a rich salmon-orange skin and a deep orange flesh. They are considerably sweeter than the pale variety and are much preferable for baking, not to mention the traditional sweet potato casserole essential to so many holiday feasts. They can be baked, steamed, boiled or fried and have a full, round, richly sweet flavour. They have a wonderful affinity with other sweet ingredients, especially brown and maple sugar, as well as butter, rich nuts and spirits such as bourbon, rum and brandy.

Caribbean and Latin markets often stock yet another tuber often confused with the sweet potato. Sometimes mistaken for the white sweet potato, the *boniato* is an unrelated species, with a flavour and texture somewhere between a common potato and a sweet potato. They are not generally used in baking and dessert cookery.

Dark sweet potatoes are generally available throughout the year, but are at their peak in the fall and winter. They can be stored for up to 3 months in a cold-storage pantry, away from light, heat and moisture, or at room temperature, ideally in a dark, aerated place, for about 2 weeks. They do not need refrigeration, but deteriorate quickly in the presence of warmth and light. Keep them away from onions as well, as they tend to accelerate each other's demise. Choose small or medium-sized sweet potatoes, with smooth, uncracked or undamaged skin. Some irresponsible grocers have a frustrating habit of lumping pale and dark sweet potatoes in the same bins, so make sure you buy potatoes of the same shade. They should be hard and smooth, with no soft or wrinkled areas.

Canned sweet potatoes are widely available, but tend to have an overly soft, mushy texture that rarely works in dessert recipes. The flavour will be more "cooked" than that of freshly prepared potatoes, and the result is usually disappointing. Sweet potatoes are too common to bother with inferior substitutes like this!

INGREDIENT
SUBSTITUTION CHART

WHEN LOOKING TO substitute one ingredient for another, you should first understand the role of the original ingredient in the final dessert in order to find a suitable replacement that will produce a similar result. See the section on ingredients (beginning on page 89) and their roles in various products before substituting any ingredient for another.

INGREDIENT	AMOUNT AND FORM	SUBSTITUTIONS
Ammonium bicarbonate	¾ teaspoon	◆ 1 teaspoon baking soda
Anise seed	whole or ground	◆ equal amount star anise
Arrowroot	1 tablespoon	◆ 2¼ teaspoons cornstarch, potato starch, rice starch ◆ 1½ to 2 tablespoons all-purpose flour to thicken
Armagnac	¼ cup	◆ ¼ cup Cognac ◆ ¼ cup brandy
Bakewell Cream	2 teaspoons Bakewell Cream plus 1 teaspoon baking soda	◆ 2 teaspoons baking powder

continued on page 336

Baking powder, double-acting	1 teaspoon	• ¼ teaspoon baking soda plus ½ teaspoon cream of tartar (plus ¼ to ½ teaspoon cornstarch, optional) • 1½ teaspoons single-action (phosphate or tartrate) baking powder • ¼ teaspoon baking soda plus ½ cup buttermilk, sour milk or yogurt to replace ½ cup non-acidic liquid in the recipe
Baking soda	1 teaspoon	• 4 teaspoons double-acting baking powder (replace acidic liquid in recipe with non-acidic liquid)
Bourbon	¼ cup	• ¼ cup Scotch or rye whiskey • ¼ cup Cognac
Brandy	¼ cup	• ¼ cup Cognac • ¼ cup Bourbon • ¼ cup Scotch whiskey • ¼ cup dark rum, if flavour is suitable
Bread crumbs, dry	1 cup	• 1⅓ cup fresh bread crumbs • ¾ cup plain cracker crumbs • ¾ cup matzoh meal • ¾ cup crushed cornflake cereal • ⅔ cup all-purpose flour, in some recipes
Buttermilk, sour milk	1 cup	• 1 tablespoon vinegar plus enough milk to make 1 cup (let stand 5 minutes) • 2 tablespoons lemon juice plus

Buttermilk, sour milk	*continued*	enough milk to make 1 cup (let stand 5 minutes) • 1 cup milk plus 1½ teaspoons cream of tartar • 1 cup plain yogurt • 1 cup sour cream • 1 cup mild-flavoured soy milk plus 1 tablespoon vinegar or lemon juice (in baked goods only)
Butter, unsalted	1 cup	• 1 cup salted butter (decrease the salt in the recipe by ½ teaspoon) • 1 cup unsalted margarine (not recommended) • 1 cup solid vegetable shortening (for pie crusts only) • 1 cup lard (for pie crusts only)
Butter, clarified, for frying	2 tablespoons	• 2 tablespoons ghee • 2 tablespoons vegetable oil • 2 tablespoons bacon fat, if flavour is appropriate • 2 tablespoons lard, if flavour is appropriate
Cardamom, ground	1 teaspoon	• ¾ teaspoon ground cinnamon plus ¼ teaspoon freshly grated lemon zest
Carob powder	3 tablespoons plus 2 tablespoons water	• 1 ounce unsweetened chocolate • 3 tablespoons unsweetened cocoa, Dutch-process or natural, plus 2 tablespoons water

continued on page 338

Cassia, ground	1 teaspoon	◆ 1 teaspoon ground cinnamon
Chocolate, bittersweet or semisweet	1 ounce	◆ ½ ounce unsweetened chocolate plus 1 to 1½ tablespoons granulated sugar
Chocolate, bittersweet or semisweet, melted	6 ounces	◆ ½ cup plus 1 tablespoon unsweetened natural cocoa plus 7 tablespoons granulated sugar plus 3 tablespoons unsalted butter
Chocolate, milk, chips or chunks	1 ounce	◆ 1 ounce bittersweet or semisweet chocolate plus 1 tablespoon granulated sugar ◆ 1 ounce sweet dark chocolate ◆ 1 ounce white chocolate
Chocolate, sweet	1 ounce	◆ 1 ounce bittersweet or semisweet chocolate plus ½ tablespoon granulated sugar ◆ 1 ounce milk chocolate ◆ 1 ounce white chocolate
Chocolate, unsweetened	1 ounce	◆ 3 tablespoons unsweetened natural cocoa powder plus 1 tablespoon unsalted butter or shortening, melted if desired ◆ 1⅔ ounce bittersweet or semisweet chocolate (reduce sugar in recipe by 4 tablespoons) ◆ 3 tablespoons carob powder plus 2 tablespoons water or milk
Chocolate, white, chips or chunks	1 ounce	◆ 1 ounce milk chocolate ◆ 1 ounce sweet dark chocolate

Cinnamon, ground	1 teaspoon	• 1 teaspoon ground cassia
Cocoa, unsweetened, Dutch-process	3 tablespoons	• 3 tablespoons natural cocoa powder plus pinch ($\frac{1}{8}$ teaspoon) baking soda • 1 ounce unsweetened chocolate plus pinch baking soda (reduce fat in recipe by 1 tablespoon) • 3 tablespoons carob powder
Cocoa, unsweetened, natural	3 tablespoons	• 3 tablespoons Dutch-process cocoa plus pinch cream of tartar or $\frac{1}{8}$ teaspoon lemon juice or vinegar • 1 ounce unsweetened chocolate (reduce the fat in the recipe by 1 tablespoon) • 3 tablespoons carob powder
Coconut, fresh	1 cup	• 1 cup dried flaked coconut • $\frac{3}{4}$ cup dried shredded coconut
Coconut, dry shredded	1 cup	• 1$\frac{1}{4}$ cups freshly grated coconut • 1$\frac{1}{4}$ cup dried flaked coconut
Coconut milk, fresh	1 cup	• 1 cup canned coconut milk (not low-fat) • 3 tablespoons canned cream of coconut plus enough hot water or milk to make 1 cup • 3 to 5 tablespoons grated creamed coconut dissolved in enough whole milk to make 1 cup • $\frac{1}{4}$ cup coconut cream powder plus 1 cup hot water or milk

continued on page 340

Coconut cream, fresh	1 cup	• 1 cup canned coconut cream • 1 cup top layer of canned coconut milk (not low-fat) • 1 cup heavy cream (36%) plus ½ cup coconut cream powder • ¼ to ⅓ cup grated creamed coconut dissolved in enough heavy cream (36%) to make 1 cup
Coffee, strong brewed	¼ cup	• 2 tablespoons instant espresso powder dissolved in 3 tablespoons hot water
Cognac	¼ cup	• ¼ cup Armagnac • ¼ cup Bourbon • ¼ cup Scotch or rye whiskey • ¼ cup dark rum, if flavour is suitable
Cornmeal, stone-ground	½ cup	• ½ cup regular milled cornmeal • ½ cup corn grits • ½ cup polenta • ½ cup maize meal
Cornstarch	1 tablespoon	• 2 tablespoons all-purpose flour • 1 tablespoon potato starch • 1 tablespoon rice starch • 1½ tablespoons arrowroot • 4 teaspoons instant (quick-cooking) tapioca
Corn syrup, light	1 cup	• 1 cup granulated white sugar (increase the amount of liquid in recipe by ¼ cup or decrease flour by ¼ cup)

Corn syrup, light	*continued*	◆ 1 cup liquid glucose ◆ 1 cup dark corn syrup
Corn syrup, dark	1 cup	◆ 1 cup light or dark brown sugar (increase the amount of liquid in recipe by ¼ cup or decrease flour by ¼ cup) ◆ 1 cup light corn syrup ◆ ¾ cup light corn syrup plus ¼ cup molasses, maple syrup or dark honey
Cream, clotted	1 cup	◆ 1 cup crème fraîche ◆ 1 cup mascarpone cheese ◆ 1 cup heavy cream (36%), whipped
Cream, light (5%) (available only in Canada)	1 cup	◆ ⅞ cup whole milk plus 1 tablespoon butter ◆ ¾ cup whole milk plus ¼ cup whipping cream (35%) ◆ ⅞ cup full-fat, mild-flavoured soy milk plus 1 tablespoon butter (in baked goods only)
Cream, half-and-half (10.5 to 18%)	1 cup	◆ ½ cup whole milk (3.5%) plus ½ cup light cream (18 to 30%) ◆ ½ cup partly skimmed milk plus ½ cup heavy cream (36%) ◆ ⅞ cup whole milk plus 2 tablespoons unsalted butter
Cream, sour	1 cup	◆ 1 cup plain yogurt ◆ ¾ cup buttermilk plus ⅓ cup butter ◆ 1 cup crème fraîche

continued on page 342

Cream, sour	*continued*	• ¾ cup whole milk combined with 1 tablespoon white vinegar, plus ¼ cup melted butter • 1 cup mild-flavoured soy milk (in baked goods only)
Cream, light (18 to 30%)	1 cup	• ⅞ cup milk plus 3 tablespoons butter
Cream, heavy (36%) (not for whipping)	1 cup	• 1 cup evaporated milk • ⅔ cup whole milk warmed with ⅓ cup unsalted butter
Cream of tartar	¼ teaspoon	• ⅛ to ¼ teaspoon white vinegar
Crème fraîche	1 cup	• 1 cup sour cream • ½ cup sour cream plus ½ cup heavy cream (36%) • 1 cup mascarpone cheese
Currants, dried	1 cup	• 1 cup raisins • 1 cup dried cranberries, blueberries or cherries • 1 cup other dried fruit, finely chopped
Eggs, whole	1 large egg (about 2 ounces)	• 2 large egg yolks plus 1 tablespoon water (in baked goods) • 2 large egg yolks (in custards, sauces, puddings and mousses) • 3½ tablespoons frozen whole egg, thawed • 3 to 4 tablespoons egg replacement substitute • 2½ tablespoons powdered whole egg plus 2½ tablespoons water

Eggs, whites	1 large white	• 2 tablespoons frozen egg whites, thawed • 2 tablespoons packaged egg whites • 1 tablespoon powdered egg white plus 2 tablespoons water
Eggs, yolks	2 large yolks	• 1 whole egg
Eggs, yolks	1 large yolk	• 3½ teaspoons frozen egg yolks, thawed • 2 tablespoons powdered egg yolk plus 2 teaspoons water
*Flour, white, all-purpose	1 cup, sifted	• 1 cup plus 2 tablespoons white cake flour (not self-rising) • ⅞ cup hard (bread) flour • ½ cup white cake flour plus ½ cup whole wheat flour • ½ cup whole wheat flour plus ½ cup oat flour (for breads, some cakes and some quick breads) • 1¼ cups whole rye flour (in some recipes) • 1 cup cornmeal (do not replace all of the flour with cornmeal) • ⅞ cup rice starch (rice flour) (do not replace all of the flour with rice starch)
Flour, white, as a thickener	4 tablespoons (¼ cup)	• 2 tablespoons cornstarch • 3 tablespoons instant tapioca

continued on page 344

Flour, white, as a thickener	*continued*	◆ 2½ tablespoons arrowroot ◆ 2 tablespoons potato starch ◆ (flour) ◆ 2 tablespoons rice starch (flour)
Flour, white, cake	1 cup	◆ ⅞ cup white all-purpose flour and 2 tablespoons cornstarch
Flour, white self-rising	1 cup	◆ 1 cup similar grade flour (all-purpose or cake) plus 1 teaspoon baking powder and ½ teaspoon salt
Flour, whole wheat	1 cup	◆ ⅞ cup white flour plus 2 tablespoons wheat germ
Gelatine, leaf (sheet)	4 leaves (4" x 9")	◆ 1 (¼-ounce) envelope powdered gelatine
Gelatine, powdered	1 envelope (¼-ounce)	◆ 4 leaves sheet gelatine ◆ ¼ ounce powdered agar-agar
Ghee	2 tablespoons	◆ 2 tablespoons clarified butter ◆ 2 tablespoons vegetable oil
Ginger root, freshly grated	2 teaspoons	◆ 2 teaspoons candied ginger, rinsed and finely minced ◆ 1½ teaspoons dried ginger plus ½ teaspoon freshly squeezed lemon juice
Glucose, liquid	1 cup	◆ 1 cup light corn syrup
Grits, corn	1 cup	◆ 1 cup cornmeal ◆ 1 cup polenta ◆ 1 cup maize meal

Honey	1 cup	• 1¼ cup granulated white or brown sugar, plus ¼ cup additional liquid plus ½ teaspoon cream of tartar • ¾ cup light molasses plus ½ cup granulated sugar • ¾ cup dark corn syrup plus ½ cup granulated sugar • ¾ cup maple syrup plus ½ cup granulated sugar • ¾ cup barley malt syrup plus ½ cup granulated sugar (increase dry ingredients by 2 to 4 tablespoons) • ¾ cup brown rice syrup plus ½ cup granulated sugar (increase dry ingredients by 2 to 4 tablespoons)
Lard	1 cup	• 1 cup solid vegetable shortening • 1 cup plus 2 tablespoons unsalted butter
Lemon juice, freshly squeezed	2 tablespoons	• 2 tablespoons bottled lemon juice • 1½ tablespoons freshly squeezed lime juice • 1 tablespoon vinegar, if flavour is not a consideration
Lemon zest, freshly grated	2 teaspoons	• 2 teaspoons orange zest • 2 teaspoons lime zest • 2 teaspoons orange or lemon marmalade • 2 teaspoons finely minced candied ginger

continued on page 346

Lime juice, freshly squeezed	2 tablespoons	• 2½ tablespoons freshly squeezed lemon juice • 3 teaspoons orange juice
Lime zest, freshly grated	2 teaspoons	• 2 teaspoons lemon zest • 2 teaspoons orange zest • 2 teaspoons finely minced candied ginger
Mace, ground	1 teaspoon	• 1 teaspoon ground nutmeg
Margarine	1 cup	• 1 cup butter • 1 cup solid vegetable shortening
Maple sugar, finely grated	½ cup	• 1 cup maple syrup (reduce liquid in recipe by ¼ cup) • ¾ cup granulated sugar plus 1 teaspoon pure maple extract
Maple syrup	1 cup	• ½ cup maple sugar (increase liquid in recipe by ¼ cup) • 1 cup honey
Mascarpone cheese	1 cup	• 1 cup crème fraîche • ¾ cup cream cheese, beaten with ¼ cup heavy cream (36%)
Milk, fresh, whole (3.5%)	1 cup	• 1 cup skim (non-fat) milk plus 2 tablespoons butter • ¼ cup powdered whole milk plus ⅞ cup water • ¼ cup powdered skim milk plus ⅞ cup water plus 1 tablespoon butter • ½ cup evaporated whole milk plus ½ cup water • 1 cup water plus 2 tablespoons unsalted butter

Milk, fresh, whole (3.5%)	*continued*	◆ 1 cup mild-flavoured soy or nut milk, in some recipes, such as baked goods ◆ 1 cup fruit juice, in some recipes
Milk, fresh, skim (non-fat)	1 cup	◆ ¼ cup powdered skim milk plus ⅞ cup water
Milk, evaporated whole	1 cup	◆ 1 cup light cream (18%) ◆ 1 cup heavy cream (36%)
Molasses	1 cup	◆ 1 cup dark honey ◆ 1 cup grade C maple syrup ◆ ¾ cup dark brown sugar heated to dissolve in ¼ cup liquid ◆ 1 cup dark corn syrup ◆ 1 cup brown rice syrup ◆ 1 cup barley malt syrup
Nuts, ground, chopped, whole	1 cup	◆ 1 cup similar nuts, prepared the same way (i.e., almonds for hazelnuts, pecans for walnuts, etc.)
Orange juice, fresh	1 cup (from about 3 oranges)	◆ 1 cup reconstituted frozen concentrate
Orange zest, freshly grated	2 teaspoons	◆ 2 teaspoons finely grated lemon zest ◆ 2 teaspoons finely grated lime zest ◆ 2 teaspoons finely chopped candied orange peel ◆ 1 teaspoon marmalade ◆ 2 teaspoons candied ginger, minced

continued on page 348

Peanut butter	1 cup, smooth or chunky	• 1 cup other nut butter, such as almond, hazelnut, etc. • 1 cup tahini (sesame paste)
Polenta (dry)	1 cup	• 1 cup cornmeal • 1 cup maize meal • 1 cup corn grits
Raisins	1 cup	• 1 cup dried currants • 1 cup dried blueberries, cranberries or cherries • 1 cup other finely chopped dried fruit
Star anise, ground	1 teaspoon	• 1 teaspoon ground anise seed • 1 teaspoon ground fennel seed
Sugar, granulated white	1 cup	• 1 cup superfine sugar • 1 cup tightly packed light or dark brown sugar • 1 cup raw sugar • 1¾ cup confectioners' sugar, sifted • 1¼ cups molasses or maple syrup plus ½ teaspoon baking soda (decrease liquid in recipe by ¼ cup or increase flour by ¼ cup) • ¾ cup honey plus ½ teaspoon baking soda (decrease the amount of liquid in recipe by ¼ cup or increase flour by ¼ cup) • 1 cup maple sugar, if flavour is appropriate, plus ½ teaspoon baking soda • 1 cup Sucanat

Sugar, granulated white	*continued*	◆ 2½ cups barley malt syrup or brown rice syrup (for some recipes only; increase dry ingredients by ½ to ¾ cup)
Sugar, brown, light or dark	1 cup tightly packed	◆ 1 cup raw sugar ◆ 1 cup granulated white sugar ◆ ⅞ cup white sugar plus ¼ cup molasses, maple syrup, dark corn syrup or honey ◆ For light brown sugar, substitute ½ cup dark brown sugar plus ½ cup granulated sugar
Sugar, raw	1 cup, tightly packed	◆ 1 cup light or dark brown sugar ◆ ⅞ cup granulated white sugar plus ¼ cup molasses
Sugar, superfine	1 cup	◆ 1 cup granulated white sugar spun in food processor
Sugar, fructose	1 cup	◆ 1½ cups superfine sugar ◆ 1½ cups granulated white sugar, spun in food processor
Tapioca, instant (quick-cooking)	2 tablespoons	◆ 4 tablespoons pearl tapioca, soaked ◆ 3 tablespoons flour ◆ 1½ tablespoons cornstarch
**Vanilla extract, pure	1 teaspoon	◆ ½ Bourbon-Madagascar vanilla bean ◆ ½ Mexican vanilla bean ◆ ¼ Tahitian vanilla bean ◆ ½ to 1 teaspoon other extract, such as almond, peppermint, lemon, orange, etc.

continued on page 350

**Vanilla bean, Bourbon-Madagascar	1 bean	♦ 1 Mexican vanilla bean ♦ ½ Tahitian vanilla bean ♦ 2 teaspoons pure vanilla extract
**Vanilla bean, Mexican	1 bean	♦ 1 Bourbon-Madagascar vanilla bean ♦ ½ Tahitian vanilla bean ♦ 2 teaspoons pure vanilla extract
**Vanilla bean, Tahitian	1 bean	♦ 2 Bourbon-Madagascar vanilla beans ♦ 2 Mexican vanilla beans ♦ 4 teaspoons pure vanilla extract
Vegetable shortening, solid	1 cup	♦ 1 cup butter ♦ 1 cup lard ♦ 1 cup margarine
Vinegar, white	¼ cup	♦ ⅓ cup lemon juice ♦ ¼ cup apple cider vinegar ♦ ¼ cup champagne vinegar ♦ ¼ cup malt vinegar
Yeast, active dry	1 envelope (¼ ounce)	♦ 1 scant tablespoon active dry yeast ♦ 1 (⅗-ounce) cake fresh compressed yeast
Yeast, fresh (compressed)	1 cake (⅗ ounce)	♦ 1 (¼-ounce) envelope active dry yeast ♦ 1 scant tablespoon active dry yeast (¼ ounce)
Yogurt, plain, (not low-fat)	1 cup	♦ 1 cup sour cream ♦ 1 cup buttermilk ♦ 1 cup crème fraîche ♦ 1 cup heavy cream (36%) plus 1 tablespoon lemon juice

* Whenever any or all of the white wheat flour in a recipe is replaced, the texture and flavour of the finished baked good is altered, sometimes significantly. Never replace more than ¼ of the total flour in a yeast bread recipe with a non-glutinous flour, such as soy or millet, or the dough will not have enough strength to support the structure of the risen loaf. In cake and pastry recipes, try to use the type of flour suggested in the recipe, or you risk a batter that is either too weak to support the structure, or one that is overly strong, resulting in a tough cake or pastry.

** Vanilla extracts are available in many different potencies and strengths, from very intense to quite dilute. Similarly, vanilla beans from different regions vary in their size, aroma, flavour and intensity. Together, these facts make an accurate standard substitution ratio difficult. The guidelines given above are those I use myself, having found them to be fairly reliable.

FLAVOUR PAIRING CHART

STRAWBERRIES AND CREAM, prunes and Armagnac, apples and caramel, maple syrup and walnuts, hazelnuts and dark chocolate. These are only a few of the heavenly marriages made when flavours in the sweet kitchen are well matched. Some pairings, such as those above, are classic and always appreciated. Others, such as strawberry and guava, almonds and Kirsch or white chocolate and mint, are a little less famous but equally rewarding.

Most desserts have one or two predominant flavours, and some have additional elements that play supporting roles. Don't complicate the final dessert with too many flavours, or the result will be significantly less than the sum of its parts.

The following chart is a listing of many of the best combinations of ingredients and flavours. Use it when you are looking to alter the flavours in a favourite recipe or when creating your own desserts. The flavours on the right-hand side of the chart can take many forms—if orange is suggested as a pairing, you could use oranges themselves in the dessert, or you could turn to orange liqueurs or brandy, orange zest or even orange oil as the flavouring. Similarly, the flavour of almonds can come from any form of the nuts or from almond extract or liqueurs; the flavour of cherries can come from the fresh fruit, as well as dried cherries, Kirsch or other cherry brandy, even cherry extract. Let the style of the dessert and the other ingredients guide you to the most effective form of an ingredient. As with any question of flavour, the highest judge is your own palate. Some of the matches on the following pages will not appeal to you and, undoubtedly, there are magnificent matches that are not represented here. I have tried to assemble a relatively comprehensive chart, taking into account both classic combinations and more unusual matches that I have found to marry particularly well. Feel free to augment it with any combinations you discover, as well!

INGREDIENT OR FLAVOUR	COMPATIBLE FLAVOURS
Almonds	Amaretto, apples, blackberries, brandy, caramel, cherries, coffee, cornmeal, cranberries, cream, currants, elderberries, dark and milk chocolate, figs, fruit liqueurs, goat's cheese, gooseberries, grapes, hazelnuts, honey, Kirsch, lemon, mascarpone cheese, marzipan, melon, nectarines, oats, orange, orange liqueurs, passion fruit, peaches, pears, plums, prunes, quince, raisins, raspberries, rhubarb, ricotta, rum, strawberries, tea, vanilla, walnuts
Anise, star anise	Almonds, apples, cinnamon, coffee, cream, dates, ginger, goat's cheese, hazelnuts, lemons, oranges, peaches, pears, pineapple, plums, prunes, quince, raisins, rhubarb, ricotta, strawberries, sweet potatoes, tea, vanilla, walnuts
Apples	Almonds, apple brandy, blackberries, blackcurrants, brandy, brown sugar, Calvados, caramel, chestnuts, cinnamon, cloves, Cognac, cranberries, cream, custard, dates, ginger, goat's cheese, gooseberries, hazelnuts, honey, kiwi fruit, lemon, maple syrup, marzipan, molasses, nutmeg, oats, oranges, pears, pecans, pine nuts, prunes, pumpkin, quince, raisins, red wine, rhubarb, rum, sherry, sour cream, sweet potato, tea, vanilla, walnuts, yogurt
Apricots	Almonds, Amaretto, apricot brandy, bananas, blackberries, blueberries, brandy, caramel, cardamom, cherries, coconut, Cognac, cranberries, cream, custard, ginger, hazelnuts, honey, Kirsch, lemon, maple syrup, mascarpone cheese, marzipan, nectarines, nut liqueurs, oats, oranges, orange liqueur, peaches, pineapple, pistachios, plums, prunes, raisins, raspberries, strawberries, sweet wine, vanilla, walnuts, white wine, yogurt

continued on page 354

Bananas	Almonds, apricots, Armagnac, blueberries, brandy, brown sugar, buttermilk, caramel, cardamom, cinnamon, coconut, coffee, Cognac, cream, cream cheese, custard, dark chocolate, dates, dried figs, ginger, guava, honey, Kirsch, kiwi fruit, kumquats, lemon, lime, mango, maple syrup, oats, oranges, papaya, passion fruit, peanuts, pecans, pineapple, pistachios, pomegranate, raspberries, raisins, rum, sour cream, strawberries, sweet potato, vanilla, walnuts, white chocolate, yogurt
Blackberries *(see also raspberries)*	Almonds, apples, apricots, berry liqueurs and brandies, buttermilk, cinnamon, cream, cream cheese, custard, dark chocolate, elderberries, goat's cheese, honey, Kirsch, lemon, mango, mascarpone cheese, melon, mint, nectarines, oats, oranges, peaches, raspberries, strawberries, white chocolate, vanilla
Blueberries	Almonds, apples, apricots, bananas, berry liqueurs, brown sugar, buttermilk, cinnamon, Cognac, cream, cream cheese, custard, elderberries, ginger, honey, lemon, lime, mango, maple syrup, mascarpone cheese, nectarines, oats, orange, orange liqueur, peaches, raspberries, sour cream, strawberries, white chocolate, yogurt
Buttermilk	Bananas, blackberries, blueberries, brown sugar, cherries, cinnamon, cornmeal, dates, ginger, honey, lemon, lime, maple syrup, mint, nectarines, nutmeg, oats, orange, peaches, plums, raisins, raspberries, rhubarb, strawberries, walnuts
Cantaloupes	Ginger, lime, port, raspberries, watermelon, yogurt
Cardamom	Cinnamon, coffee, lemon, orange, apricots, pistachios, tea, walnut
Carrots	Almonds, brandy, brown sugar, cinnamon, cloves, cream, ginger, hazelnuts, honey, lemon, maple syrup, mace, mint, nutmeg, oranges, pecans, raisins, rum, walnuts

Cashews	Almond, apricots, banana, brown sugar, caramel, cinnamon, coconut, dates, ginger, grapefruit, guava, honey, kiwi fruit, kumquats, macadamia nuts, mango, mint, nutmeg, papaya, passion fruit, persimmons, pineapple, rum, vanilla, white chocolate
Champagne	Blackberries, cherries, cranberries, melon, lemon, lime, mint, raspberries, strawberries
Cherries	Almonds, almond liqueur, apricots, Armagnac, brandy, buttermilk, caramel, Cognac, cream, cream cheese, custard, dark chocolate, goat's cheese, hazelnuts, Kirsch, kiwi fruit, lemon, marzipan, mascarpone cheese, melon, mint, nectarines, oats, oranges, orange liqueurs, peaches, pecans, plums, port, quince, sour cream, vanilla, walnuts, white chocolate
Chestnuts	Apples, Armagnac, brandy, brown sugar, caramel, cinnamon, cloves, coffee, Cognac, cream, dark chocolate, figs, ginger, honey, lemon, orange, maple syrup, plums, prunes, raspberries, raisins, ricotta, rum, sweet potato, sweet wine, tea, vanilla, white chocolate
Chocolate, dark	Almonds, apricots, bananas, berry liqueurs, brandy, caramel, cherries, cinnamon, coconut, coffee, coffee liqueurs, Cognac, cream, dates, dried cranberries, dried figs, elderberries, ginger, hazelnuts, lemon, macadamia nuts, maple syrup, marzipan, mascarpone cheese, mint, nut liqueurs, oats, orange, orange liqueurs, passion fruit, peanuts, pecans, pistachios, port, prunes, raspberries, ricotta, rum, tea (especially Earl Grey), vanilla, walnuts, whiskey, white chocolate
Chocolate, white	Almonds, apricots, bananas, berry liqueurs, blackberries, blueberries, caramel, cashews, cherries, coconut, cornmeal, cranberries, dark chocolate, dates, figs, ginger, grapes, guava, hazelnuts, kumquats, lime,

continued on page 356

Chocolate, white continued	macadamia nuts, mango, marzipan, mint, oats, oranges, papaya, passion fruit, persimmon, pistachios, pomegranate, prunes, raspberries, rhubarb, rum, strawberries, sweet potato, vanilla
Coconut	Apricots, bananas, cashews, cinnamon, cream, custard, dark chocolate, dates, dried figs, ginger, grapefruit, guava, honey, kiwi fruit, kumquats, lemon, lime, lychee fruit, macadamia nuts, mango, mint, oats, papaya, passion fruit, peanuts, pineapple, pumpkin, raspberries, rum, strawberries, sweet potato, vanilla, white chocolate
Coffee	Almonds, anise, bananas, brandy, brown sugar, caramel, cardamom, cinnamon, coffee liqueurs, Cognac, cream, custard, dark chocolate, dates, figs, hazelnuts, lemon, macadamia nuts, maple syrup, mascarpone cheese, marzipan, oats, orange, peanuts, pears, pecans, persimmon, prunes, raisins, ricotta, rum, star anise, vanilla, walnuts, white chocolate
Cornmeal	Almonds, anise, apricots, blackberries, blueberries, brandy, buttermilk, caramel, cherries, cranberries, cream, custard, figs, goat's cheese, hazelnuts, honey, Kirsch, lemon, lime, mango, maple syrup, mascarpone cheese, orange, orange liqueurs, papaya, pears, peaches, pineapple, pine nuts, pistachios, plums, quince, raisins (especially currants), raspberries, red wine, rhubarb, sour cream, sweet potatoes, sweet wine, vanilla, white chocolate, yogurt
Cranberries	Almonds, apples, brown sugar, cinnamon, cloves, cornmeal, dark chocolate, ginger, goat's cheese, hazelnuts, lemons, oats, oranges, orange liqueurs, peaches, pears, pistachios, pumpkin, quince, sweet potato, vanilla, walnuts, white chocolate

Custards	Almonds, apples, apricots, bananas, berries (all), cherries, cinnamon, coconut, coffee, cranberries, dark chocolate, ginger, hazelnuts, kumquats, lemon, mango, maple syrup, nut liqueurs, orange, orange liqueurs, passion fruit, pears, persimmon, pineapple, plums, prunes, pumpkin, quince, raisins, raspberries, rhubarb, strawberries, sweet potatoes, sweet wine, vanilla, walnuts, white chocolate
Dates, dried	Almonds, apples, apricots, Armagnac, brandy, bananas, brown sugar, buttermilk, caramel, cinnamon, coffee, cream, cream cheese, dark chocolate, figs, ginger, hazelnuts, honey, lemons, limes, marzipan, mascarpone cheese, oats, oranges, macadamia nuts, pecans, pistachios, prunes, quince, raisins, red wine, ricotta, rum, sweet wine, tea, vanilla, walnuts, white chocolate
Elderberries and elderflowers	Almonds, blackberries, blueberries, brandy, brown sugar, dark chocolate, gooseberries, honey, lemon, lime, orange, raspberries, strawberries, vanilla, white wine
Figs, dried	Almonds, anise, apples, bananas, brandy, brown sugar, caramel, chestnuts, cinnamon, coconut, coffee, Cognac, cornmeal, cream, dark chocolate, dates, ginger, goat's cheese, guava, honey, lemons, macadamia nuts, maple syrup, marzipan, mascarpone cheese, oats, oranges, pears, pecans, pistachios, prunes, quince, raisins, red wine, ricotta, sweet potatoes, sweet wine, tea, vanilla, walnuts, whiskey, white chocolate
Figs, fresh	Almond, anise, cherries, cinnamon, Cognac, cornmeal, ginger, goat's cheese, hazelnuts, honey, Kirsch, lemon, lime, mango, marzipan, mascarpone cheese, oranges, pistachios, raspberries, raspberry liqueur, red wine, sweet wine, vanilla, walnuts, white chocolate

continued on page 358

Filberts	See Hazelnuts
Ginger	Almonds, anise, apples, apricots, brown sugar, caramel, cashews, cinnamon, coconut, cornmeal, cranberries, cream, custard, dark chocolate, figs, grapefruit, guava, hazelnuts, honey, kumquats, lemon, lime, lychee fruit, mango, mascarpone cheese, melon, mint, oats, orange, papaya, peaches, peanuts, pears, persimmon, pineapple, plums, prunes, pumpkin, quince, raisins, raspberries, rhubarb, ricotta, rum, strawberries, sweet potato, sweet wine, tea, vanilla, walnuts, white chocolate
Goat's cheese (chèvre)	Almonds, anise, apples, blackberries, cherries, cinnamon, cornmeal, cranberries, cream, figs, grapes, hazelnuts, honey, lemon, orange, pears, pecans, pine nuts, port, raisins, raspberries, red wine, vanilla, walnuts
Gooseberries	Almonds, apples, brown sugar, caramel, cinnamon, cream, cream cheese, elderberries, honey, lemon, lime, orange, raspberries, strawberries, sweet wine, vanilla, white wine
Grapefruit	Bananas, blood oranges, brown sugar, Campari, caramel, cashews, champagne, coconut, gin, hazelnuts, honey, lemon, lime, macadamia nuts, melons, meringue, mint, orange, papaya, pecans, pineapple, pomegranate, poppyseeds, raspberries, rum, strawberries, walnuts
Grapes	Almonds, brandy, Cognac, cream, goat's cheese, hazelnuts, honey, lemon, marzipan, melon, mint, pecans, raspberries, red wine, rum, strawberries, walnuts, white chocolate, white wine
Guava	Bananas, cashews, coconut, cream, cream cheese, ginger, honey, lemon, lime, macadamia nuts, mascarpone cheese, orange, strawberries, vanilla, white chocolate

Hazelnuts	Almonds, almond liqueurs, anise, apples, apricots, bananas, berries (all), brandy, brown sugar, caramel, champagne, cherries, chestnuts, cinnamon, coffee, Cognac, cranberries, cream, cream cheese, custards, dates, dark chocolate, goat's cheese, grapes, grapefruit, hazelnuts, figs, ginger, honey, Kirsch, kiwi fruit, kumquats, lemon, mango, maple syrup, mascarpone cheese, nectarines, oats, oranges, orange liqueurs, peaches, pears, pecans, persimmons, plums, prunes, pumpkin, quince, raisins, raspberries, red wine, rhubarb, ricotta, rum, strawberries, sweet potatoes, sweet wine, tea, vanilla, walnuts, white chocolate, white wine
Honey	Almonds, apples, apricots, bananas, brandy, brown sugar, buttermilk, chestnuts, cinnamon, coconut, Cognac, cornmeal, cream, dark chocolate, dates, dried figs, elderberries, ginger, goat's cheese, gooseberries, grapefruit, grapes, guava, hazelnuts, kiwi fruit, kumquats, lemons, limes, lychee fruit, marzipan, mascarpone cheese, melon, mint, nutmeg, oats, oranges, papaya, peaches, peanuts, pears, pecans, persimmon, pineapple, pine nuts, pistachios, plums, prunes, pumpkin, quince, raisins, rhubarb, red wine, ricotta, rum, sweet potato, tea, vanilla, walnuts, white chocolate, white wine
Honeydew melon	Champagne, honey, lemon, lime, mint, strawberries
Kiwis	Apples, bananas, cashews, cherries, coconut, hazelnuts, honey, Kirsch, lemon, lime, lychee fruit, macadamia nuts, oranges, papaya, passion fruit, pineapple, strawberries, white chocolate
Kumquats	Bananas, blackberries, blueberries, cashews, coconut, cranberries, cream, custards, ginger, hazelnuts, honey, lemons, limes, oranges, macadamia nuts, mace,

continued on page 360

Kumquats continued	mango, mint, nutmeg, papaya, pecans, persimmon, pineapple, pistachios, pomegranate, poppyseeds, pumpkin, quince, rum, strawberries, vanilla, walnuts, white chocolate, white wine
Lemons	Almond, anise, apples, apricots, bananas, blackberries, blueberries, brown sugar, buttermilk, caramel, cardamom, cherries, chestnuts, coconut, coffee, cinnamon, cornmeal, cranberries, cream, custard, dark chocolate, dates, elderberries, figs (fresh and dried), ginger, goat's cheese, gooseberries, grapefruit, grapes, guava, hazelnut, honey, kiwi fruit, kumquat, lime, mango, marzipan, mascarpone cheese, mint, nectarines, nut liqueurs, oats, oranges, orange, liqueurs, papaya, passion fruit, peaches, pears, pecans, persimmons, pine nuts, pistachios, plums, poppyseeds, prunes, quince, raisins, raspberries, red wine, rhubarb, ricotta, rum, sour cream, strawberries, tea, vanilla, walnuts, white chocolate, white wine
Limes	Apricots, bananas, brandy, brown sugar, buttermilk, caramel, cashews, coconut, cornmeal, cream, dates, dried figs, elderberries, gin, ginger, gooseberries, grapefruit, guava, hazelnuts, honey, kiwi fruit, kumquat, lemon, lychee fruit, orange, macadamia nuts, mango, maple syrup, mascarpone cheese, papaya, passion fruit, peanuts, pineapple, pecans, raspberries, rum, strawberries, sweet potatoes, vanilla, white chocolate, yogurt
Lychees	Coconut, cream, ginger, honey, kiwi fruit, lime, pineapple
Macadamia nuts	Apricots, bananas, brandy, brown sugar, caramel, cashews, coconut, coffee, cornmeal, cream, dates, dark chocolate, dried figs, ginger, grapefruit, guava, honey, kumquats, lemon, lime, orange, mango, maple syrup, mint, papaya, passion fruit, peaches, pineapple, prunes, raspberries, vanilla, white chocolate

Mangoes	Almonds, anise (especially star anise), bananas, blackberries, blueberries, caramel, cashews, cinnamon, coconut, cornmeal, cloves, cream, ginger, honey, kumquats, lemon, lime, orange, macadamia nuts, marzipan, mint, papaya, passion fruit, pineapple, raspberries, rum, strawberries, sweet wine, vanilla, white chocolate, yogurt
Maple sugar, maple syrup	Almond, apples, apricots, bananas, blueberries, brandy, brown sugar, buttermilk, carrots, chestnuts, cinnamon, coffee, cornmeal, custard, dark chocolate, dates, dried figs, hazelnuts, lime, macadamia nuts, nectarines, oats, orange, peaches, pears, pecans, persimmons, pineapple, plums, prunes, pumpkin, quince, raisins, raspberries, rhubarb, rum, strawberries, sweet potatoes, tea, vanilla, walnuts, whiskey, white chocolate, yogurt
Marzipan	Almonds, almond liqueur, apples, apricots, blackberries, brandy, caramel, cherries, coffee, dark chocolate, dates, figs, grapes, honey, Kirsch, lemon, mango, nectarines, orange, peaches, pears, plums, prunes, quince, raspberries, strawberries, sweet wine, vanilla, white chocolate
Mascarpone cheese	Almonds, apricots, blackberries, blueberries, brandy, caramel, cherries, cinnamon, coffee, cornmeal, figs, ginger, guava, hazelnuts, honey, lemon, lime, nectarines, oats, orange, peaches, pears, pecans, pistachios, pine nuts, quince, raisins, raspberries, rhubarb, rum, strawberries, sweet wine, tropical fruit, red wine, vanilla, walnuts
Melons	Almonds, blackberries, champagne, cherries, ginger, grapefruit, grapes, hazelnuts, honey, lemon, lime, macadamia nuts, mint, orange, pears, pecans, port, raspberries, strawberries, vanilla

continued on page 362

Mint	Blackberries, buttermilk, cashews, champagne, cinnamon, coconut, dark chocolate, ginger, grapefruit, grapes, honey, kumquats, lemon, mango, melon, nectarines, orange, papaya, peaches, pineapple, pumpkin, strawberries, tea, vanilla, white chocolate, yogurt
Nectarines	Almonds, blackberries, blueberries, brandy, brown sugar, buttermilk, caramel, champagne, cherries, cinnamon, cornmeal, cranberries, custard, figs, ginger, hazelnuts, honey, Kirsch, lemon, maple syrup, marzipan, mascarpone cheese, mint, oats, oranges, orange liqueurs, peaches, pecans, pistachios, plums, raspberries, strawberries, sweet wine, vanilla, walnuts, white wine, yogurt
Oats, oatmeal	Almonds, apples, apricots, bananas, blueberries, brandy, brown sugar, buttermilk, caramel, cherries, cinnamon, coconut, coffee, cranberries, cream, dark chocolate, dates, dried figs, ginger, hazelnuts, honey, lemon, maple syrup, mascarpone cheese, nectarines, orange, peaches, peanuts, pears, pecans, persimmons, plums, prunes, pumpkin, raisins, raspberries, rhubarb, rum, strawberries, sweet potato, sweet wine, tea, vanilla, walnuts, whiskey, white chocolate, yogurt
Oranges, sweet	Almonds, almond liqueur, apples, apricots, banana, blackberries, blueberries, brandy, brown sugar, buttermilk, caramel, cardamom, chestnuts, cherries, cinnamon, cloves, coconut, coffee, Cognac, cornmeal, cranberries, dark chocolate, dates, elderberries, figs, ginger, goat's cheese, gooseberries, grapefruit, guava, hazelnuts, honey, kumquats, lemon, lime, macadamia nuts, mango, maple syrup, marzipan, mascarpone cheese, melon, mint, nectarines, oats, orange liqueurs, papaya, passion fruit, peaches, pears, pecans, persimmons, pineapple, pine nuts, pistachios, plums, pomegranate, poppyseeds, port, prunes, pumpkin,

Oranges, sweet *continued*	quince, raisins, raspberries, red wine, rhubarb, ricotta, rum, strawberries, sweet potato, sweet wine, tea, vanilla, walnuts, whiskey, white chocolate, white wine, yogurt
Oranges, blood	Brown sugar, caramel, champagne, cinnamon, cloves, grapefruit, honey, kumquats, lemon, mint, pomegranate, white chocolate
Papayas	Banana, caramel, cashews, coconut, cream, ginger, grapefruit, kiwi fruit, kumquat, lemon, lime, orange, macadamia nuts, mango, mint, passion fruit, peaches, pineapple, port, raspberries, strawberries, vanilla, white chocolate
Passion fruit	Almond, caramel, cashews, champagne, coconut, cream, dark chocolate, kiwi fruit, lemon, lime, macadamia nuts, mango, orange, papaya, pineapple, strawberries, vanilla, white chocolate
Peaches	Almonds, apricots, blackberries, blueberries, brandy, brown sugar, buttermilk, caramel, champagne, cinnamon, cloves, coconut, cornmeal, cream, custards, figs, ginger, hazelnuts, honey, Kirsch, lemon, lime, maple syrup, marzipan, mascarpone cheese, mint, nectarines, nut liqueurs, oats, orange, orange liqueurs, papaya, pecans, pistachios, plums, port, raspberries, red wine, rum, sour cream, strawberries, sweet wine, vanilla, walnuts, whiskey, white chocolate, white wine
Peanuts, peanut butter	Bananas, brown sugar, caramel, coffee, coconut, dark chocolate, ginger, honey, lime, oats, raisins, raspberries, strawberries
Pears	Almonds, almond liqueurs, anise, apples, brandy, brown sugar, caramel, cream, champagne, cherries, chestnuts, cinnamon, cloves, cranberries, custards, dark chocolate, dates, figs, ginger, goat's cheese,

continued on page 364

Pears continued	hazelnuts, hazelnut liqueur, honey, Kirsch, lemon, macadamia nuts, maple syrup, marzipan, mascarpone cheese, nutmeg, oats, oranges, pear brandy, pecans, pine nuts, pistachios, port, prunes, quince, raisins (especially golden), raspberries, red wine, sweet potatoes, sweet wine, tea, vanilla, walnuts, white chocolate, white wine
Pecans	Almonds, apples, apricots, bananas, blackberries, blueberries, brandy, brown sugar, caramel, cherries, cinnamon, coffee, Cognac, cranberries, dark chocolate, dates, ginger, goat's cheese, grapefruit, grapes, hazelnuts, honey, kumquats, lemon, lime, maple syrup, mascarpone cheese, melon, nectarines, oats, orange, orange liqueurs, peaches, pears, persimmons, plums, prunes, pumpkin, quince, raisins, raspberries, red wine, rhubarb, rum, strawberries, sweet potato, sweet wine, tea, vanilla, walnuts, whiskey (especially Bourbon), white chocolate
Persimmons	Brandy, brown sugar, caramel, cashews, cinnamon, cloves, coffee, Cognac, cream, custard, ginger, hazelnuts, honey, kumquats, lemon, mace, maple syrup, nutmeg, oats, oranges, orange liqueurs, pecans, sweet potatoes, vanilla, walnuts, white chocolate
Pineapples	Apricots, banana, brown sugar, brandy, caramel, cashews, cinnamon, coconut, ginger, grapefruit, honey, Kirsch, kiwi fruit, kumquats, lime, macadamia nuts, mango, maple syrup, mint, orange, papaya, passion fruit, raspberries, rum, strawberries, sweet potato, sweet wine, vanilla
Pine nuts	Apples, cornmeal, goat's cheese, honey, lemon, mascarpone cheese, orange, orange liqueurs, pears, prunes, raisins, raspberries, red wine, ricotta, rum, sweet wine, vanilla, walnuts

Pistachios	Apricots, bananas, cardamom, cornmeal, cranberries, dates, dried figs, fresh figs, kumquats, lemon, mascarpone cheese, nectarines, orange, orange flower water, peaches, prunes, quince, raisins (especially golden), raspberries, rose water, strawberries, white chocolate
Plums	Almonds, almond liqueur, anise, brandy (especially plum), brown sugar, buttermilk, caramel, cardamom, cherries, cinnamon, cornmeal, cream, custards, gin, ginger, hazelnuts, honey, Kirsch, lemon, mace, maple syrup, marzipan, nectarines, oats, oranges, orange liqueur, peaches, pecans, raspberries, red wine, rhubarb, strawberries, sweet wine, vanilla, walnuts, whiskey, white wine
Pomegranates	Bananas, blood oranges, cream, grapefruit, kumquats, oranges, white chocolate
Prunes	Almonds, almond liqueur, anise, apples, apple brandy, apricots, Armagnac, brandy, brown sugar, caramel, chestnuts, cinnamon, cloves, coffee, Cognac, cream, custard, dark chocolate, dates, dried figs, ginger, hazelnuts, honey, lemon, macadamia nuts, maple, marzipan, nut liqueurs, oats, orange, pears, pear brandy, pecans, pine nuts, pistachios, port, raisins, red wine, ricotta, rum, sweet wine, tea (especially Earl Grey), vanilla, walnuts, whiskey, white chocolate, white wine
Pumpkins	Apples, apple brandy, brandy, brown sugar, caramel, cinnamon, cloves, coconut, Cognac, cranberries, cream, custard, ginger, hazelnuts, honey, kumquat, mace, maple syrup, nutmeg, oats, orange, pecans, raisins, rum, sour cream, sweet potato, sweet wine, vanilla, walnuts, white chocolate, yogurt
Quinces	Almonds, apples, brandy, brown sugar, caramel, cherries (especially dried), cinnamon, cornmeal, cranberries,

continued on page 366

Quinces continued	cream, custard, dates, dried figs, ginger, hazelnuts, honey, kumquats, lemon, maple syrup, marzipan, mascarpone cheese, nut liqueurs, oranges, pears, pear brandy, pecans, pistachios, raisins, raspberries, red wine, sweet wine, vanilla, walnuts, white wine
Raisins	Almonds, anise, apples, apricots (dried), bananas, brandy, brown sugar, buttermilk, caramel, carrots, chestnuts, cinnamon, coffee, Cognac, cornmeal, custard, dark chocolate, dates, dried figs, ginger, goat's cheese, hazelnuts, honey, lemon, maple syrup, mascarpone cheese, nut liqueurs, nutmeg, oats, orange, peanuts, pears, pecans, pine nuts, pistachios, prunes, pumpkin, quince, raisins, red wine, ricotta, sweet potato, sweet wine, tea, vanilla, walnuts, whiskey, white wine, yogurt
Raspberries	Almonds, apricots, bananas, berry liqueurs and brandies, blackberries, blueberries, brandy, brown sugar, buttermilk, caramel, Champagne, coconut, cornmeal, cream, custard, dark chocolate, elderberries, fresh figs, fruit liqueurs, goat's cheese, gooseberries, grapefruit, grapes, hazelnuts, lemon, lime, macadamia nuts, mango, maple syrup, marzipan, mascarpone cheese, melon, nectarines, nut liqueurs, oats, orange, papaya, peaches, peanuts, pears, pecans, pineapple, pine nuts, pistachios, plums, quince, red wine, rhubarb, ricotta, sour cream, strawberries, sweet wine, vanilla, white chocolate, yogurt
Rhubarb	Almond, apples, brandy, brown sugar, buttermilk, caramel, cinnamon, cornmeal, cream, custard, ginger, hazelnuts, honey, Kirsch, lemon, maple syrup, mascarpone cheese, oats, orange, pecans, plums, raspberries, sour cream, strawberries, vanilla, white chocolate, yogurt

Ricotta cheese	Almonds, anise, brandy, cinnamon, chestnuts, coffee, cream, dark chocolate, dates, dried figs, ginger, hazelnuts, honey, lemon, mace, nutmeg, orange, pine nuts, prunes, raisins, raspberries, red wine, sweet wine, vanilla, walnuts
Strawberries	Almonds, anise, balsamic vinegar, bananas, berry liqueurs, blackberries, brandy, brown sugar, buttermilk, caramel, champagne, cinnamon, coconut, cream, cream cheese, custard, dark chocolate, elderberries, ginger, gooseberries, grapefruit, grapes, guava, hazelnuts, Kirsch, kumquats, lemon, lime, mango, maple syrup, marzipan, mascarpone cheese, melon, mint, oats, oranges, orange liqueurs, papaya, passion fruit, peaches, peanuts, pecans, pineapple, pine nuts, pistachios, plums, port, raspberries, red wine, rhubarb, rum, sour cream, vanilla, walnuts, white chocolate, yogurt
Sweet potato	Anise, apples, banana, brandy, brown sugar, caramel, chestnuts, cinnamon, cloves, coconut, cornmeal, cranberries, cream, custard, dried figs, ginger, hazelnuts, honey, lime, maple syrup, nut liqueurs, nutmeg, oats, orange, orange liqueurs, pears, pecans, persimmon, pineapple, pumpkin, raisins, rum, sour cream, sweet wine, vanilla, walnuts, whiskey, white chocolate
Tea, black, especially Earl Grey	Almonds, anise, apples, Armagnac, brandy, brown sugar, caramel, cardamom, chestnuts, cinnamon, cream, dark chocolate, dates, dried figs, ginger, hazelnuts, honey, lemon, maple syrup, mint, nut liqueurs, nutmeg, oats, oranges, pears, pecans, prunes, raisins, sweet wine, vanilla, walnuts, whiskey
Walnuts	Almonds, anise, apples, apricots, Armagnac, bananas, brandy, brown sugar, buttermilk, caramel, carrots, cherries, chestnuts, cinnamon, cloves, coffee, Cognac,

continued on page 368

Walnuts continued	cranberries, cream, dates, dark chocolate, dried figs, ginger, goat's cheese, grapefruit, grapes, hazelnuts, honey, kumquats, lemon, maple syrup, mascarpone cheese, nectarines, oats, orange, orange liqueur, peaches, pears, pecans, persimmons, pine nuts, plums, port, prunes, pumpkin, quince, raisins, raspberries, red wine, ricotta, rum, strawberries, sweet potato, sweet wine, tea, vanilla, white chocolate, white wine
Yams	See Sweet Potato
Yogurt	Apricots, bananas, blackberries, blueberries, brown sugar, coconut, cream, hazelnuts, honey, lemon, lime, nectarines, oats, oranges, mint, peaches, pecans, pistachios, raisins, raspberries, rhubarb, strawberries, vanilla, walnuts

the recipes

Recipes from the Sweet Kitchen

THE RECIPES I'VE INCLUDED in this book are both simple and seductive. My own desserts have never been highly structural, elaborate and precarious creations; I leave those to the frustrated architects among my professional colleagues. I think the best desserts are those that are satisfying and exciting enough to serve in the most festive situations, but not out of place on a plain old Tuesday night when you *really* need a taste of something wicked. Most of the recipes can be made in little time, with minimal equipment and by even the most novice baker. Others may take more time to prepare, but are nevertheless straightforward and easily made by the home cook.

They range from the very traditional, like the *Ultimate Soft and Chewy Chocolate Chunk Cookies*, to the unashamedly trashy, the *S'mores Roulade* cake for one, to the elegant and sophisticated, such as the *Fresh Fig and Pistachio Frangipane Tart with Honeyed Mascarpone*. There are two common threads that bind all of the recipes: they are all simple enough to be made perfectly in the home kitchen and they rely on excellent ingredients for their success. The latter condition is far from exclusive to the recipes in this book—it applies universally to all desserts, and all savoury dishes, for that matter. The better the raw materials, the more stupendous the outcome. I have also tried to incorporate some of the more exciting ingredients and products available to the home baker today: fresh guava appears in a rich and creamy cheesecake; the warm and heady flavour of star anise laces through lemon churros; tea cakes get a subtly sweet fruitiness from fresh persimmon; and dried Bing cherries punctuate the almondy filling of a sweet yeast bread. Other recipes rely on new ways of using common ingredients or are old favourites updated with the incorporation of unusual ingredients: parsnips appear unexpectedly but smashingly in a heavenly layer cake; grapefruit juice makes a thick and tangy curd for filling tarts or accompanying poppyseed angel food cake; the flavour of tapioca, a familiar nursery pudding, is rounded out by mellow vanilla bean seeds and a side of fragrant cinnamon toast.

Keep in mind that the dessert you choose to make should complement the rest of the meal, and the situation. It should be neither too heavy, nor too light; too plain or too fussy; too rich, too sweet or too insubstantial. Let the season, the menu, the occasion and the tastes of your guests suggest a suitable finale, and the result will be balanced and thoroughly enjoyable.

I love to bake what I love to eat—simple but truly seductive desserts made with the very best ingredients, and with passion and care. I hope these recipes bring you as much pleasure, both in the making and the eating, as they still bring me!

CAKES AND TEA CAKES

continued on page 374

Sweet Potato Layer Cake with Rum-Plumped Raisins and a Caramel Cream Cheese Frosting

SERVES 12 TO 14

As a layer cake, this cake is a glorious testament to flavour and fantasy over form. It is a bit of an architectural improbability: three layers of moist, delicately flavoured cake separated by gobs of a divinely wicked cream cheese frosting. It is grand, huge in fact, and even more satisfying to eat than it is to present. If, however, you prefer a more modest, homey and structurally sound dessert, try the Bundt variation that follows. It has the same rich flavour and gorgeous texture, but is slightly more understated and can be moved without fear of toppling!

CAKE:
¾ cup golden raisins

⅓ cup dark rum

2 large or 3 medium-sized sweet
   potatoes

4 large eggs

2 cups granulated sugar

1 cup mild-flavoured vegetable oil

2 teaspoons pure vanilla extract

3 cups all-purpose flour

1 teaspoon baking powder

1 teaspoon baking soda

½ teaspoon salt, plus extra for salting
   the water

1½ teaspoons cinnamon

½ teaspoon freshly grated nutmeg

¾ cup buttermilk

Additional unsalted butter, at room
   temperature, for greasing the pans

Additional all-purpose flour, for dusting
   the tins

Caramel Cream Cheese Frosting,
   page 646

1. Preheat the oven to 350°. Grease and flour three 9-inch round cake pans. In a small non-reactive bowl, soak the raisins in the rum for at least 30 minutes or several hours. Meanwhile, peel the sweet potatoes, cut them in half and then cut each half into ¾-inch slices. Place the slices into a pot of cool salted water, cover, then bring the water to a boil. Reduce to a gentle simmer and cook until the sweet potatoes are very tender when pierced with a sharp knife. Drain off the water and allow the potatoes to air-dry for a few minutes, then use a potato masher or large fork to roughly mash them. Measure out about 2 cups of the mash and set aside to cool.

Sweet Potato Layer Cake continued

2. In a large bowl with a whisk or the bowl of a stand mixer fitted with the paddle attachment, beat the eggs a little just to break them up. Add the sugar and beat until the mixture is thick and pale, about 2 minutes with a mixer, 3 if whisking by hand. Add the vegetable oil and vanilla, then beat to blend. Drain the raisins, and set aside, but add ¼ cup of the rum macerating liquid to the batter. Add the mashed sweet potatoes and mix until thoroughly combined, scraping down the sides and bottom of the bowl.

3. Into a separate bowl, sift the flour, baking powder, baking soda, salt, cinnamon and nutmeg. Add the flour mixture to the batter in three additions, alternating with the buttermilk in two additions, beginning and ending with the dry ingredients. Fold in the raisins. Divide the batter evenly between the pans and place them in the preheated oven. Bake for 35 to 45 minutes, or until a cake tester inserted into the centre of each cake comes out clean (or with only a few sweet potato particles clinging to it, if you happen to skewer a pocket of unmashed potato!). Rotate each cake at least once during the baking and switch the position of the pans so that the same cakes are not at the back or the front of the oven for the whole baking time. This will ensure the cakes bake evenly.

4. Remove from the oven and cool for 10 minutes in the pans set on wire racks. Run a thin-bladed knife around the cakes and invert them onto the racks to cool completely before frosting with *Caramel Cream Cheese Frosting*. This cake keeps very well, wrapped in plastic wrap and stored at room temperature if uniced. Once frosted, store airtight in the refrigerator.

⚜ VARIATION ⚜

Sweet Potato Bundt Cake with a Spiked Sugar Glaze

GLAZE: ½ cup tightly packed dark brown sugar, 4 tablespoon unsalted butter, 3 tablespoons whipping cream (35%), remaining rum macerating liquid from raisins.

1. Preheat the oven to 350°. Grease and flour a 10-inch fluted tube or Bundt pan. Prepare the cake as per the above recipe, but increase the amount of rum in which the raisins are soaked to ½ cup. Reserve the remaining rum for the

---

glaze. Pour the entire batter into the tube pan. Bake in the centre of the oven for 1 hour to 1 hour and 20 minutes, or until a wooden skewer inserted into the centre comes out clean, and the cake is just beginning to pull away from the sides of the pan. Cool the cake in the pan set on a wire rack for 10 minutes, then invert onto the rack. Set the rack over a baking sheet or large plate to catch the excess glaze. While the cake is cooling, prepare the glaze. This cake must be glazed while still warm, so it absorbs the maximum syrup—so don't take it out of the oven and go to the movies!

2. For the glaze, combine the brown sugar, butter and cream in a small, heavy-bottomed saucepan. Bring to a boil over medium heat, stirring until the sugar dissolves. Continue to boil until the mixture thickens somewhat, about 3 minutes, stirring often. Remove the glaze from the heat and stir in the rum. With a long wooden or metal skewer, poke holes all over the cake, concentrating on the top. Spoon about half of the warm glaze over the cake and let the cake and remaining glaze cool for 10 to 15 minutes, until it has thickened slightly. Pour over the cake, letting it dribble down the sides, then allow the cake to cool completely before cutting and serving or wrapping and storing.

Polenta-Almond Cakes with Golden Raspberries and Crème Fraîche

SERVES 8

These are beautiful golden cakes, reminiscent of traditional Italian breakfast or tea cakes. The combination of cake flour and ground almonds gives the cakes a delicate crumb, with a richness and enhanced moisture. Stone-ground cornmeal makes a great deal of difference in this recipe, adding a distinct toasted-corn taste and a subtle crunch. I have called for individual cakes rather than one large one, so that everyone gets a generous share of the crunchy-sweet exterior. Regular cornmeal will yield a much more bland and ordinary cake.

Polenta Almond Cakes continued

For a winter version, make the cakes without the berries and serve them with a selection of excellent-quality dried fruits, such as figs, pears or apricots, perhaps in a compote or soaked in Armagnac or port. Although the more unusual golden variety are wonderful with the cornmeal, the cakes can also be made with black or red raspberries, or with dried cherries or cranberries. Eat them with tea and fresh fruit for breakfast, with coffee and lightly sweetened whipped cream in the afternoon or with crème fraîche and a glass of dessert wine at the end of a rustic dinner.

1 cup whole blanched almonds
¾ cup granulated sugar
Seeds of ½ plump vanilla bean, or
   1 teaspoon pure vanilla extract
½ cup plus 1 tablespoon stone-ground
   cornmeal
1 cup plus 3 tablespoons cake flour,
   not self-rising
½ teaspoon baking powder
¼ teaspoon salt
¾ cup unsalted butter, at room
   temperature

3 large eggs, separated, whites at
   room temperature
½ pint (1 cup) fresh golden
   raspberries, dry

Soft butter, for greasing moulds
2 tablespoons granulated sugar, for
   dusting moulds
3 tablespoons stone-ground cornmeal,
   for dusting moulds
Crème Fraîche, page 651, for serving

1. Preheat the oven to 325°. Generously butter 8 6-ounce (¾-cup) aluminum cake moulds or muffin tins. In a small bowl, blend the 2 tablespoons granulated sugar and 3 tablespoons cornmeal. Dust the insides of the moulds with this mixture, returning the excess to the bowl after coating each cup, so that each mould gets the same balance of sugar and cornmeal. Tap out the excess sugar and cornmeal and set the moulds aside.

2. Combine the almonds, 2 tablespoons of the granulated sugar and the vanilla bean seeds (hold off if using extract) in the bowl of a food processor and pulse until very finely ground. Transfer the mixture to a medium bowl and add the cornmeal. Set aside 2 teaspoons of the flour for tossing with the berries. Sift the remaining flour, the baking powder and salt into the almond mixture. Stir the dry ingredients with a fork or a wire whisk to thoroughly combine everything, then set aside.

3. Place the butter in the bowl of an electric or stand mixer, or in a large mixing bowl if mixing by hand. Reserving an additional 2 tablespoons of sugar for the egg whites, add the remaining sugar to the butter and cream until very light and fluffy. Add the egg yolks one at a time, blending well after each addition and scraping down the sides of the bowl often. If you are using vanilla extract rather than seeds, blend it in now. Fold in the flour-almond-cornmeal mixture in 3 stages. The batter will be very stiff and dry, more like a cookie dough than a typical cake batter. You may find incorporating the last bit of the dry ingredients easier by hand with a wooden spoon rather than with the mixer. Try not to overwork the batter, but just mix until the dry ingredients are moistened.

4. Place the egg whites in a very clean bowl, one with no traces of grease or fat. The whites can be whipped by hand or with a mixer, but either way, be sure to use a perfectly clean whisk. Beat until soft peaks form. Gradually whisk in the reserved 2 tablespoons of granulated sugar, until the foam stands in stiff, glossy peaks. The whites should still be moist, not dry and granular-looking. Stir about ¼ of the whites into the batter to lighten it, then fold in the remaining whites in 2 stages. In a small bowl, toss the raspberries with the reserved flour, then fold them into the batter gently, distributing them evenly, but taking great care not to crush the berries. Spoon the batter into the prepared pans, filling each one ⅔ full. Set the pans on a baking sheet and place the sheet in the centre of the oven.

5. Bake the cakes for about 45 minutes, or until the tops are golden and springy and a wooden skewer inserted into the centre of each cake comes out clean or with a few moist crumbs clinging to it. Transfer the pans to a wire rack and cool for 7 to 10 minutes, then turn the cakes out of the pans. Place them right-side up on the rack and cool completely before serving or wrapping and storing. These cakes can be made a day or so ahead of time and stored at room temperature, wrapped securely in plastic wrap. They will stay fairly fresh this way for up to 3 days, or in the refrigerator for 4 or 5 days. (They can also be frozen, well-wrapped in plastic then in a freezer bag or aluminum foil, for up to 4 months. Thaw at room temperature for 3 to 6 hours without disturbing the wrapping.) Serve the cakes with a generous mound of *Crème Fraîche* and a bowl of fresh golden raspberries.

Polenta Almond Cakes continued

☙ VARIATIONS ❧

Polenta-Almond Cakes with Red or Black Raspberries: Substitute red or black raspberries for the golden berries in the master recipe. Other blackberry-type berries work beautifully as well, but make sure they are fairly small—blackberries themselves tend to be too large for the little cakes.

Polenta-Almond Cakes with Dried Figs: Bake the cakes without the berries. To serve, accompany the cakes with crème fraîche and a few of the very best quality dried figs, preferably from France, and small glasses of Vin Santo.

Pecan Toffee Coffee Cake

SERVES 12 TO 15

Rich with the flavours of pecans, sweet butter and creamy toffee, this simple coffee cake exceeds all expectations. It has a velvety fine crumb and just enough sweetness to be the perfect complement to a strong cup of espresso. Toffee bits are a fairly new addition to the baking section of many supermarkets and I have already found about two dozen uses for them (muffins, cookies, pancakes ... snacking ...). Here, they add a distinctly caramel-like flavour, without the need to go to the trouble of making butter toffee yourself.

FILLING:
- ½ cup tightly packed light brown sugar
- 2 tablespoons granulated sugar
- 1 teaspoon instant espresso powder
- 1½ tablespoons unsweetened cocoa powder, sifted
- 2 teaspoons cinnamon
- ½ teaspoon freshly grated nutmeg
- ¾ cup chopped pecans, toasted (see page 253 for tips on toasting nuts)
- ¾ cup (half of a 225-gram package) English toffee pieces for baking, such as Skor Bits

CAKE BATTER:

3 cups all-purpose flour

2 teaspoons baking powder

1 teaspoon baking soda

¾ teaspoon salt

2 teaspoons ground cinnamon

1 teaspoon freshly grated nutmeg

¾ cup unsalted butter, at room temperature

1¼ cups tightly packed light brown sugar

½ cup granulated sugar

3 large eggs, at room temperature

2½ teaspoons pure vanilla extract

1¾ cups full-fat sour cream

¾ cup (or the other half of the package) English toffee pieces for baking, such as Skor Bits

3 tablespoons confectioners' sugar, sifted, for decoration

1. Preheat the oven to 350°. Grease and flour a 10-inch fluted tube or Kugelhopf Bundt pan and tap out excess flour. Prepare the filling: in the bowl of a food processor or a clean coffee or spice mill, combine the brown and granulated sugars with the espresso powder. Pulse several times to grind the mixture quite finely and transfer to a small bowl. Add the sifted cocoa and spices and mix with a fork until well blended. Add the nuts and toffee pieces and stir to combine. Set aside.

2. Prepare cake batter: sift the flour, baking powder, baking soda, salt, cinnamon and nutmeg into a medium-sized bowl; set aside. In the bowl of an electric mixer, or a large bowl if mixing by hand, combine the butter, brown sugar and granulated sugar. Cream on medium speed for about 3 minutes, or about 5 minutes by hand, until the mixture is light and fluffy. Add the eggs, one at a time, beating well after each addition, beating in vanilla with the last egg. Scrape down the sides of the bowl periodically to make sure the mixture gets evenly blended.

3. Add the flour mixture to the batter in three additions, alternating with the sour cream in two additions, beginning and ending with the dry ingredients. Mix just to blend after each addition and be careful not to overbeat at this point, or the crumb of the cake will be tough, not delicate and fine. When the last of the flour has been incorporated, fold in the toffee bits.

4. Spoon about ⅓ of the batter into the bottom of the prepared pan. Using a teaspoon, spread the batter evenly over the bottom and make a little moat all

Pecan Toffee Coffee Cake continued

the way around in the centre to cradle the filling. Spoon ½ the filling into the groove, taking care not to have any of the filling touch the centre tube or the sides of the pan, or it could scorch, making a graceful unmoulding very difficult! Smooth the filling down a bit, then add another ⅓ of the batter. Again, spread the batter over the filling and up the sides of the pan, creating another moat. Fill this groove with the last of the filling and cover it with the remaining batter. Using the spoon or a rubber spatula, spread the batter smoothly and evenly, making sure it goes right to the edges of the pan, blanketing any exposed filling. The two layers of filling must be well-separated by batter, or the resulting cake will have an unpleasantly sugary and crunchy centre. Rap the pan on the counter once or twice to remove any trapped air bubbles.

5. Place pan on the centre rack of the preheated oven and bake for 50 to 65 minutes, or until the cake is golden brown and the centre springs back when lightly touched. A wooden skewer inserted about 2 inches into the centre of the ring should come out clean, except for any stray toffee that it may have speared. Cool the cake in the pan on a rack for 5 to 7 minutes, then invert cake onto another rack and leave to cool completely. This cake must be absolutely cool before you attempt to slice it, or you'll end up with one pile of cake and another of nutty toffee! The cake keeps very well for 2 or 3 days, well wrapped at room temperature. To serve, sift the confectioners' sugar over the top.

Old-Fashioned Glazed Lemon Bundt Cake

SERVES 10 TO 12

This velvety-crumbed lemon cake is a variation on the traditional 1-2-3-4 Cake: an all-purpose cake made by Southern bakers in the antebellum era. The numbers refer to the quantities of the main ingredients: 1 cup butter, 2 cups sugar, 3 cups flour and 4 eggs. Many recipes deviate in some way from the formula (every self-respecting baker had to have her own secret touch!) and this recipe would work perfectly well with 3 eggs. Moist, tender and bursting with bright lemon flavour, this scrumptious cake needs no adornment save a simple lemon glaze.

CAKE:

1 cup unsalted butter, at room
   temperature
2 cups granulated sugar
4 large eggs, at room temperature
3 cups all-purpose flour
½ teaspoon baking soda
½ teaspoon salt
1 cup buttermilk
Grated zest of 2 large lemons
Juice of 1 large lemon (about 2½
   tablespoons)

GLAZE:

¼ cup unsalted butter, softened
1½ to 2 cups confectioners' sugar,
   well sifted
Finely grated zest of 1 large or
   2 small lemons
Juice of 1 lemon (about 2½
   tablespoons)

Additional unsalted butter, at room
   temperature, for greasing the pan

1. Preheat the oven to 325°. Grease a 10-inch Bundt pan and set aside. Using a wooden spoon, or the paddle attachment of an electric mixer, cream the butter and sugar together in a large bowl until fluffy and pale. Add the eggs, one at a time, beating well after each addition, and scraping down the sides of the bowl.

2. Sift the flour, baking soda, and salt into a small bowl. Add the flour mixture to the creamed mixture in 3 additions, alternating with the buttermilk in 2 additions, beginning and ending with the dry ingredients. Don't overmix; just fold gently until the batter looks well blended. Fold in the lemon zest and juice. (The batter may appear curdled with the addition of the lemon juice—don't worry!)

3. Scrape the batter into the prepared pan, smoothing the top with a rubber spatula. Bake the cake for 1 hour to 1 hour and 15 minutes, or until a tester inserted into the centre comes out clean, and the cake has begun to pull away from the sides of the pan. Transfer the pan to a wire rack and cool for 10 minutes. Meanwhile, prepare the glaze.

4. For the glaze, in a medium-sized bowl, cream the butter until light and fluffy. Gradually beat in the sifted sugar and the combined zest and lemon juice, alternating one then the other, until a creamy, pourable consistency is achieved.

5. Invert cake onto a wire rack set over a baking sheet. Spoon the glaze over hot cake and allow to cool completely before cutting. Best the day it is made, it will keep fairly well, in an airtight container at room temperature, for up to 3 days.

Oatmeal Stout Cake with a Chewy Oat Topping and Orange-Date Ice Cream

SERVES 10

This unusual twist on the old-fashioned oatmeal cake smells absolutely incredible while it's baking. The chewy, almost chocolatey and coffee-like flavours of the stout and the coarse oats produce a rich but not overly sweet cake that is perfect with the date-studded ice cream. You could, of course, substitute Vanilla Bean Ice Cream (page 553) or any other good ice cream, or even eat the cake all by its glorious self. It may sound strange, but a glass of the same dark stout used in the cake is also a wonderful accompaniment!

CAKE:

1 cup old-fashioned oats (not instant), also called coarse oatmeal or Irish Oatmeal

1¼ cups oatmeal stout or other dark stout beer, such as Guinness

½ cup unsalted butter, at room temperature

1 cup tightly packed dark brown sugar

1 cup granulated sugar

2 large eggs, at room temperature

½ teaspoon pure vanilla extract

1 teaspoon finely grated orange zest

1½ cups all-purpose flour

1 teaspoon baking soda

½ teaspoon salt

½ teaspoon cinnamon

½ teaspoon freshly grated nutmeg

CHEWY OAT TOPPING:

¼ cup unsalted butter, at room temperature

½ cup tightly packed light brown sugar

¼ cup sweetened condensed milk

½ cup old-fashioned (coarse) oats

½ cup lightly toasted pecans or walnuts, coarsely chopped (see page 253 for tips on toasting nuts)

Orange-Date Ice Cream, page 555, for serving, if desired

1. Two hours before you plan to put the cake in the oven, combine the oatmeal and the stout and in a small, non-reactive bowl; cover with plastic wrap and chill.

2. Preheat the oven to 350°. Grease a 9-inch springform or other 9-inch round cake pan with 3-inch-high sides. Line the bottom with a circle of parchment paper. Lightly grease the paper, then set the pan aside. In the bowl of an electric mixer or a large mixing bowl, cream the butter and both sugars until well combined and somewhat fluffy. Add the eggs, one at a time, beating well after each addition. Beat in the vanilla and orange zest.

3. Drain the chilled oat mixture, reserving the stout. Into a separate bowl, sift the flour, baking soda, salt, cinnamon and nutmeg. Add the flour mixture to the creamed butter mixture in three additions, alternating with the reserved stout in two additions, beginning and ending with the dry ingredients. Take care at this point not to overmix; just make sure the flour is moistened and all ingredients are evenly distributed. Fold in the oats and scrape the batter, which will be quite thick, into the prepared pan. Place in the centre of the preheated oven and bake for 55 to 65 minutes, or until the centre of the cake springs back when lightly touched, and a wooden skewer inserted there comes out clean. Cool the cake completely on a rack before topping.

4. To prepare the Chewy Oat Topping, preheat the broiler. Combine all the ingredients for the topping in a small bowl and scatter over the cooled cake in its pan, pressing the mixture onto the surface evenly. Place the pan under the broiler and cook, watching closely, until the topping is bubbling and golden. This sweet stuff can burn quickly, so don't leave the pan under the heat and walk away! Cool the topped cake for at least 10 minutes, then serve warm or at room temperature with *Orange-Date Ice Cream*.

Honey-Poached Apricot Cornmeal Crunch Cake

SERVES 10 TO 12

This cake was one of my happiest experiments, and so good I've been tempted to move to a place where apricot season is longer than the blindingly short time it is in most of Canada! Heady with the flavours of honeyed ripe fruit and vanilla perfume, the cake itself is both crunchy and tender; and the syrup is to die for. Make this during the precious apricot season (June into July); the other eleven months of the year you can just fantasize about it!

Honey-Poached Apricot Cornmeal Crunch Cake continued

<table>
<tr><td>

FRUIT LAYER:

2 pounds fresh apricots, ripe, but not
    overly soft
3 cups water, preferably still spring or
    filtered water
1 cup granulated sugar
⅓ cup flavourful unpasteurized honey,
    not buckwheat
½ large vanilla bean, or the scraped-
    out hull of one bean
1 cinnamon stick
Juice of ½ large lemon
    (about 1½ tablespoons)

</td><td>

CAKE:

1½ cups stone-ground yellow cornmeal
½ cup tightly packed light brown sugar
2½ cups all-purpose flour
1 teaspoon baking powder
½ teaspoon salt
¼ teaspoon ground cinnamon
⅔ cup cold unsalted butter, cut into
    small cubes
2 large eggs, lightly beaten

</td></tr>
</table>

1. Prepare the apricots: with a small paring knife, halve the apricots, cutting the fruit along the little cleft, then continuing to slice around the entire fruit. Remove the stones; these can be cracked open with the back of a heavy cleaver or a hammer, and the little almond-shaped pit inside can be reserved for another use. (See page 277 for more information on using apricot pits).

2. Place the apricot halves in a heavy-bottomed 2-quart saucepan and add the water, sugar, honey, vanilla bean or hull, cinnamon stick and lemon juice. Set a heatproof plate directly on top of the fruit, ensuring that every piece is submerged, but none is resting on the bottom. Bring the contents of the pot to a gentle simmer over medium-low heat, reducing the heat once bubbles appear. The water should just shimmer, not boil. Poach until the apricots are very soft, to the point of extreme softness, but not quite to the point of complete collapse. The fruit should be almost a lovely jammy compote at this stage. Gently lift the fruit out of the poaching syrup with a slotted spoon and set aside to cool to room temperature. Meanwhile, return the pot to the heat and bring the syrup to a boil. Reduce the liquid until it is a medium-thick syrup, then transfer to a clean container and set aside to cool. (The fruit and the syrup can be prepared a day or two ahead of time, and stored separately in the refrigerator, in airtight containers. Bring both to room temperature before proceeding with the recipe.)

3. Preheat the oven to 350°. Grease the bottom and sides of a 10-inch spring-form pan; line the bottom with a circle of parchment paper and grease the paper. In a large bowl, stir together the cornmeal and brown sugar, using a fork to break up any lumps of the sugar. Sift in the flour, baking powder, salt and cinnamon and stir to blend well. Use a pastry blender or two knives to cut the butter into the dry ingredients until the largest lumps are about the size of large peas, then use the tips of your fingers to rub the mixture together until it looks a little like large-flake oats. Add the beaten eggs and lightly work them into the dough with your fingers until it is uniformly blended, moist and still crumbly. Press half of the mixture into the bottom of the prepared pan, pressing firmly. Don't press the dough up the sides of the pan.

4. Spoon the poached apricots over the dough in an even layer. Smooth the fruit with a rubber spatula, then crumble the remaining cornmeal mixture over the top. Pat the crumble gently so that all of the fruit is covered and there are no very large lumps of dough or thinly covered areas. Spoon about 4 tablespoons of the poaching syrup over the top of the cake and set the pan on a baking sheet.

5. Place the sheet in the centre of the oven and bake for 55 to 65 minutes, or until the fruit is just visibly bubbling around the sides of the cake and the top of the crumble is crisp and golden. A skewer inserted in the centre of the cake should come out clean. Transfer the cake tin to a rack and cool completely. When cool, run a thin-bladed knife around the cake and gently release the sides. Serve at room temperature with a generous spoonful of the thick syrup—vanilla ice cream is nice, too, but by no means necessary! The cake and syrup can be kept at room temperature, well covered, for up to 4 days, but are best if eaten within a day or two of baking. Serve any leftover (ha ha ha) syrup with pancakes, oatmeal or over ice cream or fresh apricots.

Golden New-Fashioned Dried Fruitcake with Cashews, Pistachios and Bourbon

2 LARGE LOAVES

All modesty aside, I consider this to be the best fruitcake ever! I should qualify that by saying that I detest most candied fruit and never eat those doorstop dark fruitcakes that seem to appear in multitudes every December. This cake will turn most people's notions of traditional fruitcakes on their ears, but it is, in fact, a simple and old-fashioned recipe. It is full of the rich flavours of subtly sweet dried fruit, very delicate spices and soft nuts, and is heady with the perfume of just enough bourbon. It won't keep as long as the traditional cakes made with tons of chemically treated and candied fruit, but will last a couple of weeks if stored in the refrigerator. It makes wonderful gifts, especially for people who swear they HATE fruitcake, as I have yet to find anyone who doesn't love this. Do make the effort to find unsulphured dried fruit, as the flavour is so much better. If this is impossible, try at least to buy organic fruit. The list of ingredients is long, but the cake is quickly assembled if you have all the components measured out and ready to go before you begin.

1½ cups chopped* dried peaches

1½ cups chopped dried apricots

1 cup chopped dried pears

¾ cup plump golden raisins

½ cup Muscat or Lexia raisins

3 tablespoons finely chopped candied orange zest, homemade (see page 634) or good-quality purchased

1 cup bourbon

2 cups all-purpose flour

1 teaspoon baking soda

½ teaspoon salt

1¼ teaspoons ground mace

1¼ teaspoons ground ginger

⅛ teaspoon ground cinnamon

2 cups lightly roasted unsalted cashews

2 cups shelled unsalted pistachios

1 ripe pear

1 cup unsalted butter, at room temperature

1 cup granulated sugar

4 large eggs, at room temperature

½ cup full-fat sour cream

¼ cup freshly squeezed lemon juice

1 tablespoon pure vanilla extract

¾ cup sweetened shredded coconut, optional

All of the dried fruit should be chopped to about the size of large raisins.

1. The day before you plan to bake the cakes, combine the chopped peaches, apricots, pears, both types of raisins and candied orange zest in a non-reactive jug or bowl. Add the bourbon and stir to coat the fruit. Cover tightly and leave for 7 or 8 hours, tossing occasionally to distribute the alcohol.

2. Preheat the oven to 300°. Grease two (9½ x 5½-inch) metal loaf pans and line the bottoms and up the two long sides with pieces of parchment paper. Let the paper overhang the edges of the sides by an inch or so. Lightly grease the paper, then set the pans aside. Sift the flour, baking soda, salt and spices into a small bowl and set aside. In the bowl of a food processor, finely grind 1½ cups of the cashews; add to the sifted flour mixture. Coarsely chop the remaining ½ cup cashews and the pistachios. Set these aside. Peel, core and coarsely grate the pear, then add it to the macerating fruit and bourbon mixture.

3. In the bowl of an electric or stand mixer fitted with the paddle attachment, cream the butter with the sugar until light and fluffy. Beat in the eggs, one at a time, mixing well. The batter may seem to curdle at this point, but will come together beautifully as the dry ingredients are added. Fold in the flour and ground cashew mixture in three additions, alternating with the sour cream in two additions, beginning and ending with the dry ingredients. Scrape down the bowl often, making sure you reach the very bottom. Stir in the lemon juice and vanilla.

4. If your stand mixer or other mixing bowl is too small to accommodate the batter as well as the macerating fruit and the chopped nuts, transfer to a larger bowl. Fold in the fruit and nuts, including the coconut, if using, in several stages, evenly distributing the goodies. Scrape the batter into the two prepared pans and smooth the tops.

5. Set the pans in the centre of the preheated oven and bake for about 1 hour and 45 minutes, rotating the pans several times during the baking so the cakes bake evenly. The tops of the finished cakes should be firm and slightly springy, and a wooden skewer inserted into the centre of each cake should come out clean. Cool the cakes in their pans on a rack for 10 minutes, then turn them out and cool completely before wrapping and storing. The cakes are best when aged for 2 days in the refrigerator before being cut and served. Well-wrapped and chilled, this light cake will last up to 2½ weeks. For the very best flavour, let it come to room temperature before serving.

Poppyseed Angel Food Cake with Grapefruit Curd

SERVES 8 TO 10

Angel food cake has recently become fashionable again, mostly due to its low fat content. The thing is, dreamy light angel food cake is very nice with a few slices of orange or a handful of berries, but is absolutely wicked with a big dollop of rich fruit curd beside it (diet police be damned!). Both original and simple, this is a fluffy cake with a fine moist crumb, enhanced by the delicate flavour and texture of poppyseeds. The Grapefruit Curd makes it a truly exceptional dessert, but the cake would also be wonderful with a raspberry or blackberry sauce, page 643, or with the blackberry curd on page 477. The cake and the grapefruit curd are natural partners for another reason: the curd uses the same number of yolks as the cake does whites!

1 cup cake flour (not self-rising)
1½ cups superfine sugar
1½ cups egg whites (about 10 extra large, or 12 to 13 large), at room temperature (see page 188 for tips on separating eggs)
2 tablespoons lukewarm water
1¼ teaspoon cream of tartar
½ teaspoon salt

2 teaspoons pure vanilla extract
3 tablespoons poppyseeds
1 recipe Grapefruit Curd, recipe page 569

Candied grapefruit peel, optional, for garnish (see variation on page 634)

1. Preheat the oven to 350°. Have ready a spotlessly clean 10-inch tube pan with a removable bottom, ungreased and unlined. I prefer the old-fashioned aluminum pans, as opposed to the new non-stick pans. A properly baked angel food cake will have no trouble unmoulding from an aluminum pan. Working between two sheets of parchment or waxed paper, sift the flour and ½ cup of the sugar together 3 times, then set it nearby.

2. In the very clean, grease-free bowl of an electric or stand mixer fitted with the paddle attachment, or a large mixing bowl if whipping by hand, beat the egg whites with the warm water until frothy. Make sure your whisk and any scrapers you will use are also grease-free—even a speck of fat or yolk could prevent the whites from achieving the best volume. Add the cream of tartar and the salt and whip the whites until soft peaks form. Gradually add the remaining sugar, a little at a time, whipping constantly. When all the sugar has been added, the whites should be firm, glossy and hold stiff peaks. Beat in the vanilla extract.

3. The flour-sugar mixture must be incorporated very gently, but as quickly as possible so as not to deflate the whites. I find the best way to do this is to use my bare hand. This way, I can feel exactly when the flour has been evenly distributed, and where any lumps might be. (You can also use a large rubber spatula, but I encourage you to get right in there—it feels wonderful and decadent.) Sprinkle about ¼ of the flour mixture over the whites, then use your (clean!) hand to fold the batter over onto itself, making sure you reach down to the very bottom of the bowl and scoop all the way around the sides and through the centre. When you don't see or feel lumps of flour, add another ¼ of the flour. Repeat until the final ¼ of the flour is almost incorporated, then fold in the poppyseeds. The batter should still be very fluffy, light and smooth. Scrape the batter into the pan, taking care not to bang the spatula on the bowl or the bowl on the counter, as this could deflate some of the air trapped in the whites. Smooth the top of the batter, then run a clean knife though the batter in the pan to rupture any large air bubbles.

4. Bake the cake for 40 to 45 minutes, or until a wooden skewer inserted in the centre of the cake comes out clean, and the top is cracked and golden. If your tube pan has little legs, invert the pan and cool the cake upside down right over the counter. If your pan does not have legs, invert the pan over a wine bottle neck through the centre tube. Some pans have tubes that are too narrow to accommodate the neck of a wine bottle—these pans can be inverted into a large colander and cooled right in the bowl of the colander. The holes allow the cake to cool perfectly well. Cool the cake completely, until the pan no longer feels warm.

5. To unmould, run a long, thin-bladed knife all around the outside of the cake and around the centre tube. Carefully pull the tube upwards, bringing the cake with it and leaving the sides of the pan. Run the knife between the cake and the pan bottom, then invert the cake onto a platter. Angel food cake is best served the day it is made, as it tends to lose its fluffiness and gets sticky with sitting, but well-covered leftovers can be stored for several days at room temperature.

Poppyseed Angelfood Cake continued

There are special angel food cake cutters available at kitchenware shops, and they are a great gadget if you like this type of cake! Conventional knives tear the delicate cake and make a mess of each slice. The best way to cut this cake without the special cutter is with two forks: put the forks back to back into the top of the cake, where you mean to make a cut. Gently pull the cake apart, as though you were exposing a treasure buried just beneath the surface. You will have perfect, high-standing pieces. Serve with a generous dollop of *Grapefruit Curd* and garnish with a few pieces of candied grapefruit peel, if desired.

Caramel Apple and Sweet Cream Cheesecake

SERVES 12 TO 14

Cheesecake is one of those special desserts for which fans would climb small mountains. (I married into a Dutch family and know a thing or two about dairy fanaticism ...) So many are disappointingly bland or sugary or "fake"- tasting, but this one is none of the above. Rich with a glorious cream cheese flavour, laced with vanilla and just enough Calvados to tickle the taste buds, it comes with the unusual complement of a warm, gooey, caramel apple sauce. It's a happy marriage: rich and sweet, chewy and creamy, cool and warm. This will be a favourite.

CRUST:

¼ cup crisp oatmeal cookie crumbs, from about 3 to 4 crushed cookies

¼ cup tightly packed dark brown sugar

¼ cup unsalted butter, at room temperature

1 cup all-purpose flour

FILLING:

1½ pounds Philadelphia brand cream cheese (not Light or Whipped), softened at room temperature for 30 minutes until malleable

1 cup superfine sugar

Seeds of ½ vanilla bean, hull reserved for another use

2 tablespoons all-purpose flour

4 large eggs

1 large egg yolk

½ cup heavy cream (36%)

¼ cup Calvados, or substitute Applejack or other apple-flavoured liqueur

6 tablespoons unsalted butter

7 tablespoons tightly packed light
  brown sugar

7 tablespoons heavy cream (36%)

1 cup tightly packed unsulphured
  dried apple slices, as plump and
  fresh as possible

1. Preheat the oven to 350°. Grease a 9-inch round springform pan. In the bowl of a food processor, combine the crushed oatmeal cookies, brown sugar and butter. Pulse until well blended. Add the flour and pulse just until a crumbly, moist dough forms. Spread the crumb mixture evenly onto the bottom and an inch or so up the sides of the pan, pressing firmly. Wrap the bottom and sides of the pan with several layers of heavy-duty aluminum foil, pressing the foil as tightly as possible (this is to ensure that no water from the water bath used in Step 3 seeps into the joint of the springform). Bake the crust for 10 to 12 minutes or until it feels dry to the touch. Cool completely and set aside. (The crust can be made up to 24 hours ahead of time and stored, loosely covered, at room temperature.)

2. Reduce the oven temperature to 325°. In the bowl of an electric mixer with the paddle attachment, or a large mixing bowl using a wooden spoon, beat the cream cheese just until smooth. Scrape down the sides of the bowl and add the superfine sugar and vanilla seeds. Beat this mixture until smooth, scraping down the sides of the bowl several times. Sift the flour over the cheese batter and fold in. Add the eggs and yolk, one at a time, beating well after each addition, and again, scraping the sides. When the eggs are incorporated, add the cream and Calvados and beat on low speed just to blend completely.

3. Pour the batter into the cooled crust and rap the filled pan on the counter once or twice to remove any trapped air bubbles. Place the cake pan in a baking dish large enough to accommodate it and add enough hot water to reach halfway up the sides of the pan. Carefully place the whole set-up in the centre of the preheated oven and bake for approximately 1 hour and 10 minutes, or until the centre of the cheesecake no longer looks wet and runny, but is still slightly wobbly. Don't overbake this cake—the filling will firm up further as it cools, so don't look for the centre to be completely firm. Turn the oven off, then run a thin-bladed small knife around the outside of the cake, so it doesn't stick to the sides of the pan as it cools, or crack or become uneven. Return the cake to the oven and leave it inside, with the door slightly ajar (a wooden spoon

Caramel Apple and Sweet Cream Cheesecake continued

wedged in between the door and the jamb works well if your oven door doesn't want to stay open by itself), until it has cooled to room temperature, about 2 hours. Cover the pan tightly with aluminum foil and chill at least 2 hours, preferably overnight.

4. Prepare the caramel apple topping: in a medium-sized, heavy-bottomed saucepan, combine the butter, brown sugar and cream. Place the pot over low heat and stir to melt the sugar. Increase the heat to medium and bring the caramel to a boil. Add the dried apple slices and boil for 2 to 3 minutes, until the caramel is fairly thick and the apple slices are well coated. Remove the pan from the heat and cool the caramel until it is just warm. (The caramel topping can be made up to 2 days ahead of time and stored in an airtight container in the refrigerator.)

5. To serve, rewarm the caramel sauce if it has been prepared ahead of time. If you have a microwave, place the cold caramel in a heatproof bowl and heat on medium-high power for several minutes, stirring every 30 seconds. On the stove, place the caramel in a small saucepan over medium-low heat and stir frequently. With either method, stir the caramel frequently to ensure even heating and only heat until the topping is pourable and warm, but not hot to the touch. The topping can be kept warm for an hour or so by placing it in a bowl set over a pot of barely simmering water. Check temperature before serving to make sure it is neither too thick and cold nor too hot. Just before serving, bring the cake out of the refrigerator and run a knife around the edges again. Remove the sides of the springform. Slice the cake, then ladle a generous amount of the warm caramel apple topping over each slice. Do not accept demure protestations to omit the sauce—it is not optional!

Guava Cheesecake with a Cashew Ginger Crust

SERVES 12

This may be the most unusual cheesecake you will ever make. Guavas have a powerfully floral, sweet and intoxicating aroma that perfumes this cake with as penetrating a flavour. The buttery cashew and candied ginger crust is the perfect foil. Do use fresh guavas—they are not available all year, but for a brief period in late fall and early winter they are at their best and are perfectly showcased in this spectacular but very simple cake.

CRUST:

¾ cup lightly roasted unsalted
   cashews
⅓ cup tightly packed light brown sugar
1½ cups all-purpose flour
¼ teaspoon salt
½ cup cold unsalted butter, in small
   pieces
1 large egg, cold and lightly beaten
3 tablespoons candied ginger,
   finely chopped
1 to 2 teaspoons ice water, if necessary

FILLING:

5 medium guavas, very ripe
2 pounds cream cheese, preferably
   Philadelphia brand, at room
   temperature
1½ cups granulated sugar
Seeds of ½ vanilla bean, hull reserved
   for another use, or 1½ teaspoons
   pure vanilla extract
3 large eggs, at room temperature
½ cup mascarpone cheese

GLAZE:

2 tablespoons good-quality guava jelly
1 tablespoon water

1. Prepare the crust: pulse the cashews and brown sugar in a food processor until finely ground. Add the flour and salt and pulse to blend. Pulse in the butter until the largest pieces resemble large peas, then pulse in the egg and ginger. Turn the dough into a bowl and work the egg into the mixture until a moist, crumbly dough is formed. If the mixture seems too dry, add a teaspoon or two of the ice water. Don't overwork the dough; just use your fingertips to rub the ingredients together until thoroughly blended. Press the crumble into the bottom and part-way up the sides of a 9-inch springform pan, keeping the crust about ¼-inch thick. Don't worry about getting the dough all the way up the sides. Wrap the pan in plastic wrap and chill the crust for at least 2 hours, or overnight.

2. Preheat the oven to 350°. Remove the plastic wrap from the pan, and prick the crust all over with a fork. Bake it for 15 to 25 minutes, or until partly dried and partly firm. This pre-baking is not finicky—the idea is just to give the crust a head start in baking. Cool the crust completely before filling.

Guava Cheesecake continued

3. Preheat the oven to 300°. Peel the guavas with a vegetable peeler and use a teaspoon to scoop out the seeds. Roughly chop the flesh, then purée in a food processor. Measure out 1 cup of the purée and use the remainder for another purpose (try it spooned over vanilla ice cream!). In the bowl of an electric or stand mixer fitted with the paddle attachment, or by hand with a wooden spoon, beat the cream cheese until smooth and creamy. Gradually beat in the sugar, add the vanilla seeds, if using, and continue beating until fluffy. Add the eggs, one at a time, beating well after each addition and scraping down the sides and bottom of the bowl. Stir in the vanilla extract, if using, and the mascarpone. Stir in the guava purée.

4. Pour the filling into the prepared crust and set the pan on the middle rack in the centre of the oven. Place a shallow pan of water on the rack below the pan. This will help prevent the cheesecake from forming a crust and cracking. Bake the cheesecake for 1¾ hours to 2 hours, or until set around the edges but still slightly wobbly in the centre. The edges will have coloured slightly and may have cracked a little. Immediately run a thin-bladed knife around the outside of the cake to prevent the filling from sticking and cracking as it cools and contracts. Cool the cheesecake on a wire rack for 1 hour, then refrigerate until chilled, preferably overnight. (The cheesecake can be made up to 3 days ahead of time and kept, covered, in its pan in the refrigerator.)

5. When the cake is cold, run a knife around the edges of the cake again and release the sides of the springform. Melt the guava jelly and the water in a small saucepan or non-stick skillet, then bring to a boil. Simmer for about 1 minute, then pour the glaze over the chilled cake. Spread just to distribute the glaze over the surface, then refrigerate until about 1 hour before serving. This, like all cheesecakes, keeps very well, covered with aluminum foil.

Caramelized Pineapple Upside-Down Cake

SERVES 10

Definitely not the upside-down cake your mum made! This is a fine-flavoured golden cake, made sexier by a splash of brandy and a crown of caramelized fresh pineapple. It has an absolutely incredible aroma, even the second day. The cake is rich, moist and light, and the pineapple is both tart and sweet, creating a wonderful harmony of tastes and textures. Serve it as a simply elegant dessert at a picnic, or as an elegantly simple finale to a grand evening meal. Either way, there won't be much left over.

TOPPING:

1 large, sweet ripe pineapple

⅓ cup unsalted butter

1 cup plus 2 tablespoons granulated sugar

CAKE:

1½ cups all-purpose flour

1½ teaspoons baking powder

¼ teaspoon salt

3 large eggs

4 or 5 large egg yolks (if the yolks seem small for the size of the egg, use 5 rather than 4)

1½ cups granulated sugar

3 tablespoons brandy

Seeds of ½ large vanilla bean, hull reserved for another use, or 2 teaspoons pure vanilla extract

¾ cup unsalted butter, melted and cooled

1. Preheat the oven to 350°. Grease a 10-inch springform cake pan and line the bottom and about 2 inches up the sides with a single sheet of aluminum foil. Press the foil into the inside of the pan, smoothing out the wrinkles as best as possible. Grease the foil and line the bottom with a circle of parchment paper cut to fit neatly. Grease the paper and sprinkle the bottom of the pan with a little sugar, carefully tapping out the excess while keeping a finger on the linings to hold them in place.

2. Cut the rind from the pineapple and cut away all the tough little eyes (see page 309). Cut the fruit lengthwise into four quarters, then cut out and discard the fibrous core. Set aside one quarter for another use (like snacking while your cake bakes …) and cut each of the remaining three quarters lengthwise into three pieces. Slice each of these into ⅓- to ½-inch slices. Place these in a bowl just large enough to hold the fruit and set the bowl within easy arm's reach of the stove-top.

3. Melt the ⅓ cup of butter in a large heavy pot over medium heat. As soon as the butter is liquid, add the 1 cup plus 2 tablespoons of sugar. Stir constantly over the heat with a wooden spoon until the sugar dissolves and the mixture

Caramelized Pineapple Upside-Down Cake

begins to colour. At first the mixture will be grainy and foamy, then after a few minutes of stirring, the oil will separate from the caramel and swirl around on top. Don't worry about this—the caramel will become homogeneous again. Keep stirring slowly, covering the entire surface of the bottom. At this point, the mixture should look thick and creamy and be a light tawny brown. When the spoon uncovers trails of a darker gold colour, watch closely. The caramel will darken quickly now, and you should have the bowl of pineapple ready to add, which will stop the cooking process.

4. When the caramel is a glossy dark amber, carefully slip the pineapple slices into the pot all at once, standing back to avoid the splatter. This addition will produce a great deal of hissing and spluttering from the pot, as the caramel is shocked with the cool wet fruit. Let the commotion subside a little, about 30 seconds, before using the wooden spoon to gently move the fruit around, coating it with the syrup. The caramel will most likely have seized into a few knobs of hardened toffee, making it awkward to stir, but, again, don't be concerned. The lumps will eventually melt back into the caramel. When the contents have settled down to a steady boil, keep stirring slowly, for 6 to 8 minutes depending on the juiciness of the pineapple, until the slices are golden, their edges becoming glassy-looking and almost transparent. At this point, remove the pot from the heat to a heatproof pad or folded kitchen towel beside the prepared cake tin.

5. Using a pair of tongs, remove the pineapple slices from the caramel and arrange them decoratively in the bottom of the pan. I like a pattern of concentric circles, but your design, or lack thereof, is up to you! Use a slotted spoon to remove any little bits of fruit from the syrup and return the pot to the heat. Continue boiling liquid in the pan, stirring slowly, until it is thick and syrupy. It will be very foamy, and you may need to tilt the pan from time to time, running your spoon across the bottom, to gauge the consistency. Watch closely, as the caramel can burn if left to its own devices. If you are unsure, take the pot off the heat and let the caramel sit for a minute or so. It should be about the consistency of a thick honey. Pour the hot caramel over the pineapple, then set the pan aside.

6. Into a small bowl, sift the flour, baking powder and salt. Set aside. In a larger bowl, lightly whisk the eggs and egg yolks to break them up. Whisk in the 1½ cups sugar, then blend in the brandy and vanilla seeds or extract. Add the dry ingredients to the egg mixture in two or three additions, stirring with the whisk until thoroughly incorporated. Gently stir in the cooled melted butter. The batter should be smooth and glossy and will be fairly runny. (It is also one of the yummiest batters in this book, but do try to restrain yourself—the cake is even better!) Pour the batter over the pineapple slices in the pan, taking care not to disturb the layer of fruit.

7. Place the pan on a baking sheet and set in the middle of the preheated oven. Bake for 1 hour and 10 minutes to 1 hour and 20 minutes. An evenly golden crust will have formed on the top of the cake, and the edges should be just beginning to pull away from the sides of the pan. To test for doneness, poke a wooden skewer through the centre of the crust, making a larger hole than the skewer needs, so the crust doesn't wipe it clean as you pull it out; it should come out clean or with a few moist crumbs clinging to it. Transfer the pan to a rack and cool for 7 or 8 minutes. Run a thin-bladed knife around the cake and carefully release the sides of the pan. Invert the cake onto a serving platter and remove the bottom of the pan. Peel away the foil and the parchment paper, taking care not to tear the fragile hot cake. Cool completely before serving or covering and storing. This cake is really best the day it is made, but can be stored for several days, well covered, at room temperature. For a more elegant presentation, accompany the cake with a vanilla bean crème anglaise or ice cream. The *Lychee and Coconut Milk Sorbet* on page 558 would also be lovely!

S'mores Roulade

SERVES 10

Yes, it is what you think: the favourite campfire treat updated and reworked into a decadent rolled cake. Graham flour and honey are the bases for a soft sponge cake; a sweet chocolate cream pairs with marshmallow fluff to form the filling and the whole roll is slathered in more marshmallow cream and thick chocolate curls. Trashy, gooey, satisfying and deeply nostalgic. Okay, your kids will worship the ground you walk on, but they're pushovers. It's your grown-up friends you'll surprise, and endear! No chemicals, no burnt marshmallows, no waxy chocolate, no campfire and, best of all, portions bigger than a graham cracker! Graham flour is available in natural food stores.

S'mores Roulade continued

GRAHAM SPONGE CAKE:

4 large egg yolks, at room
  temperature

1 cup granulated sugar

⅓ cup flavourful unpasteurized honey,
  such as wildflower or orange
  blossom, but not buckwheat

¼ cup water

¼ cup mild-flavoured vegetable oil,
  such as canola

¼ cup unsalted butter, melted and
  cooled

½ cup graham flour

½ cup all-purpose flour

1 teaspoon baking soda

½ teaspoon baking powder

¼ teaspoon salt

6 large egg whites, at room
  temperature

⅛ teaspoon cream of tartar

Additional unsalted butter, at room
  temperature, for greasing the pan

SWEET CHOCOLATE CREAM:

8 ounces sweet (not milk) chocolate,
  such as German's or Baker's Sweet,
  finely chopped

1 cup heavy cream (36%)

CHOCOLATE CURLS:

6 ounces semisweet or sweet
  chocolate, finely chopped

MARSHMALLOW FLUFF FILLING:

1⅓ cups granulated sugar

⅓ cup water

4 large egg whites with no flecks of
  yolk, at room temperature

¼ teaspoon cream of tartar

1 teaspoon pure vanilla extract

1. Prepare the cake: preheat the oven to 350°. Butter a 12¾ x 17½-inch jelly-roll pan and line the bottom with parchment paper. Butter the paper and set the pan aside. In a large mixing bowl, beat the egg yolks with ½ cup of the granulated sugar just to combine. Add the honey, water, vegetable oil and cooled melted butter, and stir well.

2. Into a small bowl, sift the graham flour, all-purpose flour, baking soda, baking powder and salt together, pressing out any lumps. Add the bran left in the sifter from the graham flour to the mixture. Gradually stir the dry ingredients into the egg yolk mixture a little at a time, stirring each addition in until the batter is smooth before adding another.

3. In a very clean bowl with a clean, grease-free whisk or beaters, whip the egg whites with the cream of tartar until very soft peaks form. Gradually sprinkle in the reserved ½ cup granulated sugar, whipping constantly. The finished meringue should be firm and glossy, and hold stiff peaks. Stir a spoonful of the meringue into the batter to lighten it, then fold in the remaining meringue in three additions. Don't overwork this batter, or it won't have the lightness and tenderness necessary to roll properly.

4. Scrape the batter into the prepared pan and spread it evenly with a rubber spatula. Bake the cake in the centre of the oven for 15 to 20 minutes, turning the pan once during baking. The top of the cake should be golden brown and spring back when very lightly touched in the centre, and the sides should have just started to pull away from the sides of the pan. Cool the cake for 3 to 5 minutes in the pan. Spread a piece of parchment paper larger than the cake on a table- or countertop. Gently run a knife around the sides of the cake to loosen it, then in one smooth motion invert the cake onto the parchment and let it cool completely. The cooled cake can be left for a few hours right where it is, covered with several pieces of plastic wrap.

5. Prepare the sweet chocolate cream: place the chopped chocolate in a medium-sized bowl. Scald the cream in a small pot on the stove, removing it from the heat just as it reaches the boil. Watch closely—cream has an aggravating habit of bubbling up and all over the stove! Pour the hot cream over the chocolate, then stir until the ganache is smooth. Cool to lukewarm, then refrigerate until cold, stirring occasionally so the mixture cools evenly. When you are ready to assemble the cake, remove the chocolate from the refrigerator and beat until thick and spreadable.

6. For the chocolate curls: melt the chopped chocolate in a small bowl set over a pan of barely simmering water, stirring occasionally. The bowl should not touch the water, and moisture must not come into contact with the chocolate, or it will seize. When the chocolate is mostly melted, remove it from the heat, dry the bottom of the bowl and let the residual heat finish the melting. Pour the warm chocolate onto a clean metal baking sheet (not non-stick) and chill for 5 to 10 minutes. Test the temperature of the chocolate by using a bench scraper or offset spatula to scrape the chocolate—if it is still slightly soft, the curls will be bigger and rounder; quite chilled and the curls will be smaller and tighter. Have fun! No one knows what they're supposed to look like, so anything goes! And this does take practice, so don't get discouraged. Finished curls can be stored in a cool, dry place, in an airtight container, for several days.

S'mores Roulade continued

7. Prepare the marshmallow fluff filling: no more than 4 hours before you plan to serve the cake, and just before you are ready to assemble it, combine the sugar and the water in a heavy-bottomed 2-quart saucepan. Place the pan over medium-high heat and stir gently until the sugar dissolves. Bring the syrup to a boil, then boil, without stirring, until the syrup reaches 236°F on a candy thermometer (see page 74 for sugar cookery stages). Meanwhile, beat the egg whites and the cream of tartar in the bowl of an electric or stand mixer fitted with the whip attachment until frothy. Make sure the bowl and the beaters or whip are very clean and grease-free. As soon as the syrup is the right temperature, pour it in a thin, steady stream into the egg whites, beating constantly. If you don't have a stand mixer, get someone to help you with this part! Pour the hot syrup just beside the path of the beaters—if you aim directly for the moving metal, the syrup will spray onto the sides of the bowl and harden. Done properly, the whites will puff up in a steamy foam as the hot syrup is spun into them; just keep the beaters or whip moving quickly, and the mixture will soon take on a less alarming appearance. Continue beating for 2½ or 3 minutes after the last of the syrup is incorporated. The meringue should become dense and glossy. Add the vanilla and beat for another 1 to 3 minutes. The finished mixture will still be warm. Use immediately, because as it cools, it loses its flexibility and becomes too thick and sticky to work with.

8. To assemble the cake: no more than 4 hours before you plan to serve the cake (fewer if the weather is warm and humid), prepare the Marshmallow Fluff Filling and beat the Sweet Chocolate Cream. Place a sheet of parchment paper over the cake and carefully flip the cake over onto the new sheet. Peel off the first sheet, then slide the cake and bottom sheet onto a large platter or cutting board. Position the cake so that one long side is nearest you. Spread the chocolate cream over the cake, leaving about an inch bare on the long edge closest to you. Spread half of the marshmallow mixture over the chocolate, again leaving that 1-inch strip free. Using the paper under the cake to help you, roll up the cake, starting at the edge closest to you. This will become the very inside of the roll. The cake will roll only about 1¼ or 1½ times. Ease the roll onto its seam and carefully pull the paper out from under it. Spread the remaining Marshmallow Fluff over the cake and decorate with the Chocolate Curls. Slice off half an inch or so from each end to make the cake a little neater and keep at room temperature until served. This cake should be eaten within a few hours of being assembled, but any leftovers can be stored in the refrigerator, covered.

Almond Apricot Pound Cake
with Amaretto

SERVES 16 TO 20

This huge, tender cake is laced with the perfume and flavour of sweet and bitter almonds. Marzipan, toasted almonds, almond extract and almond liqueur are used together, each supporting and enhancing the others, contributing to a great depth and complexity of flavour and aroma. Although it is a big cake, it's simple to prepare once the ingredients are assembled and keeps very well. It is rich and deeply flavoured enough to satisfy in small slices, making it perfect for a large party. A word of advice: be sure to let it cool completely before attempting to cut it—it is a dense pound cake and will crumble terribly if cut while still warm!

1½ cups blanched almonds, lightly toasted (see page 253 for tips on toasting nuts)

3 cups plus 3 tablespoons granulated sugar

1 cup unsalted butter, at room temperature

4 ounces good-quality soft marzipan, at room temperature

6 large eggs, at room temperature

2 teaspoons pure almond extract

1½ teaspoons pure vanilla extract

¼ cup Amaretto or other almond liqueur

¼ cup apricot or orange brandy

2½ cups all-purpose flour

½ cup cake flour, sifted

¾ teaspoon salt

½ teaspoon baking soda

1 cup full-fat sour cream

⅔ cup chopped dried apricots, preferably unsulphured

1. Preheat the oven to 325°. Grease and flour a 10-inch tube pan and tap out the excess flour, holding the centre tube if it is a removable bottomed pan. Process the almonds and 3 tablespoons of the sugar in a food processor until finely ground, then set aside.

2. In a large bowl, or the bowl of a stand mixer fitted with the paddle attachment, cream the butter and remaining 3 cups of sugar together for 3 or 4 minutes, or until the mixture is very fluffy and pale. Add the marzipan, and cream until well blended. There may be a few little pieces of marzipan that don't break

Almond Apricot Pound Cake continued

up in the batter—this will add a little texture and pockets of flavour to the finished cake. (If the marzipan is not soft enough to cream, grind it in the food processor with the almonds and add to the batter when the nuts are added.) Scrape down the sides of the bowl and do so frequently from now on—this is a large batter, and you want to ensure everything is properly distributed. Add the eggs, one at a time, beating well between each addition. Beat in the almond and vanilla extracts, Amaretto and apricot brandy.

3. Sift together the flours, salt and baking soda. Add the flour mixture to the creamed batter in three additions, alternately with the sour cream in two additions, beginning and ending with the dry ingredients so the batter never gets too dry, causing the flour to become overworked. Fold in the chopped apricots and scrape the batter into the prepared pan, smoothing the surface with a rubber spatula.

4. Bake the cake in the centre of the oven for 1½ hours to 1¾ hours, or until a wooden skewer inserted into the centre of the cake comes out clean and the cake is beginning to pull away from the sides of the pan. Cool the cake in the pan on a wire rack for 15 minutes. Run a thin-bladed knife around the outside of the cake and the centre tube. If the pan has a removable bottom, lift the tube out, freeing the cake. Invert the cake onto a wire rack and pull out the tube and bottom. If the pan does not have a removable bottom, simply invert the cake onto the rack. Allow the cake to cool completely before serving or storing. It keeps very well at room temperature for up to 4 days, stored in an airtight cake dome or well wrapped in plastic, and it may also be frozen for up to 2 months, wrapped securely, and thawed, without disturbing the wrapping, at room temperature. This wonderful cake really doesn't need any embellishment, but if you must, a scoop of *Vanilla Bean Ice Cream* (page 553) or a little lightly sweetened whipped cream would be a perfect accompaniment.

Chocolate Raspberry Torte

SERVES 10

In this deep, dark and extremely moist cake, raspberry extract conspires with raspberry eau-de-vie to add a wonderful depth of flavour, and just enough raspberry taste to balance the rich chocolate. Keep your eyes open for baking extracts in gourmet food stores and cake decorating supply stores—stock up when you see them. They add a wonderful dimension to your baking!

TORTE:

5½ ounces best-quality bittersweet or semisweet chocolate, chopped

3 ounces unsweetened chocolate, chopped

⅔ cup unsalted butter, cut into small pieces

7 tablespoons seedless raspberry jam (if you cannot find seedless, use a good seeded variety, forced through a sieve)

4 large eggs, at room temperature

¾ cup granulated sugar

1 tablespoon Framboise (raspberry eau-de-vie), or other raspberry-flavoured liqueur

1 teaspoon pure raspberry extract (available at specialty baking and food stores), optional, but highly recommended

½ cup plus 1 tablespoon all-purpose flour

¾ teaspoon baking powder

¼ teaspoon salt

SYRUP:

½ cup granulated sugar

1 tablespoon light corn syrup

¼ cup water

¼ cup Framboise, or other raspberry-flavoured liqueur

3 tablespoons confectioners' sugar, sifted, for serving

1. Preheat the oven to 350°. Grease a 9-inch round cake tin and line the bottom with a circle of parchment paper. Grease the paper and dust the insides of the tin with flour, tapping out the excess. Set aside. Place a large pot on the stove with about 1½ inches of water in the bottom, and bring to just below a gentle simmer. Combine the chopped chocolates and the butter in a stainless steel or

Chocolate Raspberry Torte continued

glass bowl and set this over the barely simmering water. Melt this mixture, stirring occasionally. When the mixture is almost melted, add the raspberry jam and turn off the heat. The residual heat in the chocolate and butter will melt the jam. Stir until smooth, then cool slightly.

2. Meanwhile, beat the eggs with the sugar until the mixture is thick and pale and falls from the whisk or beaters in a ribbon when lifted. Beat in the Framboise and raspberry extract. In a small bowl, sift together the flour, baking powder and salt and set aside. When the chocolate mixture has cooled to about body temperature, beat it into the egg and sugar mixture. Scrape down the sides of the bowl and make sure the mixture looks smooth and well blended. Fold in the sifted flour mixture, then scrape the batter into the prepared pan.

3. Bake the torte until the top is cracked in several places, springs back when lightly touched, and a skewer inserted through one of the cracks into the centre comes out with a few moist crumbs clinging to it, about 50 to 60 minutes. Transfer the cake to a wire rack and cool 10 minutes. Run a thin-bladed knife around the outside of the cake and invert onto the rack. Carefully peel off the parchment paper and cool the cake completely.

4. While the cake is baking, or up to 3 days ahead of time, prepare the syrup: in a small, heavy-bottomed saucepan, combine the sugar, corn syrup and water. Stir over medium-low heat until the sugar dissolves, then increase the heat and bring the mixture to a boil. Boil for 30 seconds, then remove from the heat and cool for 5 minutes. Add the liqueur and cool completely before brushing on the cooled cake or covering and refrigerating.

5. This cake keeps well for several days, covered, at room temperature. The syrup will help to keep it moist and fresh. To freeze, wrap the un-syruped cake well with plastic wrap, then with aluminum foil or a freezer bag. Thaw overnight in the refrigerator, without removing the wrapping. Bring the cake to room temperature, unwrap and brush with the syrup. To serve, dust the cake with sifted confectioners' sugar. It is wonderful with *Raspberry Coulis* (page 643) and a dollop of whipped cream or crème fraîche and, of course, a handful of fresh red raspberries.

All-in-the-Pan Chewy Chocolate Cake with Chocolate Butter Icing

SERVES 6 TO 8

This is my mother's foolproof recipe for what I think is absolutely the simplest, fastest, yet most satisfying chocolate cake there is. I must admit—as much as I love the elaborate and impressive cakes served in restaurants and great pastry shops, this is the cake I crave. (My sister and I have been known to polish off a whole cake in one sitting. No, I'm not kidding.) You can put it together in less than 10 minutes, from start to finish, pop it in the oven for half an hour, and the result is nothing short of your childhood memory of real chocolate cake: deep, dark and chewy. Sprinkle the top with sifted confectioners' sugar and cocoa, if you are really in a hurry, but for true nostalgia, mix up a batch of the simple Chocolate Butter Icing. In this recipe, the cocoa of choice is a plain American-style unsweetened cocoa powder, not the Dutch-process type. The inherent bitterness and darkness of the American cocoa is what gives this cake its rich, dark chocolate flavour. Whatever you do, do not be tempted to do anything silly to this cake, like add liqueurs or other flavourings to the batter. It is a childhood cake, and the only acceptable gilding it should receive is a side of good ice cream, and a tall glass of milk.

CAKE:

1½ cups all-purpose flour

1 cup granulated sugar

¼ cup natural unsweetened cocoa powder, such as Ghirardelli or Hershey's

1 teaspoon baking soda

½ teaspoon salt

6 tablespoons flavourless vegetable oil, such as canola

1 tablespoon white vinegar

1 teaspoon pure vanilla extract

1 cup cool water

ICING:

¼ cup unsalted butter, at room temperature

2 cups confectioners' sugar

2 to 3 tablespoons milk or water

1½ tablespoons natural unsweetened cocoa powder

1 teaspoon pure vanilla extract

All-in-the-Pan Chewy Chocolate Cake continued

1. Preheat the oven to 350°. Sift the flour into an ungreased, unfloured 8 x 8-inch square baking pan (a 9 x 9-inch pan would work too; reduce the baking time by 5 to 7 minutes). (If you wish to unmould the cake before icing and serving, butter the pan lightly and line the bottom and up two sides with a piece of parchment paper. Take care when mixing not to disturb or tear the paper. Personally, I like to leave the cake in the pan; it keeps very well that way, and is even easier!) In a small bowl, whisk together the sugar, cocoa, baking soda and salt. Add this mixture to the flour in the pan and stir well with a fork or small whisk to blend the ingredients (a flat sauce whisk works beautifully). With the back of a teaspoon, make three indentations or wells in the dry mixture: one large, one medium-sized and one small. Into the large well, pour the vegetable oil. Into the medium-sized well, the vinegar. Pour the vanilla extract into the last well and pour the water over everything. With a fork, stir the mixture until the ingredients are well blended, making sure you reach into the corners and sides to catch any dry pockets. Do not beat this batter, but mix just until most of the lumps are smoothed out, and there are no little patches of overly thick or overly runny batter. A few lumps won't hurt, and it's important not to overbeat at this point.

2. Bake the cake for 30 minutes, or until a wooden skewer inserted into the centre of the cake comes out clean and the top feels springy when lightly touched. Transfer the pan to a wire rack and cool the cake completely before cutting, turning out or icing. This is an extremely moist cake, and it will tear if cut too soon. While you're waiting for the cake to cool, whip up a batch of the Chocolate Butter Icing. If you have lined the pan with parchment, run a knife around the sides of the pan and gently lift the cake out with the help of the parchment paper.

3. In a medium bowl, cream together the butter and 1 cup of the confectioners' sugar until the butter is well distributed. The mixture will be very dry and still powdery. Stir in 1 tablespoon of milk or water, then sift the cocoa powder over the mixture and cream to blend. Mix in the vanilla, then add the second cup of confectioners' sugar. Add as much of the remaining liquid as necessary to make a thick, creamy icing. (This recipe makes more than enough to generously frost the top and sides of the cake, and if you keep the cake in the pan, as I do, you will have plenty of icing left over for greedy fingers!)

4. To serve, you can simply sprinkle the cooled cake with sifted confectioners' sugar and/or cocoa powder, but the yummy butter icing really completes it. And there is no better cake for a scoop of chocolate or vanilla ice cream. Any leftovers can be stored in the pan, at room temperature, covered with a piece of aluminum foil. The un-iced cake freezes well: wrap the whole pan securely and thaw without disturbing the wrapping, at room temperature, for 4 to 6 hours. Makes enough for 8 servings if your guests are really polite, 3 to 4 if they are honest. (Again, I'm not kidding.)

✿ VARIATION ✿

The cake recipe can be doubled and baked in 2 (8- or 9-inch) round or square baking pans (for a layer cake!), or 1 (9 x 13-inch) pan. The baking time for the two pans is the same as in the master recipe; for one 9 x 13-inch cake, increase the baking time to 35 to 40 minutes. In each case, double the icing recipe.

Valrhona Molten Chocolate Cakes with an Espresso Crème Anglaise, à la Avalon

SERVES 8

This was the signature dessert at Avalon Restaurant when we opened. Cakes similar to this began appearing on restaurant menus all over North America several years ago, all based on a recipe created by Chef Jean-Georges Vongerichten. Some of them were merely interesting, others simply arresting! Many used a plain chocolate cake batter imbedded with a piece of dark chocolate or even a truffle to achieve the molten, melting warm chocolate centre. This version uses a specially made batter that, when baked just enough, remains molten at the centre. A marvellously light and delicate cake encases a warm, thick and runny chocolate sauce with the potency of an espresso. Not cloying, or even elaborate, this is one of the most adult desserts I have ever made. Indeed, the high you may

Valrhona Molten Chocolate Cakes continued

experience after partaking of this magnificent dessert is akin to a coffee jolt! But infinitely more sensual and enjoyable. The cakes are the best of both worlds: fabulously impressive, but easy as pie to prepare. And, they can be made up to 24 hours in advance and baked just before serving.

11 ounces bittersweet chocolate, preferably Valrhona Guanaja, or another bittersweet chocolate with at least 70% cocoa solids, finely chopped

1¼ cups plus 2 tablespoons (11 ounces) unsalted butter, cut into small pieces

6 large eggs

6 large egg yolks

¾ cup granulated sugar

½ cup plus 2 tablespoons all-purpose flour

Espresso Crème Anglaise, page 650

*A note on equipment: the best vessels in which to bake these cakes are aluminum cups, 2 inches deep and about 3 inches in diameter across the top, with a capacity of 6 ounces (¾ cup). Those I find work best have slightly rounded bottoms, making turning the warm cakes out easier. Cups like these are widely available to professionals and are easily found in restaurant or baking supply shops. If you cannot find them, substitute ceramic ramekins of the same size and shape; the baking time may have to be adjusted somewhat. Just keep an eye on the cakes as they bake.

1. Thoroughly grease eight 6-ounce aluminum cups and dust the insides well with flour, tapping out the excess. Make sure the entire inner surface of each cup is completely coated. Have all ingredients measured and ready to go before proceeding to the next step.

2. Combine the finely chopped chocolate and pieces of butter in a stainless steel or glass bowl. Place the bowl over a pot containing an inch or two of barely simmering water, stirring occasionally. Remove the bowl from the heat when the chocolate and butter are almost melted, and stir to melt completely. Cool slightly. The chocolate should be just warmer than body temperature when it is added to the batter; if it seems to have cooled too much by the time it is called for, set it over the pot of barely simmering water again for a few seconds until it warms slightly.

3. While the chocolate is cooling, in an electric or stand mixer fitted with a whip attachment, beat the eggs and the yolks to combine them, then beat in the sugar. Whip the mixture at medium-high speed until very thick and pale, about 10 minutes. Gradually beat in the flour, about ⅓ of a cup at a time, making sure each addition is completely incorporated before adding the next. Unless you are blessed with a 5-quart stand mixer, at this point you may need to transfer the batter to a larger bowl, one that can accommodate the egg batter and the melted chocolate-butter mixture. Gradually pour the chocolate mixture into the batter, stirring continuously. (Wrap a long, damp towel around the base of the bowl to hold it steady while you pour with one hand and stir with the other. You may need an extra pair of hands for this stage! Just promise someone a spoon to lick, and you should have no trouble finding volunteers.) Continue to beat until the batter is thick and glossy, about 5 minutes. Divide the batter among the prepared cups. Refrigerate for 30 minutes, then cover each cup with plastic wrap and chill for at least another 4, or up to 24, hours.

4. Preheat the oven to 325°. About 25 minutes before you plan to serve dessert, remove the cups from the refrigerator and discard the plastic wrap. Set the tins on a heavy baking sheet and place the sheet in the centre of the oven. Bake the cakes until the edges are set and spring back when touched, but the centres are still wobbly and jiggle slightly when the cups are moved, about 15 minutes. Checking the cakes often after the first 10 minutes will not have any adverse effect on them and will ensure you catch them at the right moment! Cool the cakes in the pans for 1 minute, then run a thin-bladed knife gently around the top edges and invert the cakes onto individual dessert plates. The cakes should unmould intact, but are very delicate, so don't slam them onto the plates, or otherwise force the cakes out of the cups. One smooth motion should do it. Ladle some of the *Espresso Crème Anglaise* onto each plate and serve immediately!

Black Chocolate Espresso Cake with Bittersweet Glaze

SERVES 12 TO 16

Huge, heavy and heavenly, this cake is almost jet black, with a wicked chocolate flavour. It hardly needs it, but the glaze is great. The cake begins as a somewhat strange batter, as the large amount of brewed coffee seems to be too much liquid for the rest of the batter. But it contributes both a balanced flavour and a wonderful moistness and in the end the cake does work, beautifully.

CAKE:

1½ cups unsalted butter, in small pieces

7 ounces unsweetened chocolate, the best you can afford, coarsely chopped

3 ounces bittersweet chocolate, coarsely chopped

2½ tablespoons instant espresso powder dissolved in 2 cups boiling water, cooled (or 2 cups strong black coffee)

3 cups granulated sugar

10 tablespoons (5 ounces) Kahlúa or other coffee-flavoured liqueur

1½ teaspoons pure vanilla extract

3 large eggs, lightly beaten

2¼ cups all-purpose flour

½ cup cake flour, not self-rising

1½ teaspoons baking soda

½ teaspoon salt

GLAZE:

10 ounces bittersweet or semisweet chocolate, chopped

7 tablespoons unsalted butter, in small pieces

Additional unsalted butter, at room temperature, for greasing the pan

Dark chocolate-covered espresso beans or chocolate coffee bean-shaped candies, for garnish

Lightly sweetened whipped cream, optional

1. Preheat the oven to 325°. Grease a 10-inch springform pan, line with a circle of parchment paper and lightly grease the paper. Combine the butter, both chocolates and coffee in the top of a double boiler or a stainless steel or glass bowl. Set the bowl or insert over a pot of barely simmering water and stir frequently with a wooden spoon until melted. If the melted mixture appears somewhat speckled with what looks like unmelted chocolate, don't be concerned. (Different chocolates have different cocoa butter and cocoa solids content and when melted with such a large quantity of liquid may seem to separate.) Place the sugar in the bottom of a large mixing bowl, or the bowl of an electric mixer. Remove the chocolate mixture from the heat and pour over the sugar. Stir to blend and dissolve the sugar, then allow to cool for 10 minutes.

2. With a wire whisk or the paddle attachment of an electric mixer, add the Kahlúa and vanilla extract to the cooled chocolate mixture and blend well. Blend in the lightly beaten eggs, making sure they are thoroughly incorporated. The batter at this point will be extremely thin; don't worry, just make sure to work each added ingredient into it carefully.

3. Sift the flours, baking soda and salt together. Add dry ingredients to the chocolate mixture in two additions, scraping down the sides of the bowl several times. Beat on medium speed for one minute. The batter may have little lumps, but they won't affect the finished cake.

4. Place the prepared pan on a baking sheet to catch any leaks and pour the batter into the pan. Bake in the middle of the oven for 1¾ hours to 2 hours, rotating the pan several times during that time to ensure even baking. The cake bakes slowly and stays beautifully moist. A crust will form on the top of the cake and may crack. Test for doneness by inserting a wooden skewer in a fault of the crust, poking near the centre of the cake. It should come out clean, or with only a very few moist crumbs clinging to it. Remove the cake from the oven and cool completely in the pan set on a rack. (The cake may be made up to 2 days ahead of time and kept in the pan at room temperature, covered tightly with plastic wrap.)

5. To prepare the glaze, combine the chopped chocolate and butter in the top of a double boiler or a bowl set over barely simmering water. Stir frequently until melted, then remove from the heat and cool slightly, stirring occasionally. Run a thin-bladed knife around the cake and loosen and remove the sides of the pan. Using a long-bladed serrated knife, carefully even out the top of the cake, slicing off any domed or uneven part of the crust. Use long, slow strokes of the knife, keeping the blade perfectly parallel with the counter.

Black Chocolate Espresso Cake continued

6. Place a dab of the chocolate glaze on a 10-inch cardboard cake circle and invert the cake onto the board. Remove the pan bottom and the parchment paper. (If you haven't got a cake circle or other piece of cardboard cut to 10 inches round, invert the cake onto a plate and remove the pan bottom but leave the paper. Re-invert the cake onto a second plate and place the pan bottom on the top of the cake. Invert the cake a third time, ending up with the bottom-side up, top-side down on the metal pan bottom, and peel off the paper.) Brush any crumbs from the cake and pour the warm glaze onto the centre. Using a metal spatula or palette knife, coax the glaze to the edges of the cake and over the sides; quickly spread the overflow evenly onto the sides. Garnish with the chocolate-covered espresso beans. Give the glaze an hour or so to set, then serve the cake with lightly sweetened whipped cream, if desired.

Black Sticky Gingerbread

SERVES 10 TO 12

Dark, moist and not overly sweet, with that almost-burnt caramel and spice flavour, this is the ideal anytime (read: breakfast!) cake. My grandmother would never forgive me if I didn't recommend whipped cream as an accompaniment (okay, maybe not with breakfast ...).

1 cup unsalted butter
½ cup water
¾ cup unsulphured blackstrap
    molasses
¾ cup flavourful honey, such as a dark
    wildflower, berry or chestnut
1 cup tightly packed dark brown sugar
3 cups all-purpose flour
1½ teaspoons baking soda
½ teaspoon salt
2 teaspoons ground ginger

2 teaspoons ground cinnamon
½ teaspoon allspice
⅛ teaspoon ground cloves
3 large eggs, at room temperature
½ cup partly skimmed milk (2%)
1 packed tablespoon grated fresh
    ginger root

Lightly sweetened whipped cream,
    to serve

1. Preheat the oven to 325°. Lightly grease a 9 x 9 x 2-inch baking pan and line the bottom with a piece of parchment paper that has been cut to hang over two opposite edges by a couple of inches. This overhang will make removing the cake from the pan clean and simple.

2. Combine the butter, water, molasses, honey and brown sugar in a medium non-reactive saucepan and place over low heat. Stir the mixture frequently until the butter is melted, and all of the ingredients are well blended. Remove from the heat, pour into a large bowl and set aside to cool.

3. Meanwhile, sift together the flour, baking soda, salt, ginger, cinnamon, allspice and cloves, and set aside. When the molasses mixture feels just warm to the touch, add the eggs, one at a time, beating well after each addition. Add the milk and stir to combine. Fold the dry ingredients into the batter in four additions, using big, long strokes. Don't be concerned if you can't get all the lumps out—settle for most of them! Stir in the grated ginger.

4. Pour the batter into the prepared pan and bake in the centre of the oven for 1¼ to 1½ hours, or until the top of the cake springs back when touched and a cake tester inserted into the centre comes out clean. Allow to cool for 15 minutes, then, using the overhang of parchment, lift the cake out of the pan and cool completely on a wire rack before cutting. Well-wrapped in plastic, this gingerbread actually improves with age. If stored at room temperature, it will have a sponge-cakey texture and will keep for about 4 days. Refrigerated, it becomes stickier, denser and wonderfully chewy and will last at least a week. Allow the cake to return to room temperature before serving. This cake is fabulous warm, and the only adornment it needs is mounds of softly whipped cream.

Banana-Strawberry Layer Cake

SERVES 10 TO 12

I can't wait for strawberry season each year just so I can make this cake. Happily, strawberry season coincides with all sorts of cake-appropriate occasions: Mother's Day, Victoria Day, End of School Day, laundry day, Tuesday ... This is a very moist, banana-y cake, and the frosting is a great contrast: thick, extra-creamy and cheesy-sweet. It is very important that the butter, eggs and bananas be just at room temperature, or the cake will seem overly heavy. Fabulous for birthdays, picnics or for just plain celebrating how good bananas and strawberries can be together (and how much we love cake with gooey icing).

CAKE LAYERS:

¾ cup unsalted butter, at room temperature, but not overly soft

1 cup granulated sugar

2 large eggs, at room temperature

1 teaspoon pure vanilla extract

1⅓ cups mashed overripe bananas (about 3 large), at room temperature

2 cups cake flour, not self-rising

¾ teaspoon baking soda

¼ teaspoon salt

⅓ cup full-fat sour cream

Additional butter and all-purpose flour for greasing and dusting the cake pans

CREAM CHEESE ICING:

1 pound (two 8-ounce packages) Philadelphia brand cream cheese, at room temperature

½ cup unsalted butter, at room temperature

1 package (500 grams, about 4 to 4⅓ cups) confectioners' sugar, sifted

1½ teaspoons pure vanilla extract

1 teaspoon freshly squeezed lemon juice

1 quart fresh ripe strawberries, washed and dried, if necessary

1. Preheat the oven to 350°. Grease and lightly flour two 9-inch round cake pans and tap out the excess flour; set aside. In the bowl of an electric or stand mixer fitted with the paddle attachment, or a large mixing bowl if mixing by hand, cream the butter and the sugar until light and fluffy, about 1½ to 2 minutes. Add the eggs, one at a time, beating well and scraping down the sides of the bowl after each addition. If your butter is too warm, or your eggs too cold, the batter may begin to separate; don't worry, it will come together when the last ingredients are added. Add the vanilla and the mashed bananas and blend well. Again, this addition may seem to completely curdle the batter if the ingredients were not the correct temperature. No need to panic—all will be well!

2. Sift together the flour, baking soda and salt. Add ½ of this mixture to the banana mixture, blending just to moisten the flour. Scrape down the bowl and beat in the sour cream. Scrape again, then add the remaining flour mixture, stirring just until the batter is evenly mixed. Divide the batter between the two pans and smooth the tops with a rubber spatula.

3. Set the cakes on the centre rack of the oven and bake for 25 to 30 minutes, or until the tops are light golden and spring back when touched and a wooden skewer inserted into the centre of each cake comes out clean. Rotate the pans once during baking so the cakes bake evenly. Cool the cakes in the pans on wire racks for 7 minutes, then invert onto the racks and cool completely before icing or wrapping and storing. (The cakes can be made up to this point up to one day ahead, then wrapped tightly in plastic wrap and stored at room temperature. They may also be frozen up to 3 months; thaw and bring to room temperature before proceeding.)

4. Prepare the Cream Cheese Icing: in the bowl of an electric or stand mixer fitted with the paddle attachment, beat the cream cheese and butter together until they are smooth, light and creamy, about 1½ minutes. (The icing can also be made by hand (a strong one!), by beating with a wooden spoon.) Add the confectioners' sugar, a cup at a time, re-sifting it over the cream cheese mixture. Beat well and scrape down the sides of the bowl. Continue adding the sugar one cup at a time, until almost all the sugar has been smoothly incorporated. Beat in the vanilla and lemon juice, then the remaining sugar. Taste the icing: it should be rich, cheesy and sweet, but not achingly so. If necessary, add a few drops more lemon juice or vanilla to your taste. Cover the icing and refrigerate it for 15 to 30 minutes before icing the cake to firm it up enough to support the layers. (The icing may be prepared up to 2 days ahead of time, and stored covered in the refrigerator. Allow the icing to return to room temperature or near it before spreading.)

Banana-Strawberry Layer Cake continued

5. Place one layer of the cake on a cardboard cake circle or a platter. (If you are going to ice the cake directly on the platter, slip strips of waxed or parchment paper around the bottom of the cake. These will protect the platter from gobs of icing and can be pulled cleanly away when you're finished decorating.) Spread the top of the first layer with a generous amount of icing, not going over the edges. Place the cake in the refrigerator for 15 minutes, to firm up the icing again. Meanwhile, reserve 10 to 12 pretty, small strawberries, and one large one. Hull the remaining berries and cut them in thirds from hull to point. Remove the iced layer from the refrigerator and cover the top with slices of strawberry. Feel free to overlap the slices slightly, but don't pile or stack them, or your next layer will topple over! Top the strawberries with the second cake layer, centring it over the bottom tier. Press down gently to make it adhere to the berries and icing. Spread the top and sides generously with the remaining icing, then immediately place the entire cake in the refrigerator, for at least 20 minutes, or up to 24 hours, before serving.

6. If the cake has been chilled for more than a few hours, remove it from the refrigerator 30 to 45 minutes before serving so it is not too cold. Just before serving, cut the large reserved strawberry several times from point to hull, not cutting through the stem. Push down lightly on the fat part of the berry, and it will fan out. Place this in the very centre of the cake. Cut the remaining berries once from point to stem, again not severing the halves from the hull, then twist slightly, "fanning" the little berries. Settle one berry at each of ten evenly spaced places around the outside of the cake, one for each piece. Once the cake has been decorated, it should be served within 6 hours or so, as the strawberries tend to pull the moisture from the icing, creating runny pink patches in the cream cheese. If the cake is to be made ahead, keep the icing chilled until needed, the cake layers wrapped and stored separately and assemble just before serving.

Caramelized Parsnip Layer Cake

SERVES 10

Parsnips are tragically underappreciated in North America. They are delicately flavoured and highly nutritious, yet almost completely ignored! I adore them, and love to cook them simply, covered in the oven, where they both steam and caramelize to a luscious sweetness. I realized one day how close to a dessert they already are, far sweeter than the carrots traditionally used in layer cakes. This cake is a result of my epiphany: wonderful, and rich, but with delicate and beautifully blended flavours. Think of it as a white carrot cake. None of the flavours (parsnip, pear, coconut) is more distinguishable than any other, but the overall result is one of both light and luxurious tastes.

CAKE:

2 cups raw parsnips, peeled, and sliced about ¼-inch thick

1 cup lightly toasted pecans, coarsely chopped (see page 253 for tips on toasting nuts)

¾ cup finely chopped tinned pears in their own juice, drained, reserving ¼ cup liquid

1¼ cups granulated sugar

¾ cup tightly packed light brown sugar

2 cups all-purpose flour

1 tablespoon baking powder

½ teaspoon salt

1 teaspoon ground cinnamon

½ teaspoon freshly ground nutmeg

3 large eggs

1 cup mild-flavoured vegetable oil, such as canola

2 teaspoons pure vanilla extract

1 cup sweetened shredded coconut

Unsalted butter, at room temperature, for greasing the pans

Caramel Cream Cheese Frosting, page 646

1. Preheat the oven to 350°. Line a small baking dish with aluminum foil, add sliced parsnips and cover tightly with another sheet of foil. Bake for 45 minutes to 1 hour, or until the parsnips are nicely caramelized on the bottom and soft and almost custard-like on the tops. Remove from the oven and mash with a potato masher or a fork. Set aside.

2. While the parsnips are baking, toast and chop the pecans and chop the tinned pears. Butter two 9-inch round cake pans and line the bottoms with circles of parchment paper. Lightly butter the paper and set the pans aside.

3. In a large bowl, combine white and brown sugars and stir with a fork or wire whisk to blend and break up any lumps. Into the same bowl, sift the flour, baking powder, salt, cinnamon and nutmeg and stir to blend thoroughly. In a separate bowl, lightly beat the eggs, then add the vegetable oil and vanilla, whisking gently until the mixture is homogeneous. Pour the wet ingredients

Caramelized Parsnip Layer Cake continued

into the flour mixture and stir until the dry ingredients are just moistened, then fold in the parsnips, chopped pears and reserved pear liquid. Finally, fold in the chopped pecans and coconut.

4. Divide the batter evenly between the two pans, smooth the tops with a rubber spatula, then place them in the middle of the preheated oven. Bake for 35 to 45 minutes, or until a tester inserted into the centre of the cakes comes out clean and the cakes are golden and just beginning to pull away from the sides of the pans. Allow the cakes to cool in the pans set on wire racks for 15 minutes, then invert onto the racks, peel off the parchment circles and cool completely. (The cake layers can be made 1 day ahead and stored at room temperature, well wrapped in plastic wrap. They also freeze well, wrapped securely, for up to 3 months. Thaw at room temperature without disturbing the wrapping.)

5. When the layers are cool, frost with the cream cheese icing. If cake is not to be eaten immediately, refrigerate until ½ hour before serving. This cake can be assembled up to 1 day ahead of time and stored in an airtight cake dome in the refrigerator.

Fall Charlotte with Apples, Quince and Golden Raisins

SERVES 6

This is one of my all-time favourite desserts. Amazingly light, and softly flavoured with autumnal apples, quinces, vanilla and Calvados, it is perfect at the end of a rich holiday meal. The flavours are a seamless marriage—nothing jarring, nothing distinct, and yet the combined impression is rich and deeply satisfying. One bite, and everyone will find room for dessert! The mould traditionally used for this classic French dessert is a deep, straight-sided tin pan, about 7 inches across the top, with a capacity of about 1½ quarts. The sides usually have distinctive heart-shaped handles. Moulds made in France may be a little pricey, but there are perfectly good products coming out of China and Portugal for less than half the price. If you cannot find a charlotte mould, head to the Italian neighbourhood in your town and look for an equivalent-sized panettone mould—it will do nicely!

FILLING:

2 large quinces, prepared using the instructions for Poached Quince, page 596, but using only 3 cups of water and 1½ cups granulated sugar, plus cinnamon stick and vanilla bean

8 medium-sized tart, firm cooking apples, such as Northern Spy, Rome Beauty or Spartan, or use a combination of several varieties for a more complex flavour

¼ cup unsalted butter

⅔ cup granulated sugar

3 tablespoons Calvados, or other apple brandy

1-inch piece of vanilla bean, split and scraped out (you'll use both the seeds and hull)

¼ teaspoon salt

Juice of ½ lemon

2 tablespoons cornstarch mixed with 1 tablespoon cool water to form a paste

¾ cup plump, soft golden raisins

TO ASSEMBLE THE CHARLOTTE:

1½ loaves day-old brioche or challah bread (loaf-pan shaped, not decorative or braided), cut into ⅓-inch slices, with crusts removed

½ cup unsalted butter, melted and cooled

Additional unsalted butter, at room temperature, for greasing mould

Additional granulated sugar for dusting mould

Vanilla Bean Ice Cream (page 553), or good-quality store-bought vanilla ice cream, to serve

1. Prepare the filling: poach the quinces according to the method on page 595 and allow the slices to cool until they can be handled. Drain the slices and cut them into ¾- to 1-inch chunks and set aside. Boil the syrup until reduced, slightly thickened and syrupy. The syrup will thicken further as it cools. Cool to room temperature, then cover the syrup and refrigerate. (The quince and its syrup can be made up to 3 days ahead of time and stored separately in airtight containers in the refrigerator. Allow the fruit to come to room temperature before proceeding.)

2. Peel and core the apples and cut them into ¾-inch chunks. In a large skillet, melt the ¼ cup butter over medium-low heat and add the apples when the foam subsides. Add the sugar, Calvados, vanilla seeds and hull, salt and lemon juice and increase the heat to medium. Simmer the mixture, stirring just enough to combine the ingredients and cook until the apples are soft but not

Fall Charlotte continued

mushy and most of the liquid has evaporated. Take the skillet off the heat and stir in 1 tablespoon of the cornstarch paste. When the paste has been smoothly incorporated, return the pan to the heat and simmer the mixture for 30 seconds to 1 minute, until the juices are thickened. If after the first 15 or so seconds the mixture still looks too runny, add another ½ tablespoon of the paste, off the heat. Return to simmer for 30 seconds. Transfer the mixture to a bowl and add the quince and the golden raisins. Allow to cool completely. The filling may be prepared 1 day ahead and stored, covered, in the refrigerator. Allow it to return to room temperature before filling the charlotte.

3. Preheat the oven to 350°. Generously butter the mould and dust the inside with granulated sugar, tapping out the excess. With a drinking glass or a plain round biscuit cutter about 3 inches in diameter, cut 7 or 8 rounds from the slices of bread. Brush these on both sides with melted butter and arrange in an overlapping pattern in the bottom of the mould. Use a scrap piece of bread to patch the little space in the very centre of the circle. One by one, brush the remaining slices of bread on both sides and line the sides of the mould, overlapping the slices and making certain every bit of the tin is covered. With the back of a spoon, press against the bread lining to seal any spaces between the slices. Spoon the cooled filling into the mould, packing it tightly. When the filling reaches the top of the lining, smooth the top and tamp it down as much as possible. Cut three or four slices of bread to fit the opening of the tin exactly, brush both sides with melted butter and press them onto the filling, covering the whole surface. Use small scraps of buttered bread to fill in any gaps and to ensure a good seal.

4. Bake the charlotte in the centre of the oven for 20 minutes, or until the top is golden brown and toasted. Cover the surface lightly with a piece of aluminum foil, then return the charlotte to the oven for another 30 to 40 minutes. A metal skewer inserted in between two pieces of bread on the top and midway into the filling, held for 10 seconds, should feel warm when touched to your bottom lip. Let the charlotte cool in the tin for 5 to 10 minutes. Meanwhile, gently re-warm the reduced quince syrup. Invert the charlotte onto a decorative platter and serve immediately. Drizzle each portion with some of the syrup and accompany with a scoop of *Vanilla Bean Ice Cream*. You could serve crème anglaise with this dessert, but I prefer the lovely contrasts of the fragrant soft warm fruit, the buttery crunch of the bread and the rich, smooth, cold ice cream. A hint: you might find using a serrated knife the easiest way to cut through the charlotte!

Pumpkin and Orange Breakfast Cake with a Fresh Orange Syrup

MAKES 10 SERVINGS

This cake, perfect for a simple dessert, or even for breakfast, is dense and light at the same time, with a delicate and very moist crumb and a subtle autumnal flavour. It is best with the syrup ladled over the individual slices, rather than the whole cake. Also great with an afternoon cup of Earl Grey!

CAKE:

1 cup unsalted butter, at room temperature

1 cup granulated sugar

2 tablespoons finely grated orange zest

3 large eggs, two of them separated, all at room temperature

1 cup pumpkin purée, homemade (see page 331), or pure canned solid-pack pumpkin (not "Pumpkin Pie Filling")

1½ cups all-purpose flour

½ cup cake flour (not self-rising)

2 teaspoons baking powder

¼ teaspoon salt

SYRUP:

Juice of 1 large juice orange, such as Seville

½ cup granulated sugar

Additional unsalted butter, at room temperature, for greasing the pan

Thick vanilla yogurt or vanilla ice cream, to serve

1. Preheat the oven to 350°. Butter a 9-inch fluted tube pan and set it aside. Cream the butter, sugar and orange zest together until light and fluffy. Add the whole egg and the two egg yolks, one at a time, beating well and scraping down the sides of the bowl between each addition. Beat in the pumpkin purée.

2. Sift together the flours, baking powder and salt. Add to the pumpkin batter in three or four stages, blending gently but thoroughly after each. Stir in the final addition of dry ingredients by hand if you have been using a mixer, so as not to overwork the batter. In a clean, small bowl, whip the egg whites until they hold soft peaks. Fold into the batter, then scrape the batter into the prepared pan and smooth the surface. Bake in the centre of the oven for 50 to 60 minutes, or until the top of the cake is springy when lightly touched, the sides are beginning

Pumpkin and Orange Breakfast Cake continued

to pull away from the sides of the pan and a wooden skewer inserted into the-centre of the cake comes out clean. Cool in the pan for 10 minutes, then invert onto a wire rack and cool completely. This cake keeps very well for several days, well wrapped, and it freezes beautifully for up to 2 months.

3. For the syrup, combine the orange juice and sugar in a small saucepan over low heat and stir until the sugar has dissolved. Increase the heat, bringing the syrup to a boil. Boil without stirring for 2 minutes, then use immediately, or allow to cool and refrigerate for up to 3 days (re-heat gently).

4. To serve, place one slice of the pumpkin orange cake on each plate. Spoon a few tablespoons of the warm syrup over each piece, and accompany with a scoop of thick vanilla yogurt (for breakfast) or ice cream (for dessert).

Toasted Hazelnut Pound Cake

SERVES 10 TO 12

Hazelnut oil is a wonderful product, available in gourmet and specialty food stores. It is highly perishable, however, and goes rancid quickly. Buy it from a shop with a high turnover and, once opened, store it in the refrigerator and use promptly. Here, hazelnut oil contributes another dimension to the already intense flavour of the roasted nuts. I love bringing one of these fine-crumbed cakes on picnics, cutting big rough wedges for everyone after the meal. But it is just as at home as the finale for an elegant formal dinner; a glass of dessert wine or Frangelico, the hazelnut liqueur, is a lovely partner.

1½ cups hazelnuts, toasted and
   skinned (see page 262 for tips on
   toasting and skinning hazelnuts)
1 cup granulated sugar
1 cup unsalted butter, at room
   temperature
½ cup tightly packed light brown sugar
4 large eggs, at room temperature
2 teaspoons pure vanilla extract

2 cups all-purpose flour
2½ teaspoons baking powder
½ teaspoon salt
½ cup heavy cream (36%)
1 tablespoon pure hazelnut oil,
   optional, but highly recommended!

Additional unsalted butter, at room
   temperature, for greasing the pan

1. Preheat the oven to 350°. Butter and lightly flour a 9-inch springform pan and set aside. In a food processor, pulse the toasted hazelnuts with 2 table-spoons of the granulated sugar until finely ground. Take care not to overgrind the hazelnuts to the point where they become a nut butter, or the cake will be oily and heavy. Set the nut mixture aside.

2. In the bowl of an electric mixer fitted with the paddle attachment, or a large mixing bowl with a wooden spoon, cream the butter until light, then add the white and brown sugars and cream the mixture until it is light, pale and fluffy. Add the eggs, one at a time, beating well after each addition and scraping down the sides of the bowl periodically. Don't worry if the mixture looks separated and broken; it will come together perfectly when the flour is incorporated. Beat in the vanilla.

3. Sift the flour, baking powder and salt together, then stir in the nut mixture. Add this to the butter mixture in three additions, alternating with the cream in two additions, beginning and ending with the dry ingredients. Mix only enough to mostly incorporate each addition, and if you are using a mixer, switch to a rubber spatula or flat wooden spoon for the last addition of flour. Add the hazelnut oil with the last addition of cream. As soon as the dry ingredients are completely moistened, scrape the batter into the prepared pan and place the pan in the centre of the oven.

4. Bake for 1 hour and 10 minutes to 1 hour and 20 minutes, or until the top springs back when lightly touched, the sides are just beginning to pull away from the pan and a wooden skewer inserted in the centre of the cake comes out clean. Transfer the pan to a wire rack and cool 20 to 30 minutes. Run a thin-bladed knife around the outside of the cake, then remove the sides of the pan. Cool the cake on the rack completely before serving or wrapping and storing. This cake is actually better the second day, stored well wrapped at room temperature, and can be kept for up to 5 days, stored in the refrigerator. Either way, it needs no accompaniment, not even a dusting of confectioners' sugar.

Walnut Layer Cake with a Coffee Buttercream

SERVES 10 TO 12

This is another of my favourite cakes. Lots of lovely buttery walnut flavour in a fine-crumbed rich cake and a satiny, intensely coffee-flavoured buttercream. The frosting is a simple meringue buttercream: lighter and less sweet than the traditional type made with egg yolks, and much less finicky than most recipes, which often require a candy thermometer and an experienced hand.

CAKE LAYERS:

1½ cups unsalted butter, at room temperature

1⅓ cups granulated sugar

4 large eggs, at room temperature

2 tablespoons pure maple syrup, preferably grade B or C (see page 139)

1 teaspoon pure vanilla extract

1 cup finely ground fresh walnuts

2 cups all-purpose flour

2 teaspoons baking powder

½ teaspoon salt

BUTTERCREAM:

4 large egg whites, with no traces of fat or yolk

1 cup granulated sugar

1¼ cups unsalted butter, at room temperature

1 teaspoon pure vanilla extract

2½ tablespoons espresso powder dissolved in 1½ tablespoons hot water, cooled

Additional unsalted butter, at room temperature, for greasing the pans

Chocolate espresso beans, for garnish, optional

Lightly toasted walnut halves, for garnish, optional

1. Prepare the walnut cake layers: preheat the oven to 350°. Butter and lightly flour two 9-inch round cake pans, tapping out the excess flour. Set the pans aside. In the bowl of an electric or stand mixer fitted with the paddle attachment, or in a large bowl (if you are preparing the batter by hand), cream the butter and the sugar until pale, light and very fluffy. Add the eggs, one at a time, beating well and scraping down the sides of the bowl after each addition. Beat in the maple syrup and the vanilla, then mix in the ground walnuts.

2. Sift the flour, baking powder and salt together into a small bowl and add this mixture to the batter in three additions, mixing just enough to moisten the flour between each addition. Fold the last addition in by hand with a large rubber spatula. Scrape the batter into the prepared pans, smoothing the tops with the spatula. Bake the layers in the centre of the oven, on the same rack, if possible. If your oven is not large enough to accommodate two pans side by side or slightly staggered, position racks close together on two central tiers in the oven and rotate the layers several times during the baking so they bake evenly. Bake for 30 to 35 minutes, or until the cakes are just beginning to pull away from the sides of the pan and a wooden skewer inserted in the centre of each layer comes out clean. Cool the cakes in the pans on wire racks for 7 minutes, then invert onto the racks and cool completely before icing or wrapping and storing. The layers may be prepared up to 2 days ahead of time, wrapped very well in plastic wrap and stored at room temperature.

3. Prepare the Coffee Buttercream: bring an inch or two of water to a bare simmer in a large pot. In a medium bowl, lightly beat the egg whites to break them up. Add the sugar, and whisk together until frothy. Set the bowl over the water and stir the whites-sugar mixture with the whisk until the sugar is dissolved and the mixture feels quite warm, but not hot, to the touch—about 5 minutes. Quickly transfer the mixture to the clean bowl of an electric or stand mixer fitted with the whip attachment and beat the meringue on medium-high speed until the meringue feels cool to the touch, about 8 to 10 minutes. The meringue must be cool before you add the butter, or the heat will melt the butter, and the meringue will be heavy and may separate.

4. Beat in the butter, a few tablespoons at a time, making sure the last pieces are completely incorporated before adding the next. Beat well, scraping the sides of the bowl often. When all of the butter is incorporated, the buttercream is ready to be flavoured, if it is to be used immediately, or covered and refrigerated to be used later. (The buttercream can be made up to 4 days ahead of time; to use, bring the icing to room temperature and beat until spreadable before flavouring.) Add the vanilla; beat well. Add the espresso-water paste a teaspoon at a time, beating well between each addition. The final buttercream should be smooth, thick and glossy. If it separates at any point, or looks wet and

Walnut Layer Cake continued

lumpy, immerse the bottom of the bowl in hot tap water, then beat until it becomes smooth. Use the buttercream immediately.

5. To assemble the cake: place a small dollop of buttercream on a cardboard cake circle or a decorative cake platter, to anchor the first layer. Place one layer, bottom side down, on the circle or plate. Spread the top of the layer with about ½ an inch of buttercream. Place the second layer on the filling and spread the top and sides with a generous amount of buttercream. Garnish the cake as you like—I use a piping bag or a paper cone to pipe the remaining buttercream in a decorative pattern on the top and place the chocolate espresso beans and/or walnut halves to mark each piece. The finished cake is best served within a few hours of decorating, but may be made up to 24 hours ahead of time and stored at cool room temperature, under a cake dome.

Persimmon and Cashew Tea Cakes

6 SINGLE-SERVING TEA CAKES
OR 12 SMALLER CAKES

Persimmons are wonderfully sweet and luscious fruit, but can present a problem for the baker. Most recipes using fresh persimmons are for steamed puddings—dense, moist, fairly heavy desserts using the puréed flesh. Some of these are truly delicious, but many are simply damp, sticky cakes in which other flavours, such as brown sugar or spices, mask the elusive taste of the persimmon. I set out to invent something that would showcase the lovely sweetness of the fruit, but remain tender, light and cakey. The secret, I discovered, lies in the type of persimmon used. The most commonly available Hyachia variety has a good flavour, but must be jelly-soft before it can be eaten or used in baking, or it will be unpalatably tannic and rough flavoured. The pulp is too soft to chop and, once extracted, becomes more liquid than flesh. The trick is to use a variety of persimmon that is sweet and flavourful when it is still firm, such as a Fuyu or, even better, the unusual imported Vanille variety, which can be eaten very firm and is the sweetest of all, tasting of honey and vanilla. They are available for a brief time in the fall, from Italy, but you can use the Fuyu variety if you can't track these down.

Subtle, delicate and slightly tropical in flavour, these little cakes are perfect as part of an assortment of treats at afternoon tea, or a luxurious late brunch. Both persimmons and cashews have a delicate flavour, and they complement each other beautifully. I like to bake these cakes in the larger muffin tins and serve one per person, but you can also make smaller ones using a regular 12-muffin tray.

CAKES:

About 2 large, firm but slightly yielding Vanille persimmons, or 2 to 3 semi-soft Fuyu persimmons (do not substitute the Hyachia variety)

¾ cup unsalted butter, at room temperature

1 cup granulated sugar

2 large eggs, at room temperature

¼ teaspoon pure vanilla extract

1 tablespoon bourbon, optional

1½ cups all-purpose flour

1½ teaspoons baking powder

½ teaspoon salt

¼ teaspoon ground cinnamon

1 cup roasted unsalted cashews, coarsely chopped

GLAZE:

¼ cup unsalted butter, melted and cooled

⅓ cup granulated sugar

½ teaspoon ground cinnamon

Additional unsalted butter, at room temperature, for greasing the moulds

1. Preheat the oven to 350°. Butter a 6-muffin tray (1 cup each) or a regular 12-muffin tray (½ cup each) and set aside. Peel the persimmons and halve them crosswise. Take out any seeds; some persimmons have a few large, black seeds, and some have none. There's no way to tell from the outside, so make sure you buy a little extra. Cut the fruit into pieces about ¾-inch square and set aside 1 cup of these chunks. You can eat the rest standing right there in your kitchen—they're like a firm, sweet pudding. And good for you, too!

2. With an electric or stand mixer fitted with the paddle attachment, or by hand with a wooden spoon, cream the butter and sugar until very light and fluffy. Add the eggs, one at a time, beating well and scraping down the sides and bottom of the bowl after each addition. Beat in the vanilla and bourbon, if using. Sift the flour, baking powder, salt and cinnamon together into a small bowl.

Persimmon and Cashew Tea Cakes continued

Fold the flour mixture into the batter in two additions, mixing just enough to incorporate it smoothly, without overworking. When the last of the flour is almost completely blended in, fold in the chopped persimmon and cashews.

3. Divide the batter among the cups and smooth the tops with the back of a spoon. Bake large muffin-sized cakes for 35 to 40 minutes and regular muffin-sized cakes 25 to 30 minutes, or until the tops are golden brown and a wooden skewer inserted into the centres of the cakes comes out clean. Cool the cakes in the pan for 7 minutes.

4. While the cakes are baking, prepare the glaze. Melt the butter and set it aside to cool slightly. Blend the sugar and cinnamon together in a small bowl. When the cakes have cooled, turn them out of the pans and, one by one, dip the tops first in the melted butter and then in the spiced sugar, rolling them to coat the whole top. Cool the cakes on a wire rack before serving or wrapping and storing. The cakes keep well for up to 3 days, wrapped well, at room temperature. They may also be frozen for up to 3 months, and thawed overnight in the refrigerator. Serve the cakes warm or at room temperature, alone or with a little pillow of whipped cream sweetened with honey.

Vanilla Date Cupcakes with Buttermilk Fudge Frosting

SERVES 12

These sweet little cakes have a distinctly adult date and vanilla flavour and a fudge-like icing with the subtle tang of buttermilk. If you can, use Medjool dates in the cakes—the flavour is incomparable. Cake flour and buttermilk in the batter make this an extremely tender cake, and plump dates mashed to a paste contribute richness and moisture. And because they're shaped like muffins, I say you can have them for breakfast. Great with a hot cup of Earl Grey!

CUPCAKES:

½ pound plump, moist dried dates, preferably Medjool, pits removed and coarsely chopped

1 cup unsalted butter, at room temperature

¾ cup granulated sugar

¾ cup tightly packed light brown sugar

Seeds of 1 vanilla bean, hull reserved for another use

3 large eggs, at room temperature

1 teaspoon pure vanilla extract

3 cups cake flour (not self-rising), sifted

1 teaspoon baking powder

1 teaspoon baking soda

¼ teaspoon salt

¼ teaspoon nutmeg

1¼ cups buttermilk

FROSTING:

2½ cups granulated sugar

4 teaspoons light corn syrup

½ cup unsalted butter, in small pieces

1 cup buttermilk, plus an additional ¼ to ½ cup, for thinning the cooked frosting

1 teaspoon baking soda, sifted

1 teaspoon pure vanilla extract

Additional unsalted butter, at room temperature, for greasing pans

1. Preheat the oven to 350°. Butter 12 large (1-cup capacity) muffin cups or line them with large paper liners. Pour ½ cup boiling water over the chopped dates and mash with a fork to a rough paste. Set aside.

2. In a large bowl, or the bowl of an electric or stand mixer fitted with the paddle attachment, cream the butter, both sugars, and the vanilla seeds until light and fluffy. Add the eggs, one at a time, beating well after each addition and scraping down the sides of the bowl. Beat in the vanilla extract.

3. Sift the flour, baking powder, baking soda, salt and nutmeg together. Add this mixture to the batter in three additions, alternating with the buttermilk in two additions. Fold in the date paste, then scrape the batter into the muffin cups, filling each one ⅔ to ¾ full. Smooth the tops with the back of a teaspoon and place the tins in the centre of the oven. Bake the cakes for about 30 minutes, or until the tops are golden and spring back when lightly touched and a wooden skewer inserted in the centre of the cakes comes out with just a few moist crumbs clinging to it. Cool the cakes in the pans for 10 minutes, then run a thin-bladed knife around the edges of the cakes and turn them out. Cool completely, right-side up on wire racks, before icing. (The cupcakes can be prepared 1 day

Vanilla Date Cupcakes continued

ahead and stored, well wrapped in plastic, at room temperature. These cakes also freeze very well for up to 2 months. Thaw them overnight in the refrigerator, then allow them to come to room temperature before icing.)

4. Prepare the Buttermilk Fudge Frosting: combine the sugar, corn syrup, butter, buttermilk and baking soda in a large, heavy-bottomed pot. The pot should seem too large—this mixture foams to about four times its original volume as it nears the boil. (I learned this the hard way—and am still scraping bits of caramelized buttermilk candy off my stove!) Stir the mixture over medium heat until the sugar dissolves. Increase the heat slightly and bring the syrup to a boil. Stir the mixture just as it comes to the boil, then don't stir again. Boil the syrup until it reaches the soft ball stage (see the chart on page 74) or registers 236°F on a candy thermometer. Immediately pour the hot syrup into a large mixing bowl, or the bowl of an electric or stand mixer fitted with the whip attachment, and allow it to cool for a minute or two.

5. Stir in the vanilla extract, then beat the mixture on medium speed until it is thick enough to spread, about 3 to 5 minutes. Add ¼ cup buttermilk and beat just to incorporate. This frosting thickens very quickly as it cools; add more buttermilk, a few tablespoons at a time, to keep it spreadable. If the icing hardens too much, place the bowl in a pot of warm water and stir until malleable. Working quickly, slather the tops of the cupcakes with the icing and cool before serving or storing. Iced cupcakes can be stored for 2 or 3 days in an airtight container at room temperature.

Little Lime-Syrup-Soaked Coconut Cakes

7 OR 8 INDIVIDUAL CAKES, 12 SMALL CAKES OR 24 MINIATURE CAKES

These little cakes are dense and moist without being heavy, brimming with a rich coconut flavour. Laced with the fresh lime syrup, they would be perfect at the end of an Asian, Caribbean, Mexican or Middle Eastern meal. They would also be good for an al fresco dinner, as they require neither refrigeration, nor rewarming, nor anything at all to accompany them! Little paper muffin cups are perfect for serving them, pretty and simple. I like the size of one cake per person, but you could also make twelve smaller cakes and serve two to each guest, or even twenty-four tiny petit-four-sized cakes, for an especially elegant presentation or for a dessert buffet or platter. These cakes need no embellishment, but a scoop of Lychee and Coconut Milk Sorbet (page 558) couldn't hurt!

SYRUP:

½ cup plus 2 tablespoons granulated sugar

⅓ cup freshly squeezed lime juice (from about 10 large limes)

Finely grated zest of 2 large limes

¼ cup cool water

CAKES:

2 cups all-purpose flour

¾ teaspoon baking powder

1⅓ cups granulated sugar

1 cup unsweetened desiccated coconut

2 large eggs, at room temperature, lightly beaten

1 cup canned coconut milk, not low-fat: use ⅔ cup of the thick cream that sits at the top of the tin, and the remaining ⅓ cup blended cream and milk from the rest of the tin

1 cup unsalted butter, melted and cooled

2 scant teaspoons finely grated lime zest (the zest of about 2 large limes)

½ teaspoon pure vanilla extract

Additional unsalted butter, at room temperature, for greasing the moulds

1. Prepare the lime syrup: in a small saucepan, combine the syrup ingredients and heat gently, stirring just until the sugar dissolves. Increase the heat to medium and bring the mixture to a boil. Boil for 6 to 8 minutes, until the syrup has thickened slightly. Remove from the heat and set aside until the cakes are baked. (The syrup may be prepared up to 24 hours ahead; refrigerate until needed, then bring to just below the boil before proceeding with recipe.)

2. Preheat the oven to 350°. Butter seven or eight 6- to 8-ounce (¾ to 1 cup) muffin cups or individual cake moulds. If you are serving other desserts, or a heavy meal, or would like to serve two pretty little cakes per guest, this recipe can be made in 12 regular-sized muffin tins, or even 24 mini muffin tins. (These cakes may be the exception to my general rule about preferring aluminum bakeware to non-stick: I have found that darker, non-stick tins yield a better cake than light shiny aluminum ones; if you do use light shiny aluminum, increase the baking time.) Place the pans on a baking sheet and set aside.

Little Lime-Syrup-Soaked Coconut Cakes continued

3. Sift the flour and baking powder together in a large bowl. Stir in the sugar and coconut. In a small bowl, lightly beat the eggs, then add the coconut milk/cream and cooled melted butter. Stir with a whisk to blend the mixture into a thick, smooth liquid. Stir in the lime zest and vanilla extract. Add the egg mixture to the dry ingredients all at once and stir with a wooden spoon just until the flour is evenly moistened.

4. Spoon the batter into the prepared pans and place the baking sheet in the centre of the oven. Bake the large cakes for 35 to 40 minutes in dark tins or 50 to 55 minutes in light shiny tins; bake 12 small cakes for 20 to 30 minutes, and 24 mini cakes for 15 to 18 minutes, depending on the metal. The edges will darken quite quickly to a rich golden brown, but the cakes are done when the edges begin to pull away from the sides, the tops are cracked and risen, and a wooden skewer inserted in the centre of each cake comes out clean.

5. Transfer the tins to a wire rack set over a baking sheet and cool for 5 minutes. Carefully run a thin-bladed knife around each cake and turn them out onto the rack right-side up. Use a small toothpick to prick ten or twelve holes in the tops of each cake, poking down 2 inches or so. Rewarm the lime syrup over a low flame until it is just beginning to bubble at the edges of the pot. Spoon some over each cake and leave them to cool completely. Although the cakes are best eaten the same day they are baked, they keep well, tightly covered, at room temperature for 2 to 3 days.

Spice Layer Cake with Maple Meringue Frosting

SERVES 10 TO 12

Like many other pastry chefs, I began my baking career at a tender age with nothing more glamorous than an Easy-Bake Oven. Although chocolate was probably my favourite at the time, the spice cake is the one I can remember to this day—delicately spiced for a child's sweet palate and yet seductively more adult in its flavour than childish chocolate. I think that this light layer cake, topped with a wonderfully sticky frosting, is a good deal better than the add-water-and-stir variety of my youth, but I've made sure it has the same satisfying flavours as the first spice cake I loved. Using maple syrup instead of granulated sugar makes the frosting slightly less sweet than most meringue frostings and a good complement to the subtle cake. The result is not a powerfully heavy dessert, but a perfect anytime old-fashioned layer cake. Here's to Betty Crocker!

CAKE LAYERS:

3 cups all-purpose flour

1½ teaspoons baking powder

1 teaspoon baking soda

½ teaspoon salt

1½ teaspoons ground cinnamon

¾ teaspoon ground ginger

½ teaspoon ground allspice, preferably freshly ground

½ teaspoon ground mace (or substitute nutmeg)

⅛ teaspoon ground cloves, preferably freshly ground

⅔ cup unsalted butter, at room temperature

1½ cups tightly packed light brown sugar

2 large eggs, at room temperature

2 teaspoons pure vanilla extract

1 cup milk, not 1% or skim

⅓ cup sour cream

1 tablespoon dark rum, optional

½ to ¾ cup chopped walnut or pecans, lightly toasted, optional, or substitute chopped Maple Sugared Pecans, page 636

FROSTING:

1½ cups pure maple syrup, grade B or C

3 large egg whites, at room temperature

¼ teaspoon cream of tartar

Additional unsalted butter, at room temperature, for greasing the pans

Lightly toasted pecan or walnut halves or Maple Sugared Pecans, page 636, for garnish, optional

1. Preheat the oven to 350°. Butter two 9-inch round cake pans and line the bottoms with circles of parchment paper. Butter the paper and dust the insides of the pans with flour, tapping out the excess. Sift together the flour, baking powder, baking soda, salt and spices and set aside.

2. In a large bowl, or the bowl of an electric or stand mixer fitted with the paddle attachment, cream the butter until soft. Add the brown sugar and cream until light and fluffy. Add the eggs, one at a time, beating well and scraping down the sides of the bowl after each addition. Don't worry if the batter looks

Spice Layer Cake continued

a little bit curdled; when the flour and liquid are added, it will come together again. Beat in the vanilla. Add the flour mixture in three additions, alternating with the milk in two additions, beginning and ending with the dry ingredients. Don't overwork the batter and be sure to scrape down the sides and bottom of the bowl frequently. Stir in the sour cream and rum, if using; fold in the nuts, if you've chosen to use them.

3. Divide the batter evenly between the two pans and smooth the tops with a rubber spatula. Set the pans on the middle rack of the oven; if both pans do not fit on the same rack, position two racks as close together as possible and switch their positions once during the baking. Bake the cakes for 35 to 40 minutes, or until the tops spring back when lightly touched and a wooden skewer inserted in the centre of each cake comes out clean. Cool in the pans for 10 minutes, then run a thin-bladed knife around the edges of the cakes and invert them onto wire racks. Peel off the parchment paper and cool completely before wrapping and storing, or frosting. (The layers can be made ahead of time and stored, well wrapped, at room temperature for 1 day, or frozen for up to 2 months. Thaw the layers for 4 hours at room temperature in their wrappings before frosting.)

4. Prepare the Maple Meringue Frosting: in a heavy-bottomed saucepan, bring the maple syrup to a boil over medium-high heat and boil without stirring until the syrup reaches the soft ball stage or registers 236°F on a candy ther-mometer (see chart page 74). Meanwhile, beat the egg whites and cream of tartar in the very clean bowl of an electric or stand mixer fitted with the whip attachment to soft peaks. When the syrup has reached the right temperature, immediately pour it in a thin, steady stream directly onto the whites, beating constantly at medium-high speed. (Make sure the syrup lands on the whites, not the beaters, or you will end up spinning the syrup all around the sides of the bowl, making nothing even resembling a frosting.) I find this easier to do with hand-held electric beaters, securing the bowl by wrapping a damp towel around its base. Continue beating the mixture until it is thickened and spread-able. The frosting will still be warm and must be used before it cools, or it will become stiff, tacky and impossible to work with. As it is, try to work as quickly as you can and don't fuss too much with the frosting.

5. Place one of the layers on a cake circle or platter and spread the frosting about ½ an inch thick. Settle the second layer atop the first and scoop almost all

Pecan-Caramel Sandwich Cookies (page 518)

Roasted Clementine and Chocolate Tart with a Macadamia Nut Crust (page 460)

Lemon Anise Churros (page 624)

Pears Poached in Gewürztraminer with Tahitian Vanilla and Ginger (page 574)

Warm Sweet Risotto with Saffron and Dried Cherries (page 546)

Mango Ripple Ice Cream (page 556)

Poppyseed Angel Food Cake with Grapefruit Curd (page 390)

Hazelnut Crème Brûlée with a Crushed Praline Crust (page 532)

of the remaining frosting onto the centre of the top. Spread the frosting out to the edges and over the sides of the cake, spreading the overflow evenly around the sides. Use what is left in the bowl to patch any bare spots. This cake is best served within 4 hours of frosting, fewer if it is hot or humid.

Olive Oil and Sweet Wine Cake

SERVES 10

This moist and subtle cake is very simple, and tastes truly of the oil and the wine, so these ingredients should be chosen thoughtfully. A very "hot," or "peppery" olive oil wouldn't be as appropriate as a more fruity variety. I prefer a fruitier wine as well, such as a late-harvest Vidal, or even a Sauternes, to a sweet Riesling; the apricot, honey and tropical fruit flavours in the first two are more palatable in a dessert cake than the mineral and petrol overtones in many Rieslings. A sweet muscat, such as a Muscat de Beaumes de Venise would be good as well, contributing more genuine honey flavours than ripe fruit. Learn about the predominant flavours in the wine before you use it, but do experiment! Even a raisiny Vin Santo would make a good choice, if it is to your liking. I like to serve this cake with the Oven-Roasted Figs with Honey and Orange on page 584, with the fruit warm from the oven, and spoon a little of the juices from the baking dish over the cake. Another option is to serve the cake with a selection of cheeses and a bowl of roasted almonds and fresh ripe pears or figs. And, of course, glasses of the same sweet wine you used in the cake.

6 large eggs, separated, at room temperature

¾ cup plus 1 tablespoon granulated sugar

1 cup all-purpose flour

¾ cup plus 2 tablespoons cake flour (not self-rising)

¼ teaspoon salt

½ teaspoon baking powder

½ cup fruity and full-flavoured extra-virgin olive oil

⅓ cup pure light olive oil, plus extra for brushing the tin

1 teaspoon finely grated orange zest

1 teaspoon finely grated lemon zest

½ cup good-quality dessert wine, such as a late-harvest Vidal

½ teaspoon cream of tartar

Confectioners' sugar, for dusting

Olive Oil and Sweet Wine Cake continued

1. Preheat the oven to 350°. Brush a 9-inch springform pan with light olive oil and line the bottom with a circle of parchment paper. Oil the paper and set the tin aside. In the bowl of an electric or stand mixer fitted with the whip attachment, or in a large bowl with a whisk, beat the egg yolks and sugar until the mixture is thick and pale, and falls in a ribbon when the beater is lifted. In a separate bowl, sift together the flours, salt and baking powder and set aside.

2. Change to the paddle attachment if using a mixer. Beat the oils and the orange and lemon zests into the egg and sugar mixture, then stir in the wine, scraping down the sides of the bowl. Fold the flour mixture into the batter in three additions, blending gently after each.

3. In a separate bowl with very clean beaters or a whisk, whip the egg whites until frothy. Add the cream of tartar and whip to medium-stiff peaks. The whites should be able to hold a peak, but not be dry or grainy. Fold the whites into the batter in three stages, then scrape the batter into the prepared pan.

4. Bake the cake in the centre of the oven for 25 minutes, then reduce the temperature to 325° and continue baking until the surface of the cake is golden-brown, slightly cracked and springs back when lightly touched. A wooden skewer inserted through one of the cracks should come out clean. Transfer the pan to a rack and cool for 10 minutes. Run a thin-bladed knife around the edges of the cake and remove the sides of the pan. Cool the cake completely before serving or storing. The flavours in this cake actually improve if it is wrapped well and stored at room temperature overnight. Dust with confectioners' sugar before serving alone or with a fruit compote.

Chocolate Marquise

SERVES 10 TO 12

More like a cross between a dense mousse, a flourless chocolate cake and a baked pudding, this is, as my mother so eloquently put it, "a pure, direct, intense and ethereal CHOCOLATE experience!" I like to use a combination of bittersweet and semisweet chocolate for a more complex and balanced flavour, but you can use one type alone, if you prefer. Caster sugar is used because it dissolves very quickly in the mixture, leaving no doubt that the marquise will be luxuriously smooth.

9 ounces excellent-quality semisweet or bittersweet chocolate, or a combination of the two, chopped

¾ cup unsalted butter, in small pieces

¼ cup strong black coffee, or 1 heaping tablespoon espresso powder dissolved in 3 tablespoons boiling water

1 cup less 2 tablespoons superfine sugar, sifted

4 large eggs, lightly beaten

½ teaspoon pure vanilla extract

2 tablespoons Crème de Cacao, or liqueur of your choice

¾ cup very cold heavy cream (36%), for garnish

2 tablespoons superfine sugar, for garnish

Candied violets or rose petals, for garnish, optional

1. Preheat the oven to 350°. Line a 4½ x 8½-inch loaf pan with a double thickness of aluminum foil: first fold the foil to fit the pan's width, leaving a few inches overhang on each side, then fold it to fit the length, again leaving an overhang. The overhang will help unmould the marquise when it comes time to serve it. Press the foil into the corners of the pan, creating as smooth an interior as possible. Set aside.

2. In a stainless steel or glass bowl set over a pot of barely simmering water, combine the chopped chocolate, butter and coffee. Melt, stirring frequently, until the ingredients are smooth and blended. Remove the bowl from the pot and wipe the bottom with a dry cloth to prevent even a drip of moisture from settling in the chocolate. Immediately add the sugar and stir to dissolve. Let the mixture cool slightly.

3. Add the eggs and beat with a wooden spoon until thoroughly blended. The aim is to completely incorporate all the ingredients, but not to beat in too much air, so use rapid horizontal strokes, as opposed to round vertical strokes (think of blending a gravy, rather than whipping egg whites). Beat in the vanilla and Crème de Cacao, then pour the batter into the prepared pan.

Chocolate Marquise continued

4. Rap the filled pan on the counter 4 or 5 times to remove any air bubbles. Place the pan in a larger baking pan and add enough hot water to come halfway up the loaf pan to create a bain marie. Carefully set the pans in the centre of the preheated oven and bake for 1 hour and 10 minutes, or until a firm crust forms on the top. Cool the marquise on a rack until room temperature, then chill until ready to serve, at least 4 hours, or preferably overnight. (The marquise can be made up to two days ahead.)

5. To serve, invert the chilled marquise onto a serving platter and carefully peel off the strips of foil. Whip the cream with the superfine sugar until stiff peaks form, then spoon the cream into a pastry bag fitted with a star or other decorative tip. Pipe a border around the base of the marquise, and pipe decorative rosettes or coils down the centre of the terrine, one each ¾ inch or so. Place a candied violet between each rosette and serve immediately. I find using a very thin-bladed knife dipped in hot water and wiped quickly with a dry cloth the best way to slice the marquise. Serve slices of about ¾ of an inch—the taste and texture are so intense, so rich, a little can be savoured a long way!

VARIATIONS

Chocolate-Orange Marquise: Substitute Grand Marnier or other orange-flavoured liqueur for the Crème de Cacao and garnish with small strips of candied orange zest.

Chocolate-Coffee Marquise: Substitute Kahlúa or other coffee-flavoured liqueur for the Crème de Cacao and garnish with chocolate-covered espresso beans.

Chocolate-Almond Marquise: Substitute Amaretto for the Crème de Cacao and garnish with lightly toasted, coarsely chopped almonds and dark chocolate-covered almonds.

Chocolate-Raspberry Marquise: Substitute Framboise or other raspberry eau-de-vie for the Crème de Cacao and garnish with fresh raspberries.

Sticky Spiked Double-Apple Cake with a Brown Sugar-Brandy Sauce

SERVES 10 TO 12

Sticky, gooey and gorgeous for breakfast! This simple cake is packed with both fresh and dried apples for flavour and texture, just enough spice, and brown sugar for a lovely caramel sweetness. The Brown-Sugar Brandy Sauce is a scrumptious accompaniment when it's for dessert.

1 cup Lexia, Muscat or sultana raisins
⅓ cup brandy
1 cup unsulphured dried apple slices
   (if only rings are available, cut them
   in half)
½ cup granulated sugar
2 cups all-purpose flour, sifted
1½ teaspoons baking soda
⅛ teaspoon salt
¾ teaspoon ground cinnamon
½ teaspoon freshly grated nutmeg
⅛ teaspoon ground cloves (preferably
   freshly ground)
1½ cups tightly packed dark brown
   sugar
2 large eggs, lightly beaten

1 cup unsalted butter, melted and
   cooled
¾ cup coarsely chopped pecans,
   toasted (see page 253 for tips on
   toasting nuts)
2 medium-sized tart cooking apples,
   such as Northern Spy or Rome
   Beauty, one peeled, one unpeeled,
   both cored and cut into ½-inch
   pieces

Additional unsalted butter, at room
   temperature, for greasing the pan
Brown Sugar-Brandy Sauce, page 640,
   warmed slightly, to serve

1. In a small bowl, soak the raisins in the brandy for 45 minutes. Add the dried apple slices and macerate for a further 15 minutes. Do not drain!

2. Preheat the oven to 325°. Butter a 9 x 13-inch pan and line the bottom and up the two long sides with a sheet of parchment paper, letting the paper hang over the edges by an inch or so. Lightly butter the paper. In a small bowl, sift together flour, baking soda, salt, cinnamon, nutmeg and cloves together into a bowl and set aside.

Sticky Spiked Double-Apple Cake continued

3. In a large bowl with a hand-held electric mixer or whisk, or in the bowl of a stand mixer fitted with the paddle attachment, blend both sugars. Add the eggs and beat on medium speed until thickened and pale, about 2 minutes with a machine, 4 to 5 minutes by hand. Add the cooled melted butter and mix to blend. Fold in the dry ingredients in two additions, mixing just enough to moisten most but not all of the flour. Add the dried fruit and brandy mixture, chopped pecans and diced fresh apple, then fold them into the batter with long, deep strokes. Don't fret about the ratio of fruit to batter—there is a remarkable amount of fruit but it bakes into a wonderfully chewy cake.

4. Scrape the batter into the prepared pan and set in the centre of the oven. Bake for 1 hour and 10 minutes to 1 hour and 20 minutes, or until the centre springs back when lightly touched, a tester inserted into the centre comes out clean and the cake is beginning to pull away from the sides of the pan. Transfer to a wire rack and cool. This cake keeps beautifully, well wrapped, at room temperature for up to 5 days, although it is best within 2 or 3. Serve warm or at room temperature with a healthy pour of the warm *Brown Sugar-Brandy Sauce*. Makes enough for 10 to 12 people (or 2, if you give them a couple of days ...).

PIES AND TARTS

continued on page 444

Fresh Fig and Pistachio Frangipane Tart with Honeyed Mascarpone

SERVES 8 TO 10

Here is a simple recipe with two very different variations. The master recipe combines ripe black figs and pistachios in a deeply flavoured, sophisticated tart with sunny Mediterranean flavours. Paired with the sensuous Honeyed Mascarpone, it would make a lovely end to a Mediterranean or al fresco meal. When white peaches or white nectarines are substituted for the figs and red raspberries added, an entirely different dessert is created, one with very light and delicate, almost floral flavours. For a truly sensual experience, serve a fine sweet wine, such as a good Sauternes or a Muscat de Beaumes de Venise with either tart.

1 (10½- or 11-inch) Pâte Brisée tart shell, page 653, partially baked and cooled

FRANGIPANE:

1 cup shelled unsalted pistachios, skinned (see page XX for tips on skinning pistachios)

⅓ cup granulated sugar

5 tablespoons unsalted butter, at room temperature

1 large egg

1 large egg yolk

¼ teaspoon good-quality pure almond extract

3 tablespoons all-purpose flour, sifted

1 tablespoon flavourful dark honey, such as berry or wildflower, but not buckwheat

1¼ to 1½ pounds fresh ripe figs, such as Black Mission

2 tablespoons granulated sugar, for sprinkling

3 tablespoons plum or redcurrant jelly, for glazing

Confectioners' sugar, for dusting, optional

Honeyed Mascarpone, page 652, to serve

1. Prepare the frangipane: in a food processor, pulse the pistachios and the ⅓ cup of sugar together until finely ground. Add the butter and pulse until smooth, scraping down the sides of the bowl once or twice. Add the egg and egg yolk and process until thoroughly incorporated, then add the almond extract.

Fresh Fig and Pistachio Frangipane Tart continued

Process for about 45 seconds, again scraping down the sides of the bowl. Sift half the flour over the pistachio paste and pulse three or four times just to moisten it; repeat with the second half, pulsing just until the flour is incorporated. Don't over-process at this point, but make sure all the ingredients are well-blended. The frangipane may be used immediately or can be made up to 2 days ahead and stored, covered, in the refrigerator. Bring to room temperature before proceeding with the recipe.

2. Preheat the oven to 350°. Gently warm the honey over a low flame and brush it in a thin film over the entire bottom of the cooled tart crust. Spread the pistachio frangipane evenly over the honey. Wash and thoroughly dry the figs if they seem particularly dusty and cut off the tough little nib on the end of the stems. Cut each fig in half lengthwise, from stem to bottom, discarding any unripe, overripe or badly blemished fruit. Arrange the halves, cut-side up, in concentric circles over the frangipane. I like to have the stem-ends pointing towards the centre—they seem to fit better this way. Don't be concerned about covering every inch of the filling—the puffed green frangipane peeking through the baked figs is part of the beauty of this tart.

3. Sprinkle the entire surface of the tart with the 2 tablespoons of sugar and place on a baking sheet. Bake in the centre of the oven for 50 to 60 minutes, or until the frangipane is slightly puffed and golden in places and is firm to the touch in the centre of the tart. The figs should be very soft and may be tinged with black on the edges. Transfer the tart tin to a wire rack and cool completely.

4. In a small pot or saucepan, melt the jelly with 1 tablespoon of water. Use a pastry brush (I have one I reserve just for this sticky purpose) to lightly coat the figs with the glaze, returning it to the heat if it starts getting too gummy to brush thinly. The glaze should just be a thin shiny film over the fruit, not a gelatinous layer. Let cool for 5 to 10 minutes. I like to dust just the edges of this tart with a little confectioners' sugar before serving, but to dust or not to dust is up to you! The tart is best served the day it is made, as the crust absorbs the moisture from the frangipane upon sitting, and that in turn soaks up moisture from the figs. Any leftovers, however, can be stored for a day or two, wrapped, in the refrigerator and will still taste yummy—they just might not look as elegant! Serve with a scoop of *Honeyed Mascarpone* or a dollop of lightly sweetened whipped cream or crème fraîche.

White Nectarine or White Peach and Raspberry Tart with Pistachio Frangipane: Substitute 4 to 6 medium-sized white nectarines or white peaches for the figs. Wash and thoroughly dry the fruit, then cut each one in half and discard the stones. Slice each half into six slices and lay the slices slightly overlapping in concentric circles over the frangipane. Sprinkle with the granulated sugar and bake as for the fig tart. When the tart is completely cool, arrange about ⅔ cup of fresh red raspberries over the filling, placing one berry between every one or two slices of fruit. Substitute apricot or peach jam for plum or redcurrant and brush a thin glaze over the fruit. Allow to cool, then dust with confectioners' sugar, if desired, and serve. For this version, I would suggest a dollop of lightly sweetened crème fraîche, rather than the more voluptuous *Honeyed Mascarpone*, to allow the aromas and tastes to come through. The flavours here are so delicate and light, it is even wonderful all on its own.

Rhubarb Brûlée Tartlettes with Ginger

6 4½-INCH TARTS
OR 8 3-INCH TARTLETTES

Sugared, stewed rhubarb was the very first fruit I experimented with in the kitchen. A huge crop of wild rhubarb grew in the backyard of my childhood home, and one spring I decided I knew how to cook it. Into a pot along with the rhubarb went some sugar and a bit of water. After a few minutes on the heat, the hot, sweet, tangy compote that resulted was as much of a surprise to me as to my mother! In these unusual tarts, the pungent flavour of rhubarb is tempered by a rich and silky custard, accented by chewy pieces of candied ginger. And the surface of each tart is caramelized like a crème brûlée. To achieve the smooth and perfectly cooked custard, a combination of the stove-top and oven methods is used, ensuring the mixture neither curdles, nor remains too runny. A gorgeous dessert for an elegant spring dinner, these tarts need absolutely nothing to accompany them, but are wonderful with a glass of champagne!

Rhubarb Brûlée Tartlettes continued

6 (4½-inch) Pâte Brisée tartlette shells,
     page 653, or 8 3-inch tartlette
     shells, pre-baked and cooled

RHUBARB:

¾ pound fresh rhubarb stalks, leaves
     removed, washed and cut into
     ¾-inch pieces
¼ cup plus 1 tablespoon tightly
     packed light brown sugar

CUSTARD:

2 cups heavy cream (36%)
½ vanilla bean, split
4 large egg yolks

¼ cup plus 1 tablespoon granulated
     sugar
1 tablespoon unsalted butter, cut into
     small bits

1½ tablespoons redcurrant or
     plum jelly
2 scant tablespoons finely chopped
     crystallized ginger, preferably
     Australian
½ cup light brown sugar, sifted,
     for caramelizing

1. Prepare the rhubarb: combine the rhubarb pieces and the brown sugar in a saucepan and stir to coat. Place the pan over low heat and cover. After a minute or so, stir the rhubarb to help release the juices. Recover and cook gently for 5 or 6 minutes or until the rhubarb is tender, but still retains its shape. Drain the fruit and discard the juices. Cool the rhubarb to room temperature before proceeding, or chill until needed, up to 2 days.

2. Prepare the custard: fill a large pot with an inch or two of water and bring the water to a gentle simmer. Have ready a fine-mesh sieve set over a bowl to strain the cooked custard. Pour the cream into a 2-quart saucepan with a heavy bottom. Scrape the seeds out of the vanilla bean and add both the seeds and the hull to the cream. Place the pot over medium heat and bring just to the boil. Meanwhile, whisk the egg yolks lightly in a large non-reactive bowl, then pour in the granulated sugar, whisking constantly. Place the yolk-sugar mixture over the pot with the barely simmering water, until it has thickened and paled, about as long as it will take the cream to scald.

3. Remove the cream from the heat as soon as it reaches the boil and gradually whisk it into the yolk mixture (still over the barely simmering water). When all the cream is incorporated, retire the whisk and stir the custard with a wooden spoon until it thickly coats the back of the spoon, about 7 minutes. Another good test for the right consistency is called the rose test: bring the coated spoon to your lips and blow a thin stream of air onto the back. The custard is ready if a pattern resembling an unfurled rose reveals itself when you blow onto the spoon. Strain the custard through the sieve into the clean bowl and add the pieces of butter, stirring until they melt. Press a piece of plastic wrap onto the surface of the custard to prevent a skin from forming. Poke a few holes in the plastic with a paring knife to allow the steam to escape and cool the custard to room temperature. (Although it is best used as soon as it cools, the custard can be chilled at this point up to 2 days, then used to fill the shells straight from the refrigerator.)

4. To bake the tarts: preheat the oven to 325°. Melt the jelly in a small saucepan over low heat and brush a thin layer onto the bottoms of the tartlette shells. Place the shells, still in their tins, on a baking sheet. Spoon a tablespoon or two of the drained cooled rhubarb into each shell, smoothing the surface. Sprinkle with the chopped ginger, dividing it evenly among the shells. Ladle the custard into the tart shells, then place the baking sheet in the oven. Bake for 25 to 30 minutes (depending on the temperature of the custard when you filled the tarts), or until the filling is still a little wobbly in the centre and just set around the edges. The custard will set further as it cools. Make sure the custard never gets so hot it boils, or it will be unpleasantly grainy. Cool the tarts on a wire rack, or if they will not be eaten within 2 hours, place in the refrigerator, loosely covered. (Tarts may be prepared up to this point up to 5 hours ahead of time.)

5. To serve, remove the tarts from their tins and spread the top of each with an even layer of the sifted brown sugar. Using a hand-held blow torch, or a very hot broiler, glaze the tops of the tarts until the sugar melts and caramelizes. (If using a broiler, make sure it is hot enough. Many home broilers are not sufficiently hot, and you could melt or burn the tarts before the sugar has caramelized, leaving you with blackened pudding rather than burnt cream! Little blowtorches specifically designed for the kitchen are inexpensive and so very handy!) Serve immediately.

Hazelnut Frangipane Tart with Caramelized Dried Apricots

SERVES 6 TO 8

A lovely golden tart with an autumnal feel. The pairing of toasted hazelnuts and dried apricots brings out the buttery, caramel flavours in both of them. Do try to get unsulphured fruit for this tart, as the sulphur-treated variety doesn't have the same intense sweetness.

1 (10½- or 11-inch) Pâte Sucrée tart shell, page 655, pre-baked and cooled

2 cups plump dried apricots, preferably unsulphured

FRANGIPANE:

1 cup toasted, skinned hazelnuts (see page 262 for tips on toasting and skinning hazelnuts)

⅓ cup granulated sugar

¼ cup unsalted butter, at room temperature

1 large egg, at room temperature

1 large egg yolk, at room temperature

1 tablespoon Frangelico (hazelnut-flavoured liqueur)

3 tablespoons all-purpose flour, sifted

1 tablespoon unsalted butter

3 tablespoons granulated sugar, plus ¼ cup for glaze

1 tablespoon Frangelico

1. Place the apricots in a deep non-reactive bowl and pour over them enough boiling water just to cover. Soak the fruit overnight, then drain thoroughly, reserving 1 cup of the soaking liquid. Place the apricots in a single layer on a sheet of paper towel and dry in a microwave for 1 minute at 50% power, or in the oven at 200° for 10 minutes, turning once.

2. Preheat the oven to 350°. In a food processor, whir together hazelnuts and sugar until finely ground. Add the butter and process until smooth. Add the egg and egg yolk, process until blended, then add the Frangelico and process for 1 minute, scraping down the sides of the bowl once or twice. Sift the flour over the nut paste in the processor, pulse just until the flour is incorporated. The frangipane may be used immediately, or transferred into a clean container and refrigerated, covered, until needed, up to 2 days. Allow it to return to room temperature before using.

3. Spread the frangipane evenly over the bottom of the cooled tart shell. Arrange the apricots in concentric circles over the filling. Don't worry about covering every inch of the tart with fruit—the patches of frangipane showing through will puff up and become lovely and golden.

4. In a little saucepan or in the microwave, melt the tablespoon of butter with 1 tablespoon of sugar. Brush the apricots with this mixture, then sprinkle the surface of the tart with 2 tablespoons of sugar. Place the tart in the oven and bake for 35 to 40 minutes, or until the centre of the frangipane is firm to the touch and the filling is caramel-coloured. The apricots should be just beginning to caramelize. Transfer the tart to a wire rack and allow to cool.

5. Meanwhile, prepare the glaze: in a small saucepan, combine the 1 cup of reserved apricot soaking liquid with the ¼ cup of sugar. Bring to a gentle boil, stirring until the sugar is dissolved, then reduce the heat slightly and allow the liquid to reduce to a syrupy glaze. Watch closely—the syrup can burn easily. When the glaze reaches the consistency of a thin pouring syrup, remove it from the heat and stir in the Frangelico. Brush the warm tart with warm glaze and allow to cool completely. Serve at room temperature with *Vanilla Bean* or *Roasted Cinnamon Ice Cream*, page 553, or with a little lightly sweetened whipped cream. This tart is best served the day it is made, but any leftovers can be stored, loosely covered, at room temperature for up to 4 days.

Roasted Plum Tart with a Cinnamon Crème Pâtissière

SERVES 8

In this simple tart, the sweetness and complexity of fresh plums are concentrated by oven-roasting with a light dusting of sugar. The plums become soft and slightly caramelized and are then paired with a silky cinnamon custard. The tart is easy to put together at the last minute, as all the components can be made ahead of time. It doesn't store very well, however, so it should be assembled no more than a few hours before serving. A scoop of Vanilla Bean or Roasted Cinnamon Ice Cream, page 553, would be a perfect accompaniment.

Roasted Plum Tart continued

1 (10½- or 11-inch) Pâte Brisée tart
   shell, page 653, prebaked and
   cooled

PASTRY CREAM:

2 cups whole milk (3.5%)
½ cup granulated sugar
½ vanilla bean, scraped out (use both
   seeds and hull), or the hull of 1
   whole bean
1 cinnamon stick, broken into pieces

6 large egg yolks
5 tablespoons all-purpose flour
1 teaspoon ground cinnamon
2 tablespoons unsalted butter, chilled,
   cut into small pieces

20 large red plums or 40 small black
   plums, ripe but not overly soft
⅓ cup granulated sugar
2 tablespoons good-quality plum jam
   or jelly

1. Prepare the pastry cream: pour the milk and ¼ cup of the sugar into a 2-quart heavy-bottomed saucepan, then add the vanilla bean or hull and the pieces of cinnamon stick. Place the pot over low heat and stir until the sugar is dissolved. Increase the heat to medium and bring the milk just to the boil, then remove from the heat. Meanwhile, whisk the egg yolks in a large bowl to combine them, then the remaining ¼ cup of sugar. Sift the flour and cinnamon into the yolks in three additions, whisking well after each to beat out any lumps. The mixture should be thick and shiny. Place a damp towel under the bowl to keep it anchored to the counter and leave one hand free to whisk, the other to add the milk. Have a fine mesh sieve set over a clean bowl ready to strain the cooked cream.

2. Pour about ¼ cup of the hot milk into the yolk mixture, whisking vigorously to incorporate it quickly. Add another bit of milk, more this time, whisking all the while. Keep adding milk in increasing amounts until all the milk is thoroughly blended with the yolks. The cream will already have thickened noticeably. Remove the cinnamon stick. Rinse out the pot used to scald the cream and pour the contents of the bowl back into the pot without drying it. (This will help prevent the cream from scorching.)

3. Return the pot to the element over medium-low heat. Whisking constantly, making sure the whisk reaches the corners of the pot and all across the bottom, cook the pastry cream until it coats the back of a spoon thickly and the whisk reveals traces of the bottom of the pot when drawn across it quickly. This should take between 1½ and 2 minutes. Don't let the cream boil and don't let it sit in the pot for any length of time without whisking, or you risk curdling the yolks or scorching the cream. Remove the pot from the heat and whisk in the butter. Immediately strain the cream into the waiting bowl, then press a piece of plastic wrap onto the surface to prevent a skin from forming. Poke 6 or 8 slits in the plastic with a sharp knife to allow the steam to escape and cool the pastry cream to room temperature if using immediately, or chill until needed, up to 3 days.

4. Prepare the plums: preheat the oven to between 375° and 400°. Wash and dry the plums thoroughly. Slice around the pit of each plum, following the little line of indentation and continuing around until the cut is complete. Twist the two halves in opposite directions until one is released, leaving the other with the pit still embedded in it. Use a fine paring knife to carefully work around the stone. Discard it. When all the plums are stoned, place them in a large bowl and toss them with the ⅓ cup granulated sugar. Arrange the plum halves skin-side down on a large baking sheet (not non-stick) and set the sheet in the centre of the oven for 1 hour to 1 hour and 15 minutes, or until the edges of some of the plums are tipped with black and a paring knife inserted in the flesh slips in and out with no resistance. Cool the plums on the baking sheet set on a wire rack. The fruit can be roasted 1 day ahead and kept covered in the refrigerator. Let the plums return to room temperature before assembling the tart.

5. To assemble the tart: melt the plum jam or jelly in a small saucepan over low heat, stirring so it doesn't scorch. Brush a thin layer of this glaze over the bottom of the cooled tart shell. Spread a 1½-inch layer of the cinnamon pastry cream over the glaze, smoothing the surface with a spatula. Arrange the plum halves, cut-side down, on the pastry cream. A pattern of concentric circles is lovely, but stripes or even a haphazard array are every bit as scrumptious. This tart is best served immediately, but can be kept in the refrigerator, loosely covered for several hours. Store any leftovers in the refrigerator for up to 3 days.

❧ VARIATION ❧

Roasted Plum Tart with Vanilla Crème Pâtissière: Proceed exactly as for the cinnamon version above, but omit the cinnamon from the pastry cream and use 1 whole vanilla bean, split and scraped out (use both the seeds and the hull).

Rustic Apricot Galette

SERVES 8 TO 10

An ideal summer dessert to showcase absolutely ripe, big-flavoured fruit. People who never gave apricots a second glance find this tart a revelation of pure, intense yet delicate flavour. Serve with Honeyed Mascarpone, page 652, lightly sweetened whipped cream or a good vanilla ice cream. The variations that follow are other examples of the simplest types of tarts, with sweet juicy fruit and good buttery pastry creating a perfect union.

1 recipe Pâte Brisée, page 653

FILLING:

2 pounds ripe but not mushy, fresh
   apricots, preferably local
½ cup granulated sugar (or more if
   the fruit is not very sweet)
3 tablespoons cornstarch

2 tablespoons unsalted butter, cold,
   cut into small bits
1 large egg white, lightly beaten with
   1 tablespoon water
1 tablespoon granulated sugar, for
   sprinkling

1. Preheat the oven to 425°. Lay a large rectangle of parchment paper on a surface large enough to roll out your pastry. Remove the pastry from the refrigerator and let it temper slightly, until it is soft enough to roll out.

2. Meanwhile, wipe the apricots with a damp towel and dry them well. Cut each apricot in half and discard the stone. Cut each half in half again and place the quarters in a large non-reactive bowl. Add the ½ cup sugar and the cornstarch, then toss to thoroughly coat.

3. Lightly dust the sheet of parchment paper with a little flour and place the disc of pastry in the centre. Roll the pastry out to a circle about 12 inches in diameter and ¼-inch thick and brush away any excess flour. Make sure the pastry isn't sticking to the paper; periodically lift the edges and sprinkle the paper with a dash more flour if it does. (If the pastry is really sticking, slide the paper onto a cutting board or baking sheet and pop the whole thing in the refrigerator for a few minutes. Warm pastry will stick no matter what, and will absorb so much flour that it will become tough. Keep it cool and you'll have no trouble.) When you have a large enough circle, slide the paper and the pastry onto a large baking sheet.

4. Pile the apricots and their sugary syrup into the centre of the pastry circle, leaving 1½ to 2 inches around the outside free of filling or syrup. Pat the fruit together to make it as compact as possible, mounding it a little higher in the very centre. Dot the filling with the little pieces of butter, scattering them over the fruit. With clean fingers, fold up the outside edge of the pastry over the filling, gently pressing the folds together to secure the pastry. Brush the pastry with the egg white-water glaze, then sprinkle with the 1 tablespoon sugar.

5. Place the baking sheet in the centre of the oven and bake at 425° for 20 minutes, then reduce the temperature to 375° and bake another 25 to 35 minutes, or until the pastry is crisp and golden and the filling is bubbling in the centre of the tart. Cool on the sheet set over a wire rack. The galette may be served warm or at room temperature. On its own, it makes a delicate and refreshing dessert for a summer lunch or light supper; paired with one of the accompaniments suggested above, it becomes a truly celebratory finale!

✿ VARIATIONS ✿

Rustic Plum Galette: Proceed exactly as for the *Apricot Galette*, substituting 2 pounds ripe red or black plums for the apricots and increasing the sugar in the filling to ⅔ cup. Bake as for above. This variation is great with *Roasted Cinnamon Ice Cream* (page 553)

Rustic Gooseberry and Honey Galette: Substitute 3 cups (about 1 good pint) green gooseberries (these have a better flavour than the white, yellow or red varieties), with the stems and nibs removed, for the apricots. Increase the cornstarch to 4 tablespoons and add ¼ cup flavourful honey to the berry-sugar mixture. Bake as for the *Apricot Galette* and serve with *Honeyed Mascarpone* (page 652) or *Vanilla Bean* or *Roasted Cinnamon Ice Cream* (page 553).

Cornmeal-Crusted Lemon Tart

SERVES 8 TO 10

A mouth-puckering, intensely lemony version of a classic bistro dessert. The cornmeal crust adds a rich nutty flavour and acts as a crunchy contrast to the silky curd. The Lemon Blueberry Tart variation that follows is divine—these two flavours complement each other beautifully. But be sure you prepare it with fresh wild berries, or don't make it at all!

PASTRY:

1¾ cups all-purpose flour

⅓ cup yellow cornmeal, preferably
    stone-ground

⅓ cup granulated sugar

¾ teaspoon baking powder

¼ teaspoon salt

9 tablespoons (4½ ounces)
    unsalted butter, cold, cut into
    small pieces

1 large egg

1 large egg yolk

FILLING:

6 large eggs

6 large egg yolks

2 cups granulated sugar

2 tablespoons finely grated lemon zest
    (from about 2 large lemons)

1⅓ cups freshly squeezed lemon juice

1 cup unsalted butter, at room
    temperature, cut into small pieces

1 pint fresh raspberries, to garnish,
    optional

Sifted confectioners' sugar, optional

1. Prepare the tart shell: combine the flour, cornmeal, sugar, baking powder and salt in the bowl of a large food processor and whir once or twice to blend. Add the pieces of butter and pulse until the largest bits are about the size of fat peas. In a small bowl, lightly beat together the egg and egg yolk, then add this all at once to the processor. Pulse once or twice to distribute the egg, then transfer the mixture to a medium-sized bowl. (Alternatively, the dough can be prepared up to this point by hand: in a large bowl, blend the dry ingredients together, then using a pastry blender or two knives cut in butter. With a fork, gently stir the beaten egg and yolk into the flour mixture.)

2. The dough now looks nothing like you think dough should look. It is extremely dry and floury, and you are at this very moment suspecting a typo in this book, my ineptitude at pastry making, or sabotage. Actually, all is perfectly well.

Cornmeal is slow to absorb moisture and needs a little time. Using your fingers, roughly work the mixture together, crumbling the egg, butter and dry ingredients into each other until the dough becomes a uniformly moist crumble. Press it into a 10½- or 11-inch round tart tin with a removable bottom, making sure the pastry is even and firmly pressed into the bottom and up the sides. Cover the shell well with plastic wrap and chill for at least 4 hours, or up to 24. (The shell may be frozen at this point, well wrapped, and baked from frozen. Increase the baking time slightly.)

3. Preheat the oven to 350°. Prick the bottom of the shell all over with a fork. Line with aluminum foil or parchment paper and fill with dried beans or pie weights. Bake for 20 minutes, or until edges are starting to turn golden, then remove weights and foil. Continue baking until shell is golden-brown and dry, about 15 minutes more. Cool completely before filling, or pastry will be soggy. The shell can be baked up to 1 day ahead of time and stored, loosely covered, at room temperature.

4. Prepare the lemon curd filling: fill a large pot with about 2 inches of water and bring this to a gentle simmer over low heat. In a stainless steel or glass bowl, whisk together the eggs and egg yolks. Whisk in the sugar, then the lemon zest and juice. Place the bowl over the mouth of the pot, making sure the water is still just barely simmering. Using a wooden spoon, stir the mixture until it thickens enough to coat the back of the spoon and is about the consistency of pudding—about 15 to 20 minutes. Whatever you do, DO NOT BOIL, or you'll have made lemon-flavoured scrambled eggs! This may seem to take a long time to cook, but the result will be a very light, creamy and smooth curd.

5. Remove the bowl from the heat and immediately stir in the soft butter, a few tablespoons at a time, until all of it is incorporated. Immediately pour the hot curd into the cooled tart shell (this will ensure the curd cools with a shiny surface and an easy-to-cut texture). Allow the filling to set at room temperature for 4 to 6 hours before serving. I like to garnish with a little ring of fresh red raspberries around the perimeter, then dust the edges of this simple tart with a little sifted confectioners' sugar. It's best the day it is made, but any leftovers can be covered and refrigerated for several days.

Cornmeal-Crusted Lemon Tart continued

┌───┐

◦ VARIATION ◦

Lemon Blueberry Tart: Reduce the recipe for lemon curd by half, then prepare the tart as for the master recipe. Top the cooled lemon curd with 2 to 3 cups fresh wild blueberries that have been picked over. Dust the edges of the tart with confectioners' sugar.

└───┘

Cocoa, Date and Dried Fig Crostata

SERVES 12 TO 16

A crostata is a traditional rustic Italian pastry—a thick layer of cooked fruit, often a homemade preserve, spread between two layers of tender pastry. Almost confection-like, this crostata is made with a chunky paste of gloriously rich and full-flavoured dried fruit and is perfect for the holidays. Serve it in small wedges with espresso or, even better, a good brandy. The quality of the fruit will make all the difference—try to find Medjool dates and unsulphured dried black figs.

FILLING:

1 pound pitted Medjool dates
1 pound unsulphured dried black figs, moist and plump
1½ teaspoons finely grated orange zest
½ cup orange juice
½ cup whole milk (3.5%)
⅓ cup granulated sugar
½ cup top-quality unsweetened Dutch-process cocoa, sifted
3 tablespoons water
2 large eggs, at room temperature, lightly beaten

PASTRY:

¾ cup walnuts, lightly toasted (see page 253 for tips on toasting nuts)
½ cup granulated sugar
2½ cups all-purpose flour
¼ teaspoon salt
1 teaspoon baking powder
¾ cup cold unsalted butter, cut into small pieces
2 large eggs, cold, lightly beaten
½ teaspoon pure vanilla extract

1. Prepare the filling: coarsely chop the dates and set them aside. Dice the figs, discarding the tough little nib on the stem end. Combine the figs, orange zest, orange juice, milk, sugar, cocoa and water in a heavy-bottomed 2-quart sauce-pan (you'll add the 2 beaten eggs later on). Heat gently, stirring until the sugar dissolves. Bring the mixture to a simmer and cook for 5 to 7 minutes, stirring frequently, until the mixture is very thick. Remove the pot from the heat and add the dates. With a wooden spoon, roughly mash the mixture as it cools, until a thick, sticky, chunky purée is formed. Cool to room temperature, then cover and refrigerate or proceed with the recipe. (The filling can be made up to 3 days ahead of time and stored in the refrigerator, well covered. Bring the fill-ing to room temperature before proceeding with the recipe.)

2. Prepare the pastry: process the walnuts with the sugar in a food processor until finely ground. Sift in the flour, salt and baking powder and pulse just to blend. Add the butter, then pulse until the largest pieces are about the size of fat peas. Transfer the mixture to a large bowl and add the cold eggs and the vanilla. Use your fingers to lightly and quickly work the liquid into the flour. (If your processor cannot accommodate such a large batch of pastry, place the nut-sugar mixture into a large bowl, sift in the dry ingredients and stir to blend. Cut in the butter using a pastry blender, then work in the eggs and vanilla.) The dough should be uniformly moist and crumbly, with no patches of egg or flour. If the dough has become too warm, cover it with plastic wrap so it won't dry out and pop the bowl into the refrigerator for a few minutes.

3. Make the top crust of the tart: cut out a 10-inch circle of parchment paper. Place about ⅓ of the dough in the centre of this circle and press a piece of plas-tic wrap over the dough. Roll out the dough to a 10-inch circle, about ⅙ inch thick. If there is too much dough (the circle is the right thickness but is larger than 10 inches), trim the excess and add it to the remaining dough. Chill the circle of pastry on a flat plate or baking sheet until needed. Press the remaining dough into the bottom of a 10-inch springform pan and 1 to 1½ inches up the sides. Chill the lined tart tin until firm.

4. Preheat the oven to 350°. Stir the reserved eggs into the room-temperature filling, making sure they are well distributed. (The mixture is thick, but have

Cocoa, Date and Dried Fig Crostata continued

patience!) Spread the filling into the chilled crust, smoothing the top. Slide the chilled circle of pastry onto the filling, centring it and pressing out any large air bubbles. Use your finger to seal the edges all the way around the sides of the tart. Cut 4 to 6 slits in the top pastry to allow the steam to escape, then place the crostata in the centre of the oven. Bake until the crust is golden and crisp, about 1 hour and 15 minutes to 1½ hours. Cool completely on a wire rack before serving. The crostata can be kept at room temperature, lightly covered, for up to 4 or 5 days, but is best served within 2 days of baking.

Roasted Clementine and Chocolate Tart with a Macadamia Nut Crust

SERVES 8 TO 10

A rich and unusual tart to celebrate the fleeting clementine season, and the eternally wonderful marriage of oranges and chocolate! All of the elements can be prepared ahead, making it a great holiday dessert.

1 (10½- or 11-inch) Rich Nut tart shell, page 657, made with macadamia nuts, pre-baked and cooled

ROASTED CLEMENTINES:
10 medium-sized clementine oranges (also called mandarins), washed and dried, but not peeled
1 cup freshly squeezed orange juice

1 to 2 tablespoons Grand Marnier or other orange liqueur, optional
3 tablespoons plus ½ cup dark brown sugar, tightly packed

CHOCOLATE GANACHE:
8 ounces bittersweet chocolate, finely chopped
1 cup heavy cream (36%)

1. Preheat the oven to 325°. With a sharp knife slice the clementines crosswise into very thin rounds, discarding the stem and flower ends. Lay the slices overlapping in the bottom of a 9 x 13-inch glass baking dish. Pour the orange juice and Grand Marnier, if using, over the clementines and sprinkle them with 3 tablespoons brown sugar. Cover the dish with aluminum foil and roast in the centre of the oven for 60 to 70 minutes, or until the peels are tender when pierced with the tip of a knife.

2. Increase the temperature to 375°. Uncover the dish and sprinkle the clementines with the remaining ½ cup brown sugar. Return to the oven for another 30 minutes, or until the liquid has become syrupy and the oranges have begun to caramelize. Lightly cover the baking dish and allow the clementines to cool to room temperature. (They may be prepared up to 3 days in advance and stored, well covered, at room temperature until needed.)

3. To make the ganache, place the chopped chocolate in a medium-sized bowl. Bring the cream just to the simmer over medium-high heat, watching closely to see that it does not boil. Immediately pour the hot cream over the chocolate and stir until thoroughly combined. Allow the ganache to cool until it has the consistency of a soft icing, then spread it evenly over the bottom of the tart shell. (The ganache may be prepared up to 3 days in advance and stored covered in the refrigerator. When ready to use, allow it to come to room temperature, then warm it very gently in a bowl set over a pot of barely simmering water until it reaches a soft consistency.)

4. Once the tart shell has been lined with the ganache, lay the clementine slices over the chocolate in an overlapping circular pattern. I find a pair of kitchen tongs extremely useful for this, but if you have none, your fingers or a fork will work fine. Scrape the syrup from the bottom of the baking dish with a rubber spatula and spoon this liquid over the clementines. The finished tart may be assembled up to 1 day before serving and stored, lightly covered, at room temperature.

Tarte au Sucre d'Érable
(Maple Sugar Pie)

SERVES 10

When French settlers colonized what is now Quebec, they faced a harsh and most inhospitable environment. Their cuisine was tailored to the climate and was simple, hearty and rich. Maple sugar was the primary sweetener, used in everything from savoury meat dishes to decadent desserts like this tart. True to

Tarte au Sucre d'Érable continued

the original recipes, this version of maple sugar pie uses the raw sugar, not maple
syrup. Whereas sugar pie recipes made elsewhere, such as the American South,
use eggs or egg yolks to thicken and set the filling, this one does not. Eggs would
have been too valuable in colonial Quebec to waste on a simple, everyday pie, so
a mixture of flour and heavy cream was used instead. The result, surprisingly, is
a fairly light and remarkably not-too-sweet dessert. The flavour is very intensely
maple, but is neither sugary nor cloying. In keeping with the Québécois tradi-
tion, serve this tart warm, with a healthy pour of chilled heavy cream.

1 9-inch Flaky Pie Pastry shell, page
658, bottom crust only, partially
baked in a standard 1½-inch deep
metal pie tin and cooled

1½ cups granulated maple sugar
(available in gourmet or specialty
food shops and health and natural
food stores)

7 tablespoons all-purpose flour
¼ teaspoon salt
1 cup light cream (18%)
¼ cup heavy or whipping cream (36%)
plus 1 cup for serving
3 tablespoons unsalted butter, cut into
small pieces

1. Preheat the oven to 350°. Sift the sugar, flour and salt together into a small
bowl, then stir with a whisk to blend them thoroughly. Spread this mixture
evenly over the pie shell. Combine the two creams and pour over the sugar
layer. The cream will completely cover the sugar and won't blend with it at this
point, but fear not—the oven's heat does marvellous things to sugar and cream!
Run a thin-bladed knife through the filling a few times to create paths for the
cream in the sugar, taking care not to puncture the crust. Dot the surface of the
filling with the butter and place the pie on a baking sheet to catch any bubbling
overflow.

2. Bake the pie for about 1 hour, or until the filling is just set in the centre and
the surface is a rich burnished brown, speckled with dark golden patches. The
filling will set further as it cools. Cool the pie on a rack and serve warm or at
room temperature. Either way, Tarte au Sucre should be served in small slices,
with a pour of chilled, but not whipped, heavy cream. Makes enough for 10
small but rich servings, unless you are serving French Canadians, in which case
maybe 4 or 5.

Wild Blueberry Pie

SERVES 6 TO 8

There is one thing you must remember in order to make this pie: YOU NEED WILD BERRIES!! Never use the cultivated ones! They make lousy pies, and lousy everything else for that matter. This is the perfect, and my favourite, pie. Don't dress it up, and don't waste it on anyone you aren't deeply fond of! The addition of lemon juice prevents the berries from becoming too jammy-tasting, and the cinnamon lends depth and texture. Neither one will be detectable in the finished pie, but they support the full, bursting berry flavour.

1 recipe Flaky Pie Pastry, page 658, separated into 2 discs and chilled

FILLING:

6 cups (3 pints) fresh wild blueberries, picked over

½ cup granulated sugar

3 tablespoons cornstarch or instant tapioca

1 tablespoon freshly squeezed lemon juice

⅛ teaspoon ground cinnamon

1 large egg, lightly beaten

1 tablespoon milk

1 tablespoon granulated sugar

1. Preheat the oven to 400°. Remove the two discs of pastry dough from the refrigerator and let them sit at room temperature for 20 minutes or so, until they are soft enough to roll. On a lightly floured surface, roll out one of the discs to a circle about 12 inches in diameter, then line a 9½-inch glass pie dish. Gently ease the pastry into the corners and trim the overhang to about 1 inch. Cover loosely with plastic wrap and place in the refrigerator for 15 minutes.

2. In a large bowl, combine the blueberries, ¼ cup of the sugar, the cornstarch, lemon juice and cinnamon and toss to evenly coat. Let the filling sit for 5 to 10 minutes; the sugar will begin to coax the juice from the berries and create a liquid to dissolve the cornstarch.

3. Roll out the remaining disc of pastry to a circle of about 9½ inches in diameter and set aside. Remove the shell from the refrigerator and sprinkle 2

Wild Blueberry Pie continued

tablespoons of the remaining ¼ cup sugar over the bottom of the shell. Spoon the berries and their juices into the shell, making sure the filling is even over the bottom and mounding any excess in the centre. Be careful to keep the pastry edges free of berries or purple juice; you will get a better seal with a clean rim. Use a rubber spatula to scrape out all the sugary juices from the bowl— you don't want to waste a drop! Sprinkle the remaining sugar over the filling and brush the rim of the pastry with the lightly beaten egg. Settle the other pastry circle on top of the filling. Seal the rim by lightly pressing around the edges of the pie, then use a small sharp knife to trim the excess dough. Crimp the edges decoratively, if desired, or re-roll any excess dough to make cut-outs or ornamental shapes. Place the pie (and any shapes you have cut out, wrapped in plastic wrap) in the refrigerator to chill for 10 to 15 minutes. This will help to prevent the dough from shrinking during baking and to retain the shape of the edges.

4. Remove the pie (and any decorations) from the refrigerator and add the tablespoon of milk to the egg wash. Brush the top of the pie thinly with this glaze and apply any pastry decorations you have made. Brush these with the milk and egg mixture as well. Sprinkle the entire surface of the pie with the 1 tablespoon of sugar, then cut four or five 2-inch-long slits in the top pastry to allow steam to escape. Place the pie on a baking sheet and into the preheated oven. Bake for 20 minutes at 400°, then reduce the temperature to 350°, and continue baking for another 35 to 45 minutes, or until the pastry is a golden brown and the juices are visibly bubbling through the slits in the crust. Transfer the pie to a wire rack and cool at least 30 minutes before serving. This pie is best served the day it is baked (actually, it is best within an hour of baking!), but leftovers can be stored, lightly covered with a piece of waxed paper or aluminum foil, for a day or two. (Being basically flour, butter, egg and fruit, I find blueberry pie to be an entirely honourable breakfast food, and it warms up beautifully in a toaster oven.) Serve warm or at room temperature, alone or with a scoop of *Vanilla Bean* or *Roasted Cinnamon Ice Cream*, page 553.

Double-Crust Deep Red Raspberry Pie

SERVES 6 TO 8

If you love raspberries as much as I do, you'll agree: an entire pie made of them may just be the most decadent recipe there is. One raspberry is divine, a whole pie full of them is downright other-worldly. Not overly sweet, this pie is light, rich and full of a punch of true raspberry flavour. The little bit of Crème de Cassis highlights the berries' flavour and adds depth and richness, but its own flavour remains undetectable. Raspberry syrup may be substituted, or one table-spoon of a pure raspberry extract may be used instead.

1 recipe Flaky Pie Pastry, page 658, separated into two discs and chilled

FILLING:
7 cups fresh red raspberries, preferably local
⅔ to ¾ cup granulated sugar, depending on the sweetness of the berries
4 tablespoons cornstarch

3 tablespoons Crème de Cassis, Framboise or another red or black berry liqueur
1 teaspoon finely grated lemon zest
1 teaspoon freshly squeezed lemon juice

1 large egg, lightly beaten
2 teaspoons coarse white or granulated sugar

1. Preheat the oven to 400°. Take one disc of pastry dough out of the refrigerator and let it warm at room temperature for 15 minutes or so, until it is just soft enough to roll. Roll it out to a circle of about 12 inches in diameter and ⅛ inch thick, then use it to line a 9½-inch glass pie plate. Gently ease the pastry into the bottom of the plate and trim the overhang to 1 inch. Cover the pastry with plastic wrap and return to the refrigerator for at least 45 minutes, and up to 2 days if well covered.

2. Remove the second portion of dough from the refrigerator 15 to 20 minutes before you plan to bake the pie. Meanwhile, in a large bowl, combine the raspberries, sugar, cornstarch, liqueur, lemon zest and lemon juice. Using a big rubber spatula or mixing spoon, very gently fold the berries together with the

Double-Crust Deep Red Raspberry Pie continued

other ingredients, trying not to crush the fruit too badly. Remove the chilled shell from the refrigerator. Spoon the filling into the pastry, spreading it evenly, then mounding it slightly in the centre. Try to keep the edges of the shell clean. Brush the edges of the pastry with the lightly beaten egg.

3. When the remaining disc of dough is pliable, roll it out to a circle of about 10 inches in diameter and ⅛ inch thick. Use the rolling pin to help you lay this circle over the filling, centring it on the top of the shell: fold the edge of the circle of dough over the length of the rolling pin and gently roll the pin through mid-air towards you, bringing with it the pastry, now folded over the pin. When the pastry is suspended at about the mid-point, slide the filled shell underneath the hanging dough and use the rolling pin to centre the circle and ease it down onto the top of the pie. Press the edges of the pastry together, sealing the top and bottom crusts. Trim the overhang with a sharp knife, then crimp the edges decoratively, if desired. You can also use the trimmings from the edges to stamp or cut out shapes of pastry to decorate the top of the pie.

4. Allow the pie (and any decorations, wrapped in plastic wrap) to rest in the refrigerator for 15 minutes, then place it on a baking sheet. Combine the remaining beaten egg with 1 tablespoon water and brush the top of the pie with a thin glaze. Apply any decorations to the top crust and brush these with the egg wash as well. Sprinkle the entire top of the pie with the 2 teaspoons of sugar and use a thin-bladed knife to cut four 2-inch-long slits in the top of the crust to allow the steam to escape.

5. Place the baking sheet into the centre of the preheated oven. Bake for 45 minutes to 1 hour, or until the crust is golden and crisp and the filling is bubbling through the slits in the top. Transfer the pie to a rack and cool at least half an hour before cutting and serving. I don't think this pie needs anything except a fork (and I have been known to proceed without even this!), but those who wish to can add a scoop of *Vanilla Bean Ice Cream*, page 553.

Macadamia and Fresh Coconut Tart

SERVES 6 TO 8

This tart is seriously decadent, and so sophisticated. Luxurious tropical flavours and the wonderful contrasts of texture are immensely satisfying. The extra effort of using fresh coconut meat is well worth it—don't skimp and use packaged!

1 recipe Pâte Sucrée tart pastry, page 655, pressed into a 13½ x 4½-inch rectangular tart tin with a removable bottom (or a 9-inch round tin), partially baked and cooled

1¼ cups fresh coconut shavings (see below for how to crack, clean and shave a coconut)
3 large egg yolks

¼ cup tightly packed light brown sugar
3 tablespoons granulated sugar
Seeds of 1 vanilla bean, hull reserved for another use
3 tablespoons unsalted butter, melted and cooled
⅔ cup half-and-half cream (10%)
1 tablespoon bourbon, optional
1¼ cups unsalted, raw macadamia nuts

1. Preheat the oven to 375°. Working on a hard surface covered by a kitchen towel, carefully drive a nail into two of the small, indented black eyes on the coconut. Turn the coconut over a small bowl and shake out the juice. This is not coconut milk, but does taste good and makes a refreshing drink! When you can't hear any more sloshing, wrap the towel around the coconut, making a mental note of where the long seam is. With a forceful hand, a heavy hammer and a healthy burst of aggression, crack the shell. Break the resulting pieces into manageable sizes, roughly 3 to 4 inches square, but not too small, or they will be impossible to shave. I find the next step easiest with a parmesan or oyster knife: both are very short-bladed, thick little knives for prying, not cutting. If you don't own either of these knives, raid your toolbox—a good flat-head screwdriver will also do the trick nicely. The aim is to wedge the blade between the shell and the meat and pry the meat clean in large pieces, not little chips. Rinse the pieces under cool water and pat dry, and clean your work surface. You can pare away the brown covering on the white flesh if you like, but for this tart, I like to keep it on; it isn't too tough and adds a pretty colour. Using a vegetable peeler, shave the larger pieces of coconut along the edges, pulling off long strips.

Macadamia and Fresh Coconut Tart continued

When the pieces get too small to shave, eat them! Fresh coconut meat is a treat, and you have just earned it. Store the strips of coconut in an airtight container and use them as soon as possible, as they lose freshness quickly.

2. Set the tart tin on a baking sheet. In a medium-sized bowl, whisk together the egg yolks and the brown and granulated sugars. Add the vanilla seeds and whisk to distribute them as well as possible. Stir in the melted butter, then blend in the cream and bourbon, if using. Add the macadamia nuts and the coconut shavings and stir to coat. Spoon the filling into the cooled tart shell, evenly distributing the chunky bits, then spooning the custard over everything.

3. Place the baking sheet in the centre of the oven and bake the tart for about 30 minutes (turning it once so it bakes evenly), or until the custard is just set in the centre. Cool the tart completely on a rack before removing the sides and serving. This tart should be eaten the same day it is baked, but any leftovers can be stored, covered, in the refrigerator for up to 3 days.

Pear and Bittersweet Chocolate Tart

SERVES 6 TO 8

Pears and chocolate are one of the best marriages in the sweet kitchen; each enhances the other, creating a luxurious new flavour. This simple tart would be an elegant and impressive finale to a fall or winter dinner and is lovely with a fine dessert wine.

1 (10½- or 11-inch) Pâte Sucrée tart shell, page 655, partially baked and cooled

4 ounces best-quality bittersweet chocolate, finely chopped

5 or 6 medium-sized dessert pears (or more or less, depending on the size), preferably Anjou or Bartlett, ripe but still firm and unblemished

2 large eggs
2 large egg yolks
¾ cup granulated sugar, plus 2 tablespoons for sprinkling
Seeds of ½ vanilla bean, hull reserved for another use, or substitute 1 teaspoon pure vanilla extract
1½ cups heavy cream (36%)

1. Preheat the oven to 400°. Scatter the chopped chocolate evenly over the bottom of the cooled tart shell. Peel and halve the pears, then core them using a melon baller to scoop out just the round seed area. Place one pear half, cut-side down, on a cutting board. Using a sharp, thin-bladed knife, slice the pear into very thin slices across the axis (horizontally), keeping the shape intact (so even after it's sliced, it still looks like an intact pear half). Gently press your hand down upon the curve, fanning the slices back towards the wide end of the pear, like dominos. Slide a palette knife under the sliced pear half, keeping the fanned shape, and transfer to the tart shell, with the narrow end facing the centre. Repeat with the other halves until the tart shell is full. Don't worry about covering the whole surface; any space between the fanned pear halves will be filled with the custard.

2. In a small bowl, whisk together the eggs, yolks, ¾ cup sugar and the vanilla seeds. Add the cream and vanilla extract, if using, and whisk to combine. Pour the custard over the pears. (Depending on the size of your tart tin, there may be a little custard left over.) Sprinkle the surface of the tart with the remaining 2 tablespoons of sugar and set the shell on a baking sheet to catch any drips.

3. Bake the tart in the centre of the preheated oven for 10 minutes, then reduce the heat to 375°, and continue baking until the custard is just set in the centre, about 40 to 50 minutes more. Allow tart to cool completely before slicing. This rich tart needs nothing to be wonderful, but if you must, it is good with a scoop of *Vanilla Bean Ice Cream*, page 553, or a dollop of crème fraîche. Serve the tart within 6 hours of baking and store any leftovers in the refrigerator.

Caramelized Banana Tart
with a Lime Linzer Crust and a
Warm Caramel Sauce

SERVES 8

Like the original Linzer tart, this dessert is really a cross between a cake and a tart. Here, a tropical variation: a cake-like dough laced with lime surrounds a

Caramelized Banana Tart continued

layer of soft caramelized banana slices. The combination is big on flavour but not too sweet, overwhelming or heavy. Perfect for a simple dessert, or with a cup of coffee or tea.

CRUST:

1¼ cups all purpose flour

1 cup finely ground pecans

1 teaspoon baking powder

½ teaspoon ground cinnamon

½ teaspoon freshly grated nutmeg

¾ cup granulated sugar

Seeds of ½ plump vanilla bean, hull reserved for another use, or substitute 1 teaspoon pure vanilla extract

1 large egg

1 large egg yolk

Freshly grated zest of 1 lime (about 1 teaspoon)

¾ cup unsalted butter, at room temperature

FILLING:

1 cup tightly packed light brown sugar

Finely grated zest and freshly squeezed juice of 1 lime

⅓ cup dark rum

¼ cup unsalted butter, at room temperature

5 medium to large bananas, mostly but not overly ripe

1. Preheat the oven to 350°. In a large bowl, combine the flour, ground nuts, baking powder, spices, sugar and vanilla seeds, then stir with a fork or whisk to blend. In a separate bowl, whisk together the egg, the yolk, lime zest and the vanilla extract, if using. Add the soft butter in dollops to the dry ingredients and use your fingers to rub it in, kneading gently with just the tips of your fingers until a soft, sticky dough is formed. Add the egg mixture to this, mixing the dough with a wooden spoon or a stiff rubber spatula until the egg is completely and evenly incorporated. It is a strange dough! It should be very soft and floppy, and quite wet and sticky. Scoop about ⅓ of the dough into a sturdy pastry bag fitted with a medium-sized plain tip and set aside. Spread the remaining ⅔ of dough over the bottom of a 10½- or 11-inch tart pan with a removable bottom. Don't spread the batter up the sides, but concentrate on getting it relatively even across the bottom. Set the pan aside.

2. Prepare the bananas: in a medium-sized, heavy-bottomed saucepan, combine the brown sugar, lime juice and zest and rum. Stir constantly over low heat until the sugar melts and dissolves completely. Increase the heat to medium, and bring the syrup to a boil, then reduce the heat to a simmer. Simmer for about 30 seconds, then whisk in the butter by tablespoonfuls, keeping the pan over the heat. After another 30 seconds, remove the pot from the element.

3. Peel the bananas and slice them into rounds of about ⅓ to ½ inch thick. (You should have about 3½ to 4 cups of slices.) Return the syrup to the heat and add the banana slices. Gently move the bananas around with a wooden spoon or a heatproof spatula, being careful not to mash or bruise them. When all of the slices are well coated with the syrup, transfer the pot to a heatproof pad on the counter beside the tart pan. A pair of small tongs are almost essential for the next step: tenderly remove the slices one by one from their warm syrup and lay them overlapping on the layer of dough. The pattern is up to you—I like concentric circles or straight stripes, but you can create whatever design makes you happy. The grouping can be reasonably dense, especially if your slices are on the thin side. Transfer the syrup to a small container and set aside to cool.

4. With the reserved batter, pipe a circle around the perimeter of the tart, then pipe three or four stripes in a crosshatch pattern over the banana slices. The batter will spread quite a bit, so don't pipe your lines too close together. You want to be able to see the glossy bananas between the cake. Place the tart on a baking sheet to catch any escaping caramel and bake for 35 to 40 minutes, or until the batter is puffed, golden and firm to the touch in the centre. Transfer to a rack and cool 15 to 20 minutes.

5. Using a pair of oven mitts, or a couple of kitchen towels, carefully loosen the sides of the tart by pushing up the bottom every few inches, making sure the tart isn't sticking to the rim. If it is, use a small, thin knife to pry the cake away from the pan. When you're sure it is free, remove the sides and allow the cake to cool completely. The tart is best served the day it is made, but can be kept, well covered, at room temperature for up to 2 days. The cake absorbs moisture from the bananas upon sitting and will be softer and somewhat heavier the next day. Serve the tart with a healthy spoonful of the warmed caramel sauce.

Damn Fine Apple Pie

SERVES 6 TO 8

This is a super pie, full of soft, sweetly flavoured apples, with just the right amount of juice. The pure flavour of the fruit comes through, not masked by too much cinnamon or other spices or muted with the addition of cream or too much sugar. I like to make this with Northern Spy apples, but any good, tart, firm cooking apple will do. Try to taste the apples before you decide—make sure that the ones you choose have a lot of flavour and are neither too sweet, nor too soft-fleshed. When I was in cooking school, one of my instructors was an Austrian pastry chef named Chef Lippert. Austrian pastry chefs have a reputation for being rather severe, and for being very vocal proponents of the concept that when it comes to baking, things European, specifically Austrian, are infinitely better than those from anywhere else. So we were all the more astounded when Chef Lippert not only allowed, but insisted, that the very best apples in the world for apple pie were America's own Northern Spys. In fact, his Austrian pastry chef mentor had waxed poetic about those very apples when my chef was his apprentice! I have to agree; I have made good pies with other varieties, but the best have always been with Spys.

1 recipe Flaky Pie Pastry, page 658,
   separated into two discs and chilled

3 pounds Northern Spy apples, or
   other tart cooking apple
Freshly squeezed juice of ½ lemon
⅔ cup granulated sugar
1 teaspoon ground cinnamon
½ teaspoon freshly grated nutmeg

½ teaspoon ground ginger
5 teaspoons cornstarch

1 egg, lightly beaten
1 tablespoon milk

Additional granulated or crystal sugar
   for sprinkling

1. Preheat the oven to 400°. Remove the two discs of dough from the refrigerator about 15 minutes before you want to roll them out, to allow them to soften. On a lightly floured surface, roll the slightly larger portion of dough to a circle about 12 inches in diameter and use it to line a deep 9½-inch glass pie plate. Ease the dough into the plate, then cover the shell with plastic wrap and place in the refrigerator until needed. Roll out the other portion of dough between two sheets of parchment paper to a circle just larger than the top of the pie plate. This will make covering the pie very simple. Keep the circle between the sheets of paper, slide it onto baking sheet and pop this in the refrigerator as well.

2. Peel, core and thinly slice the apples and place them into a large mixing bowl. I find thin slices allow me to add more fruit, with much less space taken up with air. This makes for a thicker, denser filling and a just plain bigger pie, which is always a good thing. Sprinkle the apples with the lemon juice. In a small bowl, combine the sugar, cinnamon, nutmeg and ginger. Sift the cornstarch over this mixture and stir with a small whisk or a fork until everything is well blended. Add the sugar mixture to the apples and toss to coat well. Let the apples sit for 3 to 5 minutes; if there seems to be a great deal of juice, add an extra teaspoon of cornstarch and toss to distribute it evenly. Remove the lined pie plate from the refrigerator and spoon the apples and their juices into the shell, pressing gently on each spoonful to pack the apples in as tightly as possible. Mound the filling slightly in the centre and take care not to get any filling or juice on the edges of the shell.

3. Brush the edges of the shell with the beaten egg. Remove the other pastry circle from the refrigerator and peel off the top piece of parchment. Invert the bottom piece of paper over the pie, centring it as you do so, and settle the pastry onto the filling. Peel off the parchment and gently press the top pastry onto the filling, easing out any air bubbles, then press around the edges to seal. Trim the excess pastry with a very sharp knife and crimp the edges of the shell decoratively if desired. Be careful not to crimp the edges so much that they become very thin, or they may overcook before the pie is finished baking. You can also use the scraps of dough to cut out shapes with a paring knife or cookie cutters and secure these to the top pastry with a little more of the egg wash. Mix the milk into the remaining beaten egg and brush over the entire surface of the pie. With a sharp paring knife, make three or four long slits in the top to allow steam to escape and sprinkle the surface of the pie with ½ to 1 tablespoon granulated or crystal sugar.

4. Place the pie plate on a baking sheet to catch any drips and turn the oven down to 375°. Bake the pie for 50 minutes to 1 hour, or until the crust is a lovely golden-brown and the filling can be seen bubbling up between the slits in the

Damn Fine Apple Pie continued

pastry. If parts of the crust seem to be darkening too quickly, cover those areas with a bit of aluminum foil; this will prevent them from scorching. Transfer the pie to a wire rack and cool at least 20 minutes before cutting. This pie can be stored at room temperature, lightly covered, for up to 3 days. To reheat before serving, pop the pie in a preheated 300° oven for 15 to 25 minutes. Serve with *Vanilla Bean Ice Cream*, *Roasted Cinnamon Ice Cream*, *Crème Anglaise*, a wedge of aged cheddar cheese or a good dollop of lightly sweetened whipped cream. (It's awfully good all by itself, too!)

Cazuela Pie
(Pumpkin, Sweet Potato and
Coconut Milk Pie)

2 9½-INCH PIES,
EACH SERVING 6 TO 8

This very complex and sweet-tasting pie has a dense, dark-orange filling, a combination of cooked pumpkin and sweet potato mash. It may look similar, but it beats the pants off regular pumpkin pies! Cazuela is a traditional Puerto Rican pudding, usually baked in banana leaves. The idea to encase the filling in a flaky pie crust was my mother's, and an inspired one at that! This pie has a more refined, richer, more flavourful taste than the common pumpkin pie and has now replaced it on our Thanksgiving table! You, too, may never go back.

A few notes about the ingredients and procedure: oven-steaming the sweet potatoes with the spices and ginger infuses the flesh with the flavours and lets the water absorb the starch and flavour from the potatoes as well. The filling can be made using canned pumpkin or fresh, cooked pumpkin—the filling will be smoother if you use canned, but you can get the same effect by forcing your cooked pumpkin flesh through a ricer or mesh sieve. Make sure the pie shell is thoroughly chilled to ensure the pastry won't overbake during the long cooking time needed for the dense filling.

1 recipe Flaky Pie Pastry, page 658,
  divided and used to line 2 9½-inch
  glass pie dishes, unbaked and
  well chilled

FILLING:

2½ pounds orange sweet potatoes,
  peeled and cut into small egg-sized
  chunks
1¼ cups water
2 small or 1 large cinnamon stick(s),
  broken into pieces
5 whole cloves
1 star anise, crumbled
1½-inch-long piece of fresh ginger,
  peeled and cut into ¼-inch slices
4 cups homemade pumpkin purée
  (see page 331), or good-quality
  canned solid-pack pumpkin (not
  "Pumpkin Pie Filling")

3 large eggs, lightly beaten
¼ cup unsalted butter, melted and
  cooled
1 cup granulated sugar
1 cup plus 2 tablespoons tightly
  packed light brown sugar
¼ cup all-purpose flour
1½ teaspoons salt
1 cup good-quality canned coconut
  milk (stir the contents of the can
  well before measuring out the
  amount you need, to ensure you
  will get some of the rich cream, as
  well as the thinner milk below)

1½ cups heavy cream (36%), chilled,
  then whipped to soft peaks with
  3 tablespoons granulated sugar,
  to serve

1. Preheat the oven to 325°. Place the sweet potato chunks in a single layer in one large or two medium shallow, ceramic baking dish(es). Add the water, dividing it between the two dishes if necessary. The water should be about ½-inch deep; add more if the level is lower than this. Scatter the pieces of cinnamon stick, cloves, pieces of star anise and ginger slices among the sweet potatoes. Cover the baking dishes securely with aluminum foil and place in the preheated oven. Bake for 35 to 45 minutes, or until the sweet potatoes are very tender when pierced with the tip of a sharp knife. Remove the potatoes from the dishes and force them through a ricer, food mill or sieve. Let cool. Strain the baking liquid, discarding the solids, and measure. You want about ½ cup of liquid; if you have less, add enough fresh water to make ½ cup; if you have more, simmer the liquid in a small saucepan on the stove over high heat until it is reduced to about ½ cup. Let the liquid cool. (The pumpkin, sweet potato and spiced liquid can all be prepared up to 3 days ahead of time and stored in

Cazuela Pie continued

the refrigerator. Bring each to room temperature before proceeding with the recipe. Each of these elements can also be frozen for up to 5 months (thaw overnight in the refrigerator before bringing to room temperature).

2. Increase the oven temperature to 350°. In a large bowl, combine the pumpkin and sweet potato purées and stir to blend well. Beat in the eggs, then stir in the melted butter and reserved spice liquid. In a separate bowl, stir together the granulated and brown sugars with a wire whisk. Sift the flour and salt over the sugars and stir to blend. Add the sugar-flour mixture to the pumpkin mixture and stir well until there are no pockets of sugar visible. Blend in the coconut milk.

3. Scrape the filling into the two chilled pie shells, dividing it evenly and smoothing the tops. Place the pies in the lower half of the preheated oven and bake for 1¾ to 2 hours, turning the pies several times so they bake evenly. The point of a thin-bladed knife should come out clean when inserted into the centre of the filling, and the surface should be unevenly cracked. If the edges of the pastry seem to be darkening too much before the filling is cooked, cover them with strips of aluminum foil. Transfer the pies to wire racks and cool completely before serving with mounds of lightly sweetened whipped cream. Each pie would serve 6 to 8 people if everyone wants only one piece. This is unlikely.

Blackberry Curd Tarts with Lemon Crème Fraîche

SERVES 6

The curd in these beautiful tarts is not sugary sweet and retains that lovely mouth-puckering sweet-tartness that is so seductive about blackberries. It is not as firm as traditional lemon curd, but is thick, smooth and almost pudding-like in its consistency. Here, combined with a buttery pastry, it makes a fabulous tart filling; it would also make a wonderful filling for a white or chocolate cake. Try serving it mounded beside a thick slice of angel food cake for a riotous change to fresh fruit!

6 (4½-inch) Pâte Sucrée tartlette shells, page 655, pre-baked and cooled

CURD:

4 cups fresh blackberries, picked over
1½ tablespoons freshly squeezed lemon juice
3 large eggs, at room temperature
2 large egg yolks, at room temperature

½ cup plus 2 tablespoons granulated sugar (or more or less, depending on sweetness of berries)
5 tablespoons unsalted butter, cold, cut into small pieces

2 tablespoons finely grated lemon zest
3 to 5 tablespoons granulated sugar, to taste
1½ cups Crème Fraîche (page 651)

1. Prepare the Blackberry Curd: combine the blackberries and the lemon juice in the bowl of a food processor and purée, scraping down the sides of the bowl once or twice. Pour the purée through a fine strainer or sieve, pressing down on the solids and seeds to extract as much of the purée as possible. I use a curved rubber spatula to forcefully stir the pulp in the sieve; it takes a few minutes of vigorous elbow grease, but it works! You should end up with about 2 cups of thick purée, give or take a few tablespoons.

2. Bring a large pot containing an inch or two of water to a gentle simmer. In a large, non-reactive bowl, lightly whisk the eggs and egg yolks until frothy. Add the sugar, then beat to combine—but just enough to blend the ingredients and ensure the sugar is evenly distributed; you don't want to add too much air to this

Blackberry Curd Tarts continued

mixture. Stir the blackberry purée into the egg mixture, then switch from the whisk to a heatproof rubber spatula. Place the bowl over top of the barely simmering water and stir the mixture over low heat until the curd thickens and leaves a raised trail on the surface when the spatula is lifted. This should take about 10 to 15 minutes of constant but gentle stirring. The aim is to keep all parts of the mixture moving so the eggs don't get a chance to coagulate in large globules. Keep the spatula scraping down all the parts of the bowl, especially the very bottom and the outside edges. After about 10 minutes, you will begin to think your heat is too low, or your mixture is too runny, but have faith! A few minutes more and the curd will be thick and perfect. Keep the heat low, and your arm moving, and the result will be a smooth, creamy, pudding-like curd.

3. As soon as the curd has thickened, remove the bowl from the heat and stir in the pieces of butter, a few at a time, until completely incorporated. Scrape the curd into a clean bowl and press plastic wrap down onto the entire surface to prevent a skin from forming. With the tip of a very sharp knife, poke 6 to 8 slits in the plastic to allow steam to escape, let the curd cool to room temperature, then refrigerate until chilled, at least 4 hours or overnight. (The curd can be made up to 2 days ahead of time and kept chilled until needed.) Makes about 3 cups.

4. Prepare the Lemon Crème Fraîche: whisk the lemon zest and sugar into the crème fraîche, cover and chill until needed, up to 2 days.

5. To serve, fill each tart shell with about ½ cup of the blackberry curd and top with a fresh blackberry or two. Place one tart on each dessert plate and spoon a little mound of the Lemon Crème Fraîche beside each tart. Serve immediately. These tarts are best if assembled just before serving, but all of the components can be prepared ahead of time.

Walnut, Orange and Sweet Chèvre Tartlettes

SERVES 6

We all know people who prefer savoury to sweet, and who take one mouthful of even the best cake or pudding and seem sated. Even they will adore these nutty, earthy and creamy tarts. I like to serve the tarts in place of a fruit and cheese course, or accompanied by slices of ripe pear or fresh ripe figs and a glass of good dessert wine.

1 recipe Rich Nut Tart Pastry, page 657, made with walnuts, divided among 6 (4½-inch) tart tins and chilled at least 4 hours

FILLING:

11 ounces soft fresh goat's cheese (chèvre), such as Montrachet

½ cup full-fat ricotta

Seeds of ½ vanilla bean, hull reserved for another use, or substitute 1 teaspoon pure vanilla extract

½ cup superfine sugar, or substitute granulated sugar spun in the food processor until very fine

1 teaspoon packed finely grated lemon zest

1 teaspoon packed finely grated orange zest

3 large egg yolks

3 tablespoons all-purpose flour, sifted

¾ cup to 1 cup coarsely chopped fresh walnuts, lightly toasted

6 lightly toasted walnut halves, to garnish

1. Preheat the oven to 375°. Place the 6 pastry-lined tart tins on a baking sheet and prick the bottoms several times with a fork. Line each shell with a piece of aluminum foil or parchment paper an inch or so bigger than the tins. Fill each shell with pie weights or dried beans and place the baking sheet in the centre of the oven. Bake for 15 minutes, or until the edges of the pastry are just beginning to colour, then remove the foil or paper and weights and return the shells to the oven for a further 5 to 8 minutes, or until the bottom of the shells feels almost dry and firm. Transfer the whole sheet to a wire rack and cool completely (keep them on the baking sheet). The shells can be prepared to this point up to 2 days in advance and stored, loosely covered, at room temperature.

2. Reduce the oven temperature to 325°. In a large bowl, or the bowl of an electric mixer, using a wooden spoon or the paddle attachment of the mixer, cream the goat's cheese and ricotta together until they are partially blended. Smear in the vanilla seeds, if using. Add the sugar and the lemon and orange zests and cream until the mixture is smooth. Add the egg yolks, one at a time, beating well after each addition, making sure the yolks are thoroughly incorporated.

Walnut, Orange and Sweet Chèvre Tartlettes continued

Add the vanilla extract, if using. Sift the flour over the cheese mixture and stir to blend. The batter should be shiny and smooth. If it appears lumpy, use a wide-wired whisk to stir until it becomes fairly smooth. Don't worry about a few small lumps of cheese, but any flour lumps should be broken up.

3. Sprinkle about 2 tablespoons of chopped toasted walnuts onto the bottom of each cooled tart shell. Spoon the cheese mixture over the nuts, dividing the mixture evenly among the shells. Smooth the tops with the back of a spoon and place a walnut half in the centre of the filling of each tart. Place the filled tarts in the centre of the 325° oven and bake for 35 to 40 minutes, or until the filling is slightly puffed and just firm to the touch in the centre of each tart. Transfer to a wire rack to cool completely before unmoulding and serving. These tarts are best eaten the day they are made, kept at room temperature until serving, but any leftover tarts can be refrigerated for up to 3 days.

Nectarine Custard Tart

SERVES 8

A sexy understated little tart with a creamy custard that subtly enhances the flavour of the ripe fruit. One friend of mine, who would never have chosen this dessert but was too polite to refuse it, instantly became its biggest fan. Fruit and custard tarts such as this are very popular in France; this one can be made with peaches, apricots, plums, figs, even pears or thinly sliced apples. For these variations, feel free to substitute 1 to 2 tablespoons of a compatible fruit liqueur, such as peach schnapps, plum brandy, Calvados or even a Sauternes dessert wine for 1 teaspoon of the vanilla extract. The result is both simple and sublime.

1 (9½- to 11-inch) Pâte Sucrée tart shell, page 655, partially baked and cooled

1 large egg white, lightly beaten
4 to 6 fresh nectarines, depending on the size, ripe but not overly soft or bruised

3 large egg yolks
½ cup granulated sugar plus 2 tablespoons for sprinkling
1½ tablespoons all-purpose flour
1 cup heavy cream (36%)
Seeds of 1 vanilla bean, hull reserved for another use, or substitute 2 teaspoons pure vanilla extract

1. Preheat the oven to 325°. Brush the bottom of the cooled tart shell with the lightly beaten egg white and bake for 3 to 5 minutes, or until the film is dry. Set the shell aside. Wash and thoroughly dry the nectarines, then halve them by slicing all the way around, using the little seam on the side as a guide. Remove the stones by gently twisting the halves in opposite directions and cut each half into eight wedges. Place the lined tart tin on a baking sheet. Lay the slices of fruit in the bottom of the tart shell, arranging them in concentric circles. Don't overcrowd the shell, but use your judgement as to how much fruit to custard you prefer. Set the shell aside.

2. In a small bowl, whisk the eggs to break them up. Add the ½ cup of sugar gradually, whisking all the while. Sift the flour over the mixture, whisking to incorporate it smoothly. Whisk in the cream, then stir in the vanilla seeds, or extract and liqueur, if using. Strain the custard over the nectarine slices in the tart shell and sprinkle the filling with the 2 tablespoons of sugar.

3. Place the baking sheet in the preheated oven and bake for 35 to 45 minutes, or until the custard in the centre of the tart is just barely set when lightly touched. Transfer to a wire rack and cool completely. This tart is best served the day it is made, at room temperature, but may be stored for up to 2 days, well wrapped, in the refrigerator. This tart is lovely on its own, but a pour of crème anglaise creates a more formal dessert.

White Chocolate
and Summer Berry Tart

SERVES 8 TO 10

The flavours in this pretty tart are as satisfying as the tart is beautiful. It's gorgeous made with different kinds of berries, but is equally wonderful with a single variety—raspberries, blackberries or strawberries. And a trio of red, black and golden raspberries is spectacular. The white chocolate lets the sweetness and tang of the individual berries come through, instead of overpowering it, as can sometimes happen with dark chocolate.

White Chocolate and Summer Berry Tart continued

1 (10½- to 11-inch) Pâte Sucrée tart
    shell, page 655, pre-baked and cooled

FILLING:

8 ounces best-quality white chocolate,
    finely chopped
3 scant tablespoons heavy cream
    (36%)
6½ tablespoons unsalted butter, in
    small pieces
3 tablespoons Crème de Cassis (black-
    currant liqueur), or substitute
    Framboise or Chambord (raspberry
    liqueurs)

1½ quarts fresh ripe strawberries,
    hulled
1 pint fresh ripe blackberries or
    huckleberries
1 pint fresh red raspberries,
    or a combination of golden,
    red and/or black
2 tablespoons redcurrant jelly
1 to 2 teaspoons water

1. Combine the chopped chocolate, cream and butter in a double boiler insert or a stainless steel or glass bowl. Set over a pot containing an inch or two of hot, but not simmering, water and let sit for 2 minutes. Stir gently and keep the heat just below the simmer. White chocolate melts at a very low temperature and can scorch and seize easily, so keep the heat low and stir often to keep the mixture melting evenly. When the mixture looks about ¾ melted, remove it from the heat and stir until smooth and glossy. Stir in the liqueur. Pour the warm chocolate into the cooled tart shell and refrigerate 30 minutes to 1 hour.

2. Working from the outside of the tart, largest berries to the smallest, place the berries in concentric circles on the filling. I prefer arranging the berries in circles of the same type (a ring of strawberries, then one of blackberries, then raspberries and so on), so every slice contains some of each berry.

3. Prepare the glaze: melt the jelly in a small pot over low heat and add 1 teaspoon of water. Bring to a boil, then immediately remove from the heat. Using a soft-bristled pastry brush, brush a thin layer of the glaze on each berry, re-warming the glaze if it becomes too gloppy or stiff to paint thinly. Add an extra teaspoon of water if it still seems to be going on too thick. Refrigerate the tart until 15 minutes before serving. This tart should be served the day it is made, but any leftovers can be stored, covered, in the refrigerator for up to 3 days. Serve alone, or with a dollop of crème fraîche, if desired.

COOKIES AND BARS

continued on page 484

Chewy Oatmeal-Raisin Cookie Sandwiches with Roasted Cinnamon Ice Cream

30 LARGE COOKIES, OR 15 SANDWICHES

Intensely toffee-flavoured cookies with a lovely, crisp-chewy texture and a good oatmeal taste are sandwiched with a gorgeously rich cinnamon ice cream. An indulgently nostalgic dessert!

OATMEAL RAISIN COOKIES:

1 cup unsalted butter, at room temperature

1½ cups tightly packed light brown sugar

½ cup granulated sugar

2 large eggs

1 teaspoon pure vanilla extract

1 tablespoon honey

1½ cups all-purpose flour

¾ teaspoons baking soda

¼ teaspoon salt

¼ teaspoon cinnamon

¼ teaspoon freshly grated nutmeg

3 cups old-fashioned oats

2 cups flavourful dark raisins, such as Lexia or Muscat

Roasted Cinnamon Ice Cream, page 553, softened slightly at room temperature for 5 to 10 minutes

1. Preheat the oven to 350°. Line two or three baking sheets with parchment paper, or butter the sheets, and set aside. In the bowl of an electric mixer or a large mixing bowl, combine the butter and both sugars. Cream with the paddle attachment or a wooden spoon until fluffy and light, about 2 minutes with the mixer or 3 to 4 minutes by hand. Add the eggs one at a time, beating well after each addition. Beat in the vanilla and honey and scrape down the sides of the bowl.

2. Into a separate bowl, sift the flour, baking soda, salt and spices. Add this mixture to the creamed mixture and fold in until the dry ingredients are well incorporated. Fold in the oats and raisins. At this point, if you have been using an electric mixer, take the bowl off the frame and work the oats and raisins in

Chewy Oatmeal-Raisin Cookie Sandwiches continued

by hand. Drop the batter by heaping tablespoonfuls onto the prepared baking sheets.

3. Bake, one sheet at a time, in the centre of the oven for 15 to 18 minutes, turning the sheet two or three times during that time. The cookies are done when they are a deep golden brown and set around the edges but still puffy and soft in the centre. Cool the cookies on the sheet for 5 minutes, then transfer them to wire racks to cool completely. Repeat until all the cookies are baked and cooled. The cookies can be stored in an airtight container at room temperature for up to 1 week. To make the ice cream sandwiches, return the cooled cookies to the baking sheets and place the trays in the freezer until the cookies are frozen. Transfer them to a freezer bag or container until ready to assemble the sandwiches, up to 1 month.

4. To assemble sandwiches, place a generous scoop of the slightly softened ice cream onto the underside of a frozen cookie. Use the back of a spoon to flatten the mound a little before topping with a second cookie, underside down, and press gently to ensure a good seal. Try to make the scoops large enough, and let the ice cream soften enough to have it squoosh out to the edges of the cookies. You can then wipe off the excess with a butter knife, giving the sandwiches a neat edge. Wrap each sandwich securely in plastic wrap or waxed paper, pressing the ice cream gently into shape, and freeze until firm. The sandwiches can be made up to 1 week ahead of time and unwrapped just before serving.

White Meringues with Fresh Cream and Pomegranate Syrup

SERVES 6 TO 10

This is a simple dessert of glorious colours and textures and contrasting flavours. The crisp, sweet meringues, lots of soft, cool whipped cream, and a ruby-red, intense, tangy red reduction of fresh pomegranate juice make wonderful bedfellows! All of the components can be made ahead of time, and assembled in less than five minutes. A light, flavourful end to a rich autumn or winter dinner, and perfect after a heavy holiday meal.

MERINGUES:

4 large egg whites, preferably several
    days old, at room temperature
½ teaspoon cream of tartar
1 cup superfine sugar
Scant ½ teaspoon pure vanilla extract

1 cup heavy cream (36%),
    very cold
1 recipe Pomegranate Syrup,
    page 638
Seeds of 1 small pomegranate,
    for garnish

1. Preheat the oven to 250°. Line a large baking sheet with parchment paper and set aside. In a spotlessly clean and grease-free bowl, beat the egg whites until foamy. Add the cream of tartar and continue whipping until soft peaks form. The meringues are easiest done in a stand mixer fitted with the whip attachment or with an electric mixer, but they can be done by hand, with a very strong arm! Add the sugar, one tablespoon at a time, whipping constantly; it should take you about 3 minutes to fully incorporate the cup of sugar. The meringue should be thick, stiff and very glossy. Whip in the vanilla extract. If you want really perfectly shaped meringues, spoon the mixture into a pastry bag fitted with a medium star tip and pipe the meringue onto the prepared sheet in 2-inch rosettes. I actually prefer simply spooning the meringue mixture onto the sheet in little plump mounds—I love the look of these billowy clouds on the dessert plates.

2. Bake the meringues for 1 to 1½ hours, or until dry and crisp on the outside and slightly chewy on the inside. The colour should stay very white; if your meringues seem to be browning slightly, reduce the temperature to 225°. Cool the meringues on the baking sheet in the oven, with the heat off and the door ajar, for about an hour, then store in an airtight container for up to a week. A word of caution: do not even attempt to make meringues in hot or humid weather! You could do everything right and still end up with sticky cookies. Makes about 15 (2- to 2½-inch) meringues.

3. To assemble the dessert, whip the cream to soft peaks. Using a chilled bowl and whisk and very cold cream will make the cream easier to whip and enable it to hold its shape longer. Don't be tempted to sweeten the cream; the other components of this dessert are sweet enough. Arrange one or two meringues on each dessert plate and spoon a dollop of whipped cream beside them. Drizzle the meringues and cream with about 2 tablespoons of the Pomegranate Syrup and sprinkle each plate with some fresh pomegranate seeds.

Really, REALLY Fudgy Brownies

28 LARGE SQUARES

Very dense, very rich, very moist, very chocolatey, these brownies are not for the faint of heart. After tasting them at our house, friends who were getting married soon asked that these be the only gift at their wedding ... the ONLY gift— they had asked everyone else not to bring any gifts at all! Almost more of a confection than a cake, these are great as part of a dessert assortment, or pack- aged as a gift. In theory, these should keep very well, but I have never been able to keep them around long enough to find out.

7 ounces unsweetened chocolate,
   finely chopped

3 ounces bittersweet chocolate, finely
   chopped

1 cup plus 2 tablespoons unsalted
   butter, in small pieces

4 large eggs, at room temperature

2⅓ cups granulated sugar

1½ teaspoons pure vanilla extract

1¼ cups all-purpose flour

3 tablespoons good-quality
   unsweetened Dutch-process
   cocoa

⅛ teaspoon salt

Additional unsalted butter, at room
   temperature, or vegetable oil
   cooking spray, for greasing pan

1. Preheat the oven to 350°. Grease a 9 x 13-inch baking pan, preferably alu- minum. Line the bottom and up two sides with a single sheet of parchment paper, letting the paper overhang the two long sides by an inch or so. Not only will this prevent any sticking, but it will also make removing the cooled brown- ies from the pan easy and neat.

2. Place a large pot filled with an inch or two of water over low heat and bring the water to a very gentle simmer. Combine the two chocolates and the diced butter in a stainless steel or glass bowl and set the bowl over the pot. Stir the chocolate occasionally until it is about ¾ melted, then turn off the heat under the pot and stir until the mixture is completely melted and smooth. Remove the bowl from the top of the pot and set it aside to cool slightly.

3. Meanwhile, in a large bowl, beat the eggs slightly just to blend the yolks and the whites. Whisk in the sugar and beat until the mixture is thickened and pale, about 2 minutes if beating by hand, 1 minute if using beaters or a stand mixer. Stir in the vanilla. In a small bowl, sift the flour, cocoa and salt together.

4. When the chocolate is just warm but not hot, pour it into the egg and sugar mixture, stirring to blend well. Sift the flour mixture over the batter in three additions, using a rubber spatula or a wooden spoon to gently fold in each addition before adding the next.

5. Scrape the batter into the pan and place it in the centre of the oven. Bake for approximately 35 minutes, or until a tester inserted in the centre of the brownies comes out with a few moist crumbs clinging to it, and the surface is set, shiny, and perhaps beginning to crack slightly at the edges. Transfer the pan to a wire rack and cool completely before cutting into bars. Don't overbake these brownies! A gooey, chewy texture is part of their allure. The whole cake can be lifted out of the pan onto a cutting surface using the overhang of parchment paper, or you can cut the bars right in the pan. A thin-bladed knife dipped in hot water and wiped dry between cuts makes cutting these sticky, gooey bars much easier! Makes enough for, oh, three or four chocoholics, or several more mere mortals. Store brownies well wrapped in plastic, at room temperature for gooier brownies, or in the refrigerator for denser, fudgier bars, for up to 5 days (they'll never last that long). I find keeping the leftover bars in the pan and covering the whole pan with wrap keeps the brownies fresh and soft.

Chocolate Crisps

50 TO 55 2½-INCH
ROUND CRISPS

These very simple, crisp, flat, delicate little wafers are perfect with *stuff: ice cream, puddings, fresh berries, custards. Also great with a cup of coffee! The cocoa should be as good as you can afford—Dutch brands such as Droste or Van Houtte, or others such as Valrhona are ideal. The variations that follow are just a couple of the infinite ways you can serve or use these biscuits; for a real treat, try the ice cream sandwiches!*

Chocolate Crisps continued

10 tablespoons unsalted butter,
   at room temperature
1 cup granulated sugar
1 large egg
1 teaspoon pure vanilla extract

1½ cups all-purpose flour
5 tablespoons unsweetened Dutch-
   process cocoa powder
½ teaspoon baking soda
⅛ teaspoon salt

1. In a medium bowl, or the bowl of an electric or stand mixer fitted with the paddle attachment, cream the butter and sugar together until pale and fluffy. Add the egg and beat until it is thoroughly mixed in, then beat in the vanilla.

2. Sift together the flour, cocoa powder, baking soda and salt. Add ½ of this mixture to the creamed mixture and stir until mostly incorporated. Add the remaining flour mixture and work it into the dough, using your hands in the final stage of mixing. Make sure there are no pockets of flour in the dough. Divide into 2 equal portions and place each on a piece of plastic wrap. Use the wrap to help form the portions into flat discs, then wrap each disc securely. Chill the dough for at least 4 hours, or up to 3 days. (The dough may be frozen at this point for up to 3 months. Use additional plastic wrap and an outer wrapping of aluminum foil. Defrost the dough in the refrigerator overnight before proceeding with the recipe.)

3. Preheat the oven to 350°. Line at least two baking sheets with parchment paper. Remove one portion of dough from the refrigerator and allow it to warm just enough to be soft enough to roll out. On a lightly floured surface, and using just enough dusting flour to keep the dough from sticking to the surface or the rolling pin, roll out the disc of dough to a thickness of ⅛ to ¼ inch. Brush any excess flour from the surface of the dough. Using a biscuit or cookie cutter dipped in flour (I use a plain, round 2½-inch cutter), cut as many cookies as possible from the dough. Transfer the cookies to the prepared sheets with a palette knife, spacing them 1½ to 2 inches apart. Place the filled baking sheets in the refrigerator for at least 10 minutes, or until the cookies are chilled and firm. Meanwhile, pat the scraps of dough together and re-roll; again cut as many cookies as possible and repeat this process if necessary. Chill the cookies from this portion while the first are baking.

4. Bake each sheet of cookies in the centre of the preheated oven for 13 to 15 minutes, or until the centres are firm and the edges are just barely beginning to darken. Cool 2 minutes, then transfer the cookies to wire racks and cool completely before storing. Repeat with the remaining sheets of cookies, chilling the hot baking sheets under cold running water and drying them between bakings. These simple biscuits are actually better once they have cooled and crisped. They store very well, in an airtight container, at room temperature, for up to 1 week. Try them sandwiched with ice cream!

VARIATIONS

Chocolate-Espresso Crisps: Add 1½ teaspoons espresso powder dissolved in 1 teaspoon hot water, cooled, to the creamed mixture with the vanilla.

Chocolate-Espresso Ice Cream Sandwiches: Layer 12 Chocolate or Chocolate-Espresso Crisps between sheets of parchment or waxed paper, wrap the whole batch in plastic wrap and freeze for 1 hour, or until the crisps are frozen solid. (This will help prevent them from snapping when sandwiched with ice cream. Remove the cookies from the freezer and place one scoop of slightly softened *Vanilla Bean* or *Roasted Cinnamon Ice Cream*, page 553, on the underside of 6 of the cookies. Top each scoop with another crisp, underside down, and press to spread the ice cream and secure the cookie. Roll the sides of the sandwiches in ¾ cup miniature dark chocolate chips, or ¾ cup finely chopped toasted hazelnuts, to coat the ice cream. Wrap each sandwich securely in plastic wrap and return to the freezer until served, up to 3 days. Makes 6 ice cream sandwiches.

Sugar Cookies
with Rock Sugar Borders

30 COOKIES

Beautiful and light, with sparking crystal sugar rimming a buttery finger, these cookies are more delicate and less rich than shortbread, making them a perfect accompaniment to other desserts, such as poached pears, chocolate mousse, fruit compotes and ice creams.

Sugar Cookies continued

1 cup unsalted butter, at room
  temperature
½ cup granulated sugar
2 cups all-purpose flour, sifted

2 large egg yolks, lightly beaten
½ cup raw or crystal sugar, clear
  or golden

1. In a medium-sized bowl with a wooden spoon, or with the paddle attach-ment of an electric mixer, cream the butter and sugar together until light and fluffy. Add the flour, using your hands after the first few stokes to gently knead it into the creamed mixture. Mix quickly but lightly, so as not to overwork the flour.

2. Divide the dough into 2 portions. For long rectangular "finger" cookies, form each portion into a smooth square, about 4½ x 4½ inches, and about 1 inch thick. For round cookies, form each portion into a cylinder and use a piece of plastic wrap to help you tighten the dough into a firm roll about 12 inches long and 1 to 1½ inches in diameter. Wrap the dough tightly in plastic wrap and refriger-ate for at least 2 hours, and up to 3 days. (The dough may be frozen at this stage, wrapped securely, for up to 4 months. Thaw it overnight in the refrigerator without removing the wrapping before proceeding with the recipe.)

3. To bake the cookies, preheat the oven to 350°. Line two heavy, not non-stick, baking sheets with parchment paper. Work with one portion of dough at a time, leaving the other in the refrigerator. Brush the first slab or cylinder of cold dough with the lightly beaten egg yolks, coating all sides, corners and crevices. Spread the raw sugar on a flat plate and press or roll the dough in the sugar to coat all of the surfaces. Use your hand to press sugar into any slight hollows; it should cover the dough in a single, even layer. Gently brush off any excess sugar. With a long, thin-bladed knife, slice the dough into ⅜-inch wide slices, then lay them ¾ inch apart on baking sheets. If slicing from a log, rotate the log every few slices to avoid flattening the roll on any one side.

4. Bake the cookies for 12 to 18 minutes, or until the bottoms are just barely be-ginning to colour and the sugar borders are turning just slightly golden. Cool the cookies on the baking sheets for 10 minutes before carefully transferring with a palette knife to wire racks to cool completely. Repeat with the remaining portion of dough. The cookies may be stored for up to 1 week, in an airtight container, at room temperature.

Bittersweet Chocolate and Chestnut Truffles

ABOUT 100 1-INCH TRUFFLES

These divine chocolates are really like the soft, melting insides of other truffles. They have an elusive mellow flavour, due to the addition of sweetened chestnut purée, and the intense richness of good bittersweet chocolate. Don't use a really bitter variety of chocolate, but one that is pleasing to eat, with just enough sweetness and a rich, roasted acidity. The recipe makes a large batch, but they disappear quickly. If you want, however, the recipe can be halved (or doubled!). A tip: I use a tiny, 1-inch ice cream scoop to portion the truffles. This makes quick, easy work of it and is far less messy than rolling them between your warm palms—you waste less of the mixture and are finished in a quarter of the time.

½ cup plus 2 tablespoons heavy cream (36%)

1 cup (11 ounces) sweetened chestnut purée with vanilla (also called crème de marrons)

14 ounces bittersweet chocolate, finely chopped

1½ tablespoons Cognac or Armagnac

¼ cup unsweetened Dutch-process cocoa

¼ cup confectioners' sugar

1. Combine the cream and chestnut purée in a heavy-bottomed saucepan and place over medium-low heat. Bring the mixture just to the boil, stirring slowly. When bubbles break the surface of the mixture, remove the pot from the heat. Place the chocolate in a medium bowl and pour the hot cream mixture over the chocolate. Stir with a wide-looped whisk or a wooden spoon until the chocolate is very smooth, and the cream and chestnut mixture is completely incorporated. Blend in the Cognac or Armagnac. Cover the bowl with plastic wrap, leaving a gap for the steam to escape, and refrigerate the truffle mixture until thoroughly chilled, preferably overnight.

2. Sift the cocoa powder and confectioners' sugar together several times until thoroughly blended, then spread the mixture on a large plate or platter. Have ready

Bittersweet Chocolate and Chestnut Truffles continued

a second platter or baking dish lined with parchment or waxed paper to set the truffles on before they are rolled. Finally, have several platters, baking dishes, baking sheets or boxes ready to hold the finished chocolates. (I find the little paper or foil confection cups that are available in kitchenware and specialty shops very handy when making truffles, as they allow you to move the truffles and store them with a minimum of handling and damage. They are inexpensive and come in very plain or seasonally decorated designs. If you are using these, separate them before you start working with the truffle mixture and your hands become covered with goo.)

3. Remove the chocolate mixture from the refrigerator and use a 1-inch ice cream scoop or melon baller to form small balls. Keep the truffles small; the temptation is always to get bigger and bigger, but these are powerfully rich sweets, and it is always better to want two than wish you'd only eaten half. Form about 30 truffles at a time, then put the rest of the chocolate mixture back in the refrigerator to cool. Gently roll each truffle in the cocoa-sugar mixture and set them in the paper liners or on a platter. Don't worry about getting the truffles perfectly round, or perfectly covered; irregularity is part of their beauty. Once the platter is full, refrigerate the finished truffles. Keep forming, rolling and chilling the truffles until the entire mixture is used. Store the truffles in the refrigerator for up to 4 or 5 days. Do keep them chilled—they will quickly become soft and messy if left at room temperature for more than a few minutes. These gorgeously rich little chocolates are perfect at the holidays, as part of a dessert buffet, a sophisticated end to an elegant dinner or as gifts.

Dried Fruit Sablées

5 DOZEN COOKIES

These are pretty and very delicate biscuits, similar to shortbread, and made extra tender by the addition of cake flour. They are a wonderfully versatile cookie; flavour the dough with whatever you wish: any manner of dried fruit, finely chopped toasted nuts, even sesame seeds or poppyseeds. The finished cookies are called sablées, meaning "sandy" in French, because they have a delicate, crumbly, indeed sandy texture. They are lovely with a glass of sweet wine and a few ripe fruits, or with some aged blue cheese. The dried fruit varieties are a perfect accompaniment to a bowl of Roasted Cinnamon Ice Cream, page 553. For the quintessential tea cookie, bake them plain!

1¾ cups all-purpose flour
½ cup cake flour, not self-rising, sifted
⅛ teaspoon salt
½ cup granulated sugar
14 tablespoons unsalted butter, at room temperature
2 large egg yolks, lightly beaten
1 teaspoon vanilla extract

½ cup finely chopped dried fruit, such as pears, peaches, apricots, cherries, blueberries, currants, Muscat raisins, figs, Medjool dates, candied orange zest, cranberries, or any combination of the above

1 large egg, lightly beaten with 1 tablespoon water, for glaze
2 tablespoons granulated sugar

1. Into the bowl of a food processor, or a medium bowl, sift together the two flours and the salt. Add the sugar and whir or stir to blend. Add the butter, three or four tablespoons at a time, mixing just enough to coat the pieces of butter in flour. When all the butter has been added, cut it into the mixture with short pulses of the machine, or a pastry blender if mixing by hand. Add the lightly beaten egg yolks and vanilla and mix to moisten.

2. If you are using a food processor, turn the dough into a mixing bowl at this point. Use your hands to scrunch the dough together, kneading with your fingers, breaking up the dough and smushing it back together. This sounds like a vague and ungraceful process, but it serves to smear the butter throughout the dough, distributing it evenly and making sure there are no pockets of flour or egg yolk. The French term for it, *fraisage*, sounds much more dignified. The dough should be smooth and moist, but not too sticky. At this point, you can either add the desired fruit or other flavouring to the whole dough or divide the dough into two or more portions and flavour each one differently. If you choose the latter option, divide the dough and knead in 2 tablespoons of finely chopped dried fruit for each quarter of the dough. If working with the whole dough, add the entire ½ cup of chopped dried fruit and work this into the dough, then divide the dough into 2 portions for easier chilling, slicing and

Dried Fruit Sablées continued

baking. Place each portion of dough on a piece of plastic wrap and use the wrap to help you form the dough into a log, about 1½ inches in diameter. Twist the ends of the wrap to secure the roll and flatten the ends to form a tight cylinder. Refrigerate the logs at least 2 hours, or up to 3 days. (At this point, the logs of dough may be wrapped in additional plastic or aluminum foil and frozen for up to 3 months. Defrost the logs overnight in the refrigerator before proceeding with the recipe.)

3. Preheat the oven to 350°. Line two baking sheets with parchment paper. Remove one log of dough at a time from the refrigerator and place it on a cutting board. With a thin-bladed knife, slice the log into ¼-inch rounds using long strokes with little downward pressure, letting the sawing action of the knife do the work. Carefully transfer the rounds to the baking sheets, spacing them 1½ to 2 inches apart. Place the filled sheets in the refrigerator for 5 to 10 minutes to firm up the dough. Before placing them in the centre of the oven, brush a little of the egg mixture onto each of the rounds, then sprinkle with sugar.

4. Bake the sablées for 15 to 18 minutes, or until the tops are firm and the edges are lightly golden. Cool on the sheets for 30 seconds, then transfer to wire racks to cool completely. Repeat with the remaining logs. Store the cooled cookies in airtight containers for up to 4 days. These sablées are delicious tea cookies, but also make an elegant addition to many other desserts, such as poached or baked fruit, ice creams, sabayons and fresh fruit compotes.

Maple-Pecan Buttons

4½ DOZEN COOKIES

Some of my favourite things about the holidays are the little pecan or walnut snowball cookies, also called Russian Tea Cakes or Mexican Wedding cookies, that my mother still makes every year. These little rounds are just as tender, but even richer and more satisfying. (Even my mum says so!) The pecan and maple blend to give a much deeper, rounder flavour; the high ratio of butter and nuts to flour gives a meltingly tender texture.

1 cup unsalted butter, at room
   temperature

½ cup plus 1½ cups confectioners'
   sugar

1½ cups finely ground fresh pecans

3 tablespoons pure maple syrup,
   grade B or C

1 teaspoon pure vanilla extract

¼ teaspoon salt

2 cups all-purpose flour, sifted

1. In the bowl of an electric or stand mixer fitted with the paddle attachment, or in a large bowl with a wooden spoon, cream the butter until fluffy. Sift ½ cup confectioners' sugar over the butter and cream until light and fluffy, about 1 minute. Add the ground nuts, maple syrup and vanilla and stir until well blended. Add the salt and the flour, 1 cup at a time, stirring until thoroughly mixed. Use your hands to work in the last quantity of flour, scrunching the dough to make sure there are no pockets of flour or butter left undistributed. Scrape the dough together, wrap in plastic and chill at least 2 hours, or up to 4 days. (The dough may be frozen at this point, wrapped well in plastic and aluminum foil. Thaw the frozen dough overnight in the refrigerator before proceeding with the recipe.)

2. Preheat the oven to 325°. Line two heavy, not non-stick, baking sheets with parchment paper. Remove the dough from the refrigerator. Pinch off small pieces of dough and roll them into 1-inch balls. Place the balls 1 to 1½ inches apart on the baking sheets and pop the filled sheets into the refrigerator for 5 minutes to firm up the dough. Bake the cookies, one sheet at a time, on the centre rack of the oven for 18 to 20 minutes, or until the tops are just firm and the undersides of the balls are pale golden. Set the baking sheets on a wire rack and cool for 3 minutes.

3. Meanwhile, sift the remaining 1½ cups confectioners' sugar onto a large plate. Roll the warm cookies in the sugar, coating them well, and transfer them to a wire rack set over a tray or sheet of parchment to catch any stray sugar; cool completely. Roll the cooled balls in the confectioners' sugar once more before storing or serving. This double sugaring ensures a proper, velvety-sweet coating on the cookies. These cookies keep well in an airtight container at room temperature for up to 3 days. They can be kept longer, but are at their best within a few days of baking.

Pine Nut Lace Cookies

24 3-INCH COOKIES

These delicate cookies are really easy, but a little time consuming because only a few of them can be baked at a time. I love serving them as an accompaniment to fruit desserts, mousses and puddings, and especially ice creams, for an elegant touch. They are infinitely variable, limited only by your imagination.

3 tablespoons dark corn syrup
6 tablespoons unsalted butter
9 tablespoons tightly packed light
    brown sugar

¼ cup plus 2 tablespoons all-purpose
    flour
¼ teaspoon salt
¾ cup fresh raw pine nuts

1. Preheat the oven to 350°. Line at least two heavy, not non-stick, baking sheets with parchment paper. (Alternatively, the sheets can be lightly buttered, but the parchment paper makes removing the fragile cookies clean and easy.) In a small saucepan, combine the corn syrup, butter and brown sugar. Stir over low heat until butter has melted, then remove the mixture from the heat. Sift the flour and salt together into a medium-sized bowl. Pour the warm syrup mixture into the flour and mix well with a wooden spoon or small whisk.

2. Using a teaspoon dipped in vegetable oil, drop small spoonfuls of the batter onto the prepared trays, allowing plenty of room for spreading. Start with no more than 5 puddles of batter per baking sheet; if you are making them small enough, you may be able to fit 6 or 7 on the next sheet. Bake only one sheet at a time (or two side by side, if you have a large and very evenly heated oven) and set the sheet on the centre rack of the oven. After 2 minutes, when the cookies have begun to spread out, remove the tray from the oven and sprinkle each cookie with a small handful of pine nuts, then return the tray to the oven. Bake until the cookies are lacy, bubbling and golden brown, another 3 to 5 minutes. Cool the cookies on the tray for 1 minute before carefully transferring them to a wire rack. At this point, the hot cookies may be draped over an inverted tea cup to make a bowl or *coupe* shape, or curled around the handle of a wooden spoon, or even scrunched freehand into fanciful shapes. They are very flexible while warm, and will become brittle as they cool. Of course, you can also leave them flat and lovely! Cool completely before serving or storing. These lace cookies are best if eaten within a day of baking—they tend to absorb a lot of moisture from the air and get chewy and sticky, losing their delicate crispness. Store them layered between sheets of parchment or waxed paper, in an airtight container, at room temperature.

❦ VARIATIONS ❦

Orange Lace Cookies: Omit the pine nuts. Add 2 tablespoons finely grated orange zest to the butter-brown sugar-corn syrup mixture.

Ginger Lace Cookies: Omit the pine nuts. Add ¼ cup finely chopped candied ginger in syrup to the butter mixture before melting it and replace ½ tablespoon of the corn syrup with ½ tablespoon of the ginger syrup.

Sesame Lace Cookies: Omit the pine nuts. Add 3 to 4 tablespoons of raw white sesame seeds to the cookies after the first 4 minutes of baking. The sesame seeds should be added a minute or two later than the pine nuts would have been, because they cook much faster and could burn if baked too long.

Pistachio, Pecan or Dried Cranberry Lace Cookies: Replace the pine nuts with an equal amount of chopped, shelled pistachios or pecans, or with coarsely chopped dried cranberries.

Pistachio-Cranberry Florentines with White Chocolate and Orange

20 LARGE OR 35 SMALL
FLORENTINES

As beautiful as stained glass, and chewy, tart, sweet and rich. These perfect little petits fours are lovely served with coffee after dessert and also make exquisite holiday gifts.

Pistachio-Cranberry Florentines continued

3 tablespoons unsalted butter
¾ cup granulated sugar
½ cup heavy cream (36%)
1½ tablespoons flavourful honey, such
    as wildflower or orange blossom
    (not buckwheat)
½ cup all-purpose flour, sifted
⅔ cup plump dried cranberries,
    coarsely chopped
1 cup unsalted shelled pistachios,
    skins removed (see page 266 for
    tips on skinning pistachios) and
    coarsely chopped

½ cup whole unblanched almonds,
    lightly toasted in a 350° oven for
    5 minutes, then coarsely chopped
3 scant tablespoons finely chopped
    candied orange peel, homemade
    (see page 634), or good-quality
    purchased
Finely grated zest of ½ large orange
1 teaspoon Kirsch, optional, but
    recommended
4 ounces good-quality white chocolate,
    finely chopped

1. Preheat the oven to 350°. Line at least two, or up to four, baking sheets with parchment paper and set aside. In a heavy-bottomed, medium-sized saucepan, combine the butter, sugar, cream and honey. Stir over low heat until sugar is dissolved, then increase the heat to medium and bring the mixture to a boil. Stir at the boil for about 30 seconds, then take the pot off the heat and add the flour, sifting it over the sugar mixture. Whisk vigorously until the mixture is smooth. Return the pan to the heat and add the cranberries, chopped nuts, candied peel, grated orange zest and Kirsch, if desired, and stir just until everything is well coated; remove the pan from the heat.

2. Spoon the batter onto the baking sheets in heaping teaspoonfuls, spacing the mounds at least 3 inches apart. Use the back of a spoon dipped in water to flatten the mounds slightly. Bake the cookies, one sheet at a time, in the centre of the oven. After 5 minutes, rotate the sheet and bake another 5 minutes or until the edges of the florentines are golden, bubbling and lacy. Transfer the sheet to a rack and cool 10 minutes, then slide the parchment off the sheet directly onto the rack and cool the cookies completely. Repeat the process until all the batter is baked, and the cookies are cool.

3. Loosen the cookies from the paper and, for convenience, place them close together on fewer baking sheets. There are two ways to melt white chocolate. The easiest is in the microwave, on medium-high power for 1 to 2 minutes, stirring every 30 seconds. The second and more elaborate way is on the stove. Fill a medium-sized saucepan with one or two inches of water and bring to a boil. Place the finely chopped white chocolate in a stainless steel or thin glass bowl wide enough to fit comfortably over the top of the pot and for the chocolate to sit in a single thin layer in the bottom of the bowl. White chocolate has a very low melting point and if melted too quickly or over too high a heat can end up lumpy or grainy. To avoid this, turn the heat under the pot of water off completely before placing the bowl over it. Let the chocolate soften over the residual heat for 3 minutes, then give it a stir. Wait another minute, then stir again, repeating this process until the chocolate is melted, smooth and glossy.

4. Remove the bowl from the heat, taking care that no moisture or steam comes into contact with the chocolate, and spoon it into a pastry bag fitted with a small plain tip. If you don't have a pastry bag, scrape the chocolate into a small plastic sandwich bag, close the top and snip off a small corner, making a spout for the chocolate. Proceed as though you were using a real pastry bag. Drizzle the warm chocolate over the florentines in wavy lines, or squiggles or whatever design makes you happy. Let the chocolate firm up, either for a few hours at room temperature, or by popping the cookies into the refrigerator for 5 minutes or so. Don't leave the cookies in the refrigerator for long, though, or they'll become sticky and limp. Florentines are best eaten the same day they are baked, but may be stored for several days, layered between sheets of parchment paper in an airtight container, at room temperature.

The Ultimate Soft and Chewy Chocolate Chunk Cookies

35 LARGE COOKIES

Crisp and crunchy have their place in the world of biscuits, but not, I believe, in the best and simplest chocolate chip cookie. If you like chewy, cakey and full to the brim with chocolate, these are for you.

The Ultimate Soft and Chewy Chocolate Chunk Cookies continued

1 cup unsalted butter, at room
   temperature

1 cup tightly packed light brown sugar

½ cup granulated sugar

2 large eggs

1½ teaspoons pure vanilla extract

3 cups plus 2 tablespoons all-purpose
   flour

1 teaspoon baking soda

½ teaspoon salt

16 ounces flavourful bittersweet or semisweet chocolate, coarsely chopped

1. Preheat the oven to 350°. Line two heavy, not non-stick, baking sheets with parchment paper, or lightly butter them, and set them aside. In the bowl of an electric or stand mixer fitted with the paddle attachment, or a large bowl if mixing by hand, cream the butter and both sugars until light and fluffy. Add the eggs, one at a time, beating well and scraping down the sides of the bowl after each addition. Beat in the vanilla.

2. Sift the flour, baking soda and salt together into a small bowl. Add the dry ingredients to the butter-sugar mixture, mixing until just combined. Fold in the chocolate chunks.

3. Using your hands, shape knobs of dough about the size of a large walnut into balls and place them 2 inches apart on the baking sheets. Stagger the rows of cookies to ensure even baking. Bake 12 to 15 minutes for smaller cookies, 14 to 17 minutes for larger cookies, or until the tops are light golden brown. If the cookies are neither firm nor dark when they are removed from the oven, they will cool chewy and soft. Cool the cookies on the sheets for 5 minutes, then transfer to wire racks to cool completely. If, somehow, these don't all get inhaled immediately, they may be stored airtight at room temperature for up to 1 week.

Chocolate Fudge Cookies with Toffee and Dried Cherries

40 LARGE COOKIES

Crisp on the outside, soft and chewy in the middle and downright gooey if you get to them still warm. These cookies are great for picnics and crowds, and the dough can be frozen until you need it. The contrasting flavours and textures:

rich, dark chocolate; sweet, crunchy toffee; and chewy, tangy sour cherries, make these totally addictive—and a step up from the average chocolate cookie. Make sure the cherries are plump and soft, not dry and hard. I like to make these pretty much fist-sized, but you can make them smaller if you wish. (Don't fool yourself; it just means you'll eat more of them.) Adjust the baking time accordingly if you reduce the size of the cookies.

2¼ cups all-purpose flour

½ cup unsweetened Dutch-process cocoa powder

1 teaspoon baking soda

¼ teaspoon salt

1 cup unsalted butter, at room temperature

1 cup tightly packed dark brown sugar

¾ cup granulated sugar

2 large eggs

1½ teaspoons pure vanilla extract

1 cup plump, moist, dried sour cherries

8 ounces bittersweet or semisweet chocolate, chopped into chunks about the size of the cherries

1 cup English toffee pieces for baking, such as Skor Bits

1. Preheat the oven to 350°. Line two heavy baking sheets, not non-stick, with parchment paper and set aside. Sift the flour, cocoa, baking soda and salt together into a bowl and set aside. In a large mixing bowl, or the bowl of an electric or stand mixer fitted with the paddle attachment, cream together the butter and both sugars until light in colour and fluffy, about 3 minutes. Add the eggs, one at a time, beating well after each addition and scraping down the sides of the bowl. Beat in the vanilla. Stir in the flour-mixture in three additions, blending just until the dry ingredients are moistened. I find this part of the job easier with a wooden spoon, rather than the mixer, as I can see better which parts of the batter need more attention without overmixing. Stir in the chunky ingredients and mix until they seem evenly distributed. (The dough may be frozen at this point for up to 4 months: wrap the dough securely in plastic wrap, then in a plastic freezer bag. Thaw the dough in the refrigerator without removing its wrapping before portioning the cookies and baking.)

2. Drop the batter by heaping tablespoons onto the prepared baking sheets and place them in the centre of the oven. If you have a large and evenly tempered oven, place the two sheets in at once, on two racks positioned close to the middle of the oven. Switch the position of the trays once during baking. If your

Chocolate Fudge Cookies continued

oven is small, or tends to have hot and cold spots, bake one tray at a time so the cookies will bake evenly.

3. Bake the cookies for 15 to 18 minutes, or until barely set in the centre and just firm around the edges. Rotate the sheets once or twice. Cool the cookies on the tray for 3 to 5 minutes, then transfer to a wire rack to cool completely before storing. (Feel free to eat them at any point.) Run the hot tray under cold water to cool it, dry thoroughly and repeat with the remaining dough. Store the cookies in airtight containers, layered between sheets of parchment or waxed paper, for up to 5 days.

 VARIATION

Chocolate Fudge Brownies with Toffee and Dried Cherries

1. Preheat the oven to 350°. Grease a 9 x 13-inch baking dish and line the bottom and up the two long sides with a sheet of parchment paper, letting it hang over the two long sides by an inch or so. Follow the same recipe as above, substituting an equal amount of cake-and-pastry flour (not self-rising) for the all-purpose flour. (This dough may be frozen and thawed in the same fashion as the cookie dough above.)

2. Spread the finished batter evenly into the pan and bake in the centre of the oven for 50 to 60 minutes, or until the top is shiny and a wooden skewer inserted about 2 inches away from the centre of the brownies comes out with crumbs clinging to it. (Test in another spot if your skewer happens to hit a chocolate chunk.)

3. Cool the brownies completely in the pan set on a wire rack. Run a thin-bladed knife around the edges of the pan and use the overhang of paper to lift the whole cake out. Cut into squares and serve or store in an airtight container up to 5 days. Makes 20 to 24 brownies.

Honey and Spice Madeleines

24 LARGE OR 36 TO 48 SMALL
MADELEINES

Madeleines are really more like a delicate sponge cake than a cookie. They are traditionally flavoured with browned butter or left quite plain, but they are lovely dressed up with the gentle flavours of honey and just the right amount of sweet spice. Perfect with tea and lemon, and a selection of other not-too-sweet treats. For best results, don't use anything but melted butter and flour to prepare the moulds and watch the temperature of the oven. Make sure the honey you choose is not only fine- and full-flavoured, but also unpasteurized, as pasteurized honey will leave a slight chemical aftertaste.

2 large eggs
⅓ cup flavourful unpasteurized honey, such as lavender, wild flower or berry honey, but not buckwheat
¼ cup granulated sugar
½ teaspoon pure vanilla extract
1 cup all-purpose flour
½ teaspoon baking powder
⅛ teaspoon salt
½ teaspoon ground cinnamon
½ teaspoon freshly grated nutmeg
⅛ teaspoon ground allspice, preferably freshly ground

Scant ⅛ teaspoon ground white pepper
¾ cup unsalted butter, melted and cooled

Additional unsalted butter, melted and cooled, for brushing moulds
Additional all-purpose flour, for dusting moulds
Sifted confectioners' sugar, for dusting the finished madeleines

1. In a large bowl, break the eggs up slightly with a whisk. Add the honey and sugar, then place the bowl over a pan of simmering water. Whisk until the mixture is just warm to the touch, then remove the bowl from the heat. Using electric beaters, beat the mixture on high speed until it has tripled in volume and a thick ribbon falls from the beaters and rests on the surface of the batter for several seconds when the beaters are lifted. This should take about 10 minutes. Beat in the vanilla.

Honey and Spice Madeleines continued

2. Sift the flour, baking powder, salt and spices into a small bowl, then sift this mixture over the egg batter in three additions, folding each addition in gently before adding the next. Use long, light strokes and as few as possible to avoid deflating the egg mixture too much. Finally, fold in the cool melted butter. The batter should now be glossy, light, smooth and homogeneous. Cover the bowl with plastic wrap and allow it to rest at room temperature for 30 minutes. This resting will relax any gluten that may have developed and make the madeleines very tender and delicate.

3. Preheat the oven to 425°. Brush two trays of 12 madeleine moulds each with the additional melted butter, thoroughly coating all the little grooves. Sift enough all-purpose flour over the moulds to cover them well, then invert the trays over the sink or a garbage bin and tap hard several times to shake out any excess. All areas of the moulds must be completely coated to ensure the cakes will unmould neatly. Gently spoon the batter into the moulds, filling them ¾ or slightly more full.

4. Bake in the centre of the oven for 8 to 10 minutes (4 to 6 minutes if you are using small madeleine moulds). Immediately invert the pans over a wire cooling rack, being careful not to let the trays drop and crush the delicate cakes. Use a small palette knife or butter knife to pry any stubborn madeleines out of their shells. Dust the madeleines with confectioners' sugar and cool them shell-side up on the racks. Serve the cakes slightly warm or let them cool completely. These cakes are most moist and tender on the day they are baked, but may be kept for 2 or 3 days, in an airtight container, at room temperature.

Macadamia Nut Biscotti

ABOUT 55 BISCOTTI

The best biscotti are crisp, brittle and not too sweet. They should resist for just a moment as your teeth first bite down, then delicately shatter. They must be sturdy enough to survive a dunk in an espresso or a glass of Vin Santo, but not be rock-hard or overbaked. Traditional biscotti rarely contain butter or oil, but get all of their moisture from eggs and egg yolks, and often wine or spirits. Being so lean, they bear little resemblance to most North American-style cookies, not to mention the host of so-called biscotti so popular today in cafés. These are usually nothing more than a regular, butter-rich cookie dough, baked in a log, sliced and baked again until dry. They lack the brilliant texture of the real thing (and often completely melt into your latte if you happen to dunk!). Many biscotti recipes in Italy traditionally called for ammonium bicarbonate as the primary leavener, as it produces a more brittle, fragile cookie than either baking powder or baking soda. I have developed this recipe using it, but if you cannot find it, feel free to substitute baking soda. Biscotti are not dessert cookies the way a brownie or a meringue is, but are by their very nature an accompaniment: to a coffee, a liqueur, a sweet wine, even a few scoops of sorbet, ice cream or a granita. These simple biscotti, quite untraditionally flavoured with tropical macadamia nuts, are a fantastic partner to Lychee and Coconut Milk Sorbet, page 558, Vanilla Bean Ice Cream, page 553, or Pears Poached in Gewürztraminer with Tahitian Vanilla and Ginger, page 574.

3⅓ cups all-purpose flour

2¼ cups granulated sugar

1 teaspoon ammonium bicarbonate (see page 197) or substitute ½ teaspoon baking soda

2 teaspoons baking powder

⅛ teaspoon salt

2 to 3 large eggs

3 large egg yolks

Seeds of 1 vanilla bean, hull reserved for another use

8 ounces raw unsalted macadamia nuts, very coarsely chopped

1. Preheat the oven to 300°. In a large bowl, combine the flour, sugar, ammonium bicarbonate or baking soda, baking powder and salt. In a separate bowl, lightly beat together 2 of the whole eggs, 3 yolks and the vanilla seeds. Make a well in the flour mixture and pour in the egg mixture. Use your hand in a stirring motion to mix the wet and dry ingredients. When you no longer see rivers of egg, rub the mixture between your fingertips to moisten the flour evenly, scrunching the dough together, then crumbling it. If the mixture does not hold together when squeezed, lightly beat the remaining egg and add it a tablespoon at a time until the dough just holds together when tightly packed. This dough should feel dry and crumbly, but must be evenly moistened enough to keep its shape. Add the macadamia nuts and toss to distribute them evenly.

Macadamia Nut Biscotti continued

2. Line a heavy, not non-stick, baking sheet with parchment paper. Divide the crumbly dough into 2 relatively equal portions. Press each portion into a long log (about 2 to 2½ inches wide), packing very tightly and slightly flattening the top. Squeeze the logs very firmly, making sure there are no weak or loose areas; the biscotti will keep their shape better the more densely the logs are packed and will have a crisper more brittle texture. Too much air in the logs will cause them to spread, making them very difficult to slice without shattering.

3. Bake 1 hour to 1 hour 20 minutes, or until the logs are completely dried and feel firm when gently pressed in the centre. Transfer the logs to a wire rack and allow them to cool for 10 minutes. Line a second baking sheet with parchment paper and turn the oven down to 275°. Place one log on a cutting board. Using a serrated knife and a long, gentle sawing motion, cut the log on a slight diagonal into ¾-inch slices. Don't push down on the knife to get through the log; let the sawing motion of the knife do the work. Lay the slices on the baking sheet and repeat with the other log. You can eat (or discard) the hard ends of the logs.

4. Return the baking sheets to the oven for 10 to 15 minutes, turning the cookies over after 7 minutes. The biscotti are done when they feel dry and almost completely firm to the touch, but not browned. A shorter second bake will produce a slightly more tender cookie, good for eating with ices or on its own; a longer second bake will yield a more brittle, sturdier biscotti, perfect to dunk in a cappuccino or a late-night glass of sweet wine. Biscotti are rumoured to be a wonderful keeping cookie, able to last for weeks if stored in an airtight container at room temperature. I wouldn't know.

Double Chocolate Hazelnut Biscotti

30 TO 35 BISCOTTI

Very chocolatey, with a lovely rich taste of hazelnuts and almost imperceptibly laced with espresso, these biscotti are rich in flavour, but still light and very crisp. Chocolate, hazelnuts and espresso: one of the holy trinities of pastry! The biscotti can be made more or less brittle depending on how long they are left in the oven during the second baking. Theoretically, they keep for weeks, but this is a moot point unless they are in an empty house, or one full of toothless people.

¾ cup lightly toasted, skinned hazelnuts (see page 262 for tips on toasting and skinning hazelnuts)

2 cups all-purpose flour

1 teaspoon baking soda

⅛ teaspoon salt

¼ teaspoon ground cinnamon

1 cup granulated sugar

1 tablespoon good-quality instant espresso powder, such as Medaglia d'Oro

⅓ cup unsweetened Dutch-process cocoa powder

5 ounces bittersweet chocolate, finely chopped

2 large eggs

2 large egg yolks

1 teaspoon pure vanilla extract

2 tablespoons Frangelico (hazelnut-flavoured liqueur)

1. Preheat the oven to 300°. Line two heavy, not non-stick, baking sheets with parchment paper. Run a knife through the hazelnuts just to chop them roughly; half nuts or pieces of about that size are perfect. Set the nuts aside. Into a large bowl, sift the flour, baking soda, salt and cinnamon. Add ½ cup of the sugar and stir these ingredients together well to blend them.

2. Combine the espresso powder, cocoa and chopped chocolate in the bowl of a food processor together with the remaining ½ cup sugar. Pulse quickly until the mixture is mostly ground, with just a few bits of chocolate remaining, and set aside. Lightly beat the eggs and egg yolks together in a small bowl, then beat in vanilla and Frangelico. Pour this mixture into the flour mixture all at once. With clean hands, reach into the bowl, bringing your fingers down the outside edges of the mixture, then up towards you, using a crumbling motion to knead the ingredients together. Do this until the mixture begins to come together, then add the chocolate mixture. Keep mixing lightly and quickly until the dough becomes evenly moist and sticky. Add the hazelnuts and continue to mix until they are scattered throughout the dough, and there is no flour or loose sugar remaining at the bottom of the bowl when the dough is lifted up.

3. Clean off your sticky hands, then build two rectangular logs of the biscotti dough on one single baking sheet, leaving about 3 inches between them. Each log should be about 2½ inches wide and ¾ to 1 inch high, with straight sides and ends and a flat top. Make sure you press the dough so that it is as compact as possible, or the air trapped in the dough will cause the logs to expand too

Double Chocolate Hazelnut Biscotti continued

much during baking and the biscotti will lose their neat shape. Use as much force as is necessary to make tight, very firm logs! The rectangular shape ensures that the logs will bake evenly. Place the baking sheet on the centre rack of the oven and bake for 1 hour to 1 hour and 15 minutes, or until the logs are firm when pressed in the centre and on any cracks. Turn the baking sheet several times during the baking so the logs bake evenly. Transfer the logs to a wire rack and cool 15 minutes. Reduce the oven temperature to 275°.

4. Secure a large cutting board by placing a damp kitchen towel or paper towel underneath it. Using a long-bladed serrated knife, slice the first log on a diagonal into ½-inch wide slices. I find using long strokes and a sawing motion works best, letting the sawing motion do the work of biting through the cookie, rather than using any downward pressure that could break and chip the logs. Lay the slices on the baking sheet and repeat with the second log, using the second lined baking sheet. Return the sheets to the oven and bake for 20 to 30 minutes, flipping the biscotti halfway through. The finished cookies should feel dry and hard to the touch. A longer second bake will produce very traditional, crisp dry biscotti, while a shorter time will yield a slightly more tender cookie. If you like to dunk, err on the longer side! Store in an airtight container at room temperature.

❧ VARIATIONS ❧

Chocolate and Sun-Dried Cherry Biscotti: Omit the espresso powder and add 1 teaspoon finely grated orange zest to the egg and egg yolk mixture. Substitute 1 cup plump, coarsely chopped sun-dried cherries for the hazelnuts and substitute Kirsch or another cherry-flavoured liqueur for the Frangelico.

Chocolate Almond Biscotti: Replace the hazelnuts with lightly toasted blanched almonds that have been very coarsely chopped and substitute Amaretto for the Frangelico.

Chocolate Espresso Biscotti: Increase the espresso powder to 1½ tablespoons and use whichever type of nut you prefer. Substitute a coffee-flavoured liqueur such as Tia Maria or Kahlúa for the Frangelico.

Pine Nut, Polenta and Currant Biscotti with Red Wine

ABOUT 35 TO 40 BISCOTTI

Subtle, mature flavours and a delicate, crisp not-too-sweet biscuit. An adult cookie that shows a true marriage of flavours: none sticks out, but all intertwine to support each other and create a totally elusive and addictive taste. The dough for these biscotti is much stickier than most, but bakes tender and less brittle, making the cookies perfect for optional dunking! I love these with a glass of red wine and a selection of fruits, cheeses and nuts at the end of a rustic Italian meal.

1 cup plus 3 tablespoons all-purpose flour

1½ teaspoons baking powder

¼ teaspoon salt

½ cup yellow cornmeal, preferably stone-ground

¾ cup granulated sugar

3 large eggs

3 tablespoons dry red wine

⅔ cup fresh raw pine nuts

⅓ cup currants

1. Preheat the oven to 300°. Line a heavy, not non-stick, baking sheet with parchment paper and set it aside. Sift the flour, baking powder and salt together into a large bowl, and stir in the cornmeal and sugar. In a separate bowl, lightly beat the eggs and add them to the dry ingredients. Add the red wine, then use your hands to work the liquid into the flour mixture, adding the nuts and currants after about 20 seconds of mixing. Gently toss and knead until a shaggy, sticky dough is formed. And this dough *will* be sticky!

2. Wash your hands and divide the dough into two roughly equal portions. Form each portion into a tightly packed log, about 2½ by 8 or 10 inches, spaced about 3 inches apart on the baking sheet. Bake the logs for 60 to 75 minutes, or until dry and firm when pressed in the centre. Transfer the logs to a wire rack and cool for 10 minutes. Reduce the oven temperature to 275°.

3. Line a second baking sheet with parchment paper. Using a serrated knife in a long sawing motion, slice one log into ⅓- or ½-inch slices on the diagonal,

Pine Nut, Polenta and Currant Biscotti continued

letting the action of the knife do the cutting work. If you press down on the log, the crust may shatter, and the slices may crumble as they are cut. Eat the two end pieces (or you could, I suppose, discard them) and lay the slices on the baking sheet. Repeat with the remaining log.

4. Return the sheets to the oven for about 25 minutes, or until almost totally dry and firm. Flip the slices once during this time so both sides dry evenly. Cool the biscotti completely on wire racks. Biscotti keep beautifully, stored in an air-tight container, for up to several weeks. Serve with a glass of red wine or espresso, or a bowl of ice cream.

Scottish Shortbread in Three Variations

1 VERY LARGE OR
3 MEDIUM-SIZED BATCHES

A truly great shortbread: crisp, buttery and full of flavour. The ingredients are few, but quality and freshness are imperative. Buy the best unsalted butter, fresh, not previously frozen. Make sure your flour is also fresh—and don't forget the pinch of salt. When I bake this shortbread for holiday gifts, I usually divide the dough in three equal portions. The variations below flavour ⅓ of the dough each, so you can create three types of shortbread from a single recipe: a rich plain butter type, one with dark chocolate and espresso, and a subtle and delicate white chocolate and ginger version. Using rice flour to replace part of the all-purpose flour is an old Scottish trick that yields a very tender crumb. Fruit sugar dissolves very quickly, but caster sugar can be substituted. Both rice flour and fruit sugar can be purchased in health and natural food stores.

3 cups all-purpose flour

1 cup rice flour, or substitute cornstarch if rice flour is unavailable

1 teaspoon salt

2 cups (1 pound) good-quality,
   fresh unsalted butter, at room
   temperature, but not overly soft

1 cup fruit sugar, or substitute
   superfine sugar

1. Preheat the oven to 325°. Line at least two baking sheets with parchment paper and set aside. (Alternative baking moulds and pans are discussed in Steps 3 to 5 below.) Have ready any flavourings (see below) that you plan to add to the dough. Sift the all-purpose and rice flours together with the salt and set aside. In the bowl of a stand mixer fitted with the paddle attachment, or by hand with a wooden spoon, beat the butter until creamy. Gradually add the sugar— and cream the mixture until very light and fluffy.

2. Add the flour mixture to the creamed butter and sugar in four or five additions, creaming thoroughly between each one. I prefer to work in the dry ingredients by hand, in a bowl large enough that I can use both hands to knead in the last bit of flour. Work the final addition in by hand, squeezing the dough between your fingers. Try to keep your palms off the dough as much as possible so the heat from your hands doesn't melt the butter and cause the dough to become oily. For plain shortbread, knead the dough for 30 seconds after the last of the flour has been incorporated. For flavoured shortbread, divide the dough into three roughly equal parts and place each one in a separate bowl. Cover the portions of dough you are not working with a piece of plastic wrap to prevent them from drying out. Work the flavouring ingredients into the dough as per the recipes below.

3. There are several options for baking shortbread dough. Traditional Scottish shortbread is baked one of three ways: in round ceramic moulds, often marked with a thistle or floral design; in a square or rectangular pan, to be cut into fingers as soon as it comes out of the oven; and simply cut into biscuit shapes with decorative cutters. For the first two methods, chilling the mixed dough, plain or otherwise, is not necessary.

4. For Moulded Shortbread: if you have a ceramic shortbread mould, the dough can be pressed directly into the form and baked. I have a lovely 8-inch clay thistle mould that is a standard size and conveniently accommodates ⅓ of the full recipe above. (Moulds like this are widely available in specialty kitchenware and gourmet shops.) Prick the dough all over with a fork and bake for about 30 to 35 minutes, or until pale golden. Cool for 5 minutes, then invert the form onto a wooden board. Mark the divisions with a sharp knife to facilitate

Scottish Shortbread continued

separating the pieces once the bread has cooled and set. If you have a wooden mould, the dough will need to be pressed into the mould, chilled for ½ hour, carefully turned out and then baked. Mark the dough as for the round above.

5. For Shortbread Fingers: use an 8-inch-square baking pan lined with an overhang of parchment paper on two sides and press the dough evenly into the bottom. Prick the dough all over with a fork and bake for 30 to 35 minutes, or until the top is pale golden. This size pan will hold ⅓ of the total recipe above.

6. For Cut-Out Cookies: the dough will have to be chilled until it is cool enough to roll, about 20 to 30 minutes. The high butter content of this dough means it firms quite quickly; keep an eye on it so it doesn't become too cold to roll. Wrap the mixed dough portions in plastic wrap and flatten each one into a disc. Chill, then roll out on a very lightly floured surface to a thickness of about ¼ inch. Cut shapes from the flat of dough using sharp cookie cutters. I like simple shapes like plain or fluted circles of about 2 to 2 ½ inches in diameter, making each cookie a satisfying but not too decadent morsel. Transfer the shapes to the lined baking sheets and chill the filled sheets for 10 to 15 minutes or until the dough is firm. Prick the shapes once or twice with a fork and bake for 15 to 20 minutes. Adjust this time according to the size and thickness of the cookies. The tops of the shortbread should be just firm, and the edges should be barely colouring. Cool on the baking sheets set on wire rack for 7 minutes, then transfer the cookies to the racks. Cool the sheets under cold running water and wipe dry before reusing. Repeat with the remaining dough until all the cookies are baked and cooled.

7. Store shortbread in airtight tins for up to 2 weeks. Both shortbread dough and baked cookies may be frozen, well wrapped in plastic wrap and aluminum foil. The cut raw cookies should be separated with pieces of waxed or parchment paper to prevent them from sticking and can be baked from frozen (increase the baking time by a few minutes). Frozen baked cookies should also be layered with waxed or parchment paper and thawed in their wrappings at room temperature for several hours before being unwrapped and served. Each ⅓ of the dough makes about 24 (2 to 2½ inch) cookies, or one 8-inch round or square.

❧ VARIATIONS ❧

Note: Each variation recipe flavours ⅓ of the total dough; the flavourings may be doubled or tripled to flavour ⅔ or all of the batch.

Dark Chocolate and Marbled Mocha Shortbread: Before creaming the butter and sugar, dissolve 1 tablespoon of good-quality espresso powder in ½ teaspoon warm water to form a thick paste; set aside. Gently knead 1 teaspoon of this paste into ⅓ of the dough once the last of the flour mixture has been incorporated. Work the paste in just enough to evenly distribute it in a marbled effect throughout the dough. Wrap the mocha dough in a sheet of plastic wrap and flatten slightly into a disc. Chill for 20 to 30 minutes or until firm enough to roll. Roll and cut into 2- to 2½-inch circles (or other shapes). Transfer to lined baking sheets, chill and bake as per Step 6 of the recipe above. While the shortbread are cooling, melt 4 ounces of finely chopped semisweet chocolate in a non-reactive bowl set over a pan of barely simmering water, or in a microwave set on medium-high power for 1 minute. Stir frequently and remove the bowl from the heat or the microwave when the chocolate is almost melted. Stir to melt completely. Dip the cooled cookies, one at a time, into the warm chocolate, half-coating them. Transfer the dipped biscuits to a parchment-lined baking sheet and allow the chocolate to set completely before storing the cookies, stacked between pieces of parchment or waxed paper, in airtight tins.

Candied Ginger and White Chocolate Shortbread: Knead 2½ tablespoons of finely chopped candied ginger (preferably Australian) into ⅓ of the dough after the last of the flour mixture has been added. Wrap the dough in plastic wrap, flatten it slightly into a disc and chill until firm enough to roll. Roll, cut, chill and bake the cookies as per Step 6 of the recipe above, then cool completely. Meanwhile, melt 4 ounces of finely chopped good-quality white chocolate in a non-reactive bowl in the microwave on medium power for 1 to 1½ minutes, stirring every 30 seconds, removing the chocolate from the oven when it is about ¾ melted. Stir to melt completely. Dip the edges of the cooled shortbread in the warm chocolate, creating a rim of white around the cookies. Transfer the dipped cookies to a parchment-lined baking sheet, and allow the chocolate to set completely before storing the cookies as described in the variation for mocha shortbread, above.

Butter-Toffee Crunch Shortbread

50 3-INCH FINGERS

Perhaps the most decadent cookie I have ever had. Awfully impressive, and dead easy, this is just a good basic brown sugar Scottish shortbread recipe, enhanced with butterscotch and toffee bits. As with any shortbread, the quality and fresh-ness of the butter and flour make all the difference in the flavour and texture. Use the best, and make sure they're fresh. This makes a large batch, perfect for giving, and the shortbread keeps very well in airtight tins. If desired, the recipe can be reduced by half.

2⅓ cups all-purpose flour

⅔ cup rice flour, or substitute cornstarch if rice flour is unavailable

½ teaspoon salt

1½ cups (¾ pound) fresh unsalted
  butter, at room temperature

6 tablespoons fruit sugar or superfine
  sugar

6 tablespoons tightly packed light
  brown sugar

¾ cup miniature butterscotch chips

¾ cup English toffee pieces for
  baking, such as Skor Bits
  (available in the baking sections
  of most supermarkets)

Additional unsalted butter, for
  greasing pan

1. Preheat the oven to 325°. Butter the bottom and sides of a 9 x 13-inch metal baking pan. Line the bottom and up the two long sides with a piece of parch-ment paper. Leave about a 1-inch overhang over the sides to make removing the cooled shortbread easier. Sift the all-purpose and rice flours together with the salt and set aside.

2. In the bowl of an electric or stand mixer fitted with the paddle attachment, or in a large mixing bowl with a wooden spoon, beat the butter until very smooth. Gradually add the sugars and cream the mixture until it is very light and fluffy. If using a mixer, transfer the creamed butter-sugar mixture to a large mixing bowl. Add the flour mixture, about ½ cup at a time, fully incorporat-ing each addition before adding the next. Use your fingers to knead the final portion of dry ingredients into the dough, keeping your palms off the dough as much as possible, so the warmth doesn't turn the butter oily. When the last of the flour is fully blended, add the butterscotch and toffee bits and knead them into the dough until they are evenly distributed. I should warn you, at this point, that this dough now smells better than any cookie dough you have ever experienced. Restrain yourself; you will do yourself no favours devouring the entire mess at this point, and the baking doesn't take *that* long.

3. Press the dough firmly into the prepared pan and use the back of a metal spoon to smooth the surface. Prick the dough all over with a fork and set the pan in the centre of the oven. Bake the shortbread for about 45 minutes, then prick the dough again to release any trapped air. Return the pan to the oven for another 15 to 30 minutes, or until the edges are light golden brown, and the centre feels just firm to the touch.

4. The shortbread will set to a very firm biscuit as it cools, so it must be cut while it is still warm. Cool the pan on a wire rack for 7 or 8 minutes, then run a sharp paring knife around the outside of the dough to loosen the edges. Make two long cuts in the shortbread, dividing it evenly into three rectangles, each cut beginning and ending at a short side of the pan. Cutting from long side to long side, cut the rectangles into about ¾-inch wide fingers, wiping the knife on a clean towel between each cut, as it gets sticky and can pull and tear the cooling shortbread.

5. Leave the fingers to cool completely in the pan, then re-cut and transfer them to airtight tins. This shortbread can be frozen before or after it is baked. Freeze the dough pressed into the prepared pan, well wrapped with plastic and aluminum foil. Thaw overnight in the refrigerator, without disturbing the wrapping, and bake directly from the refrigerator. The baking time may have to be increased by a few minutes to compensate for the chilled dough. Freeze the cooled fingers in airtight bags or containers, layering between sheets of waxed or parchment paper and wrapping the whole tin or container with aluminum foil. Thaw the entire package, without removing the wrapping, at room temperature for 6 to 8 hours.

Pecan-Caramel Sandwich Cookies

40 TO 45 SMALL
SANDWICHES

The year I made these as Christmas gifts, fights literally broke out among my normally well-adjusted friends and family. Even my father claims he innocently "forgot" the batch he was supposed to deliver to my best friend; and of course after the opportunity had passed, what could he do but eat them? Well, who can blame him: buttery pecan shortbread cookies concealing a creamy, chewy caramel filling—these are indescribably good. Make them small, as they are rich, and so special.

COOKIES:

1½ cups all-purpose flour

½ cup granulated sugar

¼ cup rice flour (or substitute cornstarch)

⅛ teaspoon salt

¾ cup cold unsalted butter, cut into cubes

1 teaspoon pure vanilla extract

¾ cup fresh pecans, coarsely chopped

FILLING:

1½ tablespoons unsalted butter

6 tablespoons tightly packed light brown sugar

3 tablespoons condensed milk

1½ tablespoons dark corn syrup

¾ teaspoon pure vanilla extract

1. Prepare the cookies: preheat the oven to 325° and move the racks as close to the centre as possible. Line two heavy, not non-stick, baking sheets with parchment paper and set aside. In a food processor, combine the flour, sugar, rice flour and salt and whir just to mix. Add the butter and vanilla and pulse until the mixture resembles a rough meal. Add the pecans and process until the mixture comes together in clumps when you squish it together. Depending on the size of the processor bowl, you may have to scrape the dough down the sides several times. Turn dough out onto a large sheet of parchment paper and press into a compact disc. The final dough will be dense and crumbly, but should hold together well when pressed firmly.

2. Roll the dough between two pieces of parchment paper to a ¼-inch thickness. Using a small 1- to 1½-inch cutter (I use a little star-shaped cutter for these cookies), cut the dough into shapes and carefully transfer them to the lined baking sheets with the help of a palette knife. Space the cookies about ¾ inch apart. Chill the filled sheets for 20 to 30 minutes, or until the dough is very firm. Bake the cookies for 12 to 15 minutes, or until the tops of the cookies are just firm and the bottoms are just barely beginning to colour. Cool for 5 minutes on the baking sheets, then transfer the cookies to wire racks and cool completely. (The cookies can be made up to this point up to 2 days ahead and stored at room temperature in airtight containers.)

3. Prepare the caramel filling: in a small, heavy-bottomed saucepan, combine all of the ingredients for the filling. Bring the mixture to a gentle boil over low heat, stirring constantly, until bubbles break the surface. Keeping the mixture at a gentle boil, and stirring constantly, cook the caramel for 2 minutes from this point, then remove the pot from the heat and allow the mixture to cool completely. (The caramel can be made up to 1 day ahead of time and stored in an airtight container in the refrigerator. Return it to the stove and bring it slowly back to just below the boil, stirring constantly, then allow to cool to room temperature before proceeding.)

4. To assemble the sandwiches, spread a scant teaspoon of the room temperature caramel on the underside of a cookie with a small palette or butter knife. It can be a sticky job, and I usually end up using a finger to secure the glob of caramel onto the cookie. Keep your fingers clean and dry, and the caramel shouldn't stick too badly. Top the caramel with a second cookie, underside down, lining up any points or edges on the two cookies. Repeat until all of the cookies are sandwiched. Although they are best within a day or two, the filled sandwiches will keep in an airtight container at room temperature for up to 1 week.

Chewy Almond Macaroons

ABOUT 3½ DOZEN
BITE-SIZED MACAROONS

*A small, richly flavoured, chewy cookie with a succulent texture. The secret
lies in using almond paste, rather than ground almonds in the dough. The oils
released in the paste make the macaroons moister and more evenly tender than
those made with freshly ground nuts. Do use almond paste, and not marzipan,
as the latter contains too much sugar in relation to almonds. Almond paste is
available in specialty food stores and baking supply shops.*

8 ounces good-quality almond paste
   (not marzipan)
½ cup confectioners' sugar,
   not sifted

2 large egg whites, at room temperature,
   preferably at least several days old,
   or even frozen whites, thawed
¼ teaspoon pure almond extract

1. Preheat the oven to 325°. Line two heavy, not non-stick, baking sheets with
parchment paper and set aside. In a medium-sized bowl, break up the almond
paste and gradually knead the confectioners' sugar into the paste by hand. This
may take 6 or 7 minutes, but the mixture will eventually become homogeneous
and smooth. Lightly beat the egg whites, then add all at once to the almond mixture. Beat the mixture until the whites are fully incorporated, add the almond
extract, then continue to beat for 2 to 3 minutes until the batter is lightened.

2. Spoon the batter into a strong piping bag fitted with a medium-small (Ateco
#3 or #4) plain tip and pipe the batter in little mounds of about ¾-inch diame-
ter onto the baking sheets, spacing the macaroons 1½ to 2 inches apart. The
macaroons will not spread very much and should retain the mounded shape
well. Bake in the centre of the oven for approximately 15 minutes, or until the
edges and tips are lightly golden and the undersides are golden and firm.
Transfer the sheets to wire racks, cool for 5 minutes, then remove the macaroons to the racks themselves and cool completely. Rinse the baking sheets
under cold water and dry well before repeating with the remaining batter.
These cookies are absolutely fantastic the day they are made, but keep well
stored in an airtight container for up to 3 days.

🍃 VARIATION 🍃

Chocolate-Dipped Chewy Almond Macaroons: Melt 4 ounces of finely chopped semisweet or bittersweet chocolate in a bowl set over a pan of barely simmering water, stirring occasionally. Alternatively, melt the chocolate in a non-reactive bowl in the microwave set on medium power for about 1½ minutes, stirring every 30 seconds. With both methods, remove the chocolate from the heat when it is ¾ melted and stir to melt completely. Take care not to let any moisture, even steam, come into contact with the chocolate, or it will seize. Dip each macaroon into the warm chocolate, tip first, up to the flat bottom. Feel free to dip these any way you like, but I find leaving the bottoms free of chocolate make them easier to dip and lets a little more of the almond flavour through. Transfer the dipped macaroons to a parchment-lined baking sheet and allow the chocolate to set completely before stacking the cookies between layers of waxed or parchment paper in airtight containers. Store at room temperature.

Peanut Butter and Chocolate Shortcake Cups

30 CUPS

These are a combination of many wonderful things: cake, shortbread, peanut butter and dark chocolate. They are also a perfect example of when natural and unprocessed ingredients are not always best. I first made these with pure natural peanut butter; the result was so alarming I had to convince myself the idea was good enough to try again! The strong, sweet, rich peanut flavour of a brand-name, commercial peanut butter is what gives these tender cups their smooth, creamy taste and tender texture. For best results, try to find a brand with molasses in the ingredients.

Peanut Butter and Chocolate Shortcake Cups continued

¾ cup unsalted butter, at room
   temperature
¾ cup chunky peanut butter, not
   sugar-free or salt-free, but a good
   old-fashioned children's favourite
   supermarket brand
½ cup granulated sugar
⅓ cup tightly packed light brown sugar
2 large eggs, at room temperature
1 teaspoon pure vanilla extract
2⅓ cups all-purpose flour
1 teaspoon baking powder

¼ teaspoon salt
½ cup full-fat sour cream (14%)
⅓ to ½ cup semisweet chocolate
   chips, chunks or pieces of
   chopped chocolate

Confectioners' sugar, for dusting
   finished cups
Non-stick cooking spray,
   for greasing pans, or a mild-
   flavoured vegetable oil

1. Preheat oven to 350°. Spray or grease two mini-muffin trays, with 12 muffin cups each. I find with such small pans a good-quality cooking spray works beautifully. In the bowl of an electric or stand mixer fitted with the paddle attachment, cream the butter, peanut butter and both sugars until light and fluffy, about 1½ to 2 minutes. Add the eggs, one at a time, beating well after each addition. Scrape down the sides of the bowl, then beat in the vanilla.

2. Sift the flour, baking powder and salt together into a small bowl. Add the flour mixture to the creamed batter in three additions, alternating with the sour cream in two additions, scraping down the sides of the bowl often.

3. Scoop a heaping teaspoon of the dough into each little tin, then use clean fingertips to push the dough into the corners. Keep the tins no more than ⅔ full. Press a hazelnut-sized chunk of chocolate, or two or three chips, into each cup, keeping the chocolate suspended in the dough but buried in the centre of the cups. Top each cup with another dab of dough, and press the dough into the cups, completely covering the chocolate, sealing it in on all sides. The cups should now be full of dough—the little cakes don't rise very much.

4. Place the trays in the centre of the oven and bake for 18 to 20 minutes, rotating once or twice so the cups bake evenly. The cups are done when they are firm to the touch, and the edges are just beginning to colour. The cookies will be fairly pale when done; don't wait for them to be a deep golden brown, or you will have burnt them! Cool the trays on a wire rack for 1 minute, then gently lift the cookies from the tins and cool directly on the rack. Sprinkle the cooled cookies with sifted confectioners' sugar before serving. These are indescribably good about 10 minutes out of the oven, when they are still soft and chewy and warm, and the little surprise of chocolate is oozing and creamy. But they're perfectly scrumptious later in the day, too, if they last that long! They really are best if eaten within a day or so of baking, but can be stored airtight at room temperature for 3 or 4 days.

White Chocolate Tropical Chunk Cookies

22 TO 25 COOKIES

I love the combination of white chocolate and dried tropical fruit, and these chewy, chunky colourful cookies are positively addictive. I use dried mango in this recipe, but papaya would work, too. The freshness and quality of the dried fruit and nuts is what makes or breaks these cookies. Try to find moist, preferably unsulphured fruit, sweet-tasting nuts and make sure the white chocolate is good. For a change, substitute cashews or pistachios for the macadamia nuts and dried pineapple, banana or even dates for the mango. The cookies could be made smaller, but because there is so much good stuff in the dough, I like the hearty size!

⅓ cup unsalted butter, at room temperature

1 cup tightly packed light brown sugar

1 large egg

2 teaspoons pure vanilla extract

1¾ cups all-purpose flour

¼ teaspoon baking powder

¼ teaspoon salt

1 cup sweetened shredded coconut

1 cup good-quality white chocolate chips (or white chocolate chopped to about the size of chips)

¾ cup coarsely chopped macadamia nuts, preferably raw and unsalted

¾ cup (about 18 to 20) dried apricots, chopped about the size of chocolate chips

¼ cup chopped dried mango, sweetened or unsweetened, preferably unsulphured (or substitute chopped dried papaya), chopped about the size of chocolate chips

White Chocolate Cookies continued

1. Preheat the oven to 350°. Line a heavy, not non-stick, baking sheet with parchment paper, or lightly butter it. In the bowl of an electric or stand mixer fitted with the paddle attachment, or a large bowl if mixing the cookie dough by hand, cream the butter and brown sugar together until well blended and smooth. Beat in the egg and vanilla and scrape down the sides of the bowl.

2. Sift together the flour, baking powder and salt. Add the flour mixture to the creamed mixture in two additions, blending well after each. Fold in the coconut, white chocolate chips or chunks, macadamia nuts and dried fruit. At this point, there is nothing better with which to mix the dough than your hands. Get in there and scrunch the ingredients together until the chunky bits are evenly distributed and there are no clumps of unstudded batter.

3. Pinch off a piece of dough somewhere between the size of a walnut and a golf ball and roll it into a ball, packing tightly. Place it on the prepared baking sheet and repeat until the sheet is full, leaving 2 inches between each ball. Slightly flatten the balls with the bottom of a glass, then set the sheet on the middle rack of the oven.

4. Bake for 18 to 20 minutes, or until the edges of the cookies are golden brown, the bottoms are slightly darker and the tops still yield slightly when touched in the centre. For chewier cookies, bake for a little less time, for crunchier ones, leave them in a little longer—watch closely, though, the fruit, nuts and chocolate can burn easily if left too long. These cookies will keep in airtight containers at room temperature for up to 1 week, if they aren't devoured before then!

Blueberry and Hazelnut Bars

12 LARGE DESSERT-SIZED BARS OR
UP TO 48 BITE-SIZED BARS

Lots of punchy blueberry flavour, very tender crust and crumble, with a lovely buttery mellow taste of toasted hazelnuts, these are just the thing for picnics, kids, lunches or that 3 o'clock sugar craving, but they're not your same ol' dry crumbly fruit square! Moist, fruity and moreish, they are scrumptious enough for a dinner-party dessert.

CRUST & TOPPING:

1 cup hazelnuts, toasted and skinned
(see page 262 for tips on toasting
and skinning hazelnuts)

2 cups all-purpose flour

1 cup confectioners' sugar, sifted

2 teaspoons baking powder

1 cup cold unsalted butter, cut into
small cubes

1 large egg

1 large egg yolk

1 teaspoon pure vanilla extract

FILLING:

6 cups fresh wild blueberries, picked
over (don't substitute frozen)

⅔ cup granulated sugar

⅓ cup cornstarch

½ teaspoon ground cinnamon

½ teaspoon freshly squeezed lemon
juice

Additional unsalted butter, at room
temperature, or vegetable oil
cooking spray, for greasing pan

1. Preheat the oven to 350°. Lightly grease a 9 x 13-inch baking pan. Line the bottom and up two sides with a piece of parchment paper, leaving a few inches of the paper hanging over the edges of the two long sides to facilitate removing the first few bars. Place ½ cup hazelnuts in the bowl of a food processor and pulse in short bursts until the nuts are very coarsely chopped. Halved or quartered nuts are about right; don't go too fine. Put these nuts in a small container and set aside.

2. Process the other ½ cup hazelnuts until finely ground and transfer them to a large mixing bowl. Add the flour, confectioners' sugar and baking powder and stir with a fork to blend. Using a pastry blender or two knives, cut in the butter until the largest lumps in the mixture are about the size of fat peas. Lightly beat the egg together with the yolk and add all but 2 tablespoons of the egg to the butter-flour mixture. Add the vanilla, and use your fingertips to gently but quickly toss the mixture (rubbing it between your fingertips) until it clumps together. It should be uniformly blended, moist and crumbly. If the dough looks too dry and floury, mix in a little more of the egg. (If you have a sufficiently large food processor, the dough can be prepared in the processor. Pulse to blend the dry ingredients, then add the butter and pulse just until the largest lumps are the size of fat peas. Lightly beat the egg and the yolk together and add all but about 2 tablespoons of this liquid to the butter-flour mixture. Add the vanilla and pulse for 5 to 7 seconds; feel the dough. It should clump together when squeezed. If necessary, add a little more of the egg and pulse to combine

Blueberry and Hazelnut Bars continued

it. Transfer the dough to a large bowl and finish working the liquid into the dough with the tips of your fingers.) Divide the dough into two portions, one slightly larger than the other. Pat the larger portion of the crumble into the bottom of the prepared pan, pressing firmly, and set the pan in the refrigerator for 15 to 20 minutes. Cover the remaining portion with plastic wrap and put it in the refrigerator as well.

3. Remove the pan from the refrigerator and prick the pastry all over with a fork. Bake the base for 20 to 25 minutes, until the edges are golden, and the pastry is dry and beginning to colour slightly in the centre. Cool the base completely on a wire rack before filling, or the bottom of the bars will be soggy.

4. Prepare the filling: in a large bowl, combine the blueberries, sugar, cornstarch, cinnamon and lemon juice. Toss gently to thoroughly coat the berries and pour the filling onto the cooled crust. Spread the berries in an even layer and scrape any residual sugar or cornstarch from the bowl over the filling. Remove the reserved dough from the refrigerator and crumble it over the berries. It probably won't cover every inch of the filling, but that's fine. Bake the bars for 25 minutes, then sprinkle with the reserved chopped hazelnuts. (If you are like me, set a timer, or you'll forget!) Return the pan to the oven and continue baking for another 35 to 45 minutes, or until the topping is puffed and golden and the filling is bubbling vigorously. Cool the bars completely on a wire rack before cutting and serving or storing. These bars keep beautifully for a day or two, kept in the pan at room temperature, tightly covered. For a special dessert, warm in a low oven and top with a scoop of *Vanilla Bean* or *Roasted Cinnamon Ice Cream*.

Custards, Puddings and Mousses

continued on page 528

White Coffee Pots de Crème

SERVES 6

A good pot de crème is a looser, more creamy custard than crème caramel, not stiff enough to be turned out. This variation, called white coffee because the beans are never ground, has smoky, subtle flavours—the infusion of dark-roast coffee beans imparts a deep, complex coffee flavour, but is not overly powerful. Be sure to use good beans and experiment with your favourite blend or roast. The brown sugar is what lends this creamy custard its mocha colour; if you want a whiter coffee custard, substitute white granulated sugar for the brown. I like to make them in heatproof coffee cups, but any ceramic or porcelain ramekin will do. Chocolate-Espresso Crisps (page 491) are a lovely complement!

1½ cups plus 2 tablespoons heavy cream (36%)

1½ cups milk, whole (3.5%) or 2%, but not 1% or skim

2 strips lemon zest (about ½ inch wide and 2 to 3 inches long), with no white pith

¼ pound fresh dark-roast coffee beans (about 1½ cups)

2 large eggs

4 large egg yolks

⅔ cup tightly packed light brown sugar

Lightly sweetened whipped cream, to serve, if desired

1. Preheat the oven to 325°. Combine the cream, milk, lemon zest and coffee beans in a heavy-bottomed 2-quart saucepan and place the pan over medium heat. Bring to the boil, then turn off the flame and let the mixture infuse for 30 minutes. Return the mixture to just below the boil before proceeding.

2. In a large bowl, beat the eggs and the egg yolks together to break them up. Add the brown sugar and beat until the eggs and sugar are well blended. The object is not to create a lot of foam, but just to thoroughly combine the mixture. Wrap a damp towel around the base of the bowl to secure it and free your hands.

3. Strain the coffee bean mixture into a bowl or pitcher and discard the beans. Gradually pour the hot cream into the eggs and sugar, a little at a time, whisking constantly. If the mixture looks a little lumpy, strain it through a fine mesh

White Coffee Pots de Crème continued

sieve into a clean bowl. Ladle or pour the custard into six 6-ounce (¾-cup) ramekins or pot-de-crème pots and place the pots in a baking dish.

4. Pour enough warm water into the dish to come about halfway up the sides of the cups, then cover the whole dish tightly with aluminum foil. (If you are using classic pot-de-crème pots with lids, use the lids rather than foil.) Very carefully set the dish in the oven and bake for 30 to 45 minutes, or until the custards are still just wobbly in the centre. Remove the pots from the baking dish and cool to room temperature on a wire rack. Cover the pots with pieces of plastic wrap and poke a few holes in each to allow any residual steam to escape. Refrigerate the custards until chilled, at least 4 hours or overnight. The pots de crème can be made up to 2 days ahead of time. These luxurious desserts are best if removed from the refrigerator an hour or so before you plan to serve them. You can top each pot with a dollop of lightly sweetened whipped cream and a chocolate-covered espresso bean or leave them plain.

Gingerbread Soufflé with a White Chocolate Crème Anglaise

SERVES 6

You can walk on the kitchen floor, talk loudly, even steal a peek into the oven. Soufflés are not the finicky things we imagine, but are actually quite simple. And there is truly no more impressive and sensual dessert to be had. This recipe is best made in stages, and the custard base can even be made a day ahead.

1½ cups milk (not 1% or skim)
½ vanilla bean, split
3 large egg yolks
2 tablespoons molasses
½ cup all-purpose flour
1½ teaspoons ground ginger
1½ teaspoons ground cinnamon
¾ teaspoon freshly grated nutmeg
¼ teaspoon salt

4 large egg whites, at room temperature
¼ teaspoon cream of tartar
3 tablespoons granulated sugar

White Chocolate Crème Anglaise,
    page 651, chilled

Unsalted butter, for greasing dishes
Additional granulated sugar for coating
    dishes

1. In a heavy-bottomed 2-quart saucepan, combine the milk and vanilla bean. Bring just below the boil over medium-high heat, then remove from the heat and allow the milk to infuse for 1 hour.

2. In a medium bowl, whisk together the egg yolks and molasses and set aside. In a separate bowl, whisk together the flour, spices and salt. Add a little more than ½ cup of the infused milk to the flour mixture, whisking to form a thick paste. Add a little extra milk if the paste is unworkably thick. Scrape this paste into the remaining milk in the pot and place over medium heat. Whisking constantly, cook the mixture until thickened and smooth, about 5 to 7 minutes. (If at any time the bottom of the mixture seems overly thick, just take the pot off the heat and whisk until smooth.)

3. Pour the hot milk mixture over the egg yolks and molasses and whisk to blend. Press a piece of plastic wrap directly onto the surface of the mixture. With the tip of a sharp knife, poke a few slits in the plastic to allow steam to escape, then chill the mixture at least 2 hours or overnight.

4. Allow the soufflé base to sit at room temperature for 1 hour before proceeding. Meanwhile, preheat the oven to 375°. Generously and thoroughly butter six 6-ounce soufflé dishes, or one 2-quart soufflé dish. Coat the insides of the dishes with granulated sugar, making sure every spot is lined with butter and sugar, even the rims.

5. In a very clean bowl with very clean beaters, whip the egg whites until just foamy, then add the cream of tartar and whip until very soft peaks form. Gradually add the 3 tablespoons sugar, whipping until the whites form soft, shiny peaks. Fold the whites into the base mixture in three additions, then divide the mixture among the prepared dishes. (If using individual dishes, I find it helpful to place them on a baking sheet before putting them in the oven.)

6. Place the dishes in the centre of the oven and bake for 16 to 20 minutes for individual soufflés, or 25 to 30 minutes for one large soufflé. The edges should be slightly darkened and appear matte and cakey. Serve immediately, pouring the chilled crème anglaise into the a hole made in the centre of each soufflé.

Hazelnut Crème Brûlée with a Crushed Praline Crust

SERVES 8

Lightly toasted hazelnuts, crushed to a fine paste, are added to a classic crème brûlée custard, creating a gorgeous, voluptuously flavourful dessert. Be sure to use the freshest hazelnuts you can find, so they'll contribute a smooth, sweet, buttery flavour, not a coarse or bitter one.

PRALINE:

1½ cups granulated sugar

⅓ cup hazelnuts, lightly toasted and skinned (see page 262 for tips on toasting and skinning hazelnuts)

CUSTARD:

1½ cups hazelnuts, lightly toasted and skinned

2 tablespoons confectioners' sugar, sifted

4 cups heavy cream (36%)

1 plump vanilla bean, split

8 large egg yolks

½ cup plus 1 tablespoon granulated sugar

3 tablespoons cold unsalted butter, cut into small pieces

2 tablespoons Frangelico (hazelnut-flavoured liqueur)

Additional unsalted butter for greasing baking sheet

1. Prepare the praline: have ⅓ cup of the skinned hazelnuts ready and make sure your hands and forearms are protected by long sleeves and oven mitts or a kitchen towel wrapped securely around them. Put a small bowl of ice water on the stove in case of splattering caramel and butter a large, not non-stick, baking sheet with 1-inch sides and set nearby. Combine the granulated sugar and just enough water to moisten it in a heavy-bottomed, 2-quart saucepan. Stir the mixture over medium-low heat until the sugar melts, then increase the heat to medium-high. Boil the syrup, watching closely, as it begins turning a medium amber colour. When the syrup is a dark gold, immediately slide in the nuts and remove the pot from the heat. The addition of the hazelnuts will produce quite a commotion in the pot, and the caramel will splatter and spit as it is forced to quickly drop in temperature. Stand back and wait for the action to subside. Stir the nuts once or twice to coat them well, then pour the mixture onto the baking sheet and spread it quickly before it sets too much. Cool on the sheet in a cool, dry place, but not the refrigerator, as this will make the praline tacky and sticky.

2. When it is totally cool, carefully break it into shards, taking care not to cut your hands—this candy is as sharp as glass! Place several shards into the dry bowl of a food processor fitted with a steel blade and pulse until the praline is reduced to a relatively fine powder. Repeat with additional shards until you have about ¾ cup ground praline. Remove any obvious or large lumps of hazelnuts—these could cause the topping to scorch. Transfer the powder to an airtight container and store at room temperature in a cool, dry place until needed, up to 1 week if it's not too humid. The remainder of the praline can be stored the same way and used whole to garnish ice creams, custards, cakes and other desserts, or ground and sprinkled on sundaes, cakes, etc.

3. Prepare the custard: place the 1½ cups hazelnuts in the clean bowl of a food processor. Add the sifted confectioners' sugar and pulse until the mixture forms a smooth paste, but is not too oily, and set aside.

4. Fill a large pot with an inch or two of water and bring the water to a gentle simmer. Have ready a fine-mesh sieve set over a medium bowl. Pour the cream into a 2-quart saucepan with a heavy bottom. Scrape the seeds out of the vanilla bean and add the seeds and the hull to the pot. Bring the cream just to the boil over medium heat, watching closely so it doesn't boil over.

5. Meanwhile, whisk the egg yolks lightly in a large non-reactive bowl and pour in the granulated sugar, whisking constantly. Place the bowl over the pot with the barely simmering water and whisk the sugar and yolks until they have thickened and paled, about as long as it will take the cream to scald.

6. Remove the cream from the heat as soon as it boils and add a small amount to the yolk mixture, whisking all the while. Add the cream in increasing amounts, whisking well after each addition. When all of the cream has been in-corporated, stir the custard with a wooden spoon over the barely simmering water until it thickly coats the back of the spoon, about 10 minutes. Strain the custard into the clean bowl and add the pieces of butter, a few at a time, stirring

Hazelnut Crème Brûlée continued

until they melt. Stir in the hazelnut paste, whisking gently until it is fully blended, then stir in the Frangelico. Press a piece of plastic wrap onto the surface of the custard and poke a few holes in the plastic with a paring knife to allow the steam to escape.

7. Cool the custard to room temperature, then pour it into eight 6-ounce (¾-cup) ramekins or heat-proof custard cups and chill at least 4 hours or overnight. I like to use wider, shallower dishes for crème brûlée, so every mouthful of silky cool custard gets a bit of the crackly caramel crust.

8. To serve, spoon a layer of the praline powder onto the surface of each custard and smooth it with the back of the spoon so it evenly covers the whole area. Using a hand-held blowtorch, or a very hot preheated broiler, caramelize the praline topping until it is a dark amber and completely melted, but not burnt. A blowtorch makes easy work of this and other flash-caramelizing tasks, and a perfectly good one is well worth the few dollars it costs. If you are using the broiler of your oven, make sure it is very hot—many home broilers are not sufficiently hot and will end up curdling the custard before caramelizing the top. Serve the brûlées immediately; a little glass of Frangelico or other hazelnut liqueur is a perfect accompaniment.

Black Cherry Clafouti

SERVES 6

Easy, fresh, light, very country, but also very elegant, clafouti is a traditional rustic Provençal dessert somewhere between a baked custard, a light pancake and a cakey soufflé. This recipe is more custardy than cakey, not too sweet, with a full, ripe cherry flavour, laced with a little Kirsch. I recommend stoning the fruit; although this isn't traditionally done, it does reduce the risk of incurred dental bills from surprised guests! Traditionally made with cherries, clafouti is also wonderful made with apricots, berries, fresh figs, pears or even peaches or apricots, with like-flavoured liqueurs standing in for the Kirsch.

1½ pounds ripe sweet black cherries, washed and dried thoroughly if necessary

¾ cup whole milk (3.5%)

¾ cup heavy cream (36%)

1 vanilla bean, split

4 large eggs, at room temperature

½ cup granulated sugar

½ cup all-purpose flour, sifted

¼ teaspoon salt

1½ to 2 tablespoons Kirsch, or other cherry brandy

Unsalted butter, at room temperature, for greasing dish

Confectioners' sugar, for dusting over finished dessert, optional

1. Preheat the oven to 375°. Select a shallow, wide ceramic baking dish of about 2-quart capacity. Glass can also be used, but I have found ovenproof ceramic or glazed earthenware hold the heat much more evenly and produce an evenly baked custard. They also look quite beautiful when the clafouti is served at the table, in keeping with the rustic nature of the dessert. Generously butter the entire inside of the dish and set it aside. Pit the cherries using a little manual cherry or olive pitter. You could leave the stones in, but warn your guests! Scatter the cherries in the bottom of the buttered dish.

2. Combine the milk and the cream in a heavy-bottomed saucepan. Scrape the seeds from the vanilla bean into the pot and add the hull. Bring this mixture just to the boil, then remove from the heat.

3. Meanwhile, in a medium-sized bowl, lightly beat the eggs. Add the sugar gradually and whisk until the mixture is thickened and pale, about 1 to 2 minutes. Combine the flour and salt in a small cup or bowl and sift together over the yolk and sugar mixture in three stages, whisking each addition in gently and thoroughly. You want to add just as much sifted flour as the mixture can absorb at a time without getting lumpy. When all of the flour has been smoothly incorporated, wrap a damp kitchen towel around the bottom of the bowl to hold it steady. Pour a small amount of the hot milk and cream into the batter, whisking constantly. Slowly add the rest of the hot liquid, whisking steadily and making sure the whisk covers the whole area of the bowl. (You can remove the vanilla bean at this point, but I like to leave it in and bake it with the custard, discarding it when the clafouti is served.) Stir in the Kirsch.

Black Cherry Clafouti continued

4. Pour the custard over the cherries (they will bob up and float on the surface of the mixture) and place the baking dish in the centre of the oven. Bake for 30 to 40 minutes, or until it is evenly puffed and browned and the centre is just set when lightly touched. Allow to cool for at least 15 minutes, then serve warm or at room temperature, dusted with confectioners' sugar, if desired.

Coconut Panna Cotta with a Mango-Orange-Passion Fruit Coulis

SERVES 6

Panna cotta is a beautifully simple Italian eggless custard. It is usually made with cream, (the name panna cotta means, literally, cooked cream), but I have used a combination of cream and rich, subtly flavoured coconut milk to give the dessert a slightly tropical taste. The bright orange sauce and the pure white of the custard make a striking plate, even more satisfying on the tongue.

½ cup whole milk (3.5%), cold

2 packages (2 scant teaspoons) powdered gelatine

½ cup granulated sugar

½ cup heavy cream (36%)

3½ cups (28 ounces) tinned coconut milk

One 2-inch piece vanilla bean, or 1 vanilla bean hull, scraped out, seeds reserved for another use

Mango-Orange-Passion Fruit Coulis, page 644

½ cup fresh coconut shavings, lightly toasted (see page 260 for tips on toasting coconut), or substitute lightly toasted dried coconut flakes, for garnish, optional

Unsalted butter, at room temperature, for greasing moulds

1. Grease six 6-ounce (¾-cup) porcelain, ceramic or metal ramekins or moulds. Pour the milk into a small bowl and sprinkle powdered gelatine over top. Stir to combine, then set aside for 5 minutes to allow the gelatine to soften.

2. In a medium-sized, heavy-bottomed sauce pan, combine sugar, cream, coconut milk and vanilla bean. Bring to a boil, stirring frequently, then immediately remove from heat and let sit for 5 minutes to infuse. Don't worry about any un-dissolved lumps of coconut milk fat; they will be strained out.

3. Pour the warm coconut milk mixture through a medium-fine mesh strainer into a large bowl. Add the milk-gelatine mixture and stir gently with a wooden spoon or wipe-looped whisk to blend thoroughly. Try to incorporate as little air as possible—pockets of bubbles detract from the luscious smoothness of the panna cotta! Press a piece of plastic wrap onto the surface of the custard to prevent a skin from forming and let it cool at room temperature for 1 hour.

4. Ladle the custard into the prepared moulds, cover with plastic and chill for at least 6 hours or overnight. To serve, carefully dip the moulds in a shallow bowl of hot water for 30 to 90 seconds. Place a dessert plate over the top of the mould, invert the two together and let the panna cotta slip out of the mould. A thin, small, sharp knife can be used to carefully loosen the custard from the sides of the moulds if necessary, but be careful not to gouge them. Spoon a little pool of the *Mango-Orange-Passion Fruit Coulis* around the base of each panna cotta and garnish the plate with a sprinkle of toasted coconut.

Quince and Brioche Bread Pudding with Dried Sour Cherries

2 PUDDINGS, EACH SERVING 6 TO 8

Sinfully, seductively, sensuously good! This will immediately erase people's memory of gloppy, tasteless nursery bread-and-butter puddings. The combination of buttery brioche, silky vanilla custard, soft, fragrant poached quince and a few plump sour cherries is so satisfying, you'll probably end up warming the leftovers for breakfast. I have made this a large recipe, simply because it is as easy to prepare two puddings as one, and even happily sated guests seem to find room once they taste this dessert. Any leftovers can be stored in the refrigerator, covered, for up to 3 days, and warmed in the microwave before serving.

Quince and Brioche Bread Pudding continued

1 quantity Poached Quince, page 595
1 loaf Classic Brioche, page 619,
　　preferably a day or two old
½ cup dried sour cherries, plumped in
　　warm water if very dry, and drained

BREAD PUDDING CUSTARD:
3 cups heavy cream (36%)
3 cups whole milk (3.5%)
½ plump vanilla bean, split
6 large eggs

6 large egg yolks
1 cup granulated sugar, plus 3 table-
　　spoons for sprinkling over custard
⅛ teaspoon salt

Unsalted butter, at room temperature,
　　for greasing the baking dishes
Additional granulated sugar for dusting
　　the baking dishes
Crème Fraîche, page 651, to serve,
　　optional

1. Preheat the oven to 325°. Butter two (2½-quart) oval casseroles or baking dishes, 3 inches deep, and dust the insides with granulated sugar. Tap out the excess and set the dishes aside. Drain the quince slices from their poaching liquid, reserving the syrup. Cut each slice in half lengthwise and lay the slices in the baking dishes, covering the bottoms in a single layer.

2. Slice the ends off the brioche and discard them. Cut the loaf into ½- to ⅔-inch slices, then cut the slices in half from top to bottom, and arrange them over the quince, overlapping each other. I find that laying the brioche in a curve around the whole dish, with two or three pieces in the centre of the circle, works well for this dish. The whole loaf should provide just the right number of slices for the two puddings. Scatter ¼ cup dried cherries over each of the filled dishes.

3. Prepare the custard: in a heavy-bottomed 2-quart saucepan, bring the cream, milk and vanilla bean just to the boil, then remove the mixture from the heat. Watch closely as the mixture nears the boil—heavy cream has an uncanny knack for bubbling over onto the stove just as you turn your head! Let the mixture infuse for about 5 minutes.

4. Meanwhile, beat the eggs and egg yolks in a large mixing bowl until just combined. Whisk in the sugar and salt and beat just until well blended; you don't want a lot of froth or thickening in this mixture. Wrap a damp towel around the base of the mixing bowl to secure it. When the cream mixture has scalded and infused, gradually pour the hot liquid onto the egg mixture, a little at a time, whisking constantly so the eggs don't curdle.

5. Ladle the custard over the brioche, pushing the slices down every now and then with the back of your ladle so the custard thoroughly soaks into the bread. Make sure every bit of bread is saturated! Fill the dishes until about ½ to ¾ inches of the brioche is exposed above the level of custard. The amount of custard should be just about perfect for two puddings. Sprinkle the surface of each pudding with 1½ tablespoons of granulated sugar and set it in a larger baking dish.

6. Add enough warm water to the larger dishes to come about halfway up the sides of the pudding dishes. Place both sets of dishes in the centre of the oven and bake for 1½ to 1¾ hours, turning them several times, or until the brioche is toasted and dark golden, and no custard squeezes up through the bread when the centre of the puddings are prodded with a finger. Another way to test the custard is with a fine metal skewer—inserted into a ribbon of custard in the centre of the pudding, the skewer should come out clean. Cool the puddings on wire racks for at least 30 minutes, then serve, or cover and refrigerate.

7. Before serving, boil the reserved quince poaching liquid in a small saucepan until it is reduced to a thin syrup. Cool slightly before serving. (The syrup can be reduced up to 3 days ahead of time and stored, covered, in the refrigerator. Warm the syrup gently before serving.) I think this pudding should be served slightly warm; if it has been made ahead and refrigerated, microwave individual portions for a minute or two until warm to the touch. Serve the pudding scooped into shallow bowls, drizzled with a little of the quince syrup. (A hint: drizzle the refrigerated portions of pudding with the chilled quince syrup before microwaving and save yourself a step!) A dollop of crème fraîche would not be overkill here—we are dealing with bread pudding after all. The puddings are best within a day or two of baking, but any leftovers can be kept covered in the refrigerator for up to 4 days.

Sweet Potato Cornbread Pudding
with Maple Custard

2 PUDDINGS,
EACH SERVING 6 TO 8

The New World flavours of sweet potatoes, toasted corn and pure maple syrup conspire to create a rich, satisfying, and deeply warming take on a classic dessert. A drizzle of warm maple syrup just before serving is lovely, and I highly recommend a dollop of crème fraîche, too! All of the elements can be made ahead of time, so little or no last minute preparation is required, and I have made the recipe for two puddings, perfect for a fall or winter crowd.

MAPLE CUSTARD:

3 cups heavy cream (36%)

2⅔ cups whole milk (3.5%)

2-inch piece of vanilla bean, split

Finely grated zest of ½ orange

6 large eggs

6 large egg yolks

1 cup pure maple syrup, grade B or C, plus 1 cup for serving

⅓ cup, plus 3 tablespoons granulated sugar for sprinkling over custard

⅛ teaspoon salt

1½ to 2 loaves Sweet Potato Cornbread, page 607, preferably at least one day old

Unsalted butter, at room temperature, for greasing the pans

Additional granulated sugar, for dusting the pans

Crème Fraîche, page 651, to serve, optional

1. Preheat the oven to 325°. Butter two (2½-quart) baking dishes with 3-inch sides, preferably ceramic or stoneware. Sugar the dishes the same way you would flour a baking pan after greasing, tapping out the excess sugar.

2. In a medium-sized, heavy-bottomed saucepan, combine the cream, milk, vanilla bean and orange zest. Set the pan over medium-high heat and bring just to the boil. Watch carefully once the mixture becomes hot—cream tends to expand enormously upon reaching the boiling point, and I have lost more cream to my stove elements than I care to admit! Move the pan off the heat as soon as bubbles break the surface and leave to infuse for 5 to 7 minutes.

3. Meanwhile, whisk the eggs and yolks together to break them up, then whisk in 1 cup maple syrup, ⅓ cup sugar and the salt. Place a damp cloth or towel under the bowl to secure it and whisk in a small amount of the hot cream mixture to warm the egg mixture. Gradually pour in the remaining hot liquid, whisking constantly. Pour the custard through a strainer into a clean container. (Can be made 1 day ahead of time. If the custard is not to be used immediately, press a piece of plastic wrap onto the surface and refrigerate. To use, gently warm the custard in a pot over low heat, stirring with a wooden spoon, until just warmer than body temperature. If you heat the custard any hotter you risk curdling the eggs—you'll end up with scrambled egg in hot cream!)

4. Slice the cornbread in half, then cut each half into ½-inch slices from short end to short end. Lay the slices in the prepared baking dishes. I like to start with the first slices leaning up against the back of the dish, the next one slightly in front of that one, and so forth, overlapping the slices. You want about the same amount of custard as bread in the finished pudding, but part of the beauty of this dessert is that it is not an exact science! Ladle the warm custard over the slices, making sure all parts of the bread are coated and pushing down with the back of the ladle onto the bread to make sure it soaks up the custard. Leave about ¾ inch of the top of the bread slices above the line of custard. Let the pudding sit for 7 to 10 minutes if the bread is soft and moist, or about 15 minutes if the bread is stale.

5. Sprinkle each pudding with 1½ tablespoons sugar and place each dish in a baking pan large enough to hold it. Add hot water to the larger pans to come ⅔ of the way up the side of the pudding dishes and set the pans in the middle of the oven. Bake for 1¼ to 1¾ hours, checking after 45 minutes to make sure the exposed bread isn't browning too much; if it is, cover the pudding loosely with aluminum foil for the duration of the baking. The finished puddings should be just set in the centre, so a finger pressed onto the centre of the pudding does not provoke an ooze of liquid custard and a metal skewer inserted in the custard comes out clean. The custard will set further as it cools, however, so don't overbake. Remove the baking dishes from the water bath and transfer to a wire rack. Cool for 30 minutes, then refrigerate, covered with foil, if not serving immediately.

Sweet Potato Cornbread Pudding continued

6. To serve, warm the remaining 1 cup maple syrup slightly. Scoop portions of the pudding into shallow bowls and serve at room temperature, or even better, warmed in a 350° oven for a few minutes. An even easier way to warm the pudding is to drizzle the portions with the maple syrup first, then microwave at medium-high, partially covered, for one minute per portion. Serve each portion with a dollop of crème fraîche. Any leftover pudding can be stored in the refrigerator for up to 4 days.

Deep Chocolate Pudding (or, This Ain't No Instant Pudding)

SERVES 6 TO 8

Outrageously rich, gloriously smooth and thicker, creamier and more deeply chocolatey than any other chocolate pudding I have ever tried. Serve it in small portions, at least to begin with. A good eating chocolate is best for this recipe, one with a fine flavour and a rich, full, sweet taste. This is not the time for a very bitter, 70% cocoa solids variety.

1 cup granulated sugar

4 tablespoons cornstarch

⅓ cup plus 1 tablespoon unsweetened Dutch-process cocoa powder

⅛ teaspoon salt

2½ cups whole milk (3.5%), or substitute 2% milk

4 large egg yolks

½ cup heavy cream (36%)

1 teaspoon pure vanilla extract

4 ounces good-quality bittersweet or semisweet chocolate

Lightly sweetened whipped cream, to serve, if desired

1. Place the sugar in a large bowl. Sift over it the cornstarch, cocoa and salt. Add ½ cup of the milk and stir the mixture to make a thick paste. Lightly beat the egg yolks, then add these to the cornstarch mixture, whisking to blend well. Wrap a damp towel around the base of the bowl to prevent it from sliding around when the scalded milk is added.

2. Meanwhile, in a heavy-bottomed 2-quart saucepan, combine the remaining 2 cups milk and the cream. Bring these just to the boil, then remove the pot from the heat. Pour a small amount of the hot liquid into the cornstarch-cocoa mixture, whisking constantly. Continue to whisk the milk-cream mixture into the bowl gradually, until all of the liquid has been incorporated, and the mixture is smooth. Rinse out the pot used to scald the milk and cream, but don't dry it; this will help prevent the pudding from scorching on the bottom. Pour the custard into the clean pot and add the vanilla.

3. Have ready a clean mesh sieve over a medium-sized bowl. Return the pot to the stove and stir with a wooden spoon over low to medium-low heat until the custard thickens, about 5 to 7 minutes. It should approach, but never quite reach, the boil and be about the consistency of mayonnaise when it's done. This custard behaves very strangely—you may fear something has gone terribly wrong, but press on! It will get increasingly lumpy to the point where, just as it reaches the right thickness, it will seem downright chunky. Never mind! Quickly remove the pot from the element and pour through the sieve into the clean bowl, pressing the custard through with a rubber spatula.

4. Add the finely chopped or grated chocolate in two additions, stirring gently with a clean wooden spoon or rubber spatula until the chocolate is melted smoothly into the pudding. Spoon the pudding into 6 to 8 serving dishes or goblets and chill at least 6 hours or overnight. If you like pudding with no skin on the top, press plastic wrap onto the surface of the warm pudding in the serving dishes. If a skin on your chocolate pudding makes you happily nostalgic, wait until the puddings are cold before covering. The pudding can be made up to 2 days ahead of time. Serve just as it is, or with a dollop of lightly sweetened whipped cream for a truly decadent dessert. Definitely not instant!

Vanilla Tapioca Pudding with Cinnamon Toast

SERVES 6

I debated calling this something other than tapioca, because so many people seem to have such dreadful memories of gloppy, bland puddings they were forced to eat as children. A tragedy, as good tapioca pudding is truly wonderful:

Vanilla Tapioca Pudding continued

sweet and delicate and creamy. It is super on its own, but the cinnamon toast makes it just about the best comfort food going.

3⅓ cups whole milk (3.5%)
1 large egg yolk, lightly beaten
4½ tablespoons minute or instant
 tapioca
½ cup granulated sugar
¼ teaspoon salt
1 vanilla bean, split

¼ cup tightly packed dark brown sugar
1 teaspoon ground cinnamon

6 thick slices brioche (see page 619),
 challah (egg bread) or other soft,
 rich white bread, preferably a
 day old
Unsalted butter, at room temperature

¾ cup heavy cream (36%), whipped
 with 1 tablespoon granulated sugar,
 for garnish

1. Combine the milk, egg yolk, tapioca, sugar and salt in a 2-quart saucepan with and whisk to blend. Scrape the seeds from the vanilla bean and add the seeds and the hull to the pot. Let the mixture sit for 5 minutes, then place the pot over medium heat.

2. Whisk slowly but constantly until the mixture just barely reaches the boil, about 13 to 18 minutes. Don't let the custard truly boil, but remove it from the heat just as the bubbles begin to surface. The grains of tapioca should be plump and very soft. Pour the pudding into a clean bowl and press a piece of plastic wrap onto the surface, poking a few holes in the plastic with a sharp knife to allow the steam to escape. Refrigerate for 1 to 2 hours, until cooled. Divide the custard between 6 dessert goblets or bowls. Cover the dishes with plastic wrap and chill until set, at least 4 hours.

3. Preheat the broiler. Blend together the brown sugar and cinnamon and set aside. Lay the slices of bread on a baking sheet and place under the broiler. Watch closely and remove the sheet when the bread looks pale gold. Turn the slices over and return the sheet to the broiler until golden on this side as well. Lightly butter one side of each slice and sprinkle generously with the cinnamon sugar. Cut the slices in half or quarters and serve immediately with the tapioca, which has been topped with a dollop of the lightly sweetened whipped cream.

Ricotta Pudding with Orange, Vanilla and Almonds

SERVES 10 TO 12

This unusual pudding is similar to some traditional Italian desserts that use ricotta, flavoured with sugar and other ingredients, and served fresh or baked into a soft pudding or cheesecake. Here, the cheese is left uncooked and is infused with the delicate flavours of orange zest, a bare hint of cinnamon, rich vanilla and lightly toasted almonds. Unadorned it is creamy and delicately flavoured; accompanied with a fruit or chocolate sauce, it is the kind of dessert you want to curl up with on a cold winter evening by the fire in your flannel pajamas. The Raspberry Coulis, page 643, the Mexican Chocolate Sauce, page 641, or the Mango-Orange-Passion Fruit Coulis, page 644, would all be wonderful partners. Both rich and light, this pudding makes a glorious finale to an elegant rustic meal. A note: different brands and types of ricotta will yield different results, some thicker, some more runny. Find a product you like, and use the cream to adjust the consistency.

2 pounds whole-milk (full-fat) ricotta

Seeds of 1 vanilla bean, scraped out, hull reserved for another use

1¼ cups confectioners' sugar, sifted

½ teaspoon ground cinnamon

1 to 1⅓ cups heavy cream (36%), or more, to adjust the consistency, if necessary

2 tablespoons tightly packed finely grated orange zest

Mexican Chocolate Sauce, page 641, to serve

1 cup lightly toasted sliced almonds, preferably not blanched (but unblanched sliced almonds *are* difficult to find, so blanched ones will do just fine), to serve

1. Place the ricotta in a large bowl. Use a wide wooden spoon to soften it a little. Add the vanilla bean seeds and smear them into the cheese, using the spoon in a deep spreading motion. Sift the confectioners' sugar and cinnamon together, and add about ½ cup of the mixture to the cheese. Blend in the rest of the sugar

Ricotta Pudding continued

mixture and the cream in ½-cup increments, alternating between the two, blending well after each addition. Smear in the orange zest; the pudding should be about the consistency of whipped cream cheese. If it appears too thick, add a few more tablespoons of cream. Cover the pudding with plastic wrap and refrigerate at least 4 hours or overnight to allow the flavours of the vanilla and orange to infuse the ricotta.

2. To serve, remove the pudding from the refrigerator half an hour before serving. Ricotta, like most cheeses, is most flavourful when just slightly cooler than room temperature, but not downright cold. Transfer the pudding to a decorative serving bowl, or to individual dessert bowls, and sprinkle with the toasted almonds. If serving with a sauce, pass it around separately and allow guests to pour a little over their own portions. The pudding can be made up to 24 hours ahead.

Warm Sweet Risotto with Saffron and Dried Cherries

SERVES 4

The most divine rice pudding you have ever dreamed of. This very simple variation is made without eggs, using instead the natural creaminess in arborio rice to achieve its richness and luxurious texture. This makes the pudding both lighter and more delicately flavoured than those made with eggs. I have infused the risotto with rich vanilla, grated orange and a hint of saffron, which adds an elusive flavour. The sweet dried cherries can be replaced with any other good-quality dried sweet fruit, such as dates, figs, apricots or raisins. Make sure the fruit you choose is unsulphured, as in this delicate pudding the "off" taste of the sulphur is quite detectable.

¾ cup arborio rice (short-grain rice)

2½ to 3 cups whole milk (3.5%), do not substitute low-fat or skim milk

½ cup granulated sugar

¾ teaspoon finely grated orange zest

1 plump vanilla bean, scraped out (use both seeds and hull)

Pinch saffron threads

½ cup plump dried sweet cherries, such as Bing

1. In a heavy-bottomed 2-quart saucepan, combine all of the ingredients save the cherries. Place the pot over medium-low heat and stir until bubbles break the surface. Reduce the heat to keep the mixture at a gentle simmer. Cook for 30 to 40 minutes, stirring frequently with a wooden spoon, until the pudding is thick and creamy, and the rice is tender and soft. Add the cherries during the final 5 minutes of cooking, then serve the pudding immediately in warmed shallow bowls.

❧ VARIATION ❧

Moroccan-Spiced Rice Pudding with Dates, Orange Flower Water and Honey:
Increase the grated orange zest in the master recipe to 1½ teaspoons. Reduce the sugar to ¼ cup and add ⅓ cup flavourful honey. Add ½ teaspoon ground cinnamon and ¼ teaspoon ground cardamom. At the end of cooking, add ½ cup coarsely chopped Medjool dates instead of the cherries, as well as ½ teaspoon orange flower water. Serve this exotic pudding garnished with ¼ cup finely chopped pistachio nuts or thin strands of Candied Orange Peel, page 634, if desired.

French Bittersweet Chocolate Mousse

MAKES 6 TO 8 SERVINGS

The true French chocolate mousse. I was first introduced to this type of mousse through a recipe given to my mother by her sister. Rich and sexy, it is beautifully simple: no whipping cream, no gelatine, no fillers, but the few ingredients it does have need to be the best available. It shows off a good chocolate better than almost anything else—I love really dark, bittersweet chocolate, but some people prefer a slightly sweeter type. Experiment! You'll have no shortage of willing taste-testers! The whipped cream garnish really isn't optional—it contributes as much to the overall dessert as the chocolate or the eggs.

8 ounces best-quality bittersweet
    chocolate, chopped
2 tablespoons instant espresso
    powder dissolved in ¼ cup warm
    water
8 large egg yolks
Seeds of ½ vanilla bean, hull reserved
    for another use

¼ cup coffee- or chocolate-flavoured
    liqueur, such as Kahlúa or Crème de
    Cacao, or substitute Cognac,
    Armagnac or another spirit
6 large egg whites, at room temperature

Lightly sweetened whipped cream,
    to serve
Chocolate-covered espresso beans,
    for garnish, optional

1. Place about 1 to 2 inches of water in a large pot and bring to a gentle simmer. Combine the chocolate and espresso in a stainless steel or glass bowl and set the bowl over the mouth of the pot. Reduce the heat so the water under the bowl is just barely simmering, and melt, stirring occasionally, until the mixture is about ¾ smooth. Remove the bowl from the heat and let the residual heat in the mixture finish the melting. Set the mixture aside to cool.

2. In a medium-sized bowl, whisk yolks together to break them up, then blend in the cooled chocolate mixture. Stir in the vanilla seeds and liqueur.

3. In a clean bowl with a clean, grease-free balloon whisk, beat the egg whites until stiff, but not dry and flaky. Fold the whites into the chocolate mixture in three stages, working quickly but using as few strokes as possible. Spoon the mixture into individual dessert glasses or bowls and refrigerate for 1 hour. Cover the dishes with plastic wrap and return them to the refrigerator for at least 3 hours, or overnight. Serve the mousses cool, garnished with a dollop of lightly sweetened whipped cream and a few chocolate-covered espresso beans, if desired.

✿ VARIATIONS ✿

Chocolate-Orange Mousse: Add 2 teaspoons very finely grated orange zest to the egg yolks before adding the chocolate mixture. Use an orange-flavoured liqueur, such as Curaçao or Grand Marnier in place of the coffee or chocolate liqueur. Garnish the mousses with lightly sweetened whipped cream and finely chopped *Candied Orange Peel*, page 634.

Chocolate-Hazelnut Mousse: Prepare the mousses as for the master recipe, using Frangelico (hazelnut-flavoured liqueur) in place of the coffee or chocolate liqueur. Along with the whipped cream, the mousses may be garnished with chocolate-dipped hazelnuts or finely chopped lightly toasted skinned hazelnuts (see page 262 for tips).

Chocolate-Amaretto Mousse: Prepare as for the Chocolate Hazelnut Mousse, above, substituting Amaretto (almond-flavoured liqueur) for the Frangelico and almonds for the hazelnuts as a garnish.

Ice Creams
and Other Frozen
Desserts

Roasted Cinnamon Ice Cream, Vanilla Bean Ice Cream

ABOUT 4 CUPS

Decadently rich and smooth, with the warm and unapologetic taste of cinnamon. Roasting the ground spice in releases some of the natural oils and gives the finished custard a dark, intense flavour. I've used two forms of cinnamon, ground and stick, to layer the flavour and give a profound, complex taste to the ice cream. For a more powerful cinnamon taste, use cassia; but for a more delicate, nuanced flavour, opt for true cinnamon. The Vanilla Bean variation that follows is also lusciously flavourful, with two whole fat beans imparting a big vanilla flavour. You can vary the flavour by using different kinds of vanilla beans: Mexican beans will yield a robust, rich flavour; Bourbon-Madagascar beans will give a more mellow, sweet taste; and Tahitian beans will impart a slightly floral, delicate flavour. Either of these ice creams is excellent as an accompaniment to other desserts, but they are truly special by themselves, with a drizzle of a chocolate ganache, a fresh berry coulis or nothing at all!

2 teaspoons good-quality ground cassia or cinnamon	6 large egg yolks
2 cups half-and-half cream (10%)	¾ cup granulated sugar
1 large cinnamon or cassia stick, broken into 3 or 4 pieces	1 cup heavy cream (36%)

1. In a small, dry, non-stick skillet over low heat, toast the ground cinnamon until it is warm to the touch and fragrant, about 2 to 3 minutes. Keep the spice moving, either by shaking the pan or by stirring, to prevent scorching. Remove the skillet from the heat and set aside.

2. In a heavy-bottomed 2-quart saucepan, combine the half-and-half cream and the pieces of cinnamon stick. Place the pot over medium-high heat and bring just to the boil, watching closely so the cream doesn't boil over. As soon as bubbles break the surface, remove the pot from the heat and let the custard infuse for 5 minutes. Meanwhile, in a large bowl, lightly whisk the egg yolks, then gradually whisk in the sugar. Beat just until it pales and thickens ever so

Roasted Cinnamon Ice Cream, Vanilla Bean Ice Cream continued

slightly. Place a damp kitchen towel around the base of the bowl to keep it still and whisk in the hot cream, a little at a time, until it is all incorporated.

3. Rinse out the saucepan but don't dry it; this will help prevent the custard from sticking to the bottom. Have ready a fine strainer set over a clean bowl. Return the custard mixture to the pot over medium heat, stirring constantly until it thickens enough to coat the back of a wooden spoon, about 7 to 10 minutes. A finger drawn across the back of the spoon should leave a clean trail. Immediately pour the custard through the strainer and set aside for a moment.

4. Add 2 tablespoons of the heavy cream to the roasted cinnamon and use a rubber spatula to blend into a thick, smooth paste. Add another 2 tablespoons of the cream and work this in until the mixture is about the consistency of a spreadable icing. Whisk the cinnamon paste into the hot strained custard until smooth. Stir in the remaining whipping cream and press a piece of plastic wrap onto the surface of the custard to prevent it from forming a skin. Poke a few holes in the plastic to allow steam to escape and place the bowl in the refrigerator until very cold, at least 4 hours but preferably overnight.

5. Process the chilled custard in an ice cream maker according to the manufacturer's instructions. Transfer the softly frozen ice cream to a freezable dish and freeze until firm. This richly flavoured ice cream is wonderful on its own, but makes an exceptionally good accompaniment to many other desserts, such as *Dried Fruit Sablées* (page 494) or many fruit tarts. Although best within a few days of being made, this ice cream can be stored for up to 1 week.

❦ VARIATION ❦

Vanilla Bean Ice Cream: Omit the ground cinnamon from the above recipe and substitute 2 plump vanilla beans, split and scraped out, for the cinnamon sticks, using both the hulls and seeds. After the cream has come just to the boil, remove it from the heat and let it infuse for 10 minutes. Return the pot to the burner and bring the mixture just below the boil. Proceed with the recipe above, leaving the vanilla bean hulls in the custard until it is cold. Remove the hulls before processing the custard in the ice cream maker.

Orange-Date Ice Cream

ABOUT 1½ QUARTS

Perfumed with the scent of orange and studded with plump, chewy dates, this is a glorious ice cream all by itself for a special dessert, but also makes a wonderful and unusual accompaniment to many others, such as the Oatmeal Stout Cake, page 384, or the Olive Oil and Sweet Wine Cake, page 437. It is also perfect with the Honey and Spice Madeleines on page 505! Do use Medjool dates, as their flavour will make the difference between a good ice cream and a spectacular one.

2 cups half-and-half cream (10%)
2 cups heavy cream (36%)
3 tablespoons finely grated orange zest
6 large egg yolks

⅔ cup granulated sugar
1 cup fresh orange juice
1 cup coarsely chopped, pitted Medjool dates

1. In a heavy-bottomed 2-quart saucepan, combine the half-and-half, 1 cup of the heavy cream and 1 tablespoon of the orange zest. Place the pot over medium-high heat until bubbles just break the surface, then remove from the heat and let the flavours infuse for about 5 minutes. As the mixture nears the scalding point, watch closely, as cream inflates voluminously as it boils and can make a terrible mess of an element!

2. Meanwhile, in a large bowl whisk the yolks to break them up, then add the sugar. Whisk this mixture until it is well blended and slightly pale, about 45 seconds. Place the bowl of yolks and sugar on a damp towel to stop it from sliding around, and to free up both of your hands. When the hot cream has infused for 5 minutes, slowly whisk a small amount into the yolks. Incorporate this before adding more, then gradually add the rest of the cream. Add the orange juice.

3. Bring an inch or two of water in a large pot to a bare simmer and have ready a fine-mesh sieve set over a medium bowl. Transfer the bowl with the custard to the top of the pot, creating a double boiler. Stir with a wooden spoon until the custard thickens and leaves a trail on the back of the spoon when you draw

Orange-Date Ice Cream continued

your finger across it, about 8 to 10 minutes. Remove the bowl from the heat and strain the custard into the waiting bowl. Stir in the remaining 1 cup whipping cream and 2 tablespoons orange zest. Press a piece of plastic wrap onto the surface of the custard to prevent a skin from forming and poke a few holes in the plastic with a sharp knife to allow the steam to escape. Refrigerate the custard until well chilled, at least 4 hours or preferably overnight.

4. Process the chilled custard in an ice cream maker according to the manufacturer's instructions, adding the chopped dates during the last few minutes of the churning. Transfer the soft ice cream to a shallow, freezer-safe dish, such as a glass loaf pan or baking dish, and freeze at least 6 hours to firm the texture. Placing the ice cream in a shallow dish enables you to scoop large beautiful scoops easily, and the ice cream will stiffen evenly throughout. The ice cream is best served within 3 or 4 days of making it, but may be kept for up to a week.

Mango Ripple Ice Cream

ABOUT 1 QUART

This is a lovely, rich ice cream, with a bright and fruity mango ribbon running through it. It is a great showcase for the best mangoes of the season, or those a little overripe. Although I usually prefer the more complex flavour of the Alphonse mango, the larger Kent type (the fat, reddish orange and green variety that is most common in North American markets) seems to work best in this recipe.

CUSTARD:

2 cups half-and-half cream (10%)
1 1-inch piece vanilla bean, scraped
   out (use both hull and seeds),
   or substitute ¾ teaspoon pure
   vanilla extract
5 large egg yolks
½ cup granulated sugar
¾ cup heavy cream (36%)

RIPPLE:

1 large or two small, ripe mango(es),
   preferably of the large Kent variety
¼ cup white corn syrup
1 teaspoon freshly squeezed lemon
   juice, if necessary
1 large egg white, lightly beaten

1. Prepare the custard: combine the half-and-half cream and the vanilla bean hull and seeds in a heavy-bottomed 2-quart saucepan and place the pan over medium heat. Bring the cream just to the boil, watching closely so it doesn't boil over, then remove it from the heat and let it infuse for 3 to 5 minutes. Meanwhile, in a large mixing bowl, lightly beat the egg yolks to break them up, then whisk in the sugar. Do not be tempted to overwhisk—you don't want a very thick, pale mixture with a lot of air incorporated.

2. Wrap a damp towel around the base of the bowl to hold it steady and very slowly pour the hot cream over the egg-sugar mixture, whisking constantly so the yolks don't curdle. Wash out the pot used for the cream, but don't dry the inside; a little film of water helps prevent the custard from sticking to the bottom of the pot. Have ready a fine-mesh strainer set over a clean bowl.

3. Return the custard to the pot and place it over medium-low heat. Stirring constantly with a wooden spoon, cook the custard until it thickens enough to coat the back of the spoon, about 7 to 10 minutes. A finger drawn across the back of the spoon should leave a clean trail. Immediately pour the custard through the strainer. Stir in the heavy cream and the vanilla extract, if using, and press a piece of plastic wrap onto the surface of the warm custard to prevent a skin from forming. Poke a few slits in the plastic with the tip of a sharp paring knife to allow the steam to escape and refrigerate the custard until well chilled, at least 4 hours, but ideally overnight.

4. Prepare the mango purée: peel the mango, making sure to remove all of the skin, as it is toxic if eaten. Cut away all of the usable flesh from around the stone, following the tips on page 307 if you are not familiar with mangoes. Roughly chop the fruit and place it in the bowl of a food processor or blender. Add the corn syrup and whir until the flesh is well puréed, scraping down the sides of the bowl several times.

5. Taste the purée: if it seems somewhat flat, not bright, add the lemon juice. Some mangoes are more sweet, tangy, spicy, peppery or acidic than others, and the flavour may need a boost. Force the purée through a fine mesh strainer into a clean bowl, pressing down on the solids to extract all of the thick liquid. In a separate bowl, beat the egg white just enough to loosen and break it up, but try

Mango Ripple Ice Cream continued

to incorporate as little air as possible. (Both the corn syrup and egg white help keep the purée from crystallizing and becoming overly icy when frozen.) Stir the white into the mango mixture, cover with plastic wrap and refrigerate until thoroughly chilled.

6. To make the ice cream, process the chilled custard in an ice cream maker according to the manufacturer's instructions. There are two ways to incorporate the mango ripple: the first is to add 1 cup of the purée to the ice cream maker during the last minute or two of processing, so it gets swirled but not thoroughly blended into the mostly frozen custard. The second option is to spread half of the softly frozen custard over the bottom of a glass loaf pan that has been chilled in the freezer for an hour or so. Top with a layer of the chilled mango purée, about ½ cup. Scrape the rest of the custard over the mango, then pour another ½ cup purée over the surface. To achieve the swirled, ripple effect, draw the blade of a butter or palette knife through the layers just enough to run the mango into the custard, leaving no large pockets of purée.

7. Quickly cover the dish with heavy plastic wrap and place in the freezer to firm up the ice cream. Homemade ice creams do not keep as long as commercial varieties; they should be used within 1 week, but are really best within 6 hours to 1 day of making. Serve this refreshing ice cream after a spicy Asian or Indian meal, or on a hot, sweltering summer afternoon. The remaining mango purée can be served as a simple sauce for the ice cream, if desired. This ice cream makes a lovely and elegant dessert when paired with the *Macadamia Nut Biscotti* on page 506, or topped with lightly toasted fresh coconut shavings. For an unusual treat, pair it with the *Lychee and Coconut Milk Sorbet* below.

Lychee and Coconut Milk Sorbet

ABOUT 1 QUART

The first time I served this, it was one of eight desserts at an elaborate buffet party, and by far the plainest one there. It was also the first to go! Easy and truly original, this refreshing sorbet is perfect as the finale to an Asian or Indian meal. Cool, tropical and light, it has a powerful yet very delicate flavour—elusive and luxurious. Canned lychees are actually more reliable than fresh, not to mention much less expensive and always available. Powdered cream of coconut is available in Thai or Asian grocery stores and adds a wonderful richness and depth of flavour to the sorbet, without sacrificing the silky texture. This sorbet is lovely paired with the Macadamia Nut Biscotti on page 506 or with the Mango Ripple Ice Cream, page 556.

3 (540 ml./19-ounce) tins lychees in syrup, drained, reserving ½ cup syrup

1 (400 ml./14-ounce) tin good-quality coconut milk, not "light"

¼ cup powdered cream of coconut

¼ cup warm water

¼ cup light corn syrup

Fresh coconut shavings, (see page 467), to serve, optional

Fresh lychee fruits, to serve, optional

1. Combine the drained lychees and reserved syrup in the bowl of a food processor and whir until puréed. Open the tin of coconut milk and spoon from the top of the tin 1 cup of the thick coconut cream. Add this cream to the processor and blend into the fruit. Strain the purée in batches through a coarse mesh sieve into a clean bowl, pressing hard on the solids to extract as much liquid as possible.

2. In a small bowl, stir together the powdered coconut cream and warm water. The mixture may be lumpy, but this is normal. Strain the liquid through a fine sieve into the lychee purée, pressing down on the solids. Blend well, then stir in the corn syrup. Cover the mixture and refrigerate until well chilled, at least 3 hours or overnight. (The mixture may be prepared up to 2 days ahead of time.)

3. Process the chilled lychee-coconut mixture in an ice cream maker according to the manufacturer's instructions. Pack the soft sorbet into a freezable container and freeze until firm, about 4 hours. The sorbet can be frozen for up to 2 weeks. Serve in tall wine glasses, garnished with a handful of fresh or lightly toasted coconut shavings and a few fresh lychee fruits, if in season.

Chestnut Ice Cream with Marrons Glacés

ABOUT 1 QUART

I adore the subtly rich, autumnal flavour of chestnuts and created this smooth and simple ice cream to show it off. The marrons glacés are optional, as they are not inexpensive, but they do make an extra-special dessert, glorious enough to stand well on its own. For a truly grand affair, pair this ice cream with the Warm Compote of Winter Fruits in Red Wine on page 583.

2¼ cups whole milk (3.5%)
½ cup sweetened chestnut purée with pure vanilla, also called crème de marrons
½ cup granulated sugar

6 large egg yolks
½ cup heavy cream (36%)
¾ cup coarsely chopped marrons glacés, available at gourmet and specialty food shops, optional

1. In a heavy-bottomed 2-quart saucepan, lightly whisk together the milk, chestnut purée and ¼ cup sugar. Over medium-high heat, bring the mixture just to the boil, stirring until the sugar is dissolved. Remove the pot from the heat.

2. Meanwhile, in a medium bowl, whisk together the egg yolks and the remaining ¼ cup sugar until thickened and pale. Wrap a damp towel around the base of the bowl to secure it, freeing both hands. Whisking constantly, pour a small amount of the hot milk mixture into the yolks, making sure it is well and quickly incorporated to avoid cooking the yolks unevenly. Gradually whisk in the rest of the milk.

3. Have a fine mesh strainer set over a clean bowl nearby. Wash the pot used for scalding the milk mixture, but don't dry it; this will help prevent the custard from scorching. Transfer the custard to the pot and place it over medium-low heat. Stir with a wooden spoon until the mixture is thick enough to coat the back of the spoon, and a finger drawn across the back leaves a clean trail. Do not leave this custard on the heat without stirring! It scorches easily and must be kept moving. Immediately pour the custard through the strainer and stir in the heavy cream. Press a piece of plastic wrap onto the surface of the custard and poke several slits in the plastic with a small, sharp knife to allow the steam to escape. Cool the custard to lukewarm, then refrigerate until well-chilled, at least 4 hours, but preferably overnight. (The custard may be prepared up to 2 days ahead and kept refrigerated.)

4. Process the custard in an ice cream machine according to the manufacturer's instructions. During the final 5 minutes of processing, add the chopped marrons glacés, if using. Transfer the ice cream to a shallow container to firm up before serving. This ice cream keeps for up to 5 or 6 days in the freezer, but is best if served within a day or two. Serve alone or as an accompaniment to simple cakes or fruit compotes, such as the *Warm Compote of Winter Fruits*.

World's Sexiest Sundae

4 LARGE SUNDAES

Sundaes are for children, right? Soooo wrong! Try this one—it is, simply put, a shamelessly decadent adult dessert. All the elements can be prepared well in advance and assembled at the last minute.

1 to 1½ cups Dark Chocolate Ganache (page 647)

12 scoops Vanilla Bean Ice Cream (page 553), or any combination of Vanilla Bean, Roasted Cinnamon Ice Cream (page 553) and Chestnut Ice Cream with Marrons Glacés (page 560)

1 cup heavy cream (36%), whipped to soft peaks

About ½ cup hazelnut or almond Praline (page 633), crushed

4 Sugar Cookies with Rock Sugar Borders (page 491) or 4 Chocolate Crisps (page 489)

1. Place the ganache in a small bowl set over a pot of simmering water and stir occasionally until it is evenly melted and warm to the touch. Alternatively, the ganache can be warmed in a microwave on medium power, stirring every 30 seconds. Take care not to scorch the sauce, though.

2. Place three scoops of the desired ice cream(s) in each of four shallow glass bowls or sundae dishes. Ladle about ¼ cup of the warm ganache over the ice

World's Sexiest Sundae continued

cream in each bowl. (Be generous here—it will save you the trouble of getting up when everyone moans softly for more chocolate.) Top with a healthy dollop of whipped cream and sprinkle each portion with a tablespoon or two of the crushed praline. Place a sugar cookie or chocolate crisp at the side of each dish and serve immediately. The recipe can be doubled, tripled, as you see fit!

Frozen Chocolate Chestnut Terrine

SERVES 6 TO 8

Somewhere between an ice cream and a chocolate mousse, this terrine is very rich and smooth. Chestnut is an elusive, earthy flavour, and one that blends beautifully with dark chocolate. Too many other flavours can overpower it, and too much sugar can mask its subtlety. Unsweetened chestnut purée is used in the terrine itself for its deep chestnut taste and keeps the terrine rich, but not sweet. The flavour is echoed in the cream, in which sweetened chestnut purée is used to give a gentle sweetness and depth. Marrons glacés are a lovely accompaniment, if you want to splurge! An easy, elegant, make-ahead dessert for a fall or winter dinner party.

12 ounces bittersweet chocolate, finely chopped

¾ cup unsalted butter, at room temperature

½ cup plus 2 tablespoons superfine sugar

1 (15-ounce) tin unsweetened chestnut purée

1 heaping teaspoon good-quality espresso powder, dissolved in ½ tablespoon warm water

2½ teaspoons pure vanilla extract

2 tablespoons Crème de Cacao, or other chocolate-flavoured liqueur

CHESTNUT CREAM:

1 cup heavy cream (36%)

½ cup sweetened chestnut purée with pure vanilla, also called crème de marrons

Marrons glacés, to serve, optional

1. Pour an inch or two of water into a large pot and bring it just to a simmer. Place the chocolate in a stainless steel or glass bowl that will fit comfortably over the mouth of the pot and reduce the heat so the water continues to just barely simmer. Melt the chopped chocolate, stirring occasionally and taking care that absolutely no moisture or steam comes into contact with the chocolate at any time (or it will seize). Do not let the bottom of the bowl touch the water. When the chocolate is mostly melted, turn the heat off and let the residual heat finish the melting. Remove the bowl from the pot and set it on a dry towel, wiping off the bottom completely. Cool the chocolate to about body temperature, or just slightly warmer.

2. Meanwhile, in a large bowl, beat the butter and sugar together until light and fluffy. In a separate bowl, mash the unsweetened chestnut purée with a fork until it is well creamed. Add the purée to the butter-sugar mixture and beat until fluffy. Beat the cooled chocolate into the creamed mixture, scraping down the sides and bottom of the bowl to make sure everything is thoroughly blended. Beat in the espresso paste, vanilla and liqueur and give the mixture a final stir. Scrape the mixture into a 9 x 5-inch metal loaf pan and cover with a piece of plastic wrap. Cover the whole pan with a sheet of aluminum foil, wrapping it tightly to keep air out. Freeze the terrine overnight, or up to 1 week.

3. Within a few hours of serving the terrine, prepare the Chestnut Cream: beat the heavy cream with the ½ cup sweetened chestnut purée until the cream holds soft peaks. Cover and chill until needed.

4. Allow the terrine to temper in the refrigerator for 30 minutes to 1 hour before unmoulding. If the terrine is difficult to unmould, press a piece of plastic wrap onto the terrine itself, making sure no plastic protrudes over the sides. Invert the pan onto your hand and run the underside of the tin under lukewarm water for a few seconds; the terrine should then slip out. Invert it onto a decorative tray or plate and slice with a knife dipped in warm water and wiped dry. Serve immediately; I like to serve two thin slices per person, topped with a good dollop of the Chestnut Cream and one or two whole marrons glacés.

Armagnac Parfait with
Agen Prune and Apple Compote
in Vanilla and Earl Grey Tea

SERVES 8 TO 12

*So smooth, so luxurious, so adult, so sexy, so luscious. And so easy! Creamier
and less solid than ice cream, this dessert is velvety and rich. This is a traditional parfait, not like the layered pudding and whipped-cream desserts we in
North America have come to know as "parfaits." The traditional parfait, an
egg-yolk-and-sugar syrup custard with whipped cream folded in, is similar to
what is often called a frozen soufflé. The basic recipe is infinitely flexible. I
have given a few of my favourite variations, but feel free to experiment with
other liqueurs and fruits.*

2 cups heavy cream (36%),
   very cold

¼ cup Armagnac

1 cup plus 5 tablespoons granulated
   sugar

½ cup water

7 large egg yolks

Agen Prune and Apple Compote in
   Vanilla and Earl Grey Tea (page 582)

1. In a chilled bowl with chilled beaters, whip the cream to soft peaks. Beat in
the Armagnac. Cover with plastic wrap and set in the refrigerator until needed.
Combine the sugar and the water in a heavy-bottomed 2-quart saucepan. Heat
gently, stirring until the sugar dissolves, then increase the heat and bring the
liquid to a boil. Boil until the syrup reaches 236°F on a candy thermometer (soft
ball stage, see page 74).

2. Meanwhile, beat the egg yolks until thickened and pale. I prefer hand-held
electric beaters and a damp towel wrapped tightly around the base of the mixing bowl to secure it for this recipe; it is very difficult to pour the syrup over the
yolks while whisking by hand, and the quantity of yolks is too small for most
stand mixers.

3. When the syrup reaches the right temperature, remove it from the heat and
immediately pour it onto the yolks in a thin, steady stream, whisking constantly

and quickly. Make sure the hot syrup is poured directly onto the eggs, not onto the whisk or beaters, or the movement of the whisking will just spin the syrup around the outside of the bowl, and you will end up with beaten egg yolks and a sticky bowl, but no parfait base. When the last of the syrup is incorporated, continue beating the yolk and syrup mixture until thick and slightly cooled, about 5 minutes on medium-high heat. Fold the chilled whipped cream into the yolk and syrup mixture. Scrape the mixture into a 2-quart soufflé dish or eight to twelve (½- to 1-cup) ramekins. (The mixture can be portioned into as few as 1 or as many as about 16 moulds. For very small parfaits, use tiny paper cups such as Dixie cups.) Cover with plastic wrap and then with aluminum foil and freeze until firm, at least 6 hours or overnight.

4. Remove the parfait(s) from the freezer about 20 minutes before serving. With one large parfait, use an ice cream scoop or large serving spoon to portion the dessert onto serving plates. To unmould individual parfaits, dip the bottoms of the ramekins in warm water for a few seconds, wipe dry, then invert onto dessert plates. Serve with generous spoonfuls of *Agen Prune and Apple Compote*. (I like to gently warm the compote in the microwave or on the stove first.)

VARIATIONS

Calvados Parfait with Caramelized Griddled Apples: Substitute ¼ cup Calvados for the Armagnac and prepare the parfait as above. For the caramelized apples, peel, core and thinly slice 5 or 6 medium-sized tart, firm apples. Melt ¼ cup un-salted butter in a large skillet, then add ¼ cup tightly packed light brown sugar, stirring over medium-low heat until the sugar dissolves. Add the apples, increase the heat and cook until the apples are golden and caramelized, 5 to 7 minutes. Remove the apples from the heat and serve immediately with the parfait.

Poire Williams Parfait with Caramel Pears: Substitute Poire Williams liqueur for the Armagnac and proceed with the master recipe. Serve with *Caramel Pears*, page 594.

Fruit Desserts

continued on page 568

Grapefruit Curd

ABOUT 6 CUPS

The sweet-tart taste of grapefruit is perfectly captured in a curd—smooth, bright and tangy. If you prefer a really tart flavour, use white or yellow grapefruit for the juice. Pink or Ruby Red grapefruit will yield a mellower, slightly sweeter curd with a more gentle citrus taste. Serve as an unusual partner to plain scones or croissants, or as a wild accompaniment to angel food cake. The meringue tart variation that follows is one of the most refreshing summer desserts I know!

12 large egg yolks

1 cup superfine sugar

2 teaspoons finely grated pink or yellow grapefruit zest

¾ cup freshly squeezed pink or yellow grapefruit juice

3 tablespoons freshly squeezed lemon juice

1 cup cold unsalted butter, cut into small pieces

1. Fill a large pot with an inch or two of water and bring the water to a simmer. Have a fine-mesh sieve set over a medium-sized bowl nearby. Place the egg yolks in a separate heatproof bowl, preferably stainless steel, and whisk them until they are frothy. Whisk in the sugar, then the grapefruit zest and juice and the lemon juice.

2. Set the bowl over the pot of simmering water and adjust the heat to keep the water just barely simmering. Cook the mixture, stirring constantly with a wooden spoon, until it thickly coats the back of the spoon and a finger drawn across the back of the spoon leaves a clean trail, about 7 to 10 minutes. This curd must be kept moving or the egg yolks will cook unevenly, and the curd will be lumpy and taste of egg, not grapefruit! Make sure the spoon sweeps across the bottom of the bowl and all around the sides. As soon as the curd has thickened, pour it through the waiting strainer.

3. With a clean spoon or rubber spatula, stir the butter into the hot curd a few pieces at a time, blending well after each addition. Press a piece of plastic wrap

Grapefruit Curd continued

directly onto the surface of the curd to prevent a skin from forming and poke a few slits in the top with a sharp knife to allow the steam to escape. Cool the curd to lukewarm, then refrigerate until cold, at least 2 hours or up to 8 hours. It's best served the day it is made, but may be stored, well-covered, in the refrigerator for up to 3 days. This curd is exceptional with *Poppyseed Angel Food Cake* (page 390) and makes plain croissants or scones terribly exciting.

✤ VARIATION ✤

Grapefruit Curd Meringue Tart: Pour the hot curd into a pre-baked and cooled Pâte Sucrée tart shell (page 655) and cool to lukewarm. Chill the cooled tart for several hours. Preheat the broiler and place 6 large, room-temperature egg whites in a non-reactive bowl. Whisking gently, add ½ cup granulated sugar, then place the bowl over a pot of barely simmering water. Stir the whites and the sugar together just until the mixture feels warm to the touch. Remove the bowl from the heat and add ½ teaspoon of cream of tartar. Whip the mixture, by hand or with an electric or stand mixer fitted with the whip attachment, until the meringue holds tall, stiff, glossy peaks. Spread the meringue over the entire surface of the tart, making sure it reaches the edges of the pastry all the way around (so it won't shrink away from the edges as it bakes). Slip the tart under the broiler, for a minute or two, until the peaks and mounds of the meringue are tinged with gold. Watch carefully! Don't leave the tart under the heat and walk away. Let the topping cool before serving.

Gala Apple Fritters with a Fresh Cider Syrup

ABOUT 20 FRITTERS

A comforting, not-too-sweet fritter, with a fresh apple taste and aroma. The cider syrup makes them a little out of the ordinary! I like to use Gala apples because the flavour is so floral, sweet and delicate, and I like the fruit to retain a little crunch. If you prefer a softer apple, feel free to experiment with other varieties. Whatever you do, try to use local apples—the flavour is so much

*more intense than that of long-travelled fruit! This batter is made with milk,
but can be made with beer, or even carbonated apple cider, for a lighter, slightly
crispier texture and different flavour.*

1 cup all-purpose flour

½ teaspoon salt

½ teaspoon baking powder

2 teaspoons granulated sugar

2 large eggs, separated

½ cup milk (or substitute beer or
    sparkling cider)

1 tablespoon unsalted butter, melted
    and cooled

3 to 4 cups vegetable oil, for deep-
    frying

4 large fresh Royal Gala, or other
    sweet, firm eating apple

Confectioners' sugar, sifted, for dusting

Fresh Apple Cider Syrup (page 637),
    warmed slightly in a microwave
    or on the stove

1. Sift the flour, salt, baking powder and sugar into a medium-sized bowl. In a separate bowl, beat the egg yolks with the milk and melted butter to blend. Gradually whisk the egg mixture into the dry ingredients, keeping the batter as smooth as possible. The batter will be very thick and maybe a little gluey. Cover the bowl with plastic wrap and let the batter rest for about 30 minutes to give the gluten a chance to relax.

2. Slowly heat the oil in a deep fryer or a large, heavy Dutch oven to a temperature of 375°F. I use a big enamelled cast iron pot for deep-frying—cast iron holds the heat beautifully. Whip the egg whites to soft peaks and gently fold them into the rested batter. Core the apples (peel them if you like, but I find the skins add a good flavour). Slice the apples into rings about ¼ to ⅓ inch thick and discard the end slices. Place the rings of one apple in the bowl of batter. Coat each slice well and lower them one at a time into the hot oil. Be careful, as the fat will splatter. Don't overload the fryer; three or four slices at a time are plenty.

3. Fry the rings for about 3 or 4 minutes, turning them once for even cooking. When the slices are a deep golden-brown on both sides, transfer them with a slotted spoon to a platter covered with paper towels. Dust the fritters with confectioners' sugar and drizzle with the warm syrup. Repeat with the remaining apple slices, letting the oil return to the right temperature before adding more fritters. As soggy fritters are remarkably unappetizing, these, like all fritters, are best eaten as they come out of the fryer!

Poached Peaches
with a Sweet Wine Syrup
and Crème Fraîche

SERVES 6

For this recipe, I like to use a late-harvest Vidal, which has the right balance of sweetness, flavour and acidity. Be careful when poaching sweet fruit in sweet wine: the wine you choose must have a good acidity, not just a cloying sweetness. Also, do remember to TASTE the fruit before deciding how much sugar to add to the poaching syrup. The amount below is appropriate for fruit that is ripe and quite sweet, but if your fruit is any less ripe, increase the amount by several tablespoons. The peaches and their syrup would also be good with ice cream, or a scoop of mascarpone cheese. You can lightly sweeten the crème fraîche if you like, but I prefer the slightly tangy cool cream as a contrast to the intensely flavoured and sweet fruit and syrup. Use spring water if you can—it makes a difference!

6 medium to large, firm but fully ripe unblemished and unbruised free-stone peaches

2 cups late-harvest Vidal dessert wine, or other sweet wine with a good sugar-acid balance

3 cups water, preferably filtered or still spring water

⅓ cup granulated sugar

1 (1 inch wide, 1½ inches long) strip lemon zest, thinly pared, with no white pith

2 (1-inch wide, 2 inches long) strips orange zest, thinly pared, with no white pith

1½ tablespoons freshly squeezed lemon juice

1 small cinnamon stick

1 vanilla bean, whole

2 green cardamom pods, lightly crushed

Crème Fraîche (page 651), to serve

1. Peel the peaches by dropping them two at a time into a pot of boiling water for 30 seconds, then plunging them into a bowl of ice water to stop the cooking. With the skins still on, halve the peaches and pick the stone out of the flesh. Slip the skins off the fruit, with the help of a paring knife if necessary.

2. In a heavy-bottomed 2-quart saucepan, combine the wine, water, sugar, lemon and orange zests, lemon juice, cinnamon, vanilla bean and cardamom pods. Bring the mixture to a boil over medium heat, stirring until the sugar is dissolved. When the syrup boils, remove it from the heat and carefully add the peach halves.

3. Return the pot to the burner and bring the syrup back to a boil, gently easing the peaches down into the liquid with a wooden spoon. As soon as bubbles begin to break the surface, take the pot off the heat and press a clean small towel onto the surface of the syrup and peaches and cool the fruit in the syrup. When the contents of the pot have reached room temperature, remove the peaches from the syrup and refrigerate them until just before you serve them.

4. Wring out the towel and set it somewhere you'll remember to clean it! Return the poaching liquid in the pot to the burner over medium-high heat and bring to a boil. Simmer until reduced to a thin syrup, then cool to room temperature and strain. Split the vanilla bean and scrape the seeds into the strained syrup. Return the hull to the syrup, too—it will continue to flavour the syrup. Pour the syrup over the chilled peaches and return both to the refrigerator.

5. The peaches may be served chilled, or at room temperature. Place two peach halves in each of 6 dessert bowls and spoon some of the syrup over top, stirring to make sure each portion includes some of the vanilla seeds. Place a dollop of crème fraîche beside or atop each portion and serve. They're wonderful warmed too, over a really good vanilla ice cream. For an extra treat, serve a shortbread or sugar cookie along with the peaches.

Pears Poached in
Gewürztraminer with Tahitian
Vanilla and Ginger

SERVES 6

This is one of my favourite desserts, and it's deceptively simple—not the kind you get wildly excited fantasizing about, but the kind that seems so perfect when you eat it. Its great beauty lies in its wonderfully complementary flavours: floral, tropical and delicate. The pears are great accompanied by a scoop of vanilla ice cream and the Macadamia Nut Biscotti (page 506) or Sugar Cookies with Rock Sugar Borders (page 491). Seckel pears are small, seasonally available pears that are perfect for poaching: firm, flavourful and too hard to eat raw. The beautiful Forelle pears are similar, but slightly softer and sweeter, so won't need as long to poach. Adjust the cooking time depending on the variety, size and ripeness of the fruit.

1 bottle (750 ml.) good-quality
   Gewürztraminer wine
1 cup water, preferably filtered or still
   spring water
1 cup granulated sugar
1 plump Tahitian vanilla bean, split
   lengthwise
One (1½-inch) piece fresh ginger root,
   peeled and sliced in ¼-inch thick
   slices

2 teaspoons freshly squeezed lemon
   juice
6 medium-sized, ripe but firm pears,
   such as Bartlett or Anjou; or 10 to
   12 small firm dessert pears, such
   as Sugar, Seckel or Forelle

Vanilla Bean Ice Cream (page 553),
   to serve

1. In a heavy-bottomed 2-quart saucepan just large enough to hold the pears with about 2 inches of headspace to spare, combine the wine, water and sugar. Bring the mixture to the boil, stirring until the sugar dissolves. Remove the syrup from the heat and add the vanilla bean, ginger slices and lemon juice. Peel the pears, removing the skin as thinly as possible, leaving the stems intact. Follow the gentle curves of the pears as you peel them so they retain their beautiful shape.

2. Add the pears all at once to the pot of syrup and press a small, clean dish-cloth directly onto the surface of the mixture, soaking the cloth. Place a circle of parchment paper onto the cloth; this will prevent the pears from poaching unevenly or drying out on one side. (If you find the pears are still floating, you can place a little plate or saucer onto the cloth to weigh them down. The trick is to keep the fruit under the syrup, without having it rest on the bottom of the pot! Do your best; I have found one side plate that is the perfect size and weight—heavy enough to hold the fruit under, but not so heavy that the pears are squashed against the bottom. Experiment! Somewhere in your kitchen is the ideal dish!)

3. Return the pot to the element over medium-low heat and slowly bring the syrup to a bare simmer. Watch closely: you don't want the mixture to boil too vigorously at any point, or the fruit will cook too quickly and begin to break down in the syrup. Reduce the heat slightly and keep the syrup just below the simmer. Tiny bubbles should dance up around the pears and just break the surface. Too low is better than too high a heat; the pears may take a little longer to poach, but will remain intact and tender.

4. Poach the fruit until the tip of a very sharp knife slips in and out easily. Let the pears cool in their syrup, then refrigerate until needed. If the pears are extremely soft, carefully remove them from the syrup into a shallow container and refrigerate until cool. Cool the syrup separately, then pour it over the pears and refrigerate together until needed. (The pears can be poached up to 4 days ahead of time and refrigerated, submerged in their syrup.)

5. To serve, remove the fruit from the refrigerator about 1 hour before you plan to serve them. Pare off a little slice from the bottom of each pear to create a flat plane for the fruit to stand on and place one in each of 6 shallow dessert bowls. Spoon some of the syrup over top and accompany with a scoop of *Vanilla Bean Ice Cream* and a flavourful biscuit. Crème anglaise also makes a lovely accompaniment.

Oven-Roasted Pears
with Red Wine and a Gratin
of Goat's Cheese

SERVES 6 TO 10

This is a sensational dessert for an elegant dinner party, perfect for those who aren't overly fond of sweet finales. The softly sweet, spiced pears are the perfect foil for the tangy goat's cheese, and the mulled wine sauce wraps everything in a dark, complex flavour. Very sophisticated—and also very simple!

½ cup tightly packed light brown sugar
½ teaspoon ground cinnamon
¼ teaspoon freshly grated nutmeg
⅛ teaspoon freshly ground cloves
Pinch freshly ground black pepper
⅓ cup unsalted butter, melted and
　cooled
1 tablespoon freshly squeezed lemon
　juice

1 tablespoon orange juice
6 firm but ripe Bartlett, Bosc or
　Anjou pears
6 ounces (about ¾ cup, packed) soft
　unripened goat's cheese

Warm Mulled Wine Sauce, page 640

1. Preheat the oven to 375°. Generously butter a baking dish just large enough to hold 12 pear halves in one layer. Combine the brown sugar, cinnamon, nutmeg, cloves and black pepper in a medium bowl. Stir in the melted butter to make a paste, then add the lemon and orange juices. Peel and halve the pears and scoop out the cores with a melon baller or teaspoon.

2. Gently place the pear halves in the brown sugar mixture to coat, then place them cut-side down in the baking dish. Scrape the mixture over the pears and place the baking dish, uncovered, into the centre of the oven. Bake the pears for 35 to 45 minutes, basting every 10, or until the pears are very tender when pierced with the tip of a sharp knife and are amber-coloured and caramelized.

3. Preheat the broiler. Turn the pear halves over, exposing the cut sides. Spoon about 2 tablespoons of the goat's cheese into the core cavity of each half, mounding it in the centre. Flash the dish of cheese-filled pears under the broiler and watch closely until the cheese is slightly melted and tinged with brown. Serve immediately, with *Warm Mulled Wine Sauce*.

Peach and Mixed Berry Cobbler

SERVES 8

In this easy cobbler, a mixture of any summer berries, such as blackberries, blueberries and raspberries, would work beautifully, or you could use just one type, if you happen to have a glut (or a passion!). Either way, the result is gorgeous colours bubbling up between fluffy golden biscuits. Add a scoop of ice cream and you have a divine way of passing the time. I don't skin my peaches for this dessert, but if you prefer, you can blanch and peel them (following the directions on page 280) before proceeding.

FRUIT:

2½ pounds ripe freestone peaches (about 8 medium, or 6 very large)

2 cups mixed berries, such as blueberries, blackberries, red or black raspberries, huckleberries, etc.

½ cup plus 2 tablespoons granulated sugar

3 to 4 tablespoons cornstarch, depending on the juiciness of the fruit

2 teaspoons freshly squeezed lemon juice

BISCUIT TOPPING:

2 cups all-purpose flour

3 tablespoons granulated sugar

½ teaspoon salt

2 teaspoons baking powder

5 tablespoons unsalted butter, cold, cut into small pieces

½ cup whole milk (3.5%), cold

½ cup heavy cream (36%), cold

1 teaspoon pure vanilla extract

Additional unsalted butter, at room temperature, for greasing the dish

Additional 1½ tablespoons granulated sugar, for sprinkling

Peach and Mixed Berry Cobbler continued

1. Preheat the oven to 400°. Lightly butter the inside of a shallow 2-quart, preferably ceramic, baking dish and set aside. Wash and pat dry the peaches, then cut each one in half, discarding the stone. Cut the peach halves into 6 or 8 slices and place in a large bowl. Add the berries, sugar, cornstarch and lemon juice and use a large rubber spatula to gently toss the ingredients together until the sugar and cornstarch are evenly distributed. Don't be overly aggressive at this point, or you will bruise and crush the fruit. Let the fruit sit while you prepare the biscuit mixture.

2. Into a large bowl, sift together the flour, sugar, salt and baking powder and stir with a fork to blend well. Use a pastry blender or two knives to cut the butter into the flour mixture until the largest lumps are about the size of fat peas. (Alternatively, combine the dry ingredients in the bowl of a food processor and pulse once or twice to blend. Add the butter and pulse until the largest lumps are the size of fat peas. Transfer the mixture to a large bowl and proceed with the recipe.) At this point, give the fruit one more gentle stir, then spoon it into the prepared baking dish, scraping the juices, sugar and starch from the bottom of the bowl over the fruit and spreading the filling evenly over the bottom of the dish.

3. Combine the milk, cream and vanilla and pour this mixture into the flour-butter mixture. Use the fork to stir for the first few strokes, then use your hands to gently rub the liquid into the crumble. The dough should be very wet and sticky. Pinch off egg-sized lumps of the gooey dough and drop these dollops onto the fruit, eventually covering most of the surface of the dish. A few little cracks between the biscuits is fine; the jewel-coloured juices of the berries will bubble up and stain the white biscuits and look gorgeous. Sprinkle the top of the cobbler with the 1½ tablespoons of sugar.

4. Bake the cobbler for 50 to 60 minutes, or until the juices from the fruit are bubbling vigorously through the cracks between the biscuits and the biscuits are puffed and golden. Cool on a wire rack for at least 25 minutes before serving. Serve warm or at room temperature, alone or with a scoop of *Vanilla Bean Ice Cream*, page 553. The cobbler should be eaten within 3 or 4 hours of baking, but any leftovers can be covered and refrigerated for 2 to 3 days. (A hint: leave the serving spoon in the dish for easy access.)

Tropical Fruit Crumble

SERVES 8

A good crumble is one of the simplest, yet most satisfying desserts I know. The right combination of flavours and ingredients does all the work, letting you sit back and enjoy something truly greater than the sum of its parts. This islands-inspired crumble is infinitely variable, depending on your taste, and the availability of the different fruits. Try to get a good mix of sweetness, textures, acidity and colour. The finished dessert will be rich, complex and addictive.

TOPPING:

½ cup granulated sugar

½ cup tightly packed demerara or dark brown sugar

1 cup all-purpose flour, sifted

½ cup plus 1 tablespoon cold unsalted butter, diced

⅓ cup sweetened shredded coconut

⅓ cup raw, unsalted macadamia nuts, chopped

FRUIT:

1 ripe pineapple*, peeled, eyes removed, and cored (see page 309)

1 ripe papaya, peeled and seeded (see page 308)

1 large or 2 small ripe mangoes, peeled and oblong pit removed (see page 307)

1 large or 2 small bananas, ripe but not brown

Juice of ½ lime

½ cup granulated sugar, or more or less depending on the sweetness of fruit

2 tablespoons instant (small pearl or minute) tapioca

**or any combination to achieve 8 cups chopped tropical fruits*

1. Preheat the oven to 375°. Select a wide 2- to 2½-quart baking dish or casserole large enough to hold 8 cups of fruit and an inch or two of crumble and set aside.

2. Prepare the topping: in a large bowl, combine the sugars and stir with a fork to break up any lumps of demerara. Blend in the flour. With a pastry blender or by rubbing the mixture roughly between your fingers, cut in the butter until the crumble begins to lump together. (The crumble may also be prepared up to

Tropical Fruit Crumble continued

this point in a food processor fitted with a steel blade: whir the sugars together to break them up, then add the flour and whir just to mix. Add the diced butter and use quick pulses to reduce the mixture to a lumpy crumble. Transfer the crumble to a bowl and proceed with the rest of the recipe by hand). Add the coconut and macadamias and work these in by hand, kneading the mixture until evenly moist and crumbly, then set aside.

3. Prepare the fruit: cut the pineapple, papaya and mango flesh into roughly 1-inch chunks and combine in large non-reactive bowl. Peel and slice the banana, then add to the bowl. Sprinkle the fruit with lime juice and toss gently to coat. In a small bowl, combine the sugar and tapioca, then toss with the fruit. Don't forget to taste! If not sweet enough for your liking, add another few tablespoons of sugar. If the sweetness is more than you care for, add another squeeze of lime.

4. Spoon the fruit into the baking dish. Sprinkle the crumble mixture evenly over the top. Be generous! I like to have every bit of fruit covered with a good inch or so of the sweet crunchy topping. Set the dish in the preheated oven and bake for about 45 minutes, or until the topping is a rich golden brown in spots and the juices from the fruit are visibly bubbling up through the crumble. Remove from the oven and cool at least 20 minutes before serving. (The crumble may be baked up to 1 day ahead of time and reheated in a 350° oven for 15 minutes before serving.) Serve warm or at room temperature, with *Vanilla Bean Ice Cream*, page 553, or *Lychee and Coconut Milk Sorbet*, page 558, or with a dollop of thick yogurt, lightly sweetened with a flavourful honey.

Pear, Cranberry and Vanilla Crumble

SERVES 6 TO 8

Oh, how I love a good crumble. I think they're pretty much the most comforting and homey desserts in the world. This one pairs soft sweet pears with sparklingly tart cranberries. Real vanilla seeds lace the flavours together, and a generous crunchy topping is the "icing on the cake"! Make it only in the fall and winter, when ripe local pears and fresh cranberries abound. The secret to a fabulous crumble, in my opinion, is in the size of the dish you bake it in. A larger area means more crumble in each bite!

TOPPING:

¾ cup all-purpose flour

¾ cup old-fashioned rolled oats

¾ cup tightly packed dark brown sugar

¾ cup unsalted butter, cold, cut into small pieces

FILLING:

Seeds of 1 plump vanilla bean, hull reserved for another use

¼ cup tightly packed light brown sugar

¼ cup granulated sugar

½ tablespoon cornstarch

¼ teaspoon ground cinnamon

5 to 6 medium-sized, ripe, but not mushy, eating pears, such as Bartlett or Anjou

3 cups fresh cranberries

1. Preheat the oven to 375°. Butter a large shallow baking dish, preferably ceramic. You can prepare this crumble in any 2½-quart casserole or gratin dish, but, as I said, the wider the better. Prepare the crumble topping: combine the flour, oats, brown sugar and butter in a mixing bowl and cut together until the largest pieces are about the size of the oats. Use your fingers to rub the ingredients together until the mixture forms a crumbly dough. Cover with plastic wrap and chill until needed. The crumble can be made up to 2 days ahead of time and stored in the refrigerator.

2. In a large bowl, stir together the vanilla seeds, sugars, cornstarch and cinnamon. Peel and core the pears and cut them into sixths or eighths. Add the pears and cranberries to the mixing bowl and toss gently to thoroughly coat the fruit. Scatter the fruit mixture in the baking dish, then crumble the oat mixture over top, distributing it evenly.

3. Bake the crumble for 35 to 45 minutes for a shallow dish, 45 to 55 minutes for a deeper casserole, or until the topping is crisp and golden and the filling can be seen bubbling up through the cracks. Cool at least 15 minutes before serving so people don't burn their mouths, then serve warm or at room temperature with a scoop of *Vanilla Bean* or *Roasted Cinnamon Ice Cream* (page 553). Or dispense with ceremony and eat it with a big spoon straight from the dish while still on the cooling rack, as is my preference.

Agen Prune and Apple Compote in Vanilla and Earl Grey Tea

ABOUT 6 CUPS

This is the sort of recipe a good pastry cook should always have up their sleeve: so simple, so versatile, so few ingredients and so wonderfully satisfying! I love this over ice cream, and it is outstanding when paired with the frozen Armagnac Parfait on page 564. For the best breakfast you have ever, ever had, try it spooned over French toast—this was our Sunday brunch specialty at Delisle, and it was awfully hard for the kitchen staff not to deplete the pot of compote before service had even started! Agen prunes are reputed to be the best in the world. Imported from the Agen region of France, they are available in upscale fruit and vegetable shops, as well as gourmet and specialty shops. If you cannot find them, substitute plump, moist, unsulphured dried prunes. Twinings Earl Grey tea is by far the most fragrant and delicately flavoured variety; it is available in good supermarkets and specialty food stores throughout Canada. The recipe can be doubled, and makes lovely gifts!

¾ pound pitted Agen prunes
2 cups water, preferably filtered or still
    spring water
2 Earl Grey tea bags, preferably
    Twinings brand

3 cups water
1¼ cups granulated sugar
½ vanilla bean, split
3 to 4 firm, semi-tart apples, such as
    Cortland, about 1½ to 1¾ pounds

1. Place the prunes in a medium-sized, non-reactive bowl. Bring the 2 cups water to the boil in a saucepan with the tea bags, then pour the tea over the prunes, leaving the bags in the liquid to infuse. Let the prunes steep in the tea for about 3 hours. Strain the prunes, discarding the liquid.

2. Meanwhile, combine the 3 cups water, the sugar and the vanilla bean in a large, heavy-bottomed saucepan and heat gently, stirring until the sugar dissolves. Increase the heat, bring the syrup to a boil and boil for 4 to 5 minutes. Peel and core the apples, then cut them into eighths. Add the apples to the syrup all at once and return the liquid to the boil. Simmer for 1 minute, then transfer the apples and their syrup to a clean container. Cool to room temperature, then cover and refrigerate until the prunes are ready.

3. Add the drained prunes to the apples and stir to distribute the fruit. Refrigerate the compote for 24 hours before serving, to allow the flavours to mingle and deepen. This compote can be kept for up to 2 weeks, covered, in the refrigerator. Use it to garnish yogurt or French toast for breakfast; or ice cream, pound cake or a rich parfait for dessert.

Warm Compote of Winter Fruits in Red Wine

ABOUT 1½ TO 2 QUARTS

An easy dessert that is guaranteed to warm you up on even the coldest winter night. I devised the recipe below simply as a guide—play with the quantities and types of fruit to suite your taste and the meal. The ingredients list may seem long, but the assembly is very quick. The flavours of the fruits and spices blend, bound with the richness of the wine, to create a great harmony of flavour. Serve warm in shallow bowls or glass goblets.

½ pound dried pitted prunes, such as
    Agen prunes
½ pound moist dried Calmyrna figs
⅓ pound moist dried pear halves,
    preferably unsulphured
⅓ pound dried peaches, preferably
    unsulphured
¼ pound dried apricots, preferably
    unsulphured
½ cup golden raisins
½ cup dried cherries
¼ cup dried cranberries

1 bottle (750 ml.) dry red wine, such as
    Pinot Noir or Beaujolais Nouveau
2 cinnamon sticks, broken into pieces
8 allspice berries
6 to 8 black peppercorns
2 cardamom pods, lightly crushed
1 bay leaf
3 whole cloves
1 strip of orange zest, about 3 inches
    long and 1 inch wide
⅓ cup freshly squeezed orange juice
1½ cups granulated sugar

Warm Compote of Winter Fruits continued

1. Place all the dried fruit in a large non-reactive saucepan. Pour the wine over it all. Tie the cinnamon sticks, allspice berries, peppercorns, cardamom pods, bay leaf and cloves in a small square of cheesecloth, securing the ends with a piece of string. Pop the spice bag in the pot with the fruit and wine, then add the orange zest, juice and sugar. Over medium-low heat, bring the mixture to a gentle simmer and cook for about 5 to 10 minutes, or until the fruit is tender, but still chewy. Allow the compote to cool slightly then cover and place in the refrigerator for at least 24 hours, to allow the flavours to mature, or up to 5 days.

2. To serve, rewarm the fruit and its liquid in a saucepan set over low heat, stirring until just warm. The fruit looks like plump jewels when served in glass or crystal coupes. Slices of plain cake or a plate of pretty biscuits are lovely accompaniments, but the best partner for this highly flavoured dessert is a generous scoop of *Chestnut Ice Cream with Marrons Glacés*, (page 560) or *Roasted Cinnamon Ice Cream* (page 553). This recipe makes a large amount of compote, perfect for a holiday meal, and any leftovers will keep very well for up to 2 weeks. It also makes a great topping for pancakes or waffles!

Oven-Roasted Figs with Honey and Orange

SERVES 4 TO 6

Meltingly tender, honeyed fruit and a luscious runny sauce, this simple dessert takes literally minutes to prepare and is sensuous, hugely flavourful and versatile. Serve it right from the oven over Vanilla Bean or Roasted Cinnamon Ice Cream, or with a plain pound cake. It is sublime when paired with the Olive Oil and Sweet Wine Cake on page 437. Dried Fruit Sablées (page 494) or a plain shortbread would also make wonderful accompaniments. I prefer to use black figs, rather than green, for this and most other dessert recipes, as they are sweeter and have more of a honey flavour to them. Make sure the figs are perfectly ripe, and use a good, flavourful honey. One with a floral taste works very well with the fruit in this recipe—lavender, wildflower and orange blossom would all be wonderful choices.

14 to 18 ripe black figs, dusted off
   if necessary
1 large or 2 small cinnamon sticks,
   broken into pieces
3 cardamom pods, lightly crushed

½ cup flavourful honey
Grated zest and juice of 1 large orange
3 tablespoons unsalted butter, in
   small pieces

1. Preheat the oven to 350°. Cut off the hard little nib at the top of each fig, then cut each fig almost into quarters, not cutting through the bottom, so it opens like a flower, but remains intact. Arrange the figs, cut-side up in a stoneware or crockery baking dish just large enough to hold the fruit in one layer. The figs should be slightly opened, but not splayed. Scatter the cinnamon sticks and cardamom pods among the fruit.

2. In a small bowl, whisk together the honey, orange zest and orange juice and pour this mixture over the figs. Dot the figs with the butter and place the dish in the oven. Bake for 10 minutes, then baste the fruit with the juices in the dish and increase the heat to 375°. Bake another 10 to 15 minutes, until the figs are meltingly tender, and the juices have at least doubled. Cool the figs 10 minutes before serving. Serve 3 to 4 figs per person if no other dessert is served, 2 or 3 if the compote is poured over ice cream or served with cake or biscuits.

Sautéed Orchard Fruit with an Orange Muscat Sabayon

SERVES 6 TO 8

A marriage of beautiful flavours, colours, textures and temperatures, this is a simple, last-minute dessert that showcases the best fruits of the late season. The fruit can be a single variety, such as peaches; several types of one variety, such as orange and white peaches; or a combination of two or more fruits, such as peaches, nectarines, apricots and even plums. The muscat sabayon can be made two ways. If made at the last minute, it will be warm and dense, a luxurious topping for the hot fruit. If you want to prepare it ahead of time, whipped

Sautéed Orchard Fruit continued

heavy cream is folded into the cooled sabayon to stabilize it and enable it to be refrigerated for several hours without losing volume and deflating. This version is particularly good with the warm fruit compote—the sensuous cool frothy cream balances the warm, juicy sweetness of the fruit. If you prefer to serve your fruit absolutely fresh, not sautéed, opt for the last-minute sabayon, so the warm will contrast with the cool.

SABAYON:

6 large egg yolks

⅓ cup granulated sugar

½ cup Orange Muscat dessert wine, such as Quady's Essencia, or another sweet muscat

¾ cup heavy cream (36%), chilled, if the sabayon is to be prepared ahead and served chilled

SAUTÉED FRUIT:

About 3 pounds (about 8 large peaches) firm, ripe mixed stone fruit, such as yellow and white peaches, nectarines, apricots and plums, unblemished and unbruised

2 tablespoons unsalted butter

2 tablespoons granulated sugar, or more, depending on the sweetness of the fruit

Small squeeze of lemon juice

1. A few hours before serving, prepare the sabayon. Fill a large pot with about 1 to 2 inches of water and bring to a gentle simmer on the stove. Reduce the heat until there are only tiny bubbles almost breaking the surface. The water should not come to the boil again, or the heat could curdle the eggs. Have ready a large bowl filled with ice water to cool the sabayon as soon as it comes off the stove. In a medium-sized bowl (preferably copper, but stainless steel will do), with a fine-wired balloon whisk, lightly beat the yolks just to break them up. Have the ½ cup wine at hand. Beat in the sugar and place the bowl over the simmering water. Whisk the mixture constantly until it begins to foam, then whisk in the wine.

2. Whisk the custard over the heat until it is thickened, frothy and doubled in volume. The movement you are aiming for with the whisk is not simply a stirring motion, but a vertically circular arc; you are whipping air into the egg mixture. The sabayon should be ready in 3 to 7 minutes, depending on the heat and the type of bowl you are using. The finished sauce should fall thickly and luxuriously from the whisk, and the whisk should leave a trail when pulled through the mixture. Still whisking, immediately set the base of the sabayon bowl into the larger bowl of ice water. Stir the sabayon with the whisk until completely cool, then remove it from the ice bath.

3. Beat the chilled heavy cream until it forms soft, floppy peaks, then fold it into the cooled sabayon. (This will prevent the egg foam from deflating and enable the sabayon to be prepared ahead of time. For a warm sabayon that must be served immediately, omit the whipped cream and serve the sabayon as is, directly from the stove.) Transfer the sabayon cream to a clean bowl, cover and refrigerate for up to 4 hours.

4. Prepare the sautéed fruit: bring a pot of water to the boil and drop the peaches, nectarines, apricots—whatever fruit needs skinning—into the water in batches of 3 or 4. Remove them after 30 to 45 seconds, depending on the ripeness, and immediately plunge them into a bowl of ice water to stop the cooking. Repeat with the remaining fruit, then slip the skins off. Halve the fruit and remove the stones, then slice the halves—larger fruit like peaches and nectarines should be cut into 6 or 8 slices, apricots can be quartered. The slices should be small enough to fit comfortably on a dessert spoon.

5. Melt the butter in a large skillet over medium heat. Add the sugar and stir until it melts. Add the fruit, spreading the slices out in a single layer. If the fruit will not all fit in the skillet at once, use two skillets and add a little extra butter and sugar. Cook the fruit until it begins to caramelize and turn golden brown at the edges, then flip the fruit over and do the same on the other side. The slices should be hot and beginning to colour, but should not be cooked so long that they become mushy. Adjust the heat if they don't seem to be colouring quickly enough or are softening too quickly! In general, a higher heat is preferable, as it will promote the caramelizing, but it must not be so high that the butter and sugar burn.

6. Add the lemon juice and spoon the fruit into 6 or 8 glass or crystal dessert coupes or goblets. Top the warm fruit with generous mounds of the chilled sabayon and serve immediately, with little glasses of the remaining muscat, of course!

Baked Apples with Currants, Vin Santo and Crumbled Biscotti

SERVES 6

These are yummy and warm, with the comforting flavours of a grandmother's dessert, dressed up a bit with some distinctly adult elements. Vin Santo is a luscious Italian dessert wine, with a deep amber colour that matches its taste. It has overtones of raisins and nuts and marries beautifully with the currants and biscotti. The biscotti contribute a great deal of flavour to the final dessert and should be of good quality, either homemade or purchased from a good bakery or café. The apples should be a firm, tart baking apple. Softer apples will collapse before they are fully cooked and will not support the filling. I love to serve this with a cool crème anglaise, flavoured with a little more Vin Santo, but you could substitute Vanilla Bean Ice Cream (page 553) or lightly sweetened whipped cream if you prefer. And, of course, pour small glasses of the same dessert wine to accompany this rustic but elegant dessert.

⅓ cup Vin Santo

¼ cup dried currants

1½ cups (about 6 to 10, depending on the size) crumbled Currant Biscotti (page 511), or good-quality purchased almond biscotti

3 large egg whites, at room temperature

3 tablespoons dark, flavourful honey, but not buckwheat

6 large firm, tart cooking apples, such as Rome Beauty or Northern Spy, unblemished and unbruised

Juice of ½ lemon

¼ cup unsalted butter, melted and cooled

1 tablespoon granulated sugar, for sprinkling

Crème Anglaise (page 649), flavoured with ¼ cup Vin Santo, if desired, to serve

Additional unsalted butter, for greasing the dish

1. In a small bowl, combine the Vin Santo and the currants, cover, then set aside to macerate overnight or for up to 2 days.

2. Preheat the oven to 350°. Grease a shallow baking dish, preferably ceramic, just large enough to hold all the apples; set aside. Place the biscotti in the bowl of a food processor and whir until finely ground. Add 1 egg white and pulse just until blended. Transfer the crumbs to a medium bowl and stir in the currants and their wine, along with the honey. Let this mixture sit while you prepare the apples, giving the crumbs time to absorb the liquid.

3. Peel the apples from the middle up, leaving the lower half of each apple "au naturel." This will allow the apples to expand in the oven without bursting. With a paring knife, slice a small piece off the bottom of each apple, providing a flat base so they won't topple over. Using a melon baller, scoop out the stem and the core of the apples, hollowing out a little beyond the core to make a cavity for the filling. Make sure you do not go through the base of the apple, or the filling may erupt out the bottom and could scorch. Brush the apples inside and out with the lemon juice and then with some of the melted butter. Set them aside while you finish making the filling.

4. Whip the remaining 2 egg whites in a clean bowl until soft peaks form, then stir a spoonful of the foam into the biscotti mixture to lighten it. Add the rest of the whites in two additions, folding just until most of the whites are incorporated. Spoon the filling into the apples and place the apples in a baking dish just large enough to hold them. Brush the apples with a little more melted butter, then sprinkle with the sugar.

5. Bake the apples for 45 to 50 minutes, or until tinged with gold and a knife inserted into an apple slides in and out effortlessly. Cool the apples in the baking dish for a few minutes so no one burns themself, then serve with the chilled *Crème Anglaise*.

Peaches Baked with Frangelico and Hazelnut Frangipane with Vanilla Bean Ice Cream

SERVES 6

A rich and satisfying combination: soft, sweet hot fruit, warm crumbly nutty filling and cool, creamy ice cream. The recipe is wonderfully versatile—substitute pears for the peaches and/or almonds and Amaretto liqueur for the hazelnuts and Frangelico. A perfect late summer or early fall dessert, even after a heavy meal. Make sure the fruit, either pears or peaches, is ripe but firm, and well flavoured.

FRANGIPANE:

3 ounces (about ¾ cup) lightly toasted, skinned hazelnuts (see page 262 for tips on toasting and skinning hazelnuts)

¼ cup confectioners' sugar, sifted

1 tablespoon unsalted butter, at room temperature

1 large egg, lightly beaten

1 tablespoon all-purpose flour

2 teaspoons Frangelico (hazelnut-flavoured liqueur)

FRUIT:

6 medium-sized ripe but firm free-stone peaches

¼ cup tightly packed light brown sugar

¼ cup unsalted butter, melted and cooled

¼ cup Frangelico

¼ cup fresh orange juice

Vanilla Bean Ice Cream (page 553), Crème Anglaise (page 649) or good-quality purchased vanilla ice cream

1. Prepare the frangipane: process the hazelnuts in a food processor until finely ground. Add the confectioners' sugar and pulse until blended. Add the butter, then pulse again until the ingredients are mixed. Add the egg and pulse to blend well. Sift the flour over the nut mixture and pulse just until incorporated. Mix in the Frangelico and scrape the paste into a clean container. Cover tightly and refrigerate until chilled and firm, at least 2 hours or overnight. (The frangipane may be prepared up to 3 days ahead and stored in the refrigerator.)

2. Preheat the oven to 375°. Generously grease a ceramic baking dish large enough to accommodate the halved fruit in one layer. If the peaches have a particularly furry or thick skin, peel them before proceeding by immersing them, two at a time, in a large pot of boiling water for 30 seconds, then plunging them into ice water to halt the cooking. Halve the peaches and remove the pits, then slip the skins off. (I find keeping the skin on the blanched peaches until I have twisted them apart and plucked out the pit easier than skinning them first; that way, I have something to grip rather than a slippery naked peach!)

3. In a large bowl, combine the brown sugar and melted butter and stir to make a paste. Add the peach halves and toss gently to coat each half. Place the peaches cut-side up in the buttered baking dish, paring off a little slice of the bottom if the halves won't sit properly. Rub the edges of the fruit with some of the sugar-butter paste. Fill each peach half with a heaping teaspoon of the chilled frangipane, pressing it into each little cavity.

4. Combine the Frangelico and orange juice. Dribble half this mixture over the peaches and place the dish in the preheated oven. Bake for 30 to 40 minutes, or until the fruit is tender when pierced with a sharp knife. Remove the peaches from the dish to a plate to cool for 5 to 10 minutes. Add the remaining Frangelico and orange juice mixture to the baking dish and scrape the bottom of the dish with a wooden spoon, creating a thin sauce from the caramelized juices.

5. To serve, place two peach halves in each of 6 shallow dessert bowls. Spoon a few teaspoons of the liquid from the baking dish over the peaches and accompany with a generous scoop of *Vanilla Bean Ice Cream*. This recipe can very easily be doubled.

❧ VARIATIONS ❧

Baked Peaches with Amaretto and Almond Frangipane: Substitute almonds for the hazelnuts and Amaretto for the Frangelico.

Baked Pears with Amaretto and Almond Frangipane: Substitute 6 firm but ripe pears, such as Anjou, or 12 small dessert pears, such as Sugar, Seckel or Forelle, for the peaches. Prepare the frangipane with almonds instead of hazelnuts and Amaretto (almond-flavoured liqueur) instead of Frangelico. Halve the pears

Peaches Baked with Frangelico and Hazelnut Frangipane continued

and scoop out the core with a melon baller, creating a little round cavity to hold the frangipane. Replace the Frangelico used to drizzle the fruit and make the sauce with Amaretto. Bake as for the peaches.

Baked Pears with Frangelico and Hazelnut Frangipane: Substitute pears for the peaches in the master recipe. See above for tips on coring the pears.

Medjool Date and Spiced Ricotta Strudel

2 STRUDELS, SERVING 8 TO 12

This rich but light strudel is made crisp with phyllo pastry, rather than the time-consuming traditional strudel dough. Medjool dates impart a deep, complex flavour and the filling is laced with sweet spices. A perfect dessert at the end of a rustic Italian meal, it would be lovely with a rich dark coffee or a glass of Armagnac or port.

12 sheets of frozen phyllo pastry, thawed overnight in the refrigerator
1½ pounds whole-milk ricotta
½ cup granulated sugar
Seeds of 1 plump vanilla bean, hull reserved for another use
½ teaspoon ground cinnamon
¼ teaspoon freshly grated nutmeg
⅛ teaspoon freshly ground allspice
¼ cup flavourful honey, not buckwheat
Finely grated zest of 1 large lemon

Finely grated zest of ½ large orange
3 large egg yolks, lightly beaten
½ cup unsalted butter, melted and cooled
1 pound Medjool dates, pitted and very coarsely chopped
⅓ cup unseasoned dry bread crumbs

Confectioners' sugar, for dusting the finished strudels

1. The night before you plan to make the strudel, transfer the frozen phyllo pastry to the refrigerator. Line a stainless steel wire mesh sieve with two layers of dampened cheesecloth. Remove the ricotta from its tub and press it into the lined sieve. Gather the ends of the cheesecloth in a twist around the ricotta and twist until the cheese is tightly squeezed into a ball. Secure the knot of cheesecloth with a twist-tie or rubber band and set the ball of ricotta back in the sieve. Place the sieve over a small bowl to catch the whey that will drip away from the cheese and refrigerate overnight.

2. The following day, discard the whey and unwrap the ricotta. Preheat the oven to 375°. Transfer the cheese to a large mixing bowl and add the sugar, vanilla seeds, spices, honey and the lemon and orange zests. Stir the mixture with a wooden spoon until well blended, incorporating as little air as possible. Beat in the egg yolks, scraping down the sides and bottom of the bowl. Cover the cheese mixture and set aside.

3. Lay the stack of thawed pastry on a flat surface and cover with a slightly damp kitchen towel to prevent them from drying out. Place a large sheet of parchment paper on the work surface in front of you and place 1 sheet of pastry on the paper. Brush the entire surface with melted butter. Place another sheet of pastry over the first and repeat this process until you have 6 sheets of pastry, one on top of the other. Spoon half of the cheese mixture in a log shape along one long side of the pastry, leaving a 1½-inch margin on that long side, and on the two short sides. Keep the filling confined to one half of the sheet. Scatter half of the chopped dates over the filling, pressing them into the cheese to secure them. Sprinkle half of the bread crumbs over the filling (these will absorb any excess moisture) and brush the edges of the pastry with melted butter.

4. Fold the 1½-inch margin on the long side over the log, then fold the short sides over the ends of the filling. Roll the log lengthwise towards the other long side, keeping the cylinder firm but not super-tight, as the filling must have a little space to expand in the oven. Using the parchment paper to help you, transfer the strudel to a large baking sheet, positioning it so the seam of the roll is on the bottom. Repeat the process with the second 6 sheets of pastry, the second half of the filling and the remaining dates. Place the second strudel on the same baking sheet and brush both tops with more melted butter. Bake for 40 to 50 minutes, or until the tops are golden brown and crisp. Cool the strudels before dusting with confectioners' sugar. Serve thick slices of these strudels warm or at room temperature, ideally the day they are made, as the pastry goes soggy with time. Any leftover strudel can be covered and refrigerated for up to 4 days.

Caramel Pears

6 TO 10 SMALL PEARS

These honey-coloured, almost transparent little pears are the perfect accompaniment to many simple cakes, spice breads, biscuits and frozen desserts. Be sure to use a variety of firm fall dessert pear, so the fruit does not fall apart with the prolonged poaching. Local pears will likely be fresher, and therefore firmer than imported varieties—they'll taste better, too!

2 cups water, preferably filtered or still spring water
2½ cups granulated sugar
Juice of ½ lemon

6 to 10 very small, firm Sugar pears, unblemished, with the stems intact, or substitute another tiny firm fall cooking pear, such as Clapp, Seckel or Forelle

1. Combine the water, sugar and lemon juice in a heavy-bottomed 2-quart pot. Heat slowly, stirring until the sugar dissolves. Let the syrup cool to lukewarm.

2. Peel the pears carefully, with a vegetable peeler or paring knife that doesn't remove too much of the flesh. I find the cheap, old-fashioned, long metal peelers pare the thinnest piece of peel. Leave the stems intact for a prettier presentation. As they are peeled, place the pears in the tepid sugar syrup so they don't discolour. When all the pears are in the syrup, place a small dishcloth directly on the surface of the pears and liquid, weighing down the fruit so it poaches evenly. Press a circle of parchment paper onto the cloth.

3. Return the pot to the element over medium heat and watch closely as the syrup nears the boil. When bubbles begin to break the surface, reduce the heat and keep the liquid just below the simmer. Tiny bubbles should dance up the sides of the pot and break the surface around the pears, and the surface of the syrup should shimmer. If the syrup boils too vigorously, the pears will start to break down and turn to mush before they have a chance to caramelize. Poach the fruit for about 1 hour, checking periodically to make sure the heat is not too high, and the syrup is not too thick. If it begins to look or smell like caramel, and it is becoming quite thick, add ¼ cup of boiling water to the pot. If you find this necessary, however, the syrup has likely boiled too hard, and the pears may already be overcooked. They should be extremely tender when pierced with the tip of a sharp knife and be a pale amber in colour.

4. Cool the pears in their poaching liquid until they are room temperature, then drain, reserving the liquid. Cover them well with plastic wrap to prevent them from drying out, then place in the refrigerator. Meanwhile, transfer the poaching liquid to a small, heavy-bottomed pot and bring it to a boil over medium-high heat. Boil gently until the liquid is reduced to a moderately thick syrup, about the consistency of maple syrup, or a very runny honey. Cool, then pour over the chilled pears and refrigerate together, up to 4 days. Serve as accompaniments to any number of other desserts, including *Pain d'Épices* (page 603), *Honey and Spice Madeleines* (page 505) or a deep dish of *Roasted Cinnamon Ice Cream* (page 553).

Poached Quince with Vanilla and Cinnamon

3 TO 4 CUPS

If I were stranded on a desert island, and could choose which kind of tree grew in place of the ubiquitous coconut palm, a quince tree would be my one and only choice. This ancient golden apple-like fruit will perfume your entire kitchen just by sitting on the counter. Sweet, floral, totally intoxicating, its flavour eclipses even its aroma, but must be released with a gentle cooking. The best and simplest way to do this is to slowly poach the peeled fruit in a sugar syrup, laced here with the compatible flavours of vanilla and a little cinnamon. Prepare this preserve when quinces are plentiful, and ladle it into sterilized jars. It will keep you in tarts, toppings and strudels, not to mention bread puddings, for months to come. The recipe below is a basic one, perfect for quince that is to be used in the other recipes in this book, and produces an unadulterated flavour in the fruit. Feel free to experiment with other spices, even herbs and savoury elements, such as peppercorns, rosemary and thyme, pieces of lemon or orange zest ... the possibilities are endless.

Poached Quince continued

4 cups water, preferably filtered or still
    spring water
2 cups granulated sugar

1 large cinnamon stick
½ plump vanilla bean, split
3 to 4 large quinces

1. Combine the water, sugar, cinnamon stick and vanilla bean in a heavy-bottomed 2½- to 4-quart saucepan. Heat gently, stirring until the sugar dissolves, then bring to the boil and remove from the heat. Peel the quince with a vegetable peeler and cut them into quarters. Cut out the cores and cut each quarter in half.

2. Add the fruit all at once to the syrup. The liquid should cover the fruit with about 1 inch to spare. If you need to add more water, do so in ¼-cup increments and keep track of how much water you add. Add half that amount of sugar to the pot—the ratio of water to sugar is always 2:1 for this recipe, so you can use as many or as few quince as you like, so long as you keep the syrup balanced. Press a small, clean dishcloth directly onto the surface of the fruit and syrup to prevent the fruit from poaching unevenly and weigh the fruit down with a small plate or saucer if it continues to poke out of the syrup. Just make sure the quinces are not sitting on the bottom of the pot; add a little more water if necessary.

3. Return the pot to medium-low heat and bring the syrup to just below the boil. Reduce the heat and keep the syrup at a bare simmer for 40 minutes to 1 hour, or until a sharp paring knife slips easily into the inside curve of the slices and the quinces have turned a lovely muted rose colour. Cool the fruit in its syrup, unless it seems overly soft. In that case, cool fruit and syrup separately and combine them again once they are at room temperature. Refrigerated, the fruit and its aromatic syrup will keep for 1 week or more.

4. Use the fruit in the *Fall Charlotte with Apples, Quince and Golden Raisins* (page 420), *Quince and Brioche Bread Pudding* (page 537) or simply serve it warmed over *Roasted Cinnamon* or *Vanilla Bean Ice Cream* (page 553). If you do the latter, reduce the syrup on the stove until slightly thickened and pour this delicious nectar over the ice cream and fruit. This recipe can be doubled or even tripled, as long as the ratio of water to sugar remains the same, and the size of pot is just large enough to accommodate the syrup and the fruit without cramping the quinces against the bottom.

Port Wine Gelatines with Melon and Fresh Figs

SERVES 10 TO 12 IN SMALL
DECADENT DOSES

Gelatine desserts are delightful when prepared from scratch, and these potent jiggly mouthfuls are a great new take on some classic combinations. The deep flavour of port in a softly set dessert, paired with ripe fresh fruit (along with some roasted nuts if you like), is a perfect ending to a rich holiday meal. I like to prepare these in tiny fluted moulds—they dance and sparkle like little rubies, but you can set the whole amount into one pretty decorative mould. This recipe can be made with either leaf or powdered gelatine; I prefer working with the sheets, but I have provided recipes for both. An "adults only" treat!

WITH LEAF GELATINE:

5 tablespoons cold water, plus 2 cups
  for soaking
Finely grated zest of ½ large orange
¼ cup fresh orange juice
½ cup granulated sugar
8 sheets leaf gelatine
14 ounces (1¾ cups) good-quality port

WITH POWDERED GELATINE:

¼ cup warm water, plus ⅓ cup for
  soaking
Finely grated zest of ½ large orange

¼ cup fresh orange juice
½ cup granulated sugar
4 teaspoons powdered gelatine
  (about 1¾ envelopes)
14 ounces (1¾ cups) good-quality port

1 large or 2 small ripe cantaloupe
  melons, to serve
1 pint (about 5 or 6) ripe black figs,
  such as Mission, to serve

1. With either recipe, combine the first portion of water, the orange zest, juice and sugar in a small non-reactive saucepan. Heat gently, stirring until the sugar melts, then bring the mixture to the boil. Turn off the heat and let the mixture infuse for about 10 minutes.

2. Meanwhile, if using the sheet gelatine, soak the leaves in the 2 cups of cold water for 10 minutes while the syrup infuses. Squeeze well before proceeding.

Port Wine Jellies continued

For powdered gelatine, soak the powder in the ⅓ cup cold water during the last 2 or 3 minutes of the syrup's infusing.

3. Strain the syrup, then return it to the stove and bring it back to the boil. Remove it from the heat and add the squeezed gelatine leaves, or the powder and its soaking liquid. Stir the mixture until the gelatine is completely dissolved, about 3 minutes, then stir in the port.

4. Ladle the mixture into decorative baking moulds, such as mini fluted brioche moulds, or one 2½- to 3-cup jelly mould. Refrigerate the jellies until just set, about 2 hours for small moulds, 4 hours for one large mould. The jellies should be set but not overly firm or rubbery.

5. To unmould the gelatines, dip the bottom of the moulds in warm water for 10 to 25 seconds, then invert onto individual dessert plates or a single decorative platter. (Some gelatines may need a discreet finger to ease them out onto a plate. Just keep the mould inverted and gently push one side of the gelatine so the other side slides out.) Remember to wipe the water from the outside of the mould so you don't end up with a juicy puddle instead of a wobbly dessert. Seed the cantaloupe and cut it into thin wedges. Trim the tough nib on the stem end of each fig and cut the fig into quarters from top to bottom. Arrange the fruit around the gelatines and serve. This dessert is wonderfully potent, much like having a little nip of port after a heavy meal. Judge your portions accordingly!

Bananas in Phyllo Pastry with Dates, Pecans and Brown Sugar, with a Maple-Lime Syrup

SERVES 6

I love making these in the dead of winter when I need a dessert that is warm, soft and full of sweet fruit flavour. The ingredients are few and deceptively plain and yet the result is a perfect harmony of taste and texture. The flavours of maple and lime in the syrup may seem out of place, but are actually beautifully matched with the soft, yielding sweetness of the baked bananas. So simple, the entire dessert can be prepared ahead of time, then simply baked to order. Do use Medjool dates if you can find them; not many are called for, and the difference in flavour is remarkable.

PASTRIES:

12 sheets of phyllo pastry, thawed overnight in the refrigerator and tempered at room temperature for 1 hour, still wrapped

⅓ cup unsalted butter, melted and cooled

6 small, ripe bananas

½ cup chopped plump Medjool dates

½ cup finely chopped, lightly toasted pecans (see page 253 for tips on toasting nuts), or substitute walnuts

¼ cup tightly packed dark brown sugar

SYRUP:

¾ cup pure strong-flavoured maple syrup, preferably grade B

Juice of 2 limes

2 tablespoons dark or amber rum

Vanilla Bean Ice Cream (page 553), or good-quality store-bought vanilla ice cream, to serve

1. Work with one sheet of phyllo pastry at a time, keeping the rest covered with a damp towel to prevent them from drying out. (This type of pastry dries out extremely quickly, becoming brittle and completely unworkable.) Lay 1 sheet on a clean, dry, flat surface and brush all over with the melted butter. Place another sheet directly on top, smoothing it with your hand to eliminate most of the air bubbles. With one short side facing you, brush half the sheet with melted butter, from the short end to about the middle. Fold the pastry in half, so the unbuttered half is sealed onto the buttered half, and press gently. You should have a rectangle with what used to be the short side now being the long side.

2. Brush the whole surface of the rectangle with butter. Peel a banana and lay it about 1½ to 2 inches in from one short side of the pastry, with the inside curve facing the other short side of the pastry. There should be a border of pastry on either end of the banana that will ultimately be folded over onto it; trim the fruit if it seems too long. Nestle about 1½ tablespoons each of the chopped dates and pecans next to the curve of the banana, and sprinkle this filling with 1½ packed teaspoons of brown sugar. Fold the bit of pastry behind the banana onto it, then fold the long sides over about 1 inch, covering the ends of the

Bananas in Phyllo Pastry continued

banana and making a long fold along the sides of the pastry. Brushing with additional melted butter where necessary to seal the bundle together well, roll the banana towards the remaining short side, forming a compact package. Transfer the filled pastry to a plate or baking dish and cover with plastic wrap. Repeat this process until all of the pastries are made, then cover them with plastic wrap and chill for at least 1 hour or up to 24 hours.

3. Prepare the syrup: in a small saucepan, combine the maple syrup and the lime juice and warm over low heat, stirring to blend. Remove the syrup from the heat and add the rum. (Syrup may be prepared up to 4 days ahead of time and stored covered in the refrigerator.)

4. Preheat the oven to 375°. Line a baking sheet with parchment paper and place the pastries about 1½ to 2 inches apart on the sheet. Brush the tops with melted butter, then bake for 20 to 25 minutes, or until the pastry is golden brown and crisp and the bananas yield to the touch when the pastries are gently squeezed. Cool for 5 minutes, then serve immediately with a drizzle of the Maple-Lime Syrup and a generous scoop of Vanilla Bean Ice Cream. This recipe can be scaled up or doubled, depending on how many guests you have!

❧ VARIATION ❧

Bananas in Phyllo Pastry with Apricots, Coconut and Brown Sugar, with a Caramel-Lime Syrup: Prepare exactly as for the recipe above, substituting chopped dried apricots for the dates, sweetened shredded coconut for the pecans and light brown sugar for the dark brown sugar. For the caramel syrup, combine 1 cup of granulated sugar with ⅓ cup water in a heavy-bottomed saucepan. Heat gently, stirring until the sugar dissolves, then increase the heat and bring the syrup to a boil. Cook the syrup until it becomes a golden amber colour, watching closely as it starts to darken. Have ready a small vessel containing the juice of 2 limes. When the caramel is a deep gold, remove it from the heat and add the lime juice—stand back, as this addition will cause a great deal of commotion in the pot, and hot caramel makes a devilish burn! Once the spluttering has subsided, stir the syrup to blend and pour into a clean, heatproof container. Cool to just warm, then add 2 tablespoons of rum. Divine!

QUICK BREADS, SWEET YEAST BREADS AND FRITTERS

continued on page 602

Pain d'Épices with Crème Fraîche and Caramel Pears

ONE 9 X 5-INCH LOAF AND EITHER
ONE 8 X 4-INCH LOAF OR FOUR MINI LOAVES

Pain d'épices is a traditional spice cake from the Burgundy region of France. It is akin to other ginger and spice breads, but is made with neither fat nor eggs, relying instead on a healthy amount of honey and sometimes milk or cream for moisture and richness. I have used water instead of milk for a lighter flavour, but feel free to substitute milk. Dark, spicy and very moist, this sweet bread is lovely for breakfast, spread with sweet butter and a drizzle of honey; all by itself with a cup of afternoon tea; or with caramel-poached pears and crème fraîche as a rich and not-too-sweet ending to a fall or winter meal. The Star Anise Crème Anglaise (page 650) would also be a good accompaniment. The bread keeps brilliantly and makes great Christmas gifts, baked in little individual loaf pans. Its mellow, warm and autumnal flavour makes it perfect for the Jewish New Year, too.

1½ cups hot water, preferably still spring or filtered water, or substitute hot whole (3.5%) or partly skimmed milk (2%)

1½ cups flavourful dark honey, such as chestnut or buckwheat

⅔ cup tightly packed light brown sugar

½ teaspoon salt

⅓ cup amber or dark rum

3 cups whole rye flour, preferably organic

1½ cups unbleached all-purpose flour, preferably organic

¾ cup cake flour (not self-rising)

1 tablespoon baking soda

1½ teaspoons baking powder

1½ teaspoons freshly ground star anise

1½ teaspoons ground cinnamon

1 teaspoon ground ginger

½ teaspoon ground mace, or substitute freshly grated nutmeg

¼ teaspoon freshly ground cloves

¼ teaspoon ground white pepper

¼ cup finely chopped candied orange zest, or substitute 2 teaspoons freshly grated orange zest

¾ cup currants, optional

1¼ cups coarsely chopped lightly toasted unblanched almonds (see page 253 for tips on toasting nuts)

Crème Fraîche, page 651, to serve
Caramel Pears, page 594, to serve

Pain d'Épices continued

1. In a medium bowl, pour the hot water or milk over the honey. Add the brown sugar and stir with a whisk until the sugar is dissolved. Stir in the salt, let the mixture cool until tepid, then stir in the rum. Meanwhile, sift together the rye, all-purpose and cake flours, baking soda and baking powder. In another small bowl or cup, combine the spices.

2. Place 3 cups of the sifted flour mixture into a large bowl. Make a deep well in the centre and pour in the lukewarm honey mixture. Stir with a whisk in one direction, bringing in increasingly more of the flour from the edges of the bowl, until the batter is smooth. Exchange the whisk for a wooden spoon and stir in the rest of the flour mixture, about ½ cup at a time, keeping your strokes going in the same direction and waiting until the last addition of flour is mostly incorporated before adding the next. When all but 1 or so cups of flour remain, stir the spices into this last bit of flour, then proceed to incorporate it into the batter.

3. When all the dry ingredients have been added, the batter should be smooth, glossy and thick. Add the chopped candied orange zest and the currants and beat the batter with 25 long, smooth strokes. Transfer the batter to a slightly smaller container if you wish, cover tightly with plastic wrap and refrigerate for at least 8 hours, or up to 4 days. This aging process allows the flavours of the batter to mellow, blend and develop. Traditionally, French bakers would age their batter for 1 week or longer!

4. Preheat the oven to 400°. Thoroughly grease one 9 x 5-inch loaf pan and either one 8 x 4-inch loaf pan or four mini loaf pans. Line the bottom and up the two long sides of the larger pans with a piece of parchment paper, letting the paper hang over the edges by an inch or two. Remove the batter from the refrigerator and stir in the almonds. Scrape the batter into the prepared pans, dividing it evenly, and smooth the surfaces with a rubber spatula.

5. If baking both large and small loaves, place the larger one(s) in the oven 3 or 4 minutes before the smaller. Bake on the middle rack for 10 minutes (7 minutes for the mini loaves), then reduce the temperature to 350° and continue baking for 1 hour to 1 hour 10 minutes for the 9 x 5-inch or 8 x 4-inch loaves, 25 to 35 minutes for the mini loaves, or until a skewer inserted in the centre of each loaf comes out clean, the surface of the bread is firm, dark brown and cracked and the bread is pulling away from the sides of the pan. Cool in the pans set on wire racks for 10 minutes, then turn them out and cool completely on the racks.

6. Pain d'épices, once baked, must be aged at least 2 days, and up to 4 days, wrapped well, first in plastic wrap, then in aluminum foil, to allow the flavours to mature. This bread keeps extraordinarily well and is a perfectly acceptable treat any time of the day. If you like, bake the entire batter in mini loaf pans, in which case you will have between 10 and 12.

7. For *Pain d'Épices with Crème Fraîche and Caramel Pears*, place one or two slices of the aged pain d'épices (or one mini loaf) on each dessert plate. Dollop a generous mound of crème fraîche beside the cake and spoon some of the thickened caramel syrup from the pears onto the cream. Accompany with a single caramel pear.

Plum and Cardamom Sweet Bread

ONE 9 X 5-INCH LOAF

Cardamom is a wonderful spice, woefully underused in North America. Although its origins are in Asia and the Middle East, it appears throughout the cuisine of much of Scandinavia as well, especially in many sweet breads and pastries. Here, it pairs beautifully with rich and tangy plums. This sweet bread has a moist, cake-like crumb and a full, but not-too-sweet flavour—the cardamom adds a unique spiciness.

¾ cup unsalted butter, at room
  temperature
1 cup granulated sugar
¾ cup tightly packed light brown sugar
2 large eggs, at room temperature
1 teaspoon pure vanilla extract
½ teaspoon finely grated orange zest
3 cups all-purpose flour
1 teaspoon baking powder
½ teaspoon baking soda

½ teaspoon salt
2 teaspoons ground cardamom
¾ cup full-fat sour cream (14%)
2 cups (about 12 to 16) Italian blue
  plums, stoned and cut into
  ½-inch pieces

Additional unsalted butter, at room
  temperature, or vegetable oil cooking
  spray, for greasing the pan

Plum and Cardamom Sweet Bread continued

1. Preheat the oven to 350°. Grease a 9 x 5-inch loaf pan. If it is not non-stick, line the bottom and up the two long sides with a piece of parchment paper, letting the paper hang over the edges of the pan by an inch or two. If you haven't any parchment, lightly dust the greased pan with flour and tap out the excess. In the bowl of a stand mixer, or in a large bowl with a wooden spoon, cream the butter and sugars together until light and fluffy. Add the eggs, one at a time, beating well after each addition and scraping down the sides of the bowl. Beat in the vanilla and orange zest.

2. Reserve 2 tablespoons of the flour; sift the remaining flour together with the baking powder, baking soda, salt and cardamom. Add this mixture to the creamed mixture in three additions, alternating with the sour cream in two additions. Scrape down the sides of the bowl between each addition. Toss the plums with the reserved 2 tablespoons of flour (this will help keep them from sinking to the bottom) and fold them into the batter, mixing just until the fruit is evenly distributed. As with most cakes and quick breads, you want to avoid overworking this batter, or your loaf will be heavy and too dense. Scrape the batter into the prepared pan and smooth the top with a rubber spatula.

3. Bake the loaf in the centre of the oven for 1 hour and 30 minutes to 1 hour and 45 minutes, or until a wooden skewer inserted into the centre of the cake comes out clean. Cool the loaf in the pan on a wire rack for 15 minutes, then turn it out and cool completely before slicing, or wrapping and storing. This loaf can be made a day or two ahead of time and stored, well wrapped, at room temperature and will keep for several days longer stored in the refrigerator. It is very good spread with sweet or flavoured butter and even a few days old is wonderful toasted. For a special dessert, serve the fresh bread with a little mound of *Crème Fraîche* (page 651) or lightly sweetened whipped cream, and a few slices of fresh plum that have been macerated in sugar and brandy or other compatible alcohol for 30 minutes.

Sweet Potato Cornbread

2 9 X 5-INCH LOAVES

There are as many variations of cornbread as there are good bakers. This version combines the nutty, toasted flavour of stone-ground cornmeal with richly flavoured sweet potato to produce a moist, not-too-sweet cornbread that would be perfect for breakfast, or with a bowl of homemade soup. I love it thickly sliced and lightly toasted, spread with sweet butter and honey, and it makes a dynamite bread pudding (see recipe page 540). It would also be wonderful with chopped toasted pecans added to the batter, served with fresh summer fruit and lightly sweetened whipped cream for a simple and scrumptious dessert.

2 cups stone-ground yellow cornmeal
½ cup granulated sugar
2 cups all-purpose flour
1 tablespoon baking powder
1 teaspoon baking soda
½ teaspoon salt
4 large eggs, at room temperature
1½ cups full-fat sour cream
1½ teaspoons pure vanilla extract

½ cup unsalted butter, melted and cooled
2 cups cooked, mashed, peeled sweet potatoes, cooled (about 2 large, or 3 medium)

Additional unsalted butter, at room temperature, for greasing the pans

1. Preheat the oven to 375°. Grease two 9 x 5-inch loaf pans and set aside. Combine the cornmeal and the sugar in a large bowl, then sift in the flour, baking powder, baking soda and salt. Stir with a whisk until well combined.

2. In a separate bowl, beat the eggs just to break them up. Add the sour cream, vanilla and melted butter and whisk gently until the mixture is uniformly creamy and thick. Stir in the mashed sweet potatoes until thoroughly blended. Add the sweet potato mixture to the cornmeal mixture all at once and stir with a wooden spoon just enough to moisten the dry ingredients. Divide the batter evenly between the prepared loaf pans and smooth the tops.

3. Bake loaves in the middle of the oven for 1 hour and 5 minutes to 1 hour and 20 minutes, or until the tops are golden brown and a wooden skewer inserted

Sweet Potato Cornbread

into the centre of each loaf comes out clean. Transfer pans to a rack and cool for 10 minutes, then turn the loaves out of the pans and set right-side up on the racks to cool completely before slicing or wrapping. This bread is best made a day in advance for bread pudding, but is wonderful eaten right out of the oven, spread with butter. Store the loaves, well wrapped, at room temperature for up to 3 days or in the refrigerator up to 1 week. They freeze very well, wrapped securely in plastic and aluminum foil, for up to 2 months.

Wild Blueberry Buttermilk Cinnamon Muffins

12 REGULAR OR 6 LARGE MUFFINS

Still-warm muffins spread with sweet butter are one of the very favourite breakfasts in our house. These addictive muffins have a moist, fine crumb, closer to the texture of a cake than most rough-crumbed quick breads, because the batter is a creamed mixture rather than the traditional wet-dry muffin mix. Cake flour also contributes to the velvety texture, making the muffins lighter and more delicate. I strongly urge you to use wild blueberries, rather than the horribly bland cultivated berries so widely available today. The difference in your baking will be stunning!

TOPPING:
½ teaspoon cinnamon
2 tablespoons granulated sugar
¼ cup unsalted butter, melted and
    cooled

MUFFINS:
½ cup unsalted butter, at room
    temperature
1 cup granulated sugar
2 large eggs
1½ teaspoons pure vanilla extract

1½ cups all-purpose flour
½ cup cake flour (not self-rising)
1 teaspoon baking soda
½ teaspoon baking powder
½ teaspoon salt
¾ teaspoon ground cinnamon
½ teaspoon freshly grated nutmeg
1 cup buttermilk
1 cup fresh wild blueberries, picked
    over (or substitute same amount
    of frozen wild blueberries)

1. Preheat the oven to 350°. Grease 12 regular (½-cup) or 6 large (1-cup) muffin tins or line with paper liners. I find non-stick cooking spray works very well. Combine the cinnamon and sugar for the topping in a small bowl and set aside. In a large bowl, or the bowl of an electric mixer fitted with the paddle attachment, cream butter and sugar until light and fluffy, about 3 minutes. Add the eggs, one at a time, beating well after each addition. Scrape down the sides of the bowl, then beat in the vanilla.

2. Into a separate bowl, sift both flours, baking soda, baking powder, salt, cinnamon and nutmeg. Add the flour mixture to the batter in three additions, alternating with the buttermilk in two additions, beginning and ending with the dry ingredients. Gently fold in the blueberries. Spoon the batter into the muffin cups to about ⅔ full.

3. Bake in the centre of the oven for 15 to 20 minutes for regular-sized muffins, 25 to 30 minutes for large muffins, or until the tops are golden and spring back when lightly touched and a wooden skewer inserted into the centre of a muffin comes out clean. Cool the muffins in the pan for 5 minutes, then turn out onto a rack. Dip the crowns of each muffin first into the cooled melted butter, then into the sugar-cinnamon mixture, then cool right-side up on a wire rack. Serve warm, slathered with sweet butter, or at room temperature. To store, wrap well in plastic wrap. Muffins may be frozen for up to 1 month.

Orange, Dried Cranberry and Cornmeal Muffins with Millet

12 REGULAR OR 6 LARGE MUFFINS

I probably make this recipe, exactly as it is here, more often than any other. These muffins became a hit several years ago when my duties as pastry chef at Avalon included baking breakfast pastries for the sister restaurant, Zocalo. After weeks of the entire batch of these disappearing into the hands of the cooks and wait staff before the customers even got to them, the chef insisted everyone

Orange, Dried Cranberry and Cornmeal Muffins continued

eat breakfast at home! They are a great combination of flavours and textures. Cornmeal adds a nutty, toasted flavour; plump dried cranberries give the muffins a chewy, pleasantly tangy taste; millet adds a subtle sweetness and crunch; and freshly grated orange zest and orange juice lace it all together with a fresh, bright taste. As far as I'm concerned, the perfect muffin!

2⅔ cups all-purpose flour
4 teaspoons baking powder
1 teaspoon salt
½ cup granulated sugar
⅔ cup yellow cornmeal, preferably
    stone-ground
¼ cup millet
2 large eggs

1 teaspoon finely grated orange zest
1½ cups orange juice
⅔ cup unsalted butter, melted and
    cooled
1 cup dried cranberries, plumped
    in warm water for 30 minutes if
    necessary

1. Preheat oven to 350°. Grease 6 large (1-cup) or 12 regular-sized (½-cup) muffin tins, including rims, or line with paper liners. I find a non-stick cooking spray works very well. Sift the flour, baking powder and salt together into a large bowl. Add the sugar, cornmeal and millet and stir with a fork or whisk to blend.

2. In a separate bowl, lightly whisk the eggs, then blend in the orange zest and juice and melted butter. Add the egg mixture all at once to the dry ingredients, mixing with a rubber spatula or a wooden spoon just until the dry ingredients are moistened. While there are still a few floury patches, gently fold in the cranberries.

3. Spoon the batter into prepared tins, filling each cup to the rim, and place the tray on a baking sheet, to catch any drips. Bake 20 to 25 minutes for regular-sized muffins, 30 to 35 minutes for large ones, or until the tops are golden brown in places, spring back when lightly touched and a skewer inserted in the centre comes out clean.

4. Transfer the tray to a rack and cool 5 minutes, then turn the muffins out onto the rack. These are fabulous served warm with a little sweet butter, or may be cooled completely, then wrapped individually and stored at room temperature for up to two days. If they become slightly hard, wrap in foil and warm in a low oven before serving. These muffins also freeze beautifully, for up to 2 months.

Oatmeal Biscuit Cakes with Whiskeyed Peaches and Sweet Cream

SERVES 6

This is a gloriously messy dessert, perfect for when peaches are at their best. The oatmeal biscuits are not as light and bready as normal biscuits, but are cakey and dense, and thick-cut rolled oats make the biscuits chewier and delicious. Not many things actually taste of oats, but these scones are full of their nutty, sweet malty flavour. They're not split like traditional shortcakes, but used whole as a base for ripe peaches macerated in a splash of good whiskey and topped with a mound of sweetened whipped cream. A scrumptious summer dessert, and an absolutely divine breakfast.

PEACHES:

4 to 6 fresh ripe freestone peaches, depending on the size (or more, if desired)

3 tablespoons granulated sugar, or to taste

2 tablespoons whiskey (bourbon or single-malt scotch are perfect), or to taste

BISCUITS:

1 cup plus 1 tablespoon thick-cut, old-fashioned rolled oats

1 cup all-purpose flour

¼ cup granulated sugar

½ teaspoon salt

1 tablespoon baking powder

5 tablespoons unsalted butter, cold, cut into small pieces

6 tablespoons milk, whole or partly skimmed, but not low-fat, cold

6 tablespoons heavy cream (36%), cold

Additional 2 tablespoons granulated sugar, for sprinkling

Additional heavy cream for brushing on biscuits (about 1½ tablespoons)

SWEET CREAM:

1½ cups heavy cream (36%), beaten to soft mounds with 2 tablespoons granulated sugar

1. Preheat the oven to 400°. Prepare the peaches: if they have a particularly thick skin, you may want to peel them. (To peel peaches, drop them a few at a time into a pot of boiling water, then take them out after 30 to 45 seconds and plunge them into a bowl of ice water to stop the cooking. The skins should slip off with

Oatmeal Biscuit Cakes continued

the help of a small paring knife.) Young fresh ripe peaches don't need to be peeled. Cut each peach in half and discard the stone. Cut each half into 6 or 8 slices and place the slices in a medium-sized bowl. Add the 3 tablespoons of sugar and dribble with the whiskey, then gently stir the fruit with a large wooden spoon or rubber spatula to combine the ingredients. Let the peach slices macerate in the sugar-whiskey mixture while you prepare and bake the biscuits.

2. Line a baking sheet with parchment paper, or lightly butter it. In a large bowl, combine the oats, flour, sugar and salt. Sift the baking powder over the mixture and stir to blend. Add the cold butter pieces, then use a pastry blender or two knives to cut the butter into the dry ingredients until the largest lumps are about the size of fat peas. Combine the milk and 6 tablespoons cream in a small bowl and add all at once to the flour-butter mixture. Use your hands to quickly distribute the liquid, reaching down under the dough, then bringing small handfuls up and rubbing the crumble through your fingertips. You may think you have added too much liquid, but this dough should be extremely wet and sticky. Don't overwork it; just make sure there are no creamy or floury patches.

3. Turn the dough out onto a lightly floured surface and use floured hands to pat it into a circle of about 8 inches in diameter and ¾ to 1 inch thick. Try to use as little flour as possible so the dough remains tender and moist. With a 3- to 3½-inch biscuit cutter or an overturned glass, dipped in flour, cut as many circles as you can, about 3 or 4. Use a palette knife or lifter to transfer the rounds to the prepared baking sheet. Pat the scraps together, filling in the spaces, and continue cutting rounds until there is not enough dough to make a biscuit. You should end up with 5 or 6 biscuits. Pop the baking sheet into the refrigerator for about 10 minutes to let the gluten in the dough relax.

4. Brush the raw biscuits with the 1½ tablespoons of cream and sprinkle with the 2 tablespoons sugar. Bake the biscuits in the preheated oven for 18 to 22 minutes, or until puffed and golden brown. Transfer to a wire rack to cool while you whip the cream.

5. To assemble the dessert, place a warm oatmeal biscuit on each dessert plate. I prefer to leave the biscuits whole, letting each person have the pleasure of splitting or biting into the crusty warm pastries themselves, but you can split them if you wish. Spoon some of the sweetened peaches and their juices over or beside each biscuit and top with a generous dollop of whipped cream. (You can, of course, play with this arrangement—biscuit, cream, peaches; biscuit, peaches, cream, juices; biscuit, cream, peaches, cream ...whatever tickles your fancy.) The dessert is best served within 30 minutes of the biscuits coming out of the oven, but the components can be made up to 4 hours ahead. Any extra biscuits can be stored, wrapped, at room temperature for a day or so; they are best if rewarmed or lightly toasted before eating.

Rich Old-Fashioned Strawberry Shortcakes

SERVES 6

Some things are pretty much perfect just the way they are, and as far as I am concerned, strawberry shortcakes are one of those things. I am all for progress and individual expression but old-fashioned desserts like this one, when made properly, can often beat the pants of any "Nouvelle" skyscraper creation. This version is fabulous—just the way you imagine a great strawberry shortcake should taste. The cream scones are not heavy, not sour, not cloying, but are definitely dessert scones, rich and sweet and satisfying. The ingredients should all be as fresh as possible, including the flour and butter ... it makes all the difference in the world.

SCONES:

2 cups all-purpose flour

¼ cup granulated sugar

1 tablespoon baking powder

½ teaspoon salt

½ cup unsalted butter, cold, cut into small bits

1 large egg, lightly beaten

¼ cup whole milk (3.5%)

5 tablespoons heavy cream (36%)

Additional whipping cream for brushing scones (about 1 tablespoon)

Additional 1 tablespoon granulated sugar, for sprinkling

BERRIES:

2 quarts fresh ripe strawberries, hulled

3 to 4 tablespoons granulated sugar, depending on the sweetness of the berries

CHANTILLY CREAM:

2 cups heavy cream (36%)

1½ tablespoons granulated sugar

1 teaspoon pure vanilla extract

Strawberry Shortcakes continued

1. Prepare the scones: preheat the oven to 425°. Line a small heavy baking sheet with parchment paper and set aside. In a medium bowl, sift together the flour, ¼ cup sugar, baking powder and salt and stir with a fork to blend. Using a pastry cutter or two knives, cut in the butter until the largest pieces are no larger than fat peas. If the butter seems to be getting too warm, pop the whole bowl into the refrigerator for a few minutes to firm it up.

2. In a small bowl, lightly beat the egg, then stir in the milk and the 5 tablespoons of cream. Add this mixture all at once to the flour-butter mixture and use your fingers to incorporate the wet ingredients. The dough will be very sticky and floppy, but don't overwork it. Once the dry ingredients are evenly moistened, turn the dough out onto a lightly floured board.

3. Gently pat the dough into a rough square about 7 inches all around and ¾ to 1 inch thick. (This is where the expression "Pat-a-cake, Pat-a-cake …" came from!) Use a 3-inch biscuit or cookie cutter, or an overturned glass, to cut 4 rounds from the dough, dipping the cutter or glass rim in flour before each cut. Transfer the rounds to the baking sheet, spacing them 2 inches apart and re-pat the scraps of dough together. Cut one or two more rounds and repeat this process if necessary. You should end up with 6 rounds.

4. Brush the tops of the scones with the reserved cream and sprinkle with the tablespoon of sugar. Bake in the centre of the oven for 14 to 18 minutes, or until the tops are tinged with golden-brown and are crisp. Cool the scones on the baking sheet set on a wire rack for at least 10 minutes before splitting and filling. (The scones are best if eaten as soon after baking as possible, but can be made several hours ahead of time and re-warmed in a moderate oven for a few minutes before assembling.)

5. While the scones are baking, prepare the strawberries. Cut 1 quart of the strawberries in half and set aside. Cut the remaining quart of strawberries into rough pieces and sprinkle with the 3 to 4 tablespoons sugar, stirring to coat. Let the fruit macerate for at least 20 minutes, and up to 1 hour, at room temperature. Just before serving, use a fork or an old-fashioned potato masher to lightly crush the macerating berries, leaving some chunky pieces, but creating a rough berry sauce.

6. Prepare the Chantilly Cream: in a large bowl, combine the 2 cups cream and 2 tablespoons sugar and beat until soft peaks form. Add the vanilla and beat until the cream is in billowy mounds. Refrigerate until needed, up to 1 hour. (The cream can be prepared several hours ahead, but may need to be re-whipped slightly before serving.)

7. To assemble the shortcakes, split the scones in half horizontally and place one warm bottom on each of 6 dessert plates. Spoon some of the crushed berries over the biscuits, including the runny juices. Scoop a generous dollop of Chantilly Cream over the crushed berries and top with a handful of the reserved halved strawberries. Place a biscuit top over the whole gorgeous pile and serve at once. No one ever said it was an elegant dessert, but it is definitely one of the most satisfying.

VARIATIONS

Lemon-Poppyseed Shortcakes with Blackberries: Add 2 teaspoons tightly packed, finely grated lemon zest and 1½ tablespoons poppyseeds to the biscuit dough just after the egg-milk mixture has been added. Substitute blackberries for the strawberries, if desired, increasing the macerating sugar to 5 tablespoons.

Cardamom Shortcakes with Strawberries and Lemon Cream: Add 1 teaspoon ground cardamom to the flour mixture before adding the butter. Omit the vanilla extract from the Chantilly Cream and substitute 2 tightly packed teaspoons of finely grated lemon zest and ¼ teaspoon lemon oil, optional (available in specialty food shops).

Almond and Dried Bing Cherry Braid

ONE LARGE LOAF,
16 TO 20 THICK SLICES

A voluptuous, glossy loaf, threaded with almonds and little pockets of dried cherries. Not a difficult bread, and one that never fails to impress. I adore bread —it may be my favourite thing in the world to eat. And this slightly sweet, chewy bread is so satisfying, it needs only a small amount of filling. The filling, however, must be made with fresh nuts and plump fruit. The flavours extend to cover the whole loaf, but the bread itself isn't weighed down by gobs of almond paste. The loaf freezes extremely well; bake it when you have the time, then serve it whenever you like.

FILLING:

1½ cups blanched whole almonds

⅔ cup granulated sugar

⅓ cup unsalted butter, at room temperature

Finely grated zest of ½ large orange

1 large egg, at room temperature

½ teaspoon pure almond extract

½ teaspoon pure vanilla extract

2 teaspoons Kirsch, or other cherry-flavoured brandy or liqueur

2 teaspoons Amaretto, or other almond-flavoured liqueur

1 cup unsulphured dried Bing cherries, or other dried sweet cherries

SWEET YEAST DOUGH:

¼ cup warm (105° to 115°F) water

1 cup warm (105° to 115°F) whole milk (3.5%), or substitute partly skimmed (2%)

2 packages active dry yeast

½ cup granulated sugar

5 to 5½ cups all-purpose flour

½ cup unsalted butter, at room temperature

1 teaspoon salt

1½ teaspoons pure vanilla extract

3 large eggs, at room temperature

1 large egg white lightly beaten with 1 teaspoon water, to glaze the loaf before baking

ALMOND GLAZE:

1 cup confectioners' sugar, sifted

2 tablespoons water

¼ teaspoon pure almond extract (or substitute pure vanilla extract or Amaretto)

1. Prepare the filling: combine the almonds and the sugar in the bowl of a food processor, and pulse until very finely ground. Add the butter and pulse until it is blended into the almond paste. Add the orange zest and the egg, whizzing until thoroughly incorporated and scraping down the sides of the bowl. Whir in the extracts and the liqueurs and scrape the paste into a clean container. Refrigerate until needed, up to 2 days. Allow the filling to come to room temperature (or microwave on "defrost" for 1 minute or so) until spreadable before proceeding.

2. Prepare the dough: place the warm water and milk in the bowl of a stand mixer, or a large mixing bowl if you are preparing the dough by hand. Sprinkle the yeast over the warm liquid and stir in 1 teaspoon of the granulated sugar. Let the mixture stand until foamy and bubbling, about 5 minutes. With the paddle attachment of the mixer, or a wooden spoon, stir in 1 cup of the flour, beating to make a lumpy batter. Stir in the butter, remaining sugar, salt and vanilla and beat to blend. Add another 1½ cups flour and beat until smooth and elastic, about 5 minutes on medium-high with the mixer, or 15 minutes by hand.

3. Add the eggs, one at a time, beating well and scraping down the sides and bottom of the bowl between each addition. Add 2 more cups of flour and stir to incorporate. With the dough hook attachment of the mixer if it is large enough, or kneading on a smooth surface with your hands, knead the dough until it is very smooth and elastic, and little bubbles form just under the surface. This should take about 10 minutes with the machine, and 20 to 25 by hand (no need to visit the gym this week). A finger poked into the dough should leave an indentation that springs back immediately. Use just enough of the remaining flour to prevent the dough from sticking, but be sparing: you want a soft, tender dough, and too much flour will make it dry and tough. (As it nears the right consistency, the dough will begin to neatly come away from the sides of the bowl or the counter, reaching what is cleverly known as the "clean-up stage.") Place the dough in a large buttered bowl, cover the bowl with plastic wrap and leave in a warm, draught-free place (about 75 degrees is perfect) until the dough is doubled in bulk, about 1¼ to 1½ hours.

4. Punch the dough down once or twice to deflate it, then turn it out onto a large, clean work surface. Invert the bowl over the dough and let it rest for 10

Almond and Dried Bing Cherry Braid continued

minutes. Meanwhile, line a large (at least 12½ x 17½-inch) baking sheet with parchment paper and set aside. Deflate the dough again and divide it into 3 equal portions. Cover 2 of the portions with plastic wrap to prevent them from drying out and roll out the third portion to a rectangle about 6 or 7 by 16 or 18 inches. You may find picking the dough up by one short end and letting it hang for a few seconds helps get the dough in roughly the right shape. Be careful not to actually stretch the dough so much that it tears, however; rolling is still the safest way to handle the dough.

5. Spread ⅓ of the almond filling in a strip down the centre of the dough, leaving about a 1-inch border around the perimeter free of filling. Scatter ⅓ cup of the cherries over the filling, pressing gently to anchor them. Roll up the dough into a long cylinder, starting at one long end, trying not to trap any large air bubbles in the roll. Pinch the dough along the seam to seal it and fold the edges over, pinching them as well. Transfer the roll to the baking sheet and cover it with plastic wrap. Set aside and repeat the process with the remaining two portions of dough and the remaining filling and cherries. Don't worry at all about how the rolls look—perfection is not what bread making is all about! As long as they are well sealed, and roughly the same size, all will be glorious.

6. When all three rolls are positioned on the baking sheet, arrange the ends of the rolls together at one short end of the sheet and pinch them together gently. Braid the rolls, taking care not to stretch or tear the dough, and pinch the ends together to secure them. Cover the whole braid with plastic wrap and then with a dry dishtowel. Let the braid rise in a warm, draught-free place until plumped, risen, and not quite doubled in bulk, about 45 minutes to 1 hour.

7. Meanwhile, preheat the oven to 350°. Brush the risen loaf with the egg-white glaze and bake the braid for 45 to 55 minutes, or until deeply golden. Cool the loaf completely. For the Almond Glaze, combine all ingredients for the glaze in a small bowl and stir until a pourable icing is achieved, adding a few more drops of water if necessary. Use the glaze immediately, drizzling it over the cooled braid. The best way to store this loaf if you are not going to eat it right away is to freeze it, wrapped securely first in plastic wrap and then in aluminum foil, for up to 2 months. Thaw the braid at room temperature for 4 hours, then serve. It is divine served slightly warm!

VARIATION

Apricot and Almond Braid: Substitute chopped, unsulphured dried apricots for the Bing cherries and apricot brandy for the Kirsch.

Classic Brioche

2 9 X 5-INCH LOAVES
OR 2 8-INCH BRIOCHE À TÊTES

One of the many triumphs of the French pastry kitchen, brioche is a beautifully sweet and buttery yeast bread. It is the perfect foundation for a superb bread pudding; the perfect breakfast toast; the perfect base, spread with anything from pâté de foie gras to homemade raspberry preserves. And nothing, NOTHING, makes a better French toast! It's impressive to serve, deeply satisfying to eat and not at all difficult to prepare. Brioche is not a fussy dough, but it does take a little time. Kneading the dough thoroughly and letting it rise overnight in the refrigerator ensures a moist loaf, full of flavour, with a fine, delicate and tender crumb. As with so many other yeast breads, brioche can adapt to suit your schedule; you can prepare the dough one day, and bake it the next. Be sure to use a good-quality butter for this recipe: a poor-grade brand with a high moisture content will throw off the balance and flavour of the bread. Both the butter and the eggs should be as fresh as possible. Although brioche can be made completely by hand, I find a heavy-duty stand mixer makes the initial mixing of the ingredients and incorporation of the butter efficient and easy. I have given quantities below to make two large loaves, or two traditional fluted brioche à têtes, but the risen dough can be formed into an almost infinite number of traditional and non-traditional shapes, from tiny brioche à têtes to the filled brioche doughnuts. Best of all, baked brioche freezes beautifully!

Classic Brioche continued

2 packages (about 5 teaspoons) active
    dry yeast
1 cup warm (105° to 115°F) whole milk
    (3.5%)
1½ teaspoons granulated sugar, to
    activate yeast
5½ cups all-purpose flour
2 teaspoons salt, preferably sea salt or
    kosher salt
6 tablespoons granulated sugar

6 large eggs, at room temperature
1½ cups fresh unsalted butter, never
    frozen, at room temperature but
    not overly soft
1 egg lightly beaten with 1 tablespoon
    milk, for glaze

Additional unsalted butter, at room
    temperature, for greasing the pans

1. In the bowl of a stand mixer, or a large mixing bowl if preparing the dough by hand, sprinkle the yeast over the warm milk. Stir in the 1½ teaspoons of sugar and let the yeast proof for 5 to 7 minutes, until foamy and bubbling. Add 1 cup flour and the salt, beating with the paddle attachment or a wooden spoon to make a soft, smooth batter, about 5 minutes.

2. Beat in the remaining 4½ cups flour and the 6 tablespoons sugar in three additions, beating in 2 eggs after each addition of flour. Mix well between additions, making sure you scrape down the sides and bottom of the bowl. Beat until a smooth, soft and elastic dough is formed, about 10 minutes with the dough hook attachment, or 20 to 25 minutes by hand. I actually like to turn the dough out of the mixer at this point and hand-knead. The technique is simple (and great for relieving stress—cheaper than a therapist!). Slap the dough onto the counter, then with the heel of one hand push it through the middle into the counter. With the other hand, fold the far side of the blob towards you, over onto itself, and rotate the dough about 90 degrees. Repeat this pushing, folding and rotating cycle several times, then give the dough another good hard slap onto the counter. (Don't add any extra flour at this point, even if the dough feels sticky; just use a dough scraper to gather the dough off the work surface. As the dough becomes more elastic, it will lose its gumminess and become smooth.) Do a stretch test: pinch some of the dough and pull it upwards. When the dough is ready, it should feel springy and elastic.

3. If you have removed your dough from the stand mixer, return it to a clean mixer bowl. If you are preparing the dough entirely by hand, you may find the next step easier in a large mixing bowl with a wooden spoon. Knead or beat the butter into the dough in small portions, fully incorporating each addition before adding the next. This process is definitely easier with a dough hook, but it is not impossible by hand. Squeeze the first few additions of butter through the dough, kneading until it is absorbed, then use a wooden spoon to beat in the remaining additions to prevent the dough from getting greasy and slippery, a sign that the butter is melting and not getting properly incorporated. The butter should be malleable, but not overly soft, and the dough should not get too warm during this process.

4. When the last of the butter has been beaten in, continue beating the dough until it is very smooth, glossy and elastic, about 5 minutes with the dough hook, or 10 minutes by hand. The dough should now have reached the "clean-up stage"—it should come away from the sides of the bowl in a smooth entity, or should neatly roll on the counter, no longer sticky or tacky. Transfer the dough to a large, lightly buttered bowl and cover the bowl with a sheet of plastic wrap. Leave to rise at warm room temperature, away from any draughts (about 75 degrees is perfect), until doubled in bulk, about 1¼ to 2 hours.

5. Punch the dough down and flip it over, deflating it completely. The buttery side should now be facing up. Cover again with plastic wrap and refrigerate for 2 to 3 hours. Punch the dough down, flip it once more, cover the bowl with plastic and weigh it down with a plate or dish, making sure the dough won't be able to creep around the sides of the weight and escape the confines of its bowl. (I have seen renegade doughs running rampant over the bottles and jars on refrigerator shelves more than once, and it's not a mess that you will forget having to clean up! Not to mention the waste of time, energy and perfectly good butter.) Return the bowl to the coldest part of your refrigerator and leave there overnight. If the dough is left longer than 8 hours, check periodically to make sure it has not risen above the bowl; gently punch it down as necessary. The brioche dough may be frozen at this point, wrapped very securely. Allow the dough to thaw in the refrigerator for 4 to 7 hours, then proceed with the shaping, final rising and baking.

6. Several hours before you plan to bake the brioche, remove the dough from the refrigerator, punch it down and turn it out onto a very lightly floured surface. Invert the bowl over the dough and let the dough rest for 10 minutes. (At this

Classic Brioche continued

point, the dough can be shaped for other pastries as well, such as the *Strawberry-Filled Brioche Doughnuts* on page 623) Meanwhile, butter two 9 x 5-inch metal loaf pans, or two 8-inch fluted brioche moulds (or one of each!) and set aside.

7. To form two 9 x 5-inch loaves: divide the dough into 6 roughly equal parts and cover 5 of these with plastic wrap to prevent them from drying out. Roll the remaining portion on the counter into a smooth ball, plumping it by caressing the sides of it with your hands from top to bottom, pulling the surface taut and smooth and tucking the excess dough underneath the ball. Set the ball in the end of one of the prepared loaf pans and cover it with plastic while you repeat the process with the remaining pieces of dough. Place 3 balls in each pan, in a row.

8. To form two 8-inch brioche à têtes: divide the dough into 2 equal portions. Cover 1 portion with plastic wrap while you work with the other. Divide this half into 8 relatively equal portions, then cover 7 of them with plastic. Roll the remaining portion on the counter into a smooth ball as for the 9 x 5-inch loaves above. Place this ball in the bottom of one of the prepared fluted moulds. Repeat the rolling process with 6 of the remaining pieces of dough, setting them around the outside of the mould over the first ball. Roll the last piece into a smooth ball and nestle this into the centre of the circle of balls. Cover the pan loosely with plastic wrap and repeat with the second half of the dough.

9. Cover the pans loosely with plastic and drape a dishtowel over top. Let the shaped loaves rise in a draught-free place until plumped and risen, but not quite doubled. This last rising can take between 1½ to 2½ hours, as the dough is still chilled from the refrigerator. Keep an eye on the dough and make sure that it does not rise too much, or you will not get as good an oven-spring (the big initial rising in the oven).

10. During the last 20 minutes of the final rising, preheat the oven to between 375° and 400°. Brush the plump loaves with the egg-milk glaze and bake them for 35 to 40 minutes, or until they sound hollow when tipped out of their pans and tapped on the bottom. Be careful when handling the hot loaves, as the joints between the sections are still very soft and fragile. As the brioche cools, the loaves will become firm and less delicate.

11. Turn the loaves out and cool completely on wire racks before serving or wrapping tightly in plastic wrap and aluminum foil and storing or freezing. The baked brioche can be frozen for up to 2 months, well-wrapped. Thaw at room temperature for about 4 hours. Besides being fabulous lightly toasted, served with sweet butter and a good jam, this brioche can also be used in recipes such as *Quince and Brioche Bread Pudding* (page 537) or the *Fall Charlotte* (page 420). Or try a brioche grilled cheese!

Strawberry-Filled Brioche Doughnuts

12 TO 14 DOUGHNUTS

Brioche dough makes a perfect yeast doughnut—light, tender and airy. I adore homemade strawberry preserves, but any good jam or jelly will do just fine! Just make sure the preserves you choose aren't overly runny, or the doughnuts will be undercooked and gummy on the inside. The following recipe uses half of my brioche recipe, which means you'll have enough dough to make one large loaf, along with a mess of yummy doughnuts. Not a bad way to start the day, is it? If you prefer to save the second half of the dough, it may be frozen as per the instructions in the original recipe.

½ recipe Classic Brioche dough (page 619), prepared up to Step 6, ready for shaping and the final rising

⅓ to ½ cup good-quality strawberry jam, or other jam, jelly or preserves

Mild-flavoured vegetable oil, for deep-frying

Sifted confectioners' sugar, for dusting the finished doughnuts

1. Turn the dough out onto a very lightly floured surface and knead once or twice. Gently roll the dough out to a rough rectangle, ⅓ to ½ inch thick. Be kind to the dough, and patient. If it seems to be resisting the rolling, don't force or stretch it, but cover it with a piece of plastic wrap and let it relax for a few minutes.

2. Line a large baking sheet with parchment paper and set aside. Using a 4-inch plain round biscuit cutter dipped in flour, or an overturned glass, cut the

Strawberry-Filled Brioche Doughnuts continued

dough into rounds. Place a teaspoonful of the preserves into the centre of each round, keeping a border around the edges clean. Dip your finger into a little water and moisten the rim of dough around the filling, then pinch the edges together like a dumpling or a turnover to form a good seal. Make sure the seam is completely sealed, so none of the filling leaks out during the frying. Transfer the filled pouches to the baking sheet, spacing them about 2 inches apart. Cover the doughnuts with plastic wrap and let them rise in a draught-free place for 30 minutes.

3. Meanwhile, slowly heat about 3 inches of vegetable oil in a heavy pot or deep fryer to a temperature of 365° to 375°F. Have ready a platter lined with several layers of paper towel for draining the cooked doughnuts. Lower three dough-nuts at a time into the hot oil and fry until they are golden brown, about 1½ to 2 minutes each side. Place the doughnuts on the paper towel and let the oil tem-perature recover before frying the next batch. Repeat until all the doughnuts are cooked. Do allow the doughnuts to cool for at least 10 minutes before dusting with confectioners' sugar and serving, or the sugar will turn to paste and your overeager tongue will be scorched by molten jam! You won't have to be told this, but eat these within an hour or so of when they are made.

Lemon Anise Churros

ABOUT 20 CHURROS

Churros are traditional Mexican fritters, much like baking-powder doughnuts, usually subtly flavoured with lemon or orange zest. Like many other types of fritter, little or no sugar is added to the dough, but the warm churros are tossed in a sugar mixture, which gives them a lovely sweetness. In this variation, the churros are laced with star anise and freshly grated lemon zest. I have tried them made with regular ground anise seed, but find the rich and mellow flavour of star anise to be far superior, giving a more muted and multi-layered taste. However, feel free to experiment! Not oily or heavy, a couple of these warm and crisp fritters are the perfect accompaniment to a milky café au lait on a gen-tle morning. As with most fritters, churros should be eaten while they are still warm, as they don't keep very well. This batter, basically a simple choux pastry dough, is very quick to prepare, especially if all of your ingredients have been measured out the night before. If anise doesn't suit you, leave it out and play with the flavours: add the seeds of a vanilla bean; substitute orange zest for the lemon zest; replace the anise with cinnamon or nutmeg—the possibilities are limited only by your imagination, and your pantry!

1¼ cups all-purpose flour
⅛ teaspoon salt
1 cup granulated sugar
1 cup confectioners' sugar, sifted
1 cup water
½ cup unsalted butter, cut into small
    pieces

2 teaspoons freshly ground star anise
Finely grated zest of 1 large lemon
3 large eggs

Mild-flavoured vegetable oil, for
    deep-frying

1. About half an hour before you plan to start frying the churros, pour enough vegetable oil in a large, heavy pot to reach a depth of 3 inches and set it over low heat. The heavier the pot, the better it will retain the heat of the oil, and keep the frying temperature constant. An even temperature will ensure the pastries will absorb minimal oil and turn out light, crisp and delicate. Position the thermometer in the oil before you begin heating it. The best thermometers have a metal foot that rests on the bottom of the pot; if you are using one that clips onto the side of the pot, make sure the sensor is not touching the side or bottom, but is suspended about midway into the fat. Slowly bring the oil to 375°F, keeping a close eye on the temperature once it reaches 300°, to ensure it doesn't go above the desired temperature. The oil should never begin to smoke, a sign that it is beginning to break down. Reduce the flame under the pot as the oil nears 375°, and when it reaches that point, wait about 5 minutes, to make sure the temperature has stabilized.

2. Sift the flour and salt together into a small bowl and set it within arm's reach of the stove. Combine the sugars in a clean, strong plastic bag and set aside. Line a large plate with several layers of paper towel and place this near the stove too. In a medium-sized saucepan, combine the water, butter, ground star anise and lemon zest and bring to a boil over high heat.

3. As soon as it reaches the boil, take the pan off the heat and immediately dump in the flour mixture. Using a wooden spoon, and beating furiously, return

Lemon Anise Churros continued

the pot to the heat and cook until the mixture comes together in a ball and pulls away from the sides of the pan, about 2 minutes. Remove from heat and let the mixture cool for a minute or two. Beat in the eggs, one at a time, beating very well after each addition, until the batter is quite smooth.

4. Spoon the entire batter into a good-quality pastry bag fitted with a medium-sized star tip (about ½ inch in diameter). Check to make sure the oil is still at the desired temperature. Taking the pastry bag in one hand, and directing the nozzle with the other, pipe the batter directly into the hot oil in 5- to 6-inch lengths, cutting off the stream of dough with your finger. Don't worry too much about the shape—I like little random squiggles and "S" shapes, but by the third or fourth try you'll find your style! Pipe five or six churros per batch, one right after the other, being careful not to overcrowd the fryer. Fry for about 3 to 4 minutes, turning with a pair of tongs, or until the churros are golden brown on all sides. Remove the fritters from the oil with the tongs or a slotted spoon and place on the plate lined with paper towels. Allow the oil to recover its temperature, then continue frying until all the batter is used, ensuring the oil returns to 375° between batches.

5. While they are still warm, drop the churros a few at a time into the bag of sugar and shake to coat them generously. Serve (or eat!) immediately, as these do not improve with standing.

Buttermilk Nutmeg Drop Doughnuts

ABOUT 15 DOUGHNUTS

These are an old-fashioned, crispy, rich-textured, incredibly satisfying pastry, simply flavoured with buttermilk and freshly grated nutmeg. They are easy to prepare and can be made in as short a time as it takes the oil to come up to temperature. The batter is looser than that of rolled and cut doughnuts, making these ones faster and less tricky to prepare. Do use freshly grated nutmeg for these fritters; it is the only flavouring used and the dusty bottled stuff just can't compare.

2½ cups all-purpose flour

1 teaspoon salt

1½ teaspoons baking powder

½ teaspoon baking soda

1 teaspoon freshly grated nutmeg

⅔ cup granulated sugar

1 large egg

1 large egg white

¾ cup plus 2 tablespoons buttermilk

¼ cup unsalted butter, melted and cooled

Mild-flavoured vegetable oil, for deep-frying

1 cup granulated sugar blended with 1 teaspoon ground cinnamon, for rolling the hot fritters

1. Add vegetable oil to a large, heavy Dutch oven or deep fryer to a depth of about 3 inches. Slowly heat the oil until it registers 365° to 375° on a candy and deep-fry thermometer.

2. Meanwhile, sift 1 cup of the flour and the salt, baking powder and baking soda into a large mixing bowl. Add the nutmeg and sugar and stir well with a wire whisk to thoroughly blend. Sift the remaining 1½ cups flour into a small bowl and set aside. In a third bowl, lightly beat the egg and the egg white, then stir in the buttermilk and cooled melted butter. Add the buttermilk mixture to the dry ingredients all at once, then stir with a large-looped whisk or a wooden spoon until the batter is almost smooth. Gradually beat in the remaining flour, stirring just enough to moisten the flour and smooth out most of the lumps. Do not overbeat the batter or it may become gluey and the fritters will be tough.

3. Have a large plate lined with several layers of paper towel near the stove. Place the cinnamon sugar in a shallow bowl and have a second platter ready to hold the finished doughnuts. When the oil has reached the right temperature, gently drop spoonfuls of the batter about the size of a large egg into the hot oil in batches of three or four. Cooking more fritters at a time may cause the oil temperature to drop too severely. Keep an eye on the thermometer—the temperature will initially jump when the batter is added, then drop slightly. Try to keep it within 5 or 10 degrees of 365° by playing with the number of fritters in the pot. Too low a heat will cause the fritters to absorb too much oil, while too high a temperature will burn the outsides before the insides are properly cooked.

Buttermilk Nutmeg Drop Doughnuts continued

4. Fry the doughnuts for about 2 to 3 minutes on each side, turning once or twice so they cook evenly. When they are a deep amber brown, transfer them to the paper towels with a pair of tongs or a slotted spoon. Let the fritters cool for a minute or so, then roll them in the cinnamon sugar and set them on the platter (or, as in my house, directly into somebody's open, waiting hand). Allow the temperature of the oil to recover before adding the next batch of doughnuts and repeat until all of the batter is used. Like most fritters, these doughnuts are best eaten as soon as they are fried, as they tend to get soggy and unappetizing with standing.

Sweet Polenta Crostini with Mascarpone, Raspberries, Pistachios and Wild Forest Honey

ABOUT 24 CROSTINI

These rustic yet elegant mouthfuls are a dessert version of a popular hors d'oeuvre. A sugared crisp polenta base supports a dollop of mascarpone, fresh raspberries, chewy pistachios and gloriously fragrant honey. With their truly satisfying—though perhaps unusual—combination of flavours, textures and colours, they are perfect as part of a dessert buffet or as an end to a rich meal in place of petits fours or truffles. The polenta can be made ahead, and all the other elements can be quickly assembled at the last minute.

POLENTA:

3½ cups water, preferably still spring
   or filtered water
½ teaspoon salt
1 cup yellow cornmeal, preferably
   stone-ground

4 tablespoons unsalted butter
1 tablespoon mild-flavoured vegetable
   oil, plus extra for greasing the pan
2 to 3 tablespoons granulated sugar

¾ cup mascarpone cheese
½ pint red raspberries
⅓ cup shelled, skinned, pistachio nuts,
   lightly toasted (see page 266 for tips
   on shelling and skinning pistachios)
   and coarsely chopped
¼ cup dark, flavourful honey, such as
   wild forest or lavender honey
   (preferably not buckwheat)

1. Prepare the polenta: lightly grease an 8 x 4-inch loaf pan with vegetable oil and set aside. Bring the water to a rolling boil in a large pot. Add the salt, then gradually sprinkle in the cornmeal, stirring constantly to avoid lumps. Keep stirring after the last of the cornmeal has been added; the mixture will begin to thicken quite quickly. Reduce the heat to medium and cook the polenta for about 30 to 40 minutes, stirring frequently. Spoon a little of the polenta onto a plate and taste it: when it is no longer crunchy and granular, it's done. Scrape the polenta into the loaf pan, flattening the top and pressing the mass into a rough rectangle, ending halfway to two-thirds down the length of the pan. This sounds a little confusing, but you should now have a 2-inch-thick rectangle of polenta pressed into the loaf pan. It will be very stiff and have no trouble staying put. Cool the polenta to room temperature, then press a piece of plastic wrap onto the surface and refrigerate until chilled, at least 2 hours, or up to 3 days.

2. No more than 2 or 3 hours before you plan to serve the dessert, remove the loaf pan from the refrigerator and unmould the polenta. With a long, thin-bladed knife, slice the loaf into ¼-inch thick slices and cut each of these in half. You should end up with about 24 2-inch squares, ¼-inch thick. Heat 2 table-spoons of butter and ½ tablespoon of vegetable oil in a large frying pan (non-stick is fine) over medium heat. When the foam subsides, add half of the polenta slices and fry about 4 minutes, turning once, until golden and crisp on both sides. Carefully transfer the slices to a platter lined with paper towels and sprinkle the slices with half of the sugar. Repeat with the remaining butter, oil, polenta and sugar. Cool the sugared polenta slices to room temperature.

3. To assemble the crostini, spoon the mascarpone into a piping bag fitted with a medium star tip (about ½ inch or so). Pipe a generous amount of mascarpone on each polenta square and arrange two or three raspberries on the cheese (see photo insert). Press some pistachio pieces around the berries into the cheese and drizzle the crostini with a little of the honey (a honey dripper or even a teaspoon dipped into the jar then waved over the squares works really well—don't even bother measuring the honey!). The finished crostini should be eaten as soon as possible, but can be kept covered at room temperature for a few hours.

GARNISHES, SAUCES AND BASIC RECIPES

continued on page 632

Praline

ABOUT 2 CUPS OF PRALINE SHARDS
OR 1⅔ CUPS OF GROUND PRALINE

Praline has almost infinite uses in dessert making, from a simple shard or crushed praline garnishing a mousse, cake or goblet of ice cream to a versatile ingredient that can be substituted for toasted nuts in many recipes: icings, ice creams, even cake batters. It keeps well, as long as it is stored in an airtight container, and the weather is not too humid. This recipe doesn't make an enormous amount, but can be doubled or tripled as needed. Feel free to use whatever type of nut suits you or the dessert the praline is to accompany.

1 cup granulated sugar
3 tablespoons water
¾ cup whole, blanched almonds,* lightly toasted

*Or substitute lightly toasted, skinned hazelnuts; shelled roasted peanuts; raw unsalted macadamia nuts, or lightly toasted pecans (see page 253)

Unsalted butter, at room temperature, for greasing the pan

1. Lightly butter a baking sheet and set aside. Combine the sugar and the water in a heavy-bottomed, medium-sized saucepan. Have a bowl of ice water close at hand in case of burns from splattering caramel. Heat the sugar and water gently, swirling the pan until the sugar dissolves. Wash down the sides of the pan with a pastry brush dipped in water. Once the syrup reaches the boil, do not swirl or stir it. Boil the syrup until it reaches 300°F on a candy thermometer, also known as the hard crack stage (see page 74 for sugar cookery stages). Immediately remove the pan from the heat and carefully add the almonds. Stir to coat the nuts, then pour the hot caramel onto the prepared baking sheet and allow to set until hard. Take care when handling the baking sheet; once the caramel is poured, the pan will be as hot as the molten sugar!

2. As soon as the praline has hardened, break it into pieces and store in an airtight container. Don't leave the praline on the baking sheet too long, or the sugar from the caramel will begin absorbing moisture from the butter on the sheet

Praline continued

and from the air, and the candy will become sticky. If crushed praline is called for, break the pieces into small shards, then process in a food processor until finely ground.

Candied Orange Peel

40 TO 60 PIECES OF
CANDIED PEEL

This homemade confection is absolutely incomparable to the awful stuff available around Christmastime in supermarkets. Those brightly coloured bits are often unpleasantly artificial-tasting, not to mention distractingly bitter. This is due to the fact that they most likely are all made from the same type of citrus fruit, called a citron, and dyed various neon shades to emulate lemon, orange and grapefruit peel. Citrons do not have the subtle flavour of these other fruits, however, and the result has given candied peel a bad name. (Personally, I tend to avoid anything sporting dots and pockets of these electric-hued morsels.) Orange peel, when blanched several times to rid it of its bitterness, and long-cooked in a rich sugar syrup, can be a phenomenal addition to all sorts of baked goods, fillings, compotes and sauces, as well as a beautiful garnish. You can make this recipe using the orange peel, as below, or with the peel of 6 lemons, 2 small grapefruits or 8 to 10 limes—all are equally delicious, and will forever erase the memory of those other peels.

3 large navel oranges, washed and
   dried
2¼ cups granulated sugar, plus 1 cup
   for coating the cooked peel
1½ cups water, preferably still spring
   or filtered water

Additional water (good tap water is
   fine for this) for blanching, and for
   washing down the sides of the pot

1. Cut the oranges in quarters and juice them into a clean container. (Reserve this juice for another use, or freeze until needed.) With a teaspoon or a grapefruit spoon, scrape out the pulp and membranes from the skins and discard, leaving the clean white pith on the inside of each quarter. Place the quarters colour-side up on a cutting board and use a sharp knife to cut the skin into ¼-

to ⅓-inch-wide slices. Fill a heavy-bottomed, 2-quart saucepan with water and bring it to a boil. Add the slices of peel and simmer for about 5 minutes. Drain and discard the water, then fill the saucepan again with fresh water. Repeat this process of bringing the water to the boil, adding and simmering the peel and draining two more times. This process removes the bitterness from the peels, leaving only the pure orange flavour.

2. When the peels have been drained for the third time, combine the 2¼ cups of sugar and the 1½ cups of water in the same saucepan. Place the pan over medium-low heat and stir until the sugar melts. Add the peels, bring the mixture to a gentle boil, then reduce to a simmer. Using a pastry brush dipped in cool water, wash down the sides of the pot, to prevent burning or crystallization of the syrup. Cook the peels for 1 to 1½ hours, until they are very soft, tender and sweet. Most of their moisture will have been replaced with the rich sugar syrup, and they will be extremely hot, so take care when removing them from the syrup.

3. You have several choices at this point: you can leave the peels in their lovely syrup, in which they will stay very moist and flexible, or you can roll the peels in the reserved sugar, dry them and use for garnishing desserts, or as a confection. I usually make some of each—the recipe is generous, and I can always find uses for either! For moist peel, simply cool the peels and their syrup until just lukewarm, then transfer the whole lot to a clean container, cover and refrigerate. The peel and syrup will keep for up to 3 weeks; if any suspicious-looking white, furry or unidentified patches appear on the surface of the mixture, however, discard the batch, as it has likely been infiltrated by yeasts or moulds.

4. For dried, sugared peel, spread the reserved 1 cup of sugar on a baking sheet. Have ready a large wire rack set over another baking sheet or piece of parchment paper. Remove the strips of peel from the hot syrup and place them on the sugared tray. Roll each piece in the sugar until well coated, then transfer it to the wire rack. Make sure the peels are not touching, and that there is enough space around each one for air to circulate. When all of the pieces are sugared, leave the peels on the rack at room temperature overnight or until dry. (This should not be attempted in humid weather.) Store the sugared peel, layered between sheets of parchment or waxed paper, in an airtight container at

Candied Orange Peel continued

room temperature, for up to 2 weeks. The syrup can be kept as well, stored in a covered container in the refrigerator, for 2 to 3 weeks.

5. The peels preserved in their syrup are a wonderful addition to cake batters, muffins, cookies, biscuits and scones, compotes, ice creams, puddings—the list is endless! Finely chopped, they provide a lovely citrus flavour and a pleasantly chewy texture, similar to a plump raisin or other dried fruit. The tiny cubes look like jewels when used to garnish desserts or dessert plates, sprinkled over a fresh fruit compote or twinkling in a pool of crème anglaise. The possibilities are truly limitless. The sugared and dried peels are sweet, intensely flavoured little candies, excellent plain or with one end dipped in bittersweet or white chocolate. They are a beautiful addition to a platter of petits fours or after-dinner confections and make great holiday gifts. Finely chopped, they can also be added to batters, doughs and other desserts. I like to decorate cakes, puddings and ice creams with long strips of the sparkling peel, adding a chewy, bright-tasting counterpoint to flavours such as chocolate, nuts, other citrus fruits and tropical fruits. The thick, intensely orange-infused syrup is a rich ingredient on its own: try adding a few tablespoons to a fruit compote or warmed and ladled over a homemade ice cream or pound cake. On pancakes, French toast and even gingerbread, it adds a lovely fruity sweetness and gives a subtle citrus flavour to cakes, custards and creams, and anywhere else it is used. Be creative!

Maple Sugared Pecans

3 CUPS

A proudly Canadian version of sugared nuts, these are light, crisp and subtly sweet, laced with the pure flavour of maple. These nuts are a cinch to prepare, and make excellent gifts. They keep well and are a wonderful addition to quick breads and fruit and nut cakes, in place of lightly toasted hazelnuts or pecans, or can be a simple and unusual garnish for spice cakes or quick breads.

3 cups fresh raw pecan halves, picked over
1 large egg white, at room temperature, lightly beaten

½ cup granulated maple sugar
¼ teaspoon freshly grated nutmeg

1. Preheat the oven to 300°. Toss the pecans with the beaten egg white in a large bowl. Sprinkle the sugar and nutmeg over the nuts and toss to coat thoroughly. Spread the pecans in a single layer on a large, unlined baking sheet and bake for 30 to 40 minutes, or until the nuts feel mostly dry. Shake the pan and turn the nuts every so often so they bake evenly. They will crisp and dry further as they cool. Slide the pecans onto a cool baking sheet set on a wire rack and cool completely before using or storing. Store the nuts in an airtight container for up to 2 weeks.

⚜ VARIATIONS ⚜

The pecans can be replaced with peanuts, very lightly toasted skinned hazelnuts or walnut halves. Keep an eye on the baking, as different nuts will bake at slightly different rates. The maple sugar can be replaced with granulated white or brown sugar. To vary the spicing, use one or a combination of the following:

½ to 1 teaspoon ground cinnamon
⅛ to ¼ teaspoon freshly ground cloves
⅛ to ¼ teaspoon freshly ground allspice
¼ to ½ teaspoon freshly grated nutmeg
¼ to ½ teaspoon ground cardamom
¼ to 1 teaspoon ground ginger
pinch cayenne pepper
pinch white or freshly ground black pepper

Fresh Apple Cider Syrup

ABOUT ¾ CUP THICK SYRUP

One single ingredient, and a most intensely apple-flavoured syrup is produced. I made this quite by accident one day, as I was reducing cider for a savoury sauce for chicken. The juice became a thick, shiny syrup with a punchy apple flavour. This sauce is dynamite warmed, over Roasted Cinnamon or Vanilla Bean Ice Cream with apple slices sautéed in butter and brown sugar until

Fresh Apple Cider Syrup continued

caramelized. Try to find cider from a local orchard, or at least one without any added sugar or preservatives. The flavour of the chemicals is subtle in the cider when it is served right from the jug, but when reduced as it is here, the taste can become really intrusive.

4 cups fresh cold-pressed apple cider (non-alcoholic), without preservatives

1. Bring the cider to a boil in a non-reactive saucepan and boil until it is reduced to about ¾ cup, or is the consistency of a medium-viscosity syrup. The syrup will thicken further as it cools. Pour the syrup into a clean container and cool to room temperature before covering and storing or using.

2. The cider syrup can be used at room temperature, slightly warmed in a microwave or on the stove, or even hot over ice cream. If it seems too thick even after being warmed, thin it with a few tablespoons of hot water or fresh cider. It keeps very well; stored in the refrigerator, it should last several weeks.

❧ VARIATION ❧

Warm Cider Butter Sauce: Whisk 4 tablespoons of chilled butter, cut into small pieces, into the still warm syrup to make a warm cider sauce, perfect with *Damn Fine Apple Pie* (page 472).

Pomegranate Syrup

1 TO 1½ CUPS VERY POTENT SYRUP

This gorgeous, ruby-coloured syrup is intensely flavourful, sweet and tangy, perfectly capturing the essence of the majestic pomegranate. It is fantastic with the White Meringues and Fresh Cream on page 486, but is more versatile than one might think—try it over ice cream or a pound cake. An incredible bright fruit flavour in the dark months of winter!

2 very large or 4 small pomegranates

2 cups water, preferably still spring or
filtered water

1¼ cups granulated sugar

Juice of up to ½ large lemon

1. There is no fast, clean, technical way to seed a pomegranate. They are a glorious lot, but not for the hurried, or the obsessively neat! I have tried all sorts of shortcuts, but have decided that the old-fashioned method of painstakingly plucking the seeds out by hand is the least messy, most efficient and most fun. Spread some newspaper over your counter, set up one bowl for seeds and one for parings and tie on as large an apron as you can find! (This is a perfect time to enlist the help of spouses, children, neighbours …) A good way to begin is to lightly score the skin of the pomegranate in quarters, then pare away the tough rind, leaving the seeds and the surrounding membranes exposed. Break the fruit into sections you can work with and pry the clusters of seeds away from the membranes. When you have harvested all the seeds from the pomegranates, pick them over and discard any larger bits of membrane. Don't worry about getting all of it; the cooked syrup will be thoroughly strained.

2. Combine the seeds, water and sugar in a 2-quart, non-reactive saucepan and heat gently, stirring until the sugar dissolves. Increase the heat and bring the mixture to a boil. Reduce the heat slightly and boil the seeds in the liquid until reduced by about ⅓ and slightly thickened, about 1 to 1½ hours. The bubbles breaking the surface will become smaller and less vigorous, a sign that most of the water has evaporated and the mixture has become a syrup. (This syrup will thicken further as it cools. If, when cold, it still seems too thin, you can reduce it a little more.)

3. Strain the contents of the pot through a sieve in several batches, stirring and pressing down hard on the seeds to extract all the juice and jelly. Taste the syrup and adjust the sweetness with a squeeze or two of fresh lemon juice; it should be sweet but still quite tangy. Allow the syrup to cool at room temperature before using or refrigerating. Spoon over *Vanilla Bean Ice Cream* (page 553), *White Meringues and Fresh Cream* (page 486), *Polenta-Almond Cakes* (page 377) or even a fresh fruit salad of orange segments, pineapple, mango or papaya, banana and freshly shaved coconut.

Warm Mulled Wine Sauce

ABOUT 3 CUPS

This rich and robustly spiced sauce is just the thing to transform a simple pound cake, fruit compote or ice cream into a spectacular dessert. It is divine spooned over Roasted Cinnamon or Chestnut Ice Cream (pages 553 and 560) and makes an explosive marriage of flavours when paired with Walnut, Orange and Sweet Chèvre Tartlettes (page 478). Use your imagination—if the warm, autumnal character of mulled wine would seem to suit the dessert, try this unusual sauce! The very best wine to use is a medium-bodied red with some berry, plum and spice flavours to it. I love Pinot Noir, but feel free to experiment.

1 cup water, preferably still spring or filtered water

2 cups granulated sugar

1 cup medium-bodied red wine, such as Pinot Noir

1 cinnamon stick, broken into pieces

4 lightly crushed cardamom pods

1 2-inch-long piece of orange zest, coloured part only, not the bitter white pith

1 1-inch-long piece of lemon zest, coloured part only, not the bitter white pith

2 whole cloves

1. Combine all the ingredients for the sauce in a heavy-bottomed 2-quart sauce-pan. Place the pot over medium heat and stir until the sugar is dissolved. Increase the heat to medium-high and bring the mixture to a boil. Boil gently for 10 to 12 minutes, then remove the pot from the heat and set aside to cool slightly before serving. This sauce can be made up to 1 week ahead of time and stored airtight in the refrigerator. Warm in a small pot on the stove over low heat, or carefully in a microwave, before serving, but take care not to scorch the sauce.

Brown Sugar-Brandy Sauce

ABOUT 2¼ CUPS

A big, boozy, butterscotchy sauce to dribble generously over Sticky Spiked Double-Apple Cake (page 441) or ice cream, or gingerbread, or spice cake, or toast, or spaghetti or …

⅓ cup unsalted butter, cut into small pieces

1 cup tightly packed dark brown sugar

⅓ cup granulated sugar

⅔ cup heavy cream (36%)

2½ tablespoons brandy

1. Combine the butter, sugars and cream in a small, heavy-bottomed saucepan. Stir this mixture over low heat until the sugar dissolves, then increase the heat to medium and bring the sauce to a very gentle boil, stirring all the while. Cook 5 more minutes, then remove from the heat and stir in the brandy or other liqueur. Serve immediately, or cool to room temperature, then cover and refrigerate until needed, up to 3 days. To rewarm, either microwave the uncovered sauce on low power or transfer the cold caramel to a saucepan and stir over low heat until warm.

VARIATIONS

Substitute other liqueurs for the brandy, and the sauce becomes infinitely variable. Some particularly good twists are *Brown Sugar-Kahlúa Sauce*, *Brown Sugar-Grand Marnier Sauce* (great with a bowl of *Orange-Date Ice Cream*, page 555) and *Brown Sugar-Whiskey Sauce*, wonderful warmed and poured over the *Oatmeal Stout Cake* (page 384).

Mexican Chocolate Sauce

ABOUT 3½ CUPS

Mexican chocolate incorporates the flavours of rich dark chocolate with pungent spicy cinnamon and sweet almonds. You can buy it in some specialty food shops in the U.S. and Canada, under the brand name Ibarra, and it is a delicious eating chocolate. Due to the addition of ground almonds and cinnamon, however, its texture is quite grainy, and it has a rather muted chocolate flavour. For this reason, I developed this sauce as an homage to the wonderful trinity of flavours, but chose to use a better-quality chocolate and flavour it with rich cinnamon and pure almond extract. This sauce makes a wicked hot fudge for pouring over ice cream or beside a flourless chocolate cake or an almond pound cake.

Mexican Chocolate Sauce continued

1¾ cups heavy cream (36%)
2 cinnamon sticks, broken into pieces
⅓ cup tightly packed dark brown sugar
1 teaspoon ground cinnamon
1 teaspoon pure almond extract

8 ounces excellent-quality bittersweet
    or semisweet chocolate, finely
    chopped
2 ounces unsweetened chocolate,
    finely chopped

1. In a small, heavy-bottomed pot combine the cream and the cinnamon sticks. In a small bowl, stir together the sugar and cinnamon and add this to the cream. Place the pot over low heat and stir until the sugar dissolves. Increase the heat and bring the cream just to a boil, then remove from the heat. Let the cream infuse for 2 to 3 minutes, then stir in the almond extract. Place the combined chopped chocolate in a large bowl. Pour the hot cream over the chocolate and stir gently with a wide-pronged whisk or a wooden spoon until the mixture is smooth and shiny. Serve immediately, poured over ice cream (try it with the *Roasted Cinnamon Ice Cream* on page 553!), cakes or the *Ricotta Pudding* on page 528.

2. Alternatively, allow the sauce to cool to room temperature, transfer it to a clean container, cover and chill. To re-warm, place the container in several inches of hot water and stir the chocolate until it is warm and runny. If the container isn't tall enough or isn't heatproof, scrape the chilled chocolate into a heatproof bowl and place the bowl over a pan of barely simmering water for several minutes, until the sauce is the right temperature and consistency. This sauce can be made up to 4 days ahead of time and stored in the refrigerator.

✤ VARIATION ✤

Spiked Mexican Chocolate Sauce: Add 2 to 3 tablespoons Amaretto or Kahlúa to the hot cream mixture before pouring it over the chocolate. I highly recommend this version!

Raspberry Coulis

This berry-fresh, uncooked sauce is wonderfully simple and can be made at any time of the year, as frozen raspberries work beautifully. It has the bright, fresh, sweet-tart flavour of fresh raspberries, unlike cooked fruit sauces. Don't buy the sweetened frozen berries, as these can be a little cloying and syrupy. Framboise, the wonderful raspberry eau-de-vie, and Cassis, the sweet black-currant liqueur, both give a new depth of flavour and distinctly "adult" taste to the sauce. Serve over ice cream, a simple pound or angel food cake or even with a dark chocolate cake or torte. It is particularly good with the Chocolate Raspberry Torte on page 405.

2 packages (10 ounces each) frozen unsweetened raspberries, thawed overnight, or about 3 cups fresh raspberries, picked over

¼ to ½ cup superfine sugar

Freshly squeezed lemon juice, if necessary

2 tablespoons to ¼ cup berry-flavoured liqueur, such as Framboise or Cassis, optional

1. Thaw the raspberries overnight with their packages set in a large bowl to catch the juice. Drain the berries, reserving the liquid. Place the berries and ¼ cup juice in a food processor and add ¼ cup sugar. Whir until the berries are puréed, adding more juice if the purée seems too thick. Keep in mind, however, that any liqueur you use will also thin the sauce somewhat. Add the liqueur, if desired, whir to blend, then taste for sweetness and add more sugar if necessary. If after adding the full ½ cup sugar you still find the sauce too tart, feel free to add more. If you accidentally add too much sugar, add a squeeze of fresh lemon juice to balance the sweetness.

2. When the flavour and consistency are good, pour the sauce through a fine-mesh sieve to remove the seeds. Transfer to a clean container and refrigerate until ready to serve. Stir the sauce before serving to make sure it is well emulsified. Stored in an airtight container, this coulis keeps well for up to 3 days.

Raspberry Coulis continued

✤ VARIATIONS ✤

Blackberry Coulis: Substitute frozen blackberries for the raspberries and increase the sugar to ⅓ to ⅔ cups. As blackberries can be quite tart, you may need even more sugar before the sauce is finished. I love the flavour of Cassis with blackberries, but a good Framboise also works well. Serve this sauce with the same types of desserts as the raspberry coulis; it's particularly good with the flavours of cornmeal and almonds—try it with the *Glazed Lemon Bundt Cake* on page 382!

Chunky Fresh Berry Sauce: Prepare the coulis as in the recipe above, using raspberries alone, or a combination of raspberries, strawberries and a few blackberries. Have about 1 cup whole fresh berries, all one variety or a combination, reserved. After the coulis is sweetened to taste and strained, add the fresh berries to the sauce, then refrigerate until needed. This version is endlessly variable, wonderful with any berry in season and excellent with a combination of several types of berries. Keep in mind that some berries are more tart and acidic than others, and you will want a good balance of sweetness in the mix as well. Strawberries are generally very sweet and make a good base and contrast to the tartness of raspberries, blackberries and others. It is always preferable to derive the sweetness in the sauce from the fruit, rather than from sugar.

Mango-Orange-Passion Fruit Coulis

ABOUT 2 CUPS

This explosively flavourful sauce is good enough to be the only adornment for a bowl of Vanilla Bean Ice Cream or Lychee and Coconut Milk Sorbet and makes a perfect accompaniment for the Coconut Panna Cotta on page 536. The recipe below is a guide—you may need to add more or less sugar depending upon the sweetness of the mango and the tartness of the passion fruit.

1 large Kent mango, or two small Alphonse mangoes, ripe

Juice of ½ medium orange (you can use a sweet orange, a Seville juice orange or even a blood orange for a different twist on the final sauce)

2 ripe passion fruits, halved and scraped out

¼ to ½ cup superfine sugar (or substitute 3 to 6 tablespoons fructose)

1. Peel the mango(es) and cut the flesh away from the stone. Roughly chop it, then place in the bowl of a food processor fitted with a steel blade. Add the orange juice. Force the passion fruit pulp through a wire mesh sieve and discard the seeds. Add to the processor bowl, then add ¼ cup sugar (or 3 tablespoons fructose) and pulse the contents of the processor until it is a thick and well-blended purée.

2. Taste the sauce: if it seems overly tart, add another tablespoon or two of sugar and spin the mixture again to dissolve the sugar. When the flavour of the sauce is to your liking, transfer it to a clean container and refrigerate until needed, up to 2 days. Serve cold over ice cream, custards, pound or angel food cake or even fresh fruit salads.

VARIATIONS

Peach-Orange-Passion Fruit Coulis: Substitute 2 to 3 ripe peaches for the mango in the master recipe. Peel them by dropping them into a pot of boiling water for 30 to 45 seconds, then plunging them into a bowl of ice water to stop the cooking. The skins will then slip off easily. Halve, core and roughly chop the flesh and proceed as for the above recipe.

Papaya-Orange-Passion Fruit Coulis: Substitute 1 large ripe papaya for the mango in the master recipe. Peel and halve the papaya, then scoop out and discard the seeds. Proceed as for the above recipe.

Caramel Cream Cheese Frosting

A sexy twist on one of the world's best frostings.

1 cup granulated sugar

¼ cup cool water, plus up to ¼ cup more for thinning caramel

1 pound (2 8-ounce packages) Philadelphia brand cream cheese, at room temperature

½ cup unsalted butter, at room temperature

5½ to 6 cups confectioners' sugar, sifted

1½ teaspoons pure vanilla extract

Mild-flavoured vegetable oil for greasing measuring cup

1. Prepare the caramel: combine the granulated sugar and ¼ cup water in a heavy-bottomed saucepan that completely covers the element on your stove. Have waiting on the stove a pair of oven mitts or a cloth, a measuring cup containing ¼ cup of cool water and a bowl of ice water. (The cloth or mitt is to cover your hand as you pour in the cool water, and the bowl of ice water is a precaution—if any of the caramel should splatter on your skin, immediately plunge it into the cold water to stop the burning.) Place the pot over high heat and stir until the sugar is dissolved.

2. Bring the syrup to a rolling boil (remove the spoon!) and cook until it turns a deep golden caramel colour. This should take about 5 minutes, but watch this pot constantly! Sugar burns faster than you can stop it. When the syrup starts to turn from clear to golden, don the oven mitts and take the measuring cup in one hand. With your other hand, get ready to pull the pot off the heat. You can do this even before the desired colour is achieved, as the cooking and darkening will continue with the residual heat.

3. When the syrup is burnished-wood-coloured, but NOT dark brown or black, remove it from the heat and gently pour the ¼ cup of cool water into the pot to stop the cooking. This will cause a great deal of splattering in the pot, so stand back and have any exposed bits of skin covered! When the fury in the pot subsides, pour in another tablespoon or two of water and transfer the caramel to a heatproof bowl to cool. As it cools, keep an eye on the consistency; the room-temperature caramel should be about the consistency of corn syrup or molasses. Err on the side of too little water. If too much water is added early on, the caramel will require more cooking to thicken it, but you can always add a few tablespoons of warm water if it looks like it is cooling too thick. Set the caramel aside to cool.

4. In the bowl of an electric mixer fitted with the paddle attachment, or a large bowl if beating by hand, combine the cream cheese and butter and beat on medium-low speed until smooth and creamy. Add the sifted confectioners' sugar, one cup at a time, blending thoroughly after each addition. When the first 4 cups of sugar have been incorporated, beat in the vanilla.

5. Lightly grease a ½-cup measure with vegetable oil and fill with the caramel. With the mixer or beaters on low, gradually pour in the caramel, then return the speed to medium and beat until blended. Beat in the remaining 1½ to 2 cups of sugar, 1 cup at a time, until the frosting is thick and smooth. Chill the frosting for 15 to 30 minutes, or until it holds its shape well, but is still spreadable. The frosting can be made up to 1 day in advance, brought to room temperature and re-beaten before use.

Dark Chocolate Ganache

ABOUT 1¾ CUPS

Ganache is a classic French preparation, really nothing more than excellent chocolate melted into rich cream. It is deceptively simple, however, and its uses are almost infinite. It can be used chilled, as the centres of truffles, or lightly creamed, to thickly frost a chocolate cake. Warmed and runny, it is unparalleled as a sauce for ice cream sundaes and is the purest, richest glaze for dense chocolate tortes. It is simpler to make than a cup of tea and keeps well in the refrigerator. It can be flavoured with any liqueur for an easy variation and no matter the context will have your guests begging for more.

Dark Chocolate Ganache continued

1 cup heavy cream (36%)   2 to 3 tablespoons liqueur, if desired
8 ounces bittersweet or semisweet
   chocolate, finely chopped

1. Pour the cream into a small, heavy-bottomed pot and place over medium heat. Bring to a boil, then immediately remove from the heat. Meanwhile, place the chocolate in a medium bowl. Pour the hot cream over the chocolate and stir slowly with a wooden spoon or a wide-looped wire whisk until the ganache is smooth. Transfer to a clean container and refrigerate until the ganache is the desired consistency, or until needed.

2. For glazing cakes and confections, you want the ganache to be still liquid and smooth, so it is best to chill it for only a short time, stirring often so it cools evenly. To frost layer cakes, spread onto tart shells or use as a filling for truffles, chill the ganache until it is firm, but still malleable. The ganache can be made up to 4 days ahead of time and stored, covered, in the refrigerator. It can be gently warmed or even re-melted in the microwave or in a heatproof bowl set over a pan of barely simmering water. The recipe can easily be doubled.

❧ VARIATION ❧

White Chocolate Ganache: Substitute 8 ounces of finely chopped, very good-quality white chocolate confection for the dark chocolate, but reduce the amount of cream to ¾ cup. White chocolate is softer than dark and does not require as much liquid to thin it when melted. If, however, the ganache seems too thick for your use, heat an extra ¼ cup heavy cream and add to the warm sauce. Use and store as for *Dark Chocolate Ganache*, above.

Crème Anglaise

ABOUT 3½ CUPS

The classic French vanilla custard sauce crème anglaise can be served with cakes, pastries, pies and tarts of all sorts. It can be flavoured with nothing but rich vanilla beans, or with virtually any flavour in the sweet kitchen. It has a luxurious, creamy consistency not unlike that of melted ice cream and is just sweet enough. Serve it as an alternative whenever ice cream or whipped cream would be appropriate, or as a more elaborate cream accompaniment.

2 cups whole milk (3.5%)
½ cup granulated sugar

1 vanilla bean, split
6 large egg yolks

1. Combine the milk and ¼ cup sugar in a heavy-bottomed, 2-quart saucepan. Scrape out the seeds of the vanilla bean and add these, and the hull, to the pot. Bring the mixture just to the boil over medium heat, then remove from the heat and let it infuse for 5 minutes. Meanwhile, lightly whisk together the egg yolks and remaining sugar. Secure the bowl to the counter by wrapping a damp towel around the base, freeing up your hands. Whisking constantly, slowly pour the hot milk into the egg yolk-sugar mixture, a little at a time, until all of the milk is incorporated.

2. Rinse out the pot used to scald the milk, but don't dry it; a film of water will help prevent the custard from scorching. Have ready a fine-mesh strainer set over a medium-sized bowl. Pour the custard back into the pot and return the pot to the element over medium-low heat. Cook the custard, stirring constantly with a wooden spoon, until it coats the back of the spoon, about 7 to 10 minutes. A finger drawn across the back of the spoon should leave a clean trail. Immediately pour the custard through the strainer and discard the vanilla bean hull. Press a piece of plastic wrap onto the surface of the custard and poke a few slits in the top with a sharp knife to allow the steam to escape. Cool the sauce to lukewarm, then refrigerate until chilled, at least 2 hours, or up to 4 days.

Crème Anglaise continued

✳ VARIATIONS ✳

Espresso Crème Anglaise: Use only ½ vanilla bean. To the strained custard, add 1 heaping teaspoon to 2 teaspoons instant espresso powder dissolved in 1 tablespoon warm milk and whisk to combine. Adjust the amount of espresso powder to suit your taste and the dessert it is to accompany. Serve with *Valrhona Molten Chocolate Cakes* (page 409) or *Black Chocolate Espresso Cake* (page 412).

Orange Crème Anglaise: Use ¼ vanilla bean. Add 2 strips (2 inches long, 1 inch wide) orange zest, coloured part only, with no bitter white pith, to the milk mixture before it is scalded. Discard these after the mixture is strained, then add 2 tablespoons of finely grated orange zest to the warm custard. If desired, add 1 to 2 tablespoons Grand Marnier or other orange-flavoured liqueur to the cooled sauce before refrigerating. Serve with *Pumpkin and Orange Breakfast Cake* (page 423) or *Cocoa, Date and Dried Fig Crostata* (page 458).

Hazelnut Crème Anglaise: Process ¾ cup lightly toasted, skinned hazelnuts with ¼ cup confectioners' sugar in a food processor until a smooth paste is formed. Whisk this paste into the warm strained custard and chill. If desired, add 1 to 2 tablespoons Frangelico (hazelnut-flavoured liqueur) to the cooled sauce.

Star Anise Crème Anglaise: Use only ½ vanilla bean. Add 3 whole star anise to the milk before scalding. Discard them after straining and add 2 more to the custard before cooling. Discard these before serving. If desired, add 1 tablespoons anise-flavoured liqueur to the cooled sauce. Serve with *Pain d'Épices* (page 603).

Cinnamon Crème Anglaise: Add 1 cinnamon stick, broken into 1-inch pieces, to the milk before scalding. Add 2 teaspoons ground cinnamon to the ¼ granulated sugar before whisking it into the egg yolks. Discard the cinnamon stick after straining the custard. Serve with *Roasted Plum Tart* (page 451) or *Black Chocolate Espresso Cake* (page 412).

Chestnut Crème Anglaise: Whisk ½ cup sweetened chestnut purée into the strained custard before cooling and chilling. Serve with *Warm Compote of Winter Fruits* (page 583) or *Oven-Roasted Pears with Red Wine and a Gratin of Goat's Cheese* (page 576).

Passion Fruit Crème Anglaise: Press the pulp and juice of 2 passion fruit through a sieve to remove the seeds, if desired. (The seeds are edible, and very beautiful, but are quite tart.) Add this purée to the cooled custard before chilling. Serve with *Tropical Fruit Crumble* (page 579).

White Chocolate Crème Anglaise: Use only ½ vanilla bean. Very finely chop 5 ounces best-quality white chocolate and add this to the hot strained custard. Stir until smooth, then cover and chill until needed. Serve with the *Gingerbread Soufflé* (page 530) or *Valrhona Molten Chocolate Cakes* (page 409).

Crème Fraîche

ABOUT 2¼ CUPS

Bless the French and their beautiful cows! This is a little phrase you will begin to chant more and more often as you begin to realize the wonders and absolutely endless uses for this divine cream. Crème fraîche is a thickened heavy cream, made in France by simply allowing the naturally present lactic acid and other friendly bacteria in raw cream to multiply. The result is a very thick, faintly tangy cream, less sour than sour cream, with a slightly sweet, very rich smooth flavour. In North America, sadly, raw crème fraîche is prohibited. Many gourmet and specialty shops sell pasteurized imported French crème fraîche, but it is unreasonably expensive, considering it is dead easy to make yourself. Once you have tried it, I promise, you will find uses for it you never dreamed of: as an alternative to whipped cream, ice cream, or crème anglaise beside fresh fruit, tarts, pies, cakes, biscuits, even pancakes, waffles and French toast. If you like, sweeten it with a little honey or sugar. It can even be added to cooked sauces and stews and will not curdle the way other dairy products do. It keeps beautifully, and only gets better, thicker and more tangy as it ages.

¼ cup buttermilk
2 cups heavy cream (36%)

Crème Fraîche continued

1. In a non-reactive pitcher or bowl, stir the buttermilk into the cream. Cover the container with a piece of plastic wrap and place it in a warm, draught-free place. I often leave it on a burner (not a lit burner!) of my gas stove, where it is always a few degrees warmer than anywhere else in the kitchen. Be careful the place you put the cream is not actually hot, or the bacteria in the mixture will be killed. Think of a nice hot day; that's about the right temperature. Leave the mixture covered for about 24 hours. Don't worry about the cream going bad; the benign live bacteria in the buttermilk will multiply and protect the cream from any harmful bacteria.

2. Remove the cover and gently jiggle the pitcher or bowl. The crème fraîche should be thickened and somewhere between the consistency of jelly and sour cream. If it still looks runny, the temperature was likely too cool. Move the container to a warmer spot, cover again and leave it for another 12 hours. When the consistency looks right, re-cover the container and transfer to the refrigerator. The crème fraîche can be made up to 2 weeks ahead.

Honeyed Mascarpone

1 CUP

A luxurious accompaniment to fruit tarts, compotes and baked, grilled or poached fruit. The following recipe can be doubled, and any leftovers make a decadent breakfast of waffles, pancakes or fruit salad!

½ pound (1 cup) full-fat mascarpone cheese	3 tablespoons flavourful honey (or to taste)

1. Use a wooden spoon or the paddle attachment of a stand mixer to incorporate the honey into the cheese. Add more or less honey according to your taste and the sweetness of the dessert to be served with the mascarpone. Cover and refrigerate until needed, up to 4 days.

Pâte Brisée
(Flaky Tart Pastry)

1 10- TO 11-INCH SINGLE-CRUST TART SHELL,
6 4½-INCH SHELLS OR
12 1½- TO 2-INCH TARTLETTE SHELLS

Pâte brisée is a classic French tart pastry, traditionally used for both sweet and savoury tarts. It is made rich with butter, but is neither as rich nor as sweet as the shortbread-like pâte sucrée. For dessert pastries, pâte brisée is ideal for tarts with rich, sweet fillings, such as custards and chocolate, and is excellent for tarts filled with pre-made mixtures like fruit curds. Pâte brisée is easy to work with, but needs resting and chilling time between mixing and rolling, and rolling and baking. All ingredients should be cold; if the dough becomes too warm during the making, pop the whole thing, bowl and all, in the refrigerator for a few minutes before proceeding. As with most pie and tart pastry, it freezes beautifully, and I usually make a double or triple batch, freeze it in discs and keep it on hand in case inspiration hits or surprise guests strike.

1¼ cups all-purpose flour
½ teaspoon salt
1 teaspoon granulated sugar

½ cup unsalted butter, cold, in small cubes
3 to 5 tablespoons ice water

1. Food processor method: place the flour, salt and sugar in the bowl of a food processor fitted with a steel blade. Add the butter cubes and pulse using short bursts until the largest pieces of butter are about the size of large peas. Add the ice water through the open feed tube while using long pulses, until the dough comes together. Stop the machine and feel the dough. It should hold together well when squeezed. Add a little more water if the mixture is too dry and crumbly.

2. By-hand method: place the flour, salt and sugar in a large bowl and stir to blend. Add the butter cubes and, using a pastry blender or two knives, cut them into the dry ingredients until the largest pieces of butter are about the size of large peas. Add the water, beginning with 3 tablespoons all at once, and use the tips of your fingers to lightly and rapidly toss and rub the mixture until the dough holds together when squeezed. If necessary, add 1 or 2 more tablespoons of the ice water until the desired consistency is achieved.

3. Turn the dough out onto a piece of plastic wrap and use the plastic to help form the dough into a flattish disc. Wrap tightly, pressing the dough to the edges of the plastic packet. Chill at least 2 hours, or up to 4 days. Dough may be frozen at this point, wrapped very well, for up to 2 months. Thaw overnight in the refrigerator before proceeding.

4. Rolling out the dough: remove the chilled dough from the refrigerator and let it temper slightly. If the dough is too cold when you begin rolling it, it will resist the rolling and pull back into the disc shape. Let it sit covered with a piece of plastic or a clean kitchen towel until it is a little warmer. Roll the circle to fit the size and shape of the tart pan or tartlette tins and ease the dough into the tin(s). Trim the edges of the pastry to about a 1-inch overhang and tuck this edge under, pressing the fold gently to seal it and coax out any air bubbles. Cover the shell with plastic wrap and chill for at least 1 hour or overnight before pre-baking or filling and baking.

5. Blind baking: preheat the oven to 375°. For a *partially baked shell*, prick the chilled shell all over with a fork. Line the bottom of the chilled shell with a circle of aluminum foil or parchment paper several inches larger than the bottom of the pan and fill the liner with pie weights or dried beans. Place the shell in the centre of the oven and bake for 15 to 20 minutes, or until the edges are just colouring and the bottom of the pastry is beginning to cook. Remove the liner and the weights at this point and return the shell to the oven for another 5 to 8 minutes or until the bottom of the shell feels mostly dry but is still pale. Cool completely before filling.

6. For a *completely pre-baked shell*, bake the pastry 10 to 12 minutes from the time the liner is removed, or until the edges of the pastry are a golden brown and the bottom is completely dry and has hues of gold. Cool the shell *completely* on a wire rack before filling. The partially or fully baked pastry shells may be made up to 1 day ahead of time and stored, airtight, at room temperature.

BLIND BAKING

Blind baking refers to pre-baking the empty tart shell, either partially or completely, before filling. In the case of fillings that are to be cooked further, a partially baked shell ensures the bottom will be perfectly cooked and crisp, not damp and raw. In the case of pre-cooked or raw fillings, such as fruit curds, mousses and fresh fruit, a fully baked shell is necessary.

Pâte Sucrée
(Rich, Sweet Shortcrust Tart Pastry)

1 10 TO 11-INCH TART SHELL,
6 4½-INCH SHELLS, OR
12 1½- TO 2-INCH TARTLETTE SHELLS

Pâte sucrée is fussy, difficult to work with and sensitive. Having said that, I will add this: it also makes a dynamite tart crust! It is buttery, sweet and tender, like a good shortbread, and is perfect with fruit tarts. Don't even try to roll it out— just press the crumbs directly into the tart tin with lightly floured fingers. A tip: pop the flour in the refrigerator for 15 minutes before starting and make sure the butter is very good, and very cold.

1¼ cups all-purpose flour
½ cup confectioners' sugar, sifted
¼ teaspoon salt

8 tablespoons unsalted butter, chilled, cut into small pieces
2 large egg yolks, lightly beaten

1. By-hand method: in a medium bowl, combine the flour, sugar and salt. With a pastry blender or two knives, cut the bits of cold butter into the dry ingredients until the largest pieces of the mixture are about the size of fat peas. Add the lightly beaten egg yolks, then use the tips of your fingers to gently rub the mixture together (the heat from the palms of your hands will melt the butter); the dough should quickly come together and feel moist and crumbly. If the dough seems too dry, lightly beat a whole large egg and add half of it to the mixture. You may need the entire egg if the air is very dry.

Pâte Sucrée continued

2. Food processor method: combine the flour, sugar and salt in the bowl of a food processor fitted with a steel blade. Pulse several times just to blend the dry ingredients. Add the bits of cold butter and pulse until the largest pieces of the mixture are about the size of fat peas. Add the lightly beaten egg yolks and pulse two or three times, just until the mixture looks moist and crumbly and comes together in a clump when you squeeze it. If the mixture seems very dry, lightly beat one whole egg in a separate bowl and add half of this to the dough, pulsing until it is incorporated. The dough should be moist but still crumbly.

3. Dust your fingers with flour and press the dough evenly over the bottom and up the sides of a 10- to 11-inch tart pan with a removable bottom (or see alternative sizes, above). Wrap the whole pan and pastry carefully in plastic wrap and refrigerate for 2 to 3 hours or overnight. (The shell(s) may be made to this point and frozen up to 1 month.)

4. Blind baking (see page 655 for more on blind baking): preheat oven to 375°. For a *partially baked shell*, prick the bottom of each chilled tart shell all over with a fork. Line the bottom with a piece of parchment paper or aluminum foil. Fill the liner with dried beans or pie weights and place the shell(s) on a baking sheet. Bake for 15 to 20 minutes, or until the edges are just colouring and the bottom of the pastry is beginning to cook. Remove the foil and weights and return the shell(s) to the oven for another 10 minutes, or until lightly browned all over.

5. For a *fully baked tart shell*, return the shell to the oven for 20 minutes after removing the foil, until the bottom is golden and dry. Watch closely—every oven is slightly different, and the high butter-sugar content of pâte sucrée makes it easy to overcook! Allow the tart shell(s) to cool before filling. The partially or fully baked tart shells may be made up to 1 day ahead of time and stored, airtight, at room temperature.

Rich Nut Tart Pastry

1 10 TO 11-INCH TART SHELL, OR
6 4½-INCH TART SHELLS OR
12 1½- TO 2-INCH TARTLETTE SHELLS

This is a very rich and flavourful pastry, perfect for frangipane tarts, fresh fruit tarts and tarts with plain chocolate or mousse fillings. As with all pastry recipes, all the ingredients should be as cold as possible, and the dough must be given sufficient time to rest and chill between steps.

¾ cup nuts*
¼ cup granulated sugar
1½ cups all-purpose flour
½ cup unsalted butter, cold, cut into
    small pieces
1 large egg yolk, cold

*For Hazelnut Tart Pastry, use ¾ cup
    toasted and skinned hazelnuts (see
    page 262 for tips on toasting and
    skinning hazelnuts)

For Walnut Tart Pastry, use ¾ cup
    lightly toasted and coarsely
    chopped walnuts (see page 253 for
    tips on toasting nuts)
For Pecan Tart Pastry, use ¾ cup lightly
    toasted pecan halves or pecan
    pieces (see page 253 for tips on
    toasting nuts)
For Macadamia Nut Tart Pastry, use
    ¾ cup unsalted, raw macadamia
    nuts

1. Combine the nuts and the sugar in the bowl of a food processor. Use quick pulses to whir the mixture until the nuts are finely ground. Don't overprocess, or the nuts will release their oils and you will end up with a lovely but unusable nut butter! Add the flour and pulse once or twice just to blend. Add the cold butter pieces and pulse for 10 to 20 seconds, or until the largest pieces of butter are about the size of fat peas. Add the egg yolk and pulse for 5 to 7 seconds, until the mixture just begins to come together. Turn the crumbly dough out into a clean bowl and use your fingertips to knead it lightly, rubbing the ingredients together until the dough is uniformly moist. It should be moist, sticky and crumbly, with no dry floury patches or streaks of egg yolk. But don't overwork the dough, and be sure to use just your fingertips—there is enough heat in your hands to melt the butter, preventing it from remaining in little pockets and adding tenderness and flakiness to the baked crust.

Rich Nut Tart Pastry continued

2. Press the crumble into a 10- to 11-inch tart tin with a removable bottom (or press the dough into 6 tartlette tins or 12 mini tartlette tins). Make sure the dough is evenly pressed and that there are no bare patches. Cover the shell(s) with plastic wrap and chill at least 4 hours or overnight. (The shell(s) can be frozen at this point, well wrapped, for up to 1 month. Do not thaw, but proceed directly to blind baking.)

3. For blind baking (see page 655 for more on blind baking): preheat the oven to 375°. For a *partially baked shell*, prick the bottom of each chilled shell all over with a fork and line the bottom(s) with a piece of aluminum foil or parchment paper slightly bigger than the shell itself. Fill the liner with pie weights or dried beans reserved for this purpose and place the shell(s) on a baking sheet. Set the sheet in the centre of the oven and bake for 8 to 10 minutes for tiny shells, 12 to 15 minutes for small tarts and 15 to 18 minutes for large tarts, or until the edges of the pastry are dry and just beginning to colour. Remove the liner and weights and return the shell(s) to the oven for another 5 to 10 minutes, depending on the size of the tins, or until the floor of the shell is dry, but not coloured. Transfer the shell(s) to a wire rack to cool completely before filling and baking.

4. For a *completely baked shell*: after removing the liner and weights, return the shell(s) to the oven for 7 to 13 minutes, or until the floor of the pastry is dry and tinged with gold. Cool completely on a wire rack before filling.

Flaky Pie Pastry

2 SINGLE-CRUST 9- TO 9½-INCH
PIE SHELLS OR TOP AND BOTTOM FOR
A DOUBLE-CRUST 9-INCH PIE

A tender, flaky, yet flavourful pie crust. All ingredients should be very cold, and if the dough becomes too warm at any point during the process, pop the whole batch of ingredients in the refrigerator for a few minutes. Using lard will produce a flakier crust, but vegetable shortening will make a very close second.

2 cups all-purpose flour

¼ teaspoon salt

½ cup lard or vegetable shortening, cold, cut into small pieces

5 tablespoons unsalted butter, cold, cut into small pieces

¼ cup ice water

1 large egg, lightly beaten

1. By-hand method: sift flour and salt into a large bowl. Using a pastry blender or two knives, cut in the lard or shortening and butter until the largest lumps are about the size of fat peas. In a small bowl, combine the ice water and lightly beaten egg. Add a little more than half of this mixture to the flour mixture, then use your fingertips to gently incorporate the liquid into the dough. If the mixture appears too dry and crumbly, and does not hold together when pressed, add a little more of the egg and water. The dough should be neither sticky nor at all crumbly. Mix lightly but do mix enough to evenly distribute the moisture.

2. Food processor method: sift the flour and salt together and combine in the bowl of a food processor. Add the diced lard or shortening and butter and pulse until the largest lumps are about the size of fat peas. In a small bowl, stir together the ice water and lightly beaten egg. Add slightly more than half of this liquid to the flour mixture and pulse two or three times. Feel the dough: if it does not hold together when squished, add more of the liquid. The dough should be moist but not sticky or crumbly and dry.

3. When the dough feels soft and comes together easily, divide it into 2 portions and gently form each into a flattish disk (remember, if you are too rough with the dough, you will be rewarded with a tough crust). Wrap tightly in plastic wrap and refrigerate until needed, at least 2 hours. The dough at this point can be refrigerated up to 3 days or frozen for up to 3 months. Thaw frozen dough overnight in the refrigerator and remove from the refrigerator about half an hour before you plan to roll it.

4. For blind baking (see page 655 for more on blind baking): preheat the oven to 350°. For a *partially baked shell*, on a lightly floured board, roll out one portion of the pastry dough, then line a 9-inch pie plate with it. Prick the bottom of the shell all over with a fork. Line the pastry with a circle of parchment paper or aluminum foil large enough to hang over the shell by an inch or so and

Flaky Pie Pastry continued

fill the shell with dried beans or pie weights. Place the shell in the centre of the oven and bake for 12 to 15 minutes, until the edges appear dry and the bottom has begun to cook. Remove the weights and liner and return the shell to the oven for another 5 minutes or until the bottom looks dry, but has not coloured. Cool completely on a rack before filling.

5. For a *completely baked shell*, return the shell to the oven for 7 to 10 minutes after removing the weights and liner. The baked shell should be completely dry and lightly golden on the edges and the bottom. Cool completely on a rack before filling. The pre-baked pie shell can be prepared several hours ahead of time or even overnight, if kept uncovered in a dry place at room temperature.

Appendices

High-Altitude Baking

As ANYONE WHO has lived in both places can tell you, things just don't bake in the mountains like they do by the sea. There are several reasons for this. As one gets further from sea level, the air pressure (or atmospheric pressure) decreases because the air higher up is thinner or less dense. This means it exerts less pressure on everything in its atmosphere, including water. So, whereas water at sea level boils at 212°F, water at 5000 feet, for example, comes to the boil at about 203°F (see below for a guide to the boiling points of water at various altitudes). This 9-degree difference means foods bake and cook more slowly higher up simply because they are being cooked at a lower temperature. The second factor of lower air pressure is that water evaporates more quickly, again because of less pressure upon it. This evaporation means that recipes for baking, candy-making, deep-fat frying and preserving need to be altered in terms of baking or cooking time, temperature and even some ingredients.

Many books give brief charts citing adjustments for high-altitude baking: reducing the amount of leavening ingredients, adjusting the amount of liquid in a recipe, etc. While in principle these charts are correct, to be perfectly accurate one must consider not only the type of product one is baking, but also the particular altitude at which it is baked. Some types of cookies can be made with no alteration to the original recipe at any altitude, some need changes only higher than a certain number of feet and some should be adjusted differently at 3000, 5000 and 7000 feet respectively. Cakes in particular are finicky—at different elevations, the same recipe should be adjusted in slightly different ways, from underbeating eggs to lessen the amount of trapped air to decreasing the amounts of sugar and/or baking powder to increasing the liquid called for. For the best results and consistency, consult a good general or all-purpose cookbook with a comprehensive section on high-altitude baking (these books often divide this information according to product: cookies, cakes, quickbreads, etc.). There are also cookbooks out there written expressly for high-altitude baking. Using their detailed suggestions, you can tailor your adjustments to your own situation as well as to the specific recipe.

BOILING TEMPERATURE OF WATER AT VARIOUS ALTITUDES

ALTITUDE	BOILING POINT OF WATER	
Sea Level	212.0°F	100.0°C
2,000 feet	208.4°F	98.4°C
5,000 feet	203.0°F	95.0°C
7,500 feet	198.4°F	92.4°C
10,000 feet	194.0°F	90.0°C

Weights, Measures & Equivalents

Ounces	Grams
1 ounce	15 grams
4 ounces (¼ pound)	110 grams
8 ounces (½ pound)	230 grams
16 ounces (1 pound)	454 grams

GRANULATED SUGAR

Measurement	Ounces	Grams
1 teaspoon	⅙ ounce	5 grams
1 tablespoon	½ ounce	15 grams
¼ cup	1¾ ounces	50 grams
⅓ cup	2¼ ounces	65 grams
½ cup	3½ ounces	100 grams
⅔ cup	4½ ounces	130 grams
¾ cup	5 ounces	150 grams
1 cup	7 ounces	200 grams

CONFECTIONERS' SUGAR*

Measurement	Ounces
4 cups	1 pound (16 ounces)

*Lightly spooned into a measuring cup and levelled off

continued on page 664

BROWN SUGAR (TIGHTLY PACKED)

Measurement	Ounces	Grams
½ cup	3¾ ounces	106 grams
1 cup	7½ ounces	213 grams

HONEY, MOLASSES, MAPLE SYRUP & OTHER LIQUID SWEETENERS

Measurement	Ounces	Grams
1 tablespoon (½ fluid ounce)	⅔ ounce	20.3 grams
¼ cup (2 fluid ounces)	3½ ounces	100 grams
⅓ cup (3 fluid ounces)	4½ ounces	130 grams
½ cup (4 fluid ounces)	6½ ounces	170 grams
⅔ cup (5 fluid ounces)	8 ounces	225 grams
¾ cup (6 fluid ounces)	9½ ounces	250 grams
1 cup (8 fluid ounces)	11½–12 ounces	326–340 grams

NUTS (1 CUP, RAW, SHELLED)

	Ounces	Grams
Almonds, sliced	3 ounces	85 grams
Cashews	4½ ounces	130 grams
Hazelnuts	4½ ounces	130 grams
Macadamia nuts	4 ounces	110 grams
Peanuts	4 ounces	110 grams
Pecans	4 ounces	110 grams
Pistachio nuts	5 ounces	150 grams
Walnuts	3½ ounces	100 grams

BUTTER

Measurement	Ounces	Grams
1 tablespoon	½ ounce	14 grams
2 tablespoons	1 ounce	28 grams
¼ cup (4 tablespoons, ½ stick)	2 ounces	56 grams
½ cup (8 tablespoons, 1 stick)	4 ounces (¼ pound)	113 grams
1 cup (16 tablespoons, 2 sticks)	8 ounces (½ pound)	227 grams
2 cups (4 sticks)	1 pound (16 ounces)	454 grams

SOLID SHORTENING AND LARD

Measurement	Ounces	Grams
1 tablespoon	0.4 ounces	11.8 grams
1 cup	6.7 ounces	190 grams

EGGS (LARGE, RAW)

	Ounces	Grams	Measurement
1 large, whole (no shell)	1¾ ounces	50 grams	
1 large yolk	⅔ ounce	18 grams	1 tablespoon
16 large yolks			1 cup
1 large white	1¹⁄₁₀ ounces	30 grams	2 tablespoons
8 large whites			1 cup

LIQUID MEASUREMENTS

Measurement	Equivalent
⅛ cup (1 fluid ounce)	2 tablespoons
¼ cup (2 fluid ounces)	4 tablespoons
⅓ cup (2¾ fluid ounces)	5 tablespoons + 1 teaspoon
½ cup (4 fluid ounces)	8 tablespoons
⅔ cup (5⅓ fluid ounces)	10 tablespoons + 2 teaspoons
¾ cup (6 fluid ounces)	12 tablespoons
1 cup (8 fluid ounces)	16 tablespoons (½ pint)
2 cups (16 fluid ounces)	1 pint

DRY MEASUREMENTS

Measurement	Equivalent
3 teaspoons	1 tablespoon
2 tablespoons	⅛ cup
4 tablespoons	¼ cup
5 tablespoons	⅓ cup
8 tablespoons	½ cup
16 tablespoons	1 cup
2 cups (1 pint)	1 pound (16 ounces)

WEIGHT EQUIVALENTS

½ pound = 230 grams
1 pound = 454 grams
1 kilo = 2.2 pounds

LIQUID AND DRY MEASURE EQUIVALENTS

A pinch	slightly less than ¼ teaspoon		
A dash	a few drops		
½ teaspoon	30 drops		
3 teaspoons	1 tablespoon	½ fluid ounce	
½ tablespoon	1½ teaspoons		
2 tablespoons	1 fl. ounce	⅛ cup	
1 jigger	3 tablespoons	1½ fluid ounces	
4 tablespoons	¼ cup	2 fluid ounces	
8 tablespoons	½ cup	4 fluid ounces	
10⅔ tablespoons	⅔ cup	10 tablespoons + 2 teaspoons	
12 tablespoons	¾ cup	6 fluid ounces	
16 tablespoons	1 cup	8 fluid ounces	½ pint
⅛ cup	2 tablespoons	1 fluid ounce	
¼ cup	4 tablespoons	2 fluid ounces	
⅓ cup	5 tablespoons + 1 teaspoon (5⅓ tablespoons)		
⅜ cup	¼ cup + 2 tablespoons		
½ cup	8 tablespoons	4 fluid ounces	
⅔ cup	10 tablespoons + 2 teaspoons (10⅔ tablespoons)		
⅝ cup	½ cup + 2 tablespoons		
¾ cup	12 tablespoons	6 fluid ounces	
⅞ cup	¾ cup + 2 tablespoons		

continued on page 668

1 cup	16 tablespoons	8 fluid ounces	½ pint
2 cups	1 pint	1 pound (16 fluid ounces)	
4 cups	32 ounces	2 pints	1 quart
4 quarts	1 gallon		
8 dry gallons	1 peck		
4 dry pecks	1 bushel		

OVEN TEMPERATURE CHART

Very slow	250°–300°F
Slow	300°–325°F
Moderately slow	325°–350°F
Moderate	350°–375°F
Moderately hot	375°–400°F
Hot	400°–450°F
Very hot	450°–475°F
Extremely hot	475°–550°F++

* All oven temperatures given in this book are in Fahrenheit.

BIBLIOGRAPHY

Amendola, Joseph. *The Bakers' Manual*, 3rd edition. Rochelle Park, NJ: Hayden Book Company, 1978.

Amendola, Joseph, and Donald Lundberg. *Understanding Baking*. New York: Van Nostrand Reinhold, 1992.

Anderson, Jean, and Barbara Deskins. *Nutrition Bible*. New York: William Morrow and Co., 1995.

Armstrong, Julian. *Taste of Quebec*. Toronto: Macmillan Canada, 1990.

Baird, Elizabeth. *Apples, Peaches and Pears*. Toronto: James Lorimer and Co., 1977.

Baird, Elizabeth, and the Canadian Living Test Kitchen. *Canadian Living's Best: Muffins and More*. Toronto: Madison Press, 1994.

Beard, James. *Beard on Food*. New York: Alfred A. Knopf, 1974.

Beard, James. *James Beard's American Cookery*. Boston: Little, Brown and Co., 1972.

Beranbaum, Rose Levy. *The Cake Bible*. New York: William Morrow and Co., 1988.

Bloom, Carole. *Sugar and Spice*. New York: HPBooks for Berkley Publishing Group, 1996.

Boisvenue, Lorraine. *Le guide de la cuisine traditionnelle Québécoise*. Montreal: Alain Stanké, 1979.

Bovbjerg, Dana, and Jeremy Iggers. *The Joy of Cheesecake*. Hauppauge, NY: Barron's Educational Series, 1980.

Boxer, Arabella. *Arabella Boxer's Book of English Food*. London: Penguin Books, 1991.

Braker, Flo. *The Simple Art of Perfect Baking*. Shelburne, VT: Chapters Publishing Ltd., 1992.

Brillat-Savarin, Jean Anthelme. *The Physiology of Taste*. Translated by M.F.K. Fisher. Berkley, CA: North Point Press, 1949, 1986.

Brody, Lora. *Chocolate*. Williams-Sonoma Kitchen Library. San Francisco: Weldon Owen for Time-Life Books, 1993.

Burrell, Fiona. *Leith's Book of Cakes*. London: Bloomsbury Pub. Inc., 1995.

California Culinary Academy. *Breads*. San Francisco: Ortho Books, Chevron Chemical Company, 1985.

California Culinary Academy. *Cakes and Pastries*. Edited by Susan Lammers. San Francisco: Ortho Books, Chevron Chemical Company, 1985.

Campbell, Susan. *Cooks' Tools*. New York: Bantam Books, 1980, 1981.

Carroll, John Phillip. *Pies and Tarts*. Williams-Sonoma Kitchen Library. San Francisco: Weldon Owen for Time-Life Books, 1992.

Child, Julia. *From Julia Child's Kitchen*. New York: Alfred A. Knopf, 1975.

Child, Julia. *The Way to Cook*. New York: Alfred A. Knopf, 1989, 1995.

Child, Julia, and Simone Beck. *Mastering the Art of French Cooking*. Vol. 2. New York: Alfred A. Knopf, 1970.

Child, Julia, Simone Beck and Louisette Bertholle. *Mastering the Art of French Cooking*. Vol. 1. New York: Alfred A. Knopf, 1961.

Clayton, Bernard. *Breads of France and How to Bake Them in Your Own Kitchen*. New York: Macmillan Publishing Co., 1978.

Collister, Linda, and Anthony Blake. *The Baking Book*. New York: Smithmark Publishing, 1996.

Collister, Linda, and Anthony Blake. *The Bread Book*. Toronto: General Publishing, 1993.

Cunningham, Marion. *The Fannie Farmer Baking Book*. Avenel, NJ: Random House Value Publishing, 1984.

Cunningham, Marion. *The Breakfast Book*. New York: Wings Books, Random House Value Publishing, 1987, 1997 ed.

Dannenberg, Linda. *Paris Boulangerie Pâtisserie*. New York: Clarkson Potter, 1994.

David, Elizabeth. *English Bread and Yeast Cookery*. New York: Viking Press, 1980.

David, Elizabeth. *French Provincial Cooking*. New York: Harper and Row, 1962.

David, Elizabeth. *Spices, Salt and Aromatics in the English Kitchen*. London: Penguin Books, 1970, 1975.

DeMers, John. *Caribbean Desserts*. Freedom, CA: Crossing Press, 1993.

Dodge, Jim, with Elaine Ratner. *Baking with Jim Dodge*. New York: Simon & Schuster, 1991.

Dornenburg, Andrew, and Karen Page. *Culinary Artistry.* New York: Van Nostrand Reinhold, 1996.

Dowell, Philip, and Adrian Bailey, et al. *Cooks' Ingredients.* London: Dorling Kindersley, 1980.

Dumas, Alexandre. *Le Grand dictionnaire de cuisine.* Paris, France: Pierre Grobel, 1958.

Dupree, Nathalie. *Nathalie Dupree's Southern Memories.* New York: Clarkson Potter, 1993.

Epstein, Becky Sue, and Hilary Dole Klein. *Substituting Ingredients,* 3rd edition. Old Saybrook, CT: The Globe Pequot Press, 1996.

Fance, Wilfred J. *The New International Confectioner.* London: Virtue and Co., 1979.

Fance, Wilfred J. *The Student's Technology of Breadmaking and Flour Confectionery.* London: Routledge and Kegan Paul, 1982.

Field, Carole. *The Italian Baker.* New York: HarperCollins Publishers, 1985.

Fisher, M.F.K. *Cooking of Provincial France.* Time-Life Foods of the World series. Alexandria, VA: Time-Life Books, 1968.

Fobel, Jim. *Jim Fobel's Old-Fashioned Baking Book.* New York: Lake Isle Press, 1987, 1996.

Gisslen, Wayne. *Professional Baking.* Toronto: John Wiley and Sons, 1985.

Gotlieb, Sondra. *Gourmet's Canada.* Toronto: New Press, 1972.

Graham, Kevin. *Grains, Rice, and Beans.* New York: Artisan, 1995.

Grigson, Jane. *English Food,* revised edition. London: Penguin Books, 1974, 1992.

Grigson, Jane. *Jane Grigson's Fruit Book.* London: Penguin Books, 1982.

Grigson, Sophie. *Sophie Grigson's Ingredients Book.* London: Mitchell Beazley, 1991, 1993.

Hazan, Marcella. *The Essentials of Classic Italian Cooking.* New York: Alfred A. Knopf, 1992.

Haedrich, Ken. *The Maple Syrup Cookbook.* Pownal, VT: Garden Way Publishing, Storey Communications, 1987.

Herbst, Sharon Tyler. *The New Food Lover's Companion.* Hauppauge, NY: Barron's Educational Series, 1995.

Hilburn, Prudence. *A Treasury of Southern Baking.* New York: HarperCollins Publishers, 1993.

Hillman, Howard. *Kitchen Science.* Boston: Houghton Mifflin, 1981, 1989.

Hood, Joan, with Vivian Donald. *Will It Freeze?* For Home and Freezer Digest. Agincourt, Canada: Methuen Publications, 1976, 1980.

Johnson Gross, Kim, Jeff Stone and Cheryl Merser. *Chic Simple Cooking Tools.* New York: Alfred A. Knopf Inc., 1996.

Kidd, Kristine. *Cookies and Biscotti.* Williams-Sonoma Kitchen Library. San Francisco: Weldon Owen for Time-Life Books, 1993, 1996.

Krasner, Deborah. *Kitchens for Cooks.* New York: Viking Penguin, 1994.

Larousse Gastronomique. Various authors. London: Paul Hamlyn, 1984, 1995, 1997.

Lewis, Edna. *The Taste of Country Cooking.* New York: Alfred A. Knopf, 1976.

Luchetti, Emily. *Four-Star Desserts.* New York: HarperCollins Publishers, 1996.

Luchetti, Emily. *Stars Desserts.* New York: HarperCollins Publishers, 1991.

Maher, Barbara. *Ultimate Cake.* London: Dorling Kindersley, 1996.

Malgieri, Nick. *Great Italian Desserts.* New York: Little, Brown and Co., 1990.

Malgieri, Nick. *How to Bake.* New York: HarperCollins Publishers, 1995.

Malgieri, Nick. *Nick Malgieri's Perfect Pastry.* New York: Macmillan, 1989.

McGee, Harold. *The Curious Cook.* New York: HarperCollins Publishers, 1990.

McGee, Harold. *On Food and Cooking.* New York: Collier Books for Macmillan Publishing, 1984.

McNair, James. *James McNair's Custards, Mousses and Puddings.* San Francisco: Chronicle Books, 1992.

McQuilkin, Roxanne. *Canadian Bread Machine Baking.* Toronto: Macmillan Canada, 1996.

Medrich, Alice. *Cocolat.* New York: Warner Books, 1990.

Mistretta, Giorgio. *The Italian Gourmet.* Vancouver: Raincoast Books, 1992.

Mizer, David A., Mary Porter, and Beth Sonnier. *Food Preparation for the Professional*, 2nd edition. Toronto: John Wiley and Sons, 1978, 1987.

Neal, Bill. *Biscuits, Spoonbread, and Sweet Potato Pie.* New York: Alfred A. Knopf, 1996.

Olney, Richard. *French Menu Cookbook*, revised edition. Boston: David R. Godine, 1970, 1985.

Olney, Richard. *Simple French Food.* New York: Collier Books, Macmillan Publishing Co., 1974.

Ortiz, Elisabeth Lambert. *The Encyclopedia of Herbs, Spices and Flavorings.* London: Dorling Kindersley, 1992.

Parker, Dorian Leigh. *Doughnuts.* New York: Clarkson Potter, 1994.

Passmore, Jacki. *The Book of Ice Creams and Sorbets*. Los Angeles: HPBooks for Merehurst Ltd., London, 1986.

Peck, Paula. *The Art of Fine Baking*. New York: Simon and Schuster, 1962.

Pépin, Jacques. *La Technique: The Fundamental Techniques of Cooking*. New York: Quadrangle Books, 1976.

Prange, Cathy, and Joan Pauli. *Muffin Mania*. Kitchener, Canada: Fairway Press, 1982.

Rambali, Paul, and Maria Rudman. *Boulangerie: The Craft and Culture of Baking in France*. New York: Macmillan, 1994.

Randolph, Mary. *The Virginia Housewife*. Toronto: General Publishing for Dover Publications, 1824, 1860, 1993.

Rombauer, Irma S., and Marion Rombauer Becker. *The Joy of Cooking*. New York: Scribner, 1975.

Root, Waverley. *The Food of France*. New York: Vintage Books, 1992.

Root, Waverley. *The Food of Italy*. New York: Vintage Books, 1992.

Roux, Michel. *Michel Roux's Finest Desserts*. Translated by Kate Whiteman. Toronto: Stoddart Publishing Co., 1995.

Roux, Michel, and Albert Roux. *The Roux Brothers on Patisserie*. London: Little, Brown and Co., 1986, 1993.

Sax, Richard. *Classic Home Desserts*. New York: Chapters Publishing Ltd., 1994.

Shere, Lindsey Remolif. *Chez Panisse Desserts*. New York: Random House, 1985.

Sultan, William, J. *Practical Baking*, 5th edition. New York: Van Nostrand Reinhold, 1990.

Tenaglia, Sarah. *Cakes, Cupcakes and Cheesecakes*. Williams-Sonoma Kitchen Library. San Francisco: Weldon Owen for Time Life Books, 1995.

Teubner, Christian, and Sybil Gräfin Schönfeldt. *Great Desserts*. New York: Hearst Books, 1981, 1983, 1985.

Time-Life Good Cook Series. *Breads*. Richard Olney, chief series consultant. Alexandria, VA: Time-Life Books, 1981.

Time-Life Good Cook Series. *Cakes*. Richard Olney, chief series consultant. Alexandria, VA: Time-Life Books, 1981.

Time-Life Good Cook Series. *Candy*. Richard Olney, chief series consultant. Alexandria, VA: Time-Life Books, 1981.

Time-Life Good Cook Series. *Classic Desserts*. Richard Olney, chief series consultant. Alexandria, VA: Time-Life Books, 1979, 1980.

Time-Life Good Cook Series. *Fruits*. Richard Olney, chief series consultant. Alexandria, VA: Time-Life Books, 1983.

Time-Life Good Cook Series. *Pies and Pastries*. Richard Olney, chief series consultant. Alexandria, VA: Time-Life Books, 1981.

Underhill, J.E. (Ted). *Wild Berries of the Pacific Northwest*. Surrey, BC: Hancock House Publishers, 1974.

Walden, Hilary. *Patisserie of France*. London: McGraw-Hill, 1988.

Walton, Stuart, and Norma Miller. *The Spirits and Liqueurs Cookbook*. London, UK, Lorenz Books, 1997.

Waverman, Lucy. *Lucy Waverman's Seasonal Canadian Cookbook*. Toronto: HarperCollins Publishers, 1989.

Weber, Marcea. *Naturally Sweet Desserts*. Garden City Park, NY: Avery, 1990.

Willan, Anne. *La France Gastronomique*. London: Pavilion, 1991.

Willan, Anne. *La Varenne Pratique*. New York: Crown Publishers, 1989.

Index